THE PIE AND PASTRY BIBLE

ROSE LEVY BERANBAUM

Illustrations by Laura Hartman Maestro
Photographs by Gentl & Hyers

SCRIBNER

"O, blackberry tart, with berries as big as your thumb, purple and black, and thick with juice, and a crust to endear them that will go to cream in your mouth, and both passing down with such a taste that will make you close your eyes and wish you might live for ever in the wideness of that rich moment."
—Richard Llewellyn,
How Green Was My Valley

SCRIBNER
1230 Avenue of the Americas
New York, NY 10020

Designed by Margery Cantor
Set in Minion and Trajan
Page 4 of the photo insert, Concord Grape Pie,
styled and photographed by Rose Levy Beranbaum

Manufactured in the United States of America

1   3   5   7   9   10   8   6   4   2

Library of Congress Cataloging-in-Publication Data
Beranbaum, Rose Levy.
The pie and pastry bible / Rose Levy Beranbaum.
p.   cm.
Includes index.
1. Pies. 2. Pastry.   I. Title.
TX773.B4478   1998
641.8'65—dc21   98-42869
CIP
ISBN 0-684-81348-3

To my husband, Elliott R. Beranbaum,
for the generous brilliance of his X-ray vision

To the memory of my mother, Lillian Wager Levy,
pioneer dentist, from whom I derived my
passion for my profession

To Chefs Arthur Oberholzer and Dieter Schorner,
my pastry gurus

To my irreplaceable editor Maria D. Guarnaschelli,
nurturer of my creative center, who gives her
heart, mind, and soul 100 percent

CONTENTS

FOREWORD IX

INTRODUCTION XI

BASIC PASTRY INGREDIENTS WEIGHTS AND MEASURES 1

Crusts 3   Fruit Pies 73   Chiffon Pies 144

Meringue Pies and Tarts 177   Custard Pies and Tarts 196

Ice Cream Pies and Ice Creams 221   Tarts and Tartlets 250

Savory Tarts and Pies—and Quiche 322   Biscuits and Scones 350

Fillo 364   Strudel 385   Puff Pastry and Croissant 411

Danish Pastry 485   Brioche 515   Cream Puff Pastry 528

Fillings and Toppings 549   Sauces and Glazes 595

Techniques 613   Ingredients 624   Equipment 656

SOURCES 675

ACKNOWLEDGMENTS 678

INDEX 679

FOREWORD

The first year I was married, I lived in Amherst, Massachusetts, and spent most of my time cooking my head off. I especially liked to make desserts—the more complex, the better. I made Gâteau St.-Honoré, Zuppa Inglese, Napoleon, Dobos Torte every day of the week. No kidding. Word of my feats got out, and I was approached one day by another faculty wife at Amherst College (where my husband taught) who asked me to teach her how to make a pie crust. I was horrified. A pie crust? How in heaven's name would I ever teach anyone how to do something as elusive and as complicated as that?

Everything changed when I began to edit this book. Just as I had with Rose's book on cakes, I became mesmerized by pies. And since Rose is like Merlin in her ability to draw you in, it wasn't long before I became obsessed by pies. It took hold on a Sunday afternoon, as I left her apartment clutching a sliver of her pear pie. I saw as she sliced it how succulently juicy the pears were, yet there was no dripping of juice onto the pie plate—all the juice seemed to cling to each slice of pear. I saw the crust as she was slicing it—and it seemed crisp, crunchy, flaky—and it was the most beautiful beige-brown against the juicy, holding-the-juice-to-themselves pears. When I got home and shared the treasure with my husband (reluctantly), I realized that Rose had transformed the meaning of pie for me.

I guess I'm bound to get some people angry when I say that I've always thought pies have needed Rose to lift them out of the homey, soggy, less-than-glamorous position they've occupied in America. The fact is, nobody knows how to make them well anymore. In her ingenious, utterly meticulous way, Rose has reflected long and hard on just how to bring a pie to the level of greatness. She has devised ways that enable a crust to stay crisp beneath the most juicy fruit filling, by placing the pie plate on the oven floor. She makes a fruit more succulent by macerating it with sugar, carefully collecting the juice, and cooking it so that it caramelizes and can create a synthesis with the fruit when the pie is baked in the oven. Rose makes the most of fruit, too. She keeps whenever and wherever possible much of the fruit in her pies fresh, so that it won't lose its personality when it reaches our mouths, and she cooks just enough of the fruit to provide a juicy cushion.

I could go on in this way about each one of Rose's recipes in this book, and I know everybody would think that I was writing a press release after a while. I'll try to be as composed as I can, but who else but Rose would go to Denmark and find out what Danish pastry is all about, and come back with recipes that make you swear you'll make Danish pastry as often as you can. Who else but Rose would go to Austria, and to Hungary, zealously watching master strudel-makers stretch dough, and then come home and make it one hundred times in her apartment in New York, so she could get it just right for us? Who else but Rose would come up with a cream cheese crust whose taste and texture defy description?

I used to think, before I edited Rose's first bible, that I made cakes as well as any home baker. Rose brought me to another level I didn't know existed. I began to make my cakes differently after that, and I also began to understand how important taste was to everything. I'll never add vanilla, or a strip of lemon zest, to a recipe again, whether it's one from Rose or not, unless it smells wonderful and is of the highest quality. I'll never make pound cake unless all the ingredients are at room temperature. With this book, I'll go to the farmer's market excited to find red currants, blueberries, Marionberries, sour cherries, and know with confidence that when I put them in one of Rose's crusts, they'll lose none of their fresh, lustrous brilliance. Now finally, after thirty-three years of baking, and under Rose's tutelage, am I ready to give the woman who asked me to teach her to make a pie, and roll a crust, the class she wanted.

Maria Guarnaschelli
Vice President and Senior Editor
Scribner

INTRODUCTION

I have been thinking of this book as *The Pastry Bible* for ten years now, since the publication of *The Cake Bible*. But after much discussion, I decided to give it the title *The Pie and Pastry Bible* because I discovered that most people do not know exactly what "pastry" means or that pies *are* also pastry.

The Oxford dictionary defines pastry as: "Dough made of flour, fat and water, used for covering pies or holding filling."

The writer couldn't have known the pleasure of a fresh tart cherry pie or of a flaky, buttery croissant, or his definition would never have remained so dispassionately matter-of-fact.

I did not grow up with much of a pastry tradition. Neither my mother nor grandmother baked. Once in a while I was treated to either a bakery prune Danish or éclair but that was it. Sunday morning breakfast was a buttered bagel. My father, a cabinet maker, also provided the greater New York and New Jersey area bagel factories with wooden peels, and the fringe benefit was a weekly string of fresh bagels.

The first pie I ever attempted was cherry pie, using prepared pie filling. It was during Thanksgiving break of my freshman year at the University of Vermont. I had just learned the basic techniques of pie making in class and wanted to please and surprise my father. It turned out that everyone else in the family was surprised as well but in different and disagreeable ways! The oven in our city apartment had never been used except to store pots and pans. My mother, who was afraid of lighting an oven that had been dormant so long, made a long "fuse" from a paper towel and took me into the living room, covering her ears. A few minutes later, when the flame reached the escaping gas, there was the loud explosion she had anticipated (not to mention unnecessarily created). Minutes later, my grandmother (whose domain the kitchen actually was) came running in crying, "The soap, the soap!" It turned out she stored her bars of soap for dishwashing in the broiler under the oven. The soap, by then, was melted and bubbling (much to my amusement). But the worst surprise was yet to come. During the baking of the pie, the cherry juice started bubbling out of the pie and onto the floor of the oven where it started to burn and smoke. Apparently the steam vents I had carefully cut into the top crust had resealed from the thick juices of the sugared cherries.

At Christmas break I tried again, this time lighting the oven myself—though I did forget to remove the soap again. My creative though absurd solution to the sealed vents was to insert little straws in them so that the juices could bubble up and down without spilling. Finally, I discovered that all that is necessary is to make little cutouts, which, unlike the slits, cannot reseal. But these days I prefer a lattice crust for my cherry pies. The fruit is simply too beautiful to hide.

My next attempt at pie was two years later as a new bride. I wanted to surprise my Vermont husband with a New England specialty he claimed to enjoy: pumpkin pie. As I was emptying the contents of the can into the pie shell, I licked my finger, which confirmed my suspicion that this was not a pie I was going to like. When I presented it for that evening's dessert, I couldn't resist adding: "I don't know how you can eat this; it tastes like a barnyard." To which he answered: "It does and I can't! What did you put in it?" "Pumpkin," I said, thinking what a ridiculously obvious question. "What else?" he asked. "What else goes in?" I queried. "Eggs, brown sugar, spices, vanilla," he enumerated as I sat there feeling like a total fool. Coincidentally, I was reading James Michener's *Sayonara,* in which the Japanese bride did the same thing, making her American husband a pumpkin pie using only canned pumpkin without sweetener or flavorings, thinking that it was pumpkin pie that somehow appealed to Western taste. It made me feel a lot better. (Too bad I hadn't reached that chapter before my own misadventure!) The next week I tried again, making it from scratch. To my surprise I loved it. It took me thirty years to achieve what I consider to be the state-of-the-art pumpkin pie.

Making pie crust and other pastries was another story. Pie crust, in particular, never came out the same way twice in a row. My goal in writing this book was to delve into the mysteries of pie crusts so that they would always come out the way I wanted them to be—tender and flaky—and if not, to understand why. My goal was also to convey this knowledge in a way that would encourage and enable others to do the same. This was far more of a challenge than cake baking. When it comes to cake, if one follows the rules, perfection is inevitable. But for pastry you must be somewhat of an interpretive artist as well as disciplined technician. You have to develop a sense of the dough: when it needs to be chilled or when it needs to be a little more moist. The best way to become proficient is by doing it often. And here's the motivation: The best pastry is made at home. This is because it can receive individual attention and optimal conditions. Try making a flaky pie crust in a 100°F. restaurant kitchen and I'm sure you'll agree. Also, there is nothing more empowering than the thrill of achieving good pastry. I'll always remember my first puff pastry. My housekeeper and I sat spellbound before the oven, watching it swell open and rise. It seemed alive. It was sheer magic. I also cherish the memory of my nephew Alexander unmolding his first tartlet when he was a little boy (and didn't kiss girls). The dough had taken on the attractive design of the fluted mold and he was so thrilled he forgot the rules and kissed me!

Many people think of me as "the cake lady," but the truth is I am more a pastry person! I love cake, but I adore pastry because of its multiplicity of textures and prevalence of juicy, flavorful fruit. I have had the pleasure of developing the recipes in this book for more than ten years. All were enjoyable, but I have included only those I personally would want to have again and again.

My fondest wish is that everyone will know the goodness of making and eating wonderful pastry. Then they will walk down the street with a secret little smile on their faces—like mine.

Rose Levy Beranbaum

BASIC PASTRY INGREDIENTS WEIGHTS AND MEASURES

INGREDIENT	METHOD OF MEASURE	OUNCES PER CUP	GRAMS PER CUP
FATS			
butter		8	227
clarified butter		6.8	195
cream cheese		9	256
vegetable shortening		6.7	191
commercial lard		7.5	216
rendered beef marrow		7.3	208
SUGARS			
granulated, superfine sugar, and coarse crystal	dip and sweep	7	200
powdered sugar	lightly spooned	4	115
light brown sugar	packed	7.6	217
dark brown sugar	packed	8.4	239
FLOURS AND OTHER DRY INGREDIENTS			
cake flour	sifted lightly spooned dip and sweep	3.5 4 4.5	100 114 130
pastry flour	dip and sweep	4.5	130
all-purpose flour, bleached	sifted lightly spooned dip and sweep	4 4.2 5.2	114 121 142
all-purpose flour, unbleached	lightly spooned dip and sweep	4.5 5.2	130 148
bread flour	sifted lightly spooned dip and sweep	4.2 4.5 5.5	121 130 157
whole wheat flour	dip and sweep	5	144
Wondra rapid dissolve flour	lightly spooned	4.3	124
cornstarch	lightly spooned or sifted dip and sweep	4.2 4.8	120 138
Dutch-processed cocoa	sifted lightly spooned dip and sweep	2.6 3.2 3.3	75 92 95
NUTS			
almonds	whole slivered sliced or coarsely chopped finely ground powder fine	6.7 4.2 3 3.7 3	191 120 85 107 89
walnuts, pecans	halves coarsely chopped	3.5 4	100 114
hazelnuts (filberts)	whole coarsely chopped finely ground	5 4 3.7	142 114 107
pistachios	whole	5	142
macadamias	whole	5	142
hazelnut praline paste		10.7	308

INGREDIENT	METHOD OF MEASURE	OUNCES PER CUP	GRAMS PER CUP
smooth peanut butter		16.6	266
coconut	packaged, shredded	3	85
coconut	fresh, grated	2.7	79
LIQUIDS			
water		8.3	236
DAIRY			
sweetened condensed milk	liquid measure	11	316
heavy cream	liquid measure	8.12	232
milk, buttermilk, sour cream, half-and-half	liquid measure	8.5	242
SYRUPS			
molasses	greased liquid measure	11.2	322
refiner's syrup	greased liquid measure	12	340
corn syrup	greased liquid measure	11.5	328
honey	greased liquid measure	12	345
CITRUS			
lemon juice, strained	liquid measure	8.7	250
orange juice, strained	liquid measure	8.5	242

EGGS	OUNCES	GRAMS PER UNIT	GRAMS PER CUP
1 large, in shell	2	56.7	*
1 large, without shell (3 T + ½ t)	1.7	50	253
1 large egg white (2 T)	1	30	240
1 large egg yolk (3½ t)	0.6	18.6	255

INGREDIENT	METHOD OF MEASURE	OUNCES	GRAMS
baking powder	1 teaspoon	•	4.9
baking soda	1 teaspoon	•	5
salt	1 teaspoon	•	6.7
cinnamon	1 tablespoon	•	6.5
cream of tartar	1 teaspoon	•	3.1
gelatin	1 teaspoon	•	3.15
poppy seeds	¼ cup	1.2	36
vanilla/almond extract	1 teaspoon	•	4
citrus zest	1 teaspoon	•	2

CRUSTS

FLAKY PIE CRUSTS

My pastry odyssey began twenty-one years ago, when I started making pie crust. At first it was a complete mystery to me. Sometimes it needed just a little water and the crust came out too fragile to roll. Other times the same amount of flour required lots of water and the crust came out flaky but as tough as cardboard. I hadn't the slightest idea that in the first instance I had mixed the flour and fat too much before adding the liquid so the fat in effect moisture-proofed the flour, preventing it from absorbing water. In the second instance, I hadn't mixed the flour and fat enough so that the water could absorb into the flour readily and form gluten, resulting in a tough crust.

My dream was to turn out a flaky and tender pie crust on a regular basis. And, of course, just as for cakes, I found that the only way to have complete control is to understand the ingredients—what they contain and how they react. But that was not enough. Theory is one thing, practice another. Now, many hundreds of pie crusts later, after trying every flour, fat, liquid, and technique I could think of, I have realized my dream. Now my goal is to share this knowledge and skill with others. There is simply no commercial pie crust equal to a homemade pie crust made well. I am convinced that if pie lovers had the experience of tasting one of this quality, they would start making pies from scratch, because it's not something one is likely to forget—ever.

But even with the clearest directions, making pie crust is a craft, and one must develop a feel for the dough. The more you make dough, the better you get. The French have a saying for this: *Il faut mettre la main à la pâte,* which means, "It is necessary to put your hand to the dough"—or, to paraphrase, *hands-on experience is everything.*

COMMERCIAL PIE CRUSTS   I have tried many commercial packaged and frozen crusts over the years and find them all lacking. Most are too salty for sweet fillings. The problem with frozen crusts is that when baked blind (without filling), they tend to develop cracks that allow liquid ingredients to leak through them during baking, sticking to the pan at best and messing up the oven at worst. If I had to recommend a commercial pie crust, it would be the Betty Crocker crust in a box. Though it is salty, it has a good flavor (unfortunately not from butter). The texture is flaky and it is foolproof and easy to mix and roll. Of the frozen crusts, Pillsbury has the best flavor (it's made with lard), but don't prebake it!

THE IDEAL PIE CRUST   It has light, flaky layers, is tender and golden brown, and has a flavor good enough to eat by itself. My favorite part of the crust is the top crust, because it does not get pressed together by the weight of the filling and stays crisp. Although the most flaky texture is achieved with my all-butter crust, I often make my butter/cream cheese crust. It is a bit less crisp and flaky, but it tastes so delicious it's worth the slight loss of flakiness. I do not at all like the flavor oil imparts to a crust. Using solid vegetable shortening, however, or half shortening and half butter, is useful for making spectacular borders, as this crust doesn't soften from the heat of the oven as quickly as an all-butter crust, allowing the decoration to hold its shape better. It is also more tender and lighter than an all-butter crust, but it is less crisp and browns faster.

For savory pies, I prefer my most tender, crisp, and flaky of all crusts, the lard crust, though for some savory fillings the butter/Cheddar cheese crust is a better match. For chicken potpie, the butter/goose fat crust is a luxury, and for steak and kidney pie, the meltingly tender, flaky beef suet crust couldn't be more indulgent.

FLAKINESS   The way to achieve flaky layers of dough in a pie crust is to keep the pieces of fat large, flat, and solid. When the fat starts to soften, it is absorbed into the flour and the layering is lost. For this reason, it is essential to keep all the ingredients cold and to work quickly. I usually freeze even the flour.

TENDERNESS   Flour high in protein requires more water and forms gluten more readily, which makes the dough made from it stretchy and hard to roll thin, resulting in a chewy or tough crust. Flour low in protein, such as cake flour, will usually produce a dough that is so tender it tears when it is transferred to the pie pan and develops cracks during baking. I've succeeded in making flaky pie crust with the lowest-protein flour, cake flour, but I did not like its flavor. The trick is to leave the butter in large cold pieces so that when the water is added, all of it is absorbed into the flour, developing the maximum amount of gluten. (The usual practice of cutting the butter into the flour until mealy moisture-proofs the flour slightly, limiting gluten formation.) Pastry flour, as the name implies, contains the ideal protein content to produce a good balance of flakiness and tenderness. You can approximate the same protein content by blending together a national brand of bleached all-purpose flour and cake flour (see page 7).

BROWNING   The speed of browning is increased by high protein, sugar, and low acidity. (Cake flour, which is the lowest in protein and highest in acidity, browns the most slowly.) The higher the protein in the flour, the faster the browning. All-purpose flour and homemade pastry flour will brown faster than commercial pastry flour. A crust made with the addition of cream cheese, which contains protein, will also brown faster than an all-butter crust. My colleague Shirley Corriher recommends adding a pinch of baking soda to decrease the crust's acidity for recipes where the pie does not bake long enough to brown the crust adequately.

PIE CRUST INGREDIENTS

FLOUR   My pie dough recipes were tested with 100% Gold Medal bleached all-purpose flour, King Arthur pastry flour, and a blend of Gold Medal bleached all-purpose flour and cake flour (not self-rising).

For a whole wheat crust, since whole wheat flour weighs about the same as all-purpose flour, it is easy to replace one third the weight or volume of the all-purpose flour with whole wheat flour. This produces a tenderness similar to a crust made from pastry flour, because whole wheat flour contains very little gluten-forming protein (just a little more than cake flour). For best results, it is always a good idea to process the whole wheat flour in a food processor to reduce the size of the coarser germ and bran, which tend to cut through the dough's gluten, weakening it.

If you have a favorite recipe that uses all-purpose flour and want it to be a little more tender, you can replace the all-purpose flour with an equal weight of pastry flour. Or, if using the volume method of measure, for every cup of all-purpose flour, use 1 cup plus 1 tablespoon of pastry flour.

Wondra flour can be substituted for pastry flour. With 10 grams of protein per cup compared to pastry flour's 9.2 grams, it will make a crust that is almost, but not quite, as tender. Some of the soft Southern flours have about 9 grams of protein, a little lower than pastry flour, and therefore produce a crust that is a little more tender and a little less flaky—unless all of the fat is left in large pieces.

FAT   The fat in a pie crust not only creates flaky layers, it also tenderizes and moisture-proofs it. A crust that is high enough in fat and completely baked is not likely to become soggy even if it is not prebaked. A good ratio is 1⅓ cups flour to ½ cup (8 tablespoons) of butter. Grade A and AA butters contain only about 81 percent fat, whereas shortening and lard are 100 percent fat. This has been taken into consideration when formulating the recipes. Lower-quality butter contains more water and will produce a less tender crust. Commercial lard varies in quality and some brands have an off taste. It is always preferable to render your own (see page 42).

LIQUID   Without liquid, the proteins in the flour could not connect to form the gluten structure necessary for holding the dough together. Some liquids also provide extra fat (such as cream) or acidity (such as buttermilk). I sometimes like to substitute a small percentage of vinegar for the liquid if it has no acidity of its own. I enjoy its faint but pleasant flavor, but what is most important is that the vinegar's acidity weakens the gluten just enough to make rolling even the flakiest, most elastic dough a dream—even ¹⁄₁₆ inch thin—after resting for just 45 minutes.

It also prevents shrinkage and distortion during baking, though to ensure a perfect shape, it is always best to allow the dough to rest for 6 to 8 hours after rolling. (If you need a quick crust, the one with cream cheese shrinks least when baked without adequate resting.) I do not add vinegar to a crust that is tender on its own, such as the suet (beef-fat) crust. Using chilled beef broth to replace the water for this crust, however, is an interesting enhancement.

If your water smells of chlorine, use bottled still mineral water or allow the tap water to sit uncovered, or covered with cheesecloth, for 6 to 8 hours, and the odor and flavor will disappear.

BAKING POWDER   An eighth of a teaspoon of baking powder per cup of flour not only serves to help counteract the dough's tendency to shrink, it also helps to lift, aerate, and tenderize it, and it adds a perceptible mellowness of flavor if you use an all-phosphate product containing calcium acid phosphate, such as Rumford (see page 624). It lacks the bitter aftertaste associated with SAS baking powders, which also contain sodium aluminum sulfate. As it is a perfect balance of acid and base, it has no effect on browning. Another magnificent advantage to baking powder is that the tenderizing effect doesn't take place until baking, so there is no danger of increasing the fragility of the crust during rolling and transferring it to the pan.

SALT   A pie crust would taste flat without an adequate amount of salt. I prefer using sea salt, as it has a more aromatic, almost sweet flavor. For savory fillings, use one and a half times the salt called for in the recipe.

If you are adding baking powder to a preexisting recipe, use only half the salt called for.

MIXING THE DOUGH

In the recipes, I offer two methods for making flaky pie dough: the food processor and the hand method. The hand method produces the flakiest crust. The food processor method is easier and quicker and results in an excellent crust, though slightly less flaky, *as long as it is not overprocessed.* It's the one I choose when the kitchen is warm or if I'm in a rush. When I'm in the mood for absolute perfection, I use the hand method.

After gathering the mixed dough together and kneading it lightly, you can tell how your crust will turn out by looking at two different factors: If you see thin flakes of butter in the dough, you know it will be flaky; and if you try stretching it slightly and it seems a little elastic, you know it will be strong enough to hold up well for rolling and baking. If when you begin rolling the dough, it appears to be too fragile and tears when lifted, fold it in thirds like a business letter and refrigerate it for about 20 minutes before rolling it again. This works if the dough was not manipulated enough to develop the gluten—but not if it was too moisture-proofed by the fat.

RESTING THE DOUGH

Flattening the newly formed dough into a 5- to 6-inch disc before refrigerating it makes it easier to roll without cracking. The dough is refrigerated to relax the gluten, making it less elastic and easier to roll. (It cannot relax in the freezer, because freezing sets it too quickly, but freezing for 15 minutes before baking is a great help to set the edge and ensure flakiness.) Chilling also firms the butter, preventing it from softening, which would result in loss of flaky layering and in sticking, requiring extra flour, which would toughen it. Dough that has rested overnight before baking shrinks less and holds its shape better.

It is fine to roll out the dough, slip it onto a parchment- or plastic wrap–lined baking sheet, cover it with plastic wrap, and refrigerate it until ready to use. It will need to soften for about 10 minutes at room temperature in order to be flexible enough to line the pie or tart pan, but then it needs only brief chilling (15 minutes in the freezer) to set the edges and ensure flakiness, as opposed to the usual hour in the refrigerator needed to prevent distortion after rolling and thereby activating the gluten.

MAKING YOUR OWN PASTRY FLOUR

The major advantage of using commercial pastry flour, such as King Arthur's, is that its protein content of 9.2 grams per cup is fairly standard from batch to batch. Bleached all-purpose flour can vary from brand to brand and even harvest to harvest, from 8 to 14 grams of protein per cup, averaging 11 grams. (If your all-purpose flour has 11 grams per cup, then your homemade pastry flour will be 9.9 grams protein, compared to the 9.2 of King Arthur pastry flour—just slightly stronger.) If you find that your pie crusts made from your own blend of pastry flour are coming out too tender, either reduce the amount of cake flour or use 100 percent all-purpose flour. Conversely, if they are coming out too tough, increase the amount of cake flour slightly.

To replace the all-purpose flour in a recipe with homemade pastry flour, use a national brand of bleached all-purpose flour, such as Gold Medal or Pillsbury, and cake flour that is not self-rising, or whole wheat flour. If you are doing it by weight, then simply replace one third of the all-purpose flour in the recipe with an equal weight of cake flour or whole wheat flour. Whisk or beat them together until blended. If measuring by volume, use a ratio of 2 parts bleached all-purpose flour to 1 part cake flour.

To make your own pastry flour, if using a scale, do two thirds (bleached all-purpose flour) to one third cake flour by weight. If measuring by volume, use the following proportions: 4 cups of bleached all-purpose flour, measured by dip and sweep, and 2¼ cups of cake flour, measured by dip and sweep. (Stir the flours lightly before measuring and mix them well after combining to blend them evenly.) This will make 6¼ cups of pastry flour (almost 2 pounds). Store it airtight.

POINTERS FOR SUCCESS FOR MAKING FLAKY PIE CRUSTS

∽ For flaky crust, ingredients *must* be cold to start with and stay cold.

∽ Use the correct flour. It is practically impossible to make a flaky crust or even one that holds together using cake flour and equally difficult to make a tender crust using unbleached all-purpose or bread flour.

∽ If using baking powder, be sure not to use SAS baking powders, which contain sodium aluminum sulfate, or the crust will have a bitter aftertaste. Use an all-phosphate product containing calcium acid phosphate, such as Rumford, available in some supermarkets and most health food stores.

∽ If not weighing the flour, use the dip and sweep method: Lightly stir the flour, then dip the cup into the flour and sweep off the excess with a metal spatula or knife.

∽ Brush off any excess flour on top of the dough after shaping it, as it will taste bitter after baking.

ROLLING AND SHAPING FLAKY PIE CRUST

When determining the size of rolled-out dough you need for any pie or tart, it is necessary to consider what sort of edge or border you want. For a tart pan with fluted sides, you need extra dough to turn down to make a narrow decorative edge that extends a little past the top edge of the pan, to allow for shrinkage during baking. For a single-crust pie, you need an extra inch of dough so there is enough to tuck under at the edge for an impressive raised border. A double-crust pie does not require this extra dough, because there will be two extra layers provided by the top crust, which gets tucked under the bottom crust. If the border of the two crusts pressed together is too thick, it will droop during baking. Drooping may even occur with a thick fluted border on a single-crust pie that is baked on the floor of the oven, close to the heat source. In this instance, it is wise to choose a small border that does not extend over the edge of the pie pan.

The standard pie pan is 9 inches in diameter and 1¼ inches deep. The standard fluted tart pan is 9½ inches, measured across the top from one inside edge to the other, and 1 inch deep. Some pie and tart pans, however, measure as much as ½ inch less in diameter and the depth of the pie or tart pan may also vary by as much. To be certain that you will have a circle of dough that is the correct size, measure the pan before cutting the dough.

MEASURING THE PAN

Measure the inside of the pie or tart pan with a flexible tape measure by starting at one inside edge, going down the side, across the bottom, and up the other side. Write down these numbers for future reference. When cutting the circle of dough to line the pan, increase the measure accordingly:

For a fluted tart pan, cut the dough circle 1 inch larger.

For a single-crust pie, cut the dough circle 3 inches larger.

For a two-crust pie, cut both circles of dough 2 inches larger.

SIZES OF DOUGH CIRCLES TO CUT FOR STANDARD PANS

For 4¼-inch pielets or 7-inch half pies, see Windfall Fruit Pielets, page 78.

    For a single-crust 9-inch pie, cut the dough 13 inches (12 inches if baking on the floor of the oven).

    For a two-crust 9-inch pie, cut the bottom crust 12 inches, transfer it to the pan, and trim it almost to the edge of the pie plate. Cut the top crust 12 inches or more if the fruit is mounded high; you need enough dough to go over the mounded fruit plus a ½-inch overlap to turn under all around.

    For a two-crust 10-inch pie, cut the dough 15½ inches, transfer it to the pan, and trim it almost to the edge of the pie plate, and at least 13 inches or more if the fruit is mounded high for a top crust.

    For a 3- by ⅝-inch tartlet, cut the dough 3¾ inches.

    For a 4- by ¾-inch tartlet, cut the dough 5¾ inches.

    For a 4¾- by ¾-inch tartlet, cut the dough 6½ inches.

    For a 9½- by 1-inch tart, cut the dough 12 inches.

    If the dough has not been given a chance to relax after it has been mixed, it will usually shrink when it is transferred to the pie or tart pan. If the dough has not relaxed adequately, it will be elastic. If you don't have the time to let it relax fully, cut the dough about a half inch larger than indicated above. When the circle of dough shrinks, it becomes both smaller in diameter and thicker. Since a thin bottom crust is more desirable, it is best to plan ahead and give the dough a chance to relax.

PREPARING THE PAN

The pie crust recipes in this book, though tender, are strong enough so that after a pie made from one of them has cooled completely, you can slide it out of the pan and onto a serving plate. This makes cutting each piece easier and prevents the knife from becoming dull and the pie pan from being scratched.

    There is enough fat in these doughs to make greasing the pan unnecessary. If you would like to give added texture to the bottom crust, butter and flour the pan. To do this, use a piece of plastic wrap to spread a thin layer of softened butter onto the bottom and sides of the pan. Scoop about ¼ cup of flour into the pan and, holding it over the flour bin, rotate the pan to disperse the flour all over it. Turn it over the bin and knock out the excess flour.

THE ROLLING SURFACE

Marble covered with a pastry cloth is the ideal surface for rolling pie dough. Its coolness helps to keep the fat firm, which is essential to prevent it from being absorbed into the flour and thereby losing its flakiness or layering. A piece of marble 16 inches by 20 inches by ¾ inch (see page 669; available in gourmet stores or from a marble supply store) is a good size that is small enough to slip into your refrigerator to chill on very hot summer days. (A bag of ice applied to a marble counter or a larger piece also works to chill it.) The pastry cloth is rubbed with flour to keep the dough from sticking to it and also helps to ensure that too much extra flour is not added to the dough during rolling, because the dough picks up only as much flour as it needs. A knitted cloth sleeve that slips over the rolling pin, also rubbed with flour to prevent sticking, can also be used. Alternatively, the dough can be floured lightly on both sides, preferably with Wondra flour, and rolled between sheets of plastic wrap, overlapped if not large enough. (Waxed paper tends to be rolled into the dough more readily.)

To ensure an even and precise degree of thickness to the dough, there is a simple, clever device called Rolling Pin Rubber Rings, which slip onto each end of a rolling pin, raising it from the counter a specific distance according to the thickness of the rings selected. The thickness of the dough is determined by the space between the pin and the counter. The thinnest ring will lift the pin a mere 1/16 inch from the counter, resulting in a wonderfully thin piece of dough. It cannot be used with the pastry cloth, however, because the hem on the sides of the cloth is thicker than 1/16 inch, so the rolling pin, as it rests on the sides of the cloth, is raised too much. When I want a crust this thin, I roll the dough between sheets of plastic wrap or on one sheet of plastic wrap using a rolling pin with a floured knitted cloth sleeve.

ROLLING FLAKY PIE CRUST

Remove the dough from the refrigerator (if frozen, it is best to allow it to defrost in the refrigerator for at least 3 hours, or overnight) and allow it to sit for about 10 minutes or until it softens enough to be malleable. Thwacking it with the rolling pin also helps to ready it for rolling, but if the dough is too cold, it will crack.

Keep the dough for a lattice or upper crust refrigerated while rolling the bottom crust and remove it about 10 minutes ahead of rolling.

Always work quickly so that the dough doesn't have a chance to soften. Use a firm steady pressure to roll the dough into a circle about 1/8 inch or slightly less thick (1/16 inch for small pies, as the filling requires less baking time). As the center tends to be the thickest part, roll from the center out. Avoid the edges, as they tend to become thinner than the rest of the dough. Lift and move the dough occasionally to make sure it is not sticking and flour lightly under the dough only if it is necessary. If at any point the dough becomes too soft, slip it, still on the cloth or plastic wrap, onto a baking  sheet, cover it, and refrigerate or freeze it until firm. If using plastic wrap, you can lift the ends of it to reposition the dough so that you are always rolling away from you, which is the most effective technique. Turn over the dough, in the plastic wrap, and lift and replace the wrap as necessary to be sure that the plastic wrap is not creasing and folding into the dough.

PATCHING FLAKY PIE CRUST

If a crack should develop in the center of the dough, cut off a little piece from the edge and place it over the crack. Dust it lightly with flour, cover with the plastic wrap, if using, and roll it into the dough. When transferring the dough to the pan, have the patched side facing down so that the smooth perfect side shows.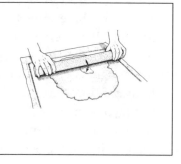

CUTTING FLAKY PIE CRUST

I find it easiest and most precise to cut out the circle of dough before transferring it to the pie or tart pan. (To determine the size, see Measuring the Pan, page 8.) Use an expandable flan ring as a guide, because it can expand to the desired diameter and then also cut through the dough. A cardboard template and the tip of a sharp knife work just as well.

Remove the top sheet of plastic wrap before cutting the dough. If the dough is very soft and sticky, replace the plastic wrap on the dough, slip the dough onto a baking sheet large enough to hold it flat, and refrigerate it for 5 to 10 minutes, until it is firm but still flexible, before fitting it into the pan.

TRANSFERRING FLAKY PIE CRUST TO THE PAN

There are three ways to accomplish this without stretching or tearing the dough. My preference is to fold it gently in fourths, center the point in the pan, and unfold it, easing it into the pan without stretching it. If the surface of the dough softens and becomes sticky, rub it very lightly with flour before folding it into fourths. The dough can also be wrapped loosely around the rolling pin and then lowered, centered, and draped into the pan. If the dough is not at all soft or sticky, you can slip your hands under it, palms down, and then lift it into the pan.

FITTING THE BOTTOM CRUST AND PLACING THE TOP CRUST

Ease the dough into the pan (or flan ring set on a baking sheet) without stretching it. Press it gently against the sides.

For a two-crust pie, trim the dough, if necessary, to about ½ inch past the edge of the pie pan. After you fill the pie, brush this edge with a little water. Place the top crust over the filling. Tuck the overhang under the bottom crust border and press down all around the top to seal it.

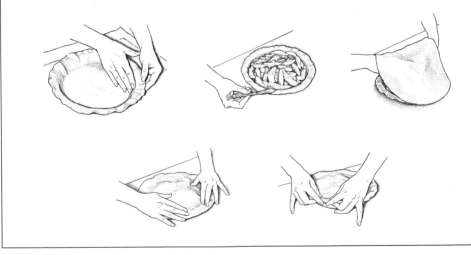

SHAPING THE BORDER

For a pie shell or flan ring, you can leave the border plain for a rustic look or create a decorative edge. If your fingers are warm, dip them occasionally in a bowl of ice water and dry them well. If the edge softens slightly, dip your fingers in flour as necessary (a little extra flour will help to hold its shape during baking, but be sure to brush off any excess loose flour after chilling, because on baking it will become bitter); if the dough becomes very soft, it is preferable to cover and chill it before proceeding.

For a two-crust pie, crimp or flute the border, using a fork or your fingers. Refrigerate the pie for 1 hour to set the crust and help hold the design of the border. (If desired, you can freeze all fruit pies, well wrapped, for at least 12 hours and up to 3 months before baking. Baking from frozen guarantees a crisp bottom crust and the best-shaped edge. Cut the steam vents just before baking.)

For a tart, press the dough against the fluted sides of the pan. Turn down the edge about ¼ inch so that it extends only about ⅛ inch above the top of the pan. Using the back edge of a knife blade, held at an angle, make decorative marks all around.

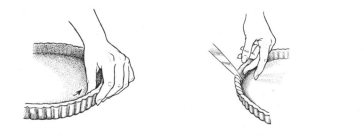

CUTTING STEAM VENTS

In a two-crust pie, the bubbling filling produces steam toward the end of baking, which, without an "escape valve," will cause the edges of the pie to burst open and some of the filling to spill out of the crust. Steam vents are cut into the top crust to control this steam pressure. For most pies with top crusts, five simple slashes, evenly achieved with a sharp knife, are enough to solve the problem. For fruits that release a lot of juice, such as cherry or grape, simple slashes reseal during baking, so it is best to use a lattice top crust or a top crust with large decorative openings that cannot reseal.

To make a top crust with decorative openings, after rolling and cutting the dough disc, use a small decorative cutter to stamp out the dough. Remove the pieces of dough with the tip of a knife or toothpick and reserve them to apply as appliqués (see Blackberry Pie, page 115), or wrap them well and freeze for future use.

Slip the top crust onto a cookie sheet and freeze it for about 5 minutes so that when you are transferring it to the pie, the cutouts do not deform.

Before baking a pie, be sure to brush off any remaining flour from the top surface of the dough, as it would give the dough a bitter taste after baking.

MAKING DECORATIVE CUTOUTS

Instead of leaving a top crust in one piece and cutting out decorative openings, the dough can be cut into decorative shapes, such as butterflies or leaves, with a knife or cookie cutter and overlapped on top of the filling before baking the pie (see Designer Cherry Pie, page 95). A few whimsical cutouts can be shaped from dough scraps and placed on the top crust (see Chicken Potpie, page 323). To make cutouts: Roll the dough ⅛ inch thick or slightly under, as for a pie crust. (If using the recommended baking powder in the crust, the cutouts will puff a bit.) Chill or freeze the dough until firm before cutting out shapes with a cookie cutter dipped in flour or free-form with the top of a sharp knife. Chill again before lifting away the trimmings.

I sometimes like to use baked cutouts to set on top of unbaked fruit fillings (with or without bottom crusts) that don't get baked, such as the Fresh Blueberry Pie (page 106). For a crunchy effect, brush the dough lightly with milk or egg white and sprinkle it with sugar before baking. Bake in a preheated 425°F. oven for 12 minutes or until golden. Cool on a rack and set on the cooked filling.

SCRAPS

Lay the pieces of dough side by side, overlapping them just enough so that there are no spaces. Wrap them in plastic and refrigerate until firm, about 30 minutes. Roll the dough between plastic wrap to avoid working in extra flour and fold it in thirds as you would a business letter. Roll lightly over it and wrap it well with plastic wrap. (Use Saran plastic wrap, which does not breathe, if you are freezing it.) Place it in a reclosable freezer bag and chill it until firm, or freeze it. I have made a pie with well-wrapped two-year-old scraps that still had excellent flavor and a flaky texture. For a full-size pie, defrost as many pieces of rolled-out leftover dough as needed: Allow them to defrost refrigerated for at least 3 hours, then remove them to room temperature until they can be rolled out. Stack one piece on top of another and roll to the size you need.

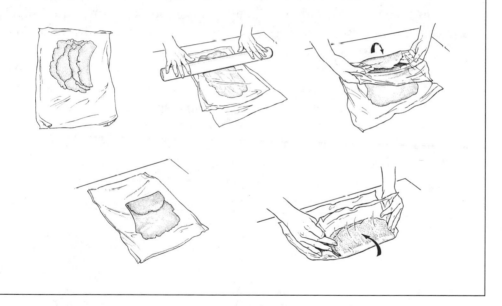

MAKING A LATTICE CRUST

A regular or open lattice crust is one in which the strips of dough are set far enough apart to show the pie filling in between. A tightly woven lattice is made essentially the same way but the strips abut each other, leaving no spaces in between. For a pie with a tightly woven lattice, make enough dough for a two-crust pie. Roll the dough for the lattice as thin as possible, as the overlapping of the tightly spaced strips will give you double the thickness of crust.

It is possible to make the lattice on a baking sheet and then to slide it onto the pie. I prefer to make it directly on the pie so it can be placed exactly where I want it to be. If you are nervous about having enough dough, you can add the scraps from the bottom crust to the dough for the lattice (see Scraps, page 15), but be sure to chill it before rolling. I find ¾-inch-wide strips, cut with a pastry jagger, to be the most attractive, as they leave enough space in between to view the pie filling without looking skimpy after slight shrinking. If not using a jagger, make them ⅝ inch instead. To make even strips, a clear plastic ruler is indispensable.

Roll the dough into an oval, 10 inches long by 8 inches wide. (Not all the strips need to be 10 inches long. As you get to the sides of the pie, the length decreases.) Starting at the left edge with a pastry jagger, pizza cutter, or sharp knife, trim off a small amount to create an even edge. Place the ruler on top so that the left edge of the pastry is ¾ inch from the right edge of the ruler. With the middle finger and thumb of your left hand, hold the ruler firmly in place toward the top and bottom and cut along the right edge. Lift away the strip and set it on the counter while cutting the remaining strips. There should be 10 (24 for a tightly woven lattice).

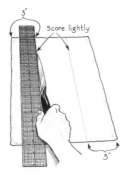

Making a Lattice Crust (cont.)

Arrange half the strips evenly over the filling. Gently curve back every other strip a little past the center and place another strip perpendicular on top. Uncurve the strips so that they lie flat on top of the perpendicular strip. Working in the same direction, curve back the strips that were not curved back the first time. Lay a second perpendicular strip on top and uncurve the strips. Continue in this manner with the third perpendicular strip, curving back the strips that were curved back the first time. Apply the remaining 2 strips to the other side of the pie, starting toward the center and working in the opposite direction toward the edge; remember always to alternate the strips that are curved back so that the strips weave in and out.

Use sharp scissors to trim the strips to a ½-inch overhang. Moisten the dough under each strip with egg white or water and tuck the overhang under the bottom crust border, pressing down to make it adhere. Leave the border plain, or crimp it if desired.

BAKING FLAKY PIE CRUST

My feeling about pie crust is that if the bottom crust is soggy, I'd just as soon not have it. Fruit pies, because of their luscious, juicy filling, often do have a soggy bottom crust, but there are ways to prevent this. When a pie does not have a top crust, I almost always fully prebake the bottom crust and brush it with a half an egg white or two tablespoons of a thick fruit preserve, strained. For custard-type pies, I sometimes sprinkle the bottom with compatibly flavored cookie crumbs, such as gingersnaps in the case of Great Pumpkin Pie (page 198).

Two-crust pies, however, require other solutions. Some bakers like to roll the bottom pie dough out on graham cracker crumbs. This helps to absorb moisture and keep the bottom from getting soggy, but I don't like the flavor graham crackers add. In many ovens, baking the pie directly on the floor of the oven will produce a crisp crust without burning it. In my oven, it works perfectly to bake it on the floor of the oven or on a baking stone set on the floor of the oven for 1 hour at 375°F. or 30 minutes at 425°F. before raising it to the lower shelf. (A large fancy raised edge will droop when so close to the heat source, so a smaller one becomes necessary in this case.) Try this the first time in a Pyrex pie plate so that you can monitor the degree of browning and move it up in the oven if it is browning too much. If the top of the pie is not browning adequately, raise it to the top shelf for the last 10 minutes of baking. Alternatively, preheating a baking stone or baking sheet on the lower rack also helps. Using a dark baking pan that absorbs and conducts the heat, a glass one that transmits it through radiant heat, or a ceramic one that retains heat well, aids in browning.

Another solution is freezing a fruit pie before baking it. The crust, which is closer to the pan than the filling, starts to bake before the fruit begins to defrost, and bakes longer than it would normally. (If you want to freeze a pie for several weeks or months and need the pie plate, line the pie plate first with plastic wrap or foil. When the pie is fully frozen, it can be lifted out and wrapped airtight. When ready to bake the pie, simply unwrap it, slash the top, and pop it into the pan in which it was formed.)

I have found that a high baking temperature of 400° to 425°F. produces the best crust. I use 425°F., but some ovens run hot and will brown too fast at this temperature. For a two-crust pie, high heat and baking on the bottom work especially well, since baking on the bottom of the oven is perfect for the bottom crust and does not overbrown the top crust (except for the edges, which need protection). I find when a crust loses its shape, it is far more a function of the recipe and insufficient resting time than of the baking temperature. If using a glass, ceramic, or dark metal pan and baking the crust blind (with weights instead of filling), start it at 425°F. but immediately turn the oven temperature down to bake at 400°F.

Almost all pastry bakes brilliantly in a convection oven. The circulating air produces an evenly golden brown crust. In order for the air to circulate around the pie, it needs to be baked directly on an oven rack, without a stone or baking sheet, and the heat needs to be reduced by 25°F.

In order to be full enough after cooking, a fruit pie needs a lot of fruit. A well-made fruit pie is, therefore, very juicy and usually bubbles over. Part of the solution is concentration of the juices, which often eliminates this problem entirely. Bubbling fruit juices are very sticky, so, to be on the safe side, if you have a Teflon-type liner (see page 666), place it on top of a sheet of foil under the pie pan for ease in cleanup. Curve up the edges of the foil slightly to keep the juices from running onto the floor of the oven. If using heavy-duty foil, you will be able to lift the pie using the foil. If using the foil alone without the liner, grease it for ease in removal, or it will stick to the bottom of the pan.

PREBAKING FLAKY PIE CRUST (BLIND BAKING)

Flaky pie crust must be weighted if baked without a filling, or the bottom puffs (especially if baking powder is used in the dough) and the sides slip down. Parchment or a coffee filter and rice or beans are best, as they do not compact the pastry or prevent it from breathing.  With foil and pie weights, the dough can end up cardboard-y in texture. The rice or dried beans can be reused many times. *Preheat the oven to 425°F. at least 20 minutes before baking.* A high temperature helps to set the crimped border before the fat in the crust starts to melt and soften.

For a large pastry shell, line the dough with parchment, pleating it as necessary to fit the shape of the pan. Cup-shaped coffee filters are even easier to use and don't stick to the dough. Large filters, the kind used for coffee urns, available through commercial equipment outlets, work perfectly for pies and tarts. Small ones, the kind sold in supermarkets, are ideal for tartlets.

Prebaking Flaky Pie Crust (cont.)

Fill the filter or parchment with rice or dried beans, making sure they are pushed up well against sides of the filter or parchment. Place it in the oven and bake for 20 minutes. Lift out the parchment or filter with the rice or beans and prick the crust all over with the tines of a fork—but only halfway through if the filling will be sticky or runny. Return the shell to the oven for 5 to 10 minutes more or until pale golden brown (or 5 minutes for a partially prebaked crust). Check after 3 minutes and prick again if the upper layer of dough has bubbled up.

BAKING TIMES FOR PREBAKED TARTLETS AND SMALL FLAN RINGS
Bake small (3- to 4-inch tartlets or flan rings) for 10 minutes at 400°F. Remove the parchment and rice or beans, prick well with a fork, and continue baking for about 3 to 5 minutes or until pale golden brown.

Bake tiny (1-inch) tartlets for about 10 minutes or until pale golden brown. Pricking is necessary only if baking powder was used in the dough. Unmold as soon as they are removed from the oven and cool on a rack.

MAKING A FOIL RING

Tear off a piece of heavy-duty foil a few inches larger than the diameter of the pie or tart pan. As a guide, use a pot lid or cardboard circle and a pencil to mark a cutout in the center that will expose the pie's surface but not the decorative edge. With scissors, cut out the circle. Leaving at least a 3-inch border, cut around the outside to form a ring. Shape it so that it will curve over the rim of the pie crust. This ring can be rinsed and reused several times. Disposable rings are available in baking stores (see page 665).

To protect the crimped edges of the crust, cover them with the foil ring after the first 15 minutes of baking (or after the first 30 minutes for a double-crust pie, as they are thicker) even if they are not overbrowning; they will continue to brown, though more slowly, beneath the foil. For very long baking pies, if the top crust becomes too brown, cover it loosely with a sheet of foil and make a vent in the center to keep the crust from steaming.

BAKING PIES FROM FROZEN

Preheat the oven to 425°. Bake for 10 minutes and then lower the temperature to 400°F. Continue baking for 25 to 35 minutes more than the specified time for a pie with 1 to 4 cups of filling, 35 to 45 minutes more than the specified time for a pie with 8 cups of filling. (Times depend on freezer temperature and will vary.)

MESSING UP

A fruit pie thickened with cornstarch must be bubbling thickly all over in order for the cornstarch to swell and do its work. (The temperature at this point will be 212°F.) If the pie has not been baked long enough and after cooling is runny, all is not lost. Spoon or pour out the juices into a saucepan (or a heatproof glass measure if using a microwave oven) and heat them until bubbling and thickened. Pour them back into the pie and let them set for about 10 minutes before serving.

MOISTURE-PROOFING THE BAKED BOTTOM CRUST

EGG WHITE GLAZE   The most effective way to moisture-proof a baked bottom crust is to brush it with a thin coating of egg white. (The yolk would toughen the dough.) The residual heat of the baked crust causes the egg white to dry to a crisp finish. Allow the baked pastry shell to cool on a rack for about 3 minutes before brushing it with lightly beaten egg white so that it isn't too hot, which would cause the egg white layer to flake off. If the baked pastry shell is no longer hot enough to set the egg white, return it to the oven for 2 to 3 minutes or until the egg white layer is dry and opaque. Half an egg white (1 tablespoon) will be enough to moisture-proof a 9-inch pie shell or 9½-inch tart shell.

FRUIT PRESERVES GLAZE   Sieved apricot or seedless raspberry preserves are another effective moisture-proofer for bottom crusts and they also provide extra flavor. You will need 2 tablespoons for a 9-inch pie shell, 3 tablespoons for a 9½-inch tart shell. For raspberry preserves: Bring them to a boil and pass them through a strainer. To thicken apricot preserves for brushing on pie crust: Put the contents of three 12-ounce jars in a food processor fitted with the metal blades and process for a few seconds to break up any solid pieces. Then place the preserves in a 4-cup heatproof glass measure in the microwave and bring them to a boil. Or place preserves in a saucepan and bring to a boil over medium heat, stirring constantly. Strain them, discarding the residue in the strainer. Return them to the measure (there should be about 2¾ cups) and microwave for about 10 minutes or until boiled down to 2½ cups (on cooling, it will settle down to 2¼ cups). Or return the strained preserves to the saucepan and boil down, over medium-low heat, stirring often, until reduced to 2½ cups. The glaze will take on a deep orange color and a texture that is considerably thicker than the preserves but still has flow. If necessary, reheat the glaze just to make it fluid. A product called Apricoture (page 638) requires no heating or straining and has very low moisture, making it ideal for professionals or those who do a lot of pie baking.

CHOCOLATE GLAZE   When compatible with the filling, chocolate creates the most effective moisture-proof glaze of all. Melt or quick-temper the chocolate (see page 615) and brush it onto the bottom and sides of the baked pie or tart shell. Very little is needed, as just a very thin coat is desirable. Couverture chocolate, with its higher amount of cocoa butter, is ideal, as it creates the thinnest coating. You will need only 2 ounces of chocolate for a 10- by 2-inch-high tart. Allow it to sit until set (it will dull) or refrigerate it briefly.

White chocolate also works perfectly as a moisture-proof glaze, but it adds sweetness. Melted cocoa butter, which is the same as white chocolate minus the milk solids and sugar, is the most neutral of chocolate glazes. Clarified butter, at room temperature, also works, because all the moisture has been removed from it.

GLAZE FOR THE TOP CRUST   Although a glaze applied to the top of pie dough can make it look shiny and very appealing, I find that it produces a tough crust, probably because the glaze seals in moisture and prevents the crust from breathing. A light sprinkling of sugar is the one exception. It gives the top crust shine and a delightful crunch, especially when applied on the border of a tart crust, which has less fruit beneath it to make it moist and soft. To help the sugar adhere to the crust, first brush the crust or border all over very lightly with milk.

The one time I do use an egg glaze is for lattice crusts, as they look so pretty and the small strips seem less susceptible to toughening. For the shiniest egg glaze, use 1 egg yolk lightly beaten with 1 teaspoon of heavy cream. Brush it onto the unbaked dough shortly before baking. This mixture not only freezes well for months, but also thickens a little on freezing, making it far easier to apply. Milk or water can be substituted for the cream but will produce a paler, less shiny glaze.

STORING BAKED PIES AND TARTS

For open-faced pies, cover the filling loosely with waxed paper. For pies with a lattice-top crust, cover only the cut openings on the two sides with plastic wrap.

Custard pies must be stored refrigerated. As they easily absorb other odors, but cannot be covered with plastic wrap without marring the surface, I store them under a large inverted bowl.

Meringue pies cannot be covered without damaging the meringue topping. Because the meringue itself contains a large amount of moisture that, if covered, would soften the crust, it is best to store meringue pies uncovered, either at room temperature or refrigerated.

TO FREEZE   Pies that have a top crust, or tarts with a firm topping, can be wrapped before freezing. Other pies or tarts should be frozen solid (about 3 hours in the freezer) before wrapping. Use Saran plastic wrap, which is airtight, to wrap the pie or tart. Then slip it into a reclosable 2-gallon freezer bag, expelling as much air as possible before sealing it. (Pies with meringue toppings should not be frozen.)

TESTING FOR DONENESS

Bottom pie crusts often seem tough because of underbaking. As long as there is water still remaining in the crust, it is not done. The water comes from both the liquid component and from what is contained in the butter. The crust may start to brown on the surface but still be unbaked on the inside. Water boils and starts to evaporate at 212°F. When the pie crust is not fully done, you can still hear the water bubbling inside it. It is difficult to take the temperature of a thin pie crust, but it is useful when working with puff pastry, as it is always difficult to tell if the inside is done. To take the temperature, insert an instant-read thermometer into the center of the pastry. If it is less than 212°F., continue baking.

BASIC FLAKY PIE CRUST

This pie crust is light, flaky, tender, and very crisp. It has a glorious butter flavor and is an ideal container for any pie or tart recipe. I strongly recommend commercial or homemade pastry flour (see page 7), as it will result in a more tender crust than one made with all-purpose flour.

PASTRY FOR A 9-INCH PIE SHELL,
A 9½- TO 10- BY 1-INCH TART SHELL,   **#1**
OR ABOUT 3 DOZEN 1-INCH TARTLETS   **MAKES: 12 OUNCES/340 GRAMS**

INGREDIENTS	MEASURE	WEIGHT	
	VOLUME	OUNCES	GRAMS
unsalted butter, cold	8 tablespoons	4 ounces	113 grams
pastry flour or bleached all-purpose flour	1⅓ cups + 4 teaspoons 1⅓ cups (dip and sweep method)	6.5 ounces	184 grams
salt*	¼ teaspoon	•	•
optional: baking powder (if not using, double the salt)	⅛ teaspoon	•	•
ice water	2½ to 3½ tablespoons	1.3 to 1.7 ounces	37 to 52 grams
cider vinegar	1½ teaspoons	0.25 ounce	7 grams

PASTRY FOR A 9-INCH LATTICE PIE,
A 9-INCH DEEP-DISH PIE, A 10-INCH PIE SHELL,   **#2**
OR A 12- TO 14-INCH FREE-FORM TART   **MAKES: 13.6 OUNCES/390 GRAMS**

INGREDIENTS	MEASURE	WEIGHT	
	VOLUME	OUNCES	GRAMS
unsalted butter, cold	9 tablespoons	4.5 ounces	128 grams
pastry flour or bleached all-purpose flour	1½ cups + 1½ tablespoons 1½ cups (dip and sweep method)	7.5 ounces	214 grams
salt*	¼ teaspoon	•	•
optional: baking powder (if not using, double the salt)	⅛ teaspoon	•	•
ice water	3½ to 4½ tablespoons	1.75 to 2.3 ounces	52 to 66 grams
cider vinegar	1½ teaspoons	0.25 ounce	7 grams

* For savory recipes, use 1¼ times the salt.

INGREDIENTS	MEASURE	WEIGHT	
	VOLUME	OUNCES	GRAMS
unsalted butter, cold	14 tablespoons	7 ounces	200 grams
pastry flour or bleached all-purpose flour	2¼ cups + 2 tablespoons 2¼ cups (dip and sweep method)	11.25 ounces	320 grams
salt*	¼ + ⅛ teaspoon	•	•
optional: baking powder (if not using, double the salt)	¼ teaspoon	•	•
ice water	5 to 7 tablespoons	2.6 to 3.6 ounces	74 to 103 grams
cider vinegar	1 tablespoon	0.5 ounce	14 grams

*For savory recipes, use 1½ times the salt.

Divide the butter into two parts, about two thirds to one third:

FOR #1, 2.5 ounces and 1.5 ounces (5 tablespoons and 3 tablespoons)
FOR #2, 3 ounces and 1.5 ounces (6 tablespoons and 3 tablespoons)
FOR #3, 4.5 ounces and 2.5 ounces (9 tablespoons and 5 tablespoons)

Cut the butter into ¾-inch cubes. Wrap each portion of butter with plastic wrap. Refrigerate the larger amount and freeze the smaller for at least 30 minutes. Place the flour, salt, and optional baking powder in a reclosable gallon-size freezer bag and freeze for at least 30 minutes.

FOOD PROCESSOR METHOD
Place the flour mixture in a food processor with the metal blade and process for a few seconds to combine. Set the bag aside.

Add the larger amount of butter cubes to the flour and process for about 20 seconds or until the mixture resembles coarse meal. Add the remaining frozen butter cubes and pulse until all of the frozen butter is the size of peas. (Toss with a fork to see it better.)

Add the lowest amount of the ice water and the vinegar and pulse 6 times. Pinch a small amount of the mixture together between your fingers. If it does not hold together, add half the remaining water and pulse 3 times. Try pinching the mixture again. If necessary, add the remaining water, pulsing 3 times to incorporate it. The mixture will be in particles and will not hold together without being pinched.

For tiny 1-inch tartlets, omit the baking powder and allow the processing to continue just until a ball forms. The additional mixing produces a dough that is slightly less flaky but ensures that it will not puff out of shape in the tiny molds.

Spoon the mixture into the plastic bag. (For a double-crust pie, it is easiest to divide the mixture in half at this point.)

Holding both ends of the bag opening with your fingers, knead the mixture by alternately pressing it, from the outside of the bag, with the knuckles and heels of your hands until the mixture holds together in one piece and feels slightly stretchy when pulled.

Wrap the dough with plastic wrap, flatten it into a disc (or discs) and refrigerate for at least 45 minutes, preferably overnight. (For a pie shell and lattice, divide it in a ratio of two thirds : one third—use about 9.5 ounces for the shell and the rest for the lattice, flattening the smaller part into a rectangle.)

HAND METHOD

Place a medium mixing bowl in the freezer to chill.

Place the flour, salt, and optional baking powder in another medium bowl and whisk to combine them. Use a pastry cutter or rub the mixture between your fingers to blend the larger portion of the butter into the flour until it resembles coarse meal.

Spoon the mixture, together with the cold butter, into a reclosable gallon-size freezer bag. Expel any air from the bag and close it. Use a rolling pin to flatten the butter into flakes. Place the bag in the freezer for at least 10 minutes or until the butter is very firm.

Transfer the mixture to the chilled bowl, scraping the sides of the bag. Set the bag aside. Sprinkle the ice water and vinegar onto the mixture, tossing it lightly with a rubber spatula. Spoon the loose mixture back into the plastic bag. (For a double-crust pie, it is easiest to divide the mixture in half at this point.)

Holding both ends of the bag opening with your fingers, knead the mixture by alternately pressing it, from the outside of the bag, with the knuckles and heels of your hands until the mixture holds together in one piece and feels slightly stretchy when pulled.

Wrap the dough with plastic wrap, flatten it into a disc (or discs) and refrigerate for at least 45 minutes, preferably overnight. (For a pie shell and lattice, divide it in a ratio of two thirds : one third—use about 9.5 ounces for the shell and the rest for the lattice, flattening the smaller part into a rectangle.)

VARIATIONS

WHOLE WHEAT FLAKY PIE CRUST   Use two thirds all-purpose flour and one third whole wheat pastry flour or whole wheat flour.

SOUR CREAM FLAKY PIE CRUST   This crust produces a lighter texture and a more buttery flavor than the basic flaky pie crust. You are never in doubt as to how much water to add, because the sour cream provides just the right amount of liquid. Simply replace the water/vinegar (use the full amount of water, not the smaller amount) with an equal measure of sour cream. Replacing the liquid with sour cream is what gives this crust exceptional lightness and tenderness because the sour cream contains milk solids, butterfat, and acidity. The milk solids help to blend the ingredients more smoothly; the extra butter contributes more tenderness; and the acidity relaxes the gluten, making the dough less elastic, easier to roll, and less prone to shrinking during baking.

SWEET CREAM FLAKY PIE CRUST   This has the purest, most buttery flavor of any crust and the most tenderness, because of all liquid dairy products, cream contains the least water and the most fats, giving it a total fat content (depending on the percentage of butterfat in the cream, which varies by brand) close to the cream cheese crust. It holds together well for rolling despite its tenderness. Use all-purpose bleached flour, not pastry flour, which would not be strong enough. Replace the water and vinegar with 5 tablespoons/2.5 ounces/72 grams of heavy cream for #1, 5 tablespoons plus 2 teaspoons/approximately 2.75 ounces/82 grams of heavy cream for #2, and 9 tablespoons/approximately 4.5 ounces/126 grams heavy cream for #3. (Use tablespoon measures rather than converting to liquid cup measures, as the cups vary according to brand.)

BUTTERMILK FLAKY PIE CRUST   This is a light, flaky, and tender crust. There is no distinctive taste from the buttermilk; its value is as a tenderizer. Replace the water and vinegar with an equal amount of buttermilk.

YOGURT FLAKY PIE CRUST   This is an exceptionally tender and very flaky crust, with a slight tang but a less buttery taste. Replace the water and vinegar with an equal amount of yogurt.

HERB FLAKY PIE CRUST   Use 1 tablespoon of fresh thyme, finely chopped, or 1 teaspoon dried, for a 1⅓ cups flour formula. This can be added to any of the doughs in this chapter.

STORE
Refrigerated, up to 2 days; frozen, up to 3 months.

UNDERSTANDING
Pastry flour (see page 7) offers the most tenderness while maintaining flakiness, but it is the addition of vinegar that relaxes the dough without losing flakiness, making it easier to roll, shrink less, and be even more tender. The baking powder lifts and aerates the dough slightly without weakening it, but it makes it seem more tender.

The secret to success is finely incorporating about two thirds of the butter into the flour, which keeps the flour from absorbing too much water and forming gluten, which would make the crust tough. The remaining one third of the butter is incorporated in larger pieces, which serve to separate the layers, resulting in the desired flakiness. This pie crust does not shrink or distort as much as the standard all-butter crust because there is less gluten development.

If, when adding the water, you find you need more than indicated in the recipe, chances are you haven't moisture-proofed the flour adequately (you haven't used the correct amount of butter or processed it fine enough), leaving the flour free to absorb more liquid. The resulting crust will be flakier but less tender.

If you find you need less water than specified in the recipe, chances are you divided the butter incorrectly and used too much of it to moisture-proof the flour, preventing it from absorbing an adequate amount of water. The resulting crust will be more tender but not very flaky.

Flattening the newly formed dough into a disc or discs before refrigerating makes it easier to roll without cracking. The dough is refrigerated to relax the gluten, making it less elastic and easier to roll. Chilling also firms the butter, preventing sticking and the need for extra flour when rolling, which would toughen it. Dough that has rested overnight before baking shrinks less.

DELUXE FLAKY PIE CRUST

This is the ultimate all-butter pie crust. It has all of the virtues of the Basic Flaky Pie Crust (page 22), also using all butter, but it is even more flaky because all of the butter is left in large pieces. The miracle of this crust is that despite its flakiness, it is just as tender as the Basic Flaky Pie Crust—but only if the correct flour is used. It doesn't hold its shape as well as the Basic Flaky Pie Crust, despite the addition of vinegar, but the extraordinary flakiness makes it worth it.

**PASTRY FOR A 9-INCH PIE SHELL OR
A 9½- TO 10- BY 1-INCH TART SHELL**   MAKES: 12.5 OUNCES/359 GRAMS

INGREDIENTS	MEASURE	WEIGHT	
	VOLUME	OUNCES	GRAMS
unsalted butter, cold	8 tablespoons	4 ounces	113 grams
pastry flour or Wondra flour*	1⅓ cups + 4 teaspoons (dip and sweep method) 1½ cups (lightly spooned)	6.5 ounces	184 grams
salt†	¼ teaspoon	•	•
optional: baking powder (if not using, double the salt)	⅛ teaspoon	•	•
ice water	4½ tablespoons	2.3 ounces	66 grams
cider vinegar	1½ teaspoons	0.25 ounce	7 grams

*Whole wheat pastry flour also works well. The Wondra flour is not quite as tender as pastry flour.
†For savory recipes, use 1½ times the salt.

**PASTRY FOR A 9-INCH LATTICE PIE,
A 9-INCH DEEP-DISH PIE,
A 10-INCH PIE SHELL,
OR A 12- TO 14-INCH FREE-FORM TART**   MAKES: 14.25 OUNCES/404 GRAMS

INGREDIENTS	MEASURE	WEIGHT	
	VOLUME	OUNCES	GRAMS
unsalted butter, cold	9 tablespoons	4.5 ounces	128 grams
pastry flour or Wondra flour*	1½ cups + 1½ tablespoons (dip and sweep method) 1¾ cups (lightly spooned)	7.5 ounces	214 grams
salt†	¼ teaspoon	•	3.3 grams
optional: baking powder (if not using, double the salt)	⅛ teaspoon	•	•
ice water	5 tablespoons	2.6 ounces	75 grams
cider vinegar	1½ teaspoons	0.25 ounce	7 grams

PASTRY FOR A TWO-CRUST 9-INCH PIE   MAKES: 21.7 OUNCES/620 GRAMS

INGREDIENTS	MEASURE	WEIGHT	
	VOLUME	OUNCES	GRAMS
unsalted butter, cold	14 tablespoons	7 ounces	200 grams
pastry flour or Wondra flour*	2¼ cups + 2 tablespoons (dip and sweep method) 2½ cups + 4 teaspoons (lightly spooned)	11.25 ounces	320 grams
salt†	¼ + ⅛ teaspoon	•	5 grams
optional: baking powder (if not using, double the salt)	¼ teaspoon	•	•
ice water	7½ tablespoons	4 ounces	110 grams
cider vinegar	1 tablespoon	0.5 ounce	14 grams

*Whole wheat pastry flour also works well. The Wondra flour is not quite as tender as pastry flour.
†For savory recipes, use 1½ times the salt.

FOOD PROCESSOR METHOD

Cut the butter into small (about ¾-inch) cubes. Wrap it in plastic wrap and freeze it until frozen solid, at least 30 minutes. Place the flour, salt, and optional baking powder in a reclosable gallon-size freezer bag and freeze it for at least 30 minutes.

Place the flour mixture in a food processor with the metal blade and process for a few seconds to combine. Set the bag aside.

Add the frozen butter and pulse until the butter becomes the size of small lima beans. (Toss with a fork to see it better.) Add the ice water and vinegar and pulse until most of the butter is the size of large peas, with some slightly larger. Spoon the mixture into the plastic bag. (For a two-crust pie, it is easiest to divide the mixture in half at this point.)

Holding both ends of the bag opening with your fingers, knead the mixture by alternately pressing it, from the outside of the bag, with the knuckles and heels of your hands until the mixture holds together in one piece and feels slightly stretchy when pulled. This dough will be very flaky, but if you adore flakiness, fold the dough in thirds like a business letter between two sheets of plastic wrap or on a pastry cloth with a rolling pin sleeve; chill briefly, well covered, if the dough begins to soften.

Wrap the dough with plastic wrap, flatten it into a disc (or discs), and refrigerate for at least 45 minutes, preferably overnight. (For a pie shell and lattice, divide it in a ratio of two thirds : one third—use about 9.5 ounces for the shell and the rest for the lattice, flattening the smaller part into a rectangle.)

HAND METHOD

Place a medium mixing bowl in the freezer to chill.

Cut the butter into small (about ¾-inch) cubes. Wrap it in plastic wrap and refrigerate it for at least 30 minutes.

Place the flour, salt, and optional baking powder in a reclosable gallon-size freezer bag and whisk to combine. Add the butter cubes, expel any air, and close the bag. Use a rolling pin to flatten the butter into large thin flakes. Place the bag in the freezer for at least 10 minutes or until very firm.

Empty the mixture into the chilled bowl, using a rubber spatula to scrape the dough from the sides of the bag. Set the bag aside. Sprinkle the mixture with the water and vinegar, tossing lightly with a rubber spatula. There will be mostly big loose crumbs but there will still be a little dry flour.

Holding both ends of the bag opening with your fingers, knead the mixture by alternately pressing it, from the outside of the bag, with the knuckles and heels of your hands until the mixture holds together in one piece and feels slightly stretchy when pulled. This dough will be very flaky, but if you adore flakiness, fold the dough in thirds like a business letter between two sheets of plastic wrap or on a pastry cloth with a rolling pin sleeve; chill briefly, well covered, if the dough begins to soften.

Wrap the dough with plastic wrap, flatten it into a disc (or discs), and refrigerate for at least 45 minutes, preferably overnight. (For a pie shell and lattice, divide it in a ratio of two thirds : one third—use about 9.5 ounces for the shell and the rest for the lattice, flattening the smaller part into a rectangle.)

STORE

Refrigerated, up to 2 days; frozen, up to 3 months.

FLAKY CREAM CHEESE PIE CRUST

This is my favorite pie crust. It took several years and over fifty tries to get it just right and is the soul of this book. It is unlike any other cream cheese pie crust because, in addition to being tender, it is also flaky. In fact, it is very similar in texture to Basic Flaky Pie Crust—almost as flaky but a little softer and more tender, and it browns more when baked, resulting in a rich golden color. The addition of cream cheese makes it even easier to prepare than basic flaky pie crust because you never have to guess at how much water to add, and it gives it a flavor so delicious it is great to eat just by itself without filling! It is well worth purchasing or making pastry flour (see page 7), as it will result in a more tender crust.

PASTRY FOR A 9-INCH PIE SHELL
OR A 9½- OR 10- BY 1-INCH TART SHELL   MAKES: 11 OUNCES/312 GRAMS

INGREDIENTS	MEASURE	WEIGHT	
	VOLUME	OUNCES	GRAMS
unsalted butter, cold	6 tablespoons	3 ounces	85 grams
pastry flour or bleached all-purpose flour	1 cup + 1 tablespoon 1 cup (dip and sweep method)	5 ounces	142 grams
salt*	⅛ teaspoon	•	•
baking powder	⅛ teaspoon	•	•
cream cheese, cold	¼ cup	2.25 ounces	64 grams
ice water	1 tablespoon	0.5 ounce	14 grams
cider vinegar	1½ teaspoons	0.25 ounce	7 grams

*For savory recipes, use 1½ times the salt.

PASTRY FOR A 9-INCH LATTICE PIE,
A 9-INCH DEEP-DISH PIE,
A 10-INCH PIE SHELL,
OR A 12- TO 14-INCH FREE-FORM TART   MAKES: 14.3 OUNCES/406 GRAMS

INGREDIENTS	MEASURE	WEIGHT	
	VOLUME	OUNCES	GRAMS
unsalted butter, cold	8 tablespoons	4 ounces	113 grams
pastry flour or bleached all-purpose flour	1⅓ cups + 4 teaspoons 1⅓ cups (dip and sweep method)	6.5 ounces	184 grams
salt*	⅛ teaspoon	•	•
baking powder	⅛ teaspoon	•	•
cream cheese, cold	one 3-ounce package	3 ounces	85 grams
ice water	1½ tablespoons	0.75 ounce	21 grams
cider vinegar	1½ teaspoons	0.25 ounce	7 grams

PASTRY FOR A TWO-CRUST 9-INCH PIE   MAKES: 22 OUNCES/624 GRAMS

INGREDIENTS	MEASURE	WEIGHT	
	VOLUME	OUNCES	GRAMS
unsalted butter, cold	12 tablespoons	6 ounces	170 grams
pastry flour or bleached all-purpose flour	2 cups + 3 tablespoons 2 cups (dip and sweep method)	10 ounces	284 grams
salt*	¼ teaspoon	•	•
baking powder	¼ teaspoon	•	•
cream cheese, cold	1½ 3-ounce packages	4.5 ounces	128 grams
ice water	2 tablespoons	1 ounce	28 grams
cider vinegar	1 tablespoon	0.5 ounce	14 grams

*For savory recipes, use 1½ times the salt.

FOOD PROCESSOR METHOD

Cut the butter into small (about ¾-inch) cubes. Wrap it in plastic wrap and freeze it until frozen solid, at least 30 minutes. Place the flour, salt, and baking powder in a reclosable gallon-size freezer bag and freeze for at least 30 minutes.

Place the flour mixture in a food processor with the metal blade and process for a few seconds to combine. Set the bag aside.

Cut the cream cheese into 3 or 4 pieces and add it to the flour. Process for about 20 seconds or until the mixture resembles coarse meal. Add the frozen butter cubes and pulse until none of the butter is larger than the size of a pea. (Toss with a fork to see it better.) Remove the cover and add the water and vinegar. Pulse until most of the butter is reduced to the size of small peas. The mixture will be in particles and will not hold together. Spoon it into the plastic bag. (For a double-crust pie, it is easiest to divide the mixture in half at this point.)

Holding both ends of the bag opening with your fingers, knead the mixture by alternately pressing it, from the outside of the bag, with the knuckles and heels of your hands until the mixture holds together in one piece and feels slightly stretchy when pulled.

Wrap the dough with plastic wrap, flatten it into a disc (or discs), and refrigerate for at least 45 minutes, preferably overnight. (For a pie shell and lattice, divide it in a ratio of two thirds : one third—use about 9.5 ounces for the shell and the rest for the lattice, flattening the smaller part into a rectangle.)

HAND METHOD
Place a medium mixing bowl in the freezer to chill.

Cut the butter into small (about ¾-inch) cubes. Wrap it in plastic wrap and refrigerate it for at least 30 minutes.

Place the flour, salt, and baking powder in a medium bowl and whisk to combine. Add the cream cheese and rub the mixture between your fingers to blend the cream cheese into the flour until it resembles coarse meal. Spoon the mixture, together with the cold butter, into a reclosable gallon-size freezer bag. Expel any air from the bag and close it. Use a rolling pin to flatten the butter into thin flakes. Place the bag in the freezer for at least 10 minutes or until the butter is very firm.

Transfer the mixture to the chilled bowl, scraping the sides of the bag. Set the bag aside. Sprinkle the mixture with the water and vinegar, tossing lightly with a rubber spatula. Spoon it into the plastic bag. (For a two-crust pie, it is easiest to divide the mixture in half at this point.)

Holding both ends of the bag opening with your fingers, knead the mixture by alternately pressing it, from the outside of the bag, with the knuckles and heels of your hands until the mixture holds together in one piece and feels slightly stretchy when pulled.

Wrap the dough with plastic wrap, flatten it into a disc (or discs), and refrigerate for at least 45 minutes, preferably overnight. (For a pie shell and lattice, divide it in a ratio of two thirds : one third—use about 9.5 ounces for the shell and the rest for the lattice, flattening the smaller part into a rectangle.)

VARIATION
MASCARPONE CHEESE CRUST   An equal weight of mascarpone cheese can be substituted for the cream cheese, but omit the vinegar and use bleached all-purpose flour, not pastry flour, or the crust will be too tender.

STORE
Refrigerated, up to 2 days; frozen, up to 3 months.

UNDERSTANDING

A classic cream cheese crust contains no water and is more tender than an all-butter crust but not at all flaky. I have found it to be so tender it is impossible to use for a lattice top and the bottom crust often develops cracks through which a filling will leak and stick to the bottom of the pan. Very little water is needed, because the cream cheese contains 51 percent water. The addition of a small amount of water connects the two gluten-forming proteins in the flour, producing the rubbery, stretchy gluten that strengthens the structure just enough to prevent cracking when the crust bakes. This pie crust does not shrink or distort as much as an all-butter crust because there is less development of gluten. The acidity of the vinegar weakens the gluten that forms, making the crust still more tender and less likely to shrink. If desired, it can be replaced with water.

Cream cheese is 51 percent water and 37.7 percent fat, so 3 ounces contain 1.53 ounces (about 3 tablespoons) of water and 1.13 ounces of fat. That means that the pie crust with 6.5 ounces of flour contains the equivalent of about 4½ tablespoons of water. Compared to the all-butter crust, this crust has about 1 tablespoon more water, 1.13 ounces more fat, and 0.34 ounce more milk solids. The extra fat in the cream cheese coats some of the proteins in the flour, limiting the development of gluten, which would make it tougher. The milk solids add both flavor and smoothness of texture.

The baking powder lifts and aerates the dough slightly without weakening it, but it also makes it seem more tender.

In developing this recipe, I found that if not using the vinegar and baking powder to tenderize the crust, it is advisable to add one quarter of the butter together with the cream cheese when using all-purpose flour. This helps to moisture-proof it but, of course, takes away a little from the flakiness, as there is less butter available to add in larger pieces to create the layers.

FLAKY WHOLE WHEAT CREAM CHEESE PIE CRUST

This variation, ideal for savory pies, possesses all of the virtues of Flaky Cream Cheese Pie Crust (page 29), enhanced by the wheaty flavor and slight crunch of whole wheat flour. Because the addition of whole wheat flour makes the dough a little more tender, be sure to knead it a little more, until you can feel a stretchy quality when you pull it.

If using this crust with a sweet filling (not my preference), use two thirds the salt.

**PASTRY FOR A 9-INCH PIE SHELL
OR A 9½- TO 10-INCH BY 1-INCH TART SHELL**   MAKES: 11 OUNCES/312 GRAMS

INGREDIENTS	MEASURE	WEIGHT	
	VOLUME	OUNCES	GRAMS
unsalted butter, cold	6 tablespoons	3 ounces	85 grams
bleached all-purpose flour	⅔ cup (dip and sweep method)	3.25 ounces	92 grams
whole wheat flour, preferably stone-ground	⅓ cup (dip and sweep method)	1.7 ounces	48 grams
salt	⅛ teaspoon + a pinch	•	•
optional: baking powder (if not using, double the salt)	⅛ teaspoon	•	•
cream cheese, cold	¼ cup	2.25 ounces	64 grams
ice water	1 tablespoon	0.5 ounce	14 grams
cider vinegar	1½ teaspoons	0.25 ounce	7 grams

**PASTRY FOR A 9-INCH LATTICE PIE,
A 9-INCH DEEP-DISH PIE, A 10-INCH PIE SHELL,
OR A 12- TO 14-INCH FREE-FORM TART**   MAKES: 14.3 OUNCES/406 GRAMS

INGREDIENTS	MEASURE	WEIGHT	
	VOLUME	OUNCES	GRAMS
unsalted butter, cold	8 tablespoons	4 ounces	113 grams
bleached all-purpose flour*	¾ cup + 2 tablespoons (dip and sweep method)	4.25 ounces	121 grams
whole wheat flour, preferably stone-ground	⅓ cup	2.25 ounces	63 grams
salt	⅛ teaspoon + a pinch	•	•
optional: baking powder (if not using, double the salt)	⅛ teaspoon	•	•
cream cheese, cold	one 3-ounce package	3 ounces	85 grams
ice water	1½ tablespoons	0.75 ounce	21 grams
cider vinegar	1½ teaspoons	0.25 ounce	7 grams

*For this amount of dough, the volume does not lend itself to dividing exactly ⅔ : ⅓ with standard measuring cups. I have divided the weights ⅔ : ⅓, but the volume of whole wheat flour to all-purpose is slightly less.

PASTRY FOR A TWO-CRUST 9-INCH PIE   MAKES: 22 OUNCES/624 GRAMS

INGREDIENTS	MEASURE	WEIGHT	
	VOLUME	OUNCES	GRAMS
unsalted butter, cold	12 tablespoons	6 ounces	170 grams
bleached all-purpose flour	1⅓ cups (dip and sweep method)	6.5 ounces	184 grams
whole wheat flour, preferably stone-ground	⅔ cup	3.3 ounces	96 grams
salt	¼ + ⅛ teaspoon	•	•
optional: baking powder (if not using, double the salt)	¼ teaspoon	•	•
cream cheese, cold	1½ 3-ounce packages	4.5 ounces	128 grams
ice water	2 tablespoons	1 ounce	28 grams
cider vinegar	1 tablespoon	0.5 ounce	14 grams

FOOD PROCESSOR METHOD

Cut the butter into small (about ¾-inch) cubes. Wrap it in plastic wrap and freeze it for at least 30 minutes. Place the all-purpose flour in a reclosable gallon-size freezer bag and freeze it for at least 30 minutes.

In a food processor with the metal blade, process the whole wheat flour with the salt and optional baking powder for about 5 minutes to break up the bran and the germ. Add the all-purpose flour and process for a few seconds to blend. Set the bag aside.

Cut the cream cheese into 3 or 4 pieces and add it to the flour. Process for about 20 seconds or until the mixture resembles coarse meal. Add the frozen butter cubes and pulse until none of the butter is larger than the size of a pea. (Toss with a fork to see it better.) Remove the cover and add the water and vinegar. Pulse until most of the butter is reduced to the size of small peas. The mixture will be in particles and will not hold together. Spoon the mixture into the plastic bag. (For a double-crust pie, it is easiest to divide the mixture in half at this point.)

Holding both ends of the bag opening with your fingers, knead the mixture by alternately pressing it, from outside of the bag, with the knuckles and heels of your hands until the mixture holds together in one piece and feels slightly stretchy when pulled. To prevent cracking, it is helpful to fold the dough in thirds like a business letter. If the dough becomes soft and sticky, refrigerate it for 5 to 10 minutes. (This dough is a little more tender than the cream cheese dough, using all white flour, so be sure to do the turns or knead a little extra till you can feel the stretch when you pull it.)

Wrap the dough with plastic wrap, flatten it into a disc (or discs), and refrigerate for at least 45 minutes, preferably overnight. (For a pie shell and lattice, divide it in a ratio of two thirds : one third—use about 9.5 ounces for the shell and the rest for the lattice, flattening the smaller part into a rectangle.)

HAND METHOD

Place a medium mixing bowl in the freezer to chill.

Cut the butter into small (about ¾-inch) cubes. Wrap it in plastic wrap and refrigerate it for at least 30 minutes.

Place the flours, salt, and optional baking powder in a medium bowl and whisk to combine. Add the cream cheese and rub the mixture between your fingers to blend the cream cheese into the flour until it resembles coarse meal. Place the mixture, together with the cold butter, in a reclosable gallon-size freezer bag. Expel any air from the bag and close it. Use a rolling pin to flatten the butter into thin flakes. Place the bag in the freezer for at least 10 minutes or until the butter is very firm.

Transfer the mixture to the chilled bowl, scraping the sides of the bag. Set the bag aside. Sprinkle the mixture with the water and vinegar, tossing lightly with a rubber spatula. Spoon it into the plastic bag. (For a two-crust pie, it is easiest to divide the mixture in half at this point.)

Holding both ends of the bag opening with your fingers, knead the mixture by alternately pressing it, from outside of the bag, with the knuckles and heels of your hands until the mixture holds together in one piece and feels slightly stretchy when pulled. To prevent cracking, it is helpful to fold the dough in thirds like a business letter. If the dough becomes soft and sticky, refrigerate it for 5 to 10 minutes. (This dough is a little more tender than the cream cheese dough, using all white flour, so be sure to do the turns or knead a little extra till you can feel the stretch when you pull it.)

Wrap the dough with plastic wrap, flatten it into a disc (or discs), and refrigerate for at least 45 minutes, preferably overnight. (For a pie shell and lattice, divide it in a ratio of two thirds : one third—use about 9.5 ounces for the shell and the rest for the lattice, flattening the smaller part into a rectangle.)

STORE

Refrigerated, up to 2 days; frozen, up to 3 months.

UNDERSTANDING

The combination of all-purpose flour and whole wheat results in a very similar gluten content to that of pastry flour. Whole wheat flour contains a small amount of gluten-forming protein, which helps hold the crust together. Whole wheat pastry flour has less and is too weak to support this crust by itself.

FLAKY VEGETABLE SHORTENING PIE CRUST

I am of the opinion that the flavor of a butter crust is so superior to that of a vegetable shortening one as to render the shortening crust *almost* pointless. Yet vegetable shortening has several things to recommend it. It is easier to work with a dough made with vegetable shortening than one with all butter because the dough stays soft even after it has been refrigerated and does not soften excessively during rolling. Also, it always holds its shape during baking, protecting any decorative border. A shortening crust is a little less crisp than a butter crust, about as flaky, but more tender, and therefore gives the illusion of being "lighter." It browns a little faster than a butter crust.

FOOD PROCESSOR METHOD

Cut the shortening into small (about ¾-inch) cubes. (This is easiest to do if using the shortening sticks and chilling them first.) Wrap them with plastic wrap and freeze them for at least 30 minutes. Place the flour and salt in a reclosable gallon-size freezer bag and freeze for at least 30 minutes.

Place the flour mixture in a food processor with the metal blade and process for a few seconds to combine. Set the bag aside. Add the frozen shortening and pulse until the shortening is in pieces the size of small lima beans. (Toss with a fork to see it better.) Add the ice water and pulse until most of the shortening is the size of large peas, with some a little larger.

For small tartlets, allow the processing to continue just until a ball forms. The additional mixing produces a dough that is slightly less flaky and will not puff out of shape in the tiny molds.

Spoon the mixture into the plastic bag. (For a two-crust pie, it is easiest to divide the mixture in half at this point.)

Holding both ends of the bag opening with your fingers, knead the mixture by alternately pressing it, from the outside of the bag, with the knuckles and heels of your hands until the mixture holds together in one piece and feels slightly stretchy when pulled. This dough will be very flaky, but if you adore flakiness, fold the dough in thirds like a business letter between two sheets of plastic wrap or on a pastry cloth with a rolling pin sleeve; chill briefly, well covered, if the dough begins to soften.

Wrap the dough with plastic wrap, flatten it into a disc (or discs), and refrigerate for at least 45 minutes, preferably overnight. (For a pie shell and lattice, divide it in a ratio of two thirds : one third—use about 9.5 ounces for the shell and the rest for the lattice, flattening the smaller part into a rectangle.) (If you used solidly frozen shortening and worked quickly, you may be able to roll it out immediately, but be sure to rest the shell for at least an hour before baking to prevent shrinkage.)

PASTRY FOR A 9-INCH PIE SHELL MAKES: 12.5 OUNCES/356 GRAMS

INGREDIENTS	MEASURE	WEIGHT	
	VOLUME	OUNCES	GRAMS
solid vegetable shortening, cold	8 tablespoons	3.3 ounces	95 grams
bleached all-purpose flour	1⅓ cups (dip and sweep method)	6.5 ounces	184 grams
salt	½ teaspoon	•	•
ice water	5 tablespoons + 1 teaspoon	2.75 ounces	78 grams

PASTRY FOR A 9-INCH LATTICE PIE,
A 9-INCH DEEP-DISH PIE,
A 9½- TO 10- BY 1-INCH TART SHELL,
OR A 10-INCH PIE SHELL MAKES: 14 OUNCES/400 GRAMS

INGREDIENTS	MEASURE	WEIGHT	
	VOLUME	OUNCES	GRAMS
solid vegetable shortening, cold	9 tablespoons	3.75 ounces	107 grams
bleached all-purpose flour	1½ cups (dip and sweep method)	7.5 ounces	214 grams
salt	½ teaspoon	•	•
ice water	6 tablespoons	approx. 3 ounces	88 grams

PASTRY FOR A TWO-CRUST 9-INCH PIE MAKES: 22 OUNCES/623 GRAMS

INGREDIENTS	MEASURE	WEIGHT	
	VOLUME	OUNCES	GRAMS
solid vegetable shortening, cold	14 tablespoons	5.75 ounces	167 grams
bleached all-purpose flour	2¼ cups (dip and sweep method)	11.25 ounces	320 grams
salt	¾ teaspoon	•	•
ice water	9 tablespoons + 1 teaspoon	approx. 4.75 ounces	138 grams

HAND METHOD

Place a medium mixing bowl in the freezer to chill.

Cut the shortening into small (about ¾-inch) cubes. (This is easiest to do if using the shortening sticks and chilling them first.) Wrap them in plastic wrap and refrigerate them for at least 30 minutes.

Place the flour and salt in a reclosable gallon-size freezer bag and whisk to combine. Add the shortening cubes, expel any air, and close the bag. Use a rolling pin to press the shortening into the flour into large thin flakes. Place the bag in the freezer for at least 10 minutes or until very firm.

Empty the mixture into the cold bowl, using a rubber spatula to scrape the dough from the sides of the bag. Set the bag aside. Sprinkle the mixture with the water, tossing lightly with a rubber spatula. There will be mostly big loose clumps, but there will still be a little dry flour.

Holding both ends of the bag opening with your fingers, knead the mixture by alternately pressing it, from outside of the bag, with the knuckles and heels of your hands until the mixture holds together in one piece and feels slightly stretchy when pulled. This dough will be very flaky, but if you adore flakiness, fold the dough in thirds like a business letter between two sheets of plastic wrap or on a pastry cloth with a rolling pin sleeve; chill briefly, well covered, if the dough begins to soften.

Wrap the dough with plastic wrap, flatten it into a disc (or discs), and refrigerate for at least 45 minutes, preferably overnight. (For a pie shell and lattice, divide it in a ratio of two thirds : one third—use about 9.5 ounces for the shell and the rest for the lattice, flattening the smaller part into a rectangle.)

VARIATION

HALF-BUTTER, HALF-SHORTENING PIE CRUST   If you love the flavor of butter but want the advantage of shortening for a more attractively crimped edge, using half butter, half shortening (by volume) is a good compromise. Because the butter (which contains water) will make this crust less tender, replace 1½ teaspoons of the water with cider vinegar (1 tablespoon for the 2¼ cups flour formula).

I do not like the flavor of the butter-flavored shortening. I found the dough to have a bitter aftertaste when I tried it.

STORE

Refrigerated, up to 2 days; frozen, up to 3 months.

POINTERS FOR SUCCESS

∿ Flour well when rolling.

UNDERSTANDING

Shortening is 100 percent fat, butter is 80 percent fat; 1 cup shortening is 191 grams, 1 cup butter is 227 grams. To replace 8 tablespoons (1 stick) of butter with shortening and maintain the same fat content, as in the Basic Flaky Pie Crust, page 22, you would need only 7½ tablespoons. As this is an awkward amount to measure, I call for 8 tablespoons, which makes the dough slightly more tender. Using pastry flour would therefore make the dough too fragile. Replacing the butter with an equal weight of shortening would require using 9½ tablespoons of shortening, which would result in a flakier but harder to handle dough.

The Basic Flaky Pie Crust, using the same amount of flour, has the equivalent of 5 tablespoons plus ½ teaspoon of liquid, including what is contained in the butter. This shortening crust has ½ teaspoon more to compensate for the tenderizing effects of the extra fat.

FLAKY CHEDDAR CHEESE PIE CRUST

Crisper than a cream cheese crust, this crust is just as flaky and tender. The flavor of Cheddar is further enhanced by cayenne pepper, which stays in the background as a nice bite. This crust is so delicious, I bake the scraps to eat by themselves as snacks. This is the crust for a meatloaf (page 331) or the Roasted Red Pepper and Poblano Quiche (page 341).

PASTRY FOR A 9½- BY 1-INCH TART
OR A 9-INCH PIE   MAKES: 14.4 OUNCES/412 GRAMS

INGREDIENTS	MEASURE	WEIGHT	
	VOLUME	OUNCES	GRAMS
unsalted butter, cold	8 tablespoons	4 ounces	113 grams
bleached all-purpose flour*	1⅓ cups (dip and sweep method)	6.5 ounces	184 grams
salt	¼ + ⅛ teaspoon	•	•
optional: baking powder (if not using, double the salt)	⅛ teaspoon	•	•
cayenne pepper	¼ teaspoon	•	•
sharp Cheddar cheese, grated, cold	¾ cup, medium packed	3 ounces	85 grams
ice water	2½ tablespoons†	1.3 ounces	36 grams
cider vinegar	1½ teaspoons	0.25 ounce	7 grams

*Pastry flour makes the dough too weak for wrapping around a meat loaf but would add desirable tenderness if using it for a tart.

†For a tart shell, use only 2 tablespoons so it will be more tender. The pastry needs to be slightly stronger to hold together when wrapping a meat loaf.

FOOD PROCESSOR METHOD

Cut the butter into small (about ¾-inch) cubes. Wrap it in plastic wrap and freeze it until frozen solid, at least 30 minutes. Place the flour, salt, optional baking powder, and cayenne pepper in a reclosable gallon-size freezer bag and freeze it for at least 30 minutes.

Place the flour mixture in a food processor with the metal blade and process for a few seconds to combine. Set the bag aside. Add the Cheddar cheese and process for about 20 seconds or until the mixture resembles coarse meal. Add the frozen butter cubes and pulse until none of the butter is larger than the size of a pea. (Toss with a fork to see it better.) Remove the cover and add the water and vinegar. Pulse until most of the butter is reduced to the size of small peas. The mixture will be in particles and will not hold together. Spoon it into the plastic bag.

Holding both ends of the bag opening with your fingers, knead the mixture by alternately pressing it, from the outside of the bag, with the knuckles and heels of your hands until the mixture holds together in one piece and feels slightly stretchy when pulled.

Wrap the dough with plastic wrap, flatten it into a disc, and refrigerate for at least 45 minutes, preferably overnight.

HAND METHOD

Place a medium mixing bowl in the freezer to chill. Cut the butter into small (about ¾-inch) cubes. Wrap it in plastic wrap and refrigerate it for at least 30 minutes.

Place the flour, salt, optional baking powder, and cayenne pepper in a medium bowl and whisk to combine. Add the Cheddar cheese and rub the mixture between your fingers to blend it into the flour until it resembles coarse meal. Spoon the mixture, together with the cold butter, into a reclosable gallon-size freezer bag. Expel any air from the bag and close it. Use a rolling pin to flatten the butter into thin flakes. Place the bag in the freezer for at least 10 minutes or until the butter is very firm.

Transfer the flour mixture to the chilled bowl, scraping the sides of the bag. Set the bag aside. Sprinkle the ice water and vinegar onto the mixture, tossing it lightly with a rubber spatula. Spoon the loose mixture back into the plastic bag.

Holding both ends of the bag opening with your fingers, knead the mixture by alternately pressing it, from the outside of the bag, with the knuckles and heels of your hands until the mixture holds together in one piece and feels slightly stretchy when pulled.

Wrap the dough with plastic wrap, flatten it into a disc, and refrigerate for at least 45 minutes, preferably overnight.

STORE

Refrigerated, up to 2 days; frozen, up to 3 months.

POINTERS FOR SUCCESS

∾ This dough needs to be kneaded until stretchy so that it is strong enough to use for wrapping around a freestanding meat loaf and not tear during baking.

MIRACLE FLAKY LARD PIE CRUST

For years I wondered why people raved about lard pastry. Mine was either falling-apart-tender or flaky and tough. But I'm glad to have persevered, because a lard crust made well has no equal. It is more tender, more flaky, and more crisp than any other and doesn't shrink even if baked only an hour after mixing. It also browns less fast than a butter crust, making it convenient for pies that require longer baking.

Lard crust is ideal for savory pastries. You can use half butter, but it is not quite as light, though very close, and for savory food, I prefer the flavor of all lard.

Pastry flour produces the most tender crust. I like to roll out the dough on whole wheat flour for extra texture and flavor, which is compatible with the lard flavor. The success of this crust depends on the quality and temperature of the lard.

PASTRY FOR A 9-INCH PIE SHELL
OR A 9½- BY 1-INCH TART SHELL   MAKES: 13 OUNCES/370 GRAMS

INGREDIENTS	MEASURE	WEIGHT	
	VOLUME	OUNCES	GRAMS
pastry flour or bleached all-purpose flour*	1⅓ cups + 4 teaspoons 1⅓ cups (dip and sweep method)	6.5 ounces	184 grams
salt	½ teaspoon†	•	•
baking powder	⅛ teaspoon	•	•
lard, cold	approx. ½ cup‡	4 ounces	113 grams
ice water	¼ liquid cup	2 ounces	59 grams
cider vinegar	4 teaspoons	0.7 ounce	20 grams
whole wheat pastry flour or whole wheat flour	approx. 2 tablespoons	•	•

*If using all purpose flour, reduce the water by 1 teaspoon for more tenderness.
†Use ⅜ teaspoon if using rendered caul fat.
‡If using commercial lard, add ½ cup plus 2 teaspoons; if using rendered caul fat, use ½ cup plus 1 tablespoon (the weight remains the same).

Place a medium mixing bowl in the freezer to chill.

Place the flour, salt, and baking powder in a reclosable gallon-size freezer bag, and whisk them together. Using a melon baller, scoop ½- to 1-inch balls of the lard directly into the flour, shaking the bag occasionally to distribute and cover them with the flour. If the room is warm and the lard starts getting very soft, place the bag in the freezer for about 10 minutes before proceeding. If it is still firm but squishable once it's all been added, using a rolling pin, roll together the lard and flour until the lard is in thin flakes. Place the bag in the freezer for at least 30 minutes.

Empty the flour mixture into the cold bowl, scraping the sides of the bag to release all of it. Set the bag aside. Sprinkle on the ice water and vinegar, tossing gently with a rubber spatula to incorporate it evenly. Spoon the mixture back into the plastic bag. (If using caul fat, which is softer, the dough will already hold together, so it's easier to empty it onto a piece of plastic wrap and knead it lightly from the outside of the wrap.)

Holding both ends of the bag opening with your fingers, knead the mixture by alternately pressing it, from the outside of the bag, with the knuckles and heels of your hands until the mixture holds together in one piece and feels slightly stretchy when pulled.

Sprinkle the dough on both sides with a little whole wheat flour, wrap it with plastic wrap, flatten it into a disc, and refrigerate for at least 45 minutes, preferably overnight.

STORE

Refrigerated, up to 2 days; frozen, up to 3 months.

NOTE

When rolling the dough, roll it directly on the counter or on plastic wrap. Sprinkle both sides of the dough and the counter or plastic wrap amply with whole wheat flour as needed to keep it from sticking. (The whole wheat flour will not toughen it and will give it extra crunch and a lovely, wheaty flavor.)

RENDERING LARD

When you render your own, you see what a beautiful creamy fat lard can be. Caul fat is easiest to render and stays the softest, but it is hard to find (see page 640). Leaf lard, the fat from around the kidneys, also has excellent flavor. A butcher will sometimes be willing to special-order it.

Caul fat is stored in brine, so rinse it thoroughly, or soak it for a few hours in cold water, and dry it. It still will be slightly saltier than leaf lard. The fat will render a little less than two thirds its weight. (If you start with a pound of caul fat or leaf lard, you will have about 10 ounces lard.) The rest will be "cracklings."

To render leaf lard, first chop it fine or process it until well broken up. For caul fat, there is no need to chop it, as it is lacy and thin, except for the edges. Place the fat in a small heavy pan. Cook the fat over the lowest possible heat—just barely simmering (to avoid browning)—for 5 minutes, covered. Then cook for 40 minutes to an hour, uncovered, until only little golden brown bits remain in the pan. Strain it into a jar. It will keep refrigerated for months and frozen for 2 years.

POINTERS FOR SUCCESS

∾ Pay particular attention to temperature, keeping the lard well chilled.

∾ When mixing the lard flakes/flour mixture with the liquid, stir gently so as to maintain large flakes of lard.

UNDERSTANDING

Compared to an all-butter flaky crust, this crust uses essentially an equal volume of lard to butter, which adds tenderness because butter is only 80 percent fat and lard is 100 percent fat.

I have tested this recipe with several different types of lard. The weight varied from 7 ounces to 7.64 ounces per cup, which is a difference of about 4 teaspoons.

FLAKY BEEF SUET PIE CRUST

This is a flaky yet meltingly tender crust with a delicate beef flavor and pebbly surface. Beef marrow made an excellent crust, but crust from rendered fat from around veal kidneys (ask the butcher to leave the fat around the kidneys), though slightly milder in flavor, was superior in texture (considerably lighter and less greasy).

PASTRY FOR 6 POTPIES
OR A 9½- TO 10- BY 1-INCH TART SHELL   MAKES: 12 OUNCES/340 GRAMS

INGREDIENTS	MEASURE	WEIGHT	
	VOLUME	OUNCES	GRAMS
unsalted butter, cold	6 tablespoons	3 ounces	85 grams
pastry flour or bleached all-purpose flour	1¼ cups +1 tablespoon 1 cup +3 tablespoons (dip and sweep method)	6 ounces	170 grams
salt	¼ + ⅛ teaspoon	•	•
beef suet or marrow, at room temperature	3 tablespoons + 2 teaspoons	1.5 ounces	42 grams
ice water	3 tablespoons	1.5 ounces	44 grams

Cut the butter into small (about ¾-inch) cubes; wrap it in plastic wrap and freeze it for at least 30 minutes. Place the flour and salt in a reclosable gallon-size freezer bag and freeze it for at least 30 minutes. Using a melon baller, scoop ½-inch balls of the suet into a bowl. Refrigerate it for at least 30 minutes.

Place the flour mixture in a food processor with the metal blade. Set the bag aside. Add the suet and process until the mixture resembles coarse meal, about 20 seconds. Add the frozen butter cubes and pulse until the butter is the size of large peas. (Toss with a fork to see it better.) Remove the cover and add the water. Pulse until most of the butter is reduced to the size of peas. The mixture will be in particles and will not hold together. Spoon it into the plastic bag.

Holding both ends of the bag opening with your fingers, knead the mixture by alternately pressing it, from the outside of the bag, with the knuckles and heels of your hands until the mixture holds together in one piece and feels slightly stretchy when pulled.

Wrap the dough with plastic wrap, flatten it into a disc, and refrigerate for at least 45 minutes, preferably overnight.

STORE
Refrigerated, up to 2 days; frozen, up to 3 months.

RENDERING SUET
Chop the suet fine or process it until it is well broken up. Place it in a small heavy pan. Cook it over the lowest possible heat (just barely simmering, to avoid browning) for about 1½ hours or until only little bits remain in the pan. (In a double boiler it will take about 8 hours, but there is no risk of burning.) Strain it into a jar. The fat from 1 kidney yields about 1½ cups, plus about ½ cup of cracklings.

RENDERING MARROW
Choose bones about 2½ inches in diameter that have a large marrow center.

Preheat the oven to 350°F. Place the bones in a baking pan with a tablespoon of water. Cover and bake for 30 minutes or until the marrow softens enough so that a skewer inserted all the way through goes in easily. Remove the bones and allow them to cool slightly. Scoop out the marrow, placing it in a small heavy saucepan with 2 tablespoons of water. Cover and simmer, leaving the cover open a crack, for 15 to 20 minutes or until all the marrow is rendered, with the solid brown bits floating on top. Be careful not to cook it too fast, or a burnt flavor will result. Strain it into a jar. Three 7-inch bones will yield about ¾ cup/5.25 ounces/150 grams of rendered marrow.

STORE
Rendered suet or marrow will keep refrigerated for months and frozen for about 2 years.

POINTERS FOR SUCCESS

∾ If using 100 percent beef suet instead of the suet/butter combination, use a total of 4 ounces/113 grams.

∾ Suet becomes very hard when refrigerated, so it needs to be at cool room temperature to make the balls. Because of this quality, I offer only the food processor method, since the hand method requires rechilling after the butter is added.

FLAKY GOOSE FAT PIE CRUST

I adore the flavor of goose fat and collect the rendered fat whenever I roast a goose. I have never encountered a recipe for a pie crust using it and correctly assumed it would be tricky to work out because it is liquid at room temperature. This causes it to coat and moisture-proof the flour, making the crust very tender and fragile. The solution was using half goose fat, half butter. Not only does it offer a lovely and unusual flavor, it is more tender than an all-butter crust, yet still flaky, and it browns faster. A pastry chef at Gundel, in Budapest, Hungary, where goose is king, told me that in years past, pastry crust was made with unrendered goose fat because it is solid at room temperature. I tried this, processing the fat, and the texture was incredibly flaky and tender, but the flavor was not as desirable, so it wasn't worth the effort.

PASTRY FOR 6 POTPIES
OR A 9½- TO 10- BY 1-INCH TART SHELL   MAKES: 12 OUNCES/342 GRAMS

INGREDIENTS	MEASURE	WEIGHT	
	VOLUME	OUNCES	GRAMS
bleached all-purpose flour	1⅓ cups (dip and sweep method)	6.5 ounces	184 grams
salt	½ teaspoon	•	•
fresh thyme, chopped fine,	1 tablespoon	•	3 grams
or dried	1 teaspoon	•	•
goose fat, cold	¼ cup	2 ounces	57 grams
unsalted butter, cold	4 tablespoons	2 ounces	57 grams
ice water	¼ liquid cup	2 ounces	59 grams

Place the flour, salt, and thyme in a reclosable gallon-size freezer bag and whisk them together. Using a melon baller, scoop ½-inch blobs of the goose fat directly into the flour. Place the bag in the freezer for at least 1 hour. Cut the butter into small (about ¾-inch) cubes; wrap it in plastic wrap and refrigerate for at least 30 minutes. Place a medium mixing bowl in the freezer to chill.

Add the cold butter cubes to the flour mixture in the bag and working quickly, using a rolling pin, roll the goose fat and butter into the flour until they are in thin flakes. Empty the mixture into the cold bowl, scraping the sides of the bag to release all of it. Set the bag aside. Sprinkle on the ice water, tossing gently with a rubber spatula to incorporate it evenly. Spoon the mixture into the plastic bag.

Holding both ends of the bag opening with your fingers, knead the mixture by alternately pressing it, from the outside of the bag, with the knuckles and heels of your hands until the mixture holds together in one piece and feels slightly stretchy when pulled.

Wrap the dough with plastic wrap, flatten it into a disc, and refrigerate for at least 45 minutes, preferably overnight.

STORE

Refrigerated, up to 2 days; frozen, up to 3 months.

POINTERS FOR SUCCESS

∽ When rolling the dough, sprinkle both sides well with flour as needed to keep it from sticking.

UNDERSTANDING

This crust is very similar to the basic flaky butter crust. The only significant difference is that half the butter is replaced with an equal weight of goose fat, which contains no water and is liquid at room temperature. This makes the crust more tender.

FLAKY PASTRY SCRAPS

Never discard leftover pie crust scraps. They are great to have in the freezer for Windfall Fruit Pielets (page 78) and, when sweetened and flavored, they make delicious, crisp cookies.

OVEN TEMPERATURE: 425°F.
BAKING TIME: 12 TO 15 MINUTES   **MAKES: ABOUT 20 COOKIES**

INGREDIENTS	MEASURE	WEIGHT	
	VOLUME	OUNCES	GRAMS
pastry scraps		8 ounces	226 grams
sugar, preferably superfine	2 tablespoons + 1 teaspoon	1 ounce	29 grams
ground cinnamon	⅛ teaspoon	•	•
optional: amber crystal (coarse granulated) sugar (see page 645) or granulated sugar			

EQUIPMENT
Cookie sheet(s)

Cut the scraps of dough into similar lengths and lay them on a piece of plastic wrap, overlapping them slightly. Sprinkle the dough lightly with flour and cover with a second piece of plastic wrap. Roll lightly to make the dough pieces adhere to one another. Then lift away the plastic wrap and use the bottom piece to help fold the dough in thirds, like a business letter. Wrap the dough well and refrigerate it while preparing the sugar mixture.

In a small bowl, stir together the superfine sugar and cinnamon until evenly mixed.

Roll out the dough between two sheets of plastic wrap into a rectangle ⅛ inch thick. Discard the top piece of plastic wrap and sprinkle the dough evenly with the sugar mixture. Use the bottom piece of plastic wrap to start rolling the pastry, and continue to roll it into a cylinder. Wrap it with the plastic wrap and refrigerate it for at least 1 hour.

Preheat the oven to 425°F. at least 20 minutes before baking. Set an oven rack at the middle level before preheating.

Remove and discard the plastic wrap. With a sharp knife, cut the cylinder into rounds, ¼ to ⅜ inch thick. For extra crunch, dip each side in amber sugar crystals or granulated sugar. Place them at least ½ inch apart on a cookie sheet.

Bake for 10 minutes or until browned. Turn each cookie and continue baking for 2 to 5 minutes or until the other side browns. Remove the cookies to racks to cool.

STORE

Airtight, room temperature, up to 3 weeks; frozen, up to 6 months.

UNDERSTANDING

Refrigerating the dough before cutting it makes it firm enough to cut evenly. It also causes the sugar to dissolve slightly, helping the layers of dough to adhere to each other.

SWEET COOKIE TART CRUST

If you love cookies, you will love this crust in all its many permutations, from plain, nut, ginger, coconut, and chocolate to peanut butter—and it's a snap to prepare! (Actually, the recipe for a sugar cookie is exactly the same.) Its French name, *pâte sucrée,* means sugar dough. The dough produces a crust that is both firmer and more tender than a flaky pie crust. The proportions of flour, butter, and liquid in the sweet cookie tart crust are almost identical to those of the flaky pie crust. The difference is in the type of liquid used. Instead of water or another liquid with a high water content, egg yolk and cream, both of which are high in fat and low in water, are added to the sweet cookie tart dough. With less water, less gluten forms, and the crust is therefore more tender. In the variations of this crust, the chocolate and peanut butter, for example, that contain more fat, I use a whole egg, as the egg white helps to bind and strengthen the dough.

The dough for a sweet cookie crust contains about ½ to 1¾ ounces sugar for a standard 9½-inch tart crust. Sugar draws liquid away from the flour, thus keeping it from developing gluten, so the more sugar, the more tender the crust.

The sweet cookie doughs in this book are formulated to be just strong enough to roll out without falling apart. Even though all of these doughs can be easily pressed into a pan with your fingers, and the scraps reused without any loss of quality, I urge you to give rolling out a try. The process takes less time and, best of all, guarantees a crust with an even thickness.

One of the charms of the sweet cookie crust is its ability to keep its crispness and tenderness even after prolonged refrigeration or freezing, unlike a flaky pie crust. This makes it the ideal container for tarts that are filled with creams that must be refrigerated as well as for ice cream pies, which must be frozen.

ROLLING AND SHAPING SWEET COOKIE TART CRUST

This dough is usually used for tarts but can also be used to line a pie pan, as for the Coconut Ice Cream Pie (page 226). It tends to absorb moisture less readily than flaky pie crust. It will hold a decorative edge, though not as well as a flaky crust, and it will droop if made too large or extended past the edge of the pan. For a large fluted tart pan, however, you need enough dough to extend a little past the top edge to allow for shrinkage during blind baking. I prefer a plain edge for tarts made with this dough.

MEASURING THE PAN

Measure the inside of the tart or pie pan with a flexible tape measure by starting at one inside edge, going down the side, across the bottom, and up the other side. Write down these numbers for future reference. When cutting the circle of dough to line the pan, increase the measure accordingly:

For a fluted tart pan, cut the dough circle the same size.

For a single-crust pie, cut the dough circle 1½ inches larger.

SIZES OF DOUGH CIRCLES TO CUT FOR STANDARD PANS

The amounts/weights are indicated to help approximate how much dough will be needed for a specific number of tarts. They are based on rolling the dough ⅛ inch thick for tarts and 1/16 inch thick for tartlets. One tablespoon of sweet cookie dough weighs 0.6 ounces/18.5 grams. One cup of sweet cookie dough weighs about 9.75 ounce/281 grams.

For a 9½- by 1-inch tart pan, cut an 11-inch dough circle (1 cup/about 10 ounces/288 grams). Trim it or push it up to ⅛-inch above the sides of the pan. From a 14-ounce/405-gram recipe, you will have about 4 ounces/117 grams of scraps.

For a 9-inch pie pan or 10- by 1- or 2-inch tart pan, cut an 11½-inch dough circle (1 cup plus 1½ teaspoons/10¾ ounces/307 grams). From a 14-ounce/405-gram recipe, you will have about 3¼ ounces/92 grams of scraps.

For a 3-inch tartlet pan, cut a 3½-inch dough circle (1 slightly rounded tablespoon/0.5 to 0.75 ounce/15 to 20 grams).

For a 3¼-inch flan ring, cut a 4½-inch dough circle (4 teaspoons/scant 1 ounce/25 grams).

For a 3½-inch tartlet pan, cut a 4-inch dough circle (about 2 tablespoons/ 1¼ ounces/36 grams).

For a 4-inch flan ring, cut a 5½-inch dough circle (about 2 tablespoons/1.3 ounces/38 grams).

For a 4-inch tartlet pan, cut a 5½-inch dough circle (about 2 tablespoons/1.3 ounce/40 grams).

For a 4- by 1¼-inch-deep or 4¾-inch standard tartlet pan, cut a 5¾-inch dough circle (3 tablespoons/about 2 ounces/55 grams).

PREPARING THE PAN

For Tender Nut Cookie Tart Crust, Sweet Peanut Butter Cookie Tart Crust, the Sweet Cookie Tart Crust coconut variation, and the Bittersweet Chocolate Cookie Tart Crust, the pan does not need greasing or flouring unless it is being used for the first time. For all other crusts, Baker's Joy is easier to apply than grease and flour because tart pans with removable bottoms can't be turned upside down to knock out excess flour. Small flan rings do not require greasing or flouring no matter what the dough.

THE ROLLING SURFACE

A cool surface, such as marble, is preferable to keep the dough from softening too quickly. A piece of marble 16 inches by 20 inches by ¾ inch (see page 669; available in gourmet stores or from a marble supply store) is a good size that is small enough to slip into your refrigerator to chill on hot summer days. (A bag of ice applied to a marble counter or a large piece also works to chill it.)

The dough should be floured on both sides and rolled between sheets of plastic wrap, overlapped if not large enough.

ROLLING SWEET COOKIE TART CRUST

I prefer rolling to pressing the dough into the pan with fingers because it's faster and gives a head start to making it even. It may tear when you transfer it to a large tart pan, but patching is very easy. Simply press scraps of dough into an empty area, using your fingers.

If the dough has been refrigerated for more than 30 minutes, it will be too cold to roll or press without cracking. It can take as long as 40 minutes at room temperature to become malleable. But if you prefer not to wait, use the coarse side of a box grater to disperse the dough evenly in the pan and then press it into place.

To roll the dough, roll it between lightly floured sheets of plastic wrap to an ⅛-inch-thick circle (1/16 inch thick for small tartlets). It is always best to work quickly so that the dough does not soften. Use a firm, steady pressure to roll the dough into a circle. As the center tends to be the thickest part, roll from the center out. Avoid the edges, as they tend to become thinner than the rest of the dough. (For perfectly even thickness, use one of the sets of rubber rings described on page 671.) Lift away the plastic wrap occasionally and if the dough seems sticky, sprinkle it lightly with flour. If at any point the dough becomes too soft, slip it, still in the plastic wrap, onto a baking sheet large enough to hold it flat and refrigerate or freeze it until firm.

CUTTING SWEET COOKIE TART CRUST

I find it easiest and most precise to cut the
dough circle before transferring the dough to
the pie or tart pan. (To determine the size, see
Measuring the Pan, page 49.) I like to use an
expandable flan ring as a guide, because it can
expand to the desired diameter and then can
be used to cut through the dough. A cardboard
template and the tip of a sharp knife also work
effectively.

Remove the top sheet of plastic wrap before
cutting. Replace it on the cut-out dough, slip the
dough onto a baking sheet, and refrigerate it for 5 to 10 minutes, until it is
firm but still flexible.

SCRAPS

Scraps can be refrigerated for about 10 minutes or until firm and rerolled
immediately, or frozen, unrolled, for future use. Lightly press together the
scraps into one piece, wrap it in plastic, flatten it, and place it in a reclosable
freezer bag before putting it in the freezer. I have made a tart with well-
wrapped frozen two-year-old scraps that still had an excellent flavor and texture. For a full-size tart, defrost as many pieces as needed in the refrigerator,
or about 4 hours at room temperature, until malleable. Knead them together
and roll the dough to the required size.

TRANSFERRING SWEET COOKIE TART CRUST TO THE PAN

The easiest way to transfer the dough neatly to a 9½- to 10-inch tart pan is to leave it between the two sheets of plastic wrap and invert it over the back of an 8-inch round cake pan so that it covers it evenly. If any cracks develop, smooth them together—or wait until you've transferred it to the pan. Peel off the top sheet of plastic wrap. (If the dough sticks to the wrap, refrigerate or freeze it just until it is firm.) Place the bottom of the tart pan evenly centered on top of the dough. Invert the sides of the tart pan over the dough. Then simply invert both pans so that the tart pan is on the bottom and the dough slips into it. Remove the cake pan and the plastic wrap and gently press the dough against the sides of the tart pan. If necessary, allow the dough to soften at room temperature for a few minutes so that it drapes comfortably into the pan.

If you do not have an 8-inch pan, another method of lining the tart pan is to remove the top sheet of plastic wrap from the dough and use the bottom sheet to lift and invert the pastry over the tart pan. Evenly drape the dough into the tart pan, pressing it gently into the convoluted sides. If the plastic wrap sticks, refrigerate or freeze the dough until it is firm enough to be removed easily.

When the tart pan has been lined, the dough should come at least ⅛ inch above the rim of the pan. It always falls a little during baking. (For 3½-inch or smaller tarts, however, it can be even with the top.) If the dough is not high enough, push it up using your fingers. If it is too high, use scissors to trim it.

Transferring Sweet Cookie Tart Crust to the Pan (cont.)

For small odd-shaped tart pans, invert the pan over the dough and cut, leaving a border of about ½ inch all around. Press the dough into the pan. With your fingers or a rolling pin, press along the top edge to remove excess dough.

For small flan rings, use a small sharp knife held parallel to the rim of the ring to trim the dough even with the top of the ring.

For large flan rings, set the flan ring on a baking sheet. Drape the dough into the flan ring, pressing it gently against the sides. The dough should come about ⅛ inch above the rim or ½ inch for a decorative border.

For a pie pan, create a small decorative edge according to the illustrations on page 13. Do not allow it to extend past the sides of the pan, or it will droop and fall off during baking. If your fingers are warm, dip them occasionally in a bowl of ice water and dry them well. If the edge softens slightly, dip your fingers in flour as you work (a little extra flour will help the edge to hold its shape during baking), but if it becomes very soft, it is best to cover and chill it briefly.

Wrap the dough-lined tart pan(s), pie pan, or flan ring(s) well and refrigerate for at least 6 hours, to make sure the crust falls the least amount possible during baking. When you are ready to bake, remove the plastic wrap and remove any dough on the outside of the tart pan to ensure that the shell will unmold well.

NOTE

Sweet cookie dough does not unmold easily from a one-piece tart pan, so it is always best to use a two-piece tart pan. The smallest two-piece tartlet pans are 4 inches, so if making ones smaller than that, fill them before unmolding to give the sides more support.

BAKING SWEET COOKIE TART CRUST

Because of the relatively short baking time of any baked tart, tart doughs always need to be fully prebaked so that the crust is crisp and slightly crunchy. Tarts are usually baked in a loose-bottomed tart pan or flan ring set on a baking sheet in the center of the oven. The shells should be chilled for at least an hour before baking.

If the dough has been frozen for at least 6 hours (in small flan rings, it only needs to be frozen for 15 minutes) or refrigerated for at least 6 hours before baking, it is not necessary to use weights (known as blind baking), except when using 10- by 2-inch tart pans. (Without weights, the slightly sloping deeper sides of these pans will cause the dough to slip down about ½ inch, making the sides thicker.)

It is not necessary to prick the dough for small tartlets. If the centers puff during baking, press them down lightly with your fingertips. For larger tarts, when the dough starts to puff in places, prick it lightly with a fork.

LINING SWEET COOKIE TART CRUST DOUGH FOR BLIND BAKING

If using parchment, pleat it as necessary to fit the shape of the pan. A round of Teflon-type liner placed on the crust under the parchment will keep it from sticking. Otherwise, a little of the crust always attaches to it. Cup-shaped coffee filters are even easier to use and don't stick to the dough. Large filters, the kind used for urns, available through commercial equipment outlets, work perfectly for tarts. Small  ones, the kind sold in supermarkets, are ideal for tartlets. Fill the filter or parchment with rice or dried beans, making sure they are pushed up well against sides of the filter.

TESTING FOR DONENESS

Plain cookie tart dough is baked when it turns a pale gold (the edges will be a deeper brown) and feels set but still soft to the touch. These crusts continue hardening while cooling, just the way cookies do. **Chocolate cookie tart dough** will deepen in color but should not start to brown, or it will take on a burnt flavor.

To bake plain sweet cookie tart dough, preheat the oven for at least 20 minutes before baking.

For 1-inch tiny tartlets, bake at 350°F. for 14 minutes or until the edges start to brown lightly but the center still feels soft to the touch. Remove the tartlets from the oven and, using the back of a wooden spoon, gently tamp down the centers. Return them to the oven and bake 1 minute more.

For tartlets, bake at 425°F. for 5 minutes. If the centers puff during baking, press them down lightly with your fingertips. Lower the heat to 350°F. and continue baking for 1 to 5 minutes. (If using weights, lift them out with the parchment and continue baking for 2 to 3 minutes.)

For large tarts or pie shells, bake at 425°F. for 5 minutes. When the dough starts to puff in places, prick it lightly with a fork, then lower the heat to 375°F. and continue baking for 10 to 15 minutes. (If using weights, bake at 425°F. for 5 minutes, lower the heat to 375°F., and bake for 15 to 20 minutes or until set. If not set, the dough will stick more to the parchment. Lift out the weights with the parchment, prick lightly, and continue baking 10 to 15 minutes more.)

To bake chocolate cookie tart dough for tartlets, bake at 375°F. for about 12 minutes. Check after the first 4 to 5 minutes; if the centers puff during baking, press them down lightly with your fingertips. (If using weights, lift them out with the parchment or filter after 10 minutes and continue baking for 2 to 3 minutes.)

For large tarts, bake at 400°F. for 5 minutes. When the dough starts to puff in places, prick it lightly with a fork. Lower the heat to 375°F. and bake 12 to 15 minutes longer. (If using weights, bake at 400°F. for 5 minutes, lower the heat to 375°F., and bake for 15 to 20 minutes or until set. If not set, the dough will stick more to the parchment. Lift out the weights with the parchment, prick lightly, and continue baking for 10 to 15 minutes more.)

To cool tarts, use a large pancake turner to slide the tart onto a wire rack. (If you used a flan ring, leave it on the baking sheet and set it on a rack.)

To unmold large tarts, it is best generally to leave the pastry in the pan until it is filled and baked or chilled, as the pan provides added support. To unmold, place the tart on top of a canister that is smaller than the opening of the tart pan rim. If the tart has been chilled, wet a towel with hot water and wring it out well. Apply it to the bottom and sides of the tart pan. Press firmly down on both sides of the tart ring. It should slip away easily. If not, apply more heat. (This technique is also sometimes helpful for tarts that have not been chilled.) Then slip the pancake turner between the crust and the bottom of the pan, loosening it all around if necessary, and slide the tart onto a serving plate.

Unmold tartlets baked in one-piece tart pans while the tartlets are still warm. As soon as the tins are cool enough to handle, slip a long thin needle between the side of the pastry and the fluted side of the tin. This does not mark the crust and the tartlet should pop out readily. If not, repeat the process, inserting the needle in another area.

STORE

The baked crust will keep at room temperature in an airtight container for up to 2 days.

MOISTURE-PROOFING THE BAKED BOTTOM CRUST

EGG WHITE GLAZE   The most effective way to moisture-proof a baked bottom crust is to brush it with a thin coating of egg white. (The yolk would toughen the dough.) The residual heat of the baked crust causes the egg white to dry to a crisp finish. Allow the baked pastry shell to cool on a rack for about 3 minutes before brushing it with lightly beaten egg white so that it isn't too hot, which would cause the egg white layer to flake off. If the baked pastry shell is no longer hot enough to set the egg white, return it to the oven for 2 to 3 minutes or until the egg white layer is dry and opaque. Half an egg white (1 tablespoon) will be enough to moisture-proof a 9-inch pie shell or 9½-inch tart shell.

CHOCOLATE GLAZE   When compatible with the filling, chocolate creates the most moisture-proof glaze of all. Quick-temper the chocolate using any method on page 615. Brush the chocolate onto the bottom and sides of the baked tart or pie shell. Very little is needed. The purpose of the chocolate is to waterproof and provide only a taste of chocolate. Any good-quality bittersweet chocolate will do, but couverture chocolate, with its higher amount of cocoa butter, is ideal, as it creates the thinnest coating. For a 9½-inch tart shell, you will need 1¼ ounces of chocolate (melt 2 ounces to be sure you have enough; any leftover can be stored and remelted). Allow the chocolate-coated tart shell to sit until the chocolate is set (it will lose its shine and dull) or refrigerate it briefly.

FRUIT PRESERVES GLAZE   Fruit glaze also performs beautifully as a moisture-proofer for baked dough. Commercial bakeries use Apricoture (see page 638), which has an excellent flavor, very low moisture, and, unlike preserves or jelly, does not need to be sieved. Apricot or seedless raspberry preserves are also effective but they need to be heated and strained. You will need 3 tablespoons of fruit glaze for a 9½-inch tart (6 tablespoons if it is 2 inches high). See page 20 for heating and straining instructions.

SWEET COOKIE TART CRUST
(Pâte Sucrée)

This easy-to-make pastry is as tender as a sugar cookie. Most cookie crusts are merely crumbly, but this one manages to maintain a bit of flakiness. It is traditionally baked in a tart pan, but because its edges hold a design so well, it can also function as a container for a pie filling.

Friends who have had problems with this type of crust swear by this recipe. In addition to its many virtues, it is surprisingly versatile. If you increase the sugar, it becomes even more tender and delicate. If you replace the egg yolk and cream with one large egg, it becomes firmer. If you want just a touch of sweetness, the sugar can be reduced to 1 tablespoon.

The fresh ginger variation provides an exciting counterpoint to fruit tarts such as peach or pear. The coconut variation is a thrilling taste against tropical aromatic fruits such as mango and passion, and it is ideal for coconut ice-cream pie as well.

PASTRY FOR A 9½- OR 10- BY 1-INCH TART,
A 10- BY 2-INCH TART, A 9-INCH PIE,
EIGHT TO TEN 4-INCH TARTLETS,
NINE 4- BY ¾-INCH FLAN RINGS
OR SEVEN 4¾- BY ¾-INCH OR
4- BY 1¼-INCH TARTLETS   **MAKES: 14 OUNCES/405 GRAMS (ABOUT 1⅓ CUPS)**

INGREDIENTS	MEASURE	WEIGHT	
	VOLUME	OUNCES	GRAMS
unsalted butter, cold, cut into 1-inch cubes	8 tablespoons	4 ounces	113 grams
sugar, preferably superfine	¼ cup	1.75 ounces	50 grams
bleached all-purpose flour	1½ scant cups (dip and sweep method)	7 ounces	200 grams
salt	⅛ teaspoon	•	•
1 large egg yolk*	1 tablespoon + ½ teaspoon	0.65 ounce	18.6 grams
heavy cream*	2 tablespoons	1 ounce	28 grams

*If using a pie pan, replace the yolk and cream with 1 whole egg, lightly beaten.

PREPARING THE PAN
See page 50.

FOOD PROCESSOR METHOD
In a food processor with the metal blade, pulse the butter and sugar about 15 times or until the sugar disappears. Add the flour and salt and pulse again about 15 times or until the butter is no larger than small peas.

In a small bowl, stir together the yolk and cream. Add it to the mixture and pulse just until incorporated, about 8 times. The dough will still be in crumbly pieces. Empty it into a plastic bag and press the dough from the outside just until it holds together.

Remove the dough from the plastic bag and place it on a very large piece of plastic wrap. Using the plastic wrap, knead the dough a few times until the dough becomes one smooth piece. Flatten it into a 6-inch disc.

Wrap the dough well and refrigerate for 30 minutes, or freeze for 10 minutes, until firm enough to pat into the pan or to roll.

HAND METHOD
In a medium bowl, stir together the flour, sugar, and salt. With a pastry cutter or two knives, cut in the cold butter until the mixture resembles coarse meal.

In a small bowl, stir together the yolk and cream. Mix it into the flour mixture until the dough comes together and can be formed into a ball. Flatten it into a 6-inch disc.

Wrap the dough well and refrigerate for 30 minutes, or freeze for 10 minutes, until firm enough to pat into the pan or roll.

VARIATIONS

GINGER COOKIE TART CRUST   Add 2 teaspoons (11.4 grams) peeled and grated fresh ginger along with the egg/cream mixture.

COCONUT COOKIE TART CRUST   Use only 1 cup (5.25 ounces/150 grams) of flour; add ¼ cup (1 ounce/30 grams) of flaked unsweetened coconut to the flour and salt. In a food processor, process the flour, salt, and coconut until the coconut is finely grated. Replace the yolk and the cream with ½ egg (1½ tablespoons), lightly beaten. (This dough weighs 12.6 ounces/361 grams.) There is no need to grease the tart pan, because the extra oil in the coconut makes the crust release easily.

ROLLING AND BAKING

See pages 50 and 54.

STORE

Refrigerated, up to 1 week; frozen, about 1 year (unbaked).

UNDERSTANDING

If the crust is baked in a tart pan, a small crack often develops just at the stress point where the bottom of the pan meets the sides. This is of no consequence since it is covered by the filling, and it could be prevented if egg white were used in place of the heavy cream (i.e., 1 whole egg in place of the yolk and heavy cream), but this would result in a slightly less tender pastry. In a pie pan, however, the stress point is just below the border, so the crack would not be covered completely by the filling. It is, therefore, advisable to use the stronger version when lining a pie pan.

Because there is very little water (only the small amount contained in the cream), very little gluten develops, making this a very tender dough that does not shrink. The scraps can be rerolled several times without toughening, but with each rolling, the crust will lose flakiness.

SWEET NUT COOKIE TART CRUST
(Pâte Sucrée)

The addition of nuts to this crust not only imparts the flavor of your favorite nut, it also makes it slightly more tender.

PASTRY FOR A 9½- OR 10- BY 1-INCH TART,
A 9-INCH PIE,
SIX TO SEVEN 4-INCH TARTLETS,
SIX 4- BY ¾-INCH FLAN RINGS   MAKES: 10.75 OUNCES/305 GRAMS
OR FIVE 4¾- BY ¾-INCH OR 4- BY 1¼-INCH TARTLETS   (1 GENEROUS CUP)

INGREDIENTS	MEASURE	WEIGHT	
	VOLUME	OUNCES	GRAMS
pecans, walnuts, or almonds*	½ cup†	1.5 ounces	43 grams
sugar, preferably superfine	3 tablespoons	1.3 ounces	37.5 grams
unsalted butter, cold, cut into 1-inch cubes	6 tablespoons	3 ounces	85 grams
bleached all-purpose flour	¾ cup (dip and sweep method)	3.75 ounces	106.5 grams
salt	⅛ teaspoon	•	•
1 large egg yolk	1 tablespoon + ½ teaspoon	0.65 ounce	18.6 grams
heavy cream	4 teaspoons	0.66 ounce	19 grams

*Preferably sliced, as they grate more uniformly, releasing the least oil. Unblanched will give more flavor.
†Use a scant ½ cup for pecans or walnuts.

PASTRY FOR A 9½- OR 10- BY 1-INCH TART,
A 10- BY 2-INCH TART, A 9-INCH PIE,
EIGHT TO TEN 4-INCH TARTLETS
NINE 4- BY ¾-INCH FLAN RINGS   MAKES: 14 OUNCES/402 GRAMS
OR SEVEN 4¾- BY ¾-INCH OR 4- BY 1¼-INCH TARTLETS   (ABOUT 1⅓ CUPS)

INGREDIENTS	MEASURE	WEIGHT	
	VOLUME	OUNCES	GRAMS
pecans, walnuts, or almonds	⅔ cup*	2 ounces	57 grams
sugar, preferably superfine	¼ cup	1.75 ounces	50 grams
unsalted butter, cold, cut into 1-inch cubes	8 tablespoons	4 ounces	113 grams
bleached all-purpose flour	1 cup (dip and sweep method)	5 ounces	142 grams
salt	⅛ teaspoon	•	•
1 large egg yolk	1 tablespoon + ½ teaspoon	0.65 ounce	18.6 grams
heavy cream	2 tablespoons	1 ounce	28 grams

*Use a scant ⅔ cup for pecans or walnuts.

PREPARING THE PAN
See page 50.

FOOD PROCESSOR METHOD
In a food processor with the metal blade, pulse the nuts and sugar until the nuts are finely ground. Add the butter and pulse about 15 times or until no loose particles of nut/sugar mixture remain. Add the flour and salt and pulse again about 15 times or until the butter is no larger than small peas.

In a small bowl, stir together the yolk and cream. Add it to the mixture and pulse just until incorporated, about 8 times.

Dump the mixture into a plastic bag and press it together. Remove the dough from the plastic bag and knead it lightly until it holds together. Flatten it into a 6-inch disc, wrap the dough well, and refrigerate for 30 minutes, or freeze for 10 minutes, until firm enough to pat into the pan or roll.

HAND METHOD
Finely grate the nuts. In a medium bowl, stir together the nuts, flour, sugar, and salt. With a pastry cutter or two knives, cut in the cold butter until the mixture resembles coarse meal.

In a small bowl, stir together the yolk and cream. Mix it into the flour mixture until the dough comes together and can be formed into a large ball. Flatten it into a 6-inch disc, wrap the dough well, and refrigerate for 30 minutes, or freeze for 10 minutes, until firm enough to pat into the pan or roll.

VARIATION
TENDER NUT COOKIE TART CRUST   For a more crumbly and sweeter cookie-like crust, eliminate the egg and cream and double the sugar. This crust is particularly delicious with a bittersweet chocolate filling. There is no need to grease the tart pan. Eliminating the egg makes the crust release easily from the pan.

ROLLING AND BAKING
See pages 50 and 54.

STORE
Refrigerated, up to 1 week; frozen, about 1 year.

UNDERSTANDING
Replacing about one quarter the weight of the flour in the basic cookie tart crust dough with nuts makes a slightly more tender and flavorful dough.

BITTERSWEET CHOCOLATE COOKIE TART CRUST
(Pâte Sucrée au Chocolat)

This crust tastes just like a fantastic chocolate cookie. The dough rolls like a charm and the tart shell unmolds perfectly from the pan without greasing or flouring. This crust is used to line flan rings or tart pans.

I particularly recommend the walnut variation, because walnut has a way of accentuating the flavor of chocolate.

PASTRY FOR A 9½- OR 10- BY 1-INCH TART,
TEN 4- BY ¾-INCH FLAN RINGS,
OR EIGHT 4¾- BY ¾-INCH OR 4- BY
1¼-INCH TARTLETS   **MAKES: 1 POUND/455 GRAMS (1½ CUPS)**

INGREDIENTS	MEASURE	WEIGHT	
	VOLUME	OUNCES	GRAMS
bleached all-purpose flour	approx. 1¼ cups (dip and sweep method)	6.5 ounces	185 grams
unsweetened cocoa	¼ cup (lightly spooned)	0.8 ounces	23 grams
salt	a pinch	•	•
unsalted butter, cold, cut into 1-inch cubes	8 tablespoons	4 ounces	113 grams
powdered sugar	¾ cup	3 ounces	86 grams
1 large egg, lightly beaten	3 tablespoons + ½ teaspoon	1.75 ounces	50 grams

PREPARING THE PAN
See page 50.

FOOD PROCESSOR METHOD
In a small bowl, whisk together the flour, cocoa, and salt.

In a food processor with the metal blade, pulse the butter and sugar until the sugar disappears. Add the flour/cocoa mixture and pulse until the mixture resembles coarse meal. Add the egg and pulse just until incorporated.

Dump the mixture into a plastic bag and press it together. Remove the dough from the plastic bag and knead it lightly until it holds together. Flatten it into a 6-inch disc, wrap the dough well, and refrigerate for 30 minutes, or freeze for 10 minutes, until firm enough to pat into the pan or roll.

HAND METHOD

In a medium bowl, stir together the flour, cocoa, sugar, and salt. With a pastry cutter or two knives, cut in the cold butter until the mixture resembles coarse meal. Mix in the egg until the dough comes together and can be formed into a large ball. Flatten it into a 6-inch disc, wrap the dough well, and refrigerate for 30 minutes, or freeze for 10 minutes, until firm enough to pat into the pan or roll.

VARIATION

CHOCOLATE WALNUT COOKIE TART CRUST   Place ½ cup (1.75 ounces/50 grams) of walnuts on a baking sheet and bake for 7 minutes in a preheated 350°F. oven, stirring occasionally, until slightly deeper in color. Empty them onto a towel and rub off and discard as much of the skin as possible.

When the nuts are completely cool, place them in the food processor with the cocoa and powdered sugar and process until they are finely ground. Add the butter and pulse until the cocoa mixture is absorbed by the butter. Add the flour and salt and pulse until there are a lot of little moist crumbly pieces and no dry flour particles remain. Add the egg and pulse just until incorporated.

Dump the mixture into a plastic bag and press it together. Remove the dough from the plastic bag and knead it lightly until it holds together. (To use the hand method, simply grind the walnuts fine and add them to the dry ingredients.)

ROLLING AND BAKING

See pages 50 and 54.

STORE

Refrigerated, up to 1 week; frozen, about 1 year.

POINTERS FOR SUCCESS

∾ Don't overbake the chocolate dough, or it will have a burnt flavor.
∾ If you make a large tart shell and any cracks develop after baking, they can be sealed with some melted chocolate.

UNDERSTANDING

Compared to the basic cookie tart crust, by weight, this dough contains almost double the sugar to an equivalent amount of flour. This higher amount of sugar compensates for the addition of the bitter cocoa. If you prefer a very bitter chocolate flavor, you can reduce the powdered sugar to as little as ½ cup/ 2 ounces/57 grams.

Because the addition of cocoa tends to toughen dough, a tender but strong texture is more difficult to achieve. To solve the problem, powdered sugar is substituted for granulated. Powdered sugar lacks the sharp crystals of granulated sugar, which results in a tender but less airy crust. It also prevents cracking during baking.

A whole egg replaces the yolk and cream in the basic recipe because the white helps bind the fragile crust. The cocoa butter in the cocoa results in a similar fat content to that of the sweet tart dough.

SWEET PEANUT BUTTER COOKIE TART CRUST

I f you love peanut butter cookies, this is your crust. It is actually my peanut butter cookie baked in a tart pan. It makes a sensational crust for the Chocolate Peanut Butter Mousse Tart (page 316).

PASTRY FOR A 9½- OR 10- BY 1-INCH TART   MAKES: 12.7 OUNCES/363 GRAMS
OR EIGHT TO TEN 4-INCH TARTLETS   (1½ CUPS MINUS 1 TABLESPOON)

INGREDIENTS	MEASURE	WEIGHT	
	VOLUME	OUNCES	GRAMS
bleached all-purpose flour	½ cup (dip and sweep method)	2.5 ounces	71 grams
baking soda	½ teaspoon	•	2.5 grams
salt	1/16 teaspoon	•	•
light brown sugar	¼ cup, packed	approx. 2 ounces	54 grams
sugar, preferably superfine	2 tablespoons	0.8 ounce	25 grams
unsalted butter, cold, cut into 1-inch cubes	4 tablespoons	2 ounces	57 grams
smooth peanut butter, preferably Jif, at room temperature	½ cup	4.6 ounces	133 grams
½ large egg (beat before measuring)	1½ tablespoons	0.8 ounce (weighed without the shell)	25 grams
pure vanilla extract	¼ teaspoon	•	•

PREPARING THE PAN
See page 50.

FOOD PROCESSOR METHOD
Into a small bowl, sift together the flour, baking soda, and salt, then whisk to mix evenly.

In a food processor with the metal blade, process the sugars for several minutes or until very fine. With the motor running, add the butter cubes. Add the peanut butter and process until smooth and creamy, about 10 seconds. With the motor running, add the egg and vanilla extract and process until incorporated. Scrape the sides of the bowl. Add the flour mixture and pulse just until incorporated.

ELECTRIC MIXER METHOD

Soften the butter.

Into a small bowl, sift together the flour, baking soda, and salt. Whisk to combine well.

In a mixing bowl, beat the sugars until well mixed. Add the butter and peanut butter and beat for several minutes or until very smooth and creamy. Add the egg and vanilla extract and beat until incorporated, scraping the sides of the bowl. At low speed, gradually beat in the flour mixture just until incorporated.

FOR BOTH METHODS

Scrape the dough into a bowl and refrigerate for at least 1 hour, or overnight.

Press the dough evenly into the tart pan. (It is a little more challenging, but faster and neater, to roll it out between sheets of plastic wrap to about 11½ inches in diameter.* Remove one piece of plastic, invert the dough into the pan, easing the border into the sides of the pan so that the sharp top surface does not cut it off, and use the remaining plastic wrap to press it evenly into the pan, pressing it well against the sides. If the dough softens, refrigerate it until the plastic wrap can be removed easily. If it tears, simply press it together or use the scraps to press into any empty areas.) Cover it with plastic wrap and refrigerate for at least 1 hour. If using a 9½-inch tart pan, I usually have about 2 tablespoons (1 ounce/30 grams) of excess dough, which can be baked as cookies.

Bake the tart shell, without weights, in a preheated 375°F. oven for 10 to 12 minutes or until golden. It will puff at first and then settle down toward the end of baking. The sides will be soft but spring back when touched gently with a finger. Cool it on a wire rack.

STORE

Unbaked: refrigerated, up to 1 week; frozen, about 1 year.

UNDERSTANDING

The baking soda is used to impart a golden brown color to the dough. Decreasing it will not lessen the puff.

---

*The dough will be between ¹⁄₁₆ and ⅛ inch thick and rise to ¼ inch thick during baking.

CRUMB PIE CRUSTS

Crumb crusts are the easiest of all crusts to make. They are indispensable for pies that need to be refrigerated because they stand up well against moist fillings and they don't harden significantly on chilling. Their slightly sweet cookie-like flavor and texture provide a good balance for light pies such as Key lime, for chiffon pies, and for ice cream pies.

If you are using a prepared crust, for recipes calling for a 9-inch pie crust, be sure to buy one that measures 9 inches by 1½ inches deep. (The package will read 10-inch size/9 ounces/255 grams.) I encourage you to make your own, however, because these crusts are so easy to make and the flavor and texture of a homemade crumb crust is superior to any crust you can buy.

ADDITIONS TO CRUMB CRUSTS   I've put graham crackers in the cookie category, but a graham cracker crust needs a little sugar added because graham crackers are not a true cookie. Otherwise, crumb crusts require extra sugar only when nuts are added.

I like to add nuts, despite the fact that they don't impart much flavor, because crumb crusts with nuts are less brittle. Toasting the nuts brings out more flavor in a crust that will not be baked. In all the crumb crust recipes, a pinch of salt and a little pure vanilla extract work wonders to accentuate flavors.

PREPARING THE PAN   Don't grease the pie pan if you are planning to bake the crust, because it would cause it to slip down a bit. (If this should happen, you can use the back of a spoon to press it back up.) Do grease the rim, however, if you are planning to create a raised edge on top.

BAKED CRUMB CRUSTS VERSUS UNBAKED   In general, baking a crumb crust blends and brings out the flavor and makes it firmer, crisper, and more resistant to becoming soggy from very liquid fillings. If the filling needs to be baked, it is best not to prebake the crust because even with a foil collar, the exposed edge will become overbaked.

The chocolate wafer crust is darker in color, better in texture, and more delicious in flavor when not baked and is slightly more sturdy than the other crumb crusts. The Nabisco Famous chocolate wafers make a *delicious* crumb crust, much better tasting than the cookies themselves, because the addition of butter wakes up the chocolate flavor.

TO BAKE THE NONCHOCOLATE CRUMB CRUSTS   Chill the crust for at least 30 minutes to keep it from sliding down the sides of the pie pan. Preheat the oven to 350°F. at least 15 minutes ahead of baking.

Bake the crust for 8 to 10 minutes or until it puffs very slightly and colors lightly. Cool it completely before filling it.

If you are filling the pie with a filling that will not be baked, you must be sure to refrigerate the crust for at least 30 minutes before adding the filling to maintain a firm container.

STANDARD COOKIE SIZES AND WEIGHTS FOR 1½ CUPS OF CRUMBS/
6.3 OUNCES/180 GRAMS

12½ double graham crackers (6 ounces/170 grams)
25 2-inch gingersnaps, 3 scant cups whole
39 1¾-inch Sunshine Vanilla Wafers, 1¾ cups whole
46½ 1½-inch Keebler Golden Vanilla Wafers, 1½ cups whole
46½ 1½-inch Nabisco Nilla wafers, 1½ cups whole
27 2¼-inch Nabisco Famous chocolate wafers, 3 scant cups whole

CRUMB CRUST FOR 5-INCH PIELETS   You will need a scant ½ cup (1.75
ounces/50 grams) of any crumb crust, lightly spooned into the measuring
cup. For a prebaked crust, bake in a preheated 350°F. oven for 5 minutes or until
slightly puffed.

GRAHAM CRACKER CRUMB CRUST FOR A 9-INCH PIE

INGREDIENTS	MEASURE	WEIGHT	
	VOLUME	OUNCES	GRAMS
1 package (11 double crackers) graham crackers (4⅞ by 2⅜ inches)*	1⅓ cups crumbs, lightly packed	5.3 ounces	151 grams
sugar	2 tablespoons	scant 1 ounce	25 grams
optional: ground cinnamon	½ teaspoon	•	•
unsalted butter, melted	5 tablespoons	2.5 ounces	71 grams

*In the past, I have used 1½ cups/6 ounces/170 grams (12½ double crackers), but when the packaging
changed, I found that it was fine and convenient to use the slightly smaller amount.

GRAHAM CRACKER CRUMB CRUST FOR A 10-INCH PIE

INGREDIENTS	MEASURE	WEIGHT	
	VOLUME	OUNCES	GRAMS
14½ double graham crackers (4⅞ by 2⅜ inches)	1¾ cups crumbs, lightly packed	7 ounces	200 grams
sugar	2½ tablespoons	1 full ounce	31 grams
optional: ground cinnamon	½ + ⅛ teaspoon	•	•
unsalted butter, melted	6½ tablespoons	3.25 ounces	92 grams

GRAHAM CRACKER NUT CRUMB CRUST FOR A 9-INCH PIE

INGREDIENTS	MEASURE	WEIGHT	
	VOLUME	OUNCES	GRAMS
8½ double graham crackers (4⅞ by 2⅜ inches)	1 cup crumbs, lightly packed	4 ounces	113 grams
pecans*	½ cup	1.75 ounces	50 grams
sugar	3 tablespoons	1.3 ounces	38 grams
optional: ground cinnamon	½ teaspoon	•	•
unsalted butter, melted	4 tablespoons	2 ounces	56 grams

GRAHAM CRACKER NUT CRUMB CRUST FOR A 10-INCH PIE

INGREDIENTS	MEASURE	WEIGHT	
	VOLUME	OUNCES	GRAMS
1 package (11 double crackers) graham crackers (4⅞ by 2⅜ inches)†	1⅓ cups crumbs, lightly packed	5.3 ounces	151 grams
pecans*	⅔ cup	2.3 ounces	66 grams
sugar	¼ cup	1.75 ounces	50 grams
optional: ground cinnamon	½ + ⅛ teaspoon	•	•
unsalted butter, melted	5 tablespoons	2.5 ounces	71 grams

VANILLA, CHOCOLATE, OR GINGERSNAP CRUMB CRUST FOR A 9-INCH PIE

INGREDIENTS	MEASURE	WEIGHT	
	VOLUME	OUNCES	GRAMS
vanilla wafers, Nabisco Famous chocolate wafers,‡ or gingersnaps	1½ cups crumbs, lightly packed	6.3 ounces	180 grams
salt	2 pinches	•	•
unsalted butter, melted	5 tablespoons	2.5 ounces	71 grams
pure vanilla extract	½ teaspoon	•	•

*Lightly toasted, if not prebaking the crust.

†In the past, I have used 1½ cups/6 ounces/170 grams (12½ double crackers), but when the packaging changed, I found that it was fine and convenient to use the slightly smaller amount.

‡Do not use Nabisco Chocolate Nillas; the consistency will be too dry.

VANILLA, CHOCOLATE, OR GINGERSNAP CRUMB CRUST FOR A 10-INCH PIE

INGREDIENTS	MEASURE	WEIGHT	
	VOLUME	OUNCES	GRAMS
vanilla wafers, Nabisco Famous chocolate wafers,* or gingersnaps	2 cups crumbs, lightly packed	8.5 ounces	240 grams
salt	2 pinches	•	•
unsalted butter, melted	6½ tablespoons	3.25 ounces	92 grams
pure vanilla extract	¾ teaspoon	•	•

VANILLA, CHOCOLATE, OR GINGERSNAP NUT CRUMB CRUST FOR A 9-INCH PIE

INGREDIENTS	MEASURE	WEIGHT	
	VOLUME	OUNCES	GRAMS
vanilla wafers, Nabisco Famous chocolate wafers,* or gingersnaps	1 cup crumbs, lightly packed	4.25 ounces	120 grams
pecans or walnuts†	½ cup	1.75 ounces	50 grams
sugar	1 tablespoon	scant 0.5 ounce	12.5 grams
salt	2 pinches	•	•
optional: ground cinnamon	½ teaspoon	•	•
unsalted butter, melted	4 tablespoons	2 ounces	56 grams

*Do not use Nabisco Chocolate Nillas; the consistency will be too dry.

†Lightly toasted, if not prebaking the crust.

VANILLA, CHOCOLATE, OR GINGERSNAP NUT CRUMB CRUST FOR A 10-INCH PIE

INGREDIENTS	MEASURE		WEIGHT	
	VOLUME	OUNCES	GRAMS	
vanilla wafers, Nabisco Famous chocolate wafers,* or gingersnaps	1⅓ cups crumbs, lightly packed	5.6 ounces	160 grams	
pecans or walnuts†	⅔ cup	2.3 ounces	66 grams	
sugar	4 teaspoons	0.3 ounce	8 grams	
salt	2 pinches	•	•	
optional: ground cinnamon	¾ teaspoon	•	•	
unsalted butter, melted	5 tablespoons	2.5 ounces	71 grams	

*Do not use Nabisco Chocolate Nillas; the consistency will be too dry.
†Lightly toasted, if not prebaking the crust.

FOOD PROCESSOR METHOD

Process the cookies with the nuts, if using them, the sugar, salt, and the cinnamon or vanilla, if using, until the cookies become fine crumbs, about 20 seconds. Add the melted butter and pulse about 10 times, just until incorporated.

HAND METHOD

Place the cookies in a freezer bag and use a rolling pin to crush them into fine crumbs. (If using nuts, grind them fine but not powder-fine.) In a medium bowl, combine all the ingredients but the butter and toss with a fork to blend. Stir in the melted butter and toss to incorporate it.

FOR BOTH METHODS

Using your fingers or the back of a spoon, begin by pressing the mixture into the bottom of the pie pan and partway up the sides. To keep the crumbs from sticking to your fingers, it helps to place a piece of plastic wrap over the crumbs and press them through the wrap. Then switch to a flat-bottomed straight-sided measuring cup or glass to smooth the crumbs over the bottom and all the way up the sides. Be sure to press the bottom thoroughly so that the crumbs are evenly distributed.

To create an attractive top edge: As you press the crumbs against the sides, they will rise above the rim. Use your left index finger to press against them from the other direction, forming a little ridge or peak. (Chilling the crust for a few minutes firms the butter and makes this task easier.)

SERVING

The finished pie can be cut in the pan or slid out of the pan and onto a serving plate. Either way, it is necessary to loosen the crust from the pan. This can be accomplished by using a dish towel dipped in hot water and wrung well to wipe around the bottom and sides of the pie plate, two or three times. Or, the pie plate can be dipped carefully into a pan of warm water. The butter on the outside of the crust will start to melt and the entire pie or individual slices will come out intact.

STORE

Refrigerated, up to 1 week; frozen, up to 6 months.

POINTERS FOR SUCCESS

∾ Softened butter will work in place of melted butter, but I find that the melted butter is incorporated more evenly and quickly.

UNDERSTANDING

You will see many basic recipes for crumbs crusts using 5 tablespoons of butter but the amount of crumbs will vary between 1¼ cups and 1⅔ cups. That is because crumbs are very difficult to measure. Don't be concerned, as within that range the crust will still work: fewer crumbs, and it will be less firm; more, and it will be stronger and harder.

For baked crusts, too much butter produces a very hard crust. Too little butter produces a very fragile crust, not advisable for pies with meringue toppings. Meringue needs to be anchored to the crust to keep it from shrinking when it bakes. If the crumb crust is too fragile, it will come apart as the meringue contracts.

Graham crackers and gingersnaps contain 3.4 grams of fat per 32 grams. Butter cookies generally contain considerably more fat (always be sure to check the box), so they cannot be used to replace the cookies indicated in these recipes because, during baking, the crust will slide down the sides of the pan. Less butter is used when nuts are added because they contain more fat than the cookie crumbs.

DELUXE CHOCOLATE WAFER CRUMB CRUST

This crust is one of the easiest pie crust recipes in this book. Bittersweet chocolate, heavy cream, and vanilla conspire with store-bought chocolate wafers to produce an intensely fudgy crust. For years I made this crust simply by adding chocolate and water to chocolate wafer crumbs. Then the cookie manufacturers decided to produce only low-fat chocolate wafers, except for the Nabisco Famous chocolate wafers, which are often difficult to find. The Chocolate Nillas contain only 4.5 grams fat per 32 grams. The lower fat produced a dry and crumbly crust. My solution was to add the missing fat in the form of heavy cream and butter. Just as well that they removed their tasteless shortening! The crust has never tasted better.

This crust is tender but firm enough for a spectacular presentation, especially when removed from the pan.

PASTRY FOR A 9-INCH PIE — MAKES: 12.25 OUNCES/247 GRAMS

INGREDIENTS	MEASURE	WEIGHT	
	VOLUME	OUNCES	GRAMS
42 1⅝-inch chocolate wafers (such as Nabisco Chocolate Nilla)*	1½ cups crumbs	5.5 ounces	156 grams
fine-quality bittersweet chocolate, broken into squares	one 3-ounce bar	3 ounces	85 grams
unsalted butter	6 tablespoons	3 ounces	85 grams
heavy cream	1½ tablespoons	0.75 ounce	22 grams
pure vanilla extract	½ teaspoon	•	•

PASTRY FOR A 10-INCH PIE — MAKES: 16.25 OUNCES/460 GRAMS

INGREDIENTS	MEASURE	WEIGHT	
	VOLUME	OUNCES	GRAMS
56 1⅝-inch chocolate wafers (such as Nabisco Chocolate Nilla)*	2 cups crumbs	7.25 ounces	205 grams
fine-quality bittersweet chocolate, broken into squares	1⅓ 3-ounce bars	4 ounces	113 grams
unsalted butter	8 tablespoons	4 ounces	113 grams
heavy cream	2 tablespoons	1 ounce	29 grams
pure vanilla extract	¾ teaspoon	•	•

*Do not use Nabisco Famous chocolate wafers; the consistency will be too soft and gritty.

PREPARING THE PAN
See page 50.

FOOD PROCESSOR METHOD
In a food processor with the metal blade, process the wafers and chocolate until the wafers become fine crumbs and the chocolate is finely grated.* Melt the butter.

*If you need to measure the crumbs after processing them, the chocolate can be added after the wafers are processed, but it must be processed until fine or it will not melt completely.

With the processor on, pour in the hot butter, processing for a few seconds or until it is fully incorporated. Add the cream and vanilla and pulse a few times until incorporated.

HAND METHOD

Place the chocolate wafers in a freezer bag and use a rolling pin to crush them into fine crumbs. Place them in a medium bowl. Finely grate the chocolate and combine it with the crumbs.

Melt the butter. Stir in the hot melted butter and toss to incorporate it well, so that it melts the chocolate and blends it into the wafer crumbs. Stir in the cream and vanilla.

FOR BOTH METHODS

Empty the mixture into the pie plate. Using your fingers or the back of a spoon, begin by pressing the mixture into the bottom of the pie pan and partway up the sides. To keep the crumbs from sticking to your fingers, it helps to place a piece of plastic wrap over the crumbs and press them through the wrap. Then switch to a flat-bottomed straight-sided measuring cup or glass to smooth the crumbs over the bottom and all the way up the sides. Be sure to press the bottom thoroughly so that the crumbs are evenly distributed.

To create an attractive top edge: As you press the crumbs against the sides, they will rise above the rim. Use your left index finger to press against them from the other direction, forming a little ridge or peak. (Chilling the crust for a few minutes firms the butter and makes this task easier.)

Cover the crust with plastic wrap and refrigerate for at least 30 minutes to set the chocolate.

SERVING

The finished pie can be cut in the pan or slid out of the pan and onto a serving plate. Either way, it is necessary to loosen the crust from the pan. This can be accomplished by using a dish towel dipped in hot water and wrung well to wipe around the bottom and sides of the pie plate two or three times. Or, the pie plate can be dipped carefully into a pan of warm water. The butter on the outside of the crust will start to melt and the entire pie or individual slices will come out intact.

STORE

Refrigerated, up to 1 week; frozen, up to 6 months.

POINTERS FOR SUCCESS

∿ Do not bake this crust, because the chocolate will lose flavor.

FRUIT PIES

There are two kinds of people: cake people and pie people. I love cake, but I am really partial to pie. I even love the word. *Pie* sounds so substantial and friendly—full of possibility. I particularly love the way Southerners pronounce it: *Paaah,* sort of like a sigh. And it appeals to my love of fresh tart/sweet fruit, bursting with juices, and the textural contrast of it in combination with a crisp, buttery crust.

My ideal fruit pie has a crisp bottom and top crust and a fresh juicy filling that is set enough to cut into slices that hold their shape but is still just the tiniest bit runny. As these three goals tend to be contradictory, I have, over the years, developed techniques to accomplish them.

I usually like fruit pies to contain just one variety of fruit, but seasonal mixtures are often splendid together, such as the classic combination of strawberry and rhubarb. Other more unusual combinations also make great pairings, such as apricots and raspberries, currants and raspberries, currants and cherries, and nectarines and raspberries.

I don't generally like an entire pie of cooked berries because they are often too seedy and become bitter when cooked (the natural sugars break down and the bitter component is released). Uncooked berries, in contrast, require only about half the sugar. Certain combinations, however, such as currant/raspberry, can work to distract from the seed problem. Two effective techniques I discovered are to bind uncooked berries together with a glaze, as in the Glazed Strawberry Pie (page 102), and to cook only one quarter of the berries and leave the rest uncooked, such as in the Fresh Blueberry Pie (page 106).

To my taste, butter added to the filling dulls the flavor of the fruit (with the exception of apples), so I prefer to have the wonderful flavor of butter only in the crust.

Just about any flaky pie crust is suitable for a fruit pie, though I prefer the all-butter, part–cream cheese variety. As the cream cheese crust is the richest and most full flavored, I choose it to go with fillings that complement it with substantial texture and rich full flavor, such as apple. It's fun to experiment with different combinations of crust and filling to see what excites your own taste.

Fruit pies are at their best the day of baking. The crust is most crisp and the texture of the filling at its most juicy with just a little desirable flow. Fruit pies are most delicious eaten slightly warm, but if they are hot, the filling will not hold together well, unless it is a very shallow layer as in the Open-Faced Apricot Pie (page 120). Most fruit pies are still excellent in flavor and texture on the second and third day after baking. I keep them at room temperature and cover only the exposed filling, so the crust does not become soggy.

I was not born a pie baker. In fact, in all my childhood I can remember only one homebaked pie, and it was made by my grandmother. She made an apple pie and I remember vividly telling her it was good and hearing her answer, "It wasn't worth the trouble." Maybe not for her, but I'm here to tell you that if you love to bake, and love to eat well, it is always worth the effort to make your own pie, because there is nothing like it. At the very least, you'll never want for friends!

My own first apple pie was applesauce pie, and not because that was what I had intended. It was because I used my favorite eating apples: McIntosh. I envisioned a pie looking like those I had seen in photographs where the crust was highly domed and dimpled from the abundance of apple slices piled high within, so I peeled, cored, sliced, and mounded as many apples as would fit into the crust without sliding out, and carefully draped the top crust over them. The baked pie turned out beautifully golden and majestically high. I could hardly wait for it to cool to slice into it. But when I did, I was shocked and disappointed to see that the crust stood alone, towering above a thin layer of melted apples. Apparently, the apples stayed firm long enough for the crust to set and hold its shape and then the high moisture content of the apples (which makes them so delightfully juicy to eat raw) caused them to soften and dissolve. That was when I learned my first lesson about apple pie: Much depends on the type of apples, and a juicy apple like a McIntosh is not a good baking apple.

Years later, my husband, Elliott, and I bought a country house that had only three quarters of an acre of land, but on it resided a magnificent hundred-year-old Baldwin apple tree. We were warned by the previous owners that this old tree produced apples that were perfect for pies, but only every third year, and that when this third year arrived, the tree would produce so lavishly we would not know what to do with all the apples that would end up dropping from the tree and rotting, only to be crushed underfoot.

I waited anxiously for that third year of my apple tree's season. I turned on the huge upright freezer in the basement weeks in advance in anticipation of filling it with unbaked apple pies. And the moment the apples started turning from solid green to a faint blush of pink, I made my second apple pie. The Baldwins kept their shape beautifully, but they were sitting in a puddle of juices that soaked the bottom crust of the baked pie, despite the tapioca I had sprinkled on it before adding the apples. I considered adding more cornstarch to the filling but disliked the idea of corrupting the texture and flavor of the apples. That was when inspiration struck. Why not boil down and concentrate the juices! I had noticed that the apple slices had already begun to exude liquid while sitting with the sugar and spice mixture. I surmised correctly that concentrating this liquid would caramelize the sugars slightly and make the liquid syrupy, resulting in a baked filling that would be juicy but not runny. Since this discovery, I have found that this technique works not only for apples, it also is excellent for peaches and nectarines or any other juicy fruit, so now my fruit pies all have crisp bottom crusts. Another benefit to this technique is that because the juices are concentrated, only about half the usual amount of thickener is required, which results in a more pure and intense fruit flavor.

I went on to make twenty-four apple pies the season of our first Baldwin tree, some with Cheddar cheese in the crust, the rest with just a plain flaky butter crust, which in the end we all preferred. When I baked the first of these frozen pies, I discovered the third great secret: *Fruit pies baked from frozen have crisper bottom crusts!* This is because the bottom crust, which comes into direct contact with the hot pan, starts to bake before the fruit filling begins to defrost, giving the bottom crust extra time to become crisp. (The average pie, when baked frozen, requires about 30 minutes more baking time.)

Three years later, when the next bumper apple crop appeared, I went back into production, but time allowed only making six pies, so I offered baskets of apples as gifts. Then we found our dream house a few miles away, up in the mountains, surrounded by acres of hemlock, pine, and maple but no apple trees. Now for my fall apple pies I buy local apples from the farm stands.

Three years after selling the old house, we decided to take a ride over to see if the new owners had changed the landscaping. As we drove by, we both gasped and cried out in unison, "The Baldwin apple tree!" The beloved old apple tree had disappeared. Not even a stump remained. I guess the new owners must have had enough of rotting apples underfoot. In any event, they sure couldn't have been pie bakers.

QUANTITIES OF INGREDIENTS IN MY FRUIT PIES

FRUIT	PEAK SEASON	QUANTITY	SUGAR	CORNSTARCH	WEIGHT PER CUP
apple	September through November	8 cups 32 ounces 907 grams	½ cup 3.5 ounces 100 grams	4 teaspoons*	4 ounces
apricot	June to early August	4 cups 22 ounces 624 grams	6 tablespoons 2.6 ounces 75 grams	2 tablespoons	5.5 ounces
blackberry	late July through August	4 cups 16 ounces 454 grams	½ cup 3.5 ounces 100 grams	2 tablespoons + 1½ teaspoons	4 ounces
blueberry	June through August	4 cups 20 ounces 567 grams	½ cup 3.5 ounces 100 grams	2 tablespoons	5 ounces
cherry (sour)	late June to early July	3½ cups 20 ounces 567 grams	14 tablespoons 6 ounces 175 grams	2 tablespoons + 1½ teaspoons	5.75 ounces
Concord grape	September to October	4 cups 24 ounces 680 grams	14 tablespoons 6 ounces 175 grams	2 tablespoons + 1½ teaspoons	6 ounces
cranberry	October through December	3½cups 12.25 ounces 347 grams	1¼ cups 8.75 ounces 250 grams	•	3.5 ounces
currant	July	3½ cups 19 ounces 540 grams	1⅓ cups 9.25 ounces 266 grams	3 tablespoons	5.5 ounces
goose-berries	November through December, April to July	4 cups 21 ounces 600 grams	18 tablespoons 8 ounces 225 grams	2 tablespoons + 2 teaspoons	5.25 ounces
peach	June through September	6 cups 34 ounces 964 grams	9 tablespoons 4 ounces 112 grams	4 teaspoons*	5.6 ounces
pear	August through February	5¾ cups 32 ounces 907 grams	6 tablespoons 2.6 ounces 75 grams	4 teaspoons*	5.5 ounces
plum	late June through August†	4 cups 24 ounces 680 grams	½ cup 3.5 ounces 100 grams	2 tablespoons	6 ounces
nectarine	July through August	8 cups 45 ounces 127.5 grams plus 1 cup/ 4 ounces /113 g raspberries	¾ cup 5.25 grams 150 grams	2 tablespoons (5.3 teaspoons with just nectarines)	5.6 ounces
rhubarb	late winter through June	4 cups 16 ounces 454 grams	⅔ cup 4.5 ounces 132 grams	4 teaspoons cornstarch (or 2 eggs)	4 ounces

*The fruit's juices are concentrated, requiring less than the usual amount of thickener.
†Italian prune plum, September through early October.

THE AMOUNT OF CORNSTARCH AND SUGAR FOR 4 OUNCES OF FRUIT†

4 OUNCES OF FRUIT	CORNSTARCH‡	SUGAR (WEIGHT)	SUGAR (VOLUME)
apple*	½ teaspoon	12.5 grams	3 teaspoons
apricot	1 teaspoon	13.6 grams	3¼ teaspoons
blackberry	2 teaspoons	25 grams	3 teaspoons
blueberry	1¼ teaspoons	20 grams	4¾ teaspoons
cherry	1½ teaspoons	35 grams	8½ teaspoons
Concord grape	1¼ teaspoons	28 grams	6¾ teaspoons
cranberry	•	80 grams	19¼ teaspoons
currant	2 teaspoons	56 grams	13½ teaspoons
gooseberry	1¼ teaspoons	42.8 grams	10¼ teaspoons
peach*	scant ½ teaspoon	13 grams	3⅛ teaspoons
pear*	½ teaspoon	9 grams	2⅛ teaspoons
plum	1 teaspoon	16.6 grams	4 teaspoons
nectarine*	scant ½ teaspoon	13.3 grams	3⅛ teaspoons
rhubarb	1 teaspoon	33 grams	8 teaspoons

THE AMOUNT OF CORNSTARCH AND SUGAR FOR 4 CUPS OF FRUIT†

4 CUPS OF FRUIT	CORNSTARCH‡	SUGAR (WEIGHT)	SUGAR (VOLUME)
apple*	2 teaspoons	50 grams (1.75 ounces)	¼ cup
apricot	2 tablespoons	75 grams (2.6 ounces)	6 tablespoons
blackberry	2½ tablespoons	100 grams (3.5 ounces)	½ cup
blueberry	2 tablespoons	100 grams (3.5 ounces)	½ cup
cherry	2 tablespoons + 2½ teaspoons	100 grams (3.5 ounces)	1 cup
Concord grape	2½ tablespoons	175 grams (6 ounces)	14 tablespoons
cranberry	•	285 grams (10 ounces)	1⅓ cups + 1½ tablespoons
currant	3 tablespoons + 1⅓ teaspoons	304 grams (10.7 ounces)	1½ cups + 1 teaspoon
gooseberry	2 tablespoons + 2 teaspoons	225 grams (8 ounces)	1 cup + 2 tablespoons
peach*	2⅔ teaspoons	75 grams (2.6 ounces)	6 tablespoons
pear*	2¾ teaspoons	51 grams (1.8 ounces)	¼ cup
plum	2 tablespoons	100 grams (3.5 ounces)	½ cup
nectarine*	2⅔ teaspoons	75 grams (2.6 ounces)	6 tablespoons
rhubarb	4 teaspoons	132 grams (4.5 ounces)	⅔ cup

* The fruit's juices are concentrated, requiring less than the usual amount of thickener.

† The amount of cornstarch per 4 ounces of fruit varies from 1 to 2 teaspoons; per cup of fruit varies from 1½ to 2½ teaspoons. The amount of sugar for 4 ounces of fruit varies from 1 to 4½ tablespoons. Most of these pies bake at 425°F. for between 40 and 60 minutes.

‡ For pies without bottom crusts: If reducing the fruit juices, omit the cornstarch or decrease it by one third.

POINTERS FOR SUCCESS FOR FRUIT PIES

∾ Make the dough the day before and let it rest for 1 hour refrigerated after rolling and shaping to prevent distortion and for the best shape.

∾ If making the pie to eat the day after baking, decrease the cornstarch by 1 teaspoon.

∾ Use dark heavy metal, ceramic, or Pyrex pie plates for the crispest crust.

∾ For the flakiest crust with the most attractive border, preheat the oven for at least 20 minutes before baking.

∾ For a crisp bottom crust, try baking directly on the floor of the oven for the first 30 minutes of baking, or on an oven stone set on the bottom rack.

∾ The pie's juices must be bubbling thickly all over to ensure that all of the cornstarch can absorb liquid and thicken the filling.

∾ Single-crust pies need to have the edges protected from overbrowning after the first 15 minutes of baking; double-crust pies, after 30 minutes.

∾ If the top of the pie is browning too much, tent it with foil, but be sure to make a steam hole in the center for moisture to escape so the crust stays crisp.

∾ Allow the pie to cool on a rack to room temperature, or until barely warm, before slicing to ensure that the filling is set and will not run. This will take between 2 to 4 hours, depending on the thickness of the pie.

∾ If you spray the pie pan lightly with nonstick vegetable shortening before lining it with the pastry, or if you grease and flour it, it is usually possible to slide out and unmold the whole pie after it has cooled completely. This makes cutting it easier and is better for both the knife and the pie plate! Greasing and flouring also gives a pleasant, slightly rough texture to the bottom crust.

STORING FRUIT PIES

Fruit pies are at their best the day of baking. The crust is most crisp and the filling most juicy with just a little desirable flow. Pies are especially delicious when eaten slightly warm; if they are hot, the filling will not hold together well.

Many fruit pies are still excellent in flavor and texture on the second and third day after baking. I keep them at room temperature and cover only the exposed fruit, so the crust does not become soggy. For open-faced pies, cover the fruit filling lightly with waxed paper. For pies with a lattice crust, cover only the cut openings with plastic wrap. If the weather is very humid, or if I am storing the pie in the country on a porch without screens, I cover the pie with a large inverted bowl.

WINDFALL FRUIT PIELETS

When a sudden windfall brings a very small amount of fruit your way, perhaps a perfect peach or a handful of wild berries or Concord grapes, and you happen to have some flaky pie dough scraps in the freezer, a pielet for two is the perfect solution for close-to-instant gratification. If you don't have enough scraps for even an open-faced pielet, bake decorative cutouts (see page 14) and place them on the cooked or baked filling. Use a piece of foil with a 1-inch-long steam vent cut into the center, if baking the filling, to prevent it from drying.

FILLING AMOUNTS FOR STANDARD 4¼-INCH PIELETS   For an open-faced pielet, there is room for a maximum of 13½ tablespoons of filling if filled right to the top, so a ballpark amount to calculate is ¾ cup of filling for each pielet. For a double-crust pielet, the fruit can be piled higher than the crust, so it's fine to use 1 to 1½ cups. (Keep in mind that the fruit settles down to less volume after sitting with the sugar. One cup of apple slices, for example, becomes about ⅔ cup.)

The fillings for Blackberry Pie, Concord Grape Pie, and Peach Pie are enough to make 4 pielets. The filling for the Cherry Pie is enough to make 5 pielets. The filling for the Best All-American Apple Pie is enough to makes 6 pielets.

PIE CRUST AMOUNTS FOR STANDARD 4¼-INCH PIELETS   The dough for the bottom crust should be rolled about ⅟₁₆ inch thick to ensure that it will bake in the shorter time required to bake the smaller amount of filling. The upper crust can be rolled slightly thicker.

For a single-crust open-faced pielet, you will need about 2 ounces/58 grams of dough. Roll it large enough to cut a 7½-inch circle. Transfer it to the pan and turn under the edge. If desired, crimp the edge (see page 13).

For a single-crust pielet baked in a 4⅝-inch Emile Henry ceramic pan, you will need about 3 ounces/85 grams of dough. Roll it large enough to cut an 8½-inch circle. Turn the border under and press firmly to conform to the scalloped edges.

For a two-crust pielet, you will need about 4.5 ounces/127 grams of dough. Roll the bottom crust large enough cut a 6½-inch circle. It will extend about ¼ inch past the edge of the pan. Roll the top crust large enough to cut a 6-inch circle, or a little larger if the fruit is mounded.

For a two-crust pielet baked in a 4⅝-inch Emile Henry ceramic pan, you will need about 5.5 ounces/156 grams of dough. Roll the bottom crust large enough to cut a 7½-inch circle and the top crust to 6½ inches in diameter, or a little larger if the fruit is mounded. After filling, brush the edges of the bottom crust with lightly beaten egg white or water and apply the top crust. It will extend a little past the bottom crust. Press down firmly on it. Then fold under the edge and crimp the border (see page 13). Cut one or more steam vents into the dough.

A fluted tart pan also provides a charming container for a double-crust pielet.

For a 4- by 1-inch tart pan with a removable bottom, you will need about 4 ounces/113 grams of dough. Roll the bottom crust large enough to cut a 5½-inch circle. When lining the pan, allow the dough to extend past the edge—do not turn it down. Brush the edges with lightly beaten egg white or water. Roll the top crust large enough to cut a 4¾-inch circle (5 inches if the filling is mounded). Set it on top and press it together with the bottom crust. Form a scalloped border by pressing against the dough, from the inside, with your left index finger and pressing the dough around this finger using the thumb and index finger of your right hand.

BAKING THE PIELETS   Small pies really benefit from being baked frozen, as otherwise they bake only for between 30 and 40 minutes, which does not give the crust as much time to get as crisp as I like. If you are not freezing the pielet first, black or ceramic mini pie pans set directly on the oven floor for 30 minutes or on the lowest rack in the oven on a preheated baking stone or baking sheet are the best options. If you are freezing the pies before baking, they will take about an hour to bake (10 minutes at 425°F. and 50 minutes at 400°F.) and it is best to set them on a preheated baking stone or baking sheet on the bottom rack.

For all pielets, make a foil ring (see page 19) to protect the edges of the crust from overbrowning after 15 minutes of baking.

COOLING THE PIELETS   A pielet with ¾ cup of filling takes about 45 minutes to cool. One with more than 1 cup of filling takes about 1½ hours. Once lukewarm or room temperature, it can be unmolded by tilting the pan and sliding it out. If it sticks, slip a small metal spatula between the crust and pan to dislodge any congealed juices that may be keeping it in place.

HALF PIES

A half-size 7-inch pie is a very appealing size and serves four perfectly. Antique pie plates are often 7 inches, as are some small skillets. A 7¾- by 1-inch tart pan with a removable bottom also works well. A half-size pie requires a half- to three-quarters recipe of filling and a half-recipe of dough (about 6.5 ounces/184 grams) for an open-faced pie. Roll it large enough to cut an 11-inch circle.

A two-crust half pie requires 11 ounces/312 grams of dough (6 ounces/170 grams for the bottom and 5 ounces/142 grams for the top). Roll the bottom crust to 10 inches in diameter and the top dough to 8½ inches in diameter, or 9 inches if the filling is mounded. After filling the pie, brush the edges of the bottom crust with water and apply the top crust. It will extend a little past the bottom crust. Press down firmly on it. Then fold under the edge and crimp the border. Cut one or more steam vents into the dough.

Half-size pies take about the same amount of time to bake as full-size pies.

THE BEST ALL-AMERICAN APPLE PIE

Pie does not get better than this. Reducing and concentrating the juices of the apples make it necessary to use only about half the usual amount of thickener, resulting in a more pure apple flavor, a juicy filling, and a crisp bottom crust. Make apple pie in the fall, at the height of the apple season, or whenever you have the yearning. If ever you want to sell your house, have an apple pie baking in the oven as prospective buyers come to visit. The aroma of apples, butter, and cinnamon emanating from the oven permeates the house like none other and makes anyone feel truly at home.

OVEN TEMPERATURE: 425°F. • BAKING TIME: 45 TO 55 MINUTES   **SERVES: 8**

INGREDIENTS	MEASURE	WEIGHT	
	VOLUME	OUNCES	GRAMS
Flaky Cream Cheese Pie Crust for a 2-crust 9-inch pie (page 30)		22 ounces	624 grams
2½ pounds baking apples (see page 635; about 6 medium), peeled, cored, and sliced ¼ inch thick	8 cups (sliced)	2 pounds (sliced)	907 grams
freshly squeezed lemon juice	1 tablespoon	0.5 ounce	16 grams
light brown sugar	¼ cup, packed	scant 2 ounces	54 grams
granulated sugar	¼ cup	1.75 ounces	50 grams
ground cinnamon	½ to 1½ teaspoons	•	•
nutmeg, preferably freshly grated	¼ teaspoon	•	•
salt	¼ teaspoon	•	•
unsalted butter	2 tablespoons	1 ounce	28 grams
cornstarch	1 tablespoon + 1 teaspoon	0.5 ounce	13 grams

EQUIPMENT
A 9-inch pie pan

Make the dough (page 30).

Remove the dough for the bottom crust from the refrigerator. If necessary, allow it to sit for about 10 minutes or until it is soft enough to roll.

On a floured pastry cloth or between two sheets of lightly floured plastic wrap, roll the bottom crust ⅛ inch thick or less and 12 inches in diameter. Transfer it to the pie pan. Trim the edge almost even with the edge of the pan. Cover it with plastic wrap and refrigerate it for a minimum of 30 minutes and a maximum of 3 hours.

In a large bowl, combine the apples, lemon juice, sugars, cinnamon, nutmeg, and salt and toss to mix. Allow the apples to macerate at room temperature for a minimum of 30 minutes and a maximum of 3 hours.

Transfer the apples and their juices to a colander suspended over a bowl to capture the liquid. The mixture will release at least ½ cup of liquid.

In a small saucepan (preferably lined with a nonstick surface), over medium-high heat, boil down this liquid, with the butter, to about ⅓ cup (a little more if you started with more than ½ cup of liquid), or until syrupy and lightly caramelized. Swirl the liquid but do not stir it. (Alternatively, spray a 4-cup heatproof measure with nonstick vegetable spray, add the liquid and butter, and boil it in the microwave, 6 to 7 minutes on high.) Meanwhile, transfer the apples to a bowl and toss them with the cornstarch until all traces of it have disappeared.

Pour the syrup over the apples, tossing gently. (Do not be concerned if the liquid hardens on contact with the apples; it will dissolve during baking.)

Roll out the top crust large enough to cut a 12-inch circle. Use an expandable flan ring or a cardboard template and a sharp knife as a guide to cut the circle.

Transfer the apple mixture to the pie shell. Moisten the border of the bottom crust by brushing it lightly with water and place the top crust over the fruit. Tuck the overhang under the bottom crust border and press down all around the top to seal it. Crimp the border using a fork or your fingers (see page 13) and make about 5 evenly spaced 2-inch slashes starting about 1 inch from the center and radiating - toward the edge. Cover the pie loosely with plastic wrap and refrigerate it for 1 hour before baking to chill and relax the pastry. This will maintain flakiness and help to keep the crust from shrinking.

Preheat the oven to 425°F. at least 20 minutes before baking. Set an oven rack at the lowest level and place a baking stone or baking sheet on it before preheating. Place a large piece of greased foil on top to catch any juices.

Set the pie directly on the foil-topped baking stone and bake for 45 to 55 minutes or until the juices bubble through the slashes and the apples feel tender but not mushy when a cake tester or small sharp knife is inserted through a slash. After 30 minutes, protect the edges from overbrowning with a foil ring (see page 19).

Cool the pie on a rack for at least 4 hours before cutting. Serve warm or at room temperature.

VARIATIONS

BRANDIED RAISIN APPLE PIE   My cousin Susan Butterfass's superb apple pie, which I have enjoyed many a Thanksgiving, has a special touch. She uses three different varieties of apples for contrast in texture and flavor. She also macerates ½ cup of raisins in 3 tablespoons of warm brandy for 20 minutes, drains them, and adds the plumped raisins to the apple mixture just before placing them in the pie crust.

PURE PEAR PIE   I use no spices in this pie filling, opting to make the pear the star. Aside from eliminating the cinnamon, nutmeg, and brown sugar, and decreasing the sugar a little, all the other ingredients remain the same. If the pie is stored at room temperature for 3 days, the pear flavor actually intensifies but the crust remains crisp.

Replace the apples with an equal number or weight of firm but ripe Bartlett or Bosc pears. Cut them in half and core them. Slice them lengthwise into sixteenths, ⅜ inch to ½ inch thick. (Pears are softer than apples, so they can be sliced thicker.) You will have 6 scant cups/32 ounces/907 grams. Sprinkle them with the 1 tablespoon of lemon juice, 6 tablespoons (2.6 ounces/75 grams) of sugar, and the ¼ teaspoon of salt. Boil down the juices with the butter as for the apples. Toss the pears with the cornstarch, and proceed as for the Best All-American Pie.

STORE

Room temperature, up to 3 days.

POINTERS FOR SUCCESS

∽ Some of my favorite pie apples are Macoun, Stayman-Winesap, Cortland, and Jonathan. Other great baking apples I've discovered that are available around the country are listed on page 635. In the winter, I use Granny Smith or Golden Delicious apples from the supermarket, which also make a marvelous pie.

∽ To core and slice the apples, cut them in half and use a melon baller to scoop out the core. Slice each half into eighths and then each piece into 3 pieces or 4 if the apples are very large. The slices must be no thicker than ¼ inch.

∽ As you slice the raw apples, toss them occasionally with the sugar mixture to coat them, to prevent them from turning brown.

∽ If you adore cinnamon, use the full amount. For a milder flavor, use ½ to 1 teaspoon.

∽ As the pie bakes, the bubbling juices are very sticky. If you have a Teflon-type liner (see page 666), place it on top of the foil-topped baking stone under the pie pan for ease in cleanup.

UNDERSTANDING

The apples must be sliced fairly thin so that they can lie closely together. Thick slices mean more air space between them. As they cook and soften, the air space disappears and the apples sink lower in the pan, leaving a gap between them and the crust.

OPEN-FACED DESIGNER APPLE PIE

Arranging the apple slices in a flower petal formation may be work for the cook, but it sure provides luxurious eating for your lucky guests. This pie has an exceptionally crisp bottom crust under a juicy filling of caramelized, cinnamony apples made tangy and glistening with a gilding of apricot preserves. The border is a wreath of leaves cut from the pie crust.

OVEN TEMPERATURE: 425°F. • BAKING TIME: 65 TO 75 MINUTES   **SERVES: 8**

INGREDIENTS	MEASURE	WEIGHT	
	VOLUME	OUNCES	GRAMS
Flaky Cream Cheese Pie Crust for a 9-inch lattice pie (page 30)		22 ounces	624 grams
½ egg white, lightly beaten	1 tablespoon	0.5 ounce	15 grams
2½ pounds baking apples (see page 635; about 6 medium), peeled, cored, and sliced ⅛ inch thick	8 cups (sliced)	2 pounds (sliced)	907 grams
freshly squeezed lemon juice	1 tablespoon	0.5 ounce	16 grams
light brown sugar	¼ cup, packed	2 ounces	54 grams
granulated sugar	¼ cup	1.75 ounces	50 grams
ground cinnamon	½ to 1½ teaspoons	•	•
nutmeg, preferably freshly grated	¼ teaspoon	•	•
salt	¼ teaspoon	•	•
unsalted butter	2 tablespoons	1 ounce	28 grams
cornstarch	1 tablespoon + 1 teaspoon	0.5 ounce	13 grams
1 large egg, lightly beaten	3 tablespoons	2 ounces	56 grams
apricot preserves	¼ cup	3 ounces	85 grams

EQUIPMENT
A 9-inch pie pan; optional: a rose leaf cutter

Make the dough (page 30).

Remove one piece of dough from the refrigerator. If necessary, allow it to sit for about 10 minutes, until it is soft enough to roll.

On a floured pastry cloth or between two sheets of lightly floured plastic wrap, roll the pastry ⅛ inch thick or less and large enough to cut a 12-inch circle. Use an expandable flan ring or a cardboard template and a sharp knife as a guide to cut out the circle. Transfer it to the pie plate. Trim the edge if necessary so that it extends ¼ inch past the edge of the pie plate. Cover the pastry lightly with plastic wrap and refrigerate it for a minimum of 1 hour and a maximum of 24 hours.

Roll out the second piece of dough ⅛ inch thick and cut about twenty-six 2½-inch leaves, using a cutter or small sharp knife. Use a small sharp knife to make veins. Cover and refrigerate.

Preheat the oven to 425°F. at least 20 minutes before baking.

Line the pastry with parchment, pleating it as necessary so it fits into the pan, and fill it with dried beans or peas. Bake for 20 minutes. Carefully lift out the beans with the parchment. With a fork, prick the bottom and sides and bake 5 to 10 minutes more or until the crust is pale golden. Check after 3 minutes and prick any bubbles that may have formed.

Cool the crust on a rack for 3 minutes, so it is no longer piping hot, then brush the bottom and sides with the egg white.

In a large bowl, combine the apples, lemon juice, sugars, cinnamon, nutmeg, and salt and toss to mix. Allow the apples to macerate for a minimum of 30 minutes and a maximum of 3 hours at room temperature.

Transfer the apples and their juices to a colander suspended over a bowl to capture the liquid. The mixture will release at least ½ cup of liquid.

In a small saucepan (preferably lined with a nonstick surface), over medium-high heat, boil down this liquid, with the butter, to ⅓ cup (a little more if more than ½ cup of liquid), or until syrupy and lightly caramelized. Swirl the liquid but do not stir it. (Alternatively, spray a 4-cup heatproof measure with nonstick vegetable spray, add the liquid and butter, and boil it in the microwave, about 7 minutes on high.) Meanwhile, transfer the apples to a bowl and toss them with the cornstarch until all traces of it have disappeared.

Pour the hot syrup over the apples, tossing gently. (If the liquid hardens on contact with the apples, allow them to sit at room temperature for about 20 minutes or until the moisture from the apples dissolves it.)

Arrange the apples, overlapping the slices in concentric circles in the pie shell, starting from the outside edge. Keep adding more apples, using the tip of a knife to help insert them in between the other slices, until you have used all the slices. Pour any remaining apple juices evenly over the apples.

Brush the baked pie crust rim with the egg. Brush the bottom of each leaf with egg and place the leaves on the border, tilting them and overlapping them slightly. Brush the top of the leaves with egg. Cover the pie loosely with plastic wrap and refrigerate it for 30 minutes before baking to chill the pastry. This will maintain flakiness.

Preheat the oven to 425°F. at least 20 minutes before baking. Set an oven rack at the lowest level and place a baking stone or baking sheet on it before preheating. Place a large piece of greased foil on top to catch any juices.

Set the pie directly on the foil-topped baking stone and bake for 15 minutes. Cut a round of foil to fit over the apples and the edge of the crust and crimp it in 3 or 4 places to create a dome. Cover the pie with the foil and cut 3 steam vents in the foil, about 3 inches long. Continue baking for 45 to 50 minutes or until the juices bubble and the apples feel tender but not mushy when pierced with a cake tester or small sharp knife. Remove the foil and bake for 5 to 10 minutes or until the top of the apples is golden brown. Remove the pie to a rack.

In a small saucepan or microwave oven, heat the apricot preserves until melted and bubbling. Strain them into a small cup. Brush them over the top of the apples. Serve warm or at room temperature.

STORE
Room temperature, up to 2 days.

NOTE
For a different look, a 10- by 2-inch tart pan can be used. The fluted sides provide the decoration instead of the pastry leaf border. The apples should be covered when you put the pie in the oven, as there is no exposed pastry to brown.

POINTERS FOR SUCCESS
~ See Best All-American Apple Pie, page 81.

APPLE CRUMB PIE

This variation of the classic apple pie is absolutely irresistible because of its many different textures. A thick layer of caramelized apples is set in a crisp crust and topped with a crunchy streusel.

EQUIPMENT
A 9-inch pie pan

Make the dough (page 29).

Remove the dough from the refrigerator. If necessary, allow it to sit for about 10 minutes or until it is soft enough to roll.

Using a pastry cloth and sleeve rubbed with flour or two sheets of plastic wrap lightly sprinkled with flour, roll out the pastry ⅛ inch thick or less and large enough to cut a 13-inch circle. Use an expandable flan ring or a cardboard template and sharp knife as a guide to cut out the circle. Transfer the dough to the pie pan. Fold under the excess and crimp the border using a fork or your fingers (see

OVEN TEMPERATURE: 425°F., THEN 400°F • BAKING TIME: 75 TO 80 MINUTES   SERVES: 8

| INGREDIENTS | MEASURE | WEIGHT | |
	VOLUME	OUNCES	GRAMS
Flaky Cream Cheese Pie Crust for a 9-inch pie (page 29)		11 ounces	312 grams
½ large egg white, lightly beaten	1 tablespoon	0.5 ounce	15 grams
3 pounds baking apples (see page 635; about 7 medium), peeled, cored, and sliced ¼ inch thick	9½ to 10 cups (sliced)	2 pounds 6 to 9 ounces (sliced)	1 kg 90 to 162 grams
freshly squeezed lemon juice	1 tablespoon	0.5 ounce	16 grams
light brown sugar	⅓ cup, packed	2.5 ounces	72 grams
granulated sugar	¼ cup	1.75 ounces	50 grams
ground cinnamon	½ to 1½ teaspoons	•	•
nutmeg, preferably freshly grated	¼ teaspoon	•	•
salt	¼ teaspoon	•	•
unsalted butter	2 tablespoons	1 ounce	28 grams
cornstarch	2 teaspoons	•	6 grams
Streusel Topping (page 592)	1 to 1⅔ cups	6 to 9 ounces	170 to 255 grams

page 13). Cover it loosely and refrigerate for a minimum of 1 hour and a maximum of 24 hours.

Preheat the oven to 425°F. at least 20 minutes before baking.

Line the pastry with parchment, pleating it as necessary so it fits into the pan, and fill it with rice or dried beans. Bake for 20 minutes. Carefully lift out the rice or beans with the parchment. With a fork, prick the bottom and sides and bake 5 to 10 minutes more or until the crust is pale golden. Check after 3 minutes and prick any bubbles that may have formed.

Cool the crust on a rack for 3 minutes, so it is no longer piping hot, then brush the bottom and sides with the egg white.

In a large bowl, combine the apples, lemon juice, sugars, cinnamon, nutmeg, and salt and toss to mix. Allow the apples to macerate for a minimum of 30 minutes and a maximum of 3 hours at room temperature.

Transfer the apples and their juices to a colander suspended over a bowl to capture the liquid. The mixture will exude at least ⅔ cup of liquid.

In a small saucepan (preferably lined with a nonstick surface), over medium-high heat, boil down this liquid, with the butter, to ⅓ cup (a little more if more than ⅔ cup of liquid), or until syrupy and lightly caramelized. Swirl the liquid but do not stir it. (Or spray a 4-cup heatproof measure with nonstick vegetable spray, add the liquid and butter, and boil it in the microwave, about 8 minutes on high.) Meanwhile, transfer the apples to a bowl and toss them with the cornstarch until all traces of it have disappeared.

Pour the hot syrup over the apples, tossing gently. (Do not be concerned if the liquid hardens on contact with the apples; it will dissolve during baking.)

Preheat the oven to 425°F. at least 20 minutes before baking. Set an oven rack at the lowest level and place a baking stone or baking sheet on it before preheating. Place a large piece of greased foil on top to catch any juices.

Transfer the apple mixture to the pie shell. The apples will mound well above the top of the pie pan but will settle down somewhat during baking. Cut a round of foil to fit over the apples and the edge of the crust and crimp it in 3 or 4 places to create a dome. Cover the top of the pie with the foil and cut 3 steam vents in the foil, about 3 inches long.

Set the pie directly on the foil-topped baking stone and bake for 1 hour. Remove the pie from the oven and remove and discard the foil dome. Lower the oven temperature to 400°F. Sprinkle the top of the apples all over with the streusel, pressing it lightly if necessary for it to adhere to the moist apples. Place a ring of foil over the edges to protect them from overbrowning (see page 19) and return the pie to the oven. Bake for 15 to 20 minutes or until the juices bubble and the apples feel tender but not mushy when a cake tester or small sharp knife is inserted into them and the streusel is golden brown. Cool on a rack.

Serve warm or at room temperature.

STORE
Room temperature, up to 2 days.

POINTERS FOR SUCCESS
∾ See Best All-American Apple Pie, page 81.
∾ The apples should still feel a little firm when removed from the oven, as they are such a deep layer they will continue cooking for several minutes.

UNDERSTANDING
A high oven temperature is needed to set the streusel and keep it from being greasy.

Proportionately less than half the thickener is added for this pie as for the double-crust apple pie because the absence of a top crust allows additional liquid to evaporate during the last 15 minutes of cooking. This results in a pure apple flavor.

CRUSTLESS APPLE CRUMB PIE

This pie is for those who eat their apples in the form of a crisp, which is a crustless pie with crumb topping. No thickener is used in the filling, because the juices are concentrated and there is no bottom crust to get soggy, so the apples can be more juicy. Also, a little less sugar is added to the filling because without the bottom crust, less sugar provides a better flavor balance. This crumb pie is at its best when served warm, accompanied by caramel or vanilla ice cream (page 243 or page 232).

OVEN TEMPERATURE: 400°F. • BAKING TIME: 50 TO 55 MINUTES   SERVES: 6

INGREDIENTS	MEASURE	WEIGHT	
	VOLUME	OUNCES	GRAMS
1½ pounds baking apples (see page 635; about 3 large), peeled, cored, and sliced ½ inch thick	4½ to 5 cups (sliced)	20 ounces (sliced)	567 grams
freshly squeezed lemon juice	1½ teaspoons	0.25 ounce	8 grams
light brown sugar	2 tablespoons, packed	1 ounce	27 grams
granulated sugar	2 tablespoons	scant 1 ounce	25 grams
ground cinnamon	¾ teaspoon	•	•
nutmeg, preferably freshly grated	⅛ teaspoon	•	•
salt	⅛ teaspoon	•	•
unsalted butter	1 tablespoons	0.5 ounce	14 grams
Topping light brown sugar	(1½ cups) 2 tablespoons + 2 teaspoons, packed	(8.3 ounces) 2 ounces	(236 grams) 56 grams
sugar	1 tablespoon	0.5 ounce	12.5 grams
walnut halves	½ cup	1.75 ounces	50 grams
salt	1/16 teaspoon	•	•
ground cinnamon	¾ teaspoon	•	•
bleached all-purpose flour	½ cup (dip and sweep method)	2.5 ounces	72 grams
unsalted butter, slightly softened	¼ cup	2 ounces	57 grams
pure vanilla extract	¾ teaspoon	•	•

EQUIPMENT
A 9-inch pie pan

Preheat the oven to 400°F. at least 20 minutes before baking time. Set an oven rack on the second level from the bottom.

In a large bowl, combine the apples, lemon juice, sugars, cinnamon, nutmeg, and salt and toss to mix. Allow the mixture to sit for 30 minutes to 1 hour.

MAKE THE TOPPING

In a food processor fitted with the metal blade, pulse together the sugars, nuts, salt, and cinnamon until the nuts are coarsely chopped. Add the flour, butter, and vanilla and pulse until the mixture is coarse and crumbly, about 20 times. Empty it into a small bowl and with your fingertips, lightly pinch together the mixture to form little clumps. (Or, in a medium bowl, whisk all the topping ingredients except for the butter, using your fingers to get rid of any lumps in the sugar if necessary. Add the butter and cut it in, using a pastry cutter or two knives, until the mixture resembles coarse meal. Lightly pinch the together to form little clumps.)

Transfer the apples and their juices to a colander suspended over a bowl to capture the liquid. The mixture will exude about ¼ cup of liquid.

In a small saucepan (preferably lined with a nonstick surface), reduce this liquid, over medium-high heat, with the butter, to 2 tablespoons. (Or spray a 4-cup heatproof measure with nonstick vegetable spray, add the liquid and butter, and reduce it in the microwave, about 4 minutes on high.) Pour the hot liquid over the apples, tossing them gently.

Transfer the apples to the baking dish. Pour in all the remaining juice. Cover the dish with foil and make a 1-inch slash in the middle. Bake the apples for 30 minutes.

Remove the foil and sprinkle the surface evenly with the topping. Continue baking for 20 to 25 minutes or until the topping is crisp and golden brown, the fruit juices are bubbling thickly around the edges, and the apples feel tender but not mushy when a cake tester or small sharp knife is inserted. Cool on a rack.

Serve the crumb pie warm or at room temperature.

STORE

Room temperature, up to 2 days; refrigerated, up to 3 days.

NOTE

If a deeper filling is desired, you can increase the filling by 1½ times and the initial baking time to 40 minutes. Set a greased foil-lined baking sheet under the pie to catch bubbling juices.

ROSY APPLE CRANBERRY PIE

This pie is a thing of beauty. During baking, the apples become rose-tinted by the cranberries. Golden raisins add more color and a welcome sweetness against the tart apple and cranberry. Though the fruit sinks below the top crust, the cranberries leave their charming round impressions in it as an intriguing clue to the berries beneath.

OVEN TEMPERATURE: 425°F. • BAKING TIME: 50 TO 60 MINUTES   **SERVES: 8**

INGREDIENTS	MEASURE	WEIGHT	
	VOLUME	OUNCES	GRAMS
Flaky Cream Cheese Pie Crust for a 2-crust 9-inch pie (page 30)		22 ounces	624 grams
1⅔ pounds baking apples (see page 635; about 4 medium), peeled, cored, and sliced ¼ inch thick	6 cups (sliced)	1½ pounds (sliced)	680 grams
freshly squeezed lemon juice	1 tablespoon	0.5 ounce	16 grams
granulated sugar	¾ cup	5.3 ounces	150 grams
light brown sugar	¼ cup, packed	2 ounces	54 grams
ground cinnamon	1 teaspoon	•	•
salt	⅛ teaspoon	•	•
unsalted butter	4 teaspoons	0.66 ounce	18 grams
cornstarch	2½ tablespoons	approx. 0.75 ounce	24 grams
fresh (or frozen) cranberries, rinsed, picked over, and dried	2 cups	7 ounces	200 grams
optional: golden raisins or 2 extra tablespoons granulated sugar	½ cup	2.5 ounces	72 grams

EQUIPMENT
A 9-inch pie pan

Make the dough (page 30).

Remove the dough for the bottom crust from the refrigerator. If necessary, allow it to sit for about 10 minutes or until it is soft enough to roll.

On a floured pastry cloth or between two sheets of lightly floured plastic wrap, roll out the bottom crust ⅛ inch thick or less and 12 inches in diameter. Transfer it to the pie pan. Trim the edge almost even with the edge of pan. Cover it with plastic wrap and refrigerate it for a minimum of 30 minutes and a maximum of 3 hours.

In a large bowl, combine the apples, lemon juice, sugars, cinnamon, and salt and toss to mix. Allow the apples to macerate for a minimum of 30 minutes and a maximum of 3 hours at room temperature.

Transfer the apple mixture to a colander suspended over a bowl to capture the liquid. The mixture will exude at least 6 tablespoons of liquid.

In a small saucepan (preferably lined with a nonstick surface), over medium-high heat, boil down this liquid, with the butter, to ¼ cup, or until syrupy and lightly caramelized. Swirl the liquid but do not stir it. (Or spray a 4-cup heatproof measure with nonstick vegetable spray, add the liquid and butter, and boil it in the microwave, about 8 minutes on high.) Meanwhile, transfer the apples to a bowl and toss them with the cornstarch until all traces of it have disappeared.

Pour the hot syrup over the apples, tossing gently. (Do not be concerned if the liquid hardens on contact with the apples; it will dissolve during baking.) Add the cranberries and optional raisins and toss gently to mix them.

Roll out the top crust large enough to cut a 12-inch circle. Use an expandable flan ring or a cardboard template and a sharp knife as a guide to cut the circle.

Transfer the apple mixture to the pie shell. Moisten the border of the bottom crust by brushing it lightly with water and place the top crust over the fruit. Tuck the overhang under the bottom crust border and press down all around the top to seal it. Crimp the border using a fork or your fingers (see page 13). Cover the pie loosely with plastic wrap and refrigerate it for 1 hour before baking to chill and relax the pastry. This will maintain flakiness and help to prevent distortion.

Preheat the oven to 425°F. at least 20 minutes before baking. Set an oven rack at the lowest level and place a baking stone or baking sheet on it before preheating. (Place a large piece of greased foil on top to catch any juices.)

Use a small cutter, the bottom of a pastry tube, or a knife to cut a small hole (about 1 inch) in the middle of the top crust. Lift out the cut round of pastry and discard it. Set the pie directly on the foil-topped baking stone and bake for 50 to 60 minutes or until the juices are bubbling out through the hole and the apples feel tender but not mushy when a cake tester or small sharp knife is inserted through the center opening into the apples. After 30 minutes, protect the edges from overbrowning with a foil ring (see page 19).

Cool the pie on a rack for at least 4 hours before cutting.

STORE

Room temperature, up to 2 days.

POINTERS FOR SUCCESS

∾ See Best All-American Apple Pie, page 81.

UNDERSTANDING

Each cup of apples requires 1 tablespoon of sugar. Two cups of cranberries need ¾ cup of sugar. The raisins add a little extra sweetness. They are added after the sugar syrup, as it would tend to cause them to stick together if added with the apples.

CHERRY LATTICE PIE

When I think of Michigan, my immediate association is cherry pie, because Michigan is the nation's sour cherry capital. Cherry pie is America's favorite pie. It is also my father's and my husband's favorite pie. Fortunately for both of them, it is also my favorite pie, although my father has always maintained that no one has ever made one as good as his mother's.

There is something about sour cherries. Their tart flavor is as pure and joyful as the piercingly clear song of a cardinal. Classic cherry pie is made only with bright red sour cherries. For the truest flavor and texture, use fresh or frozen cherries. You can freeze your own and they will be every bit as good as the fresh, or you can purchase them (see page 639).

Never a cherry season goes by, no matter how busy I am, without my baking at least one cherry pie. And over the past twenty years, every time I made my father a cherry pie, my husband would have a ritual of asking him, "Well? Is it as good as your mother's?" The answer was always the same: a polite pause, and then the unflinchingly honest answer, "Not quite. I don't know *what* it was that made hers so special." It wasn't until after my mother died two years ago that Dad answered the question differently. To my utter astonishment, he said simply, "It's better." With these words, I knew I had finally come into my own.

Classic cherry pie is baked with a lattice crust. When cherries are not in season, or when you want a very quick and easy cherry pie filling with an incredibly pure and intense flavor, try the Fruit Perfect™ Cherry Pie variation on page 95.

It's also fun to make a designer version using leaf-shaped pie crust cutouts (see page 129).

EQUIPMENT
A 9-inch pie pan

INGREDIENTS	MEASURE	WEIGHT	
	VOLUME	OUNCES	GRAMS
Flaky Cream Cheese Pie Crust for a 9-inch lattice pie (page 30)		14.3 ounces	406 grams
sugar	¾ cup + 2 tablespoons	approx. 6 ounces	175 grams
cornstarch	2½ tablespoons	approx. 0.75 ounce	24 grams
salt	a pinch	•	•
1½ pounds fresh sour cherries	3½ cups (pitted and juices reserved)	1¼ pounds	567 grams (pitted)
pure almond extract	¼ teaspoon	•	•
Optional Glaze			
1 large egg yolk	1 tablespoon	•	•
heavy cream	1 teaspoon	•	•

Make the dough (page 30).

Remove the larger piece of dough from the refrigerator. If necessary, allow it to sit for about 10 minutes or until it is soft enough to roll.

Using a pastry cloth and sleeve rubbed with flour or two sheets of plastic wrap lightly sprinkled with flour, roll the dough ⅛ inch thick or less and large enough to cut a 13-inch circle. Use an expandable flan ring or a cardboard template and a sharp knife as a guide to cut out the circle. Transfer the dough to the pie pan. It should extend about ¾ inch past the side of the pie plate. Fold this dough under so that it is flush with the outer edge of the pie plate. Cover the pastry with plastic wrap and refrigerate it for a minimum of 30 minutes and a maximum of 3 hours.

In a medium bowl, stir together the sugar, cornstarch, and salt. Stir in the cherries along with any juice and the almond extract. Allow the mixture to macerate for a minimum of 10 minutes and a maximum of 3 hours.

Stir the cherry mixture well and transfer it to the pie shell.

Roll the remaining smaller piece of dough into an oval 10½ inches by 8 inches wide (and about 1⁄16 inch thick). Using a ruler and pastry jagger, cut ten ¾-inch strips.

To create a woven lattice decoration (see page 16), arrange half the strips evenly over the cherries. Gently curve back every other strip a little past the center and place another strip perpendicular on top. Uncurve the strips so that they lie flat on top of the perpendicular strip. Working in the same direction, curve back the strips that were not curved back the first time. Lay a second perpendicular strip on top and uncurve the strips. Continue in this manner with a third perpendicular strip, curving back the strips that were curved back the first time. Apply the remaining 2 strips to the other side of the pie, starting toward the center and working toward the edge. Remember always to alternate the strips that are curved back so that the strips weave in and out.

Use sharp scissors to trim the strips to a ½-inch overhang. Moisten the dough under each strip with water and tuck the overhang under the bottom crust border, pressing down to make it adhere.

For the optional glaze, lightly beat the egg yolk and cream together. Brush it on the lattice and border. If time allows, refrigerate the pie for 1 hour, lightly covered with plastic wrap, to keep the crust from shrinking when it bakes.

Preheat the oven to 425°F. at least 20 minutes before baking. Set an oven rack at the lowest level and place a baking stone or baking sheet on it before preheating.

Set the pie directly on the baking stone and bake for 40 to 50 minutes or until the filling is *thickly* bubbling all over and the center is slightly puffed. Cover the edges with a foil ring (see page 19) after 15 minutes of baking. If the lattice starts to become too dark toward the last 10 minutes of baking, cover it lightly with a piece of foil with a vent hole in the center.

Cool the pie on a rack for at least 3 hours before serving.

VARIATIONS

FRUIT PERFECT™ CHERRY PIE   2 jars (13.5 ounces each) Fruit Perfect Cherries (see page 639), 1 tablespoon cornstarch (0.3 ounce/9.5 grams), 1 tablespoon water, and ¼ cup sugar (1.75 ounces/50 grams). Empty the cherries, with their thickened juices, into a medium bowl. In small bowl, stir together the cornstarch and water to dissolve the cornstarch. Gently and evenly stir this mixture into the cherries with the sugar. Bake as for Cherry Lattice Pie, but at 400°F. for 30 to 35 minutes.

DESIGNER CHERRY PIE   Make enough pastry for a 2-crust 9-inch pie. Prebake the bottom crust (see page 18). Instead of making a lattice crust, roll the remaining dough out ⅛ inch thick and use a sharp knife to cut out about 18 leaf shapes, 3 inches long. Drape them over little clumps of aluminum foil set on a baking sheet. Brush them with the egg glaze if desired and bake them at 425°F. for 10 to 15 minutes or until golden. Set them aside.

You will need to increase the filling by one and a third: Use 2 pounds sour cherries (4½ cups pitted/26 ounces/737 grams), 1 cup plus 2 tablespoons plus 2 teaspoons sugar (8 ounces/227 grams) 3 tablespoons plus 1 teaspoon cornstarch (1 ounce/31 grams), a pinch of salt, and a generous ¼ teaspoon almond extract.

Place all of the above ingredients except for the almond extract in a nonreactive medium saucepan and allow them to sit for about 10 minutes or until the cherries exude enough juice to moisten the sugar. Stir gently until evenly mixed and bring to a full boil over medium heat, stirring constantly. Lower the heat and simmer for 1 minute or until the juices thicken and become translucent, stirring gently. Remove from the heat and stir in the almond extract.

Pour the cherry mixture into the prebaked pie shell. Place a foil ring (see page 19) on the pie and bake in a preheated 400°F. oven for 15 to 20 minutes or until bubbling all over. Remove to a rack and while the pie is still hot, arrange the reserved pastry leaves over the cherries.

CHERRY PIELETS   The filling for this recipe is enough to make 5 individual 4¼-inch pies. You will need enough dough for a two-crust pie, divided into 5 pieces. Roll each piece into a 7½-inch circle (¹⁄₁₆ inch thick). Reroll the scraps for the lattice ¹⁄₁₆ inch thick into an oval 6 inches long and cut thirty ½-inch-wide by 6-inch-long strips. Use 6 strips for each little pie. Proceed as for the standard 9-inch pie, baking the pielets for 25 to 35 minutes or until the juices thickly bubble. Cover the edges with a foil ring after 15 minutes of baking to prevent overbrowning.

EQUIPMENT

Five mini 4¼-inch pie pans

STORE

Room temperature, up to 2 days.

POINTERS FOR SUCCESS

∾ Sour cherries start to deteriorate very quickly after picking, especially if the stems have been removed. They freeze magnificently, however, but should be prepared for freezing and frozen as soon as possible for the best quality. To freeze cherries for future pies, pit them, saving all the juices, add ¼ cup sugar for each 3½ cups (20 ounces/567 grams) of cherries, and freeze in glass canning jars or heavy storage containers. In a freezer that maintains a temperature below 0°F., they will last for 3 years or even longer. (I have some that are still good after 6 years! After 2 years, their color will gradually fade. To restore it, add ¼ teaspoon red food color with the rest of the ingredients.)

When ready to bake a pie, defrost the cherries until they separate. Empty them into a large bowl and add the remaining ingredients, remembering that you have already added ¼ cup of sugar. Allow them to sit until they have thawed and the sugar and thickener have formed a syrup from the defrosting cherry juices and dissolved completely. (If any cherries are still frozen, parts of the pie may overcook before the filling has thickened evenly.)

∾ A large heavy hairpin is the ideal cherry pitter. Insert the looped end into the stem end, hook it around the pit, and pull it out.

∾ If you have a very sweet tooth, you can use a total of 1 cup of sugar.

∾ The egg glaze is easiest to apply if frozen and defrosted before using, as it thickens.

UNDERSTANDING

Adding butter directly to the cherries would take the edge off their flavor. Using an all-butter pastry crust, however, infuses the cherries with a rich buttery flavor. For the brightest color, it is best not to cook a cherry filling before baking the pie.

Egg glazing delivers a gorgeous lacquered finish but also toughens the crust slightly. This toughening effect is much less noticeable on lattice strips or pastry cutouts than on a solid upper crust.

I've made the 1-hour relaxing period for the finished unbaked pie optional because with a lattice crust, shrinking is not as noticeable.

Almond extract combines almost magically with the cherries, yielding a more intense cherry flavor.

PURE RHUBARB LATTICE PIE

One of my earliest childhood memories is the sharp, aromatic smell of rhubarb my grandmother used to cut on the back porch of our house. When properly sweetened, these lively reddish green stalks, which are actually in the vegetable family, make a tasty dessert. This recipe displays rhubarb in its purest form.

Rhubarb also makes a good companion for a custard filling (see variations below). The most popular rhubarb pie filling, however, is strawberry rhubarb, (see Fresh Strawberry and Rhubarb Tart, page 256).

OVEN TEMPERATURE: 425°F. • BAKING TIME: 30 TO 40 MINUTES   **SERVES: 6**

INGREDIENTS	MEASURE	WEIGHT	
	VOLUME	OUNCES	GRAMS
Flaky Cream Cheese Pie Crust for a 9-inch lattice pie (page 30)		14.3 ounces	406 grams
rhubarb, cut into ½-inch pieces	4 cups	1 pound	454 grams
sugar	⅔ cup	4.6 ounces	132 grams
cornstarch	4 teaspoons	approx. 0.5 ounce	12.5 grams
finely grated lemon zest	1 teaspoon	•	2 grams
salt	pinch	•	•
Optional Glaze			
1 large egg yolk	1 tablespoon	•	•
heavy cream	1 teaspoon	•	•

EQUIPMENT
A 9-inch pie pan

Make the dough (page 30).

Remove the dough from the refrigerator. If necessary, allow it to sit for about 10 minutes or until it is soft enough to roll.

Using a pastry cloth and sleeve rubbed with flour or two sheets of plastic wrap lightly sprinkled with flour, roll the dough ⅛ inch thick or less and large enough to cut a 13-inch circle. Use an expandable flan ring or a cardboard template and a sharp knife as a guide to cut out the circle. Transfer the dough to the pie pan. It should extend about ¾ inch past the side of the pie plate. Fold this dough under so that it is flush with the outer edge of the pie plate. Cover with plastic wrap and refrigerate for a minimum of 30 minutes and a maximum of 3 hours.

In a medium bowl, combine the rhubarb, sugar, cornstarch, lemon zest, and salt and toss to coat the rhubarb evenly. Allow it to macerate for about 10 minutes or until the sugar is moistened fully. Scrape the mixture into the pie crust.

Roll the smaller piece of dough into an oval 10½ inches by 8 inches wide (by about ⅟₁₆ inch thick). Using a ruler and pastry jagger, cut ten ¾-inch strips.

To create a woven lattice decoration (see page 16), arrange half the strips evenly over the cherries. Gently curve back every other strip a little past the center and place another strip perpendicular on top across the center. Uncurve the strips so that they lie flat on top of the perpendicular strip. Working in the same direction, curve back the strips that were not curved back the first time. Lay a second perpendicular strip on top and uncurve the strips. Continue in this manner with a third perpendicular strip, curving back the strips that were curved back the first time. Apply the remaining 2 strips to the other side of the pie, starting toward the center and working toward the edge. Remember always to alternate the strips that are curved back so that the strips weave in and out.

Use sharp scissors to trim the strips to ½-inch overhang. Moisten the dough under each strip with egg white or water and tuck the overhang under the bottom crust border, pressing down to make it adhere.

For the optional glaze, lightly beat the egg yolk and cream together. Brush the lattice and border with the egg glaze and, if time allows, refrigerate the pie for 1 hour, covered loosely with plastic wrap, to keep the crust from shrinking when it bakes.

Preheat the oven to 425°F. at least 20 minutes before baking. Set an oven rack at the lowest level and place a baking stone or baking sheet on it before preheating.

Set the pie directly on the baking stone and bake for 30 minutes or until the filling is *thickly* bubbling all over. After the first 15 minutes of baking, protect the edges with a foil ring (see page 19) to prevent overbrowning.

Cool the pie on a rack for at least 1 hour before serving.

VARIATIONS

LIGHT CUSTARD RHUBARB PIE   To my taste, adding two eggs to the filling in place of the usual cornstarch thickener adds a more interesting dimension. The eggs mingle with the rhubarb's juices to form just enough silken gold custard between the pieces of rhubarb to bind them together and to gentle without taming the rhubarb's tangy bite.

Replace the cornstarch with 2 large eggs (3 fluid ounces/3.5 ounces/100 grams), lightly beaten. In a medium bowl, combine the rhubarb, sugar, lemon zest, and salt and toss to coat the rhubarb evenly. Allow it to macerate for about 10 minutes or until the sugar is moistened fully. Scrape the mixture into the pie crust and pour the eggs over it.

Set the pie on the stone and bake at 425°F. for 10 minutes. Reduce the temperature to 400°F. and continue baking for 30 minutes or until the filling is bubbling lightly and set. After the first 15 minutes of baking, protect the edges with a foil ring to prevent overbrowning.

CUSTARD PIE WITH RHUBARB   Omit the lattice and stir together 1 tablespoon of cornstarch, 1 cup of cream, and 2 eggs. Proceed as above for Light Custard Rhubarb Pie but bake for about 10 minutes longer or until the edges of the filling bubble, the surface is puffed and golden, with little bits of the red rhubarb peeking through, and the center is set. (A knife inserted near the center should come out clean.)

STORE

Room temperature, up to 2 days. (The Custard Pie with Rhubarb can be held at room temperature for 3 hours but then must be refrigerated, loosely covered.)

NOTE

The Pure Rhubarb Pie and the Light Custard variation can both be frozen before baking and baked for an extra 20 minutes at 400°F.

POINTERS FOR SUCCESS

∾ When buying rhubarb, select bright, firm stalks. Discard the leaves, which contain poisonous oxalic acid. Strawberry rhubarb has a beautiful deep rose and green color and a less astringent flavor. Store rhubarb refrigerated in an open plastic bag for up to a week.

∾ Any leftover rhubarb can be cut and frozen for several months. Freeze the pieces on a cookie sheet for about 2 hours or until frozen solid. Then transfer them to a freezer-weight storage bag or canning jar.

CHERRY RHUBARB LATTICE PIE

T he classic combination of strawberry and rhubarb for a pie probably came
into being because they share the same season and the sweetness of strawberries offsets the tartness of rhubarb. Since rhubarb is still in season in
July, when cherries are in season, I have discovered that with a judicious amount
of sugar and extra liquid to give them a chance to blend, the intermingling of tart
rhubarb with sour cherries is more exciting still.

OVEN TEMPERATURE: 425°F. • BAKING TIME: 30 TO 40 MINUTES   **SERVES: 6 TO 8**

INGREDIENTS	MEASURE	WEIGHT	
	VOLUME	OUNCES	GRAMS
Flaky Cream Cheese Pie Crust for a 9-inch lattice pie (page 30)		14.3 ounces	406 grams
sugar	⅔ cup	4.6 ounces	132 grams
cornstarch	2 tablespoons	0.66 ounce	19 grams
salt	a pinch	•	•
water	¼ liquid cup	2 ounces	59 grams
10 ounces fresh sour cherries	1½ cups (pitted and juices reserved)	8 ounces (pitted)	227 grams
rhubarb, cut into ½-inch pieces	2 cups	8 ounces	227 grams
Optional Glaze 1 large egg yolk	1 tablespoon	•	•
heavy cream	1 teaspoon	•	•

EQUIPMENT
A 9-inch pie pan

Make the dough (page 30).

Remove the larger piece of dough from the refrigera-
tor. If necessary, allow it to sit for about 10 minutes or until it is soft enough to
roll.

Using a pastry cloth and sleeve rubbed with flour or two sheets of plastic wrap
lightly sprinkled with flour, roll the dough ⅛ inch thick or less and large enough
to cut a 13-inch circle. Use an expandable flan ring or a cardboard template and a
sharp knife as a guide to cut out the circle. Transfer the dough to the pie pan. It

should extend about ¾ inch past the side of the pie plate. Fold this dough under so that it is flush with the outer edge of the pie plate. Cover the pastry with plastic wrap and refrigerate it for at least 30 minutes and up to 3 hours.

In a medium saucepan, stir together the sugar, cornstarch, and salt. Stir in the water, then stir in the cherries, along with any juice, and the rhubarb. Allow the mixture to macerate for at least 15 minutes.

Over medium heat, stirring constantly, bring the mixture to a boil. Simmer for 1 minute, stirring gently. Scrape the mixture into a bowl and allow to cool completely, without stirring, at room temperature or refrigerated.

Spoon the mixture into the prepared crust, making sure to distribute the cherries and rhubarb evenly.

Roll the remaining smaller piece of dough into an oval 10½ inches by 8 inches wide (and about 1/16 inch thick). Using a ruler and pastry jagger, cut ten ¾-inch strips.

To create a woven lattice decoration (see page 16), arrange half the strips evenly over the cherries. Gently curve back every other strip almost to the center and place another strip perpendicularly on top. Uncurve the strips so that they lie flat on top of the perpendicular strip. Working in the same direction, curve back the strips that were not curved back the first time. Lay a second perpendicular strip on top and uncurve the strips. Continue in this manner with a third perpendicular strip, curving back the strips that were curved back the first time. Apply the remaining 2 strips to the other side of the pie, starting toward the center and working toward the edge. Remember always to alternate the strips that are curved back so that the strips weave in and out.

Use sharp scissors to trim the strips to a ½-inch overhang. Moisten the dough under each strip with water and tuck the overhang under the bottom crust border, pressing down to make it adhere.

For the optional egg glaze, lightly beat the egg yolk and cream together. Brush the lattice and border with the egg glaze and, if time allows, refrigerate the pie for 1 hour, loosely covered with plastic wrap, to keep the crust from shrinking when it bakes.

Preheat the oven to 425°F. at least 20 minutes before baking. Set an oven rack at the lowest level and place a baking stone or baking sheet on it before preheating.

Set the pie directly on the baking stone and bake for 30 to 40 minutes or until the filling is *thickly* bubbling all over and the center is slightly puffed. After 15 minutes of baking, protect the edges from overbrowning with a foil ring (see page 19).

Cool the pie on a rack for at least 3 hours before serving.

STORE
Room temperature, up to 2 days.

POINTERS FOR SUCCESS
∾ See Cherry Lattice Pie, page 93.

UNDERSTANDING

Water is added to the filling to form more liquid filling and decrease the concentration of the intense cherries and rhubarb. The juice serves to blend the two flavors more deeply, much the way sauces work with savory dishes.

The cherries and rhubarb are cooked together before baking to thicken the increased amount of liquid, which would otherwise make the bottom crust soggy.

It is best not to stir the mixture after cooking, to maintain the firm texture of the rhubarb.

GLAZED STRAWBERRY PIE

The Beranbaum family fell in love with this pie at a diner called Big Boy in Stroudsburg, Pennsylvania. We were addicted to this pie, consisting of a crisp crust filled only with fresh strawberries held together by a fruit juice glaze. We would drive fifty miles to Big Boy every weekend just to have it. When I tried to duplicate it in my kitchen, I discovered that a fruit glaze also works well with fresh raspberries or a mixture of raspberries and currants. The glaze preserves the freshness of the fruit for two days.

SERVES: 6 TO 8

INGREDIENTS	MEASURE	WEIGHT	
	VOLUME	OUNCES	GRAMS
Basic Flaky Pie Crust for a 9-inch pie (page 22)		12 ounces	340 grams
½ large egg white, lightly beaten	1 tablespoon	approx. 0.5 ounce	15 grams
sugar	¼ cup	1.75 ounces	50 grams
cornstarch	3 tablespoons	1 ounce	28.5 grams
cran/raspberry concentrate, thawed, undiluted	1 cup liquid	10 ounces	282 grams
water	¾ cup liquid	6.25 ounces	177 grams
strawberries, rinsed, hulled, dried, and halved	4 cups	1 pound	454 grams

EQUIPMENT
A 9-inch pie pan

Make the dough (page 22).

Remove the dough from the refrigerator. If necessary, allow it to sit for about 10 minutes or until it is soft enough to roll.

Using a pastry cloth and sleeve rubbed with flour or two sheets of plastic wrap lightly sprinkled with flour, roll the dough ⅛ inch thick or less and large enough to cut a 13-inch circle. Use an expandable flan ring or a cardboard template and a sharp knife as a guide to cut out the circle. Transfer the dough to the pie pan. Fold under the excess and crimp the border using a fork or your fingers (see page 13). Cover it loosely and refrigerate for a minimum of 1 hour and a maximum of 24 hours.

Preheat the oven to 425°F. at least 20 minutes before baking.

Line the pastry shell with parchment, pleating it as necessary so it fits into the pan, and fill it with rice or dried beans. Bake for 20 minutes. Carefully lift out the rice or beans with the parchment. With a fork, prick the bottom and sides and bake 5 to 10 minutes more or until the crust is pale golden. Check after 3 minutes and prick any bubbles that may have formed.

Cool the crust on a rack for 3 minutes, so it is no longer piping hot, then brush the bottom and sides with the egg white.

In a 2-quart saucepan, mix together the sugar and cornstarch. Gradually stir in the cran/raspberry concentrate and water until smooth. Over medium heat, bring to a boil, stirring constantly. Boil for 1 minute. Remove the pan from the heat and cool completely.

Gently fold in the strawberries and spoon the filling into the baked pastry shell. Refrigerate for 4 hours or until set.

VARIATIONS

GLAZED RASPBERRY PIE   Use 1 pound of raspberries (4 cups) and ¼ cup plus 2½ tablespoons of sugar for the glaze.

GLAZED RASPBERRY CURRANT PIE   Use 12 ounces (3 cups) of raspberries, 4 ounces (¾ cup) of fresh red currants, and ½ cup of sugar for the glaze. Fresh blueberries make a stunning garnish.

STORE

Refrigerated, up to 2 days.

OPEN-FACED DOUBLE STRAWBERRY PIE

This luscious dessert consists of a baked pie shell that is first filled with a layer of white chocolate, sour cream, and cream cheese, over which is placed a layer of cooked strawberries that is topped with a layer of whole fresh glazed strawberries. The cream cheese layer keeps the crust crisp and sets off the flavor of the strawberries.

As in the Open-Faced Fresh Blueberry Pie (page 107), I cook a small proportion of the strawberries to accentuate the flavor of the fresh ones.

SERVES: 6 TO 8

INGREDIENTS	MEASURE	WEIGHT	
	VOLUME	OUNCES	GRAMS
Basic Flaky Pie Crust for a 9-inch pie (page 22)		12 ounces	340 grams
½ large egg white, lightly beaten	1 tablespoon	approx. 0.5 ounce	15 grams
strawberries, rinsed, hulled, and dried	5 cups	1¼ pounds	567 grams
water	½ liquid cup	4 ounces	118 grams
sugar	⅓ cup	2.3 ounces	67 grams
cornstarch	2 tablespoons	0.66 ounce	19 grams
salt	a pinch	•	•
freshly squeezed lemon juice	1 teaspoon	•	5 grams
Cream Cheese Layer white chocolate, preferably Lindt's confectionery bar, broken into pieces	one 3-ounce bar	3 ounces	85 grams
cream cheese	½ of an 8-ounce package	4 ounces	113 grams
sour cream	2 tablespoons	1 ounce	30 grams
Topping currant jelly	¼ cup	2.7 ounces	77 grams
Chambord or water	1 tablespoon	0.5 ounce	16 grams

EQUIPMENT
A 9-inch pie pan

Make the dough (page 22).

Remove the dough from the refrigerator. If necessary, allow it to sit for about 10 minutes or until it is soft enough to roll.

On a floured pastry cloth or between two sheets of lightly floured plastic wrap, roll the dough ⅛ inch thick or less and large enough to cut a 13-inch circle. Use an expandable flan ring or a cardboard template and a sharp knife as a guide to cut out the circle. Transfer it to the pie pan, fold the excess under, and crimp the border using a fork or your fingers (see page 13). Cover it loosely with plastic wrap and refrigerate for a minimum of 1 hour or a maximum of 24 hours.

Preheat the oven to 425°F. at least 20 minutes before baking.

Line the pastry shell with parchment, pleating it as necessary so it fits into the pan, and fill it with rice or dried beans. Bake for 20 minutes. Lift out the rice or beans with the parchment. With a fork, prick the bottom and sides and bake 5 to 10 minutes more or until the crust is pale golden. Check after 3 minutes and prick any bubbles that may have formed.

Cool the crust on a rack for 3 minutes, so it is no longer piping hot, and then brush the bottom and sides with the egg white.

In a small heavy saucepan, place 1 cup of the strawberries and crush them lightly with a fork. Add the water, sugar, cornstarch, salt, and lemon juice and stir until the dry ingredients have dissolved. Bring the mixture to a boil and simmer for 30 seconds, stirring constantly. Immediately pour the mixture into a bowl and cool, stirring very gently once or twice.

In a double boiler over hot, not simmering, water,* melt the white chocolate, stirring constantly until smooth. Remove the upper container from the lower one and allow the chocolate to cool completely.

In a mixer bowl, on high speed, beat the cream cheese until smooth and light, about 3 minutes. Pour in the cooled white chocolate all at once and beat for 1 minute. Add the sour cream and beat until well blended.

Scrape the cream cheese mixture into the baked pie shell and top with the cooled strawberry mixture. Arrange the remaining strawberries on top, points up.

MAKE THE TOPPING

In a small saucepan or microwave oven, heat the currant jelly until melted and bubbling. Strain it into a small cup and stir in the Chambord or water. Brush it onto the strawberries.

---

*The water in the lower container must not touch the bottom of the upper container. The chocolate can also be melted in a microwave oven if stirred every 10 seconds. Remove it before it is fully melted and stir until melted.

STORE

Room temperature, up to 6 hours; refrigerated, uncovered, up to 2 days.

FRESH BLUEBERRY PIE

When I was growing up, our family spent a month of each summer at a family-owned hotel called Spring Lake in Parksville, New York. The two activities I remember best were sharpening stones into various shapes by the brook and going into the Catskill Mountains in the sunny afternoons to pick blueberries. We would get large empty cans from the kitchen and wouldn't stop until they were filled.

We always ate the fresh blueberries with sour cream. It wasn't until I married a New Englander that I ate them cooked in a pie.

Blueberries become bitter on cooking. The addition of lemon zest and a judicious amount of sugar, however, makes this pie retain the sweetness of fresh blueberries.

OVEN TEMPERATURE: 425°F. • BAKING TIME: 40 TO 50 MINUTES   **SERVES: 6**

INGREDIENTS	MEASURE	WEIGHT	
	VOLUME	OUNCES	GRAMS
Basic Flaky Pie Crust for a 2-crust 9-inch pie (page 23)		approx. 21 ounces	595 grams
sugar	½ cup	3.5 ounces	100 grams
cornstarch	2 tablespoons	0.66 ounce	19 grams
finely grated lemon zest	2 teaspoons	•	4 grams
freshly squeezed lemon juice	2 tablespoons	1 ounce	31 grams
salt	a pinch	•	•
blueberries, rinsed and dried	4 cups	1¼ pounds	567 grams

EQUIPMENT
A 9-inch pie pan

Make the dough (page 23).

Remove the dough for the bottom crust from the refrigerator. If necessary, allow it to sit for about 10 minutes or until it is soft enough to roll.

On a floured pastry cloth or between two sheets of lightly floured plastic wrap, roll the bottom crust ⅛ inch thick or less and 12 inches in diameter. Transfer it to the pie pan. Trim the edge almost even with the edge of the pan. Cover it with plastic wrap and refrigerate it for a minimum of 30 minutes and a maximum of 3 hours.

In a medium bowl, stir together the sugar, cornstarch, lemon zest, lemon juice, and salt. Add the blueberries and toss to coat them. Transfer the blueberry mixture to the pie shell.

Roll out the top crust large enough to cut a 12-inch circle. Use an expandable flan ring or a cardboard template and a sharp knife as a guide to cut out the circle.

Moisten the edges of the bottom crust with water and place the top crust over the fruit. Tuck the overhang under the bottom crust border and press down all around the top to seal it. Crimp the border using a fork or your fingers (see page 13) and make about 5 evenly spaced 2-inch slashes starting about 1 inch from the center and radiating toward the edge (see page 14). Cover the pie loosely with plastic wrap and refrigerate it for 1 hour before baking to chill and relax the pastry. This will maintain flakiness and help to keep the crust from shrinking.

Preheat the oven to 425°F. at least 20 minutes before baking. Set an oven rack at the lowest level and place a baking stone or baking sheet on it before preheating. Place a large piece of greased foil on top to catch any juices.

Set the pie directly on the foil-topped baking stone and bake for 40 to 50 minutes or until the filling is *thickly* bubbling. After 30 minutes, protect the edges from overbrowning with a foil ring (see page 19).

Cool the pie on a rack for at least 4 hours before cutting. When set, the berries will remain very juicy but will not flow out of the crust.

STORE

Room temperature, up to 3 days.

OPEN-FACED FRESH BLUEBERRY PIE

In this pie, one cup of berries is cooked to form a syrup. The remaining three cups of berries are heated in this syrup just enough to turn the blueberries a midnight blue with overtones of purple. The filling is then spooned into a prebaked crust. If you've made the crust ahead, this pie comes together in minutes. By dessert time, the filling is set.

EQUIPMENT
A 9-inch pie pan

SERVES: 6

INGREDIENTS	MEASURE	WEIGHT	
	VOLUME	OUNCES	GRAMS
Basic Flaky Pie Crust for a 9-inch pie (page 22)		12 ounces	340 grams
½ large egg white, lightly beaten	1 tablespoon	0.5 ounce	15 grams
blueberries, rinsed and dried	4 cups	1¼ pounds	567 grams
water	½ liquid cup + 2 tablespoons, divided	approx. 5 ounces	148 grams
cornstarch	2 tablespoons	0.66 ounce	19 grams
sugar	½ cup	3.5 ounces	100 grams
freshly squeezed lemon juice	1 teaspoon	•	•
salt	a pinch	•	•
optional decor: 1½ cups whipped cream (pages 551–53)			

Make the dough (page 22).

Remove the dough from the refrigerator. If necessary, allow it to sit for about 10 minutes or until it is soft enough to roll.

Using a pastry cloth and sleeve rubbed with flour or two sheets of plastic wrap lightly sprinkled with flour, roll the dough ⅛ inch thick or less and large enough to cut a 13-inch circle. Use an expandable flan ring or a cardboard template and sharp knife as a guide to cut out the circle. Transfer the dough to the pie pan. Fold under the excess and crimp the border using a fork or your fingers (see page 13). Cover it loosely and refrigerate for a minimum of 1 hour and a maximum of 24 hours.

Preheat the oven to 425°F. at least 20 minutes before baking.

Line the pastry with parchment, pleating it as necessary so it fits into the pan, and fill it with rice or dried beans. Bake for 20 minutes. Carefully lift out the rice or beans with the parchment. With a fork, prick the bottom and sides and bake 5 to 10 minutes more or until the crust is pale golden. Check after 3 minutes and prick any bubbles that may have formed.

Cool the crust on a rack for 3 minutes, so it is no longer piping hot, then brush the bottom and sides with the egg white.

Measure out 1 cup of the blueberries, choosing the softest ones. Place them in a medium saucepan together with the ½ cup water. Cover and bring them to a boil.

Meanwhile, in a small bowl, whisk together the cornstarch and the remaining 2 tablespoons of water. Set it aside.

When the water and blueberries have come to a boil, lower the heat and simmer, stirring constantly, for 3 to 4 minutes or until the blueberries start to burst and the juices begin to thicken. Stirring constantly, add the cornstarch mixture, the sugar, lemon juice, and salt. Simmer for a minute or until the mixture becomes translucent. Immediately remove it from the heat and quickly fold in the remaining 3 cups of blueberries.

Spoon the mixture into the baked pie shell and allow to sit at room temperature for at least 2 hours before serving. When set, the berries will remain very juicy but will not flow out of the crust.

Just before serving, if desired, pipe or spread the whipped cream around the sides of the pie, leaving the center unadorned and brilliantly glistening.

STORE

Room temperature, up to 2 days (without the whipped cream).

NOTE

The low amount of sugar in this pie maintains the tart freshness of the berries. Taste the berries before you begin. If they are very tart, increase the sugar by a few tablespoons.

DEEP-DISH BLUEBERRY/CRANBERRY
INTERNET PIE

My cousin Sue brought this pie to our family Thanksgiving. She said she got the recipe on the Internet. A little research turned up that it was the first pie to appear on the Internet and that the recipe was created by Sarah Leah Chase. This was no surprise, as I have long admired Sarah's daring taste sensibilities.

Because there is so much juicy fruit filling in this pie, it will flow a little if served the same day. I prefer to bake the pie the day before to make serving easier and avoid adding more starch thickener, but no one seems to object either way.

This is a very exciting pie. The crust remains crisp and crunchy for three days. The colors are brilliant and the flavors incredibly bright, clear and intense.

EQUIPMENT
A 9½-inch Pyrex deep-dish pie plate

INGREDIENTS	MEASURE	WEIGHT	
	VOLUME	OUNCES	GRAMS
Basic Flaky Pie Crust for a 2-crust 9-inch pie (page 23)		approx. 21 ounces	595 grams
sugar	1½ cups	10.5 ounces	300 grams
cornstarch	⅓ cup (dip and sweep method)	1.6 ounces	46 grams
finely grated lemon zest	1 tablespoon	0.25 ounce	6 grams
freshly squeezed lemon juice	3 tablespoons	1.6 ounce	47 grams
salt	a pinch	•	•
frozen blueberries	2 packages	1½ pounds	680 grams
fresh or frozen cranberries, rinsed, picked over, and dried	1 package* (3½ cups)	12.25 ounces	347 grams
Glaze heavy cream or milk	1 tablespoon	0.5 ounce	15 grams
sugar	1 tablespoon	0.5 ounce	12 grams

*Although the package states 12 ounces, there are actually 12¼ ounces.

Make the dough (page 23).

Remove the dough for the bottom crust from the refrigerator. If necessary, allow it to sit for about 10 minutes or until it is soft enough to roll.

On a floured pastry cloth or between two sheets of lightly floured plastic wrap, roll the bottom crust ⅛ inch thick or less and large enough to cut a 13-inch circle. Transfer it to the pie pan, easing it in to fit up against the sides. Trim, if necessary, to ¼ inch past the edge of the pan. Cover it with plastic wrap and refrigerate it for a minimum of 30 minutes and a maximum of 3 hours.

In a large nonreactive saucepan, stir together the sugar, cornstarch, lemon zest, lemon juice, and salt. Add the blueberries and cranberries and toss to coat them well. Allow the mixture to sit for about 30 minutes or until a little liquid starts to form.

Cook the berries over medium heat, stirring constantly, until very thickened and some of the berries are just beginning to burst, about 8 to 10 minutes after it comes to a boil. Remove the pan from the heat and allow the mixture to cool completely, without stirring, about 1 hour.

Transfer the berry mixture to the pie shell.

Roll out the top crust large enough to cut a 12-inch circle. Use an expandable flan ring or a cardboard template and a sharp knife as a guide to cut the circle.

Moisten the edges of the bottom crust with water and place the top crust over the fruit. Tuck the overhang under the bottom crust border and press down all around the top to seal it. Reroll the scraps no more than ⅛ inch thick and cut them into decorative shapes. Brush the top crust with the cream or milk and arrange the decorative pieces on top of it, overlapping them slightly. Brush them with the remaining cream or milk and sprinkle all over with the sugar.

Cover the pie loosely with plastic wrap and refrigerate it for 1 hour before baking to chill and relax the pastry. This will maintain flakiness and help to keep the crust from shrinking.

Preheat the oven to 375°F. at least 20 minutes before baking. Set one oven rack at the lowest level and one at the highest level and place a baking stone or baking sheet on the lower rack before preheating.

To make a steam vent use a small cutter, the bottom of a pastry tube, or a knife to cut a small hole (about 1 inch) in the middle of the top crust. Lift out the cut round of pastry and discard it. Set the pie directly on the stone and bake for 40 minutes. Transfer the pie to the upper rack and continue baking for 20 to 30 minutes or until the crust is golden brown. (The filling will not bubble.) After 1 hour, protect the edges from overbrowning with a foil ring (see page 19).

Cool the pie on a rack for at least 6 hours before serving.

STORE

Room temperature, up to 3 days.

NOTE

I find that in my oven it works well to bake this pie for the first 40 minutes directly on the floor of the oven instead of the bottom shelf.

POINTERS FOR SUCCESS

∽ For ease in cutting the decorative scraps, flour both sides of the pastry well. If the dough is not firm enough to hold the shapes well, cover it with plastic wrap and freeze or refrigerate it briefly. Flour the cutter before cutting each piece. Cutters that are open on both ends are easiest for releasing the dough.

∽ This pie is baked at a lower temperature than most to keep the raised decorations from burning. If the decorations are not used, the pie can be baked at 425°F. for 45 minutes. (Transfer it to the upper oven rack when the bottom crust is nicely browned.)

UNDERSTANDING

Frozen blueberries work well for this filling because they release their juices more quickly than fresh ones, but fresh blueberries are fine to use as well.

RED CURRANT PIE

T here is no fruit more beautiful to behold than currants ripening on a bush. The tiny, translucent bright red orbs glow in the sunlight, revealing their clusters of seeds within. Most people find currants disappointingly bitter when eaten off the bush, which is why the nursery where I buy my trees offered me the hundred-year-old currant bush that came with their property! Most people don't know what to do with this tempting fruit, so they leave it for the appreciative birds. But once you taste this juicy pie, with clear red fruit that seems to explode in your mouth with wild flavor, you will look forward to currant season each summer with as much excitement as I do. The juiciness of this pie causes enough buildup of steam during baking to open the steam vent slashes in the top, creating a flower petal effect.

OVEN TEMPERATURE: 425°F. • BAKING TIME: 40 TO 50 MINUTES   SERVES: 6

INGREDIENTS	MEASURE	WEIGHT	
	VOLUME	OUNCES	GRAMS
Flaky Cream Cheese Pie Crust for a 2-crust 9-inch pie (page 30)		22 ounces	624 grams
sugar	1⅓ cups	9.3 ounces	266 grams
cornstarch	3 tablespoons	1 ounce	28 grams
salt	a pinch	•	•
red currants, rinsed, stems removed, and dried	3½ cups (four ½-pints)	19 ounces	540 grams

EQUIPMENT
A 9-inch pie pan

Make the dough (page 30).

    Remove the dough for the bottom crust from the refrigerator. If necessary, allow it to sit for about 10 minutes or until it is soft enough to roll.

    On a floured pastry cloth or between two sheets of lightly floured plastic wrap, roll the bottom crust ⅛ inch thick or less and large enough to cut a 12-inch circle. Transfer it to the pie pan. Trim the edge almost even with the edge of the pan. Cover it with plastic wrap and refrigerate it for a minimum of 30 minutes and a maximum of 3 hours.

    In a medium bowl, stir together the sugar, cornstarch, and salt. Add the currants and toss to coat them. Allow them to macerate for at least 10 minutes or until the sugar mixture is completely moistened.

Transfer the currant mixture to the pie shell.

Roll out the top crust large enough to cut a 12-inch circle. Use an expandable flan ring or a cardboard template and a sharp knife as a guide to cut the circle.

Moisten the edges of the bottom crust with water and place the top crust over the fruit. Tuck the overhang under the bottom crust border and press down all around the top to seal it. Crimp the border using a fork or your fingers (see page 13). Make six to eight 2-inch slashes in the top crust, starting about 1 inch from the center and radiating toward the edge (see page 14), wiggling the knife to ensure that they open a bit to prevent resealing from the juices released by the currants during baking. Cover the pie loosely with plastic wrap and refrigerate it for 1 hour before baking to chill and relax the pastry. This will maintain flakiness and help to keep the crust from shrinking.

Preheat the oven to 425°F. at least 20 minutes before baking. Set an oven rack at the lowest level and place a baking stone or baking sheet on it before preheating. Place a large piece of greased foil on top to catch any juices.

Set the pie directly on the foil-topped baking stone and bake for 40 to 50 minutes or until the filling is *thickly* bubbling. After 30 minutes, protect the edges from overbrowning with a foil ring (see page 19).

Cool the pie on a rack for about 4 hours before cutting.

STORE

Room temperature, up to 2 days.

POINTERS FOR SUCCESS

෴ If using frozen currants, they must defrost before baking in order to dissolve the thickener and sugar.

෴ Some varieties of currants have a lot more seeds than others, which makes them better suited to currant jelly. A good pie currant will have no more than four little seeds. I have seen as many as 11 in one tiny berry!

RED CURRANT–RASPBERRY LATTICE PIE

Raspberries, when baked alone in a pie, lose their character and become too cloyingly intense. When combined with currants, however, the flavors and textures blend together brilliantly, making each fruit even more delicious than either would be alone. I've chosen a lattice crust for this pie because the color of the baked fruit is so appealing.

INGREDIENTS	MEASURE	WEIGHT	
	VOLUME	OUNCES	GRAMS
Flaky Cream Cheese Pie Crust for a 9-inch lattice pie (page 30)		14.3 ounces	406 grams
½ large egg white, lightly beaten	1 tablespoon	approx. 0.5 ounce	15 grams
sugar	¾ cup	5.25 ounces	150 grams
cornstarch	2 tablespoons	0.66 ounce	19 grams
salt	a pinch	•	•
red currants, rinsed, stems removed, and dried	1½ cups (two ½-pints)	8.25 ounces	234 grams
red raspberries	2½ cups	10 ounces	284 grams
freshly squeezed lemon juice	2 teaspoons		
Optional Glaze 1 large egg yolk	•	•	•
heavy cream	1 teaspoon	•	•

EQUIPMENT
A 9-inch pie pan

Make the dough (page 30).

Remove the larger piece of dough from the refrigerator. If necessary, allow it to sit for 10 minutes or until it is soft enough to roll.

Using a pastry cloth and sleeve rubbed with flour or two sheets of plastic wrap lightly sprinkled with flour, roll the dough ⅛ inch thick or less and large enough to cut a 13-inch circle. Use an expandable flan ring or a cardboard template and a sharp knife as a guide to cut out the circle. Transfer the dough to the pie pan. It should extend about ¾ inch past the side of the pie plate. Fold this dough under so that it is flush with the outer edge of the pie plate. Cover the pastry with plastic wrap and refrigerate it for a minimum of 30 minutes and a maximum of 3 hours.

In a medium bowl, stir together the sugar, cornstarch, and salt.

Place half the currants evenly over the bottom of the pie shell. Then place half the raspberries evenly over them. Sprinkle half the sugar mixture over the berries. Repeat with the remaining currants and raspberries and sprinkle on the remaining sugar mixture and the lemon juice.

Roll the remaining smaller piece of dough into an oval 10½ inches by 8 inches wide (and about ⅟16 inch thick). Using a ruler and a pastry jagger or pizza cutter, cut ten ¾-inch strips.

To create a woven lattice decoration (see page 16), arrange half the strips evenly over the currants and raspberries. Gently curve back every other strip a little past the center and place another strip perpendicular on top. Uncurve the strips so that they lie flat on top of the perpendicular strip. Working in the same direction, curve back the strips that were not curved back the first time. Lay a second perpendicular strip on top and uncurve the strips. Continue in this manner with a third perpendicular strip, curving back the strips that were curved back the first time. Apply the remaining 2 strips to the other side of the pie, starting toward the center and working toward the edge. Remember always to alternate the strips that are curved back so that the strips weave in and out.

Use sharp scissors to trim the strips to a ½-inch overhang. Moisten the dough under each strip with egg white or water and tuck the overhang under the bottom crust border, pressing down to make it adhere.

For the optional glaze, lightly beat egg and cream. Brush the lattice and border with the egg glaze and, if time allows, refrigerate the pie for 1 hour, loosely covered with plastic wrap, to keep the crust from shrinking when it bakes.

Preheat the oven to 425°F. at least 20 minutes before baking. Set an oven rack at the lowest level and place a baking stone or baking sheet on it before preheating.

Set the pie directly on the baking stone and bake for 40 to 50 minutes or until the filling is *thickly* bubbling all over and the center is slightly puffed. After 15 minutes, protect the edges from overbrowning with a foil ring (see page 19). If the lattice starts to become too dark toward the last 10 minutes of baking, cover it loosely with a piece of foil with a vent hole in the center.

Cool the pie on a rack for at least 3 hours before serving.

STORE

Room temperature, up to 2 days.

BLACKBERRY PIE

Varieties of blackberries that are sweet and juicy are a treasure. They are excellent both baked in a pie and used fresh to top a tart. Taste them before you use them. If they are not sweet and full-flavored, no amount of sugar will counteract the bitterness.

Blackberries are the first berry I ever tasted. When I was three years old, living with my grandparents in Far Rockaway, New York, near the ocean, my grandfather took me for a walk and just a block from our house, we discovered a wild blackberry patch. I still remember eagerly picking the luscious sun-warmed berries and popping them into my mouth, until I looked down at my legs and noticed that they were covered with a dark red, sticky substance I thought to be berry juice. My grandfather was a very tall man and would never have noticed had I not called his attention to it. He realized immediately that it was not berry juice at all but blood from multiple scratches from the large thorns on the berries' stems. I had been so entranced by the flavor of the berries, I never felt a thing. "We have to go back," he said. "It doesn't hurt, Grandpa," was my bravely hopeful reply. Clearly I loved the blackberries enough to overlook any possible discomfort and did not want to leave. "No, we have to go; Grandma will be very angry and think I didn't take good care of you." Which is exactly what transpired. And the only pain I remember is of having to leave those still unpicked berries and of the removal of Grandma's bandages a few days later (it was before the advent of nonstick Band-Aids).

This is a pure, straightforward fruit pie, entirely dependent on the quality of the blackberries you use.

OVEN TEMPERATURE: 425°F. • BAKING TIME: 30 TO 40 MINUTES   SERVES: 8

INGREDIENTS	MEASURE	WEIGHT	
	VOLUME	OUNCES	GRAMS
Basic Flaky Pie Crust for a 2-crust 9-inch pie (page 23)		approx. 21 ounces	595 grams
sugar	½ cup	3.5 ounces	100 grams
cornstarch	2½ tablespoons	approx. 0.75 ounce	24 grams
finely grated lemon zest	2 teaspoons	•	4 grams
salt	a pinch	•	•
freshly squeezed lemon juice	2 tablespoons	1 ounce	31 grams
blackberries (fresh or frozen, undefrosted)	4 cups	1 pound	454 grams

EQUIPMENT
A 9-inch pie pan

Make the dough (page 23).

Remove the dough for the bottom crust from the refrigerator. If necessary, allow it to sit for about 10 minutes or until it is soft enough to roll.

On a floured pastry cloth or between two sheets of lightly floured plastic wrap, roll the bottom crust ⅛ inch thick or less and 12 inches in diameter. Transfer it to the pie pan. Trim the edge almost even with the edge of the pan. Cover it with plastic wrap and refrigerate it for a minimum of 30 minutes and a maximum of 3 hours.

In a medium bowl, combine the sugar, cornstarch, lemon zest, and salt and whisk to blend. Whisk in the lemon juice. Add the berries and toss very gently to coat them with the mixture without crushing them. Allow them to sit for 15 minutes, until they start to release some of their juices and the dry ingredients are moistened completely.

Toss the berries gently again and transfer the blackberry mixture to the pie shell.

Roll out the top crust large enough to cut a 12-inch circle. Use an expandable flan ring or a cardboard template and a sharp knife as a guide to cut out the circle. Use a small round scalloped cutter to make many small berry-like cutouts from the circle. (If desired, these rounds can be used to decorate the top crust.)

Moisten the edges of the bottom crust with water and place the top crust over the fruit. Tuck the overhang under the bottom crust border and press down all around the top to seal it. Crimp the border using a fork or your fingers (see page 13). If using the pastry cutouts, brush the undersides lightly with water before placing them on the crust. Cover loosely with plastic wrap and refrigerate for 1 hour before baking to chill and relax the pastry. This will maintain flakiness and help to keep the crust from shrinking.

Preheat the oven to 425°F. at least 20 minutes before baking. Set an oven rack in the lowest level and place a baking stone or baking sheet on it before preheating. Place a large piece of greased foil on top to catch any juices.

Set the pie directly on the foil-topped baking stone and bake for 30 to 40 minutes (45 minutes if using frozen berries) or until the crust is golden brown and the filling is *thickly* bubbling. After 30 minutes, protect the edges from overbrowning with a foil ring (see page 19).

Cool the pie on a rack for at least 4 hours before serving.

STORE

Room temperature, up to 2 days.

UNDERSTANDING

Fresh blackberries often have tough seeds, but there are some varieties that seem practically seedless. I have not found that adding vinegar, purported to help, makes any difference. The best solution for the tough seed variety is avoidance. The seeds in commercial frozen blackberries are consistently softer and the berries are never bitter, because of the variety of berries chosen. They make a luscious, juicy, and flavorful pie.

DEEP-DISH MARIONBERRY PIE

The Marionberry is a hybrid from Marion County, Oregon—a happy marriage of the red raspberry and the blackberry, a velvety, intensely flavorful berry that resembles the long variety of blackberry in shape, with a reddish purple hue. The Marionberry is far less bitter than the raspberry and far less seedy than the blackberry, with a perfect balance of sweet/tart reminiscent of an earthy cabernet. The most remarkably distinctive characteristic of the Marionberry is that if frozen and defrosted, it is the only berry that maintains its texture, softening only very slightly as it releases some of its purple juices. This makes it possible to have a taste of the joy of fresh summer berries all year round.

Cooked berries in general become jammy and seedy in texture and lose much of their sweetness, necessitating as much as six times more sugar than uncooked berries. Cooking some of the Marionberries, however, and folding in some of the defrosted uncooked berries when they are cool is the solution. It is possible to do this because they hold their shape so well.

The crust is placed on top, so it stays crisp, but if a bottom crust is desired, the filling can be made a day ahead to give it a chance to thicken and placed in a baked pie shell shortly before serving. Alternatively, an extra teaspoon of cornstarch can be added to the filling so that it can be served the same day. Passion or lemon ice cream (page 237 or 235) would be the perfect accompaniment for this fruit.

EQUIPMENT
A 9-inch pie plate or a 4-cup casserole (the filling is a little under 3 cups)

Make and bake the pastry cutouts and balls, sprinkling them with sugar before baking (see page 14).

Measure out 1½ cups (6 ounces) of the Marionberries and set aside. Allow all the berries to defrost completely.

In a medium saucepan, place the orange and lemon zest and cover with several inches of cold water. Bring to a boil and boil for 15 minutes. Drain the zest in a strainer and rinse it well under cold running water. Return it to the saucepan.

Drain all the juice from the berries onto the zest (there should be about 9 tablespoons). Add ¾ cup of the water, the sugar, and syrup. Bring the mixture to a boil, stirring constantly. Cover and simmer it for 15 minutes. Add the 1½ cups of Marionberries. Bring the mixture to a boil.

Meanwhile, in a small bowl, whisk together the cornstarch, salt, and the remaining 3 tablespoons of water. Set it aside.

When the Marionberries are boiling, lower the heat and simmer, stirring constantly, for 3 to 4 minutes or until they have fallen apart. Stirring constantly, add the cornstarch mixture. Simmer for 1 minute, stirring gently, or until the mixture

SERVES: 6

INGREDIENTS	MEASURE	WEIGHT	
	VOLUME	OUNCES	GRAMS
Baked decorative pastry cutouts and little balls, sprinkled with sugar before baking (see page 14)			
frozen Marionberries	6 cups, divided	1½ pounds	681 grams
zest of ¾ orange, cut in fine julienne strips*		0.6 ounce	18 grams
zest of ¾ lemon, cut in fine julienne strips*		0.3 ounce	8 grams
water	¾ liquid cup + 3 tablespoons, divided	•	•
sugar	1½ cups	10.5 ounces	300 grams
Lyle's Golden Syrup (refiner's syrup) or light corn syrup	1 tablespoon	0.7 ounce	21 grams
cornstarch	4 tablespoons + 1½ teaspoons	1½ ounces	42 grams
salt	a pinch	•	•

*With a vegetable peeler, remove only the colored portion of the skin, not the white pith, which is bitter, in long strips. With a sharp knife, cut into julienne strips.

becomes translucent and thick. Immediately remove it from the heat and quickly but gently fold in the remaining 4½ cups of berries. Empty the mixture into the pie plate and allow it to sit at room temperature for at least 2 hours before serving.

When cool, garnish the pie with the baked pastry cutouts and pastry balls.

STORE

Uncovered, room temperature, up to 2 days.

OPEN-FACED APRICOT PIE

When ripe, fresh apricots have a velvety-soft deep golden skin with a faint blush and the most delicate flavor. When picked before maturity, the flavor is less than exciting, but baking surprisingly intensifies the flavor even of the pallid ones, bringing them more toward the piquancy of dried apricots. Since baked apricots are so vivid, I always bake them entirely open-faced in a pie. Glazing them with strained apricot preserves adds extra flavor and makes them glisten.

OVEN TEMPERATURE: 425°F. • BAKING TIME: 50 TO 60 MINUTES   SERVES: 6

INGREDIENTS	MEASURE	WEIGHT	
	VOLUME	OUNCES	GRAMS
Basic Flaky Pie Crust for a 9-inch pie (page 22)		12 ounces	340 grams
½ egg white, lightly beaten	1 tablespoon	0.5 ounce	15 grams
1½ pounds fresh apricots, rinsed	4 cups (halved and pitted)	22 ounces (halved and pitted)	624 grams
sugar	6 tablespoons	2.6 ounces	75 grams
cornstarch	2 tablespoons	0.66 ounce	19 grams
raspberries	½ cup	2 ounces	57 grams
apricot preserves	⅓ cup	4 ounces	113 grams

EQUIPMENT
A 9-inch pie pan

Make the dough (page 22).

Remove the dough from the refrigerator. If necessary, allow it to sit for about 10 minutes or until it is soft enough to roll.

Using a pastry cloth and sleeve rubbed with flour or two sheets of plastic wrap lightly sprinkled with flour, roll the dough ⅛ inch thick or less and large enough to cut a 13-inch circle. Use an expandable flan ring or a cardboard template and a sharp knife as a guide to cut out the circle. Transfer the dough to the pie pan, fold under the excess, and crimp the border using a fork or your fingers (see page 13). Cover it loosely and refrigerate it for at least 1 hour and up to 24 hours.

Preheat the oven to 425°F. at least 20 minutes before baking. Set an oven rack at the lowest level and place a baking stone or baking sheet on it before preheating.

Line the pastry with parchment, pleating it as necessary so it fits into the pan, and fill it with rice or dried beans. Bake for 20 minutes. Carefully remove the parchment with the rice or beans. With a fork, prick the bottom and sides and bake 5 to 10 minutes or until the crust is pale golden. Check after 3 minutes and prick again if the upper layer of dough bubbles up.

Cool the crust on a rack for 3 minutes, so it is no longer piping hot, then brush the bottom and sides with the egg white. Leave the oven on.

Cut the apricots in half and remove their pits.

In a medium bowl, stir together the sugar and cornstarch. Add the apricots and toss to coat them. Allow them to macerate for about 15 minutes or until the dry mixture is fully moistened.

Arrange the apricots decoratively in the baked pastry shell, cut side up. Place a foil collar around the border to protect the edge from overbrowning (see page 19) and bake for 50 to 60 minutes or until the liquid bubbles and the apricots are tender when pierced with a skewer. Cool the pie on a rack until warm or room temperature.

When the pie is cool, arrange the raspberries in the spaces between the apricots.

In a small saucepan or microwave oven, heat the apricot preserves until melted and bubbling. Strain them into a small cup. Use a pastry brush or the back of a spoon to paint the apricots and raspberries with the preserves.

STORE

Room temperature, up to 3 days.

UNDERSTANDING

I do not use my usual technique of sugaring the fruit first and reducing the liquid because the condensing process caramelizes the juices slightly and the combination of the caramel and natural acidity of this particular fruit produces an undesirable bitterness.

NECTARINE-RASPBERRY PIE

This pie rivals peach pie for flavor and texture. The double-crust pie is piled high with lush, tart nectarines interspersed with raspberries. The flesh of a nectarine is slightly firmer than that of a peach, producing a pie with an excellent texture.

OVEN TEMPERATURE: 425°F. • BAKING TIME: 45 TO 55 MINUTES   SERVES: 8

INGREDIENTS	MEASURE	WEIGHT	
	VOLUME	OUNCES	GRAMS
Flaky Cream Cheese Pie Crust for a 2-crust 9-inch pie (page 30)		22 ounces	624 grams
3 pounds nectarines, rinsed (5 to 6 large),* pitted and sliced but not peeled	8 cups (sliced)	2 pounds 13 ounces (sliced)	1 kg 275 grams
freshly squeezed lemon juice†	1 tablespoon	0.5 ounce	16 grams
sugar	¾ cup	5.3 ounces	150 grams
salt	a pinch		
finely grated lemon zest	1 tablespoon	0.25 ounce	6 grams
cornstarch	2 tablespoons	0.6 ounce	19 grams
kirsch	1 tablespoon	0.5 ounce	14 grams
raspberries	1 cup	4 ounces	113 grams

*The nectarines should be ripe but firm so that they maintain some of their texture on baking.
†Finely grate the lemon zest before juicing.

EQUIPMENT
A 9-inch pie pan

Make the dough (page 30).

Remove the dough for the bottom crust from the refrigerator. If necessary, allow it to sit for about 10 minutes or until it is soft enough to roll.

On a floured pastry cloth or between two sheets of lightly floured plastic wrap, roll the bottom crust ⅛ inch thick or less and large enough to cut a 12-inch circle. Transfer it to the pie pan. Trim the edge almost even with the edge of the pan. Cover it with plastic wrap and refrigerate it for a minimum of 30 minutes and a maximum of 3 hours.

Place the sliced nectarines in a large bowl and sprinkle them with the lemon juice. Sprinkle on the sugar and salt and toss them gently to mix evenly. Allow to macerate for a minimum of 30 minutes and a maximum of 1 hour.

Transfer the nectarines and their juices to a colander suspended over a bowl to capture the liquid. The mixture will exude a full cup of juice.

In a small saucepan (preferably lined with a nonstick surface), over medium-high heat, boil down this liquid to ½ cup, or until syrupy and lightly caramelized.

Swirl the liquid but do not stir it. (Alternatively, spray a 4-cup heatproof measure with nonstick vegetable spray, add the liquid, and boil it in the microwave, about 12 minutes on high). Allow it to cool for about 10 minutes or until warm.

Meanwhile, transfer the nectarines to a bowl and toss them with the lemon zest and cornstarch until all traces of the cornstarch have disappeared. Stir the Kirsch into the cooled syrup and pour it over the nectarines, tossing gently. Transfer the nectarine mixture to the pie shell and top with the raspberries.

Roll out the top crust large enough to cut a 12-inch circle. Use an expandable flan ring or a cardboard template and a sharp knife as a guide to cut out the circle.

Moisten the edges of the bottom crust with water and place the top crust over the fruit. Tuck the overhang under the bottom crust border and press down all around the top to seal it. Crimp the border using a fork or your fingers (see page 13) and make about 5 evenly spaced 2-inch slashes starting about 1 inch from the center and radiating toward the edge (see page 14). Cover the pie loosely with plastic wrap and refrigerate it for 1 hour before baking to chill and relax the pastry. This will maintain flakiness and help to prevent distortion.

Preheat the oven to 425°F. at least 20 minutes before baking. Set an oven rack at the lowest level and place a baking stone or baking sheet on it before preheating. Place a large piece of greased foil on top to catch bubbling juices.

Set the pie directly on the foil-topped baking stone and bake for 45 to 55 minutes or until the juices bubble *thickly* through the slashes and the nectarines feel tender but not mushy when a cake tester or small sharp knife is inserted through a slash. After 30 minutes, protect the edges from overbrowning with a foil ring (see page 19). Cool the pie on a rack for at least 3 hours before cutting.

STORE

Room temperature, up to 2 days.

POINTERS FOR SUCCESS

✿ The nectarines should be ripe but firm so they maintain their texture in a pie. If squishy, they lose their character.

✿ As you slice the nectarines, toss them occasionally with the sugar mixture to coat to prevent them from turning brown.

✿ The liquid must not be hot when added to the nectarines because it could cause the cornstarch to lump.

✿ Be sure to put a sheet of foil under the pie pan, as there is always a little spillover with this much fruit.

✿ For a truly crisp bottom crust, bake the pie directly on the floor of the oven for the first 30 minutes (see page 17).

PERFECT PEACH PIE

For me, there is no fruit more desirable than a fresh ripe peach. Keeping this prejudice in mind, I created my peach pie to taste of nothing but peach save for a hint of almond and the scoop of passion fruit ice cream on the side (page 237).

OVEN TEMPERATURE: 425°F. • BAKING TIME: 40 TO 50 MINUTES   **SERVES: 6**

INGREDIENTS	MEASURE	WEIGHT	
	VOLUME	OUNCES	GRAMS
Flaky Cream Cheese Pie Crust for a 2-crust 9-inch pie (page 30)		21 ounces	595 grams
2¾ pounds peaches (about 8 medium), peeled, pitted, and sliced into 16ths	6 cups (sliced)	2 pounds 2 ounces (sliced)	964 grams
freshly squeezed lemon juice	1 tablespoon	0.5 ounce	16 grams
sugar	½ cup + 1 tablespoon	4 ounces	112 grams
salt	a pinch	•	•
cornstarch	4 teaspoons	approx. 0.5 ounce	12.5 grams
pure almond extract	½ teaspoon	•	•

EQUIPMENT
A 9-inch pie pan

Make the dough (page 30).

Remove the dough for the bottom crust from the refrigerator. If necessary, allow it to sit for about 10 minutes or until it is soft enough to roll.

On a floured pastry cloth or between two sheets of lightly floured plastic wrap, roll the bottom crust ⅛ inch thick or less and 12 inches in diameter. Transfer it to the pie pan. Trim the edge almost even with the edge of pan. Cover it with plastic wrap and refrigerate it for a minimum of 30 minutes and a maximum of 3 hours.

Place the sliced peaches in a large bowl and sprinkle them with the lemon juice. Sprinkle on the sugar and salt and toss them gently to mix evenly. Allow to macerate for a minimum of 30 minutes and a maximum of 1 hour.

Transfer the peaches and their juices to a colander suspended over a bowl to capture the liquid. The mixture will release almost 1 cup of juice.

In small saucepan (preferably lined with a nonstick surface), over medium-high heat, boil down this liquid to about ⅓ cup, or until syrupy and lightly caramelized. Swirl the liquid but do not stir it. (Alternatively, spray a 4-cup heat-proof measure with nonstick vegetable spray, add the liquid, and boil it in the microwave, about 12 minutes on high). Meanwhile, transfer the peaches to a bowl and toss them with the cornstarch and almond extract until all traces of the cornstarch have disappeared.

Pour the syrup over the peaches, tossing gently. (Do not be concerned if the liquid hardens on contact with the peaches; it will dissolve during baking.) Transfer the peach mixture to the pie shell.

Roll out the top crust large enough to cut a 12-inch circle. Use an expandable flan ring or a cardboard template and a sharp knife to cut the circle.

Moisten the edges of the bottom crust with water and place the top crust over the fruit. Tuck the overhang under the bottom crust border and press down all around the top to seal it. Crimp the border using a fork or your fingers (see page 13) and make about 5 evenly spaced 2-inches slashes starting about 1 inch from the center and radiating toward the edge (see page 14). Cover the pie loosely with plastic wrap and refrigerate it for 1 hour before baking to chill and relax the pastry. This will maintain flakiness and help to prevent distortion.

Preheat the oven to 425°F. at least 20 minutes before baking. Set an oven rack at the lowest level and place a baking stone or baking sheet on it before preheating. Place a large piece of greased foil on top to catch any juices.

Set the pie directly on the foil-topped baking stone and bake 40 to 50 minutes or until the juices bubble *thickly* through the slashes and the peaches feel tender but not mushy when a cake tester or small sharp knife is inserted through a slash. After 30 minutes, protect the edges from overbrowning with a foil ring (see page 19).

Cool the pie on a rack for at least 3 hours before cutting. (The pie will still be warm after 4 hours.)

STORE
Room temperature, up to 2 days.

POINTERS FOR SUCCESS
∿ See Nectarine-Raspberry Pie, page 121.

UNDERSTANDING
Concentrating the peach juices before baking keeps the pie juicy and requires only a small amount of starch to bind them.

Only 6 cups of sliced fruit are used for this pie compared to the 8 cups used in the apple and nectarine pies because peaches are a little softer and don't hold up as well in a thicker layer.

CRUSTLESS PEACH-GINGER PIE

When fresh peaches are in season, this tart, juicy peach pie, without a bottom crust and topped with crisp pie crust cutouts, is a marvelous way to enjoy them. They are also delicious as a crustless crumb pie (see the Crustless Apple Crumb Pie on page 89; simply substitute the peach filling and almonds for the walnuts in the crumb topping).

OVEN TEMPERATURE: 400°F. • BAKING TIME: 30 TO 40 MINUTES   SERVES: 6

INGREDIENTS	MEASURE	WEIGHT	
	VOLUME	OUNCES	GRAMS
baked decorative pastry cutouts, sprinkled with sugar before baking (see page 14)		•	•
1¾ pounds peaches (about 5 medium), peeled,* pitted, and sliced into 16ths	4 cups (sliced)	22.5 ounces	635 grams (sliced)
light brown sugar	⅓ cup, packed	2.5 ounces	72 grams
salt	a pinch	•	•
cornstarch	2 teaspoons		6 grams
grated fresh ginger	2 teaspoons	•	6 grams
finely grated lemon zest	1 teaspoon	•	2 grams
ground cinnamon	¾ teaspoon	•	•

*To peel peaches, bring a pot of water to a boil, add the peaches, and blanch for 1 minute. Drain at once and rinse with cold water. If the peaches are ripe, the peels will slip off easily.

EQUIPMENT
A 9-inch pie pan (preferably clear glass)*

Make and bake the pastry cutouts, sprinkling them with sugar before baking (see page 14).

In a medium bowl, place the peaches, brown sugar, and salt. With a rubber spatula, toss them gently to mix evenly. Allow them to macerate for a minimum of 30 minutes and a maximum of 1 hour.

* I like to use clear glass because it is attractive to see the fruit through the sides.

Preheat the oven to 400°F. at least 20 minutes before baking. Set an oven rack at the middle level before preheating.

Transfer the peaches to a colander suspended over a bowl to capture the liquid. The peaches will exude ⅔ cup of juice.

In a small saucepan (preferably lined with a nonstick surface), over medium-high heat, boil down this liquid to about ⅓ cup, until syrupy and lightly caramelized. Swirl but do not stir it. (Alternatively, spray a 4-cup heatproof measure with nonstick vegetable spray, add the liquid, and boil it in the microwave, about 6 minutes on high.) Meanwhile, transfer the peaches to a bowl and toss them with the cornstarch, ginger, lemon zest, and cinnamon until all traces of the cornstarch have disappeared.

Pour the syrup over the peaches, tossing gently. (Do not be concerned if the liquid hardens on contact with the peaches; it will dissolve during baking.)

Empty the peaches into the pie pan. Cover it with foil and make a 1-inch slash in the middle. Bake for 30 to 40 minutes or until the juices bubble thickly and the peaches feel tender when pierced with a skewer or knife. Cool on a rack until warm or room temperature.

Up to 12 hours before serving the pie, garnish with the baked pastry cutouts.

STORE

Covered tightly with plastic wrap, without the pastry cutouts, room temperature, up to 2 days; refrigerated, up to 3 days.

NOTE

If a deeper filling is desired, you can increase the filling by 1½ times and increase the baking time by 5 minutes. Set a greased foil-lined baking sheet under the pie to catch bubbling juices.

CONCORD GRAPE PIE

My first Concord grape pie was brought to me as a gift from one of my former husband's students when he was a teacher at Pennsbury High School in Pennsylvania. I knew the gift of the pie meant she had a crush on him, but I didn't mind at all because she included an index card on which the recipe was perfectly printed, so I knew the gift was for me too!

Her recipe was made with a lattice crust, which was handsome because it showcased the beautiful purple fruit, but I found it difficult to apply a lattice crust to such a juicy mixture without first freezing the filling. My solution was to make round vents in the top crust so that they resembled a cluster of grapes.

Serve this pie à la mode with peanut butter ice cream (page 246).

INGREDIENTS	MEASURE	WEIGHT	
	VOLUME	OUNCES	GRAMS
Basic Flaky Pie Crust for a 2-crust 9-inch pie (page 23)		approx. 21 ounces	595 grams
1¾ pounds Concord grapes (to allow for bad grapes and stems)*	4 cups	1½ pounds	680 grams
sugar	¾ cup + 2 tablespoons	approx. 6 ounces	175 grams
cornstarch	2½ tablespoons	approx. 0.75 ounce	24 grams
freshly squeezed lemon juice	1½ tablespoons	0.75 ounce	22 grams
unsalted butter, softened	1 tablespoon	0.5 ounce	15 grams

*Twenty-five ounces of good grapes, stemmed, equal 24 ounces. Grapes can be frozen in quart canning jars for as long as 3 years in a freezer that maintains 0°F. or below.

EQUIPMENT

A 9-inch pie pan; optional: a number 8 (⅝-inch) plain pastry tube

Make the dough (page 23).

Remove the dough for the bottom crust from the refrigerator. If necessary, allow it to sit for about 10 minutes or until it is soft enough to roll.

On a floured pastry cloth or between two sheets of lightly floured plastic wrap, roll the bottom crust ⅛ inch thick or less and large enough to cut a 12-inch circle. Transfer it to the pie pan. Trim the edge almost even with the edge of the pan. Cover it with plastic wrap and refrigerate it for a minimum of 30 minutes and a maximum of 3 hours.

Rinse the grapes well and drain thoroughly. Stem them and remove the skins from the grapes by pressing them between your thumb and forefinger. Reserve the skins.

In a medium saucepan, place the grapes and squeeze the liquid from the peels into them; reserve the skins. Bring to a boil and simmer, covered, for 5 minutes. Remove the pan from the heat and cool completely.

Press the grapes through a fine sieve and discard the pits. Add the grape peels and all the remaining ingredients. (The pulp is 1⅓ cups; the pulp with the skins is 2 cups plus 2 tablespoons.) Transfer the grape mixture to the pie shell.

Roll out the top crust large enough to cut a 12-inch circle. Use an expandable flan ring or a cardboard template and a sharp knife as a guide to cut out the circle. To create a grape motif, use the pastry tube to cut little circles from the crust to form one or two grape clusters. (Stay within an 8½-inch-diameter circle, as the rest of the dough will become the raised border.) Save the scraps to make a decorative leaf if desired. To maintain the design best, slip the dough onto a flat baking sheet, cover it with plastic wrap, and refrigerate it for about 10 minutes.

Moisten the edges of the bottom crust with water and place the top crust over the fruit. Allow the crust to soften for a few minutes or until it is flexible. Then tuck the overhang under the bottom crust border and press down all around the top to seal it. Crimp the border using a fork or your fingers (see page 13).

Cover the pie loosely with plastic wrap and refrigerate it for 1 hour before baking to chill and relax the pastry. This will maintain flakiness and help to keep the crust from shrinking.

If desired, roll the scraps and use a cardboard template to cut out a grape leaf. Using a photocopier, enlarge the illustration by 200 percent. Use a small sharp knife to make the veins. Brush the bottom lightly with egg white or water and place it on the crust. Add a small strip of dough for the stem.

Preheat the oven to 425°F. at least 20 minutes before baking time. Set an oven rack at the lowest level and place a baking stone or baking sheet on it before preheating.

Set the pie directly on the baking stone and bake for 40 to 50 minutes or until the filling is *thickly* bubbling through the holes. After 30 minutes, protect the edges from overbrowning with a foil ring (see page 19).

Cool the pie on a rack for at least 2 hours before cutting. When set, the filling will remain juicy with just a little flow.

STORE

Room temperature, up to 2 days.

NOTE

For a lattice version, after pouring the fruit into the pie shell, freeze it for about 1 hour or until firm before applying the lattice. For an attractive glaze, brush the lattice with an egg yolk and cream glaze (see page 21). You will need to add a few minutes more to the baking time if the fruit is still frozen.

CRANBERRY WINDOW PIE

This pie has a wonderfully tart cranberry flavor with a tangy edge of orange in the background and a crunchy sugar-glazed crust. The center of the crust is cut open and unfolded to form a square window of glistening cranberries. The best part about this pie is that the cranberries *seem* whole. The secret is that each cranberry is cut in half, which prevents them from bursting and losing their shape during baking. Instead, they burst in the mouth, releasing more of their clear red sweet/tart juices. Don't be daunted by having to cut the berries in half; the results are more than worth the effort.

This recipe was a gift from my beloved editor, Maria Guarnaschelli. It has been a family holiday favorite for over twenty years. (Now mine too!)

OVEN TEMPERATURE: 425°F.,
THEN 375°F., THEN 325°F. • BAKING TIME: 50 TO 60 MINUTES   SERVES: 6

INGREDIENTS	MEASURE	WEIGHT	
	VOLUME	OUNCES	GRAMS
Basic Flaky Pie Crust for a 2-crust 9-inch pie (page 23)		approx. 21 ounces	595 grams
fresh or frozen cranberries, rinsed, picked over, and dried	1 package* (3½ cups)	12.25 ounces	347 grams
sugar	1¼ cups, divided	8.75 ounces	250 grams
freshly grated orange zest	1 tablespoon	•	6 grams
Lyle's Golden Syrup (refiner's syrup)† or light corn syrup	3 tablespoons, divided	2.25 ounces	64 grams
freshly squeezed orange juice	2 tablespoons	1 ounce	30 grams
Glaze			
milk	1 tablespoon	0.5 ounce	15 grams
sugar	1 tablespoon	0.5 ounce	12 grams

*Although the package states 12 ounces, there are actually 12¼ ounces.
†Lyle's Golden Syrup adds a special mellow flavor.

EQUIPMENT
A 9-inch pie pan

Make the dough (page 23).

Remove the dough for the bottom crust from the refrigerator. If necessary, allow it to sit for about 10 minutes or until it is soft enough to roll.

On a floured pastry cloth or between two sheets of lightly floured plastic wrap, roll the bottom crust ⅛ inch thick or less and large enough to cut a 12-inch circle.

Transfer it to the pie pan. Trim the edge almost even with the edge of the pan. Cover it with plastic wrap and refrigerate it for a minimum of 30 minutes and a maximum of 3 hours.

Cut each cranberry in half and place in a medium bowl. Mix the cranberries with ¾ cup (about 5¼ ounces/150 grams) of the sugar, the orange zest, and 1 table-spoon of the golden or corn syrup. Pour the mixture into the pie shell.

Roll out the top crust large enough to cut a 12-inch circle. Use an expandable flan ring or a cardboard template and a sharp knife as a guide to cut out the circle.

Moisten the edges of the bottom crust with water and place the top crust over the fruit. Tuck the overhang under the bottom crust border and press down all around the top to seal it. Crimp the border using a fork or your fingers (see page 13). With a sharp knife, cut a 3-inch-long plus sign in the center of the crust and pull back the pieces of dough to form a window. Cover the pie loosely with plastic wrap and refrigerate it for 1 hour before baking to chill and relax the pastry. This will maintain flakiness and help to keep the crust from shrinking.

Preheat the oven to 425°F. at least 20 minutes before baking. Set an oven rack at the lowest level and place a baking stone or baking sheet on it before preheating. Place a Teflon-type liner or a large piece of greased foil on top to catch any juices.

Brush the crust with the milk and sprinkle with the sugar. (For a very even coating of sugar, place the sugar in a strainer and tap the rim of the strainer.)

Set the pie directly on the foil-topped baking stone and bake for 10 minutes. Lower the heat to 375°F. and continue baking for 30 minutes.

Meanwhile, in a small saucepan or a microwave, combine the remaining ½ cup (3.5 ounces/100 grams) sugar, 2 tablespoons golden or corn syrup, and the orange juice. Bring to a boil, stirring constantly, and simmer over low heat for 2 minutes. The liquid will be reduced to ½ cup.

Pour the liquid into the center of the pie. Lower the heat to 325°F. and continue baking for 10 to 20 minutes or until the center bubbles.

Cool the pie on a rack for at least 3 hours before serving.

STORE

Room temperature, uncovered, up to 2 days.

UNDERSTANDING

The syrup is added partway through the baking time because while the cranber-ries are still very firm, they cannot absorb the liquid, and the filling would be too runny.

SHAKER LEMON PIE

This is one of the great American pies and well overdue for a revival. Who would believe that paper-thin slices of lemon—rind, pith, and pulp—could be baked into a pie and taste fantastic! For those who are looking for the greatest intensity of lemon flavor, this is the way to get it. The bitterness of the pith and acidity of the pulp are softened by a long maceration in sugar, similar to the preparation for marmalade. The lemon juices are thickened with eggs, which form a lovely, soft, clumpy custard during baking.

The first time I ever made this pie, I didn't notice the necessity for advance preparation and ended up having to carry it hot from the oven on a bus, praying that no one would trip and fall in my lap! That is why I put the advance preparation at the beginning of the recipe, where it's hard to miss!

OVEN TEMPERATURE: 450°F., THEN 350°F.
BAKING TIME: 40 TO 45 MINUTES   SERVES: 6 TO 8

INGREDIENTS	MEASURE	WEIGHT	
	VOLUME	OUNCES	GRAMS
2 large lemons (2½-inch diameter), washed well		12 ounces	340 grams
sugar	2 cups	14 ounces	400 grams
Flaky Cream Cheese Pie Crust for a 2-crust 9-inch pie (page 30)		22 ounces	624 grams
4 large eggs	¾ liquid cup	7 ounces	200 grams
1 large egg yolk	•	•	•

EQUIPMENT
A 9-inch pie pan

Make the dough (page 30).

Advance preparation: Twenty-four hours ahead, cut the lemons in half the long way. Slice off a piece from the end on each half, just to the point where the pulp begins, and discard these ends. With a sharp thin-bladed knife, slice the lemons paper-thin, collecting all the juice but picking out and discarding the seeds. When you get to the end where the white pith begins, stop slicing, and discard these end pieces too. You should have 2 cups of lemon slices (10.75 ounces/305 grams).

In a medium bowl, stir together the lemon slices, their juices, and the sugar and set aside, covered, at room temperature for 24 hours.

The next day, remove the dough for the bottom crust from the refrigerator. If necessary, allow it to sit for about 10 minutes or until it is soft enough to roll.

On a floured pastry cloth or between two sheets of lightly floured plastic wrap, roll the bottom crust ⅛ inch thick or less and large enough to cut a 12-inch circle. Transfer it to the pie pan. Trim the edge almost even with the edge of the pan. Cover it with plastic wrap and refrigerate it for a minimum of 30 minutes and a maximum of 3 hours.

In a small bowl, beat the eggs and the yolk until they are well mixed. Stir them into the lemon mixture. Transfer the lemon mixture to the pie shell.

Roll out the top crust large enough to cut a 12-inch circle. Use an expandable flan ring or a cardboard template and a knife as a guide to cut out the circle.

Moisten the edges of the bottom crust with water and place the top crust over the fruit. Tuck the overhang under the bottom crust border and press down all around the top to seal it. Crimp the border using a fork or your fingers (see page 13). Make about 5 evenly spaced 2-inch slashes starting about 1 inch from the center and radiating toward the edge. Cover the pie loosely with plastic wrap and refrigerate it for 1 hour before baking to chill and relax the pastry. This will maintain flakiness and help to keep the crust from shrinking.

Preheat the oven to 450°F. at least 20 minutes before baking. Set an oven rack at the lowest level and place a baking stone or baking sheet on it before preheating.

Set the pie directly on the baking stone and bake for 15 minutes. Lower the oven temperature to 350°F. and continue baking for 25 to 30 minutes or until a thin knife blade inserted into one of the slashes comes out fairly clean and the crust is golden. (The temperature in the center will be 165°F.; 1 inch from the side, it will be 194°F.)

Cool the pie on a rack for at least 2 hours before serving.

STORE
Room temperature, up to 2 days.

NOTE
For a half-size pie, bake it in a 7¾-inch fluted tart pan or 3-cup capacity pie pan at 450°F. for 15 minutes, then at 350°F. for 20 minutes.

POINTERS FOR SUCCESS
∾ Meyer lemons, from California, offer the mildest lemon flavor.

UNDERSTANDING
Allowing the lemons to macerate for 24 hours in the sugar enables the sugar to penetrate and sweeten the bitter white pith. It also works to let them sit for 2 hours and then hold the baked pie overnight.

The acidity of the lemons raises the temperature at which the eggs coagulate, preventing curdling in the hot oven.

One extra yolk is added to absorb the little bit of liquid that forms when using only the traditional 4 whole eggs.

This filling seems just like lemon curd interrupted by the texture of lemon slices. But it is lighter in texture and more lemony in flavor because it contains mostly whole eggs instead of just yolks and no butter.

FRUIT TURNOVERS
(*Basic Recipe*)

Turnovers are for those who adore pie dough, because this pastry contains the highest proportion of flaky golden crust to fruit filling. For this reason as well, I prefer to keep them small in size; in fact, for me, the miniatures offered below as a variation are perfect. I also like to roll the dough as thin as possible. Sprinkling the top of the dough with sugar makes it crackly/crunchy.

In a turnover, I prefer a cream cheese or basic flaky pie crust to puff pastry. Not only is there a better proportion of filling to crust, but no matter how you seal and vent the puff pastry, it always opens at some point along the seam, spewing out some of the filling. I asked one of my favorite pastry chefs how she managed to keep the fruit in the puff pastry turnover she served me. Her answer: "Are you kidding? It always leaks out—I spooned it back in!" It's always great to know you're not alone.

This recipe contains specific directions for making a wide variety of fruit and berry turnovers.

EQUIPMENT
A 17- by 12-inch baking sheet (half-size sheet pan) lined with aluminum foil or parchment

APPLE, NECTARINE, AND PEACH TURNOVERS

APPLES   14 ounces (3½ cups/400 grams) of fruit, ¼ cup (1.75 ounces/50 grams) of sugar, 1¾ teaspoons (5.5 grams) of cornstarch

NECTARINES OR PEACHES   14 ounces (2½ cups/400 grams) of fruit, ¼ cup (1.75 ounces/50 grams) of sugar, 1¾ teaspoons (5.5 grams) of cornstarch

Make the dough (page 30 or 23).

MAKE THE FILLING
In a large bowl, combine the fruit, lemon zest, lemon juice, sugar, cinnamon, and salt and toss to mix. Allow the mixture to sit for at least 30 minutes and up to 1 hour (apples can sit for up to 3 hours).

OVEN TEMPERATURE: 400°F. • BAKING TIME: 20 TO 30 MINUTES   SERVES: 10

| INGREDIENTS | MEASURE | WEIGHT | |
	VOLUME	OUNCES	GRAMS
Flaky Cream Cheese Pie Crust (page 30) or Basic Flaky Pie Crust (page 23) for a 2-crust pie		18 ounces	510 grams
½ large egg white, lightly beaten	1 tablespoon	0.5 ounce	14 grams
apples, nectarines, or peaches, peeled, cored or pitted, and sliced ⅜ to ½ inch thick	2½ to 3½ cups (sliced)	14 ounces (sliced)	400 grams
finely grated lemon zest	1 teaspoon	•	2 grams
freshly squeezed lemon juice	1 teaspoon	•	•
sugar	¼ cup or more, depending on the fruit*	•	•
ground cinnamon	½ teaspoon	•	•
salt	a pinch	•	•
unsalted butter	1 tablespoon	0.5 ounce	28 grams
¼ teaspoon almond extract or 1 teaspoon Kirsch			
cornstarch	1¾ teaspoons	0.2 ounce	12.5 grams
Optional Glaze 1 large egg, lightly beaten	3 tablespoons	1.75 ounces (weighed without the shell)	50 grams
sugar	approx. 2 teaspoons	•	•

*The recommended amounts of sugar will result in a slightly tart filling. If a sweeter filling is preferred, add 1 to 2 tablespoons more sugar.

Transfer the fruit to a colander suspended over a bowl to capture the liquid. The apple mixture will exude about 4 tablespoons of liquid; the nectarines and peaches will exude about 6 tablespoons.

In a small saucepan (preferably lined with a nonstick surface), reduce this liquid, with the butter, to about 2 tablespoons. (Or spray a 2-cup heatproof measure with nonstick vegetable spray, add the liquid and butter, and reduce it in the microwave, about 3 minutes on high.) Allow the liquid to cool for about 10 minutes or until warm. Add the almond extract or Kirsch.

Meanwhile, toss the fruit with the cornstarch. Pour the liquid over the fruit, tossing gently.

CHERRY AND BERRY TURNOVERS

The same technique of leaching out some of the fruit's liquid can be used for cherries and berries (except for blueberries, whose skin, if unbruised, is more impermeable) to make it less messy for filling the dough. It also makes it possible to use about three quarters of the thickener that would otherwise be required.

I prefer, however, to cook these fruits (except for blueberries) just to thicken the juices and cool them before filling the dough, as the filling holds together better. The filling should be very thick, because the cherries and berries will release more liquid during baking. If you are doing this, there is no need to leach out the liquid first.

CHERRIES   14 ounces (2½ cups/400 grams) of fruit, ⅔ cup (4.6 ounces/132 grams) of sugar, 1½ tablespoons (14 grams) of cornstarch if reducing the liquid, 1 tablespoon plus 2¼ teaspoons (16.5 grams) if not

BLUEBERRIES   14 ounces (2¾ cups/400 grams) of fruit, ¼ cup plus 2 tablespoons (2.6 ounces/75 grams) of sugar, 1 tablespoon plus 1¼ teaspoons (13.5 grams) of cornstarch

BLACKBERRIES   14 ounces (3½ cups/400 grams) of fruit, ¼ cup plus 3 tablespoons (3 ounces/88 grams) of sugar, 2 tablespoons plus ½ teaspoon (20.5 grams) of cornstarch if reducing the liquid, 1 tablespoon plus 2 teaspoons (16 grams) if not

CURRANTS   14 ounces (2.6 cups/400 grams) of fruit, 1 cup (7 ounces/200 grams) of sugar, 1 tablespoon plus 2½ teaspoons (17 grams) of cornstarch if reducing the liquid, 2 tablespoons plus ½ teaspoon (20.5 grams) if not

MAKE THE FILLING

In a medium bowl, whisk together the sugar and salt (omit the cinnamon). Add the fruit and lemon juice and, using a rubber spatula, toss together gently to coat the fruit. Allow it to sit for at least 30 minutes.

If reducing the liquid, place the fruit in a colander and drain it, reserving the juices.

Spray a 2-cup heatproof glass measure with nonstick vegetable spray or grease lightly, add the juices, and reduce by half in a microwave oven, 5 to 6 minutes. Or reduce in a small saucepan, preferably lined with a nonstick surface. Allow the liquid to cool until no longer hot. Add the kirsch or extract.

Meanwhile, add the lemon zest and cornstarch to the fruit and toss lightly to blend. Add the cooled juices and toss lightly again.

If cooking the cherries or berries, transfer the berries and their juices to a saucepan. Stir the lemon zest and cornstarch into the fruit until the cornstarch is dissolved and bring the mixture to a boil, stirring gently. Allow it to boil for 30 seconds to a minute, until the juices become clear and very thick. Gently stir in the Kirsch or extract. Empty the mixture into a bowl and allow it to cool completely, without stirring.

SHAPE THE TURNOVERS

Divide the dough into 10 equal pieces (1.75 ounces/50 grams each).

Using a floured pastry cloth and sleeve or two sheets of lightly floured plastic wrap, roll out one piece of dough slightly less than ⅛ inch thick and large enough to cut out a 6-inch circle. Using a cardboard template and a sharp knife, cut out the circle. Transfer it to the bottom end of a 9-inch-long piece of plastic wrap. Brush the bottom half of it with the egg white. Spoon 3 to 4 tablespoons of the fruit onto this section, leaving a 1-inch border. Using the plastic wrap if the dough is at all sticky, fold the top part of the dough over the fruit, so that the edges are flush. With your fingers, firmly press the 1-inch border to seal it. Fold the edge up over itself, pressing again to seal it. Cover the turnover with the top section of the plastic wrap and lift the turnover onto the foil-lined sheet. Repeat with the remaining turnovers. Refrigerate them for 1 hour or freeze them for at least 30 minutes.

Preheat the oven to 400°F. at least 20 minutes before baking. Set the oven rack in the lowest position and place a baking stone or large cookie or baking sheet on it before preheating.

Unwrap the turnovers and space them evenly on the foil-lined sheet. If desired, brush them lightly with the egg glaze and sprinkle lightly with the sugar. Use a small sharp knife to cut 3 steam vents through the dough into the top of each turnover.

Place the sheet directly on the stone and bake for 20 to 30 minutes or until the filling is bubbling thickly out of the vents and the pastry is golden. Remove the baking sheet to a wire rack to cool for 20 to 30 minutes. These are best eaten warm.

VARIATION

MINI-TURNOVERS   For 24 mini-turnovers, you will need about 0.75 ounce/21 grams dough for each. I prefer to roll one at a time so that there is no need to reroll the scraps. Divide the dough into 24 pieces and roll each one slightly less than ⅛ inch thick and large enough to cut out a 6-inch circle, using a cardboard template and a sharp knife. Alternatively, roll the dough into a large rectangle and cut out 4-inch circles. Then lay the scraps, side by side and slightly overlapping, in a few layers; roll them between plastic wrap, doing a turn (see page 15) if necessary to make them adhere. Refrigerate this dough for at least 15 minutes, while shaping the first batch of turnovers.

Brush the bottom half of each turnover with egg glaze, as above, and spoon 1 to 1½ tablespoons of fruit onto the bottom, leaving a ½-inch border. Seal, vent, and chill as above and bake for 12 to 15 minutes or until the pastry is golden and the filling is bubbling thickly out of the vents. Cool for 15 minutes before eating.

STORE
Room temperature, up to 2 days.

UNDERSTANDING
The same weight of apples has a greater volume than the peaches and nectarines before leaching out the liquid. But once the liquid is released, despite the fact that the apples leach out less liquid, the volume of all three fruits will be the same.

Turnovers are baked at 400°F. instead of at 425°F., as pies are, because of the egg glaze and sugar topping. If this is omitted, it's fine to use the higher temperature.

UN-RUGELACH MINI TURNOVERS

These tiny turnovers have the same balance of filling to dough as my number one favorite cookie, rugelach, but they are easier to prepare because they aren't rolled. *Rugelach* means rolled; therefore, I have dubbed these "un-rugelach." The buttery cinnamon/walnut flavors fill your mouth with opulent pleasure, but despite their richness, they are easy to keep on eating because of the fresh tanginess from the apricot jam filling.

EQUIPMENT
Two 12- by 17-inch cookie sheets or inverted half-size sheet pans, lined with parchment or foil

FOOD PROCESSOR METHOD
In a food processor with the metal blade, place the cream cheese and butter and process until smooth and creamy, scraping the sides once or twice. Add the sugar and vanilla and process for a few seconds to incorporate them. Add the flour and salt and pulse just until the dough starts to clump together.

ELECTRIC MIXER METHOD
In a mixing bowl, beat the cream cheese and butter until blended. Beat in the sugar and vanilla extract. On low speed, beat in the flour and salt just until incorporated.

OVEN TEMPERATURE: 350°F.
BAKING TIME: 15 TO 20 MINUTES

MAKES: ABOUT TWENTY-TWO
3½-INCH TURNOVERS

INGREDIENTS	MEASURE	WEIGHT	
	VOLUME	OUNCES	GRAMS
Dough			
cream cheese, softened	½ of an 8-ounce package	4 ounces	113 grams
unsalted butter, softened	8 tablespoons	4 ounces	113 grams
granulated sugar	2 tablespoons	1 ounce	25 grams
pure vanilla extract	½ teaspoon	•	2 grams
bleached all-purpose flour	1 cup (sifted into the cup and leveled off)	4 ounces	114 grams
salt	⅛ teaspoon	•	•
Filling			
granulated sugar	approx. 3 tablespoons	1.25 ounces	35 grams
light brown sugar	2 tablespoons, packed	1 ounce	27 grams
ground cinnamon	¼ teaspoon	•	•
golden raisins	¼ cup + 2 tablespoons	2 ounces	57 grams
coarsely chopped walnuts	½ cup	2 ounces	57 grams
Apricot Lekvar (page 512) or preserves (well stirred)	⅓ cup	approx. 3.5 ounces	102 grams
Topping			
granulated sugar	1 tablespoon	0.5 ounce	14 grams
ground cinnamon	½ teaspoon	•	•
milk	2 tablespoons	1 ounce	30 grams

BOTH METHODS

Scrape the dough onto a piece of plastic wrap and press it together to form a ball. Place the dough in a bowl, cover it well, and refrigerate for at least 2 hours, or overnight.

MAKE THE FILLING

In a medium bowl, with a fork, stir together the sugars, cinnamon, raisins, and walnuts until well mixed.

Using a 1¼-inch cookie scoop or a tablespoon measure, scoop out level measures of dough, placing them on a cookie sheet. Refrigerate the dough. Remove one piece of dough and roll it quickly between floured palms to form a ball. Dust it well with flour and place it between two sheets of plastic wrap. Use the flat bottom of a tumbler to press the ball flat and then a light rolling pin to roll it into a 3½-inch circle. Remove the top sheet of plastic wrap and spread rounded ½ tablespoons of Apricot Lekvar or preserves evenly over the dough, almost to the edge. Carefully place 2 teaspoons of the nut mixture on one half of the dough circle, leaving a narrow border. Use the plastic wrap to lift the other half of the dough up and over the filling to encase it. Leaving the plastic wrap in place, press along the border of the dough to seal in the filling. Remove the plastic wrap, brush away any excess flour, and place the turnover on a prepared cookie sheet. Repeat with the remaining dough and filling, leaving at least 1½ inches between each turnover. For the best shape, cover the turnovers with plastic wrap and refrigerate for at least 30 minutes before baking.

Preheat the oven to 350°F. at least 15 minutes before baking. Set the oven racks so that they divide the oven into thirds.

In a small bowl, stir together the sugar and cinnamon for the topping.

With a pastry brush or feather, brush each turnover with milk and sprinkle evenly with the sugar and cinnamon topping.

Bake for 15 to 20 minutes or until lightly browned. For even baking, rotate the cookie sheets from top to bottom and back to front halfway through the baking period. Use a small pancake turner to transfer the turnovers to wire racks to cool completely.

STORE

Airtight, room temperature, up to 5 days; frozen, up to 3 months.

UNDERSTANDING

This cream cheese dough can be more fragile and tender than the one used for pies and tarts (it contains no water to develop gluten), because it does not need strength due to the small size of the pastries.

APPLE DUMPLINGS

What a wonderful word—*dumpling.* And what a delicious and dramatic way to encase fruit. Actually, it's a turnover that takes on the shape of the fruit because the fruit is left whole.

My preference for this dumpling is for a cream cheese or basic flaky dough, rather than the lighter, flakier fillo, because its texture seems more compatible with the heartiness of the apple. The baked apple within the dough is very juicy, while the dough is crunchy because of the sugar sprinkling. If desired, the apples can be wrapped in the pastry the night before and refrigerated, covered. The next morning, they can be glazed and sugared, baked, and ready to eat in forty minutes.

OVEN TEMPERATURE: 425°F. • BAKING TIME: 30 TO 35 MINUTES　　　　　　**SERVES: 6**

INGREDIENTS	MEASURE	WEIGHT	
	VOLUME	OUNCES	GRAMS
Flaky Cream Cheese Pie Crust for a 2-crust 9-inch pie (page 30)		22 ounces	624 grams
6 apples, preferably Rome or Cortland (approx. 7½ ounces each)		approx. 3 pounds	1 kg 360 grams
freshly squeezed lemon juice	2 tablespoons	1 ounce	30 grams
unsalted butter, softened	2 tablespoons	1 ounce	56 grams
light brown sugar	½ cup, packed	approx. 3.75 ounces	108 grams
ground cinnamon	¾ teaspoon	•	•
walnuts, coarsely chopped	2 tablespoons	0.5 ounce	14 grams
Glaze 2 large egg whites, lightly beaten	¼ liquid cup	2 ounces (weighed without the shell)	60 grams
granulated sugar	2 tablespoons	approx. 1 ounce	25 grams
optional: unsweetened Crème Fraîche (page 558) or lightly sweetened softly whipped cream (page 551)	1 cup	•	•

EQUIPMENT
A 17- by 12-inch baking sheet (half-size sheet pan),* lined with parchment or aluminum foil

Make the dough (page 30).

Core the apples, starting at the stem end and leaving a little of the bottom end so that the filling does not leak out. Peel the apples and brush them with the lemon juice.

In a small bowl, stir together the butter, brown sugar, and cinnamon until well blended. You will have 6 tablespoons (1 tablespoon for each apple). Use a pastry bag or spoon to fill the cavities of the apples with the butter mixture and top each with ½ teaspoon of the chopped walnuts.

Divide the dough into 6 equal pieces. Keep the dough you are not working with covered and refrigerated.

Using a floured pastry cloth and sleeve or two sheets of lightly floured plastic wrap, roll each piece of dough into an 8-inch square, or a little larger. It will be under ⅛ inch thick, which is desirable since the dough will be overlapped and thicker in spots. Trim the edges to even them, saving the scraps, refrigerated, for the leaf decorations.

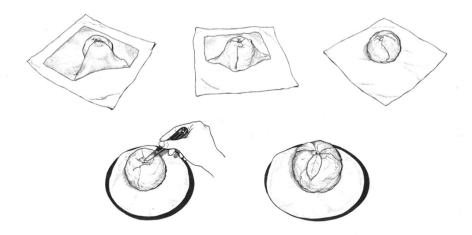

Place an apple, right side up, in the center of a dough square. Brush the edges of the dough lightly with egg white. Bring a corner of the dough up to the top of the apple and press it gently against the apple. Bring the corner next to it up to the top, overlapping the dough, and press it gently into place. Continue with the remaining two corners. Brush the dough lightly with egg white. Holding the

---

*An edge is necessary to keep any leaking juices from flowing onto the floor of the oven, but it must be low enough to allow the pastry to brown, not steam.

dumpling gently in the palm of your hand, sprinkle it all over with sugar (1 tea-spoon for each dough-wrapped apple). Set it on the prepared baking pan. Using a small sharp knife, cut a small steam vent in the center, about ¼ inch in diameter. Continue with the remaining apples, spacing them at least 1½ inches apart.

Roll the dough scraps about ⅛ inch thick and cut about 18 ovals, 2 inches long by 1 inch wide. If desired, mark vein lines with the tip of a small sharp knife. Brush the underside of each leaf lightly with egg white and press the leaf against the side of a wrapped apple, starting at the top and using 3 leaves per apple. If time allows, for the flakiest dough, refrigerate, lightly covered, for 1 hour or freeze for 15 min-utes before baking.

Preheat the oven to 425°F. at least 20 minutes before baking.

Bake for 30 to 35 minutes or until the pastry is golden and the apples feel ten-der when pierced with a skewer. The leaves tend to brown faster than the rest of the pastry, so after 15 minutes of baking, tent each apple with a 6-inch square of foil with a vent hole in the center. Remove the baking sheet to a wire rack to cool for 20 to 30 minutes before serving warm.

Use a pancake turner to lift the apple dumplings to serving plates. If desired, pass crème fraîche or whipped cream.

STORE

These are best eaten shortly after baking.

CHIFFON PIES

Here's proof of the Shakespearean quote "What's in a name?": Most people love chiffon pies, but offer them a piece of something called Bavarian cream pie and they'll probably refuse it. Yet the two pies are practically interchangeable. Chiffon filling is actually the American name for the European Bavarian filling. The only difference is that sometimes chiffon pie fillings are made without cream and sometimes Bavarians are made without egg whites. But most of the time, both chiffon and Bavarian fillings consist of a creamy custard (liquid thickened with egg), lightened with either stiffly beaten egg white and/or whipped cream and firmed into sliceable consistency by gelatin (usually 1 teaspoon per cup of liquid, including egg white).

My culinary historian friend Stephen Schmidt tells me that the name chiffon pie first started to appear in magazines in the 1950s. The name stuck, no doubt, because it is an accurate reflection of the filling's light and airy texture.

The many versions of this pie are ideally suited to entertaining. Chiffon pies are elegant and easy to make, and they can be prepared several days ahead and even frozen for several weeks. Perhaps the best thing about chiffon pies, especially for holiday entertaining, is that they are richly creamy and flavorful enough to satisfy yet sit lightly after an elaborate meal.

POINTERS FOR SUCCESS FOR CHIFFON PIES

∾ The custard filling must be heated to 160° to 170°F. to ensure that the amylase enzyme in the yolk, which would cause it to thin out after cooling, is destroyed.

∾ The real secret to success with chiffon pies is controlling the gelatin. Since gelatin continues to thicken a mixture for up to 24 hours, if you are preparing a pie 24 hours or more ahead, I recommend using only three quarters of the gelatin indicated.

The custard mixture containing the gelatin must be chilled until a small amount dropped onto the surface mounds slightly before folding in the whipped cream and meringue, in order to make a smooth and even mixture and prevent them from separating. When the custard mixture is chilled over ice water, it usually takes between 15 and 20 minutes, and it needs to be stirred occasionally for the first 10 minutes and then stirred slowly but constantly, because once it begins to set, it will continue setting at a rapid pace and therefore needs either to have other ingredients added or to be removed from the ice water at the first sign of setting. If it is chilled in the refrigerator, it needs to be stirred occasionally during the first 10 minutes and then every few minutes. The gradual chilling gives you more leeway, as when the filling begins to jell, it continues at a more gradual pace than when chilling in an ice-water bath.

If the mixture becomes too stiff, it will not be possible to incorporate the whipped cream and meringue smoothly. Should this happen, place the bowl over a larger bowl filled with hot water for just a few seconds, folding constantly with the whisk until the mixture has softened slightly. Remove the bowl from the hot water and continue stirring for a few seconds. If necessary, return it very briefly to the hot water bowl or to the ice-water bath. The mixture can be heated and chilled many times without harm as long as neither the meringue nor the whipped cream has been added. Heating would cause them to lose their airy lightness.

↷ Because chiffon pies are served chilled, to release the crust from the pan, you must wipe the bottom and sides of the pan with a dish towel dipped in very hot water and wrung out, or lower the pie carefully into a bowl of hot water. For attractive slices, cut with a sharp thin-bladed knife that has been dipped in hot water between each slice.

STRAWBERRY LOVER'S CHIFFON PIE

R educing the juices of the strawberries is what gives this filling a concentrated strawberry flavor. Fresh sliced strawberries make a beautiful topping and provide still more strawberry flavor.

SERVES: 8

INGREDIENTS	MEASURE	WEIGHT	
	VOLUME	OUNCES	GRAMS
Vanilla or Chocolate Crumb Crust for a 9-inch pie (page 67), pressed into the pan and chilled		•	•
Strawberry Chiffon frozen whole strawberries, with no added sugar*	one 20-ounce bag	20 ounces	567 grams
freshly squeezed lemon juice	2 teaspoons	0.3 ounce	10 grams
water	3 tablespoons	1.5 ounces	44 grams
gelatin	2 teaspoons	•	6 grams
heavy cream	½ cup	4 ounces	116 grams
sugar	6 tablespoons, divided	2.6 ounces	75 grams
1 large egg white	2 tablespoons	1 ounce	30 grams
cream of tartar	⅛ teaspoon	•	•
Fresh Strawberry Topping 7 cups fresh strawberries, rinsed, hulled, dried, and sliced	(3½ cups) 4½ cups	28 ounces (unhulled)	794 grams
sugar	2 scant tablespoons	1 ounce	25 grams
optional: liquid red food color	4 drops	•	•
cassava†	1¾ teaspoons	•	4.5 grams

*If fresh berries are in season, you can use 1¼ pounds (5 cups), but they must be frozen for at least 48 hours and thawed to release their juices.

†Or 1½ teaspoons arrowroot or cornstarch.

EQUIPMENT
A 9-inch pie pan

Make the crust (page 67). Press it into the pan (see page 69) and chill it.

MAKE THE STRAWBERRY FILLING

Chill a small bowl for the whipped cream.

The night before (in the refrigerator) or several hours ahead (at room temperature): In a colander suspended over a deep bowl, thaw the strawberries completely. (To speed thawing, place in an oven with a pilot light.) Press on the berries several times to force out a total of 1¼ cups of juice. Reserve the strawberries and the juices separately.

In a small saucepan over medium heat, boil the strawberry juice, stirring often, until it is reduced to ¼ cup. (Or microwave the juice on high in a 2-cup heatproof measure, lightly sprayed with nonstick vegetable spray, until reduced to ¼ cup.)

In a food processor, purée the strawberries until smooth, about 30 seconds. You will have 1 full liquid cup of purée. Transfer to a bowl. Stir in the reduced strawberry juice and the lemon juice. There will be 1¼ cups of strawberry purée. Chill the purée until it is cold, at least 30 minutes.

Place the water in a small custard cup and sprinkle the gelatin over it. Allow it to soften for at least 5 minutes.

In the chilled bowl, beat the heavy cream with 2 tablespoons of the sugar until soft peaks form when the beater is raised. Chill.

In a small mixing bowl, beat the egg white until foamy. Add the cream of tartar and beat at medium speed, gradually adding 2 tablespoons of the sugar, until soft peaks form when the beater is raised slowly. Gradually beat in the remaining 2 tablespoons of sugar and continue beating on high speed until stiff peaks form when the beater is raised. Set aside briefly.

Heat the gelatin mixture in the microwave for a few seconds, stirring once, or in a small custard cup set in simmering water, stirring once or twice, until it is hot and smooth. Whisking constantly, add the hot gelatin mixture to the cold strawberry purée. Continuing with the whisk, fold in first the egg white, then the whipped cream. Finish by using a rubber spatula, reaching down to the bottom of the bowl, where the heavier strawberry purée tends to settle. The mixture should be well incorporated but still a little streaky, to avoid overmixing and loss of air. You will have 3½ cups of filling. Pour it at once into the prepared pie crust and refrigerate until the surface is set, at least 30 minutes, before adding the fresh topping. (The filling must set for at least 4 hours before serving.)

MAKE THE FRESH STRAWBERRY TOPPING

At least 2 hours and up to 6 hours before serving: Gently stir together the sliced strawberries, sugar, and optional food color. Cover and allow it to sit for 1 hour at room temperature or up to 5 hours in the refrigerator.

Place the berries in a strainer suspended over a small saucepan and allow them to stand for about 30 minutes to drain all the syrup, stirring the berries gently with a rubber spatula several times to help release the syrup. There should be about ⅔ cup of syrup. The strawberries will measure only about 3½ cups. Set them aside.

In a small saucepan over medium heat, boil the syrup, stirring often, until it is reduced to ⅓ cup. (Or microwave the juice on high power in a 2-cup heatproof measure, lightly sprayed with nonstick vegetable spray, until reduced to ⅓ cup.) Allow it to cool completely.

Stir the cassava (or arrowroot or cornstarch) into the reduced strawberry syrup and cook over medium heat until clear and thickened. If you use cassava, this will happen just after boiling; if you use arrowroot, this will happen just before boiling. With cornstarch, the liquid needs to be simmered for about 30 seconds after reaching a boil. Remove the thickened syrup from the heat and set aside.

Spoon or arrange the berries evenly over the strawberry chiffon filling, placing as many of the bright red end pieces skin side up as possible, and brush each one all over with the thickened syrup.

Refrigerate until shortly before serving.

STORE

Refrigerated, up to 3 days; frozen (without the topping), up to 3 weeks.

POINTERS FOR SUCCESS

∾ Spraying or greasing the heatproof measuring cup prevents the strawberry syrup from bubbling over the top during microwaving.

∾ The gelatin mixture must be hot because the purée is cold from the refrigerator; the heat of the mixture keeps the gelatin from setting prematurely.

∾ Egg whites are usually folded in at the end of preparing a mixture to maintain the airy texture, but in this filling they are folded in before the cream because the cold temperature of the cream might cause the mixture to set prematurely.

UNDERSTANDING

Compared to the raspberry chiffon filling, this filling has about 9 tablespoons more purée because strawberries are less intense. This extra purée, together with the 3 tablespoons of water for the gelatin, equals ¾ cup more liquid, necessitating ¾ teaspoon more gelatin. Only half the amount of sugar used for the raspberries is necessary because strawberries are so much sweeter.

If the strawberries are at the height of their season and a bright red, no food color is necessary.

RASPBERRY CHIFFON PIE

This filling captures the lilting/lush freshness of raspberries without being overpowering. The secret is adding Italian meringue, the super-smooth and billowy meringue made with a hot sugar syrup. Fresh raspberries adorn the top and provide juicy texture and more raspberry flavor.

SERVES: 8

INGREDIENTS	MEASURE	WEIGHT	
	VOLUME	OUNCES	GRAMS
Sweet Nut Cookie Tart Crust, made with almonds, for a 9-inch pie (page 59), prebaked, or Crisp Meringue Shell for a 10-inch pie (page 575), baked	1 generous cup	10.75 ounces	307 grams
Raspberry Chiffon frozen raspberries, with no added sugar	3 cups (one 12-ounce bag)	12 ounces	340 grams
freshly squeezed lemon juice	1 teaspoon	•	5 grams
sugar	⅓ cup	2.3 ounces	66 grams
heavy cream	½ liquid cup	4 ounces	116 grams
Light Italian Meringue gelatin	1¼ teaspoons	•	4 grams
water	3 tablespoons, divided	•	•
sugar, preferably superfine	7 tablespoons, divided	3 ounces	87 grams
2 large egg whites	¼ liquid cup	2 ounces	60 grams
cream of tartar	¼ teaspoon	•	•
Fresh Raspberry Topping fresh raspberries	4 cups	1 pound	454 grams
powdered sugar	•	•	•

EQUIPMENT

A 9-inch pie pan, or a 10-inch pie pan if using the meringue shell; optional: a number 7 star pastry tube and a pastry bag or a reclosable quart-size freezer bag

Make the dough (page 59) or meringue shell (page 575). Roll and shape the dough and transfer it to the pan and prebake it (see pages 50–54) or pipe the meringue into the pan and bake it (see page 621).

MAKE THE RASPBERRY FILLING

Chill a small bowl for the whipped cream.

The night before (in the refrigerator) or several hours ahead (at room temperature): In a strainer suspended over a deep bowl, thaw the raspberries completely. (To speed thawing, place in an oven with a pilot light.) Press on the berries to force out all the juice. There should be about ½ cup of juice.

In a small saucepan over medium heat, boil the raspberry juice, stirring often, until it is reduced to 2 tablespoons. (Or microwave the juice on high power in a 1-cup heatproof measure, lightly sprayed with nonstick vegetable spray, until reduced to 2 tablespoons.) Pour it into a lightly oiled heatproof cup to stop the cooking and to cool.

In a food processor, purée the raspberries. To remove all the seeds, pass them through a food mill fitted with the fine disc, or a fine strainer, suspended over a medium bowl. You should have ½ liquid cup of purée. Stir in the reduced raspberry syrup and the lemon juice. There should be about ⅔ cup of purée (5 ounces/145 grams). Stir in the sugar. Let the raspberry purée cool.

In the chilled bowl, beat the cream just until it mounds softly when dropped from a spoon. Add the raspberry purée and, with a whisk or rubber spatula, fold the two together until they become completely uniform. (You will have 3¾ cups of filling.) Cover the bowl tightly with plastic wrap and refrigerate it.

MAKE THE LIGHT ITALIAN MERINGUE

Have ready a 1-cup heatproof liquid measure by the range.

In a small heatproof measuring cup, place the gelatin and 1 tablespoon of the water and allow the mixture to sit for 5 minutes. Set the cup in a pan of simmering water for a few minutes, stirring occasionally, until the gelatin is dissolved. (This can also be done in a few seconds in a microwave on high power, stirring once or twice.)

In a small heavy saucepan, preferably with a nonstick lining, stir together 6 tablespoons of the sugar and the remaining 2 tablespoons of water until the sugar is completely moistened. Heat, stirring constantly, until the sugar dissolves and the syrup is bubbling. Stop stirring and turn down the heat to the lowest setting. (If using an electric range, remove the pan from the heat.)

In a mixing bowl, using the whisk beater, beat the egg whites until foamy. Add the cream of tartar and beat until soft peaks form when the beater is raised slowly. Gradually beat in the remaining 1 tablespoon of sugar and beat until stiff peaks form when the beater is raised slowly.

Increase the heat under the syrup and boil the syrup until a thermometer registers 248° to 250°F. (firm ball stage). Immediately pour the syrup into the glass measure to stop the cooking.

If using an electric hand-held mixer on high speed, beat the syrup into the whites in a steady stream. To keep syrup from spinning onto the sides of the bowl, do not allow it to fall directly on the beaters. If using a stand mixer, pour a small amount of syrup over the whites with the mixer off. Immediately beat at high speed for 5 seconds. Stop the mixer and add a larger amount of syrup. Beat at high speed for 5 seconds. Continue with the remaining syrup. With the last addition, use a rubber scraper to remove the syrup clinging to the measuring cup.

Lower the speed to medium, add the gelatin mixture, and beat at medium speed until cool, about 2 minutes.

Use a large balloon whisk or rubber spatula to fold the Italian meringue into the raspberry mixture in two parts. Finish by using a rubber spatula to reach to the bottom. (You will have 3¾ cups of filling.) Pour the filling at once into the prepared pie crust or shell and refrigerate until the surface is set before topping with the raspberries, at least 30 minutes.

MAKE THE RASPBERRY TOPPING

Arrange the raspberries on top of the pie and dust lightly with powdered sugar. The filling needs to set for at least 6 hours before serving. Refrigerate until shortly before serving.

STORE

Refrigerated, up to 3 days; frozen (without the topping), up to 3 weeks.

POINTERS FOR SUCCESS

∾ Spraying or greasing the heatproof measuring cup prevents the raspberry syrup from bubbling over the top during microwaving.

UNDERSTANDING

Raspberry is so intense that compared to the strawberry chiffon filling, this needs Italian meringue to lighten it, and only about half the berries.

CRANBERRY CHIFFON PIE

This pie has the tart intense flavor of cranberry combined with the light texture of the classic chiffon filling. It makes a cold refreshing finale for a holiday feast.

EQUIPMENT
A 9-inch pie pan; optional: a number 7 large star pastry tube and a pastry bag or a reclosable quart-size freezer bag

Make the crust (page 67). Press it into the pan (see page 69) and chill it.

MAKE THE CRANBERRY CHIFFON
Chill a small bowl for the whipped cream.

Wash and drain the cranberries well. Discard any stems or soft berries.

In a medium saucepan, combine the cranberries, the cran/raspberry concentrate, ½ cup of the sugar, and the salt. Bring it to a boil, stirring often. Simmer for 5 minutes, stirring often, or until the berries burst and soften and a pink froth covers the top. Remove the pan from heat and cool slightly.

Press the entire mixture through a fine sieve placed over a bowl, and add the lemon juice. You should have about 1 cup of purée (9.35 ounces/267 grams). Discard any residue remaining in the sieve. Set the bowl near the range with the fine sieve suspended over it.

MAKE THE CUSTARD FILLING
In a small heavy nonreactive saucepan, stir together ¼ cup of the remaining sugar, the gelatin, and the yolks.

Scald the milk* and stir a few tablespoons into the yolk mixture; then gradually add the remainder, stirring constantly. Heat the mixture, stirring constantly, to just before the boiling point (170° to 180°F.). Steam will begin to appear and the mixture will be slightly thicker than heavy cream. It will leave a well-defined track when a finger is run across the back of the spoon. Immediately remove it from the heat and pour it into the strainer, scraping up the thickened custard that has settled on the bottom of the pan. Stir the mixture until it is uniform in color and add the optional Chambord. Set it aside.

In a chilled bowl, beat the heavy cream with 2 tablespoons of the remaining sugar until it mounds softly when dropped from a spoon. Chill until ready to use.

---

*Use a small saucepan, or a heatproof glass measure if using a microwave on high power, and heat until small bubbles form around the perimeter.

INGREDIENTS	MEASURE	WEIGHT	
	VOLUME	OUNCES	GRAMS
Vanilla or Chocolate Crumb Crust for a 9-inch pie (page 67), pressed into the pan and chilled		•	•
Cranberry Chiffon			
cranberries, fresh or frozen	2 heaping cups	8 ounces	227 grams
frozen cran/raspberry concentrate, undiluted	⅓ cup	3.33 ounces	94 grams
sugar	1 cup, divided	7 ounces	200 grams
salt	a pinch	•	•
freshly squeezed lemon juice	2 teaspoons	0.3 ounce	10 grams
Custard Filling gelatin	2 teaspoons	•	6 grams
2 large egg yolks 1 egg white (reserved)	2 tablespoons + 1 teaspoon	1.3 ounces	37 grams
milk	½ liquid cup	4.25 ounces	121 grams
optional: Chambord (black raspberry liqueur)	1 tablespoon	0.5 ounce	16 grams
heavy cream	½ liquid cup	4 ounces	116 grams
Meringue 1 large egg white (reserved)	2 tablespoons	1 ounce	30 grams
cream of tartar	⅛ teaspoon	•	•
Cran/Raspberry Glaze frozen cran/raspberry concentrate, undiluted	(scant ¼ cup) ¼ liquid cup	(2.5 ounces) •	(71 grams) •
cornstarch or arrowroot*	1 teaspoon	•	3 grams
optional: Chambord	¾ teaspoon	•	•
optional: ½ recipe Whipped Cream (see page 556) for Piping	1 cup	4.3 ounces	122 grams

*Or 1⅓ teaspoons cassava.

A MAXIMUM OF 20 MINUTES BEFORE
USING IT, MAKE THE MERINGUE

In a mixing bowl, beat the egg white until foamy. Add the cream of tartar and beat until soft peaks form when the beater is raised slowly. Gradually beat in the remaining 2 tablespoons of sugar and continue beating until stiff peaks form when the beater is raised slowly. Set the meringue aside briefly.

Chill the custard by placing the bowl in a bowl of ice water with about a tablespoon of salt added to speed chilling. Stir occasionally for the first 10 minutes and then slowly but constantly for about 10 minutes longer. (If you prefer, you can refrigerate the mixture, stirring occasionally for the first 10 minutes and then every few minutes.) When a small amount dropped from the spoon mounds very slightly on the surface before disappearing, immediately remove the bowl from the water bath and, using a whisk, fold in first the meringue, then the whipped cream. The mixture should be well incorporated but still streaky. (You will have 3¾ cups of filling.) Pour it at once into the prepared pie crust and refrigerate until the surface is set before glazing, at least 30 minutes.

MAKE THE GLAZE

In a small heavy saucepan, stir together the cran/raspberry concentrate and the cornstarch or arrowroot (or cassava). Cook over medium heat, stirring constantly, until clear and thickened. If you use cassava, this will happen just after boiling; if you use arrowroot, this will happen just before boiling. With cornstarch, the liquid needs to be simmered for about 30 seconds after reaching a boil. Remove it from the heat and stir in the optional Chambord. Pour the glaze into a heatproof measuring cup with a spout and drizzle it over the surface of the pie.

Refrigerate for at least 6 hours before serving. To serve: If desired, decorate with a border of piped whipped cream.

STORE

Refrigerated, 3 to 4 days; frozen (*without* whipped cream border), up to 3 weeks.

UNDERSTANDING

Less gelatin (2 teaspoons instead of 2½ teaspoons) than the usual 1⅛ teaspoons per cup of liquid is used in this filling because of the natural pectin in the cranberries, which causes the mixture to thicken.

PUMPKIN CHIFFON PIE

P eople who love pumpkin pie—and even those who don't—adore this airy, more subtle version, especially after a filling holiday dinner. I especially enjoy the strong hit of ginger in the crust echoing the ginger in the filling. In my pumpkin pie recipe, I line the pie crust with a scattering of gingersnap crumbs and ground pecans, but for this chiffon pie, the entire crust is made with them.

SERVES: 8

| INGREDIENTS | MEASURE | WEIGHT | |
	VOLUME	OUNCES	GRAMS
Gingersnap Nut Crumb Crust, made with pecans, for a 9-inch pie (page 68), pressed into the pan and chilled		•	•
Pumpkin Chiffon			
water	¼ liquid cup	2 ounces	59 grams
gelatin	2¼ teaspoons	0.25 ounce	7 grams
fresh or canned pumpkin purée	1¼ cups (15-ounce can is 1¾ cups)	10.7 ounces	303 grams
sugar	¾ cup, divided	5.3 ounces	150 grams
ground ginger	½ teaspoon	•	•
ground cinnamon	½ teaspoon	•	•
nutmeg, preferably freshly grated	½ teaspoon	•	•
salt	½ teaspoon	•	•
milk	½ cup	4.25 ounces	121 grams
3 large eggs, separated yolks whites	 1.75 fluid ounces 3 fluid ounces	 2 ounces 3 ounces	 56 grams 90 grams
cream of tartar	⅜ teaspoon	•	•
Optional Garnish			
½ recipe whipped cream (see page 556), for piping	1 cup	4.3 ounces	122 grams
coarsely chopped pecans, toasted	¼ cup	1 ounce	26 grams

EQUIPMENT
A 9-inch pie pan; optional: a pastry bag or reclosable
quart-size freezer bag and a number 7 star pastry tube

*Make the crust (page 68). Press it into the pan (see page
69) and chill it.*

MAKE THE CUSTARD FILLING
In a small bowl, place the water and sprinkle the gelatin
on top. Set it aside for at least 3 minutes.

In a small heavy saucepan, stir together the pumpkin, ½
cup of the sugar, the spices, and the salt. Over medium heat,
bring the mixture to a sputtering simmer, stirring constantly. Reduce the heat to low and cook, stirring constantly, for 3 to 5 minutes or until thick and shiny. Scrape
the mixture into a food processor fitted with the metal blade and process for 1
minute. Scrape the sides of the work bowl. With the motor on, add the milk, processing until incorporated. Add the egg yolks one at a time, processing just to incorporate, about 5 seconds after each addition. Add the gelatin mixture and pulse in.

Return the mixture to the saucepan and heat, stirring constantly, for about 3
minutes or until thickened slightly (160° to 170°F.). Pour the mixture into a
medium bowl and set it aside.

**A MAXIMUM OF 20 MINUTES BEFORE USING IT,
MAKE THE MERINGUE**
In a mixing bowl, beat the egg whites on low speed until foamy. Add the cream of
tartar and beat at high speed until soft peaks form when the beater is raised
slowly. Gradually beat in the remaining ¼ cup of sugar, beating until stiff peaks
form when the beater is raised. Set the meringue aside.

Chill the pumpkin custard by placing the bowl in a bowl of ice water with
about a tablespoon of salt added to speed chilling. Stir occasionally for the first 10
minutes and then slowly but constantly for about 10 minutes longer. (If you prefer, you can refrigerate the mixture, stirring occasionally for the first 10 minutes
and then every few minutes.) When a small amount dropped from the spoon
mounds very slightly on the surface before disappearing, immediately remove the
bowl from the water bath and, using a whisk, fold in the meringue just until
blended. (This custard is very thick, so it does not need to set fully in order to keep
the meringue evenly dispersed.) There will be about 5 cups of filling, so it will
mound nicely in the pie shell. Pour it at once into the prepared pie shell and
refrigerate until set, at least 2 hours.

To serve: If desired, pipe rosettes of whipped cream on top of the pie (see page
620) and garnish with the coarsely chopped pecans.

STORE

Refrigerated, 2 to 3 days.

NOTE

The filling can be poured into small hollowed-out pumpkin shells or bowls instead of into a crust. It will keep in a bowl, refrigerated, for up to 5 days.

UNDERSTANDING

This pie uses the same special method of cooking and processing the pumpkin and spices to create a mellow flavor and silky texture as does Great Pumpkin Pie (page 198). But instead of being baked, gelatin and a meringue of the egg whites are folded into it to create a lighter, airier texture. The pumpkin is slightly decreased, the spices significantly decreased, and the brown sugar replaced by white to harmonize better with the lighter texture.

The filling is heated to 160° to 170°F. to ensure that the amylase enzyme in the yolk, which would cause it to thin out after cooling, is destroyed, as—unlike Great Pumpkin Pie—this pie does not get baked.

LEMON ANGEL CHIFFON PIE

In this pie, a crisp meringue serves as the pie shell to contain a lilting, refreshing, intensely lemony, and creamy filling. It's fun to think of it as an upside-down lemon meringue pie with crunchy meringue.

This is an excellent fancy dessert for entertaining, as the finished pie freezes for up to six weeks. The optional raspberry sauce can also be made way ahead.

As a variation, any of the citrus curd variations, such as lime or orange, or the passion fruit (page 568), can be used in place of the lemon. If you choose passion, replace the raspberry sauce with strawberry sauce. If you choose an orange curd filling, make a chocolate meringue (page 575) or chocolate cookie crust (page 61) as the pie shell and replace the raspberry sauce with a chocolate lace topping (page 303).

EQUIPMENT

A 10-inch pie pan if using the meringue shell, or a 9-inch pie pan; optional: a number 7 large star pastry tube and a pastry bag or a reclosable quart-size freezer bag

INGREDIENTS	MEASURE	WEIGHT	
	VOLUME	OUNCES	GRAMS
Crisp Meringue Shell for a 10-inch pie (page 575, 4-egg-white meringue), baked, or Sweet Nut Cookie Tart Crust, made with almonds, for a 9-inch pie (page 59), prebaked	1 generous cup	10.75 ounces	307 grams
heavy cream	½ liquid cup	4 ounces	116 grams
Lemon Curd finely grated lemon zest	1 teaspoon	•	2 grams
2 large eggs yolks (2 egg whites reserved)	2 tablespoons + 1 teaspoon	1.25 ounces	37 grams
sugar	2 tablespoons	0.75 ounce	25 grams
freshly squeezed lemon juice	3 tablespoons	1.6 ounces	46 grams
unsalted butter, softened	2 tablespoons	1 ounce	28 grams
salt	a pinch	•	•
Light Italian Meringue gelatin	½ teaspoon + ⅛ teaspoon	•	•
water	3 tablespoons, divided	•	•
sugar, preferably superfine	7 tablespoons, divided	3 ounces	87 grams
2 large egg whites (reserved)	¼ liquid cup	2 ounces	60 grams
cream of tartar	¼ teaspoon	•	•
Optional Garnish Raspberry Sauce (page 603)	1¼ cups	•	•
heavy cream	½ liquid cup	4 ounces	116 grams

Make the meringue shell (page 575) or dough (page 59). Pipe the meringue into the pan and bake it (see page 621) or roll and shape the dough and transfer it to the pan and prebake it (see pages 50–54).

In a large mixing bowl, place the heavy cream and refrigerate it for at least 15 minutes. Chill the whisk beater alongside the bowl.

MAKE THE LEMON CURD

Put the lemon zest in a medium bowl, suspend a strainer over it, and set it aside near the range.

In a heavy nonreactive saucepan, beat the yolks and sugar until well blended. Stir in the remaining ingredients except the lemon zest (and whites). Cook over medium-low heat, stirring constantly, until the mixture is thickened and resembles hollandaise sauce—it should thickly coat a wooden spoon but still be liquid enough to pour. The mixture will change from translucent to opaque and begin to take on a yellow color on the back of the spoon. It must not be allowed to come to the boil, or it will curdle. Whenever steam appears, remove the pan briefly from the heat, stirring constantly, to keep the mixture from boiling. When the curd has thickened (196°F.), pour it at once into the strainer. Press with the back of a spoon until only the coarse residue remains, and discard it. Stir gently to mix in the zest and allow the lemon curd to cool completely.

When the lemon curd has cooled, beat the cream in the chilled bowl just until the cream mounds softly when dropped from a spoon. Add the lemon curd and, with a whisk or rubber spatula, fold the two together until completely uniform. Finish by using a rubber spatula to reach to the bottom. Cover the bowl tightly with plastic wrap and refrigerate it.

MAKE THE LIGHT ITALIAN MERINGUE

Have ready a 1-cup heatproof liquid measure by the range.

In a small heatproof measuring cup, place the gelatin and 1 tablespoon of the water and allow it to sit for 5 minutes. Set the cup in a pan of simmering water for a few minutes, stirring occasionally until the gelatin is dissolved. (This can also be done in a few seconds in a microwave on high power, stirring once or twice.)

In a small heavy saucepan, preferably with a nonstick lining, stir together 6 tablespoons of the sugar and the remaining 2 tablespoons of water until the sugar is completely moistened. Heat, stirring constantly, until the sugar dissolves and the syrup is bubbling. Stop stirring and turn down the heat to the lowest setting. (If using an electric range, remove the pan from the heat.)

In a mixing bowl, using the whisk beater, beat the egg whites until foamy. Add the cream of tartar and beat until soft peaks form when the beater is raised slowly. Gradually beat in the remaining 1 tablespoon of sugar and continue to beat until stiff peaks form when the beater is raised slowly.

Increase the heat under the sugar syrup and boil the syrup until a thermometer registers 248° to 250°F. (firm ball stage). Immediately pour it into the glass measure to stop the cooking.

If using an electric hand-held mixer, beat the syrup into the whites in a steady stream. To keep the syrup from spinning onto the sides of the bowl, do not allow it to fall directly on the beaters. If using a stand mixer, pour a small amount of syrup over the whites with the mixer off. Immediately beat at high speed for 5 seconds. Stop the mixer and add a larger amount of syrup. Beat at high speed for 5 seconds. Continue with the remaining syrup. With the last addition, use a rubber scraper to remove the syrup clinging to the measure.

Lower the speed to medium, add the gelatin mixture, and beat at medium speed until cool, about 2 minutes.

Use a large balloon whisk or rubber spatula to fold the Italian meringue into the lemon cream mixture in two parts. (You will have about 3¾ cups.) Spoon the mixture into the prepared pie shell, smoothing the surface to make it even. The filling needs to set for at least 4 hours before serving.

MAKE THE OPTIONAL GARNISH

Just before serving, or up to 4 hours ahead, drizzle some of the raspberry sauce over the surface of the pie. In a cold bowl, whip the cream until stiff peaks form when the beater is raised and pipe a shell or star border (see page 621) or spoon it around the edge of the lemon curd filling. Pass the rest of the sauce.

STORE

Uncovered, refrigerated, up to 1 day; frozen (*without* the whipped cream border), up to 6 weeks.

POINTERS FOR SUCCESS FOR THE LEMON CURD

∾ See page 570.

POINTERS FOR SUCCESS FOR THE ITALIAN MERINGUE

∾ See page 578.

UNDERSTANDING

If the egg whites are not cooked, the acidity from the lemon in combination with the cream of tartar will keep the gelatin from thickening the chiffon filling.

If using the meringue shell, the pie must be refrigerated uncovered to prevent the meringue from softening.

FROZEN LIME CHIFFON PIE

This is another easy and impressive pie for entertaining. The filling, reminiscent of an airy lime ice cream, is set off by a nut cookie or crumb crust. It can be made three months ahead, but it is most delicious served partially defrosted (like a semifreddo), to soften the texture and enhance the flavor.

SERVES: 8

INGREDIENTS	MEASURE	WEIGHT	
	VOLUME	OUNCES	GRAMS
Sweet Nut Cookie Tart Crust, made with walnuts, for a 9-inch pie (page 59), prebaked, or Graham Cracker Nut Crumb Crust for a 9-inch pie (page 67), pressed into the pan and chilled	1 generous cup	10.75 ounces	307 grams
2 large eggs, separated			
yolks	2 tablespoons + 1 teaspoon	1.25 ounces	37 grams
whites	¼ liquid cup	2 ounces	60 grams
sugar	⅓ cup, divided	2.3 ounces	66 grams
salt	a pinch	•	•
finely grated lime zest*	2 teaspoons	•	4 grams
freshly squeezed lime juice	3 tablespoons	1.6 ounces	47 grams
heavy cream	⅔ liquid cup	5.3 ounces	153 grams
cream of tartar	¼ teaspoon	•	•
optional: ½ recipe whipped cream (see pages 551–53), for piping	1 cup	4.3 ounces	122 grams

* If making a piped whipped cream border, grate an extra teaspoon of lime zest to use as garnish.

EQUIPMENT
A 9-inch pie pan

Make the dough, page 59. Roll and shape the dough and transfer it to the pan and prebake it (see pages 50–54), or press it into the pan and chill it (see page 69).

Chill a medium bowl and beaters for whipping the cream.

Have a fine strainer suspended over a medium mixing bowl ready near the range.

In a double boiler suspended over boiling water (the bottom of the upper container should not touch the water), stir together the yolks, 3 tablespoons of the sugar, and the salt, lime zest, and lime juice until blended. Heat the mixture, stirring constantly, to just below the boiling point (170° to 180°F.), stirring constantly. Steam will begin to appear and the mixture will be slightly thicker than heavy cream. It will leave a well-defined track when a finger is run across the back of the spoon. Immediately remove from the heat and pour into the strainer, scraping up the thickened custard that has settled on the bottom of the pan. Chill the mixture until cold.

In the chilled bowl, beat the cream just until stiff peaks form when the beater is raised. Using a large whisk or rubber spatula, fold the whipped cream into the chilled custard.

In a medium bowl, beat the egg whites on low speed until foamy. Add the cream of tartar, raise the speed to medium, and beat until soft peaks form when the beater is raised slowly. Continue beating while adding about 1 tablespoon of the remaining sugar. Raise the speed to high, beat in the remaining sugar, and continue to beat until stiff peaks form when the beater is raised. Using a whisk or rubber spatula, fold the beaten whites into the egg yolk mixture in two parts until uniform in color. Finish by using a rubber spatula to reach to the bottom.

Pour the mixture into the prepared pie crust, smoothing the surface to make it even. Freeze for at least 6 hours. Cover tightly with plastic wrap after the surface is frozen solid, about 1 hour. Transfer the pie from the freezer to the refrigerator 1 to 2 hours before serving. If desired, decorate with a border of piped whipped cream sprinkled lightly with lime zest.

STORE

Frozen (*without* the whipped cream border), up to 3 months.

UNDERSTANDING

The filling is very similar to the Lemon Angel Chiffon Pie, except that instead of butter, it has a little more cream in the filling and instead of using gelatin to set the texture completely, it is frozen.

GINGERY PEAR CHIFFON TART

This pie is a symphony of contrasting textures: A billowy filling of pear chiffon is nestled in a crisp ginger cookie tart crust and topped with a spiral of pear slices, accentuated by a fine dark line of peel and glistening with a glaze of pear syrup. This pie would be ideal for a gala dinner. It is not very difficult to prepare and the crust and poached pears can be made a day ahead.

INGREDIENTS	MEASURE	WEIGHT	
	VOLUME	OUNCES	GRAMS
Sweet Ginger Cookie Tart Crust for a 9½-inch tart (page 58), prebaked	1 cup	10 ounces	288 grams
Poached Pears			
2 large ripe but firm Bartlett pears, unpeeled*		1 pound	454 grams
water	1½ liquid cups	12.5 ounces	354 grams
freshly squeezed lemon juice	2 teaspoons	0.3 ounce	10 grams
Poire William eau-de-vie	2 tablespoons	1 ounce	28 grams
sugar	¼ cup	1.75 ounces	50 grams
vanilla bean, split lengthwise	1 inch	•	•
Custard Filling			
sugar	2 tablespoons	1 ounce	25 grams
salt	a pinch	•	•
gelatin	1½ teaspoons	•	5 grams
3 large egg yolks	3½ tablespoons	2 ounces	56 grams
reserved syrup from poaching pears	(¾ cup)	(7 ounces)	(200 grams)
heavy cream	½ cup	4 ounces	116 grams
Meringue			
1 egg white	2 tablespoons	1 ounce	30 grams
cream of tartar	⅛ teaspoon	•	•
sugar	2½ tablespoons	1 ounce	31 grams
Poire William eau-de-vie	1 tablespoon	0.5 ounce	14 grams
Glaze			
reserved syrup from poaching pears	(¾ cup)	•	•
arrowroot†	1 teaspoon	•	•

*Bosc pears can be substituted, but they must be peeled.

†Cornstarch can be substituted, but the glaze will be slightly cloudy. If using cornstarch, the glaze must reach a full boil and simmer for 1 minute. Alternatively, do not reduce the syrup but add ¾ teaspoon gelatin. Allow to sit for 5 minutes, then heat until the gelatin has dissolved. Stir over ice water until syrupy and glaze the pie at once. This glaze is thicker of necessity to adhere to the pears, but it is also very clear.

EQUIPMENT

A 9½-inch tart pan with a removable bottom

Make the dough (page 58). Roll and shape it and transfer it to the pan and prebake it (see pages 50–54).

POACH THE PEARS

Halve and core the pears just before poaching so that they do not darken.

In a 10-inch skillet just large enough to hold the pears in a single layer, combine the water, lemon juice, and eau-de-vie. In a small bowl, place the sugar and vanilla bean and, using your fingers, rub the seeds into the sugar. Add the vanilla sugar and the vanilla pod to the skillet and stir until the sugar is dissolved. Place the pears, hollow side down, in the skillet and bring the liquid to a boil. Place a round of parchment on top of the pears. Simmer over low heat, tightly covered, for 8 to 10 minutes or until a cake tester inserted in the thickest part of a pear enters easily. The pears should still be slightly firm. Remove the pan from the heat and cool to room temperature, covered only by the parchment. It will take about 1 hour to cool completely.

Transfer the pears and their syrup to a bowl. Cover them tightly and refrigerate until ready to use.

Drain the pears, reserving the liquid (about 1¾ cups). Remove the vanilla bean. Cover the pears and refrigerate them. Pour the liquid into a small saucepan. Boil down the liquid to 1½ cups.

MAKE THE CUSTARD FILLING

Chill a mixing bowl for whipping the cream.

Have a fine strainer suspended over a small mixing bowl ready near the range.

In a small heavy nonreactive saucepan, using a wooden spoon, stir together the sugar, salt, gelatin, and yolks until well blended.

In another small saucepan (or a heatproof glass measure, if using a microwave on high power), heat ¾ cup of the reduced pear poaching liquid to the boiling point. (Refrigerate the remaining ¾ cup for the glaze.) Stir a few tablespoons of the hot poaching liquid into the yolk mixture; then gradually add the rest of it, stirring constantly.

Heat the mixture to just before the boiling point (180° to 190°F.). Steam will begin to appear and the mixture will be slightly thicker than heavy cream. It will leave a well-defined track when a finger is run across the back of the spoon. Immediately remove it from the heat and pour it into the strainer, scraping up the thickened custard that has settled on the bottom of the pan. Set it aside.

In the chilled bowl, whip the cream until it mounds softly when dropped from a spoon. Refrigerate while preparing the meringue.

**A MAXIMUM OF 20 MINUTES BEFORE USING IT,
MAKE THE MERINGUE**

In a mixing bowl, beat the egg white until foamy. Add the cream of tartar and beat until soft peaks form when the beater is raised slowly. Gradually beat in the sugar and continue beating until stiff peaks form when the beater is raised slowly. Set the meringue aside.

Chill the pear custard by placing the bowl in a bowl of ice water with about a tablespoon of salt added to speed chilling. Stir occasionally for the first 10 minutes and then slowly but constantly for about 10 minutes longer. (If you prefer, you can refrigerate the mixture, stirring occasionally for first 10 minutes and then every few minutes.) When a small amount dropped from the spoon mounds very slightly on the surface before disappearing, and the mixture has started to set around the edges but is still very liquid, immediately remove the bowl from the ice-water bath and whisk in the pear eau-de-vie. Continuing with the whisk, fold in the meringue and then the whipped cream until just incorporated. The mixture will be billowy but soupy like melted ice cream. Finish by using a rubber spatula to reach to the bottom. (There will be 3 cups of filling.) Pour it at once into the pastry shell. Cover tightly and refrigerate for at least 30 minutes.

MAKE THE PEAR DECORATION

Use a sharp thin knife to slice the pears lengthwise into thin slices. Place a fan of overlapping slices on top of the filling with the pointed ends at the center. To form a pear-shaped decoration, trim 2 slices to make them shorter but maintain the pear shape and place them, slightly overlapping, curved sides out, in the center of the pie. Cut a small piece of stem or vanilla bean and place it on the pointed end of this "pear."

MAKE THE GLAZE

In a small saucepan, or a 4-cup heatproof liquid measure if using a microwave on high power, boil down the reserved ¾ cup of poaching syrup to ¼ cup. Cool it to room temperature, then add the arrowroot. Heat, stirring constantly, until thickened; with arrowroot, this will happen before the liquid comes to a boil. Remove it from the heat and, using a clean artist's brush or pastry feather, coat the pears with glaze. Refrigerate and allow to set for at least 4 hours before serving.

STORE

Refrigerated, up to 3 days; frozen, up to 3 weeks.

POINTERS FOR SUCCESS

∽ For the glaze, the reduced pear syrup must cool completely before you add the thickener, or it will lump.

APPLE WEINCREME CHIFFON TART
(*winekrehm*)

This exquisitely elegant and flavorful tart is unique to Swiss/German/ Austrian pastry. It consists of a Bavarian cream filling made with lemon juice and white wine. The type of wine used greatly affects the finished cream, making it fun to experiment. A Riesling, preferably Spätlese (just off-dry), produces a clean, slightly mineral quality. Sauternes offers a subtle honey background, while Muscadet suggests the poignant nectar of honeysuckle droplets experienced when you bite off the stem end of the blossom. But I enjoy making it with one of my favorite dessert wines: Far Niente's Dolce. Half the bottle provides just the right taste for the filling and the other half just enough for six people to enjoy drinking in small fancy glasses with the tart.

In this recipe, most of the weincreme is combined with whipped cream for a mellow, creamy effect, but a small amount is reserved to float on top, forming an intensely flavored gilded-mirror finish for the poached apples. Tiny champagne grapes, when in season from July to mid-November, or small round Ruby Red grapes add an attractive touch of color. I like to make this tart in the fall because the apples are at their best for poaching.

EQUIPMENT
A 10-inch fluted tart pan with a removable bottom

Make the dough (page 59). Roll and shape it and transfer it to the pan and prebake it (see page 50–54).

POACH THE APPLES
Peel, halve, and core the apples just before poaching so that they do not darken.

In a saucepan or skillet just large enough to hold the apples in a single layer, stir together the wine and water. In a small bowl, place the sugar and vanilla bean, and, using your fingers, rub the seeds into the sugar. Add the vanilla sugar and the vanilla pod to the skillet and stir until the sugar is dissolved. Add the apples to the pan, rounded sides down, and bring the liquid to a boil. Place a round of parchment on top of the apples. Simmer over low heat, tightly covered, for 6 minutes. Turn the apples and continue simmering for 4 to 6 minutes or until a cake tester inserted in the thickest part of an apple enters easily. The apples should still be slightly firm. Remove the pan from the heat and cool, covered only by the parchment. It will take about an hour to cool.

Transfer the apples and their liquid to a bowl. Cover it tightly and refrigerate until ready to use. The apples become more flavorful if allowed to sit in the poaching syrup for at least 24 hours.

SERVES: 8

INGREDIENTS	MEASURE	WEIGHT	
	VOLUME	OUNCES	GRAMS
Sweet Nut Cookie Tart Crust, made with walnuts, for a 10-inch tart (page 59), prebaked	1 generous cup	10.75 ounces	305 grams
Poached Apples 3 medium tart apples, such as Greening or Granny Smith*		1¼ pounds	567 grams
Dolce, Spätlese Riesling, Sauternes, or Muscadet	¾ liquid cup	6.25 ounces	177 grams
water	¾ liquid cup	6.25 ounces	177 grams
sugar	⅓ cup	2.33 ounces	66.6 grams
vanilla bean, split lengthwise	1 inch	•	•
Weincreme Chiffon sugar	1⅓ cups, divided	9.3 ounces	266 grams
gelatin	2¼ teaspoons†	0.25 ounce	7 grams
5 large egg yolks, lightly beaten	3 fluid ounces	3.25 ounces	93 grams
reserved syrup from poaching apples	(1 cup)	•	•
lemon zest‡	1 tablespoon	0.25 ounces	6 grams
freshly squeezed lemon juice	⅔ liquid cup	5.7 ounces	163 grams
heavy cream	½ liquid cup	4 ounces	116 grams
Garnish champagne grapes, left whole, or small red grapes, sliced in half and seeded	•	•	•

*You will actually need only about 2½ apples, but it's nice to have extra so that the most attractive pieces can be selected.

†One package = 2¼ + ⅛ teaspoons (7.5 grams), and it can be used in its entirety.

‡As the zest is added to impart flavor and is then strained out, there is no need to chop it very fine. Simply remove with a zester or peeler.

Drain the apples, reserving the liquid (there will be about 1⅓ cups). Cover the apples and refrigerate. Remove the vanilla bean. In a saucepan over high heat (or a 2-cup heatproof glass measure, lightly greased, if using a microwave on high power), reduce the liquid to 1 cup, about 8 minutes.

MAKE THE FILLING

Chill the mixing bowl for whipping the cream.

Have a fine strainer suspended over a small mixing bowl ready near the range.

In a small heavy nonreactive saucepan, using a wooden spoon, stir together ⅔ cup of the sugar, the gelatin, and the yolks until well blended.

In another small saucepan (or a heatproof 4-cup glass measure, if using a microwave on high power), heat the remaining ⅔ cup of sugar, the reduced apple poaching liquid, the lemon zest, and the lemon juice to the boiling point. Stir a few tablespoons into the yolk mixture; then gradually add the remaining liquid, stirring constantly. Heat the mixture to just before the boiling point (190° to 200°F.). Steam will begin to appear and the mixture will be just slightly thicker. It will not leave a well-defined track when a finger is run across the back of the spoon. Immediately remove it from the heat and pour into the strainer. There will be 2½ cups. Remove ⅓ cup of this mixture and set it aside for the glaze.

In the chilled bowl, whip the cream until it mounds softly when dropped from a spoon. Refrigerate.

Chill the wine custard by placing the bowl in a bowl of ice water with about a tablespoon of salt added to speed chilling. Stir occasionally for the first 10 minutes and then slowly but constantly for about 10 minutes longer. (If you prefer, you can refrigerate the mixture, stirring occasionally for the first 10 minutes and then every few minutes.) When a small amount dropped from the spoon mounds very slightly on the surface before disappearing and the mixture starts to feel thicker but is still very liquid, remove it at once from the water bath. Using a whisk, fold in the whipped cream until just incorporated. Finish by using a rubber spatula to reach to the bottom. (You will have slightly more than 3 cups.) Pour the filling into the pastry shell. Refrigerate the tart for at least 30 minutes.

MAKE THE APPLE DECORATION

Use a sharp thin-bladed knife to slice the poached apples lengthwise into thin slices, placing them on paper towels. Starting at the outer edge of the tart, place one row of overlapping slices all around on top of the filling. Have the rounded edge of the slices facing to the right and work counterclockwise. Continue overlapping the apples in rings, but change the direction so that the cored sides face the center, forming a flower-petal effect.

MAKE THE GLAZE

Stir the reserved ⅓ cup of filling over ice water until syrupy. Remove at once and, using a clean artist's brush, pastry feather, or spoon, coat the apples with some of the glaze. Arrange little clusters of champagne grapes or groupings of three larger grape halves over the apples and brush lightly with the remaining glaze.

Refrigerate and allow to set for at least 4 hours before unmolding (see page 145). When the tart is moved, the apples will shimmy slightly.

To serve: Cut with a sharp thin-bladed knife.

VARIATION

APRICOT WEINCREME   Odessa Piper, chef/owner of L'Etoile Restaurant in Madison, Wisconsin, marinates apricots in Scheurebe Auslese as a dessert. She suggested trying the combination in a weincreme. The wine and apricots intermingle in a tangy/sweet way and produce a gloriously flavorful and unusual weincreme. She warned me, however, that only high-quality dried apricots can be used. I tried the supermarket variety and although they still added a wonderful taste to the wine, they developed a bitter edge unless allowed to sit for several weeks out of the wine after soaking, refrigerated. When I used Turkish apricots, however, the taste of the apricots was delicious without the wait, and they also provided a beautiful garnish. You will need 9 ounces/255 grams of apricots (1½ cups tightly packed). Soak them in 3 cups of wine, tightly covered in a glass bowl, for 5 days to a week at room temperature. They will grow to 3 cups, absorbing some of the liquid. Use 1 cup of the resulting apricot wine and omit the water when making the chiffon filling. (You should have about ¼ cup wine left. That's known as the cook's dividend!) Drain the apricots on waxed paper before placing them on the tart, overlapping them slightly.

STORE

Refrigerated, up to 3 days; frozen (without the garnish), up to 3 weeks.

POINTERS FOR SUCCESS

∾ See Apple Tart with Walnut Cream, page 263.

HONEYCOMB CHIFFON PIE

I fell in love with the extraordinarily realistic honeycomb design imprinted into a cream in an Albert Uster catalogue featuring imported Swiss pastry products. I called Andreas Galliker, who created it, and asked him for the secret. To my profound astonishment, he told me the special effect was created with bubble wrap. I had to travel to Maryland to believe it, but it was well worth the trip. We worked together to create this enchanting pie, which contains a Bavarian cream made with honey and swirls of apricot, glazed with golden apricot (the color of honey), and decorated with adorable, easy-to-make honey ganache bees sporting almond wings.

EQUIPMENT

A 9-inch pie pan; bubble wrap with small bubbles cut in a circle; a pastry bag or a reclosable quart-size freezer bag; and a number 12 (¼-inch) round decorating tube.

Make the dough (page 56) or crust (page 68). Roll and shape the dough and transfer it to the pan and prebake it (see pages 50–54), or press the crumb crust into the pan (see page 69) and chill it.

MAKE THE APRICOT FILLING AND GLAZE

Place the apricot preserves in a food processor and pulse to break up the whole pieces of apricot. Remove ⅓ cup to use for the filling and set it aside. Place the remaining preserves in a 1-cup heatproof glass measure and microwave for 2 to 3 minutes or until bubbling thickly. (Or heat them in a small saucepan, stirring often.) Strain them into a small bowl. You should have ⅓ cup of glaze and a scant tablespoon of pulp. If there is more glaze, reheat the glaze and reduce it to ⅓ cup or it won't coat as well. Allow the glaze to cool to room temperature, then cover it and set it aside for the topping.

Spread little dabs of the pulp evenly onto the baked pie crust.

MAKE THE CUSTARD FILLING

Chill a small bowl for the whipped cream.

Have ready a fine strainer suspended over a small mixing bowl near the range.

In a small heavy nonreactive saucepan, whisk together the egg yolks, gelatin, salt, and honey.

In another small saucepan (or a heatproof glass measure, if using a microwave on high power), scald the milk.* Stir a few tablespoons into the yolk mixture; then

*Use a small saucepan, or a heatproof glass measure if using a microwave on high power, and heat until small bubbles form around the perimeter.

INGREDIENTS	MEASURE	WEIGHT	
	VOLUME	OUNCES	GRAMS
Sweet Cookie Tart Crust for a 9-inch pie (page 56), prebaked, or Vanilla Nut Crumb Crust, made with walnuts, for a 9-inch pie (page 68), pressed into the pan and chilled	1 generous cup	10.75 ounces	307 grams
Apricot Filling and Glaze			
apricot preserves	¾ cup	9 ounces	255 grams
Honey Chiffon			
4 large egg yolks (1 egg white reserved)	2 full fluid ounces	2.6 ounces	75 grams
gelatin	2¼ teaspoons	0.25 ounce	7 grams
salt	a pinch	•	•
wildflower honey	⅓ cup	4 ounces	115 grams
milk	1 liquid cup	8.5 ounces	242 grams
heavy cream	¾ liquid cup	approx. 6 ounces	174 grams
1 large egg white (reserved)	2 tablespoons	1 ounce	30 grams
cream of tartar	⅛ teaspoon	•	•
Optional Honey Ganache Bees			
bittersweet chocolate	one 3-ounce bar	3 ounces	85 grams
cream	⅓ liquid cup	2.75 ounces	77 grams
honey	2 teaspoons	0.5 ounce	14 grams
white chocolate, chopped	⅓ of a 3-ounce bar	1 ounce	28 grams
16 unblanched almond slices	•	•	•

gradually add the remainder, stirring constantly. Heat the mixture, stirring constantly with a whisk and scraping the sides, to just before the boiling point (170° to 180°F.). Steam will begin to appear and the mixture will be slightly thicker than heavy cream. It will leave a well-defined track when a finger is run across the back of the spoon. Immediately remove it from the heat and pour it into the strainer, scraping up the thickened custard that has settled on the bottom of the pan. Stir the mixture until it is uniform in color. Set it aside.

A MAXIMUM OF 20 MINUTES BEFORE USING IT, MAKE THE MERINGUE

In the chilled bowl, beat the heavy cream until it mounds softly when dropped from a spoon. Chill.

In a mixing bowl, beat the egg white until foamy. Add the cream of tartar and beat until stiff peaks form when the beater is raised slowly. Set the meringue aside briefly.

Chill the honey mixture by placing the bowl in a bowl of ice water with a tablespoon of salt added to speed chilling. Stir occasionally for the first 10 minutes and then slowly but constantly for about 10 minutes longer. (If you prefer, you can refrigerate the mixture, stirring occasionally for the first 10 minutes and then every few minutes.) When a small amount dropped from the spoon mounds very slightly on the surface before disappearing, immediately remove the bowl from the water bath and, using a whisk, fold in first the egg white, then the whipped cream. The mixture should be well incorporated but still streaky. Fold in the reserved ⅓ cup of whole apricot preserves until streaky but not fully incorporated. Finish by using a rubber spatula to reach the bottom of the bowl, as the heavier part tends to settle. (You will have about 4 cups of filling.) Pour it at once into the prepared pie crust and press the bubble wrap against the surface, bubbles down. Freeze for at least 3 hours, or until the bubble wrap can be removed without sticking to the cream.

Stir the apricot glaze topping until smooth. It should be very thick but still fluid. If it is not fluid, add a tiny amount of water but do not heat it. Brush or spoon it on the filling while the surface is still frozen solid, to maintain the honeycomb design. Refrigerate the pie for at least 1 hour, to thaw, before serving. If desired, decorate with honey ganache bees.

MAKE THE OPTIONAL HONEY GANACHE BEES

Break the chocolate into pieces and process it in a food processor with the metal blade until very fine.

In a small saucepan, heat the cream and honey to the boiling point. With motor running, pour it through the feed tube in a steady stream. Process for a few seconds or until smooth. Scrape the ganache into a bowl and allow it to cool until it is thick enough to pipe.

Spoon the ganache into a pastry bag or plastic bag fitted with the number 12 tube and pipe eight 1-inch-long bees (see illustration; you will only need about a quarter of the mixture): On a sheet of waxed paper, pipe a round ball for the head and, leaving the tube in place, continue piping a teardrop shape for the body, pulling the tube toward you gradually so that it tapers to a point. In the upper container of a double boiler, over hot water, stirring often, or in a microwave oven, stirring every 10 seconds, melt the white chocolate. Scrape it into a parchment cone or plastic bag and cut off a very small piece of the tip. Pipe 3 narrow horizontal lines on the ganache body. Attach an almond slice to each side of the body, pointed end down, to form the wings. If the ganache is too soft to hold them in place, freeze or refrigerate the bees for a few minutes first. Slip the waxed paper with the bees onto a flat surface (a plate or piece of cardboard) and place the finished bees in the freezer until firm enough to lift with a small metal spatula. They will stay flexible even when frozen solid, so the pointed tail end can be curved down slightly, using your fingers. Place the bees evenly around the edge of the pie so that the bodies rest on the crust and the heads touch the glazed chiffon filling, or place them randomly on top of the filling.

STORE

Refrigerated, 3 to 4 days; frozen, up to 3 weeks.

POINTERS FOR SUCCESS

∾ The type of honey used in the filling will determine the flavor. Experiment and use your favorite one (see page 650).

UNDERSTANDING

The usual amount of gelatin, 1⅛ teaspoons per cup of liquid, is used, taking into consideration the 2 tablespoons of egg white and the 1 tablespoon of liquid contained in the ⅓ cup of honey. The substitution of honey for sugar calls for decreasing the liquid in the recipe by one fourth, which indicates that the honey will be contributing in this case 4 teaspoons of liquid that needs to be taken into consideration for jelling.

BLACK FOREST CHIFFON PIE

I created this pie for *Cook's* magazine several years ago and received lots of enthusiastic feedback. Who wouldn't love brandied burgundy cherries suspended in a chocolate Bavarian filling, topped with ganache, and encased in a bittersweet chocolate cookie crust?

EQUIPMENT

A 9-inch pie pan; optional: a pastry bag or a reclosable quart-size freezer bag (with coupler) and a number 22 star piping tip

INGREDIENTS	MEASURE	WEIGHT	
	VOLUME	OUNCES	GRAMS
Chocolate Crumb Crust (or Deluxe Chocolate Wafer) for a 9-inch pie (page 67 or 70), pressed into the pan and chilled		•	•
Brandied Cherries (page 594)	2 cups	12 ounces	340 grams
Chocolate Chiffon fine-quality bittersweet chocolate, grated	⅔ of a 3-ounce bar	2 ounces	56 grams
sugar	½ cup, divided	3.5 ounces	100 grams
½ vanilla bean,* split lengthwise and scraped (seeds reserved)	•	•	•
salt	a pinch	•	•
gelatin	1½ teaspoons	•	5 grams
3 large egg yolks	3½ tablespoons	2 ounces	56 grams
milk	1 liquid cup	8.5 ounces	242 grams
heavy cream	⅔ liquid cup	5.5 ounces	153 grams
1 large egg white	2 tablespoons	1 ounce	30 grams
cream of tartar	⅛ teaspoon	•	•
optional: kirsch	4 teaspoons	0.6 ounce	19 grams
Glaze fine-quality bittersweet chocolate, grated	2⅓ 3-ounce bars, divided	7 ounces	200 grams
heavy cream	½ liquid cup + 2 tablespoons	approx. 5 ounces	145 grams
corn syrup	approx. 1 tablespoon	0.7 ounce	20 grams

*Preferably Tahitian, or ½ teaspoon pure vanilla extract.

Make the crust (page 67 or 70). Press it into the pan (see page 69 or 72) and chill it.

Drain the cherries well on paper towels. Reserve 6 of the most attractive ones for the garnish and place the remaining cherries evenly in the bottom of the pie crust. Cover and refrigerate the pie shell and reserved cherries.

MAKE THE CUSTARD FILLING

Chill a small bowl for the whipped cream.

Place the grated chocolate in a large bowl and set a strainer over it.

In a small heavy nonreactive saucepan, place ¼ cup of the sugar and the vanilla bean and, using your fingers, rub the seeds into the sugar. Stir in the salt, gelatin, and yolks until well combined.

Scald the milk.* Stir in 2 tablespoons of the sugar, then stir a few tablespoons of milk into the yolk mixture; then gradually add the remainder, stirring constantly. Heat the mixture, stirring constantly, to just before the boiling point (170° to 180°F.). Steam will begin to appear and the mixture will be slightly thicker than heavy cream. It will leave a well-defined track when a finger is run across the back of the spoon. Immediately remove it from the heat and pour it into the strainer, scraping up the thickened custard that has settled on the bottom of the pan. (Rinse and dry the bean for future use.) Whisk until the chocolate has melted completely and the mixture is uniform in color. (If the vanilla bean was not used, stir in the vanilla extract.) Set it aside.

In the chilled bowl, beat the heavy cream until it mounds softly when dropped from a spoon. Chill.

A MAXIMUM OF 20 MINUTES BEFORE USING IT,
MAKE THE MERINGUE

In a mixing bowl, beat the egg white until foamy. Add the cream of tartar and beat until soft peaks form when the beater is raised slowly. Gradually beat in the remaining 2 tablespoons of the sugar and continue beating until stiff peaks form when the beater is raised slowly. Set the meringue aside.

Chill the chocolate custard by placing the bowl in a bowl of ice water sprinkled with a tablespoon of salt added to speed chilling. Stir for the first 10 minutes and then slowly but constantly for about 5 minutes longer. (If you prefer, you can refrigerate the mixture, stirring occasionally for the first 10 minutes and then every few minutes.) When a small amount dropped from the spoon mounds very slightly on the surface before disappearing, immediately remove the bowl from the ice-water bath and whisk in the optional Kirsch. Continuing with the whisk, fold in the meringue and then the whipped cream just until incorporated. Finish

---

*Use a small saucepan, or a heatproof glass measure if using a microwave on high power, and heat until small bubbles form around the perimeter.

by using a rubber spatula to reach to the bottom. (You will have 4 cups of filling.) Pour the filling at once into the prepared pie crust (it will come almost to the top) and refrigerate, uncovered (as plastic wrap will stick to the surface), for at least 2 hours before glazing, so that the surface has set firmly. (The pie needs to be refrigerated for at least 6 hours before serving.)

MAKE THE GLAZE

Place 6 ounces of the grated chocolate in a small heavy saucepan with a lid. Place the cream in a small saucepan, or a heatproof glass measure if using a microwave, and bring it to the boiling point. Pour it over the chocolate, cover it tightly, and allow it to rest for 5 minutes to melt the chocolate. Gently stir the mixture together until uniform in color, trying not to create air bubbles. If necessary, heat it slightly, stirring. Pass the glaze through a fine strainer and allow it to cool until just tepid. There will be about 1 cup of glaze.

Pour about half of the glaze onto the pie, tilting it quickly to spread the glaze evenly before it sets. (You can also use a long metal spatula to spread the glaze.) Refrigerate the pie for at least 1 hour until the glaze is set, or until shortly before serving before decorating it.

DECORATE THE PIE

Melt the remaining 1 ounce of chocolate and stir it into the remaining glaze. Set the glaze over ice and stir gently until it is thick enough for piping. (Do not beat the glaze, or it will lighten in color.)

Fill the pastry bag fitted with the decorating tip with the glaze and pipe a border around the edge of the crust and a decorative design on top. If the glaze starts to become too soft to pipe well, chill your hands on the ice.

Brush the reserved cherries with the corn syrup and arrange them on top of the pie. Pipe decorative leaf shapes around the cherries. Refrigerate for at least 1 hour to set.

To serve: The pie can be unmolded, if desired. Wipe the bottom and sides of the pan with a dish towel that has been dipped in very hot water and wrung out, or lower the pie carefully into a bowl of hot water. For attractive slices, cut with a sharp thin-bladed knife that has been dipped in hot water and wiped dry between each slice. Support the rim of the pie with one hand while cutting.

STORE

Refrigerated, 3 to 4 days; frozen, up to 3 weeks.

UNDERSTANDING

This custard filling takes less time to set than other chiffon fillings because of the addition of chocolate.

MERINGUE PIES
AND TARTS

People seem either to love or hate pies and tarts topped with meringue. Those who love meringue enjoy the airy delicate foam that contrasts with the denser, creamy filling and crisp crust beneath. Those who hate it generally object to the sweetness. Meringue, however, does not have to be cloyingly sweet. Even a plain white meringue, made with only egg white and sugar, does not require as high an amount of sugar for stability as one often encounters. In fact, a high proportion of sugar weights it down, making it less airy.

A judicious amount of sweetness, however, is an excellent contrast to a tart filling, as in the Lemon Meringue Pie or "Key Lime" Pie. Folding the meringue into the lemon filling, as in the Pucker Pie, blends the sweet/tartness ahead of eating it and also offers a delightfully fluffy texture.

For a meringue tart where the meringue is not predominantly sweet at all, choose the Aurora Blood Orange Tart with its speckled meringue topping. The unsweetened chocolate folded into the meringue completely balances the sugar. Or try the Bisou, an orange curd tart topped with cocoa meringue piped as kisses, drizzled with bittersweet chocolate. The same cocoa meringue, when baked until crisp and broken into pieces resembling small boulders, achieves a totally different effect as a light crunchy topping for the Grand Canyon Pie.

LEMON MERINGUE PIE

T his is many people's number one pie (myself included). The creamy fresh tartness of the lemon, coupled with the buttery, flaky pie crust and airy sweet meringue, is just one of those perfect things that causes people to sigh with appreciation and delight.

I prefer a filling that is just firm enough to cut cleanly—neither rubbery nor so soft it flows. The consistency is easy to adjust to your own taste: It is a function of the amount of cornstarch you use to thicken the filling.

I love a deep lemon filling and a high billowy meringue, as long as it is not too sweet. The Italian meringue in this recipe has an unusually low amount of sugar and the lightest texture of all meringues, and it does not weep or puddle on sitting.

EQUIPMENT
A 9-inch pie pan

Make the dough (page 22). Roll (see page 8), shape (see page 13), and prebake it (see page 18); while it is still warm, brush it with the egg white (see page 20). Or make the crust (page 66) and press it into the pan (see page 69).

Preheat the oven to 350°F. at least 15 minutes before baking. Set an oven rack at the middle level before prebaking.

MAKE THE FILLING
In a small bowl, lightly whisk the egg yolks.

In a heavy nonreactive saucepan (or double boiler), combine the cornstarch and sugar and gradually whisk in the water until smooth. Cook over low heat, whisking constantly (or occasionally if using the double boiler) until thick, smooth, and translucent, about 5 minutes. (A thermometer will register 190°F.)

Whisk a few spoonfuls of this hot mixture into the egg yolks, then add the yolks to the remaining mixture, whisking constantly. Remove from the heat and whisk in the salt, lemon zest, lemon juice, and butter until the mixture is smooth. Scrape it into the prepared pie shell. Cover with plastic wrap to keep it hot.

MAKE THE ITALIAN MERINGUE
Have ready a 1-cup heatproof liquid measure by the range.

In a small heavy saucepan, preferably with nonstick lining, stir together the sugar and the water until the sugar is completely moistened. Heat, stirring constantly, until the sugar dissolves and the syrup is bubbling. Stop stirring and turn down the heat to the lowest setting. (If using an electric range, remove the pan from the heat.)

In a mixing bowl, using the whisk beater, beat the egg whites until foamy. Add the cream of tartar and beat until stiff peaks form when the beater is raised slowly.

OVEN TEMPERATURE: 350°F. • BAKING TIME: 5 MINUTES
(PLUS ABOUT 1 MINUTE BROILING)   SERVES: 8

| INGREDIENTS | MEASURE | WEIGHT | |
	VOLUME	OUNCES	GRAMS
Basic Flaky Pie Crust for a 9-inch pie (page 22), pre-baked and still warm, or Graham Cracker Crumb Crust (page 66), pressed into the pan		12 ounces	340 grams
½ large egg white, lightly beaten	1 tablespoon	0.5 ounce	15 grams
Filling			
8 large eggs, separated yolks (4 egg whites reserved)	scant ⅔ liquid cup	5.25 ounces	149 grams
cornstarch	½ cup + 1½ tablespoons (dip and sweep method)	3 ounces	85 grams
sugar	1½ cups	10.5 ounces	300 grams
water	2½ liquid cups	20.75 ounces	590 grams
salt	¼ teaspoon	•	•
finely grated lemon zest	1½ tablespoons	•	9 grams
freshly squeezed lemon juice	½ cup	approx. 4.5 ounces	125 grams
unsalted butter	3 tablespoons	1½ ounces	42.5 grams
Light Italian Meringue Topping	(6½ cups)	•	•
sugar, preferably superfine*	½ cup	3.5 ounces	100 grams
water	2 tablespoons	1 ounce	30 grams
4 large egg whites (reserved)	½ liquid cup	4.25 ounces	120 grams
cream of tartar	½ teaspoon	•	•
optional: powdered sugar	about 1 tablespoon	•	•

*To make your own superfine sugar, simply place granulated sugar in a food processor with the metal blade and process for a few minutes or until fine.

Increase the heat under the syrup and boil until a thermometer registers 236°F. (soft ball stage). Immediately pour the syrup into the glass measure to stop the cooking.

If using an electric hand-held mixer, beat the syrup into the whites in a steady stream, avoiding the beaters to keep the syrup from spinning onto the sides of the bowl. If using a stand mixer, pour a small amount of syrup over the whites with the mixer off. Immediately beat at high speed for 5 seconds. Stop the mixer and add a larger amount of syrup. Beat at high speed for 5 seconds. Continue with the remaining syrup. With the last addition, use a rubber scraper to remove the syrup clinging to the measure. Continue beating on high speed for about 2 minutes or until the outside of the bowl is no longer too hot to touch comfortably.

Spread the meringue on top of the filling, starting from the outside edge and covering the border of the crust about halfway. Use a small metal spatula to make attractive swirls and peaks. If desired, for extra crunch, dust the meringue with powdered sugar.

Bake the pie for 5 minutes. Then turn the oven to broil and brown the meringue for 20 seconds to 1 minute, watching carefully to prevent burning, until the meringue is golden. Cool in a place away from drafts for 2½ to 3 hours.

Serve at room temperature. Cut with a wet knife.

STORE

Uncovered, room temperature, up to 1 day; refrigerated, up to 3 days.

POINTERS FOR SUCCESS

If you measure the cornstarch, dip the cup into it and level it off. If the cornstarch is lightly spooned into the cup, you will have only 2 ounces/60 grams.

For the most stable (one that does not form teardrops or water out) yet lightest meringue topping, it is best to make the Italian meringue, but an uncooked meringue is fine if you are planning to consume the entire pie shortly after preparing it.

TO MAKE A SIMPLE SOFT MERINGUE TOPPING

In a large mixing bowl, beat the egg whites until foamy. Add the cream of tartar and beat at medium speed, gradually adding 2 tablespoons of the sugar, until soft peaks form when the beater is raised slowly. Gradually beat in the remaining sugar and continue beating on high speed until stiff peaks form when the beater is raised. (There will be about 6 cups of meringue.)

TO MAKE A SIMPLE "SAFE" SOFT MERINGUE ACCORDING TO THE EGG BOARD GUIDELINES

It is necessary to use 6 egg whites to arrive at almost the same volume (6 cups) as the Italian meringue. It will be tear-free and light, but a little less so than the Italian meringue or simple soft meringue.

TOP: OPEN-FACED DESIGNER
APPLE PIE (PAGE 84)

MIDDLE: CRUSTLESS APPLE
CRUMB PIE (PAGE 89)

BOTTOM: CHERRY LATTICE PIE
(PAGE 93)

1

TOP: DESIGNER CHERRY PIE (PAGE 95)

LEFT: GLAZED STRAWBERRY PIE (PAGE 102)

BOTTOM: OPEN-FACED DOUBLE
STRAWBERRY PIE (PAGE 104)

MIDDLE: Open-Faced Fresh Blueberry Pie
(PAGE 107); TOP LEFT: Slice with Crème Fraîche
(PAGE 558)
BOTTOM: Open-Faced Apricot Pie
(PAGE 120)

3

TOP: PERFECT PEACH PIE (PAGE 124)

MIDDLE: BLUEBERRY TURNOVERS (PAGE 136)

BOTTOM: CONCORD GRAPE PIE (PAGE 127)

4

TOP LEFT: RASPBERRY CHIFFON PIE
(PAGE 149)

MIDDLE: APPLE DUMPLING (PAGE 141)

BOTTOM: GINGERY PEAR CHIFFON TART
(PAGE 162)

5

TOP: APPLE WEINCREME CHIFFON TART
(PAGE 166)

BOTTOM: HONEYCOMB CHIFFON PIE
(PAGE 170)

TOP RIGHT: LEMON MERINGUE PIE
(PAGE 178); MIDDLE: SLICE

BOTTOM: NADÈGE TART (PAGE 185)

GREAT PUMPKIN PIE (WITH GINGERSNAP CRUST)
(PAGE 198); INSET: SLICE

TOP: Apricot Cheesecake Tart
(PAGE 208)

BOTTOM: Banner Banana Cream
Pie (PAGE 201)

9

TIRAMISÙ BLACK BOTTOM TART
(PAGE 212); INSET: SLICE

TOP: FIG TART WITH MASCARPONE CREAM
(PAGE 210)

MIDDLE: COCONUT ICE CREAM PIE (PAGE 226)

BOTTOM: FRESH STRAWBERRY AND
RHUBARB TART (PAGE 256)

TOP RIGHT: LOVE FOR THREE ORANGES (PAGE 267)

BOTTOM: LEMON TARTLET (PAGE 260)

TOP: KIWI TART WITH LIME CURD
(PAGE 271)

MIDDLE: CHRISTMAS CRANBERRY
GALETTE (PAGE 286)

BOTTOM LEFT: MANGO PASSION
TART (PAGE 272)

TOP LEFT: Gâteau Engadine (page 291)

BOTTOM: Brownie Puddle (page 297);
MIDDLE: Slice with Perfect Whipped
Cream (page 551)

TOP LEFT: CHOCOLATE OBLIVION TARTLETS (PAGE 308)
WITH RASPBERRY SAUCE (PAGE 603)

MIDDLE: BIG CHOCOLATE PECAN BLAST (PAGE 313)

BOTTOM: MOLTEN CHOCOLATE SOUFFLÉ TARTLET
(PAGE 311)

15

TOP LEFT: HOLIDAY PECAN STRIP (PAGE 304)

BELOW: CHOCOLATE PEANUT BUTTER MOUSSE SEVEN-TIER TART (PAGE 318)

16

MEAT LOAF IN A FLAKY CHEDDAR CRUST (PAGE 331)

DEEP-DISH CHICKEN POTPIE (PAGE 323)

ABOVE: MOROCCAN BISTEEYA TRIANGLES (PAGE 382)

LEFT: ROASTED RED PEPPER AND POBLANO QUICHE (PAGE 341)

17

TOP LEFT: CURRANT SCONES
(PAGE 359)

TOP RIGHT: MARIONBERRY
SHORTCAKE (PAGE 358) WITH
CRÈME FRAÎCHE (PAGE 558)

BOTTOM: PISTACHIO BAKLAVA
(PAGE 367)

TOP: GASCON APPLE PIE (PAGE 370)

MIDDLE: HUNGARIAN POPPY SEED
STRUDEL (PAGE 401)

BOTTOM RIGHT: APPLE STRUDEL
(PAGE 394)

19

TOP LEFT: PEACH TARTE TATIN (PAGE 426)

TOP RIGHT: RED CURRANT AND APRICOT TARTLETS WITH ALMOND CREAM (PAGES 431 AND 429)

BOTTOM LEFT: TWO MINIATURE GOLDEN APPLE GALETTES (PAGE 434)

BOTTOM RIGHT: CRÈME BRÛLÉE TARTLET (PAGE 440)

TOP: TWELFTH NIGHT GALETTE
(GALETTE DES ROIS) (PAGE 446)

MIDDLE: CLASSIC NAPOLEON
(PAGE 453)

BOTTOM: CHOCOLATE MOUSSE
NAPOLEON (PAGE 457) WITH PISTACHIO
CUSTARD SAUCE (PAGE 610)

TOP RIGHT: WHOLE WHEAT CROISSANT (PAGE 477)

TOP LEFT: CHOCOLATE CROISSANTS (PAIN AU CHOCOLAT) (PAGE 483)

BELOW: THE DANISH BRAID (PAGE 490)

THE DANISH BRAID BEFORE BAKING

BAKING

TOP: DANISH TRIANGLE TWISTS
(PAGE 495)

BOTTOM: DANISH ENVELOPES (SPANDAU)
(PAGE 493)

TOP LEFT: DANISH PASTRY TWISTS (PAGE 504)

TOP RIGHT: STICKY BUN (PAGE 519)

MIDDLE: BRIOCHE (PAGE 516)

BOTTOM RIGHT: PROFITEROLES (PAGE 536) WITH HOT FUDGE SAUCE (PAGE 596)

24

SIMPLE SAFE MERINGUE

INGREDIENTS	MEASURE	WEIGHT	
	VOLUME	OUNCES	GRAMS
6 large egg whites	¾ liquid cup	6.3 ounces	180 grams
water	2 tablespoons	1 ounce	30 grams
sugar	¾ cup	5.3 ounces	150 grams
cream of tartar	¾ teaspoon	•	•

In a large mixer bowl, combine all of the ingredients except the cream of tartar and place over simmering water. Stir constantly with a whisk until a thermometer registers 160°F. Immediately remove the bowl from the heat. Add the cream of tartar and beat on high speed until stiff peaks form when the beater is raised.

To ensure that the bottom of the meringue cooks and will not water out, spread the meringue on top of hot filling. (If necessary, place the pie in the oven for 3 to 5 minutes to reheat the filling.) Bake the pie for 15 minutes for a simple meringue, 20 minutes for a safe meringue (because of the 2 extra whites), or until most of the meringue is golden. (The Italian meringue is baked for 5 minutes only to dry it slightly, to keep it from being too moist. Longer baking would overcook it and cause it to deflate.)

UNDERSTANDING

Compared to lemon curd, the lemon filling of this classic pie is lighter in texture and less intense, though still delightfully lemony.

The acidity of the lemon juice can break down the cornstarch if it is added before the swelling and thickening effect has taken place.

When the yolks are added to the hot thickened cornstarch mixture, they reach a temperature of 160°F., which destroys the amylase enzyme and keeps them from watering out.

Egg whites coagulate at 144° to 149°F., but adding sugar and diluting the whites with a little water raises the coagulation temperature, making it possible to heat the whites to 160°F. safely. Adding the acidic cream of tartar after heating also delays the coagulation process.

The Italian meringue does not "weep" on the bottom because it is fully cooked to 236°F. (Uncooked meringue only reaches about 115°F. when baked for 15 minutes, but would shrink if baked longer.)

The simple meringues do not water out because the hot filling cooks the bottom. None of the meringues beads or forms tears because the sugar dissolves fully before baking.

"KEY LIME" PIE

This simple pie has demanded more of my attention than many more complex ones. I have tried countless experiments with the filling, crust, and topping and this, my absolute final version, suits my taste perfectly.

My preference is for a classic graham cracker crust and a meringue topping. I like to lighten the filling very slightly by folding the equivalent of one egg white from the meringue topping into it. If you prefer a whipped cream topping, see the variation below.

The secret to the famous Key Lime Pie from Joe's Stone Crab Restaurant in Miami, I suspect, is that they serve it partially frozen.

OVEN TEMPERATURE: 350°F. • BAKING TIME: 20 MINUTES
(PLUS ABOUT 1 MINUTE BROILING)   SERVES: 8

INGREDIENTS	MEASURE	WEIGHT	
	VOLUME	OUNCES	GRAMS
Graham Cracker Crumb Crust for a 9-inch pie (page 66), pressed into the pan		•	•
Filling 4 large eggs, separated yolks (4 egg whites reserved)	⅓ scant liquid cup	2.5 ounces	74 grams
sweetened condensed milk	1¼ liquid cups (one 14-ounce can)	14 ounces	400 grams
finely grated lime zest	1½ teaspoons	•	3 grams
freshly squeezed lime juice	¾ liquid cup	6.6 ounces	188 grams
Light Italian Meringue Topping sugar, preferably superfine*	½ cup	3.5 ounces	100 grams
water	2 tablespoons	1 ounce	30 grams
4 large egg whites (reserved)	½ liquid cup	4.25 ounces	120 grams
cream of tartar	½ teaspoon	•	•
optional: powdered sugar	about 1 tablespoon	•	•

*To make your own superfine sugar, simply place granulated sugar in a food processor with the metal blade and process for a few minutes or until fine.

EQUIPMENT
A 9-inch pie pan

Make the crust (page 66) and press it into the pan (see page 69).

Preheat the oven to 350°F. at least 15 minutes before baking. Set an oven rack at the middle level before preheating.

MAKE THE FILLING

In a medium mixing bowl, lightly whisk the egg yolks with the sweetened condensed milk. Gradually beat in the lime juice. (It will cause the mixture to thicken.) Beat in the zest.

MAKE THE ITALIAN MERINGUE

Have ready a 1-cup heatproof liquid measure by the range.

In a small heavy saucepan, preferably with nonstick lining, stir together the sugar and the water until the sugar is completely moistened. Heat, stirring constantly, until the sugar dissolves and the syrup is bubbling. Stop stirring and turn down the heat to the lowest setting. (If using an electric range, remove the pan from the heat.)

In a mixing bowl, using the whisk beater, beat the egg whites until foamy. Add the cream of tartar and beat until stiff peaks form when the beater is raised slowly.

Increase the heat under the syrup and boil until a thermometer registers 236°F. (soft ball stage). Immediately pour the syrup into the glass measure to stop the cooking.

If using an electric hand-held mixer, beat the syrup into the whites in a steady stream. To keep syrup from spinning onto the sides of the bowl, do not allow it to fall directly on the beaters. If using a stand mixer, pour a small amount of syrup over the whites with the mixer off. Immediately beat at high speed for 5 seconds. Stop the mixer and add a larger amount of syrup. Beat at high speed for 5 seconds. Continue with the remaining syrup. With the last addition, use a rubber scraper to remove the syrup clinging to the measure. Continue beating on high speed for about 2 minutes or until the outside of the bowl is no longer too hot to touch comfortably.

Remove a scant 2 cups of the meringue and cover the remainder with plastic wrap. Set it aside.

Fold the scant 2 cups of meringue into the lime mixture and pour it into the crust. Bake for 15 minutes (to set the filling more firmly). Remove the pie from the oven and spread the remaining meringue on top of the filling, starting from the outside edge of the crust and covering the border about halfway. Use a small metal spatula to make attractive swirls and peaks. If desired, for extra crunch, dust the meringue with powdered sugar.

Return the pie to the oven for 5 minutes more. Then turn the oven to broil and brown the meringue for 20 seconds to 1 minute, watching carefully to prevent burning, until the meringue is golden. Cool in a place away from drafts for at least 30 minutes, then refrigerate for at least 4 hours before serving. (The pie can be cut after 2 hours but the slices hold their shape better after 4.)

Cut with a wet thin-bladed knife.

VARIATION

WHIPPED CREAM TOPPING   Instead of making the Italian meringue, place one of the large egg whites (2 tablespoons) in a medium mixing bowl and beat until foamy. (Freeze the remaining 3 egg whites for future use, or discard.) Add ⅛ teaspoon of cream of tartar and beat at medium speed, gradually increasing to high speed, until stiff peaks form when the beater is raised. Fold this meringue into the lime mixture and proceed as above.

Shortly before serving, whip ½ cup of heavy cream with 1½ teaspoons of sugar until it mounds softly when dropped from a spoon. Pass it to serve on the side. Or, to cover the entire pie, make one recipe of Stabilized Whipped Cream (page 553) and spread it on top of the cooled filling.

STORE

Uncovered, refrigerated, up to 3 days.

POINTERS FOR SUCCESS

∾ For the most stable (one that does not form teardrops or water out) yet lightest meringue topping, it is best to make the light Italian meringue, but an uncooked meringue is fine if you are planning to consume the entire pie shortly after preparing it. Fold a scant 2 cups of meringue into the filling and immediately spread the remainder on top. Bake the pie for 15 minutes or until the meringue is golden. (Do not bake the Italian meringue for 15 minutes; if it bakes for more than 5 minutes, it will overcook and deflate.)

TO MAKE A SIMPLE SOFT MERINGUE TOPPING

See page 180.

TO MAKE A SIMPLE "SAFE" SOFT MERINGUE ACCORDING TO THE EGG BOARD GUIDELINES

See page 180.

UNDERSTANDING

After performing a blind tasting, I found that I strongly preferred the flavor of the Persian lime (the ordinary supermarket variety) to that of the Key lime, whose bitterness seemed to penetrate the sweetness, or to the bottled Key lime juices, which had a metallic aftertaste.

In past years, when uncooked egg yolk was not a problem, some Key lime pie recipes did not call for baking them but relied on the reaction of the acidic lime juice with the condensed milk to thicken the filling. Baking, however, is not only safer, it also thickens the texture to make the slices firmer.

NADÈGE TART

This lemon tart, with a deep layer of lemon curd and a thin crown of intricately piped meringue, was born at my friend Nadège Brossllet's farmhouse in the Loire Valley in France. My goal was to make a lemon meringue pie as a tart and to replace the cornstarch-thickened lemon custard with a more intense and starchless lemon curd. I also wanted the tart to have less meringue for a better balance of sweetness to tartness.

Several years later, I attended a class given by chef Dieter Schorner, who is currently dean of the pastry program at the French Culinary Institute. He demonstrated a lemon tart that contained a very thin, barely perceptible cake layer between lemon curd and meringue. He explained that the cake kept the meringue from slipping against the lemon curd filling and also absorbed any moisture released by the meringue. I have adopted the technique for all my meringue tarts.

OVEN TEMPERATURE: 300°F., THEN 500°F. •
BAKING TIME: 10 TO 15 MINUTES   SERVES: 6 TO 8

INGREDIENTS	MEASURE	WEIGHT	
	VOLUME	OUNCES	GRAMS
Basic Flaky Pie Crust for a 9½-inch tart shell (page 22), prebaked and still warm		12 ounces	340 grams
½ large egg white, lightly beaten	1 tablespoon	0.5 ounce	15 grams
1 recipe Classic Lemon Curd (page 568)	1 cup + 2½ tablespoons	11 ounces	312 grams
optional: one 8½- to 9-inch by ⅛- to ¼-inch Light Sponge Cake Layer (page 583)		•	•
½ recipe Meringue for Piping (made with 2 egg whites; page 577)*	•	•	•

*If not using the cake layer, you will need a three-quarter recipe (a 3-egg-white meringue).

EQUIPMENT

A 9½-inch fluted tart pan with a removable bottom; optional: a number 8 (⅜-inch) decorating tube, coupler, and reclosable gallon-size freezer bag or pastry bag

Make the dough (page 22). Roll (see page 8), shape (see page 13), and prebake it (see page 18). While it is still warm, brush it with the egg white (see page 20). Let cool.

Preheat the oven to 300°F. at least 15 minutes before baking. Set an oven rack in the middle of the oven before preheating.

ASSEMBLE THE TART

Spread the lemon curd smoothly into the prepared tart shell and bake the tart for 7 to 10 minutes. The curd should not begin to color. It should barely jiggle when the pan is moved gently from side to side.

Remove the tart to a rack and *increase the oven temperature to 500°F.* Allow the tart to cool until no longer hot so that the filling will be firm.

If using, place the cake layer or sprinkle cake or cookie crumbs evenly on top of the filling. Spread a smooth layer of meringue even with the top edge of the crust,* then, using the decorating tube and bag, pipe a lattice design: Pipe lines ⅛ to ¼ inch apart. Start at the center and work to the right, then turn the tart 90 degrees and finish the other half, again working to the right. Turn the tart 45 degrees and do the same. Pipe a small border close to the outside edge of the crust, as the meringue will shrink slightly during browning. Alternatively, use a small metal spatula to create swirls and peaks with the extra meringue, instead of a lattice, and use a small artist's brush to bring the edges out to cover the pastry. Bake the tart at 500°F. for 3 to 5 minutes, watching closely, or brown it under the broiler for about 20 seconds. Allow the tart to cool for at least 1 hour before unmolding (see page 251). To serve, cut with a wet thin-bladed knife.

STORE

Uncovered, room temperature, up to 1 day; refrigerated, up to 2 days.

POINTERS FOR SUCCESS

∽ If using the cake layer, an ⅛-inch layer is barely perceptible, while a ¼-inch layer is more appreciable.

UNDERSTANDING

The tart is baked briefly in order to set the curd so that it will slice neatly. (The stirring process during cooking separates the protein molecules in the yolk, and the undisturbed baking heat allows them to reconnect.) This additional heat does not change the silkiness of the texture.

The function of the fine cake layer is to make it easier to apply the meringue and to ensure that the meringue does not separate and slide off the filling.

---

*If using an ⅛-inch cake layer, you will need about 1½ cups of meringue. If using a ¼-inch cake layer, the cake will come almost to the top of the pan, so you will only need about 1 cup of meringue.

Because the meringue layer is so thin, the meringue cooks through and does not weep. Should any moisture happen to form, however, the cake layer or cookie crumbs would absorb it.

Piping the meringue creates a texture that offers a very special, delicate feel in the mouth.

LEMON PUCKER PIE™

This recipe is so easy to make and so utterly delicious, I seriously considered producing it commercially and have actually trademarked the name.

In this filling, meringue is folded into the lemon curd and baked. The result is lemony, tart, and moist and fluffy, like a chiffon in texture. It also works perfectly baked in a tart shell.

High-quality commercial lemon curd, such as Tiptree, can be excellent. One 11-ounce/312-gram jar is the exact right amount for this pie, so this makes it easier still. I chose a yogurt flaky pie crust because it is light and slightly tangy, providing a perfect counterpoint to the lemon filling. Powdered sugar adds a delicate adornment and a touch of added sweetness. Amazingly, the baked tart freezes magnificently.

OVEN TEMPERATURE: 375°F. • BAKING TIME: 20 MINUTES   **SERVES: 6 TO 8**

INGREDIENTS	MEASURE	WEIGHT	
	VOLUME	OUNCES	GRAMS
Yogurt Flaky Pie Crust for a 9-inch pie shell or a 9½-inch tart shell (page 25), prebaked and still warm		12 ounces	340 grams
½ large egg white, lightly beaten	1 tablespoon	0.5 ounce	15 grams
1 recipe Classic Lemon Curd (page 568)	1 cup + 2½ tablespoons	11 ounces	312 grams
Meringue			
4 large egg whites	½ liquid cup	4.25 ounces	120 grams
cream of tartar	½ teaspoon	•	•
sugar, preferably superfine*	¼ cup	1.75 ounces	50 grams
powdered sugar	approx. 1 tablespoon	0.25 ounce	7 grams

*To make your own superfine sugar, simply place granulated sugar in a food processor with the metal blade and process for a few minutes or until fine.

EQUIPMENT
A 9-inch pie pan or a 9½-inch tart pan with a removable bottom

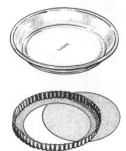

Make the dough (page 25). Roll (see page 8), shape (see page 13), and prebake it (see page 18) While it is still warm, brush it with the egg white (see page 20).

Make the lemon curd. Let it cool before folding in the meringue.

Preheat the oven to 375°F. at least 20 minutes before baking. Set an oven rack toward the top of oven before preheating.

MAKE THE MERINGUE

In a large mixing bowl, beat the egg whites until foamy. Add the cream of tartar and beat at medium speed, gradually adding 2 tablespoons of the sugar, until soft peaks form when the beater is raised slowly. Gradually beat in the remaining 2 tablespoons of sugar and continue beating on high speed until stiff peaks form when the beater is raised.

ASSEMBLE THE PIE OR TART

Fold the meringue into the lemon curd and spread it smoothly into the prepared pie or tart shell. It can come up to the top of the pastry, as it will not overflow. Protect the edges with a greased foil ring cut large enough so it does not come in contact with the filling (see page 19). Bake for 20 minutes or until puffed and golden. Allow to cool for at least 1 hour. Baked in a tart shell, the filling will sink to the level of the crust and a little below, except at the very edges.

Serve at room temperature. Lightly sprinkle the surface with powdered sugar just before serving. If desired, use a stencil to apply colored granulated sugar. I like to use golden yellow. Cut with a wet thin-bladed knife.

STORE

Uncovered, room temperature, up to 1 day; refrigerated, up to 2 days; frozen, up to 3 months (well wrapped after freezing solid).

POINTERS FOR SUCCESS

∽ Sprinkle the powdered sugar onto the pie shortly before serving so that it is not absorbed into the filling, or use dextrose (corn sugar; see page 648), which can be applied as much as 12 hours ahead. It is much less sweet as well.

AURORA BLOOD ORANGE TART

T his is a very special orange meringue tart. Blood orange has a more intense flavor than any other kind of orange except for bitter Seville orange. It also has a stunning color, which can vary from deep rose to purple. The grated zest is a stunning mélange of orange and crimson. It is so beautiful I freeze any extra zest for other recipes.

The meringue is spangled with unsweetened grated chocolate, which provides warmth and sweetness against the tart orange.

OVEN TEMPERATURE: 300°F., THEN 350°F. •
BAKING TIME: 17 TO 25 MINUTES   **SERVES: 6 TO 8**

INGREDIENTS	MEASURE	WEIGHT	
	VOLUME	OUNCES	GRAMS
Basic Flaky Pie Crust for a 9½-inch tart shell (page 22), prebaked and still warm		12 ounces	340 grams
½ large egg white, lightly beaten	1 tablespoon	0.5 ounces	15 grams
1 recipe Blood Orange Curd (page 569)	1 cup + 2 tablespoons	10.75 ounces	311 grams
optional: one 8½- to 9-inch by ⅛- to ¼-inch Light Sponge Cake Layer (page 583)		•	•
1 recipe Bitter Chocolate–Speckled Meringue (made with 4 egg whites; page 576)	4 cups	13.5 ounces	382 grams

EQUIPMENT
A 9½-inch fluted tart pan with a removable bottom

Make the dough (page 22). Roll (see page 8), shape (see page 13), and prebake it (see page 18). While it is still warm, brush it with the egg white (see page 20).

Preheat the oven to 300°F. at least 15 minutes before baking. Set an oven rack in the middle of the oven before preheating.

Spread the blood orange curd smoothly into the prepared tart shell. Bake the tart for 7 to 10 minutes. The curd should not begin to color. It should barely jiggle when the pan is moved gently from side to side. Remove the tart from the oven to a rack and *increase the oven temperature to 350°F.*

Allow the tart to cool until no longer hot so that the filling becomes more firm, to better support the cake and meringue.

If using, place the cake layer or sprinkle the cake or cookie crumbs evenly on top of the filling. Spread a smooth layer of the meringue even with the edge of the crust. Use the remaining meringue and a small metal spatula to create swirls and peaks. Use a small artist's brush to bring the edges of the meringue out to cover the pastry.

Bake for 10 to 15 minutes or until the meringue just begins to brown. Allow the tart to cool on a rack for at least 1 hour before unmolding (see page 251).

Serve at room temperature. Cut with a wet thin-bladed knife.

STORE

Uncovered, room temperature, up to 1 day; refrigerated, up to 2 days.

POINTERS FOR SUCCESS

∾ Usually the more red the outside of the blood orange, the deeper the color of the fruit within.

∾ If using the cake layer, an ⅛-inch-thick layer is barely perceptible, while a ¼-inch-thick layer is more appreciable.

UNDERSTANDING

See Nadège Tart, page 185.

The meringue is baked at a lower temperature than usual because the chocolate is more susceptible to burning. More meringue is used than for the lemon tart because the unsweetened chocolate keeps it from being overly sweet.

GRAND CANYON PIE

The concept of a pie resembling the striations of the Grand Canyon was inspired by a pie my husband and I enjoyed at El Tovar Inn on the Canyon's rim. Their version consisted of a graham cracker crust filled with chocolate amaretto mousse, topped with raspberries and toasted almonds.

In my version, I created the edible striations with a dark chocolate crumb crust, a layer of dark ganache topped with raspberries, and then a layer of speckled chocolate chip whipped cream, topped with "mini boulders" of cocoa meringue.

This is a fun party pie but also of an indulgent bent. The layers are all easy and enjoyable to make. All the components can be made ahead and the entire pie assembled up to three days ahead, but for the meringue to stay crunchy, it should not be placed on the filling until three hours ahead of serving.

SERVES: 8

INGREDIENTS	MEASURE	WEIGHT	
	VOLUME	OUNCES	GRAMS
Chocolate Crumb Crust for a 9-inch pie (page 67), pressed into the pan		•	•
Dark Chocolate Ganache	(1 cup)	(8.75 ounces)	(250 grams)
bittersweet chocolate	1⅓ 3-ounce bars	4 ounces	113 grams
heavy cream	½ liquid cup	4 ounces	116 grams
optional: Chambord (black raspberry liqueur)	2 teaspoons	•	•
Chocolate Chip Whipped Cream	(3 cups)	(12.25 ounces)	(350 grams)
bittersweet chocolate, finely grated	½ cup	2.5 ounces	71 grams
finely ground blanched almonds	¼ cup	1 ounce	27 grams
gelatin	1 teaspoon	•	3 grams
water	1½ tablespoons	0.75 ounce	22 grams
heavy cream	1 liquid cup	8 ounces	232 grams
sugar	1 tablespoon	0.5 ounce	12 grams
pure vanilla extract	½ teaspoon	•	•
fresh raspberries	1 cup	4 ounces	113 grams
Boulders Cocoa Meringue (page 575), ½ recipe unsweetened cocoa	1 teaspoon	•	•

EQUIPMENT

A 9-inch pie pan; a pastry bag or reclosable gallon-size freezer bag and a number 9 (¾-inch) plain tube; and a half-size sheet pan (12 by 17 inches) or cookie sheet, lined with a Teflon liner or parchment

Make the crust (page 67) and press it into the pan (see page 69).

Chill a mixer bowl and beater for the whipped cream.

MAKE THE DARK CHOCOLATE GANACHE

Break the chocolate into pieces and process in a food processor until very fine.

Heat the cream in a saucepan or microwave on high power until small bubbles form around the periphery. With the motor running, pour the cream through the feed tube in a steady stream. Process for a few seconds or until smooth.

Transfer the ganache to a bowl and stir in the optional Chambord. Cool for 20 to 30 minutes, until room temperature but still fluid.

Pour the ganache into the prepared crust and refrigerate it for at least 2 hours.

For an interesting effect, when the ganache has partially set, run a spoon or spatula over the surface to create an uneven surface, which will look great when sliced.

MAKE THE CHOCOLATE CHIP WHIPPED CREAM

In a small bowl, stir the grated chocolate and ground almonds together until evenly mixed. Cover and refrigerate. (The mixture needs to be cold when added to the whipped cream so that the chocolate doesn't melt into the cream.)

In a small heatproof glass measuring cup, place the gelatin and water. Allow the gelatin to soften for at least 5 minutes.

Set the cup in a pan of simmering water and stir occasionally until the gelatin is dissolved. (This can also be done in a microwave on high power, stirring once or twice.) Remove the cup and cool the liquid to room temperature, about 7 minutes. The gelatin must be liquid but not warm when added to the cream.

In the chilled bowl, beat the cream and sugar just until traces of the beater marks begin to show distinctly. Add the gelatin mixture in a steady stream, beating constantly. Add the vanilla and beat just until soft peaks form when the beater is raised. Fold in the chilled chocolate and almond mixture until evenly incorporated.

Scatter the raspberries on top of the ganache layer.

Place dollops of the chocolate chip whipped cream on top of the raspberries and, with a metal or rubber spatula, smooth the top. Chill the pie for at least 4 hours.

MAKE THE COCOA MERINGUE BOULDERS

Preheat the oven to 200°F.

Fill the pastry bag or freezer bag, fitted with the number 9 tube, with the cocoa meringue. Hold the tube at a slight angle away from you, with the tube several inches above the prepared sheet pan. Starting at the top of the pan, squeeze the meringue with a steady pressure, allowing it to drop from the tube while moving the bag forward toward you. Pipe 4 lines of meringue evenly spaced lengthwise down the pan, about 1½ inches apart. Don't worry if the lines of meringue are not perfectly straight, as they will be broken up after baking and, in any case, rustic is what you're after here.

Bake the meringues for 1½ hours or until dry. If a tiny bit of stickiness remains in the center, it will harden on cooling. Allow the meringues to cool completely, then break them into ¾-inch pieces or, using a serrated knife, make partial cuts through the top of the meringue columns and then, using your fingers, snap each cut all the way through. (The cocoa meringue boulders can be made as long as 6 months ahead, if stored, airtight, away from humidity.)

Three hours before serving, heap the meringue boulders on top of the whipped cream.

Place the cocoa in a fine strainer and hold it over the top of the pie. Tap it lightly with a spoon to dust lightly over the cocoa boulders.

STORE

Refrigerated, up to 3 days.

POINTERS FOR SUCCESS:

∾ The gelatin mixture must not be hot when added to the cream, as the cream must be cold in order to incorporate air. Do not overbeat the cream, as it will continue to stiffen after folding in the chocolate and nuts. Chilling the chocolate and nut mix prevents it from softening and discoloring the whipped cream.

∾ The meringue boulders are best when placed on top of the whipped cream about 3 hours ahead so that they get a chance to soften slightly yet still stay crunchy.

THE BISOU
(*beeZOO*)

*B*isou is French for kiss. The image came to me because the chocolate meringue crowning this orange tart is piped to resemble a chocolate candy kiss. The lightly baked chocolate meringue is crunchy on the outside but soft and creamy in the center, echoing the silken texture of the orange curd beneath it.

EQUIPMENT

A 9½-inch fluted tart pan with a removable bottom; optional: a number 6 (½-inch) plain round pastry tube and reclosable gallon-size freezer bag or pastry bag (optional); a ½ teaspoon or a reclosable quart-size freezer bag

OVEN TEMPERATURE: 300°F., THEN 350°F. •
BAKING TIME: 17 TO 29 MINUTES   SERVES: 6 TO 8

INGREDIENTS	MEASURE	WEIGHT	
	VOLUME	OUNCES	GRAMS
Basic Flaky Pie Crust for a 9½-inch tart shell (page 22), prebaked and still warm		12 ounces	340 grams
½ large egg white, lightly beaten	1 tablespoon	0.5 ounce	15 grams
1 recipe Orange Juice Curd (page 569) or Bitter Seville Orange Curd (page 569)	scant 1½ cups 1 cup + scant 2 tablespoons	14 ounces approx. 10.5 ounces	400 grams 296 grams
optional: one 8½- to 9-inch by ⅛- to ¼-inch Light Sponge Cake Layer (page 583)		•	•
1 recipe Cocoa Meringue (page 575)	approx. 4 cups*	12 ounces	342 grams
Optional Chocolate Lace Topping bittersweet or semisweet chocolate	⅓ 3-ounce bar	1 ounce	28 grams
flavorless vegetable oil	1 teaspoon	•	4.5 grams
optional: unsweetened cocoa, preferably Dutch-processed	approx. 1 teaspoon	•	•

*If using the cake layer, you will need only about 3 cups of cocoa meringue (a three-quarter recipe).

Make the dough (page 22). Roll (see page 8), shape (see page 13), and prebake it (see page 18); while it is still warm, brush it with the egg white (see page 20).

Preheat the oven to 300°F. at least 15 minutes before baking. Set an oven rack in the middle of the oven before preheating.

Spread the orange curd smoothly into the prepared tart shell. Bake the tart for 7 to 10 minutes. The curd should not begin to color. It should barely jiggle when the pan is moved gently from side to side. Remove the tart from the oven to a rack and *increase the oven temperature to 350°F.*

Allow the tart to cool until no longer hot so that the filling becomes more firm, to better support the cake and meringue.

Place the optional cake layer or sprinkle the cake or cookie crumbs evenly on top of the filling. Spread a smooth layer of meringue even with the edge of the crust, then, using the pastry tube and bag, pipe ½-inch-high kisses (see illustration). Alternatively, use a small metal spatula to create swirls and peaks with the extra meringue. Use a small artist's brush to bring the edges out to cover the pastry.

Bake for 10 to 15 minutes or until the meringue just begins to brown. Allow the tart to cool on a rack for at least 1 hour before unmolding (see page 251).

MAKE THE OPTIONAL CHOCOLATE LACE TOPPING

Break the chocolate into squares and place them, together with the oil, in the top of a double boiler set over very hot water (but no hotter than 160°F.). The water must not touch the bottom of the double-boiler insert. Stir until the chocolate begins to melt. Return the pan to low heat if the water cools, but be careful that it does not get too hot. The water must not simmer. (The chocolate may be melted in a microwave oven *if stirred every 15 seconds*.) Remove the chocolate from the heat before it is fully melted and stir, using the residual heat to complete the melting.

Dry any moisture that has formed on the bottom of the chocolate container. Pour the melted chocolate into a reclosable quart-size freezer bag, close it securely, and cut off a very small piece from one corner of the bag, or use a ½ teaspoon. Let the chocolate mixture stand at room temperature until cooled and slightly thickened.

Drizzle the chocolate all over the meringue. Dust it lightly with cocoa, if desired, by placing the cocoa in a fine strainer and tapping the side with a spoon.

Serve at room temperature.

STORE

Room temperature, up to 1 day; refrigerated, up to 2 days.

POINTERS FOR SUCCESS

∽ If using the cake layer, a ⅛-inch-thick layer is barely perceptible, while a ¼-inch-thick layer is more appreciable.

UNDERSTANDING

See the Nadège Tart, page 185.

The meringue is baked at a lower temperature than usual because the chocolate is more susceptible to burning.

CUSTARD PIES AND TARTS

Custard pies and tarts include cream pies, such as banana and chocolate, pumpkin pie, buttermilk, and even tiramisù and cheesecake tarts. And, of course, frozen custard pies are ice cream pies.

A custard is a liquid that is thickened with egg. The liquid is usually some form of milk or cream, but in the case of lemon meringue pie filling it is lemon juice. Some custards contain whole eggs, and others have added yolks or even all yolks for an exceptionally smooth, rich, and satiny texture.

If given a choice between a pie bursting with colorful luscious fruit and a creamy custard pie such as banana cream pie or chocolate cream pie, I would have to think long and hard, but the custard pie would probably win. Some cream pies, however, like coconut cream, and mincemeat, are so rich and sweet, I prefer them frozen as ice cream pies. Let's face it: Custard pies are a celebration of self-indulgent bliss!

BUTTERMILK CHESS PIE

I have tried many versions of this classic Southern custard pie. Some derive their slight tartness from buttermilk, some from lemon, others from vinegar. I find that the most intriguing and satisfying flavor comes from mostly buttermilk and a little lemon juice. Nutmeg does wonders to wake up the custard. For my Northern palate, I lowered the sugar just a bit, but there is still plenty left in the filling to form a lovely, slightly crunchy top as it bakes.

OVEN TEMPERATURE: 325°F. • BAKING TIME: 1 HOUR   SERVES: 8

INGREDIENTS	MEASURE	WEIGHT	
	VOLUME	OUNCES	GRAMS
Buttermilk Flaky Pie Crust for a 9-inch pie shell (page 25), prebaked and still warm		12 ounces	340 grams
½ large egg white	1 tablespoon	0.5 ounce	15 grams
3 large eggs	scant ⅔ liquid cup	5.25 ounces	150 grams
cornstarch	1½ teaspoons	•	5 grams
sugar	1 cup	7 ounces	200 grams
buttermilk	1½ liquid cups	12.7 ounces	363 grams
unsalted butter, melted and cooled until no longer hot	8 tablespoons	4 ounces	113 grams
finely grated lemon zest	2 teaspoons	•	4 grams
freshly squeezed lemon juice	1 tablespoon	0.5 ounce	16 grams
nutmeg, preferably freshly grated	½ teaspoon	•	•
salt	a pinch	•	•

EQUIPMENT
A 9-inch pie pan

Make the dough (page 25).

On a floured pastry cloth or between two sheets of lightly floured plastic wrap, roll the dough ⅛ inch thick and large enough to cut a 13-inch circle. Use an expandable flan ring or cardboard template and sharp knife as a guide to cut out the circle. Transfer it to the pie pan, folding the excess under and decoratively crimping the edge. Cover the pastry with plastic wrap and refrigerate it for a minimum of 30 minutes and a maximum of 3 hours.

Prebake the crust (see page 18). While it is still warm, brush it with the egg white (see page 20).

Preheat the oven to 325° F. at least 15 minutes before baking. Set an oven rack at the lowest level and place a baking stone or cookie sheet on it before preheating

In a large bowl, beat the eggs, cornstarch, and sugar until well mixed. Beat in the buttermilk, alternating it with the melted butter, in 4 parts. Beat in the lemon zest, lemon juice, nutmeg, and salt. (You will have almost 3 cups of filling.)

Pour the filling into the pie shell and place it in the oven directly on the baking stone. Bake for 1 hour or until the surface is lightly browned and the filling is set. It will jiggle slightly when moved and a knife inserted between sides and center will come out clean.

Serve warm or at room temperature.

STORE

Room temperature; this is best eaten the same day.

GREAT PUMPKIN PIE

Pumpkin is one of those tastes you either love or hate, so there is no point in half-measures. Its earthy flavor should not be overwhelmed by molasses or too much spice, particularly mace. If you're a pumpkin lover, when you bite into a piece of pumpkin pie, you want to taste pumpkin.

In this recipe, I cook the pumpkin and spices before baking, which makes for a more mellow and pleasing flavor. Puréeing the pumpkin in a food processor produces an unusually silky texture.

The crunchy bottom crust is the result of creating a layer of gingersnaps and ground pecans to absorb any excess liquid from the filling, and also of baking the pie directly on the floor of the oven.

EQUIPMENT
A 9-inch pie pan, preferably Pyrex

Make the dough (page 22).

OVEN TEMPERATURE: 375°F. • BAKING TIME: 50 TO 60 MINUTES   SERVES: 8

INGREDIENTS	MEASURE	WEIGHT	
	VOLUME	OUNCES	GRAMS
Basic Flaky Pie Crust for a 9-inch pie (page 22)		12 ounces	340 grams
4 (2-inch) gingersnaps		1 ounce	29 grams
pecan halves	¼ cup	1 scant ounce	25 grams
Pumpkin Filling	(3¾ liquid cups)	(34.5 ounces)	(984 grams)
unsweetened pumpkin purée	1¾ cups (one 15-ounce can)	15 ounces	425 grams
light brown sugar, preferably raw (see page 646)*	¾ cup, packed	5.75 ounces	163 grams
ground ginger	2 teaspoons	•	•
ground cinnamon	1½ teaspoons	•	•
salt	½ teaspoon	•	•
milk	⅔ liquid cup	5.6 ounces	160 grams
heavy cream	⅔ liquid cup	5.5 ounces	153 grams
3 large eggs	scant ⅔ liquid cup	5.25 ounces (weighed without the shell)	150 grams
pure vanilla extract	½ teaspoon	•	•

*Dark brown sugar adds a delicious butterscotch flavor but masks some of the pumpkin flavor.

Using a floured pastry cloth and rolling pin sleeve, or two sheets of lightly floured plastic wrap, roll the pastry ⅛ inch thick or less and large enough to cut a 13-inch circle. Use an expandable flan ring or a cardboard template and a sharp knife as a guide to cut out the circle. Transfer it to the pie pan and tuck the overhanging pastry under itself. If desired, reroll the scraps, chill, and cut out decorative designs such as leaves. (Bake them separately on a small baking sheet at 400°F. for 6 to 10 minutes or until golden brown. Remove to a rack to cool.)

Cut the border into a checkerboard design or use a fork or spoon to make a flat but decorative border (see page 13). Do not make a high raised border or extend it over the sides of the pan, as it will not hold up baked so close to the heat source. Refrigerate, covered with plastic wrap, for at least 1 and up to 24 hours.

Preheat the oven to 375°F. at least 20 minutes before baking. Plan to bake directly on the floor of the oven, or set an oven shelf at the lowest level and place a baking stone or cookie sheet on it before preheating.

Process the gingersnaps and pecans until finely ground. Sprinkle them over the bottom of the pie crust and, using your fingers and the back of a spoon, press them into the dough to coat the entire bottom, going about ½ inch up the sides.

MAKE THE PUMPKIN FILLING

In a small heavy saucepan, stir together the pumpkin, brown sugar, spices, and salt. Over medium heat, bring the mixture to a sputtering simmer, stirring constantly. Reduce the heat to low and cook, stirring constantly, for 3 to 5 minutes or until thick and shiny.

Scrape the mixture into a food processor and process for 1 minute. With the motor on, add the milk and cream, processing until incorporated. Scrape the sides of the work bowl. Add the eggs one at a time, processing just to incorporate, about 5 seconds after each addition; add the vanilla along with the last egg.

Pour the mixture into the pie shell and set it directly on the floor of the oven (or on the baking stone). Bake the pie for 50 to 60 minutes or just until a knife inserted between the sides and center comes out almost clean. The filling will have puffed and the surface dulled, except for the center. (The filling will shake like jelly when moved. This will happen before it has finished baking, so it cannot be used as a firm indication of doneness; conversely, if it does not have this jelly-like consistency, you can be sure that it is not baked adequately.) If the crust appears to be darkening too much on the bottom, raise the pie to the next rack. After 30 minutes, protect the edges with a foil ring (see page 19).

Place the baked pie on a rack to cool. When cool, the surface will be flat. If you have made decorative designs, place them on it now.

VARIATION

MINI PUMPKIN PIELETS   This filling is enough to make four 4¼-inch pielets. There will be about 6 tablespoons left over, which can be baked in a small custard cup in a water bath for the same time as the pielets. You will need 8½ ounces (240 grams) of dough. Divide the dough into quarters, roll each piece of dough ¹⁄₁₆ inch thick and large enough to cut a 7½-inch circle, and proceed as above.

Bake the pielets, preferably directly on the bottom of the oven, or on a baking stone set on the lowest shelf, in a preheated 375°F. oven for 35 minutes or until they test done as above.

STORE

Room temperature, up to 3 days.

UNDERSTANDING

Canned pumpkin purée is more consistent in flavor and texture than homemade.

The crust border should not be too raised or extend past the pie plate because when baked so close to the heat source, and at the lower temperature required for the custard filling, a raised border would not set quickly enough and would droop over the edge and break off. Since the border does not extend past the edge, it is not necessary to shield the edges until after 30 minutes, instead of the usual 15 minutes for a one-crust pie.

Characteristic star-burst cracking is the result of overbaking. If desired, cover any crack(s), should they develop, with baked pastry cutouts.

BANNER BANANA CREAM PIE

This visually appealing pie also has great mouth-filling texture: chunks of sweet bananas and billowing creaminess set in a crunchy cookie crust.

The pie features a large quantity of thick banana slices with just enough pastry cream filling to bind them together. I have added a layer of whipped cream for contrast on the top. For an extra fancy touch, crown it with curls of white chocolate.

SERVES: 8

INGREDIENTS	MEASURE	WEIGHT	
	VOLUME	OUNCES	GRAMS
Sweet Cookie Tart Crust (page 56) or Sweet Cream Flaky Pie Crust (page 25) for a 10-inch pie, prebaked*	1 generous cup	10.75 ounces 13.6 ounces	307 grams 390 grams
freshly squeezed orange juice	2 tablespoons	1 ounce	30 grams
freshly squeezed lemon juice	1 tablespoon	0.5 ounce	16 grams
6 ripe but firm medium bananas (7 inches long)		34 ounces	964 grams
Topping heavy cream†	2 liquid cups	16.25 ounces	464 grams
optional: Cobasan (see page 644)	½ rounded teaspoon	•	•
sugar	2 tablespoons	approx. 0.5 ounce	12.5 grams
pure vanilla extract	2 teaspoons	0.25 ounce	8 grams
Pastry Cream (page 560)‡	1½ cups	11.3 ounces	325 grams
optional: Crème de Banana (banana liqueur)	2 tablespoons	1.2 ounces	34 grams
optional garnish: white chocolate curls (page 617)	•	6 ounces	170 grams

*If making the pie a day ahead, it is preferable to brush the baked shell with white chocolate (see page 627) to keep it crisp. You will need to melt about 3 ounces and will have about ⅔ ounce left over. Chill the chocolate-brushed shell until the chocolate has hardened before filling it.

†Replacing 1 cup of the cream with 1 cup Crème Fraîche (page 558) makes a lilting variation.

‡Replace the half-and-half with half heavy cream and half milk.

EQUIPMENT
A 10-inch pie pan

Make the dough (page 56 or 25). Roll, shape if using the cookie crust, and transfer it to the pan and prebake it (see pages 50–54. If using the flaky crust, roll (see page 8), shape (see page 13), and prebake it (see page 18). Let cool.

Chill a large bowl for whipping the cream. In a medium bowl, place the orange and lemon juices. Peel and slice the bananas ½ inch thick. You will have almost 4 cups (20.3 ounces/577 grams). Add them to the juices and toss lightly to coat them.

MAKE THE TOPPING

In the cold bowl, combine the heavy cream, optional Cobasan, and sugar and beat until soft peaks form when the beater is raised slowly. Add the vanilla and optional crème de banane and beat until stiff peaks form.

Remove ¼ cup of the whipped cream and fold it into the cold pastry cream.

Drain the bananas and dry them on paper towels. Gently fold them into the pastry cream mixture. Scrape the mixture into the prepared pie shell.

Mound the remaining whipped cream on the surface of the pie, using a rubber spatula to make generous swirls.

If desired, using a wooden skewer to lift them, gently place the chocolate curls on the whipped cream. Refrigerate until ready to serve.

STORE

Refrigerated, up to 1 day. (If the crust is brushed with white chocolate and the whipped cream is stabilized, it will keep for 2 to 3 days.)

UNDERSTANDING

I am indebted to baker and cookbook author Jim Dodge for the idea of cutting the intensity of the lemon juice with orange juice, providing sufficient liquid to protect the banana slices but less acidity. Coating the bananas with the juices prevents oxidation, or browning.

CHOCOLATE CREAM PIE

The mere sight of this pie weakens my resolve! The filling is a satiny-rich chocolate pudding, the crust a flaky butter crust made with heavy cream to make it incredibly tender and light. An optional garnish of dark chocolate curls and a few bright red raspberries makes this a stunningly sumptuous dessert.

INGREDIENTS	MEASURE	WEIGHT	
	VOLUME	OUNCES	GRAMS
Sweet Cream Flaky Pie Crust, for a 9-inch pie (page 25), prebaked*		12 ounces	340 grams
Filling	(4 cups)	(38 ounces)	(1076 grams)
2 large eggs	3 fluid ounces	3.5 ounces	100 grams (weighed without the shells)
unsweetened cocoa, preferably Dutch-processed	¼ cup (lightly spooned)	approx. 1 ounce	24 grams
cornstarch	3 tablespoons	1 ounce	28 grams
milk	3 liquid cups, divided	25.5 ounces	726 grams
sugar	⅔ cup	4.6 ounces	132 grams
salt	a pinch	•	•
fine-quality bittersweet chocolate, grated or chopped	two 3-ounce bars	6 ounces	170 grams
unsalted butter	2 tablespoons	1 ounce	28 grams
pure vanilla extract	1 teaspoon	•	•
Topping			
heavy cream	1 liquid cup	8 ounces	232 grams
optional: Cobasan (see page 644)	¼ rounded teaspoon	•	•
sugar	1 tablespoon	approx. 0.5 ounce	12.5 grams
pure vanilla extract	1 teaspoon	•	4 grams
optional garnish: chocolate curls (page 617) and fresh raspberries	• ¼ cup	3 ounces 1 ounce	85 grams 28 grams

*If making the pie a day ahead, it is preferable to brush the baked shell with white chocolate (see page 627) to keep it crisp. You will need to melt about 3 ounces and will have about ⅔ ounce left over. Chill the chocolate-brushed shell until the chocolate has hardened before filling it.

EQUIPMENT
A 9-inch pie pan and a piano wire whisk (one with 10 loops of wire; see page 627)

Make the dough (page 25). Roll (see page 8), shape (see page 13), and prebake it (see page 18). Let cool.

MAKE THE FILLING

Chill a bowl for the whipped cream. Have ready near the range a strainer set over a medium bowl. In a small bowl, whisk together the eggs, cocoa, cornstarch, and ¼ cup of the milk until smooth.

In a medium nonreactive heavy saucepan, stir together the remaining 3¾ cups of milk, the sugar, and salt. Over medium heat, bring the mixture to a full boil. With the piano whisk, whisk ¼ cup of this hot mixture into the egg mixture. Whisk the egg mixture into the milk mixture. Cook, continuing to whisk rapidly, being sure to go into the edge of the pan, until the mixture thickens and pools a little when dropped on the surface.

Remove it from the heat and whisk in the chocolate and butter. Continue whisking until the chocolate has melted and the mixture is smooth. Whisk in the vanilla extract. Using a rubber spatula, immediately press the mixture through the strainer and place a piece of plastic wrap directly on top of the cream to prevent a skin from forming. Allow it to cool to room temperature, or refrigerate until cold, about 1 hour and 15 minutes.

Pour the chocolate filling into the baked pie shell. It will fill the shell up to the top. Place a piece of greased plastic wrap directly on the surface and refrigerate the pie for at least 3 hours.

MAKE THE TOPPING

In the chilled bowl, combine the heavy cream, optional Cobasan, and sugar and beat until soft peaks form when the beater is raised slowly. Add the vanilla and beat until stiff peaks form. Remove the plastic wrap from the pie and mound the topping evenly over the chocolate filling.

If desired, using a wooden skewer to lift them, gently place the chocolate curls on the whipped cream. Garnish with a few raspberries.

VARIATION

For a less bittersweet, more milk chocolate filling, replace the milk with half-and-half, decrease the sugar to ½ cup (3.5 ounces/100 grams), omit the cocoa, and increase the chocolate to 10 ounces/284 grams.

STORE
Refrigerated, up to 3 days (without the whipped cream, unless the whipped cream has been stabilized with Cobasan).

POINTERS FOR SUCCESS
~ A heavy well-insulated pan is essential to keep the filling from scorching.

~ A 10-loop piano wire whisk is practically indispensable to prevent lumps from forming in the finished chocolate cream

~ Do not beat the filling vigorously after cooling, or it will break down.

~ This pie does not travel well unless the whipped cream is mounded after reaching the destination.

UNDERSTANDING
This filling is actually a pastry cream with two thirds the usual amount of cornstarch and eggs, as the cocoa and the chocolate, which hardens on refrigeration, add substantial thickening. Unlike ordinary pastry cream, the filling is strained after thickening because the chocolate is added at the end, and the chocolate particles become smoother after straining. Less sugar is added because it is not being combined with tart fruit.

TAHITIAN VANILLA CHEESECAKE TART

The filling for this tart is a heavenly cheesecake batter prepared with crème fraîche and the floral Tahitian vanilla bean. It is poured into a deeply fluted high tart pan that has been lined with a sugar cookie crust. During the long slow baking required to set the filling to creamy perfection, the crust becomes nut-brown and crisp. This tart is at once elegant, subtle, and powerful. Though rich, it cuts cleanly, making it possible to serve as many as twenty portions for a dessert party or after a filling holiday meal.

EQUIPMENT
A 10- by 2-inch tart pan with a
removable bottom

OVEN TEMPERATURE: 350°F. • BAKING TIME: 45 MINUTES
(PLUS 1 HOUR WITH THE OVEN OFF)   SERVES: 8 TO 20

INGREDIENTS	MEASURE	WEIGHT	
	VOLUME	OUNCES	GRAMS
Sweet Cookie Tart Crust for a 10- by 2-inch tart (page 57), prebaked and cooled*	1 generous cup	10.75 ounces	307 grams
Lemon Curd (page 568), or store-bought, preferably Tiptree, or apricot preserves	3 tablespoons	1.75 ounces	50 grams
one 8½- to 9-inch by ¼-inch Light Sponge Cake Layer (page 583)†		•	•
Cheesecake Filling cream cheese, softened	1 cup + 2½ tablespoons	10.5 ounces	300 grams
sugar	⅔ cup	4.6 ounces	132 grams
cornstarch	2 teaspoons	•	6 grams
2 large eggs	3 fluid ounces	3.5 ounces	100 grams (weighed without the shells)
freshly squeezed lemon juice	4 teaspoons	0.75 ounce	21 grams
pure vanilla extract	1 teaspoon	•	4 grams
salt	⅛ teaspoon	•	•
1 recipe Crème Fraîche (page 558), made with the vanilla bean, vanilla bean reserved for garnish	2 cups	16.25 ounces	464 grams

*A 10-inch springform pan can be substituted, but the tart will be less attractive. The baked shell must be a minimum of 1¼ inches high to contain all the filling.

†Either yellow or chocolate. You can replace this with packaged angel food or sponge cake.

Advance preparation: The tart needs to chill for at least 6 hours before unmolding.

Make the dough. Roll, shape, transfer it to the pan, and prebake it (see pages 50–54). Let cool.

Preheat the oven to 350°F. at least 15 minutes before baking. Set an oven rack just below the middle level before preheating.

Brush the Lemon Curd evenly onto the bottom and ¼ inch up the sides of the baked cookie crust. Place the sponge cake layer, crust side down, into the crust.

ELECTRIC MIXER METHOD

In a large mixer bowl, preferably with the whisk beater, beat the cream cheese, sugar, and cornstarch until very smooth (about 3 minutes). Beat in the eggs one at a time, beating until smooth and scraping down the sides of the bowl once or twice. Add the lemon juice, vanilla, and salt and beat until incorporated. Beat in the crème fraîche just until blended.

FOOD PROCESSOR METHOD

In a food processor fitted with the metal blade, process the cream cheese, sugar, and cornstarch for about 30 seconds or until smooth. Scrape down the sides. With the motor running, add the eggs and process for a few seconds until smooth. Scrape down the sides. Add the remaining ingredients, including the crème fraîche, and pulse to combine.

Pour the batter on top of the cake layer in the prepared tart shell. It will reach almost to the top, but the center will settle slightly after baking and cooling.

Bake the cheesecake for 45 minutes. Turn off the oven, without opening the door, and let the cheesecake cool for 1 hour.

Remove it to a rack and cool to room temperature, about 1 hour. Cover with plastic wrap and refrigerate it 6 hours before unmolding (see page 251).

To serve, remove the vanilla bean and cut the tart with a knife that has been wiped and dipped in hot water between each slice.

STORE

Refrigerated, up to 4 days. (The filling changes texture, becoming less smooth and creamy, on freezing.)

POINTERS FOR SUCCESS

∾ Don't be tempted to use the more expensive "natural" cream cheese. Philadelphia brand (available even in Japan) offers the best and most consistent flavor and texture for this cake. Cream cheese without gums will aerate more, yielding more volume and less creaminess.

UNDERSTANDING

The gossamer-thin layer of sponge cake, attached with a dab of lemon curd between crust and filling, absorbs any liquid from the filling and keeps the bottom crust crunchy.

Using the whisk beater ensures even mixing. This is a dense batter, so there is no risk of beating air into it, which would cause it to puff up and crack during baking.

Baking the cheesecake in a crust serves as a perfect insulation, replacing a water bath, to keep the cheesecake filling evenly soft and creamy.

APRICOT CHEESECAKE TART

This tart is refreshing because of the juiciness of the apricots and the creamy-smooth unsweetened cheesecake filling. The sweetness is supplied by the apricots and the apricot glaze. Although it is delicious the day it is made, I enjoy this tart even more the following day as the flavors blend and become more mellow.

This is a terrific dessert to make in June and July, at the height of the fresh apricot season, but is equally delicious made with canned apricots.

OVEN TEMPERATURE: 375°F. • BAKING TIME: 30 TO 35 MINUTES   SERVES: 8

INGREDIENTS	MEASURE	WEIGHT	
	VOLUME	OUNCES	GRAMS
Flaky Cream Cheese Pie Crust for a 10- by 1-inch tart shell (page 30), prebaked and still warm		11 ounces	312 grams
1 large egg separated + 1 yolk: yolk	2 tablespoons + 1 teaspoon	0.6 ounce	18 grams
white (use 1 tablespoon, lightly beaten, to brush on crust)	2 tablespoons	1 ounce	30 grams
1½ pounds fresh apricots (about twelve 2-inch), poached (see page 587), or two 15- to 17-ounce cans apricots in syrup	4½ cups	21 ounces	595 grams
apricot preserves	1 cup	12 ounces	339 grams
Grand Marnier	2 teaspoons, divided	•	•
cream cheese, at room temperature	3½ tablespoons	2 ounces	57 grams
ground cinnamon	a pinch	•	•
nutmeg, preferably freshly grated	a pinch	•	•
Crème Fraîche (page 558) or heavy cream	¾ cup	6 ounces	174 grams

EQUIPMENT
A 10-inch tart pan with a removable bottom

Make the dough (page 30). Roll (see page 8), shape (see page 13), and prebake it (see page 18). While it is still warm, brush it with the egg white (see page 20).

Preheat the oven to 375°F. at least 20 minutes before baking. Set an oven rack at the lowest level and place a baking stone or cookie sheet on it before preheating.

Place the apricot halves on paper towels, cut sides down, to drain well.

Place the preserves in a 2-cup heatproof glass measure and microwave for 2½ to 3 minutes or until bubbling. (Or heat them in a small saucepan, stirring often.) Stir in 1 teaspoon of the Grand Marnier and strain them into a small bowl.

Brush 2 tablespoons of this glaze onto the bottom of the crust and set the remainder aside.

In a food processor with the metal blade, process the cream cheese, cinnamon, and nutmeg until smooth. Scrape down the sides. Add the crème fraîche or the cream, egg yolk and white, and the remaining 1 teaspoon of Grand Marnier. Process with 3 short pulses, just to mix. The mixture will be lumpy, but do not process longer. (You will have about 1⅓ cups of filling.)

Pour about half of the filling into the prepared crust. Place the apricots on it, rounded sides up, in a single layer. Carefully pour the remaining filling around the apricots so that it doesn't coat the tops.

Set the tart directly on the stone and bake for 30 to 35 minutes or until the cheese filling is puffed and lightly browned. Cool on a rack to room temperature.

Reheat the remainder of the strained apricot preserves and spoon evenly over the top of both the apricots and the filling. Chill for at least 1 hour before unmolding (see page 251).

STORE
Refrigerated, up to 3 days. Remove to room temperature for about 30 minutes before serving.

FIG TART WITH MASCARPONE CREAM

Fresh figs and marsala-perfumed mascarpone cream, the filling of the popular dessert tiramisù, struck me as a natural combination. I created this tart for the fresh fig lover as a variation of the Tiramisù Tart. The addition of pecans to the sweet cookie crust provides a nutty accent for the succulent figs.

EQUIPMENT
A 10-inch tart pan with a removable bottom

Make the dough (page 59). Roll, shape, transfer it to the pan, and prebake it (see pages 50–54). Let cool.

MAKE THE FILLING

Chill a small mixing bowl for the whipped cream.

Have ready near the range a rubber scraper and medium bowl.

In a large copper bowl or the upper container of a double boiler, whisk together the egg yolks, 2 tablespoons of the sugar, and the marsala. If using a copper bowl, set it directly on the burner over low heat. If using a double boiler, place the upper container over simmering water (the water should not touch the bottom of the upper container). Whisk constantly until the mixture approximately triples in volume and begins to thicken, 3 to 5 minutes. Be careful not to overcook the yolks, or they will scramble!

Immediately scrape the mixture into the medium bowl. Cover tightly with plastic wrap and refrigerate for at least 15 minutes or until completely cool.

In a large mixer bowl, preferably with the whisk beater, on low speed, beat the mascarpone for about 10 seconds or until creamy. Raise the speed slightly and gradually beat in the cooled egg yolk mixture until completely incorporated, scraping the sides of the bowl once or twice with a rubber spatula. Set it aside.

In a small heatproof measuring cup, place the gelatin and water and allow it to sit for 5 minutes. Set the cup in a pan of simmering water for a few minutes, stirring occasionally until the gelatin is dissolved (or microwave on high power for a few seconds, stirring once or twice). Set it aside briefly, while you beat the cream. (The mixture must still be warm or it will lump when added to the cold cream; reheat it if necessary.)

In the chilled mixing bowl, combine the heavy cream and the remaining 2 teaspoons of sugar. Beat until the cream begins to thicken. Add the vanilla extract and warm gelatin mixture and beat just until stiff peaks form when the beater is raised.

With a large rubber spatula, fold the whipped cream into the mascarpone mixture. (You will have almost 2 cups.) Scrape the mixture into the baked tart shell and refrigerate for at least 1 hour to set.

Starting at the outside edge, place the fig slices, pointed ends upward, in concentric circles on the filling, tilting the slices so they lean slightly toward the edge

INGREDIENTS	MEASURE	WEIGHT	
	VOLUME	OUNCES	GRAMS
Sweet Nut Cookie Tart Crust, made with pecans, for a 10- by 1-inch tart (page 59), prebaked	1 generous cup	10.75 ounces	307 grams
Filling 3 large egg yolks	3½ tablespoons	2 ounces	56 grams
sugar	2 tablespoons + 2 teaspoons, divided	approx. 1.2 ounces	33 grams
sweet marsala	1 tablespoon	2 ounces	56 grams
mascarpone, preferably imported, at room temperature	⅔ cup	5.75 ounces	165 grams
gelatin	½ teaspoon	•	•
water	1½ teaspoons	•	•
heavy cream	⅓ liquid cup	2.75 ounces	77 grams
pure vanilla extract	¾ teaspoon	•	•
Topping fresh black figs (about 21), cut lengthwise into ¼-inch slices	approx. 4 cups	17.3 ounces	495 grams
Glaze freshly squeezed lemon juice	1 tablespoon	0.5 ounce	16 grams
water	1 tablespoon	0.5 ounce	15 grams
sugar	2 tablespoons	approx. 1 ounce	25 grams
cassava or cornstarch or arrowroot	¾ teaspoon 1 teaspoon	• •	2 grams 3 grams

of the crust in a petal-like fashion. Begin by placing the end slices of the figs around the first circle, skin side out.

MAKE THE GLAZE

In a small saucepan, combine the lemon juice, water, sugar, and cassava (or cornstarch or arrowroot) and stir until the sugar and starch are dissolved. Heat the mixture over medium heat, stirring constantly, until thickened. With arrowroot, this will happen before the boiling point; with cassava, it will start to thicken within a few seconds of reaching the full boil; with cornstarch, the mixture needs to simmer for 30 seconds to 1 minute after reaching the boiling point. Immediately pour the glaze into a heatproof glass measure or bowl. Using a pastry brush or feather, brush the glaze onto the figs. Refrigerate for at least 1 hour before unmolding (see page 251).

VARIATION

For an eggless version of the filling, which is somewhat less airy and a shade less delicious, decrease the sugar to 2 tablespoons and briefly whisk it together with the softened mascarpone. Prepare the gelatin and whipped cream as above. Fold it together with the marsala into the mascarpone mixture. (Makes 1½ cups.)

STORE

Refrigerated, up to 2 days.

UNDERSTANDING

This filling is actually very similar to Bavarian cream. The difference is that about two thirds the volume of thick, slightly tangy mascarpone, which is a triple cream cheese, replaces the usual milk, so no gelatin is required to thicken the filling. A very small amount, however, is used to make the filling firm enough to withstand the pressure of cutting through the figs.

Double the cornstarch, cassava, or arrowroot normally used is needed for the glaze because of the high acidity of the lemon juice.

TIRAMISÙ BLACK BOTTOM TART

Tiramisù, Italian for "pick me up," consists of savoiardi biscuits dipped in strong espresso, topped with a gloriously rich custard of egg yolks, mascarpone, and marsala, and sprinkled with cocoa.

This version has the same luscious filling but is contained in a sweet cookie crust lined with melted chocolate. The crust adds an extra dimension, providing a desirable container and foundation for the creamy, custardy, voluptuous texture of the classic tiramisù. Instead of the usual dried biscuits, a slim round layer of sponge cake (store-bought or homemade) serves as the sponge to hold the coffee syrup. This is an impressive and fabulous dessert, raising "pick me up" to a new level.

| INGREDIENTS | MEASURE | WEIGHT | |
	VOLUME	OUNCES	GRAMS
Sweet Cookie Tart Crust for a 10-inch tart (page 57), prebaked, cooled, and painted with 2 ounces of bittersweet chocolate (see page 56)	1 generous cup	10.75 ounces	307 grams
Filling 4 large egg yolks	2¼ fluid ounces	2.6 ounces	75 grams
sugar	6 tablespoons, divided	2.6 ounces	75 grams
sweet marsala	2 tablespoons, divided	1 ounce	28 grams
Medaglia d'Oro instant espresso powder	4 teaspoons	•	5 grams
water	⅔ liquid cup + 1 tablespoon, divided	6 ounces	173 grams
pure vanilla extract	1 teaspoon, divided	•	•
one 8½- to 9-inch by ¼-inch Light Sponge Cake Layer (page 583)*		•	•
mascarpone, preferably imported, at room temperature	1 cup	8.75 ounces	250 grams
gelatin	1 teaspoon	•	3 grams
heavy cream	½ liquid cup	4 ounces	116 grams
Garnish 2 ounces of chocolate curls (page 617) or 2 teaspoons unsweetened cocoa	•	•	•

*Either yellow or chocolate. You can replace this with commercial packaged angel food or sponge cake.

EQUIPMENT
A 10-inch tart pan with a removable bottom

Make the dough (page 57). Roll, shape, and transfer it to the pan and prebake it (see page 50–54). Let cool, then brush it with the chocolate (see page 56).

MAKE THE FILLING

Chill a small mixing bowl for the whipped cream.

Have ready near the range a rubber scraper and medium bowl.

In a large copper bowl or the upper container of a double boiler, whisk together the egg yolks, 3 tablespoons of the sugar, and 1½ tablespoons of the marsala. If using a copper bowl, set it directly on the burner over low heat. If using a double boiler, place the upper container over simmering water (the water should not touch the bottom of the upper container). Whisk constantly until the mixture approximately triples in volume and begins to thicken, 3 to 5 minutes. Be careful not to overcook the yolks, or they will scramble!

Immediately scrape the mixture into the medium bowl. Cover tightly with plastic wrap and refrigerate for at least 15 minutes or until completely cool.

Meanwhile, prepare the espresso syrup: In a small saucepan, stir together the espresso powder, 2 tablespoons of the sugar, and ⅓ cup of the water. Bring it to a boil, stirring constantly to dissolve the espresso and sugar. Remove it from the heat and add ⅓ cup more water, ½ teaspoon of the vanilla, and the remaining 1½ teaspoons of marsala.

Place the cake layer on a sheet of plastic wrap and brush the top with half the syrup. Cover it with plastic wrap and set it aside.

In a large mixer bowl, preferably with the whisk beater, on low speed, beat the mascarpone for about 10 seconds or until creamy. Raise the speed slightly and gradually beat in the cooled egg yolk mixture until completely incorporated, scraping the sides of the bowl once or twice with a rubber spatula. Set it aside.

In a small heatproof measuring cup, place the gelatin and the remaining 1 tablespoon of water and allow to sit for 5 minutes. Set the cup in a pan of simmering water for a few minutes, stirring occasionally until the gelatin is dissolved (or microwave it on high power for a few seconds, stirring once or twice). Set it aside briefly while you beat the cream. (The mixture must still be warm, or it will lump when added to the cold cream; reheat it if necessary.)

In the chilled mixing bowl, combine the heavy cream and the remaining 1 tablespoon of sugar. Beat until the cream begins to thicken. Add the remaining ½ teaspoon of vanilla extract and the warm gelatin mixture and beat just until stiff peaks form when the beater is raised.

With a large rubber spatula, quickly fold the whipped cream into the mascarpone mixture (you will have about 3 cups). Spoon half of this mixture into the prepared tart crust, spreading it evenly with an offset spatula. Place the cake layer, syrup side down, on top. Brush with the remaining syrup. Spread the remaining mascarpone cream evenly on top. Garnish with the chocolate curls, or dust with cocoa by placing the cocoa in a fine strainer held over the surface of the tart and stirring the cocoa with a spoon. Refrigerate the tart to set for at least 3 hours before serving.

Allow the tart to sit at room temperature for about 30 minutes before unmolding (see page 251).

STORE

Refrigerated, up to 5 days.

POINTERS FOR SUCCESS

⌒ The whipped cream must be folded into the mascarpone mixture quickly, and as soon as it has been prepared, because the gelatin will begin to set, making even blending difficult.

UNDERSTANDING

The chocolate layer painted onto the crust moisture-proofs it and keeps it crunchy.

SHOOFLY PIE

Having lived near the Pennsylvania Dutch country for several years, I have sampled many versions of this eggless gingerbread cake within a pie crust, but this one, from the food historian Will Weaver, is in a class by itself. The bottom of the filling has a nice gooey layer and then it metamorphoses into a very moist cakey top. The filling contains both coffee and spices, additions that balance the sweetness of the molasses while giving it a depth of flavor.

Shoofly pie is a pie with a history. Will's recipe is from his grandmother, who got it in the 1930s from the label on a bottle of Shoofly molasses. The recipe was the creation of a Mrs. Miles Fry of Ephrata, Pennsylvania. In researching his book *Pennsylvania Dutch Country Cooking* (Abbeville, 1993), Will discovered that it was one of the original recipes handed out at the U.S. Centennial in Philadelphia in 1876. His grandmother, now ninety-seven years old, carries the recipe in her purse so she can be ready to make it on demand!

Traditionally, shoofly pie is served at breakfast as a coffee cake. Still warm from the oven and served with a scoop of coffee ice cream or a dollop of coffee whipped cream on top to complement the coffee in the filling is my favorite way to enjoy this pie.

OVEN TEMPERATURE: 425°F., THEN 350°F. • BAKING TIME: 45 MINUTES   SERVES: 6 TO 8

INGREDIENTS	MEASURE	WEIGHT	
	VOLUME	OUNCES	GRAMS
Flaky Cream Cheese Pie Crust for a 9-inch pie shell (page 29)		11 ounces	312 grams
Medaglia d'Oro instant espresso powder*	1 teaspoon	•	•
boiling water	¾ liquid cup	6.25 ounces	177 grams
bleached all-purpose flour	approx. 1¼ cups (lightly spooned)	5.5 ounces	155 grams
sugar	½ cup	3.5 ounces	100 grams
ground cinnamon	1 teaspoon	•	•
nutmeg, freshly grated	½ teaspoon	•	•
salt	¼ teaspoon	•	•
unsalted butter, cut into 1-inch pieces and chilled	8 tablespoons	4 ounces	113 grams
baking soda	½ teaspoon	•	2.5 grams
dark *unsulfured* molasses, preferably Grandma's	¾ liquid cup, lightly greased	8.5 ounces	241 grams
optional: coffee ice cream or Perfect Whipped Cream (page 551)	•	•	•

* Or use ¾ cup strong coffee instead of the water and espresso powder.

EQUIPMENT
A 9-inch pie pan

Make the dough (page 29) and chill it.

Remove the dough from the refrigerator. If necessary, allow it to sit for about 10 minutes until it is soft enough to roll. Using a pastry cloth and sleeve rubbed with flour or two sheets of plastic wrap lightly sprinkled with flour, roll the pastry ⅛ inch thick and large enough to cut a 13-inch circle. Use an expandable flan ring or a cardboard template and a sharp knife as a guide to cut out the circle. Transfer the dough to the pie pan. Fold under the excess and crimp the border using a fork or your fingers (see page 13). Cover it loosely and refrigerate for a minimum of 30 minutes and a maximum of 24 hours.

Preheat the oven to 425° F. at least 20 minutes before baking. Set an oven rack at the lowest level and place a baking stone or baking sheet on it before preheating.

In a liquid measure or small bowl, place the espresso powder and stir in the boiling water until it has dissolved. Set it aside to cool to warm.

In a food processor with the metal blade, process the flour, sugar, cinnamon, nutmeg, and salt for a few seconds to mix well. Add the butter and pulse until the mixture resembles coarse meal. (Alternatively, combine the ingredients in a medium bowl and, using a pastry cutter or your fingertips, rub together until the mixture resembles coarse meal.)

In a medium bowl, place the baking soda. If necessary, warm the coffee but do not add it hot. Stir in the coffee until the baking soda has dissolved. Stir in the molasses.

Pour the molasses mixture into the pastry-lined pan. Evenly sprinkle the flour mixture over it. At first it will sink in, but gradually a fine layer of crumbs will accumulate on the surface.

Bake for 15 minutes. Lower the oven temperature to 350°F., protect the edges from overbrowning with a foil ring (see page 19), and continue baking for 30 minutes or until the top springs back when pressed lightly in the center.

Cool the pie on a rack. Serve warm or at room temperature.

STORE

Room temperature, up to 3 days (but after the first day, the cake part becomes less moist unless the pie is reheated). Reheat in a 350°F. oven for 10 minutes.

POINTERS FOR SUCCESS

∾ Use unsulfured molasses; the sulfured variety tastes bitter.

UNDERSTANDING

The coffee is cooled to warm before adding it to the baking soda because hot coffee would activate the baking soda, thereby losing much of its leavening power.

PERSIMMON PIE

This pie is an exciting alternative to pumpkin pie at Thanksgiving, which is the height of the persimmon season. It was inspired by chef Tony Marano's persimmon pudding, which I fell in love with at the Majestic Hotel in San Francisco. It works well as a pie because the custardy texture benefits from a crunchy gingersnap crust. The persimmon itself has a puckery quality that offsets the spicy ginger and cinnamon flavorings in the filling. Whole bits of persimmon in the filling add concentrated flavor and bright bits of orange color, which contrast nicely against the deep brown filling. The persimmon slice on the top stays bright orange and tells your guests what kind of pie they are about to eat.

Serve this pie à la mode with ginger ice cream (page 241).

SERVES: 6 TO 8

INGREDIENTS	MEASURE	WEIGHT	
	VOLUME	OUNCES	GRAMS
Gingersnap Nut Crumb Crust for a 9-inch pie (page 68), pressed into the pan		•	•
2 small Fuyu persimmons (2½ inches in diameter)		7 ounces	200 grams
2 ripe Hachiya persimmons		14 ounces	400 grams
milk	⅔ liquid cup	5.6 ounces	160 grams
light brown sugar	½ cup, packed	3.75 ounces	108 grams
1 large egg	3 tablespoons + ½ teaspoon	1.75 ounces 50 grams (weighed without the shell)	
bleached all-purpose flour	⅔ cup (dip and sweep method)	3.3 ounces	94 grams
baking soda	¼ teaspoon	•	•
ground cinnamon	¼ teaspoon	•	•
nutmeg, preferably freshly grated	⅛ teaspoon	•	•
salt	¼ teaspoon	•	•
unsalted butter, melted	1 tablespoon	0.5 ounce	14 grams
raisins	3 tablespoons	1 ounce	27 grams
walnut halves, toasted (page 641) and chopped medium-coarse	⅓ cup	approx. 1.25 ounces	33 grams
candied orange peel, finely chopped	2 teaspoons	1 ounce	28 grams
candied ginger, finely chopped	2 teaspoons	0.3 ounce	9 grams
optional: 14 Crunchy Pecan Halves (page 593)	•	•	•
optional: unsweetened Crème Fraîche (page 558) or softly whipped cream (see page 551)	•	•	•

EQUIPMENT
One 9-inch pie plate and a foil crust shield, bottom lightly greased

Make the crust (page 68) and press it into the pan (see page 69).

Preheat the oven to 350°F. (325°F. if using a Pyrex pie plate) at least 15 minutes before baking. Set an oven rack just below the middle of the oven before preheating.

Peel and slice the Fuyu persimmons ¼ inch thick. Wrap one attractive center slice and set it aside for the decor. Cut enough of the remainder into ¼-inch dice to measure ⅔ cup (4.75 ounces/138 grams). Cover and set aside any extra slices to garnish the plates.

Cut away the stem from the Hachiya persimmons. Cut them in half and place them in a food processor fitted with the metal blade. Process for a few seconds until puréed. Measure the purée. You will need 1 cup (8.5 ounces/247 grams). (Any extra can be frozen up to 6 months for another pie.)

Process the Hachiya persimmon purée with the milk, brown sugar, and egg for about 8 seconds or until smooth.

In a small bowl, whisk together the flour, baking soda, cinnamon, nutmeg, and salt. Add it to the food processor and pulse about 8 times or until incorporated. Add the butter and pulse about 4 times or until incorporated. Add the chopped persimmon, raisins, walnuts, candied orange peel, and candied ginger and pulse twice, just to incorporate. (You will have about 3½ cups of filling.)

Immediately pour the filling into the prepared pie crust (the acidity in the persimmon reacting with the baking soda will cause the mixture to stiffen quickly). The filling will reach almost to the top of the crust. Smooth the surface and, if you have prepared one, set the persimmon slice in the center, pressing it lightly into the surface. Place a greased foil ring (see page 19) on the pie to shield the exposed crust edge.

Bake for 35 to 45 minutes or until a thin knife blade inserted about an inch from the center comes out clean. The filling will darken and puff slightly and the rim of the crust will spread slightly. On cooling, the filling will settle. Cool on a rack.

When the pie is cool, arrange the optional pecan halves around the edge, pointed ends out. If desired, brush a little corn syrup on the bottom of each to attach it to the filling, and press it in gently. Also brush a little corn syrup on the persimmon slice to make it shiny and prevent drying.

Serve warm or at room temperature, accompanied with crème fraîche or whipped cream and a few slices of persimmon if desired. (The pie can be reheated for 10 minutes in a 350°F. oven. Be sure to keep the crust shielded with aluminum foil.)

STORE
Room temperature, up to 1 day; refrigerated, up to 3 days.

NOTE
The filling can be prepared by hand or with an electric mixer, but the persimmon must be puréed using a food processor, blender, or food mill in order to have a smooth texture.

POINTERS FOR SUCCESS
∾ The Hachiya variety of persimmon is plump and pear-shaped, while the Fuyu variety is squat. Hachiya persimmons are ripe when they are very soft and almost jelly-like. To speed ripening, place them in a brown bag or fruit ripening bowl with an apple. Do not buy underripe Hachiyas if you do not have time to ripen them, as they will taste bitter. Fuyus can be substituted but must be peeled.
∾ Fuyus are preferable for adding to the filling and for the garnish because they keep their shape. They are ripe when still very firm and bright orange in color. A Fuyu does not have the astringency of the Hachiya but has a tough skin that must be removed. If desired, buy extra and garnish each plate with a few slices.
∾ Overcooking custard will cause the proteins in the egg to contract and squeeze the liquid from them, resulting in a curdled custard. But if the filling has not cooked sufficiently, the amylase in the egg yolk will cause it to thin out and also to become watery. When the custard has almost set, the very center will still be soft enough to leave a trace on the knife blade, but on removal from the oven, the residual heat will gently finish the cooking. With this pie, you cannot test for doneness by seeing if it will shimmy, because the thickening effect of the persimmon keeps it from moving even when not yet fully baked.

UNDERSTANDING
The cookie crust must be shielded with foil during baking. Care must be taken to maintain a temperature no higher than 325°F. if you use a glass pie plate, because it allows the heat to penetrate more easily and since the cookies have already been baked before being pulverized into crumbs, they could burn without this precaution.

Walnuts are used in the filling because they are crunchier than pecans, but pecans are used in the crust and for the garnish because their flavor is complementary to the persimmons.

ICE CREAM PIES AND ICE CREAMS

Pie and ice cream were meant for each other. I think that *à la mode* was the first French phrase I heard, and I remembered it because it meant ice cream slowly melting on top of a wedge of warm pie. Of course, vanilla ice cream goes with everything. But passion fruit ice cream with peach pie is blissful. Peanut butter ice cream with a chocolate tart is obviously wonderful, but with cherry pie it is stunning. The refreshing tang of buttermilk or lemon ice cream is extraordinarily complementary to fruit pies and tarts. Caramel ice cream is a natural with apple, pear, or peach pies and tarts and it is also wonderful with chocolate tarts.

This chapter contains recipes for ice creams not available store-bought. They all have a creamy texture without being cloyingly rich, because of the proportion of cream to milk (3 parts cream to 1 part milk). This is just enough butterfat to keep the ice crystals small.

Since ice cream is America's number one dessert, it stands to reason that a pie bible should present ways to serve it for special occasions. A pie crust, however, does more than offer a formal and attractive presentation. A crust makes it possible to introduce other elements, such as bananas, walnuts, hot fudge, and caramel, as in the Banana Split Pie. When serving an ice cream pie, be sure to transfer it from the freezer to the refrigerator for at least thirty minutes to soften it. When it is frozen too solid, the flavors hide, but when it is soft and creamy, you couldn't ask for a better dessert.

UNDERSTANDING ICE CREAM

I like to add a small amount of optional liqueur (1½ teaspoons of 80-proof liqueur for every cup of cream/milk) to all my ice cream recipes. The alcohol acts as an antifreeze, lowering the freezing point of the mixture so that it takes longer to freeze. During the freezing process, the dasher or beater in the ice cream machine is constantly turning to break up the ice crystals as they form. The longer the freezing takes, the smaller the ice crystals will be and the more evenly they will be distributed throughout the ice cream. This makes the ice cream feel creamy rather than icy. (Industrial machines have more powerful motors and beaters, so they can freeze ice cream faster and still produce small, evenly distributed ice crystals.) Ice cream has the most creamy texture within three days of freezing, but with the liqueur will maintain its texture for up to a week. The alcohol also keeps the ice cream from freezing quite as hard when it sits in the freezer. Aromatic liqueurs such as Chambord add a touch of extra flavor. Vodka does not impart any taste to the ice cream.

Cobasan (see page 644), the emulsifier that works wonders with whipped cream, also works beautifully with ice cream, making it just as smooth as it can possibly be. A rounded half teaspoon of Cobasan can be added to any of the ice creams, but it is essential in the buttermilk ice cream, where a lower proportion of cream is used in order to get more buttermilk flavor, and in the red wine ice cream, where the milk is replaced with the wine.

Heavy cream (which has already been pasteurized) does not need to be heated before adding it to the custard mixture. This maintains more of its lovely pure, floral flavor and also makes it convenient to make a fruit curd ice cream, because all you have to do is add it to the already prepared curd. According to my colleague Shirley Corriher, milk should be heated to 175°F. (just under scalding) because heating causes something in the proteins in milk to undergo a change, resulting in more smoothness in the finished ice cream. Curd-based ice creams, however, are so smooth there is no perceptible difference whether or not the milk is heated. When replacing the milk with another liquid that has no protein, as in the red wine ice cream, it is possible to add the protein in the form of nonfat dry milk to achieve a smooth texture. As milk has 3.5 percent protein, ¾ cup contains 6.35 grams, equal to about 4 teaspoons of nonfat dry milk.

All of my ice creams contain egg yolks (1 large yolk for every ½ cup of cream/milk). In addition to contributing flavor, they are great emulsifiers and, after being cooked to form the custard, offer significant body to the ice cream. Too high a temperature and they would curdle, but bringing them close to the maximum temperature produces a desirable body that feels good in one's mouth as it melts. A pinch of salt also does wonders to enhance the flavor of the ice cream without being perceived as saltiness.

After the custard is made, it should be chilled for at least 2 hours, or until cold, before adding it to the ice cream maker. For the smoothest texture and best flavor, it should sit overnight.

Some ice cream machines introduce more air into the ice cream than do others, so the yields will vary slightly. If you have one that can make very small quantities, it is possible to divide any of these recipes by 6 and make about ⅔ cup of ice cream. For the standard ice cream base, the proportions are:

1 large egg yolk: 1½ tablespoons sugar: 6 tablespoons heavy cream: 2 tablespoons milk: ¾ teaspoon 80-proof alcohol

For 1 cup of ice cream, perfect for two, multiply the base by one and a half:

1½ tablespoons egg yolk: 2 tablespoons plus ¾ teaspoon sugar: 9 tablespoons heavy cream: 3 tablespoons milk: 1⅛ teaspoons 80-proof alcohol

If you wish to speed freezing, don't add the alcohol or vanilla (which is distilled in alcohol) until after the ice cream has started to harden.

POINTERS FOR SUCCESS FOR ICE CREAM

◡ Use a wooden spoon or high-heat rubber spatula, not a whisk, to stir if not using an accurate thermometer (and you can also use it for the coating test), because the foam caused by a whisk makes it difficult to see when the mixture is getting close to boiling.

◡ Be sure to scrape the sides of the pan when stirring.

◡ The custard mixture must be heated adequately (to at least 160°F.) to thicken and prevent the amylase in the egg yolks from thinning it out on cooling, but for a silky-smooth sauce that does not curdle, the mixture must not be allowed to boil. (The boiling point of water is 212°F., but the ingredients in the custard lower the boiling point to 180°F.) If the custard is overheated and *slight* curdling does take place, pour it instantly into a blender and blend until smooth before straining it.

◡ The vodka or liqueur acts as antifreeze, preventing the formation of large ice crystals. Do not add more than the recommended amount of vodka or liqueur, or it will lower the freezing point so much that the ice cream will not freeze at all.

BANANA SPLIT PIE

This is an American ice cream parlor classic in a pie. Eating a slice of this pie is like diving into a treasure trove of goodies. A cross-section of the pie reveals a thin crumb crust topped with two layers each of vanilla ice cream and banana slices, interrupted by a scattering of chopped walnuts, topped with lacings of caramel and hot fudge and large rosettes of whipped cream, and garnished with more chopped walnuts and banana slices.

This is a fun, easy to make pie, yet the caramel and hot fudge lacing on top give it an elegant appearance. It would make a great hit at any special occasion from a children's birthday party to a Fourth of July picnic or even a New Year's dinner.

| INGREDIENTS | MEASURE | WEIGHT | |
	VOLUME	OUNCES	GRAMS
Vanilla Crumb Crust for a 10-inch pie (page 68), pressed into the pan and frozen		•	•
3 large firm bananas, cut into ½ -inch slices	3 cups (sliced)	1 pound 5 ounces (1 pound peeled)	595 grams (454 grams peeled)
Crème de Banana	1 cup	9.5 ounces	270 grams
freshly squeezed lemon juice	1 tablespoon	0.5 ounce	15 grams
1 recipe Bourbon Butterscotch Caramel (page 598)	½ cup + extra for passing	•	•
walnuts, toasted and coarsely chopped	¾ cup, divided	2.6 ounces	75 grams
Triple Vanilla Ice Cream* (page 232) or good-quality commercial ice cream, softened	3 cups (1½ pints)	•	•
1 recipe Hot Fudge Sauce (page 596)	¼ cup + extra for passing	•	•
optional garnish: 1 baby banana or ½ small banana		•	•
Whipped Cream Garnish heavy cream	1½ liquid cups	12.25 ounces	348 grams
sugar	1½ tablespoons	0.66 ounce	19 grams
optional: Cobasan	⅜ teaspoon	•	•

*If making your own ice cream, use 2 tablespoons plus 1 teaspoon of Crème de Banana (banana liqueur) in place of the optional vodka. (More is needed as "antifreeze" because Crème de Banana is only 50 proof, whereas vodka is 80 proof.) You will have a little more than the 3 cups needed for the pie.

EQUIPMENT
A 10-inch pie pan; three pastry bags or reclosable quart-size freezer bag and a number 8 large star pastry tube

Make the crust (page 68). Press it into the pan (see page 69) and freeze it.

In a medium bowl, place the banana slices and add the Crème de Banana and lemon juice. With a rubber spatula, mix gently to coat the bananas. Cover with plastic wrap and allow them to sit for 1 hour at room temperature.

Drain the bananas well, reserving the liquid for the optional banana garnish and the whipped cream.

Use a plastic squeeze bottle or a reclosable quart-size freezer bag with a small piece of one corner cut off to lace about ¼ cup of the caramel over the bottom of the prepared crust. Place half the banana slices evenly over the caramel and sprinkle ¼ cup of the walnuts on top. Spread half the ice cream over them. (If the ice cream starts to melt, place the pie in the freezer for about 15 minutes or until it is firm.) Repeat with the remaining bananas, another ¼ cup of the walnuts, and the remaining ice cream. Cover the pie with plastic wrap and freeze for at least 24 hours.

Chill a large bowl for the whipped cream.

The caramel and hot fudge can be swirled on top any time after the ice cream has set firmly (at least 3 hours or more, depending on the freezer temperature), but it can also be done 30 minutes before serving, while allowing the ice cream to soften. (When serving, pass any remaining caramel and hot fudge in the plastic bottles or reclosable bags and let the guests help themselves to extra.)

At least 1 hour before serving, if using the optional baby banana, slice it and macerate it in the reserved Crème de Banana mixture for 30 minutes. Drain the slices well, again reserving the macerating liquid.

Thirty minutes before serving,* combine the cream, sugar, optional Cobasan, and 1½ tablespoons of the macerating liquid in the chilled mixing bowl. Beat the mixture until it forms stiff peaks when the beater is raised. Cover and refrigerate. Remove the pie from the freezer to the refrigerator, to soften slightly.

Just before serving, fill a pastry bag or freezer bag, fitted with the number 8 star tube, with the whipped cream and pipe large rosettes around the border of the pie. Garnish with the remaining ¼ cup of chopped walnuts and the baby banana slices.

To serve, run a towel or sponge under hot water and wring it out well, then run it over the sides and bottom of the pie plate to help release the crust. (Do this two or three times.)

STORE
Frozen, up to 1 week.

NOTE
For a 9-inch pie, you will need a Vanilla Crumb Crust for a 9-inch pie (page 67) and three quarters of the recipe.

---

*The whipped cream can be made ahead, refrigerated, and rebeaten slightly. If Cobasan is used, it will not require rebeating.

POINTERS FOR SUCCESS

∾ The caramel should be at room temperature when laced onto the pie so that it does not melt the ice cream.

UNDERSTANDING

The banana slices do not become icy on freezing because they have been macerated in the banana liqueur.

Adding the macerating liquid to the whipped cream not only flavors it but also keeps it from becoming icy if returning the pie to the freezer.

COCONUT ICE CREAM PIE
(with Crème Fraîche Variation)

This is my answer to coconut cream pie. I love the flavors but find it too sweet. Freezing the cream component (i.e., making ice cream) and decreasing the sugar in both crust and whipped cream was the solution. This simple classic is beautiful to behold, no doubt due to its ethereal blizzard of freshly grated coconut on top.

EQUIPMENT
A 9-inch pie pan

Make the dough (page 58). Roll, shape, transfer it to the pan, and prebake it (see pages 50–54).

MAKE THE ICE CREAM

Have a fine strainer suspended over a medium mixing bowl ready near the range.

In a small heavy nonreactive saucepan, place the sugar and vanilla bean and, using your fingers, rub the seeds into the sugar. Remove and reserve the pod. Using a wooden spoon, stir in the yolks, cream of coconut, and salt until well blended.

In another small saucepan (or a heatproof glass measure if using a microwave on high power), place the reserved vanilla pod, the cream, milk, and shredded coconut and scald.* Let sit for 1 to 1½ hours.

Strain the milk mixture and squeeze the coconut to remove all the liquid. Discard the coconut.

Heat the milk. Stir a few tablespoons of the milk into the yolk mixture, then gradually add the remainder, stirring constantly. Heat the mixture, stirring constantly, to just below the boiling point (170° to 180°F.). Steam will begin to appear and the mixture will be slightly thicker than heavy cream. If a finger is run across

*Heat until small bubbles form around the perimeter.

SERVES: 6

| INGREDIENTS | MEASURE | WEIGHT | |
	VOLUME	OUNCES	GRAMS
Sweet Coconut Cookie Tart Crust (page 58), made with only 2 tablespoons sugar, for a 9-inch pie, prebaked, and cooled*	1 generous cup	10.75 ounces	307 grams
Coconut Ice Cream sugar	3 tablespoons	1.3 ounces	37.5 grams
1 Tahitian vanilla bean,[†] split lengthwise	•	•	•
4 large egg yolks	scant ⅓ liquid cup	2.6 ounces	74 grams
cream of coconut	1 tablespoon	•	•
salt	a pinch	•	•
heavy cream	1½ liquid cups	12.25 ounces	348 grams
milk	½ liquid cup	4.25 ounces	121 grams
shredded sweetened coconut	1 rounded cup	3 ounces	85 grams
optional: Cocoribe	2 tablespoons	1.2 ounces	34 grams
Whipped Cream heavy cream	1 liquid cup	approx. 8.25 ounces	232 grams
superfine sugar[‡]	1 tablespoon	0.5 ounce	12.5 grams
Cocoribe	1 tablespoon	0.6 ounces	17 grams
Garnish grated fresh coconut (see page 643)	1 cup	2.6 ounces	75 grams

*If rolling, roll the dough ¼ inch thick and large enough to cut a 12-inch circle, using an expandable flan ring or cardboard template and sharp knife. Turn under the edge and crimp, but don't flute the edges too far away from the edge of the pie pan, or it will droop. If possible, freeze overnight before baking.

†If Tahitian vanilla beans are unavailable, use 1½ ordinary (Madagascar) vanilla beans.

‡If using sweetened coconut, omit.

the back of the spoon, it will leave a well-defined track. Immediately remove it from the heat and pour it into the strainer, scraping up the thickened cream that has settled on the bottom of the pan. Cool in an ice-water bath or the refrigerator until cold, at least 2 hours, or overnight.

Remove the vanilla pod and stir in the optional Cocoribe. Freeze in an ice cream maker.

Spread the ice cream into the pie crust and freeze for at least 4 hours.

Chill a bowl for the whipped cream.

About 30 minutes before serving, whip the cream with the sugar (if not using sweetened coconut) until soft peaks form when the beater is raised. Add the Cocoribe and beat until stiff peaks form. Spread onto the ice cream and sprinkle with the coconut. Allow the pie to sit for 30 minutes refrigerated before serving.

To serve, run a sponge or dish towel under hot water and apply it several times to the bottom and sides of pie plate to release the crust.

VARIATION

PIÑA COLADA ICE CREAM PIE   Replace the coconut ice cream with Pineapple Ice Cream (page 239), made with rum.

STORE

Frozen, up to 1 week.

POINTERS FOR SUCCESS

∾ See page 223.

BRANDIED MINCEMEAT ICE CREAM PIE

I developed this holiday pie for Breyers ice cream about twenty years ago. I have always loved mincemeat but found the taste to be too cloyingly sweet. Relieving that sweetness by swirling it through vanilla ice cream and setting it in a bittersweet chocolate wafer crust will convert many to the flavor of mincemeat. The candied fruit decoration on top is reminiscent of a Della Robbia wreath, with fruit woven together to look like a garland—a very festive ending to Christmas dinner. The brandy and rum in some brands of mincemeat keep the ice cream a perfect creamy consistency even when made several days ahead.

EQUIPMENT

A 10-inch pie pan

Make the crust (page 68). Press it into the pan (see page 69) and freeze it.

In a large chilled bowl, stir together the softened ice cream and mincemeat until well blended but not melted.* Spoon this mixture into the prepared pie shell. Cover with plastic wrap and freeze for at least 24 hours.

---

* If making your own ice cream, simply add the mincemeat to the base before freezing it.

INGREDIENTS	MEASURE	WEIGHT	
	VOLUME	OUNCES	GRAMS
Chocolate Crumb Crust for a 10-inch pie (page 68), pressed into the pan and frozen		•	•
Triple Vanilla Ice Cream* (page 232) or good-quality commercial ice cream, softened	4 cups (1 quart)	•	•
fine-quality mincemeat, preferably with brandy and rum, such as Postilion (see page 641)	1 cup	9.5 ounces	269 grams
optional garnish: red and green candied cherries, angelica, and coarsely chopped toasted pecans	•	•	•

*Omit the vodka if using mincemeat with brandy.

The optional garnish can be added any time after the ice cream has set firmly (at least 3 hours or more, depending on the temperature of your freezer). Cut the candied cherries in half and cut little slivers of angelica. Working quickly, place the cherries about 1 inch from the edge of the pie, alternating the colors. Place the angelica radiating out from the cherries like leaves. Scatter a few pecans in between the cherries. Cover tightly with plastic wrap and return the pie to the freezer.

Transfer the pie from the freezer to the refrigerator about 30 minutes before serving to soften slightly.

To serve, run a towel under hot water and wring it out well, then run it along the sides and bottom of the pie plate to help release the crust. (Do this two or three times.)

STORE

Frozen, up to 1 week.

NOTE

For a 9-inch pie, you will need a Chocolate Crumb Crust for a 9-inch pie (page 67), 3 cups of vanilla ice cream, and ¾ cup of mincemeat.

BURNT ALMOND ICE CREAM TARTLETS

I could never resist the Häagen-Dazs coffee ice cream pop coated with bittersweet chocolate and chopped roasted almonds. At first, I was relieved when it disappeared from the East Coast market, because it had posed such a threat to my self-control. But I began to crave it and set out to duplicate it in the form of a tartlet. With a chocolate pastry crust holding the filling, these have a few advantages over their cousin on a stick. One is that you can hold a piece of it in your hand and not have it melt. Another advantage to this tartlet: The chocolate/almond topping always stays slightly soft and chewy, even when frozen.

MAKES: EIGHT 4- BY ¾-INCH TARTLETS

INGREDIENTS	MEASURE	WEIGHT	
	VOLUME	OUNCES	GRAMS
Bittersweet Chocolate Cookie Tart Crust (page 61), baked in eight 4-inch flan rings, cooled, and frozen	1 recipe	1 pound	455 grams
coffee ice cream, preferably Häagen-Dazs, softened	2⅔ cups	•	•
Topping	(2 cups)	(1 pound)	(458 grams)
slivered almonds	¾ cup	3 ounces	85 grams
bittersweet chocolate, preferably Lindt Excellence or Valrhona Caracque	two 3-ounce bars	6 ounces	170 grams
heavy cream	¾ liquid cup + 2 tablespoons	7 ounces	203 grams

EQUIPMENT
Eight 4-inch flan rings and a cookie sheet large enough to hold them with at least an inch of space between each*

Make the dough (page 61). Roll, shape, and prebake it (see pages 50–54). Let cool, then place in the freezer, covered.

*Seven fluted tart molds measuring 4¾ inches at their widest part can be substituted.

Spread ⅓ cup of the ice cream in each of the 8 tartlet shells. Cover them with plastic wrap and return them to the freezer for several hours or until very hard.

Remove the flan rings and return the covered tartlets to the freezer.

MAKE THE TOPPING

Preheat the oven to 350°F.

Place the nuts on a baking sheet and toast them in the oven for 10 to 15 minutes, stirring occasionally, until deep golden brown. Cool and then coarsely chop them.

In the top of a double boiler over hot, not simmering, water, melt the chocolate, stirring often, until fully melted. (Or melt the chocolate in the microwave on high power, stirring every 20 seconds.) Remove from the heat, add the cream, and stir until smooth. Stir in the nuts.

Remove the tartlets, one at a time, from the freezer and, using a small metal spatula, spread about ¼ cup of the chocolate mixture on top of the ice cream so that it is even with the top of the pastry. Working quickly, smooth the surface evenly before the chocolate mixture sets, and return the tartlet, covered, to the freezer.

About 5 minutes before serving time, remove the tartlets from the freezer.

STORE

Frozen, up to 3 weeks.

POINTERS FOR SUCCESS

∾ Leave the tartlet shells in the flan rings after cooling to serve as support for the filling.

∾ The nuts should be deeply browned but not too dark, to achieve an intense flavor without being burnt.

UNDERSTANDING

I prefer good-quality commercial coffee ice cream to homemade because manufacturers use freshly roasted coffee beans, which make an enormous difference to the purity and intensity of the coffee flavor.

TRIPLE VANILLA ICE CREAM
(with Crème Fraîche Variation)

The secret to having intensely pure vanilla flavor without bitterness is to use vanilla beans in combination with vanilla extract. Since I love the flavor differences contributed by the Madagascar and the Tahitian bean, I use both. The optional vodka is flavorless but keeps the ice cream velvety even after a week in the freezer. If serving the ice cream the same day it is made, it's fine to omit it. The Crème Fraîche variation provides a delightful tangy edge that wonderfully complements the acidity of fruit tarts. Because the crème fraîche is thicker than heavy cream, it also delivers a fuller consistency in the semimelted stage.

MAKES: ABOUT 4 CUPS (DEPENDING ON THE ICE CREAM MAKER)

INGREDIENTS	MEASURE	WEIGHT	
	VOLUME	OUNCES	GRAMS
sugar	½ cup + 1 tablespoon	4 ounces	112 grams
¾ Tahitian vanilla bean,* split lengthwise		•	•
¾ Madagascar vanilla bean, split lengthwise		•	•
6 large egg yolks	7 tablespoons	4 ounces	112 grams
salt	a pinch	•	•
heavy cream or Crème Fraîche (page 558)	2¼ liquid cups	18.3 ounces	522 grams
milk	¾ liquid cup	6.5 ounces	182 grams
pure vanilla extract	1½ teaspoons	•	6 grams
optional: vodka	1½ tablespoons	0.75 ounce	21.5 grams
optional: Cobasan	rounded ½ teaspoon	•	•

*If Tahitian vanilla beans are unavailable, use a total of 2 regular (Madagascar) vanilla beans.

Have a fine strainer suspended over a medium mixing bowl ready near the range.

In a heavy nonreactive saucepan, place the sugar and vanilla beans and, using your fingers, rub the seeds into the sugar. Remove and reserve the pods. Using a wooden spoon, stir in the yolks and salt until well blended.

In a small saucepan (or a heatproof glass measure if using a microwave on high power) place the cream, milk, and reserved vanilla pods and scald.* Stir a few tablespoons into the yolk mixture, then gradually add the remainder, stirring constantly. Heat the mixture, stirring constantly, to just below the boiling point (170° to 180°F.). Steam will begin to appear and the mixture will be slightly thicker than heavy cream. If a finger is run across the back of the spoon, it will leave a well-defined track. Immediately remove it from the heat and pour it into the strainer, scraping up the thickened cream that has settled on the bottom of the pan. Return the vanilla pods to the sauce until you are ready to freeze the ice cream.

Cool by setting the bowl in a larger bowl of ice water or in the refrigerator until cold, at least 2 hours, preferably overnight.

Stir in the vanilla extract and the optional vodka and Cobasan. Remove the vanilla pods (rinse and dry them for future use) and freeze the mixture in an ice cream maker. Allow the ice cream to ripen for at least 2 hours in the freezer before serving. If it has been held longer and is very hard, allow it to sit refrigerated or at room temperature until softened and creamy.

STORE

Frozen, up to 1 week. The ice cream has the best texture within 3 days of freezing but with the vodka will maintains its texture for up to a week.

POINTERS FOR SUCCESS

∽ See page 223.

BUTTERMILK ICE CREAM

My friend Andreas Galliker, executive chef for Albert Uster Imports, created this fantastic ice cream. Cobasan, the same flavorless emulsifier that stabilizes whipping cream, works its magic with ice cream! Without it, you will have the slightly icy consistency of ice milk instead of creamy ice cream. The fresh orange juice accentuates the buttermilk flavor without imparting more than a subtle one of its own.

A scoop of this ice cream is refreshing, tangy, and zippy, perfect on top of blueberry pie and all other fruit pies and tarts.

*Heat until small bubbles form around the perimeter.

MAKES: ABOUT 4 CUPS (DEPENDING ON THE ICE CREAM MAKER)

INGREDIENTS	MEASURE	WEIGHT	
	VOLUME	OUNCES	GRAMS
3 juice oranges, zested* and juiced	1 liquid cup	8.5 ounces	242 grams
heavy cream (not ultrapasteurized)	1⅓ liquid cups	12 ounces	348 grams
4 large egg yolks	scant ⅓ liquid cup	2.6 ounces	74 grams
sugar	¾ cup	5.25 ounces	150 grams
buttermilk	1½ liquid cups	12.7 ounces	363 grams
Cobasan	1 teaspoon	•	•
optional: vodka	2½ tablespoons	1.25 ounces	36 grams

*Remove the orange portion of the peel only. Wide strips of zest are fine, as they are used to infuse flavor and are discarded. Taste the zest to be sure it is not bitter; don't use it if it is. The ice cream will still have a lovely flavor. A few drops of orange oil (see page 638), added just before freezing, can be used in its place.

Have a fine strainer suspended over a medium mixing bowl ready near the range.

In a 4-cup heatproof glass measure sprayed with nonstick vegetable oil or lightly greased, microwave the orange juice for about 15 minutes on high power or until reduced to ⅓ cup (or place it in a small saucepan and boil, stirring constantly until reduced). Stir in the heavy cream and orange zest. Set it aside.

In a heavy nonreactive saucepan, with a wooden spoon, beat the yolks with the sugar until well blended.

Heat the orange juice mixture to the boiling point. Stir a few tablespoons into the yolk mixture, then gradually add the remainder, stirring constantly. Cook over medium-low heat, stirring constantly, to just below the boiling point (170° to 180°F.). Steam will begin to appear and the mixture will be slightly thicker than heavy cream. If a finger is run across the back of the spoon, it will leave a well-defined track. Immediately remove it from the heat and pour it into the strainer, scraping up the thickened cream that has settled on the bottom of the pan. Discard the orange zest.

Cool by setting the bowl in a large bowl of ice water or in the refrigerator until cold, at least 2 hours, preferably overnight.

Stir in the buttermilk, Cobasan, and the optional vodka. Freeze in an ice cream maker. Allow the ice cream to ripen for at least 2 hours in the freezer before serving. If it has been held longer and is very hard, allow it to sit refrigerated or at room temperature until softened and creamy.

STORE

Frozen, up to 1 week. The ice cream has the best texture within 3 days of freezing but with the vodka will maintain its texture for up to a week.

POINTERS FOR SUCCESS

∾ See page 223.

∾ Be sure to use heavy cream that has not been ultrapasteurized, or the Cobasan will not be effective.

UNDERSTANDING

No salt is added to the base because buttermilk contains salt.

The buttermilk is added shortly before freezing instead of being heated in the custard because high heat causes it to curdle.

Doubling the quantity of Cobasan prevents ice crystals from forming.

LEMON-LUSCIOUS ICE CREAM

Lemon curd has the purest, most intense, and full-flavored lemon flavor I know, so I use it as a base for lemon ice cream. All that's added is heavy cream and a little milk.

MAKES: ABOUT 3½ CUPS (DEPENDING ON THE ICE CREAM MAKER)

INGREDIENTS	MEASURE	WEIGHT	
	VOLUME	OUNCES	GRAMS
4 large egg yolks	scant ⅓ liquid cup	2.6 ounces	74 grams
sugar	1 cup, divided	7 ounces	200 grams
finely grated lemon zest	2 teaspoons	•	4 grams
freshly squeezed lemon juice	3 fluid ounces (6 tablespoons)	3.25 ounces	94 grams
unsalted butter, softened	4 tablespoons	2 ounces	57 grams
salt	a pinch	•	•
heavy cream	1½ liquid cups	12.2 ounces	348 grams
milk	½ liquid cup	4.25 ounces	121 grams
optional: vodka	4 teaspoons	0.66 ounce	19 grams
optional: Cobasan	½ teaspoon	•	•

Have ready near the range a strainer suspended over a medium bowl.

In a heavy nonreactive saucepan, with a wooden spoon, beat the yolks and ¾ cup of the sugar until well blended. Stir in the lemon zest, juice, butter, and salt. Cook over medium-low heat, stirring constantly, until the mixture is thickened and resembles hollandaise sauce; it should thickly coat the wooden spoon but still be liquid enough to pour. The mixture will change from translucent to opaque and begin to take on a yellow color on the back of the spoon. (An accurate thermometer will register 196°F.) The mixture must not be allowed to boil or it will curdle. Whenever steam appears, remove the pan briefly from the heat, stirring constantly to keep the mixture from boiling.

When the mixture has thickened, pour it at once into the strainer. Press with the back of a spoon until only a coarse residue remains. Discard the residue (or consider it the cook's dividend!).

In a medium bowl, combine the cream and milk. Whisk in the sugar until dissolved. Whisk this mixture into the curd. Cover tightly and refrigerate it for at least 1 hour or until well chilled.

Stir in the optional vodka and Cobasan. Freeze in an ice cream maker. Allow the ice cream to ripen for at least 2 hours in the freezer before serving. If it has been held longer and is very hard, allow it to sit refrigerated or at room temperature until softened and creamy.

STORE

Frozen, up to 1 week. The ice cream has the best texture within 3 days of freezing but with the vodka will maintain its texture for up to a week.

POINTERS FOR SUCCESS

∾ For finely grated zest, use a zester, a vegetable peeler, or a fine grater to remove the yellow portion only of the peel. The white pith beneath is bitter. If using a zester or peeler, finish by chopping the zest with a sharp knife.

∾ If you heat a lemon (about 10 seconds in a microwave oven on high power) and roll it around on the counter while pressing on it lightly, it will release a significantly greater quantity of juice.

∾ To prevent curdling, be sure to mix the sugar with the yolks before adding the lemon juice.

UNDERSTANDING

The lemon zest is discarded to maintain the uninterrupted creaminess of the ice cream.

A quarter cup more sugar is used than for lemon curd alone to balance the addition of the cream and milk and to compensate for the decrease in sweetness perception caused by freezing. Only part of the sugar is added directly to the curd to keep it from becoming too thick. If using a fine-quality commercial lemon curd, such as Tiptree, add this extra ¼ cup sugar to the cream/milk mixture.

PURE PASSION ICE CREAM

My version of this ice cream involves making a passion fruit curd and then stirring in heavy cream, milk, and vanilla—as simple as that. The vanilla magically rounds off any of the slightly metallic astringency usually associated with passion fruit. Fresh passion fruit pulp requires a food mill or strainer to purée. Commercial frozen purée is easier to work with and my preferred choice. (If you have already made the passion fruit curd, simply add 3 tablespoons of sugar to the cream/milk.)

This ice cream is glorious served with peach pie or simply with slices of banana and a sprinkling of macadamia nuts. It can also be served with a fresh passion fruit sauce.

MAKES: ABOUT 3½ CUPS (DEPENDING ON THE ICE CREAM MAKER)

INGREDIENTS	MEASURE	WEIGHT	
	VOLUME	OUNCES	GRAMS
sugar	14 tablespoons, divided	6.2 ounces	175 grams
¾ Tahitian vanilla bean,* split lengthwise		•	•
4 large egg yolks	scant ⅓ liquid cup	2.6 ounces	74 grams
6 to 7 passion fruit (1½ pounds), puréed†	⅔ liquid cup	approx. 5.25 ounces	146 grams
unsalted butter, softened or cut into pieces	4 tablespoons	2 ounces	56 grams
salt	a pinch	•	•
heavy cream	1½ liquid cups	12.25 ounces	348 grams
milk	½ liquid cup	4.25 ounces	121 grams
optional: passion fruit liqueur	5 teaspoons	approx. 0.75 ounce	25 grams
or vodka	1 tablespoon	0.5 ounce	14 grams
optional: Cobasan	½ teaspoon	•	•

*If Tahitian vanilla beans are unavailable, use 1½ ordinary (Madagascar) vanilla beans, or 1 teaspoon pure vanilla extract (added just before freezing).

†Commercial passion fruit purée can be substituted. Use 9 tablespoons (the same weight: 146 grams/5.25 ounces) if using Albert Uster's. Use 6½ tablespoons (108 grams/3.75 ounces) if using Perfect Purée, which is concentrated, and increase the sugar to 1 cup.

Have ready near the range a strainer suspended over a medium bowl.

In a heavy nonreactive saucepan, place 11 tablespoons of the sugar and the vanilla bean and, using your fingers, rub the seeds into the sugar. Remove the pod and drop it into the cream. Add the yolks to the sugar mixture and, with a wooden spoon, mix until well blended. Stir in the passion fruit purée, butter, and salt. Cook over medium-low heat, stirring constantly, until the mixture is thickened and resembles hollandaise sauce; it should thickly coat the spoon but still be liquid enough to pour. The mixture will change from translucent to opaque and begin to take on a yellow color on the back of the spoon. It must not be allowed to boil, or it will curdle (an accurate thermometer will read 180°F.). Whenever steam appears, remove the pan briefly from the heat, stirring constantly to keep the mixture from boiling. When the mixture has thickened, pour it at once into the strainer. Press it with the back of a spoon until only a coarse residue remains. Discard the residue (or consider it the cook's dividend!).

In a medium bowl, place the cream and milk. Whisk in the remaining 3 tablespoons of sugar until dissolved and whisk this mixture into the curd. Cover tightly and refrigerate for at least 1 hour or until well chilled.

Stir in the optional passion fruit liqueur or vodka and Cobasan. Remove the vanilla bean and freeze in an ice cream maker. Allow the ice cream to ripen for at least 2 hours in the freezer before serving. If it has been held longer and is very hard, allow it to sit refrigerated or at room temperature until softened and creamy.

STORE

Frozen, up to 1 week. The ice cream has the best texture within 3 days of freezing but with the liqueur will maintain its texture for up to a week.

NOTE

If desired, the ice cream can be garnished with a passion fruit sauce. (Leaving in the little black seeds offers a flavor clue as well as an exotic decoration.) For ½ cup sauce, in a small saucepan, stir together the pulp from 4 passion fruit (about ⅓ cup), 2 teaspoons of sugar, and ¼ cup of water. Bring to a boil, stirring constantly until thickened. Allow to cool to room temperature, and spoon a few teaspoons around each serving of ice cream.

POINTERS FOR SUCCESS

∾ See page 223.

∾ For the best flavor, choose passion fruit that are very wrinkled. They will not have an aroma until cut.

∾ To prevent curdling from the acidity of the fruit, be sure to mix the sugar with the yolks before adding the passion fruit purée.

PINEAPPLE ICE CREAM

This ice cream makes a marvelous Piña Colada Ice Cream Pie (page 228). It is also an unusually flavorful accompaniment to fruit pies such as strawberry and blueberry.

MAKES: ABOUT 4 CUPS (DEPENDING ON THE ICE CREAM MAKER)

INGREDIENTS	MEASURE	WEIGHT	
	VOLUME	OUNCES	GRAMS
Pineapple Purée	(3 cups)	(10.5 ounces)	(300 grams)
sugar	2 cups	14 ounces	400 grams
water	1 liquid cup	8.25 ounces	236 grams
1 pineapple, preferably "golden" variety, peeled, cored, and cut into chunks	4 cups	1 pound 7 ounces	652 grams
Pineapple Ice Cream sugar	½ cup	3.5 ounces	100 grams
vanilla bean, split lengthwise*	2-inch piece	•	•
5 large egg yolks	3 fluid ounces	3.25 ounces	93 grams
salt	a pinch	•	•
heavy cream	2 liquid cups	16.25 ounces	464 grams
milk	⅔ liquid cup	5.6 ounces	160 grams
optional: light rum	1 tablespoon + 2 teaspoons	approx. 0.75 ounce	23 grams
optional: Cobasan	rounded ½ teaspoon	•	•

*Or 1 teaspoon pure vanilla extract, added just before freezing.

Advance preparation: Make the pineapple purée 1 day ahead.

MAKE THE PINEAPPLE PURÉE

In a medium nonreactive saucepan, combine the sugar and water and bring to a boil, stirring constantly. Add the pineapple and, without stirring, return to a boil. Cover, cool, and let sit overnight at room temperature.

Use at once, or leave the pineapple in the syrup and refrigerate it, tightly covered, for up to 1 week.

Drain the pineapple and purée it in a food processor with the metal blade or a food mill fitted with a fine disc. Remove ⅔ cup (2.3 ounces/66 grams) for the ice cream. (Place the remaining 2⅓ cups in an airtight jar and freeze for up to 6 months.)

MAKE THE ICE CREAM

Have a fine strainer suspended over a medium mixing bowl ready near the range.

In a heavy nonreactive saucepan, place the sugar and vanilla bean and, using your fingers, rub the seeds into the sugar. Remove and reserve the pod. Using a wooden spoon, stir in the yolks and salt until well blended.

In a small saucepan (or a heatproof glass measure if using a microwave on high power), combine the cream, milk, and reserved vanilla pod and scald.* Stir a few tablespoons into the yolk mixture, then gradually add the remainder, stirring constantly. Heat the mixture, stirring constantly, to just below the boiling point (170° to 180°F.). Steam will begin to appear and the mixture will be slightly thicker than heavy cream. If a finger is run across the back of the spoon, it will leave a well-defined track. Immediately remove it from the heat and pour it into the strainer, scraping up the thickened cream that has settled on the bottom of the pan. Discard the vanilla pod (or rinse and dry it for future use).

Cool in an ice-water bath or the refrigerator until cold, at least 2 hours, preferably overnight.

Stir in the pineapple purée and the optional rum and Cobasan. Freeze in an ice cream maker. Allow the ice cream to ripen for at least 2 hours in the freezer before serving. If it has been held longer and is very hard, allow it to sit refrigerated or at room temperature until softened and creamy.

STORE

Frozen, up to 1 week. The ice cream has the best texture within 3 days of freezing but with the rum will maintain its texture for up to a week.

POINTERS FOR SUCCESS

∾ See page 223.

---

*Heat until small bubbles form around the perimeter.

GINGER ICE CREAM

This pale golden ginger ice cream delivers an intriguing counterpoint on the palate: creamy cold with a fiery background bite. Fresh ginger is first used to infuse in the syrup for the base and then strained, cut, puréed, and added to the chilled base for further intensity.

This ice cream is a sensational accompaniment to pear, peach, nectarine, and persimmon pies.

MAKES: ABOUT 3 CUPS (DEPENDING ON THE ICE CREAM MAKER)

INGREDIENTS	MEASURE	WEIGHT	
	VOLUME	OUNCES	GRAMS
sugar	½ cup, divided	3.5 ounces	100 grams
Tahitian vanilla bean, split lengthwise*	1-inch piece	•	•
fresh ginger, peeled and finely chopped	¼ cup (loosely packed)	1 ounce	28 grams
water	⅓ liquid cup	2.75 ounces	78 grams
4 large egg yolks	⅓ scant liquid cup	2.6 ounces	74 grams
salt	a small pinch	•	•
heavy cream or Crème Fraîche (page 558)	1½ liquid cups	12.25 ounces	348 grams
milk	½ liquid cup	4.25 ounces	121 grams
optional: Canton ginger liqueur or vodka	1 tablespoon	•	•
optional: Cobasan	½ teaspoon	•	•

*If Tahitian vanilla beans are unavailable, use 2 inches of regular (Madagascar) vanilla bean (or ¼ teaspoon pure vanilla extract, added just before freezing).

In a small saucepan, place 6 tablespoons of the sugar and the vanilla bean and, using your fingers, rub the seeds into the sugar. Drop in the pod. Add the ginger and water and stir until the sugar is dissolved. Heat over medium-high heat, stirring constantly, until the mixture comes to a boil. Stop stirring, reduce the heat to low, and simmer for 5 minutes, without stirring. Remove the ginger syrup from the heat, cover, and allow to cool for about 30 minutes or until room temperature.

Have a fine strainer suspended over a medium mixing bowl ready near the range.

In a heavy nonreactive saucepan, using a wooden spoon, stir together the yolks, the remaining 2 tablespoons of sugar, and the salt until well blended.

In a small saucepan (or a heatproof glass measure if using a microwave on high power), place the cream and milk. Stir a few tablespoons into the yolk mixture, then gradually add the remainder, stirring constantly. Heat the mixture, stirring constantly, to just below the boiling point (170° to 180°F.).* Steam will begin to appear and the mixture will be slightly thicker than heavy cream. If a finger is run across the back of the spoon, it will leave a well-defined track. Immediately remove it from the heat and pour it into the strainer, scraping up the thickened cream that has settled on the bottom of the pan.

Cool by setting the bowl in a large bowl of ice water or in the refrigerator until cold, at least 2 hours, preferably overnight.

Meanwhile, strain the ginger, reserving the syrup. Remove the vanilla pod (rinse and dry it for future use). Place the ginger in a mini chopper along with 2 tablespoons of the syrup and purée until the ginger is very fine. Add this mixture together with the syrup to the ice cream base.

When chilled, stir in the optional liqueur and Cobasan, and freeze in an ice cream maker. Allow the ice cream to ripen for at least 2 hours in the freezer before serving. If it has been held longer and is very hard, allow it to sit refrigerated or at room temperature until softened and creamy.

STORE

Frozen, up to 1 week. The ice cream has the best texture within 3 days of freezing but with the liqueur will maintain its texture for up to a week.

NOTE

To make this ice cream without a mini processor, instead of chopping the ginger, to start, grate it finely using a fine grater with small rough holes (as opposed to a shredder with oval openings). You will need 1 tablespoon plus 2 teaspoons to equal 1 ounce. After simmering it in the sugar syrup, let cool, then add the entire mixture to the ice cream base.

POINTERS FOR SUCCESS

∾ See page 223.

UNDERSTANDING

The total amount of sugar for the basic ice cream base is increased by 2 tablespoons to balance the sharpness of the ginger. Three quarters of the sugar is used in a poaching syrup for the ginger to soften its bite and prevent curdling of the cream mixture from direct contact with the acidity in the ginger.

*Heat until small bubbles form around the perimeter.

CARAMEL ICE CREAM

This ice cream will have the best caramel flavor of any you have ever tasted if you bring the caramel to a 20 to 25 degrees higher temperature than usual (380°F.). This increases its intensity. But you have to walk a fine line: too high, and it will taste burnt and bitter.

This ice cream has one and a half times more sugar than my vanilla ice cream both because caramelization decreases sweetness to some degree and because more is needed to intensify the caramel flavor. More milk is needed than for the vanilla ice cream because some of it evaporates and concentrates when added to the caramel.

Caramel ice cream is the ideal accompaniment to any apple pie or tart. It is also great with pear, peach, or nectarine pie and with chocolate tarts such as the Chocolate Oblivion Tartlets or the Brownie Puddle. And for the true caramel lover, it would make a fabulous replacement for the vanilla ice cream in the Banana Split Pie.

MAKES: ABOUT 3½ CUPS (DEPENDING ON THE ICE CREAM MAKER)

INGREDIENTS	MEASURE	WEIGHT	
	VOLUME	OUNCES	GRAMS
½ Tahitian vanilla bean,* split lengthwise		•	•
heavy cream	2¼ liquid cups	18.3 ounces	522 grams
milk	1 liquid cup	8.5 ounces	242 grams
sugar	1 cup	7 ounces	200 grams
water	2 tablespoons	1 ounce	27 grams
6 large egg yolks	7 tablespoons	4 ounces	112 grams
salt	a pinch	•	•
optional: vodka	4 teaspoons	0.66 ounce	19 grams

*If Tahitian vanilla beans are unavailable, use 1 ordinary (Madagascar) vanilla bean, or ½ teaspoon pure vanilla extract (added just before freezing).

EQUIPMENT
A heavy saucepan, at least 5-cup capacity, ideally with a nonstick lining

Scrape the seeds from the vanilla bean into the cream and drop in the pod. Chill until ready to add it to the custard mixture.

In a small saucepan (or a heatproof glass measure if using a microwave on high power) scald the milk.* Remove from heat and cover to keep it warm.

In the heavy saucepan, stir together the sugar and water until the sugar is completely moistened and bring to a boil, stirring constantly. Cook, without stirring, until deep amber (380°F.). Remove it from the heat and slowly pour in the hot milk. It will bubble up furiously for about a minute. Return it to low heat and cook, stirring constantly, until the caramel is totally dissolved and the mixture is reduced to ¾ cup. Remove from heat. (If any undissolved caramel remains in the saucepan, set it aside until you finish the custard mixture. Then return the custard mixture to the saucepan and refrigerate it for a few hours or until the caramel has dissolved completely.)

Have a fine strainer suspended over a medium mixing bowl ready near the range.

In a heavy nonreactive saucepan, with a wooden spoon, stir together the yolks and salt until well blended. Stir a few tablespoons of the hot caramel mixture into the yolk mixture, then gradually add the remainder, stirring constantly. Return the mixture to the saucepan and heat it, stirring constantly, to just below the boiling point (170° to 180°F.). Steam will begin to appear and the mixture will be slightly thicker than heavy cream. If a finger is run across the back of the spoon, it will leave a well-defined track. Immediately remove it from the heat and pour it into the strainer, scraping up the thickened custard that has settled on the bottom of the pan. Add the heavy cream and vanilla pod.

Cool the mixture by setting the bowl in a larger bowl of ice water or the refrigerator until cold, at least 2 hours, preferably overnight.

Stir in the optional vodka. Remove the vanilla pod (rinse and dry for future use) and freeze the mixture in an ice cream maker. Allow the ice cream to ripen for at least 2 hours in the freezer before serving. If it has been held longer and is very hard, allow it to sit refrigerated or at room temperature until softened and creamy.

STORE

Frozen, up to 1 week. The ice cream has the best texture within 3 days of freezing but with the vodka will maintain its texture for up to a week.

POINTERS FOR SUCCESS

∾ See page 223.

∾ Heating the syrup to 380°F. makes a very deep caramel without being bitter. Avoid going higher. If you don't have an accurate thermometer, a porcelain spoon will show you just how dark the caramel is getting (it's difficult to discern against most other surfaces). Taking caramel to a temperature this high requires the right equipment and/or experience with making caramel.

---

*Heat until small bubbles form around the perimeter.

UNDERSTANDING

The extra sugar, fat, and protein from the milk give this ice cream an exceptionally creamy texture.

PISTACHIO ICE CREAM

When I was a child, we went to Howard Johnson's for ice cream, and pistachio was always my choice. Of course the secret to making the most full flavored pistachio ice cream is using the finest-quality pistachio nuts and making a custard base with the right proportion of cream to milk. Here is the recipe. Serve it with the chocolate soufflé tartlets or with the apricot pie or tart.

MAKES: ABOUT 4 CUPS (DEPENDING ON THE ICE CREAM MAKER)

INGREDIENTS	MEASURE	WEIGHT	
	VOLUME	OUNCES	GRAMS
pistachio paste (see page 643) or finely ground unsalted blanched pistachio nuts (see page 642)	4½ tablespoons*	2.25 ounces	64 grams
sugar	¾ cup	5.25 ounces	150 grams
6 large egg yolks	7 tablespoons	4 ounces	112 grams
heavy cream	2 liquid cups	16.3 ounces	464 grams
milk	1 liquid cup	8.5 ounces	242 grams
green food color	6 drops	•	•
optional: Pistacha (pistachio liqueur) or kirsch	2 tablespoons + 2 teaspoons 1½ tablespoons	approx. 1 ounce 0.75 ounce	32 grams 21 grams
optional: Cobasan	½ rounded teaspoon	•	•

*½ cup whole nuts (2.6 ounces/76 grams).

In a heavy nonreactive saucepan, mix the pistachio paste, sugar, and yolks.

In a small nonreactive saucepan (or a heatproof glass measure if using a microwave on high power), scald the cream and milk.* Stir a few tablespoons into the pistachio mixture, then gradually add the remainder, stirring constantly. Heat

*Heat until small bubbles form around the perimeter.

the mixture, stirring constantly, to just below the boiling point (170° to 180°F.). Steam will begin to appear and the mixture will be slightly thicker than heavy cream. If a finger is run across the back of the spoon, it will leave a well-defined track. Immediately remove it from the heat and pour it into a bowl, scraping up the thickened cream that has settled on the bottom of the pan. (I like having the texture of the pistachio pieces in the ice cream, but if you prefer it totally smooth, strain it at this point. Either way, the ice cream will still have the pistachio flavor.) Add the green food color.

Cool the mixture in an ice-water bath or the refrigerator until cold, at least 2 hours, preferably overnight.

Stir in the vanilla and the optional Pistacha or kirsch, and Cobasan. Freeze it in an ice cream maker. Allow the ice cream to ripen for at least 2 hours in the freezer before serving. If it has been held longer and is very hard, allow it to sit refrigerated or at room temperature until softened and creamy.

STORE

Frozen, up to 1 week. The ice cream has the best texture within 3 days of freezing but with the liqueur it will maintain its texture for up to a week.

POINTERS FOR SUCCESS

∾ See page 223.

UNDERSTANDING

Two-thirds cream to milk is used instead of the usual three-quarters cream to milk because the pistachio contributes 34 grams of fat, bringing the total to slightly higher than the "plain vanilla" version, even with the decrease in cream.

PEANUT BUTTER ICE CREAM

This ice cream is, of course, for peanut butter lovers—in other words, almost every American—and especially for those who don't like peanut butter's propensity to stick to the roof of one's mouth! There's no way this intensely peanutty, smooth, and creamy ice cream can. The optional Chambord, suggested by my husband, adds a very subtle flavor accent, much in the way that jelly so perfectly complements peanut butter. This ice cream is great with Concord grape pie, cherry pie, and chocolate tarts alike.

MAKES: ABOUT 4 GENEROUS CUPS (DEPENDING ON THE ICE CREAM MAKER)

INGREDIENTS	MEASURE	WEIGHT	
	VOLUME	OUNCES	GRAMS
smooth peanut butter, preferably Jif	9 tablespoons	5 ounces	144 grams
6 large egg yolks	7 tablespoons	4 ounces	112 grams
sugar	¾ cup	5.25 ounces	150 grams
salt	a pinch	•	•
heavy cream	1½ liquid cups	approx. 12 ounces	348 grams
milk	1½ liquid cups	12.7 ounces	363 grams
optional: Chambord (black raspberry liqueur)	3 tablespoons	1.7 grams	49 grams

Place the peanut butter in a medium mixing bowl. Suspend a fine strainer over it, and have it ready near the range.

In a small heavy nonreactive saucepan, using a wooden spoon, stir together the yolks, sugar, and salt until well blended.

In another small saucepan (or a heatproof glass measure if using a microwave on high power), scald the cream and milk.* Stir a few tablespoons into the yolk mixture, then gradually add the remainder, stirring constantly. Heat the mixture, stirring constantly, to just below the boiling point (170° to 180°F.). Steam will begin to appear and the mixture will be slightly thicker than heavy cream. If a finger is run across the back of the spoon, it will leave a well-defined track. Immediately remove it from the heat and pour it into the strainer, scraping up the thickened cream that has settled on the bottom of the pan.

Whisk the peanut butter into the cream mixture. Set the bowl in a larger bowl of ice water or in the refrigerator until cold, at least 2 hours, preferably overnight.

Stir in the optional Chambord. Freeze in an ice cream maker. Allow the ice cream to ripen for at least 2 hours in the freezer before serving. If it has been held longer and is very hard, allow it to sit refrigerated or at room temperature until softened and creamy.

STORE

Frozen, up to 1 week. The ice cream has the best texture within 3 days of freezing but with the Chambord it will maintain its texture for up to a week.

*Heat until small bubbles form around the perimeter.

POINTERS FOR SUCCESS

◣ See page 223.

UNDERSTANDING

Half cream, half milk is used instead of the usual three-quarters cream to milk because the peanut butter contributes 72 grams of fat, bringing the total to slightly higher than the vanilla ice cream even with the decrease in cream.

Twice the amount of Chambord is used in order to arrive at the same level of alcohol as vodka because vodka is twice the proof.

RED WINE ICE CREAM

I tasted this pale pink, positively haunting ice cream at Vau, one of Berlin's top restaurants, owned by chef–cookbook writer Viehauser, and was utterly intrigued. The chef used Côte-Rôtie, for its body and flavor intensity. The cream base and cold temperature softened its slightly rough edges yet held its perfumed glow. The 25-proof wine also served to keep the texture softer than usual.

This splendid and sophisticated ice cream would enhance many pies and tarts, but its flavor and color would be particularly lovely with currant pie, Concord grape pie, and plum tart.

MAKES: ABOUT 4 CUPS (DEPENDING ON THE ICE CREAM MAKER)

INGREDIENTS	MEASURE	WEIGHT	
	VOLUME	OUNCES	GRAMS
6 large egg yolks	7 tablespoons	4 ounces	112 grams
sugar	½ cup	3.5 grams	100 grams
salt	a pinch	•	•
heavy cream or Crème Fraîche (page 558)	2¼ liquid cups	18.3 ounces	522 grams
nonfat dry milk	1 tablespoon + ½ teaspoon	0.2 ounce	6 grams
optional: Cobasan	½ rounded teaspoon	•	•
red wine, preferably Côte-Rôtie, cabernet, or zinfandel	¾ liquid cup	6 ounces	173 grams

Have a fine strainer suspended over a medium mixing bowl ready near the range.

In a heavy nonreactive saucepan, with a wooden spoon, stir together the yolks, sugar, and salt until well blended.

In a small saucepan (or a heatproof glass measure if using a microwave on high power), stir together the cream and dry milk and scald the mixture.* Stir a few tablespoons into the yolk mixture, then gradually add the remainder, stirring constantly. Heat the mixture, stirring constantly, to just below the boiling point (170° to 180°F.). Steam will begin to appear and the mixture will be slightly thicker than heavy cream. If a finger is run across the back of the spoon, it will leave a well-defined track. Immediately remove it from the heat and pour it into the strainer, scraping up the thickened cream that has settled on the bottom of the pan.

Cool by setting the bowl in a larger bowl of ice water or in the refrigerator until cold, at least 2 hours, preferably overnight.

Stir in the optional Cobasan and the red wine. Freeze in an ice cream maker. Allow the ice cream to ripen for at least 2 hours in the freezer before serving. If it has been held longer and is very hard, allow it to sit refrigerated or at room temperature until softened and creamy.

STORE

Frozen, up to 1 week. The ice cream has the best texture within 3 days of freezing but with the red wine will maintain its texture for up to a week.

POINTERS FOR SUCCESS

∾ See page 223.

UNDERSTANDING

To re-create the ice cream I tasted in Berlin, I simply made my vanilla ice cream base, omitting the vanilla and replacing the milk with an equal volume of red wine. The wine, though not sweet on its own, seemed to make the ice cream sweeter than usual, so I decreased the sugar slightly. The texture was ever so slightly icy because of the absence of the milk protein. I tried adding protein in the form of nonfat dry milk, which helped a great deal, but it was still just the tiniest bit icy, though perfectly acceptable. Adding the Cobasan as well emulsified it perfectly, eliminating the problem completely.

---

*Heat until small bubbles form around the perimeter.

TARTS AND TARTLETS

When people think of tarts, they usually think of a filled bottom crust baked in a fluted tart pan, but actually the tart category encompasses many more shapes and varieties. A tart can indeed be baked in a fluted tart pan, but it can also be baked in a flan ring or free-form on a cookie sheet, in which case it is referred to in French as a *galette* and in Italian as a *crostata*. A long strip of puff pastry baked on a sheet is also referred to as a *tart*. When the pastry is baked in a round pan, it is sometimes referred to as a *gâteau*, French for cake, even though it is made up of filled pastry dough, such as the Gâteau Basque. Other times, it may be referred to as a *torte*. The Engadine Nut Torte (which I call Gâteau Engadine) and the Linzertorte, for example, are also tarts, made up of filled pastry dough, baked in a round pan.

In short, it would seem that any flaky crust, sweet cookie crust, or puff pastry that is not baked in a pie pan falls into the category of tarts. (I refer to small tarts as tartlets to distinguish them from the 9½-inch or larger size.)

Certain desserts that we know as pies, such as Pecan Pie, are difficult to think of as tarts, but there is no reason they can't be baked in a tart pan. A 9-inch pie pan and a 9½-inch tart pan each can contain 4 cups (including the crust, which takes up a little of this volume, depending on how thin it is rolled) and can be used interchangeably.

A tart pan, with its short, straight fluted sides, especially one with a removable bottom, makes it easier to serve a tart than a pie, which is baked in a deeper pan with sloping sides. There are also other advantages to using a tart pan. The fluted sides create an attractive design, whereas with a pie pan, it is necessary to crimp the border to have an attractive appearance. Also, because the sides of the tart pan are essentially vertical as opposed to sloping, the outer edge of a tart has the same amount of filling from bottom to top. In a pie, the sloping side causes the outer edge to contain more crust than filling.

When it comes to ease in serving, however, it is the free-form tart, or galette (or crostata) that wins, because it is entirely flat. When warm or cool, you can simply slide it off the pan onto a cutting board and use a pizza cutter or sharp knife to cut it.

To unmold a tart or tartlet baked in a two-piece tart pan, generally it is best to leave the crust in the pan until it is filled and baked, or chilled, as the pan gives the crust support. When ready to unmold the tart, place it on top of a canister that is smaller than the opening of the tart pan rim. A flaky crust unmolds easily, but a sweet cookie crust unmolds most neatly when heated slightly. Wet a towel with hot water and wring it out well. Apply it to the bottom and sides of the tart pan. Press firmly down on both sides of the tart ring. It should slip away easily. If not, apply more heat. Slip a large pancake turner between the bottom crust and the pan and slide the tart onto a serving plate.

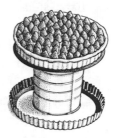

ROLLING, SHAPING, AND PREBAKING FLAKY PIE CRUST FOR 9½- AND 10-INCH TARTS

ROLL THE DOUGH   Remove the dough from the refrigerator. If necessary, allow it to sit for about 10 minutes or until it is soft enough to roll. Using a pastry cloth and sleeve rubbed with flour or two sheets of plastic wrap lightly sprinkled with flour, roll the dough ⅛ inch thick or less and large enough to cut a 12-inch circle, for a 9½-inch tart pan, or 12½ inches for a 10-inch tart pan.

SHAPE THE DOUGH   Use an expandable flan ring or a cardboard template and a sharp knife as a guide to cut the circle. Transfer the dough to the pan by rolling it around the rolling pin, by slipping your hands underneath it, palm sides down, and lifting it into the pan, or by folding it into quarters (see page 12). Press the dough against the fluted sides of the pan. Turn down the edge about ¼ inch so that it extends about ⅛ inch above the top of the pan. Using the back edge of a knife blade held on an angle, make decorative marks all around (see illustrations, page 13). Cover the pastry lightly with plastic wrap and refrigerate it for a minimum of 1 hour and a maximum of 24 hours.

BLIND BAKE THE DOUGH   *Preheat the oven to 425°F. at least 20 minutes before baking.* Line the dough with parchment, pleating it as necessary to fit the pan, or use a large cup-shaped coffee filter. Fill with rice or dried beans, making sure they are pushed up well against the sides of the liner. Place it in the oven and bake for 20 minutes. Lift out the parchment with the rice or beans and prick the bottom of the tart shell all over with the tines of a fork; if using a sticky or runny filling, prick only halfway through the dough. Return it to the oven for 7 to 10 minutes more or until pale golden brown (5 minutes for a partially prebaked crust). Check after 3 minutes and prick again if the upper layer of dough bubbles up.

ROLLING, SHAPING, AND PREBAKING SWEET
COOKIE CRUST FOR 9½- AND 10-INCH TARTS

Spray the pan with Baker's Joy or grease and flour it.

ROLL AND SHAPE THE DOUGH OR PRESS THE DOUGH INTO THE PAN   If the dough has been refrigerated for more than 30 minutes, it will be too cold to roll or press without cracking. It will take at least 40 minutes at room temperature to become malleable. But if you prefer not to wait, use the coarse side of a box grater to disperse the dough evenly into the pan and then press it into place.

Otherwise, let the dough sit until is is malleable, then roll it ⅛ inch thick and large enough to cut an 11-inch circle, for a 9½-inch tart pan, or 11½ inches for a 10-inch tart pan (see page 49) and fit it into the pan (see page 52), or press the dough into the pan.

When the tart pan has been lined, the dough should come to about ⅛ inch above the rim of the pan, as it always falls a little during baking. If necessary, push it up using your fingers.

BAKE THE DOUGH (FREEZE OR BLIND BAKE, PAGE 54)   If the dough is frozen for at least 2 hours or refrigerated for at least 6 hours before baking, it is not necessary to use weights. Make sure that there isn't any dough on the outside of the tart pan to ensure that it will unmold well.

TO BAKE PLAIN SWEET COOKIE TART DOUGH   *Preheat the oven to 425°F. at least 20 minutes before baking.* Bake at 425°F. for 5 minutes. When the dough starts to puff in places, prick it lightly with a fork, then lower the heat to 375°F. and continue baking for 10 to 15 minutes longer or until it turns a pale gold (the edges will be a deeper brown) and feels set but still soft to the touch.

BLIND BAKING   *If using weights,* bake at 425°F. for 5 minutes, then lower the heat to 375°F. and bake for 15 to 20 minutes longer or until set. Lift out the weights with the parchment, prick lightly, and continue baking for 10 to 15 minutes more.

TO BAKE CHOCOLATE COOKIE TART DOUGH   *Preheat the oven to 400°F. at least 20 minutes before baking.* Bake at 400°F. for 5 minutes. When the dough starts to puff in places, prick it lightly with a fork. Lower the heat to 375°F. and bake for 12 to 15 minutes. The dough will deepen in color but should not start to brown, or it will take on a burnt flavor.

If using weights, bake at 400°F. for 5 minutes, then lower the heat to 375°F. and bake for 15 to 20 minutes or until set. (If not set, the dough will stick more to the parchment.) Lift out the weights with the parchment, prick lightly, and continue baking for 10 to 15 minutes more.

ROLLING, SHAPING, AND PREBAKING SWEET COOKIE CRUST FOR 10- BY 2-INCH TART PANS OR 10-INCH SPRINGFORM PANS

Spray the pan with Baker's Joy or grease and flour it.

ROLL AND SHAPE THE DOUGH OR PRESS THE DOUGH INTO THE PAN   If the dough has been refrigerated for more than 30 minutes, it will be too cold to roll or press without cracking. It will take at least 40 minutes at room temperature to become malleable. But if you prefer not to wait, use the coarse side of a box grater to disperse the dough evenly into the pan and then press it into place.

Otherwise, let the dough sit until it is malleable, then roll it ⅛ inch thick (see page 49) and fit it into the pan (see page 52), or press the dough into the pan.

When the tart pan has been lined, the dough should come just to the rim of the pan. Refrigerate or chill the dough for at least 1 hour.

BAKE THE DOUGH   *Preheat the oven to 425°F. at least 20 minutes before baking.* Bake at 425°F. for 5 minutes, then lower the heat to 375°F. and bake for 15 to 20 minutes or until set. Lift out the weights with the parchment, prick lightly, and continue baking for 10 to 15 minutes more, until the crust turns a pale gold (the edges will be a deeper brown) and feels set but still soft to the touch.

ROLLING, SHAPING, AND BAKING SWEET COOKIE CRUST FOR 4-INCH FLAN RINGS

Set the ungreased flan rings on a baking sheet, at least 1 inch apart.

ROLL THE DOUGH   If the dough has been refrigerated for more than 30 minutes, it will be too cold to roll without cracking. It will take at least 40 minutes at room temperature to become malleable.

Roll the dough between lightly floured sheets of plastic wrap to ¹⁄₁₆ inch thick. With a template and knife, cut 5½-inch circles. Or divide the dough and roll each piece separately.

SHAPE THE DOUGH   Drape a circle of dough into each flan ring, easing it in and pressing it gently against the sides. Use a small sharp knife held parallel to the rim of the ring to trim the dough even with the top of the ring (see

illustration.) Cover with plastic wrap and freeze for a minimum of 15 minutes and a maximum of 24 hours before baking.

BAKE THE DOUGH

To bake plain sweet cookie tart dough, *preheat the oven to 425°F. at least 20 minutes before baking.* Bake at 425°F. for 5 minutes. If the centers puff during baking, press them down lightly with your fingertips. Lower the heat to 350°F. and continue baking for 1 to 5 minutes, until the dough turns a pale gold (the edges will be a deeper brown) and feels set but still soft to the touch.

To bake chocolate cookie tart dough, *preheat the oven to 375°F. at least 20 minutes before baking.* Bake at 375°F. for 12 minutes. Check after the first 4 to 5 minutes; if the centers have puffed during baking, press them down lightly with your fingertips. The dough will deepen in color but should not start to brown, or it will take on a burnt flavor.

COOLING TART SHELLS   Use a large pancake turner to slide the tart onto a wire rack to cool. (If you used a flan ring or rings, leave on the baking sheet and set it on a rack.)

FRESH BERRY TART
(*Basic Recipe*)

When fresh berries are at the peak of their season, this tart is the time-honored way to make the most of them. I usually choose the sweet cookie tart crust because it keeps its crumbly/crisp texture so nicely when refrigerated and blends well with the whipped cream–lightened pastry cream and firm, juicy fresh berries. If you are planning to assemble the tart more than an hour ahead, a thin glaze of strained preserves adds a lovely flavor while helping to preserve the crispness of the crust and also provides an attractive sheen. If the fruit is perfectly ripe and sweet, the fruit topping glaze can be omitted.

SERVES: 6 TO 8

INGREDIENTS	MEASURE	WEIGHT	
	VOLUME	OUNCES	GRAMS
Sweet Cookie Tart Crust for a 9½-inch tart (page 56), prebaked and cooled	1 cup	10 ounces	288 grams
optional crust glaze: strained fruit preserves, such as apricot, raspberry, or currant	3 tablespoons	2 ounces	57 grams
Whipped Cream Pastry Cream (page 562)	2 full cups	15.5 ounces	440 grams
fresh berries, rinsed, hulled if necessary, and dried	3 to 4 cups	12 to 16 ounces	340 to 454 grams
optional fruit glaze: strained fruit preserves, such as apricot, raspberry, or currant	⅓ cup	3.5 ounces	100 grams

EQUIPMENT
A 9½-inch fluted tart pan with a removable bottom

Make the dough (page 56). Roll, shape, and prebake it (see pages 50–54). Let cool.

GLAZE THE CRUST (OPTIONAL)

If using preserves with whole fruit or seeds, start with ¼ cup to result in 3 tablespoons of strained glaze, ½ cup to result in ⅓ cup of strained glaze. In a microwave oven, stirring once or twice, or in a small saucepan, stirring constantly, melt the preserves until liquid and bubbling, and strain them.

Brush 3 tablespoons of glaze evenly onto the bottom and sides of the cooled tart crust.

FILL THE TART

A minimum of 1 hour and a maximum of 3 hours ahead, spread the pastry cream evenly into the cooled tart crust. Place the fresh berries decoratively on top.

GLAZE THE BERRIES (OPTIONAL)

Shortly before serving or up to 1 hour ahead, if necessary, reheat the strained preserves slightly to make them fluid enough to brush on the berries.

Brush the glaze evenly over the top of the berries. Unmold the tart (see page 251) and serve.

STORE

Refrigerated, up to 3 hours (without the fruit glaze).

POINTERS FOR SUCCESS

ᔇ If you need to prepare the entire tart several hours ahead of serving, the best glaze to use would be a cassava lemon glaze (page 612).

FRESH STRAWBERRY AND RHUBARB TART

Strawberry and rhubarb is a time-honored combination in a pie, but my husband, Elliott, feels that when the strawberries are cooked, both the wonderful fresh flavor of strawberry and the acerbic wildness of the rhubarb are diminished. I developed this version, which delights us both.

EQUIPMENT
A 9½-inch fluted tart pan with a removable bottom

INGREDIENTS	MEASURE	WEIGHT	
	VOLUME	OUNCES	GRAMS
Basic Flaky Pie Crust for a 9½-inch tart (page 22), prebaked and still warm		12 ounces	340 grams
½ large egg white, lightly beaten	1 tablespoon	0.5 ounce	15 grams
currant jelly	⅓ cup	3.6 ounces	103 grams
rhubarb, preferably strawberry rhubarb, cut into ½-inch pieces*	4 cups	1 pound	454 grams
sugar	⅔ cup	4.6 ounces	132 grams
salt	a pinch	•	•
cornstarch	1 tablespoon	•	9.5 grams
strawberries, rinsed, hulled, dried, and sliced	2 cups (sliced)	8 ounces (sliced)	227 grams

*Or 4 cups individually quick-frozen rhubarb with no added sugar, thawed, liquid reserved. Increase the cornstarch to 2 tablespoons.

Make the dough (page 22). Roll, shape, and prebake it (see page 251). While the crust is still warm, brush it with the egg white (see page 20).

In a small saucepan or a microwave oven, heat the currant jelly until melted and bubbling. Strain it into a small cup. Allow it to cool until no longer hot.

In a heavy medium saucepan, combine the rhubarb, sugar, salt, and cornstarch. Let it stand at room temperature for at least 15 minutes or until the rhubarb exudes some juice.

Bring the mixture to a boil over moderately high heat, stirring constantly. Reduce the heat to low, cover, and simmer, stirring occasionally, until the rhubarb is tender and the liquid thickened, 7 to 10 minutes. Remove it from the heat and allow it to cool without stirring.*

Pour the rhubarb into the pie shell. Arrange the strawberry slices on top in concentric circles, using the smaller slices for the center rings. Up to 1 hour before serving, brush with the reserved currant jelly to glaze the top of the berries. If necessary, warm the jelly to make it slightly fluid.

Unmold the tart (see page 251) and serve.

*I like the rhubarb to have a slight texture. If you prefer a smooth texture, stirring at this point will accomplish it.

STORE

Room temperature, up to 6 hours; refrigerated, up to 2 days.

POINTERS FOR SUCCESS

∽ The currant jelly glaze adds a lovely sweet/tart flavor to the berries, but it will start to liquefy when brushed on cut slices of berries if it is left to stand too long. If you need to glaze the berries several hours ahead of serving, the best glaze to use would be a cassava lemon glaze (page 612).

BLUEBERRY TART WITH LEMON CURD

I n addition to being delicious, this tart also provides several textural contrasts: a flaky, crunchy crust; creamy lemon filling; and burst-in-the-mouth berry topping. It is also beautiful to behold because though the berries do not cook or begin to break down, they turn dark blue from contact with the hot glaze.

OVEN TEMPERATURE: 300°F. • BAKING TIME: 7 TO 10 MINUTES   SERVES: 6

INGREDIENTS	MEASURE	WEIGHT	
	VOLUME	OUNCES	GRAMS
Basic Flaky Pie Crust for a 9½-inch tart (page 22), prebaked and still warm		12 ounces	340 grams
½ large egg white, lightly beaten	1 tablespoon ·	0.5 ounce	15 grams
1 recipe Classic Lemon Curd (page 568)	1 cup + 2½ tablespoons	11 ounces	312 grams
Blueberry Topping fresh blueberries, rinsed and dried	(3 cups) 3 cups	14 ounces	400 grams
arrowroot or cornstarch	1 tablespoon	0.33 ounce	9.5 grams
sugar	⅓ cup	2.3 ounces	66 grams
water	½ liquid cup	4 ounces	118 grams
freshly squeezed lemon juice	1½ teaspoons	•	8 grams

EQUIPMENT

A 9½-inch fluted tart pan with a removable bottom

Make the dough (page 22). Roll, shape, and prebake it (see page 251). While the crust is still warm, brush it with the egg white (see page 56).

Preheat the oven to 300°F. at least 15 minutes before baking the tart. Set an oven rack in the middle of the oven before preheating.

Spread the lemon curd smoothly in the prebaked tart shell and bake for 7 to 10 minutes. The curd should not begin to color, but should barely jiggle when the pan is moved gently from side to side. Remove the tart to a rack and cool.

PREPARE THE BLUEBERRY TOPPING

Place the berries in a bowl.

In a medium saucepan, stir together the arrowroot or cornstarch and sugar. Stir in the water and lemon juice and heat, stirring constantly, until the mixture is clear and thickened. With arrowroot, this will happen before the boil; with cornstarch, the mixture must reach a full rolling boil and boil for 30 seconds. Remove the pan from the heat and add the blueberries all at once, tossing until coated with glaze. The berries will turn a bright blue. Empty the berries into a colander or strainer suspended over a bowl, to drain away any excess glaze. (Save this glaze in case more is needed.)

Gently spoon the glazed berries evenly on top of the lemon curd. Cool completely. If there are any dry spots on the berries, touch them up with the reserved glaze.

Unmold the tart (see page 251) and serve.

STORE

Room temperature or refrigerated, up to 2 days.

NOTE

For a 9-inch pie, use the same amount of lemon curd but two thirds the recipe for the blueberry topping, as follows:

INGREDIENTS	MEASURE	WEIGHT	
	VOLUME	OUNCES	GRAMS
Blueberry Topping	(2½ cups)	•	•
fresh blueberries, rinsed and dried	2½ cups	10 ounces	284 grams
arrowroot or cornstarch	2 teaspoons	•	6 grams
sugar	¼ cup	1.75 ounces	50 grams
water	⅓ liquid cup	2.75 ounces	79 grams
freshly squeezed lemon juice	1 teaspoon	•	5 grams

UNDERSTANDING

The tart is baked briefly to set the curd for ease in slicing. (The stirring process when cooking the curd separates the protein bonds in the yolk, and the undisturbed baking heat allows them to reconnect.) This additional heat does not change the silkiness of the texture.

VARIATION

Lemon Tartlets: use six 4-inch flan rings (cut the dough circles 5½ inches) and prebake. Make 1½ times the lemon curd and omit the blueberry topping. Garnish with thin lemon slices before baking 5 minutes until the curd barely jiggles. (For a 9½-inch tart, triple the lemon curd.)

PEAR TART WITH ALMOND CREAM

I n this luscious tart, juicy slices of poached pear, glistening with the reduced pear poaching syrup glaze, are nestled in baked almond cream and encased in flaky pastry. This tart is easy to make and heavenly to eat.

EQUIPMENT
A 10-inch fluted tart pan with a removable bottom

Make the dough (page 23). Roll, shape, and prebake it (see page 251). Let cool.

POACH THE PEARS
Peel, halve, and core the pears just before you poach them so that they do not darken.

In a nonreactive 10-inch skillet just large enough to hold the pears in a single layer, combine the water, lemon juice, eau-de-vie, sugar, and vanilla bean and stir to dissolve the sugar. Place the pears, hollow side down, in the pan and bring the liquid to a boil. Place a round of parchment on top of the pears. Simmer over low heat, tightly covered, for 8 to 10 minutes or until a cake tester inserted in thickest part of a pear enters easily. The pears should still be slightly firm. Remove the pan from the heat and cool, covered only by the parchment. It will take about 1 hour to cool completely.

The pears can be used immediately, but they develop more flavor if allowed to sit in the poaching liquid for at least 24 hours and up to 3 days. Transfer the pears and their liquid to a bowl small enough so that the pears are covered with liquid. Cover it tightly and refrigerate until ready to use.

MAKE THE ALMOND CREAM FILLING
In a food processor fitted with the metal blade, place the almonds, sugar, and flour and process until the almonds are very fine. Empty the mixture into a bowl and set aside.

In a medium mixing bowl, beat the butter until creamy. Beat in about ½ cup of the nut mixture until incorporated. Beat in 1 egg along with another ½ cup of the nut mixture. Then beat in the second egg along with the remaining nut mixture

OVEN TEMPERATURE: 350°F. • BAKING TIME: 30 MINUTES   SERVES: 6

INGREDIENTS	MEASURE	WEIGHT	
	VOLUME	OUNCES	GRAMS
Basic Flaky Pie Crust for a 10-inch tart (page 23), prebaked and cooled		12 ounces	340 grams
Poached Pears 3 large ripe but firm pears, such as Bartlett or Bosc		approx. 1¾ pounds	794 grams
water	2¼ liquid cups	18.75 ounces	531 grams
freshly squeezed lemon juice	1 tablespoon	0.5 ounce	15.6 grams
Poire William eau-de-vie	3 tablespoons	1.5 ounces	42 grams
sugar	¼ cup + 2 tablespoons	2.6 ounces	75 grams
vanilla bean, split lengthwise	1½ inches	•	•
Almond Cream	(1¾ cups)	(14 ounces)	(400 grams)
sliced blanched almonds	1 generous cup	3.5 ounces	100 grams
sugar	½ cup	3.5 ounces	100 grams
bleached all-purpose flour	2 tablespoons	0.6 ounce	18 grams
unsalted butter, softened	7 tablespoons	3.5 ounces	100 grams
2 large eggs, at room temperature	3 fluid ounces	3.5 ounces (weighed without the shells)	100 grams
pure vanilla extract	½ teaspoon	•	•
Pear Glaze reserved syrup from poaching pears	¾ cup	•	•
cassava or arrowroot or cornstarch	1 teaspoon ¾ teaspoon	• •	2.5 grams •

until incorporated. Beat in the vanilla. Refrigerate until about 10 minutes before assembling the tart.

   Preheat the oven to 350°F. at least 15 minutes before baking. Set an oven rack at the middle level before preheating.

ASSEMBLE THE TART

Drain the pears well on paper towels, rounded sides up, reserving the poaching liquid and vanilla bean. Using a thin sharp knife, slice each pear crosswise into thin slices, without slicing all the way through to the bottom. Press gently on top of each pear to fan the slices slightly.

Spread the almond cream evenly in the cooled baked tart shell.

Use a triangular tart cutter or pancake turner to lift each pear and position it on top of the almond cream, pointed ends facing in and meeting at the center.

Bake for 30 minutes or until the almond cream puffs slightly, surrounding the pears, and turns golden brown. When pressed very lightly with a fingertip, the almond cream will spring back. Remove the tart to a wire rack to cool.

MAKE THE GLAZE

Measure out ¾ cup of the poaching syrup. Remove the vanilla bean and scrape the seeds into the syrup.

In a small saucepan, or a 4-cup heatproof liquid measure in a microwave on high (about 10 minutes), reduce the syrup to ¼ cup. Cool to room temperature.

Add the cassava, arrowroot, or cornstarch to the reduced poaching liquid. Stir until dissolved; then cook briefly over medium heat, stirring constantly, until thickened and translucent. With arrowroot, this will happen before the liquid comes to a boil; with cassava, the liquid must come to a full boil and simmer for a few seconds; with cornstarch, the liquid must reach a full boil and simmer for about 20 seconds. Remove the pan from the heat and immediately pour the glaze into a small cup. Use a clean artist's brush or pastry feather to coat the pears well with glaze. Brush the remaining glaze onto the almond filling.

Unmold the tart (see page 251) and serve. The center will be slightly creamy.

STORE

Room temperature, up to 1 day; refrigerated, up to 3 days; allow the tart to come to room temperature before serving. (The almond cream can be made ahead and refrigerated for 1 week or frozen for 1 month.)

POINTERS FOR SUCCESS

ↄ The parchment keeps the tops of the pears moistened while cooking and cooling and prevents browning from oxidation (exposure to air).

ↄ The tart shell must be fully baked to ensure that even the bottom stays crisp after baking with the almond cream.

ↄ To prevent separation while mixing, the butter and eggs for the almond cream must not be cold.

ↄ A trick to ensure that, when slicing the pears, the knife will not go all the way through is to place two thin pieces of cardboard on either side of the pear so that the knife blade cannot quite reach the slicing surface.

APPLE TART WITH WALNUT CREAM

Apple and walnut have a natural affinity the way pear and almond do. In this tart, the apples are poached, sliced, and set into the walnut cream, which is encased in flaky pastry. A light touch of cinnamon, added to the poaching syrup for the apples and the walnut cream, adds yet another compatible dimension. The tiny vanilla seeds in the glaze made from the reduced poaching syrup lend a natural and lovely design element when brushed on the apples.

OVEN TEMPERATURE: 350°F. • BAKING TIME: 30 MINUTES   SERVES: 6

INGREDIENTS	MEASURE	WEIGHT	
	VOLUME	OUNCES	GRAMS
Basic Flaky Pie Crust for a 10-inch tart (page 22), prebaked and cooled		12 ounces	340 grams
Poached Apples 3 large firm-textured tart baking apples, such as Golden Delicious, Greening, or Granny Smith		approx. 1¼ pounds	567 grams
water	2¼ liquid cups	18.75 ounces	531 grams
freshly squeezed lemon juice	1 tablespoon	0.5 ounce	16 grams
sugar	¼ cup + 2 tablespoons	2.6 ounces	75 grams
vanilla bean, split lengthwise	1½ inches	•	•
½ cinnamon stick	•	•	•
Walnut Cream Filling	(1¾ cups)	(14 ounces)	(400 grams)
walnut halves, lightly toasted	1 cup	3.5 ounces	100 grams
sugar	½ cup	3.5 ounces	100 grams
bleached all-purpose flour	2 tablespoons	0.6 ounce	18 grams
ground cinnamon	½ teaspoon	•	•
unsalted butter, softened	7 tablespoons	3.5 ounces	100 grams
2 large eggs, at room temperature	3 fluid ounces	3.5 ounces (weighed without the shells)	100 grams
pure vanilla extract	½ teaspoon	•	•

EQUIPMENT
A 10-inch fluted tart pan with a removable bottom

Make the dough (page 22). Roll, shape, and prebake it (see page 251). Let cool.

POACH THE APPLES
Peel, halve, and core the apples just before you poach them so that they do not darken.

In a nonreactive skillet just large enough to hold the apples in a single layer, combine the water, lemon juice, sugar, vanilla bean, and cinnamon stick and stir to dissolve the sugar. Add the apples, rounded sides down, and bring the liquid to a boil. Place a round of parchment on top of the apples. Simmer over low heat, tightly covered, for 6 minutes. Turn the apples and continue simmering for 4 to 6 minutes or until a cake tester inserted in thickest part of an apple enters easily. The apples should still be slightly firm. Remove the pan from the heat and cool, covered only by the parchment. It will take about an hour to cool.

The apples can be used immediately, but they develop more flavor if allowed to sit in the poaching liquid for at least 24 hours and up to 3 days. Transfer the apples and their liquid to a bowl small enough so that the apples are covered by the liquid. Cover it tightly and refrigerate until ready to use.

MAKE THE WALNUT CREAM FILLING
In a food processor fitted with the metal blade, place the walnuts, sugar, flour, and cinnamon and process until the walnuts are very fine. Empty the mixture into a bowl and set it aside.

In a medium mixing bowl, beat the butter until creamy. Beat in about ½ cup of the nut mixture until incorporated. Beat in 1 egg along with another ½ cup of the nut mixture. Then beat in the second egg along with the remaining nut mixture until incorporated. Beat in the vanilla. Refrigerate until about 10 minutes before assembling the tart.

Preheat the oven to 350°F. at least 15 minutes before baking. Set an oven rack at the middle level before preheating.

ASSEMBLE THE TART
Drain the apples well on paper towels, rounded sides up, reserving the poaching liquid and vanilla bean. Discard the cinnamon stick. Using a sharp thin knife, slice each apple crosswise into thin slices, without slicing all the way through to the bottom. Press gently on the top of each apple to fan the slices slightly.

Spread the walnut cream evenly in the cooled baked tart shell.

Use a triangular tart cutter or pancake turner to lift each apple and position it on top of the walnut cream.

Bake for 30 minutes or until the walnut cream puffs slightly, surrounding the apples, and turns golden brown. When pressed very lightly with a fingertip, the walnut cream will spring back. Remove the tart to a wire rack to cool.

MAKE THE GLAZE

INGREDIENTS	MEASURE	WEIGHT	
	VOLUME	OUNCES	GRAMS
Apple Glaze reserved syrup from poaching	¾ cup	•	•
cassava or arrowroot or cornstarch	1 teaspoon ¾ teaspoon	• •	2.5 grams •

Measure out ¾ cup of the poaching syrup. Remove the vanilla bean and scrape the seeds into the syrup.

In a small saucepan, or a 4-cup heatproof liquid measure if using a microwave on high power (about 10 minutes), reduce the liquid to ¼ cup. Cool to room temperature. Add the cassava, arrowroot, or cornstarch to the reduced poaching liquid. Stir until dissolved; then cook, stirring constantly, over medium heat until thickened and translucent. With arrowroot, this will happen before the liquid comes to a boil; with cassava, the liquid must come to a full boil and simmer for a few seconds; with cornstarch, the liquid must reach a full boil and simmer for about 20 seconds. Remove from the heat and immediately pour the glaze into a small cup. Use a clean artist's brush or pastry feather to coat the apples well with glaze. Brush the remaining glaze onto the walnut filling.

Unmold the tart (see page 251) and serve. The center will be slightly creamy.

STORE

Room temperature, up to 1 day; refrigerated, up to 3 days; allow the tart to come to room temperature before serving. (The walnut cream can be made ahead and refrigerated for 1 week or frozen for 1 month.)

POINTERS FOR SUCCESS

∾ See also Pear Tart with Almond Cream, (page 260).

∾ The apples are turned halfway through poaching because when the rounded tops are down, less of the sides come into contact with the pan, so they don't cook as evenly. The apples cool in the syrup top sides up to keep them from flattening. They do not continue to soften during cooling, so they should be cooked just until tender but not undercooked.

PEACHES AND CREAM TART

Thus elegant yet homey tart has long been a favorite and is as good a reason as any I know to look forward to peach season. The filling is full of the fresh flavor of peaches and rich complexity of juicy, creamy, and crispy textures. The cream and egg yolk topping cloaks the peaches with a film of creamy golden brown custard.

OVEN TEMPERATURE: 400°F. • BAKING TIME: 35 TO 45 MINUTES   SERVES: 6

INGREDIENTS	MEASURE	WEIGHT	
	VOLUME	OUNCES	GRAMS
Sweet Nut Cookie Tart Crust, made with almonds, for a 9½-inch tart (page 59), partially prebaked	1 cup	10 ounces	288 grams
peach or apricot preserves	3 tablespoons	2.25 ounces	64 grams
sugar	⅔ cup	4.5 ounces	132 grams
ground cinnamon	1½ teaspoons	•	•
1½ pounds firm ripe peaches (4 to 5), peeled, pitted, and sliced*	approx. 3½ cups (sliced)	1¼ pounds (sliced)	567 grams
2 large egg yolks	2 tablespoons + 1 teaspoon	1.25 ounces	37 grams
heavy cream	½ liquid cup	4 ounces	116 grams
sour cream	½ cup	4.25 ounces	121 grams
pure vanilla extract	½ teaspoon	•	2 grams

*Or one 20-ounce bag individually quick-frozen peach slices, with no added sugar (such as Big Valley); do not defrost. To peel fresh peaches, place them in boiling water for 1 minute. Drain and rinse with cold water. The peels should slip off easily.

EQUIPMENT
A 9½-inch fluted tart pan with a removable bottom

Make the dough (page 59). Press it into the pan (be sure that it is at least ⅛ inch higher than the sides of the pan) and partially prebake it (see page 252).

Preheat the oven to 400°F. at least 20 minutes before baking the tart. Set an oven rack just below or at the middle of the oven before preheating.

In a small saucepan or in a small heatproof glass measure, if using the microwave, heat the preserves until they are melted and bubbling. Strain them into a small bowl. Brush the preserves onto the bottom and sides of the baked pastry shell.

Mix together the sugar and cinnamon.

Arrange the peaches in overlapping circles in the tart shell, sprinkling the sugar mixture on top of each layer. (Reserve any juice from the peaches.) Protect the pastry edges with a foil ring (see page 19). Bake for 15 minutes. (If using frozen peaches, bake for 25 to 30 minutes or until juices are exuded and the peaches are almost tender when pierced with a skewer.)

In a small bowl, whisk together the egg yolks, heavy cream, sour cream, vanilla, and any reserved peach juice. Pour this mixture on top of the peaches and continue baking for 20 to 30 minutes more or until the custard is golden brown.

Unmold the tart (see page 251) and serve warm or at room temperature. (Do not unmold the tart while still hot.)

STORE

Refrigerated, up to 2 days.

UNDERSTANDING

The acid in the peach juices keeps the custard from curdling at the higher than usual baking temperature.

LOVE FOR THREE ORANGES
(Fresh Orange Tart)

The name for this tart comes from the Prokofiev opera, which I remember going to as a child with my mother. The memory of it came back to me when I discovered that three different varieties of oranges were necessary to create the intense sweet/sour, tangy orange sour ball flavor I was searching for in this tart: Seville, a bitter orange, is ideal for the curd; navel, with its thick skin, provides the best zest for the curd and the firmest, most attractive slices; and Valencia provides the most juice for making the glaze.

The tart consists of a cookie crust filled with a layer of orange curd, topped with a thin layer of sponge cake, and adorned by overlapping thin slices of fresh orange. The sponge cake keeps the orange sections from sliding on the curd and catches all of the delicious juices. Caramelized sugar deglazed with orange liqueur gives a rich burnished red-tinged glaze to the orange slices.

This tart is very refreshing but rich and satisfying at the same time. It is a production of complexity but worth every moment of work. The different components can be made ahead over the space of several days. If you want to make a time-saving compromise, use canned mandarin orange segments instead of peeling, sectioning, and slicing the fresh oranges, the most time-consuming part of this dessert.

My friend Caryl Lee, on first tasting this tart, called to tell me afterward that the taste lasted for three hours! She didn't want to eat anything more because she didn't want to lose the taste. There is no testament better than that.

SERVES: 8 TO 10

INGREDIENTS	MEASURE	WEIGHT	
	VOLUME	OUNCES	GRAMS
Sweet Cookie Tart Crust for a 10-inch tart (page 56), prebaked and cooled	1 generous cup	10.75 ounces	307 grams
4 navel oranges*		2⅔ pounds	1 kg 206 grams
Caramel Syrup			
sugar	½ cup	3.5 ounces	100 grams
water	2 tablespoons	1 ounce	30 grams
Cointreau	¼ liquid cup	approx. 2 ounces	61 grams
freshly squeezed orange juice (from about 3 Valencia oranges)	1 liquid cup	8.5 ounces	242 grams
grenadine	2 teaspoons	•	•
Orange Curd Cream One 8½- to 9-inch by ¼-inch Light Sponge Cake Layer (page 583)†		•	•
gelatin	1 teaspoon	•	3 grams
water	1 tablespoon	0.5 ounce	15 grams
Bitter Orange Curd (page 569)	1 cup + 2 tablespoons	10.25 ounces	296 grams
heavy cream	½ cup	4 ounces	116 grams

*Or two 15-ounce cans of Mandarin orange segments, drained.

†Either yellow or chocolate. You can replace this with packaged angel food or sponge cake.

EQUIPMENT
A 10-inch fluted tart pan with a removable bottom

Make the dough (page 56). Roll and shape it or press it into the pan and prebake it (see page 252). Let cool.

Advance preparation: Macerate the oranges for 24 hours and up to 3 days ahead.
Suggested work plan
Day 1: Make the caramel syrup. Slice and marinate the oranges. Make the cake.
Day 2: Make the orange curd. Make, roll out, and freeze or chill the crust.
Day 3: Prebake the crust. Drain the orange slices and make the glaze. Make the orange curd cream. Assemble the tart.

Chill a 4-cup bowl for the orange curd cream.

Using a zester or grater, remove enough of the zest from one of the navel oranges to equal 4 teaspoons. Set this aside, covered, to use for the orange curd.

MAKE THE ORANGE SLICES

Peel the oranges. With a small very sharp paring knife, cut the ends from the 3 navel oranges and cut away all the peel and white pith from the outside of the oranges. Remove the individual sections of oranges by slicing along either side of each membrane, starting at the outside of the orange and ending at the center. Slice each section into slices no thicker than ¼ inch, preferably ⅛ inch, working over a nonreactive 4-cup or larger bowl to collect the juice. You should have about 3 cups of sliced orange sections. Carefully, so that they stay whole, place them in the bowl. Set aside.

MAKE THE CARAMEL SYRUP

In a medium saucepan, stir together the sugar and water until all of the sugar is moistened and then bring the mixture to a boil, stirring constantly. Stop stirring and continue cooking until the syrup is a deep amber (360°F.). Remove it at once from the heat, preferably to the sink, and, using a long ladle held at arm's length in case of splattering, slowly pour in the Cointreau. When the liquid stops fizzling, add the orange juice and grenadine. Return it to the heat and simmer for 3 to 5 minutes, stirring occasionally to dissolve any hardened syrup. (There will be about 1⅓ cups of syrup.)

Pour the hot syrup over the orange slices. Cover the bowl tightly with plastic wrap and cool to room temperature. Refrigerate for at least 24 hours and up to 3 days.

MAKE THE GLAZE

At least 1 hour and up to 2 hours before assembling the tart, drain the liquid from the orange slices into a greased 4-cup heatproof measure, if using a microwave, or a medium saucepan. There will be 1½ to 1¾ cups. Set the orange slices on waxed paper, in a single layer, and leave uncovered.

In the microwave, on high power, reduce the liquid to ½ cup, about 20 minutes, or, if using a saucepan, cook over medium-high heat, swirling the pan occasionally to prevent scorching. The syrup will darken and become full of thick bubbles. Cool completely.

ASSEMBLE THE TART
Have the baked sponge layer ready.

**AT LEAST 3 HOURS BEFORE SERVING,
MAKE THE ORANGE CURD CREAM**
In a small heatproof measuring cup, place the gelatin and water and allow to sit for 5 minutes. Set the cup in a pan of simmering water for a few minutes, stirring occasionally, until the gelatin is dissolved (or microwave on high power for a few seconds, stirring once or twice). Set aside briefly, only while you beat the cream, so that it stays warm, or it will lump when added to the cream.

Place the orange curd in a large bowl. In the chilled mixing bowl, beat the cream until it begins to thicken and the beater marks begin to appear distinctly. Gradually beat in the warm gelatin mixture and beat just until stiff peaks form when the beater is raised. With a wire whisk, immediately fold the whipped cream into the orange curd until uniform in color. (You will have almost 2 cups of orange curd cream.)

Pour the cream into the prebaked pastry crust. With a small angled spatula, spread it evenly in the baked tart shell. Place the cake layer gently on top. Arrange overlapping circles of orange slices on top of the cake, starting at the outside perimeter and having the rounded edge of each slice almost touching the crust. Stir the glaze until smooth and, using a pastry feather or pastry brush, paint the orange slices with the glaze. There will be about 3 tablespoons of glaze left over. Set it aside at room temperature. Refrigerate the tart for at least 2 hours and up to 2 days.

Up to 2 hours before serving time, remove the tart from the refrigerator and apply the remaining glaze. Refrigerate until shortly before serving.

Unmold (page 251) and slice with a sharp thin knife.

STORE
Refrigerated, up to 2 days.

POINTERS FOR SUCCESS
∾ Heat the Valencia oranges (15 seconds in a microwave or 10 minutes in a low oven) and roll them several times back and forth on a counter, pressing them as you roll, before squeezing to release more juice.

∾ Canned mandarin orange sections can be used in place of the fresh with excellent results. As they sometimes vary in thickness, slice any thicker ones in half to make them uniform.

∾ Fold the whipped cream into the orange curd as soon as it is whipped so that the gelatin, which will begin setting from the cold cream, will incorporate smoothly.

UNDERSTANDING
Seville orange zest is unpleasantly bitter and should not be used.

Navel oranges have no seeds and hold together well for slicing. Their skin is thick, making it easier to grate.

For an interesting variation, use blood oranges in place of the Valencia (juice) oranges for the juice and the zest. They will lend their unique, aromatically tart flavor to the glaze and turn the navel orange slices deep red. You will need to brush on the glaze while it is still hot, however, as it will be thicker because of the higher acidity of the juice.

A small amount of gelatin is needed to make the curd cream more firm because the density of the orange slices creates pressure on the cream when the tart is sliced.

KIWI TART WITH LIME CURD

The first time I ate a kiwi was twenty-four years ago in a sailboat off the coast of Maryland. I was astonished by their astringent but luscious flavor—and the fact that they immediately cured my seasickness. The kiwi has so many virtues—it is beautiful to behold, tangy in flavor, and plentiful—that it just about self-destructed through overuse. Time to give kiwis another chance, and this kiwi-lime tart is the perfect place to start. The combination of these two fruits, accented by a fresh blueberry garnish, is an exciting synergy of flavor and color.

SERVES: 6 TO 8

INGREDIENTS	MEASURE	WEIGHT	
	VOLUME	OUNCES	GRAMS
Sweet Cookie Tart for a 9½-inch tart (page 56), prebaked and cooled	1 cup	10 ounces	288 grams
Lime Curd Cream (page 568)	scant 2 cups	approx. 9 ounces	approx. 255 grams
5 kiwis		13.3 ounces	380 grams
blueberries, rinsed and dried	2 tablespoons	•	•
Glaze freshly squeezed lime juice	1 tablespoon	0.5 ounce	16 grams
water	1 tablespoon	0.5 ounce	15 grams
sugar	1 tablespoon + 2 teaspoons	0.75 ounce	21 grams
cassava or arrowroot or cornstarch	¾ teaspoon ½ teaspoon	•	•

EQUIPMENT

A 9½-inch fluted tart pan with a removable bottom

Make the dough (page 56). Roll and shape it or press it into the pan and prebake it (see page 252). Let cool.

Pour the lime curd cream into the prebaked pastry crust and chill for at least 30 minutes.

Peel and slice the kiwis into ¼-inch rounds. Arrange them in slightly overlapping circles over the lime curd cream, starting from the outer edge. Place the blueberries between and on top of the kiwi slices.

MAKE THE GLAZE

In a small saucepan, combine the lime juice, water, sugar, and arrowroot, cassava, or cornstarch and stir until the sugar and starch are dissolved. Cook over medium heat, stirring constantly, until thickened. With arrowroot, this will happen before the liquid comes to a boil; with cassava, this will happen within a few seconds of reaching the boil; with cornstarch, the liquid must come to a boil and simmer for about 20 seconds. Pour the glaze immediately into a heatproof glass measure or bowl. Using a pastry brush or feather, brush the glaze onto the kiwi and blueberries. Refrigerate for at least 1 hour or until shortly before serving.

Unmold (see page 251) and slice with a sharp thin knife.

STORE

Refrigerated, up to 2 days.

MANGO PASSION TART

This is a lush, hearty tart with substantial flavor and texture. Uncut, it resembles a giant rose encased in a golden fluted crust. A cross-section reveals a crisp coconut crust, a layer of passion curd cream, and a scant-half-inch layer of sponge cake, topped with ripe but firm slices of mango, the color of the passion curd. Reddish purple Marionberries make a beautiful and intensely flavorful garnish. This tart would also be delicious made with lemon curd cream and garnished with blackberries.

EQUIPMENT

A 10-inch fluted tart pan with a removable bottom

Make the dough (page 58). Roll and shape it or press it into the pan and prebake it (see page 252). Let cool.

SERVES: 8

INGREDIENTS	MEASURE	WEIGHT	
	VOLUME	OUNCES	GRAMS
Sweet Coconut Cookie Tart Crust for a 10-inch tart (page 58), prebaked and cooled	1 generous cup	10.75 ounces	307 grams
apricot preserves	½ cup	6 ounces	170 grams
Passion Curd Cream (page 571)	scant 2 cups	15.5 ounces	444 grams
one 9- by ½-inch Light Sponge Cake Layer (page 583)*		•	•
dark rum, preferably Myers's	2 tablespoons†	1 ounce	28 grams
1½ mangoes (each weighing about 14 ounces), sliced ½ inch thick or slightly under at their thickest center portion‡	scant 3 cups (sliced)	16.75 ounces (sliced)	475 grams
optional garnish: Marionberries, fresh or frozen	approx. ¼ cup	4 ounces	113 grams

*You can replace this with packaged angel food or sponge cake.

†This results in a very subtle flavor. If you prefer a more pronounced rum flavor, you can use up to ¼ cup without overpowering the other flavors.

‡Use a thin-bladed sharp knife, preferably flexible, and slice the mango directly on the pit.

In a small saucepan over medium-low heat, or in a microwave oven, heat the apricot preserves until melted and bubbling. Strain into a small cup. You will have about ⅓ cup. Use a pastry brush or feather to paint 3 tablespoons of the apricot glaze onto the bottom and sides of the pastry shell. Set the remainder aside, covered.

Pour the passion curd cream into the pastry shell. Spread it evenly.

With a serrated knife, remove the upper crust from the sponge cake. Set the cake in the pastry shell, top side up. Use a pastry brush or feather to brush the rum evenly onto the cake.

Arrange the mango slices in overlapping circles over the cake, starting from the outer edge and placing the curved edges toward the edge of the crust, so the slices resemble a rose. Use the smaller slices for the center. For the very center, curve 1 or 2 slices, making the ends meet, and slip them into the remaining space.

GLAZE THE TART

Reheat the reserved apricot glaze until fluid (a few seconds in the microwave, or, stirring constantly, in a small saucepan). Using a pastry brush or feather, brush the glaze onto the mangoes. Garnish, if desired, with the Marionberries. Refrigerate for at least 1 hour, or until shortly before serving.

Unmold the tart (see page 251) and slice with a sharp thin knife.

STORE

Refrigerated, up to 3 days.

UNDERSTANDING

There is no need to let the curd cream set before placing the cake on top; the curd cream is firm enough to support the cake and fruit but needs to set and firm up before cutting into perfect slices.

PLUM FLAME TART

In this tart, quartered plums are arranged to resemble petals or rich purple flames with flashes of gold from the inside of the fruit. The crust is slightly sweetened, perfumed with lemon, and nicely crunchy, the fruit moist and tart. This is a seasonal dessert, as Italian prune plums are available only in the fall. Choose firm plums that yield only slightly to pressure.

EQUIPMENT
A 9½-inch fluted tart pan with a removable bottom

Make the dough (page 56). Roll and shape it or press it into the pan and prebake it for 7 to 10 minutes or until golden and set but still soft (see page 252), so the plums can be pressed slightly into it.

Preheat the oven to 350°F. at least 15 minutes before baking the tart. Set an oven rack at the lowest level and place a baking stone or baking sheet on it before preheating.

Sprinkle the crust with the cornstarch. Starting at the outside edge, arrange the plums in a circle so that they stand upright, with one pointed end pressing into the base of the crust, the other pointed end up, and the skin side leaning against the side of the crust. After completing one circle, continue in concentric circles,

OVEN TEMPERATURE: 350°F. • BAKING TIME: 45 MINUTES   SERVES: 6

INGREDIENTS	MEASURE	WEIGHT	
	VOLUME	OUNCES	GRAMS
Sweet Cookie Tart Crust for a 9½-inch tart (page 56), partially prebaked	1 cup	10 ounces	288 grams
cornstarch	1 teaspoon	•	•
Italian prune plums, cut lengthwise into quarters and pitted	6 cups (quartered)	2 pounds (quartered)	907 grams
sugar	⅓ cup*	2.3 ounces	66 grams
ground cinnamon	½ teaspoon	•	•
nutmeg, preferably freshly grated	⅛ teaspoon	•	•
apricot preserves	⅓ cup	4 ounces	113 grams
optional: heavy cream, whipped (see pages 551–53)	½ liquid cup	4 ounces	116 grams

*The exact amount depends on the tartness of the fruit. You may want to increase the sugar to ½ cup if the plums are very tart.

fitting in as many plums as possible. If any spaces remain at the end, cut any extra pieces in half to fit into the smaller spaces.

Sprinkle the plums with the sugar, cinnamon, and nutmeg. Bake for 45 minutes or until the edges of the crust are golden brown and the plums are tender when pierced with a skewer. Remove the tart to a rack to cool.

GLAZE THE TART

In a small saucepan, or in a microwave oven, heat the apricot preserves until melted and bubbling. Strain into a small cup. Allow them to cool until no longer hot.

Brush the plums with the melted apricot preserves. Unmold (see page 251) and serve. Garnish with whipped cream, if desired.

STORE

Room temperature or refrigerated, up to 2 days. If desired, the tart can be wrapped tightly before baking and frozen for up to 3 months. Bake the tart still frozen, adding about 15 minutes extra to the baking time.

RASPBERRY AND GRAND MARNIER
CREAM CAKE TART
(*The Hiroko*)

This is a tart with a flaky crust that is filled with whipped cream–lightened pastry cream and fresh fruit, sandwiched between two gossamer sponge cake layers. It is a formal and beautiful dessert whose flavor lives up to its appearance.

My dear Japanese friend and former student Hiroko Ogawa created this stunningly elegant and delicious recipe. She learned the idea of using cake in combination with pastry from a French pastry chef who was living in Japan. I was so taken with the concept I used it to create several other tarts, including Love for Three Oranges (page 267) and Tiramisù Tart (page 212).

SERVES: 8

INGREDIENTS	MEASURE	WEIGHT	
	VOLUME	OUNCES	GRAMS
Sweet Cream Flaky Pie Crust for a 9½-inch tart (page 25), prebaked and cooled		12 ounces	340 grams
seedless raspberry jam	3 tablespoons	2.2 ounces	63 grams
one 8½- to 9-inch by ½-inch Light Sponge Cake Layer (page 583)*		•	•
Grand Marnier†	¼ liquid cup, divided	2 ounces	60 grams
½ recipe Chiboust Cream (page 565)	2¾ cups	14.7 ounces	420 grams
raspberries	1¾ cups, divided	7 ounces	200 grams
heavy cream	1 liquid cup	approx. 8 ounces	232 grams
optional: Cobasan (see page 644)	rounded ¼ teaspoon	•	•
sugar	1 tablespoon	0.5 ounce	12.5 grams
pure vanilla extract	½ teaspoon	•	•
toasted sliced almonds	2 tablespoons	0.3 ounce	10 grams

*Either yellow or chocolate. You can replace this with packaged angel food or sponge cake.

†Framboise (raspberry eau-de-vie) can be substituted if a heightened raspberry flavor is desired.

EQUIPMENT

A 9½-inch fluted tart pan with a removable bottom; optional: a pastry bag or reclosable quart-size freezer bag and a number 7 large star pastry tube

Make the dough (page 25). Roll, shape, and prebake it (see page 251). Let cool.

Chill a large bowl for the whipped cream.

In a microwave oven, stirring once or twice, or in a small saucepan over medium-low heat, stirring constantly, melt the raspberry jam until liquid and bubbling; strain. Brush it evenly onto the bottom and sides of the prebaked pastry.

With a serrated knife, remove the top crust from the cake. Slice the cake horizontally into two ¼-inch-thick layers. Use sharp shears to trim a small amount from the sides of the bottom cake layer (the smaller side, as it tapers) so that it just fits snugly into the pastry shell (this ensures that it will adhere well when cutting and serving). Brush the crust side of the cake bottom with 1 tablespoon of the Grand Marnier and place it crust side down in the pastry shell. Brush the top of the layer with 1 more tablespoon of Grand Marnier.

Spread half of the Chiboust cream evenly over the cake. Arrange 1 cup of the raspberries on top and spread the remaining pastry cream over them, mounding it slightly in the middle.

Trim the second cake layer, measuring to determine the exact size, as the upper part of the tart pan is slightly larger. Brush the side that did not have the crust with 1 tablespoon of the Grand Marnier, place it Grand Marnier side down on top of the pastry cream, and press down gently. Brush the top with the remaining tablespoon of Grand Marnier.

In the chilled bowl, combine the cream, optional Cobasan, and the sugar. Beat the cream until it starts to thicken and the beater marks become visible. Add the vanilla and beat until it forms peaks when the beater is raised.

With a spatula, frost the top of the cake with an even layer of the whipped cream, almost up to, but not touching, the pastry. Spoon the remaining whipped cream into a pastry bag or plastic bag fitted with a number 7 star tube, and pipe two rows of half shells (see page 621) around the border. Place a row of toasted almond slices vertically between the whipped cream decoration and the side of the pastry. This will help keep the pastry crisp. Arrange the remaining ¾ cup of raspberries in the center of the tart. Unmold (see page 251) and slice with a sharp thin knife.

STORE

Room temperature, up to 4 hours; refrigerated, up to 3 days. This tart is best eaten the same day but is still good on the third day.

APPLE GALETTE

This paper-thin, tart, buttery free-form apple pastry, gilded with golden apricot glaze, is a classic of French pastry. The apples are overlapped like the petals of a giant rose. The tart is simple, elegant, light, crisp, and delicious and makes a spectacular centerpiece.

OVEN TEMPERATURE: 400°F. • BAKING TIME: 40 MINUTES   **SERVES: 6 TO 8**

INGREDIENTS	MEASURE	WEIGHT	
	VOLUME	OUNCES	GRAMS
Flaky Cream Cheese Pie Crust for a 14-inch free-form tart (page 30)*		14.3 ounces	406 grams
4 firm-textured tart baking apples (1⅔ pounds), such as Greening, Granny Smith, or Golden Delicious, peeled, cored,† and sliced ⅛ inch thick	5⅓ cups (sliced)	21.25 ounces (sliced)	604 grams
freshly squeezed lemon juice	2 teaspoons	•	•
sugar	¼ cup	1.75 ounces	50 grams
unsalted butter, cut into small pieces	2 tablespoons	1 ounce	28 grams
Optional Glaze apricot preserves	½ cup	6 ounces	170 grams
apricot eau-de-vie (Barack Palinka) or Calvados (apple brandy)	1 tablespoon	0.5 ounce	14 grams

*Omit the baking powder and increase the salt to ¼ teaspoon.
†For attractive slices, first cut the apples in half and use a melon baller to scoop out the cores.

EQUIPMENT
A 12- to 14-inch flat round heavy steel pizza pan or an inverted baking sheet (preferably black)

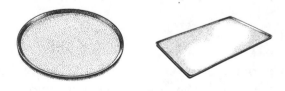

Make the dough (page 30).

Preheat the oven to 400°F. at least 20 minutes before baking. If not using a black pan, plan to bake the galette directly on the oven floor; alternatively, set an oven rack at the lowest level and place a baking stone or cookie sheet on it before preheating.

Using a floured pastry cloth and sleeve rubbed with flour or two large sheets of plastic wrap lightly sprinkled with flour,* roll the dough ⅛ inch thick or less and large enough to cut a 16-inch circle. Use an expandable flan ring or a cardboard template and a sharp knife to cut the circle. If the dough softens, slip it (still on the cloth or plastic wrap) onto a baking sheet and refrigerate it, covered, for about 30 minutes or until firm before lining the pan. The pastry is too large to slip your hands under and support it adequately. To transfer it to the pan, roll it loosely over the rolling pin or dust it lightly with flour and fold in quarters. Leave the overhang.

Sprinkle the apple slices with the lemon juice to keep them from browning. Arrange the apple slices, cored sides facing toward the center, overlapping in concentric circles, starting from the outer edge of the pan. If you run out of room, push a few slices of the fruit closer together and insert the remaining slices evenly in between. Fold the overhanging border of dough over the outer edge of the apples, helping it to pleat softly at even intervals, and brush this dough rim with a little milk or water. Sprinkle the apples and the dough rim with the sugar. (This will give the border a crunchy texture.)

Dot the apples with the pieces of butter and bake for 40 minutes or until the apples are tender when pierced with a skewer and the dough is crisp. Toward the end of baking, with a metal spatula, carefully lift up the crust and check to make sure it is not burning. If it is very dark, lower the heat to 375°F. or remove the tart (without the stone) to a higher rack to finish cooking.

Cool the tart on the pan on a rack until warm, then glaze if desired.

MAKE THE GLAZE (OPTIONAL)

In a saucepan over medium-low heat, heat the apricot preserves until boiling and strain them. Stir in the liqueur and brush the glaze onto the apples. (This creates a shiny finish and piquant taste.)

VARIATION

PEAR GALETTE   Replace the apples with 2 large firm but ripe Bartlett pears (about 12 to 14 ounces total); they should have a pronounced pear aroma. Peel, halve lengthwise, and core the pears. Slice lengthwise into ⅛-inch slices. Arrange the slices, pointed ends toward the center, in overlapping circles on the pastry. To form a center pear-shaped decoration, trim 2 slices to make them shorter but maintain the pear shape and place them, slightly overlapping, curved sides out.

---

*You may have to overlap sheets of plastic wrap to roll the dough large enough.

Cut a small piece of stem or vanilla bean and place it on the pointed end. Use only 2 tablespoons of sugar to sprinkle on top.

STORE

Room temperature, up to 2 days.

NOTE

A half-size galette can be made using a 9-inch pan. Roll the dough less than ⅛ inch thick and large enough to cut an 11-inch circle.

UNDERSTANDING

The flaky cream cheese pie crust is ideal for this tart because of its mellow, buttery flavor and its texture, which is slightly softer than the Basic Flaky Pie Crust (page 22), but the flaky pie crust or one of its variations can be substituted. For the crispiest, flakiest effect of all, puff pastry (page 417) is your dough!

THREE TATINS
(Caramelized Upside-down Tarts)

The Tatin sisters, in their hotel in the Loire Valley of France, made apple tarte Tatin famous at the beginning of the century. Since that time, it has become synonymous with a method of tart baking in which the fruit is caramelized and baked beneath the crust, then inverted before serving. But there are many ways to slice an apple, and I have joined my baking colleagues in trying to achieve a perfect tarte Tatin. I like the apples to be in thick, substantial slices, but not quartered, and the caramel to penetrate them.

When I made my first Tatin, thirty years ago, the prescribed method was to place a layer of sugar and butter in the bottom of a pan, slice in the apples, cover it with the pastry, and bake it, leaving the sugar to caramelize on its own. Then a French chef from Limousin told me making it on top of the stove was the preferred method. He was right. For one thing, caramelizing the sugar before adding the apples enables you to control the degree of caramelization. In addition, basting the apples as they cook in a skillet with the caramel syrup means the caramel will penetrate the fruit, as opposed to merely coating the bottom of it.

I prefer a flaky pie crust to the traditional puff pastry because the steam of the apples destroys the texture of the puff pastry, and puff pastry is not in keeping with the rustic texture of the fruit in this version.

The meltingly tender apples are enough on their own, yet the traditional dollop of crème fraîche brings just the right tang to the buttery richness of the tart. But here's the surprise: Pears make a still more delicious version (see page 282). And wait until you try the peach version (page 426)!

APPLE TATIN

OVEN TEMPERATURE: 425°F. • BAKING TIME: 30 MINUTES   SERVES: 8

INGREDIENTS	MEASURE	WEIGHT	
	VOLUME	OUNCES	GRAMS
½ recipe Basic Flaky Pie Crust for a 9-inch pie and lattice (page 22)		6.8 ounce	195 grams
3 pounds apples, preferably Golden Delicious* (about 7 medium), peeled, cored, and sliced 1 inch thick†	9½ to 10 cups (sliced)	2 pounds 6 to 9 ounces (sliced)	1 kg 90 to 162 grams
freshly squeezed lemon juice	1 tablespoon	0.5 ounce	16 grams
sugar	½ cup	3.5 ounces	100 grams
unsalted butter	4 tablespoons	2 ounces	56 grams
optional: Crème Fraîche (page 558)	1 cup	•	•

*A firm apple that holds its shape is essential. If using Granny Smiths, increase the sugar by 2 tablespoons.

†To core and slice the apples, cut them in half and use a melon baller to scoop out the core. Slice each half into eighths. As you slice the apples, toss occasionally with the sugar mixture to coat.

EQUIPMENT

A 9½-inch copper Tatin pan or 10-inch ovenproof skillet, preferably nonstick, with a domed cover, and a poultry baster

Make the dough (page 22).

In a large bowl, combine the apples, lemon juice, and sugar and toss to mix. Allow to sit for 30 minutes to 1 hour.

Transfer the apples to a colander suspended over a bowl to capture the liquid. The mixture will exude about ½ cup of liquid. Place this liquid and the butter in the pan or skillet and heat over medium heat, stirring often, until bubbling. Continue cooking, stirring often, until the liquid caramelizes and turns a deep amber, about 5 minutes; immediately remove the pan from the heat. (If using a cast-iron pan, remove it from the heat when the liquid turns a light amber, as it will retain the heat and continue cooking.*)

* Use a white porcelain spoon or drop a small amount onto a white plate to check the color, as it will look darker in the pan.

Taking care not to touch the caramel, as it is very hot, arrange the apples in slightly overlapping circles over the caramel, heaping them in the middle. They may be slightly higher than the sides of the pan, but they will sink during cooking. Cook, covered, over medium heat for 10 minutes. Uncover and continue cooking, adjusting the heat to as high as possible to evaporate the juices without letting them spatter out of the pan. Cook, basting constantly with the juices, for 10 minutes or until the apples are almost tender when pierced with a skewer and the juices bubble thickly. (Use a pot holder to hold the baster, as even the rubber bulb becomes very hot.) Use a pancake turner to press down the apples gently to close up large gaps.

Remove the pan from the heat and allow to cool for 20 to 30 minutes so that the sides of the pan are not too hot when you place on the crust.

Preheat the oven to 425°F. at least 20 minutes before baking. Set an oven rack in the middle position before preheating.

Using a pastry cloth and sleeve rubbed with flour, or two sheets of lightly floured plastic wrap, roll the crust to a circle 1¼ inches larger than the diameter of the pan (about 10¾ inches). Fold it in half or fourths and position it evenly over the apples. Tuck the edges down into the apples, using a small metal spatula if necessary. Work quickly before the pastry warms and softens. Cut about 6 steam vents near the center of the crust.

Place the tart in the oven and bake for 30 minutes or until the pastry is golden brown. Allow it to cool 10 minutes before unmolding. The tart will stay warm for about 1 hour after unmolding. If you find it more convenient to bake the tart ahead, it can stay in the pan for several hours and then be reheated and unmolded shortly before serving. To reheat, place it either directly on the stovetop over medium heat for about 3 minutes or in a preheated 350°F. oven for about 10 minutes or until the juices are bubbling around the sides of the tart.

UNMOLD THE TART

Have ready a serving plate with a slight lip to catch any hot juices. Run a small metal spatula around the sides of the pan. Place the serving plate on top and hold the bottom of the tart pan with a pot holder in your strongest hand. With one decisive motion, invert the tart. Allow the pan to rest in place for a few minutes. Then remove the pan; if using a Tatin pan without handles, slip a small metal spatula under one edge and lift off the pan. If a few apple slices have stuck to the bottom of the pan, lift them off with the spatula and place them on the tart.

Serve the tart warm or at room temperature, accompanied by the crème fraîche, if desired.

VARIATIONS

PEAR TATIN   Replace the apples with an equal weight of firm but ripe Bartlett pears; they should have a pronounced pear aroma. Peel the pears, halve lengthwise, core, and slice lengthwise into eighths. Use 1 less tablespoon sugar (total 3 ounces/87.5 grams).

PEACH TATIN   See page 426.

STORE
Room temperature, up to 2 days.

POINTERS FOR SUCCESS
∿ Constant basting causes the caramel syrup to permeate the apples. The juices must reduce to the point where they are bubbling thickly to maintain a crisp pastry crust and to coat the apples thickly.
∿ If desired, after the apples have caramelized, allow them and the pan to cool completely before topping with the crust. When the crust is in place, cover the Tatin tightly with plastic wrap and refrigerate up to 8 hours before baking.

UNDERSTANDING
Apricot does not produce a successful Tatin because the combination of the caramel and natural acidity of the fruit produces an undesirable bitterness. Also, unlike apples and pears, which hold their shape even when slightly overcooked, apricots break down and release too much liquid. Peaches, however, which have the same textural difficulties, meld beautifully with the caramel and make a magnificent Tatin if the fruit is cooked entirely separately from the pastry.

LINZERTORTE

This classic pastry known as Linzertorte, from the town of Linz in Austria, has a pronounced nut flavor because it is made with a nut cookie crust that contains almost double the nuts of the Sweet Nut Cookie Tart Crust (page 58). It is filled with raspberry jam and topped with a lattice and decorative border of small balls made of the same dough. It was originally called a torte because it was baked in a round cake pan, but I like to bake it in a tart pan to give it the fluted edge.

Traditionally, this pastry is made with unskinned almonds (the skin is left on for extra flavor), but I find the more intense hazelnuts (filberts) more exciting. Homemade raspberry jam is tarter than most commercial varieties and makes the most delicious filling.

EQUIPMENT
A 10-inch fluted tart pan with a removable bottom or a 10-inch springform pan, well buttered

INGREDIENTS	MEASURE	WEIGHT	
	VOLUME	OUNCES	GRAMS
unblanched hazelnuts	1 cup	5 ounces	142 grams
unsalted butter	12 tablespoons	6 ounces	170 grams
bleached all-purpose flour	2 cups (dip and sweep method)	10 ounces	284 grams
sugar	⅔ cup	4.6 ounces	132 grams
baking powder	1 teaspoon	•	5 grams
ground cinnamon	1 teaspoon	•	6.5 grams
2 large egg yolks	2 tablespoons	1.3 ounces	37 grams
pure vanilla extract	1 teaspoon	•	4 grams
Raspberry Conserve (page 589) or seedless raspberry jam*	1 cup	10.5 ounces	300 grams
optional: ½ large egg white, lightly beaten	1 tablespoon	0.5 ounce	15 grams

*If using commercial jam, add 2 teaspoons of freshly squeezed lemon juice to it. Seedless raspberry jam still contains a few small seeds that offer desirable texture.

Preheat the oven to 350°F. 15 minutes before baking.

Place the hazelnuts on a baking sheet and bake them, stirring occasionally, for 10 to 12 minutes or until they are golden where the skins have cracked. Cool them to room temperature. Leave the oven on.

FOOD PROCESSOR METHOD

Cut the butter into 1-inch cubes, wrap in plastic wrap, and refrigerate.

In a food processor with the metal blade, process the nuts with ½ cup of the flour until the nuts are finely ground but not powder-fine. Add the rest of the flour, the sugar, baking powder, and cinnamon and process for a few seconds, until evenly mixed. Pulse in the butter until the mixture has the consistency of fine crumbs. Add the egg yolks and vanilla extract and pulse just until the dough begins to hold together (do not allow it to form a ball).

ELECTRIC MIXER METHOD

Allow the butter to soften until it yields to pressure (cut it into pieces so that it softens faster). Finely grate the nuts.

In a medium bowl, whisk together the flour, baking powder, and cinnamon. In a mixing bowl, cream the butter and sugar for about 3 minutes or until light and fluffy. Beat in the egg yolks, then the vanilla extract. At low speed, gradually beat in the flour mixture just until the dough begins to hold together.

FOR BOTH METHODS

Gather the dough into a mass and divide it in two unequal pieces, one slightly larger than the other. Refrigerate the smaller half and press the remainder evenly into the tart pan up to the top edge. If using the springform pan, it should come ¾ inch up the sides. (If the dough is too soft, refrigerate it briefly.) Spread the jam over the pastry (the dough will be about ½ inch higher than the jam). Make a lattice with the refrigerated dough by rolling it between sheets of waxed paper to a rectangle 10 inches by about 5½ inches and cutting it into ten ½-inch strips. Leaving the strips in place, invert a 9-inch pie pan over them, and, using a small sharp knife, cut around the pan. Remove the excess dough and refrigerate it, well wrapped.

Place the strips, still between the waxed paper, on a cookie sheet and freeze for 5 minutes or until firm.

Remove the top sheet of waxed paper and, using a long metal spatula, carefully slide it under the strips to release them. Then carefully lift the strips onto the tart (this will be easy to do as long as the dough remains firm): Lay 5 strips, evenly spaced, across the torte, then turn it a quarter turn and lay 5 more strips across the first strips.

Roll the reserved dough into small balls, using a level measuring teaspoon for each; you will need about 26. Press all along the perimeter of the pastry to form a flat surface for the pastry balls. Place the balls slightly apart around the edge of the pastry, using a fingertip to press a shallow indentation in the pastry beneath each ball and hold them more securely in place. You can also brush a drop of lightly beaten egg white into each indentation to help the balls adhere.

Bake the tart for 35 minutes or until the pastry is golden brown. Allow it to cool until warm before unmolding it (page 251). Linzertorte is especially delicious if served warm.

STORE

Room temperature, up to 1 week; refrigerated, up to 2 weeks; frozen, up to 3 months.

CHRISTMAS CRANBERRY GALETTE

This is a free-form tart with a crisp flaky crust topped with crunchy walnuts and sweet/tart cranberries. It is easy to make and an attractive dessert on a holiday table.

Serve the galette with crème anglaise or vanilla ice cream.

OVEN TEMPERATURE: 400°F. • BAKING TIME: 40 MINUTES   **SERVES: 6 TO 8**

INGREDIENTS	MEASURE	WEIGHT	
	VOLUME	OUNCES	GRAMS
Flaky Cream Cheese Pie Crust for a 14-inch free-form tart (page 30)*		14.3 ounces	406 grams
sugar, preferably superfine[†]	¾ cup, divided	5.25 ounces	150 grams
light brown sugar	¼ cup, packed	2 ounces	54 grams
fresh or frozen cranberries, picked over	3 cups	10.5 ounces	300 grams
walnuts, coarsely chopped	¾ cup	3 ounces	85 grams
powdered sugar	•	•	•

*Omit the baking powder and increase the salt to ¼ teaspoon.

[†]To make your own, simply place granulated sugar in a food processor with the metal blade and process for a few minutes or until fine.

EQUIPMENT
A 12- to 14-inch flat round heavy steel pizza pan or an inverted baking sheet, preferably black

Make the dough (page 30).

MACERATE THE CRANBERRIES
A minimum of 1½ hours and a maximum of 24 hours ahead of baking, in a medium bowl, place the superfine sugar (reserve 1 teaspoon for the border) and the light brown sugar and use your fingertips to combine them and rub out any lumps of brown sugar. Cut each cranberry in half and add them to the sugar mixture. Stir the mixture well and set it aside for 1 hour at room temperature or, preferably, overnight in the refrigerator.

Stir the cranberry mixture well, then stir in the walnuts.

Preheat the oven to 400°F. at least 20 minutes before baking. If not using a black pan, plan to bake the galette directly on the oven floor; alternatively, set an oven rack at the lowest level and place a baking stone or cookie sheet on it before preheating.

Using a floured pastry cloth and rolling pin sleeve rubbed with flour, or two sheets of lightly floured plastic wrap,* roll the pastry to a circle roughly 18 inches in diameter. Using an expandable flan ring or a cardboard template and a sharp knife as a guide, cut out a 16-inch circle. If the dough softens, slip it (still on the cloth or plastic wrap) onto a baking sheet and refrigerate it for about 30 minutes, covered, until firm before lining the pan. The pastry is too large to slip your hands under and support adequately. To transfer it to the pan, roll it loosely over the rolling pin or dust it lightly with flour and fold in quarters. Leave the overhang.

Scatter the cranberry mixture evenly over the dough, covering a 13-inch area and leaving a 1½-inch border. Fold the overhanging border of dough over the outer edge of the cranberries, using your fingers to pleat it loosely at even intervals. Brush this border with a little milk or water and sprinkle on the reserved sugar. (This will give the border a crunchy texture.)

Cut a 10-inch round of foil and place it gently over the cranberries, leaving the crust uncovered. Bake the galette for 30 minutes.

Place a second round of foil large enough to cover the filling and the crust border loosely over the tart and continue baking for about 10 minutes more or until the bottom crust is golden brown. (Slip a small angled metal spatula or flexible knife under the edge of the tart, lifting it slightly, to check doneness.) Cool the tart on the pan on a rack for about 20 minutes or until warm. Dust with powdered sugar.

STORE

Room temperature, up to 2 days.

NOTE

A half-size galette can be made using a 9-inch pan. Roll the dough less than ⅛ inch thick and large enough to cut an 11-inch circle.

UNDERSTANDING

The challenge with this particular berry tart is to keep the cut cranberries from drying out without underbaking the crust, which would make it soggy. The solution is to make a temporary top "crust" from foil and to bake the tart on a baking stone or directly on the floor of the oven.

Cutting the cranberries in half and allowing them to sit with the sugar allows them to absorb the sugar. With their tough outer peel, whole cranberries would retain most of their juices, so they would not dissolve the sugar fully. This would cause the bitterness of the cranberry to stand apart from the sugar, rendering the final effect too bitter and too sweet simultaneously.

The crust must be prepared without baking powder, as the weight of the cranberry/nut mixture would not be sufficient to keep it from puffing.

---

*You may have to overlap sheets of plastic wrap to roll the dough large enough.

DRIED CRANBERRY (OR CHERRY) WALNUT CROSTATA

A sweet cookie crust is wrapped free-form around a filling of dried cranberries and walnuts, leaving a small window in the center through which to view the bright red berries. This foolproof recipe is from my dear friend Marcel Desaulniers, chef-owner of the Trellis Restaurant in Williamsburg, Virginia, and author of several excellent dessert cookbooks.

Dried cherries make a tasty substitute for the cranberries. Since both are readily available, this is an excellent dessert to make any time of year.

OVEN TEMPERATURE: 375°F. • BAKING TIME: 30 MINUTES   **SERVES: 6 TO 8**

INGREDIENTS	MEASURE	WEIGHT	
	VOLUME	OUNCES	GRAMS
Cranberry Walnut Filling walnuts*	1½ cups	5.25 ounces	150 grams
heavy cream	1 liquid cup	approx. 8 ounces	232 grams
sugar	¼ cup	1.75 ounces	50 grams
dried cranberries†	1 cup	3.75 ounces	106 grams
ground cinnamon	¼ teaspoon	•	•
Walnut Crostata Crust walnuts	½ cup	1.75 ounces	50 grams
bleached all-purpose flour	1 cup (dip and sweep method)	5 ounces	142 grams
sugar	1 tablespoon + 1 teaspoon, divided	0.5 ounce	16.6 grams
salt	½ teaspoon	•	•
unsalted butter, cut into 1-tablespoon pieces and chilled	4 tablespoons	2 ounces	57 grams
1 large egg yolk	1 tablespoon + ½ teaspoon	0.65 ounce	18.6 grams
ice water	3 tablespoons	1.5 ounces	44 grams
Glaze 1 large egg yolk, beaten	approx. 1 tablespoon	0.65 ounces	18.6 grams

*Do not be tempted to substitute almonds or pistachios for the walnuts. Almonds are too hard and pistachios too soft.

†Substitute an equal amount of dried cherries, if desired.

EQUIPMENT

A 9-inch pie pan; a 12- to 14-inch round heavy steel pizza pan or an inverted baking sheet; and a sheet of parchment

Preheat the oven to 300°F.

Place the walnuts for both the filling and the crust (2 cups/7 ounces/200 grams) on a cookie sheet and bake them for about 10 minutes or just until they start turning a deeper gold. Place two layers of paper towels on the counter and transfer the nuts to the towels. Use the towels to rub the nuts to remove as much of the outer skins as possible. Allow them to cool completely, then divide them into two batches of ½ cup and about 1½ cups. Set aside the larger amount for the filling and the remaining ½ cup for the dough and topping.

MAKE THE CRANBERRY WALNUT FILLING

Break or coarsely chop the 1½ cups of walnuts.

In a medium saucepan, over medium heat, bring the cream and sugar to a boil, stirring until the sugar is dissolved. Lower the heat and simmer for 6 to 8 minutes, stirring occasionally, until slightly thickened. Remove the pan from the heat and add the cranberries, walnuts, and cinnamon. Stir to combine thoroughly.

Line a 9-inch pie pan with plastic wrap. Transfer the hot filling to the pie pan and spread the mixture evenly over the bottom. Refrigerate until you are ready to assemble the crostata, for a minimum of 2 hours and a maximum of 24 hours. (The mixture seems liquid but firms on chilling and as the walnuts absorb some of the liquid.)

FOOD PROCESSOR METHOD

In a food processor fitted with the metal blade, pulse the ½ cup of walnuts until finely chopped. Remove 2 tablespoons of them, add 1 tablespoon of sugar, and reserve to sprinkle on top of the dough. To the nuts remaining in the processor, add the flour, the remaining teaspoon of sugar, and the salt. Process for a few seconds until mixed. Add the cold butter and pulse until the texture is like coarse meal with some larger pieces of butter.

In a small bowl, whisk together the egg yolk and ice water. Add it to the dough mixture and pulse about 8 times or until the dough begins to come together and there are no dry floury particles.

ELECTRIC MIXER METHOD

Finely chop the ½ cup of nuts. Remove 2 tablespoons of them, add 1 tablespoon of sugar, and reserve to sprinkle on top of the dough. Place the remaining finely chopped walnuts in a mixer bowl, together with the flour, the remaining teaspoon of sugar, and the salt. Mix on low for 30 seconds to combine the ingredients. Add the cold butter and mix on low for 1½ to 2 minutes or until the texture is mealy with some large particles.

In a small bowl, whisk together the egg yolk and ice water. Add it to the dough mixture. Mix on low for 30 seconds to 1 minute or until the dough begins to come together and there are no dry floury pieces.

FOR BOTH METHODS

Empty the dough onto a piece of plastic wrap and knead it, using the plastic wrap, to form a smooth dough. Wrap the dough in the plastic wrap and flatten it into a disc. Refrigerate for 30 minutes, or freeze it for 10 minutes, until firm enough to roll. If it has been refrigerated for several hours, allow it to soften at room temperature for at least 20 minutes or until malleable, to prevent cracking when rolling.)

Preheat the oven to 375°F. at least 20 minutes before baking. Set an oven rack at the middle level before preheating.

Transfer the chilled crostata dough to a sheet of parchment lightly sprinkled with flour. Sprinkle the top of the dough lightly with flour and roll it into a circle about 14 inches in diameter and ¹⁄₁₆ inch thick. If the dough sticks to the rolling pin, cover the dough with a piece of plastic wrap. Slip the dough, still on the parchment, onto the pizza pan or baking sheet. (Remove and discard the plastic wrap.) Invert the chilled cranberry/walnut mixture onto the center of the dough and remove and discard the plastic wrap. Use the parchment to help lift sections of the border of dough, draping it over the filling to enclose all but the center section, which will be about 3½ to 4 inches in diameter. The dough will pleat attractively as it falls into place. Trim away any excess parchment that may extend beyond the baking sheet and refrigerate the crostata for 10 minutes.

GLAZE THE CROSTATA

Brush the top of the dough with the beaten egg yolk. Then sprinkle the dough with the reserved finely chopped walnuts and sugar.

Bake for 30 minutes or until the crust is golden brown and the center cranberry/walnut mixture is bubbling. Remove the crostata to a rack and allow it to cool for 15 minutes before serving. To serve, cut with a sharp thin-bladed knife.

STORE

Room temperature, 2 to 3 days. To reheat, place it in a preheated 350°F. oven for 5 minutes.

POINTERS FOR SUCCESS

∾ The thin outer skins of walnuts are bitter, so removing them results in a purer, more delicious flavor.

∾ Pulsing the nuts instead of processing them keeps them from turning into a paste.

UNDERSTANDING

The walnut crostata crust has less sugar and less butter than the sweet cookie tart dough. It also has 3 tablespoons of water in place of the 2 tablespoons of cream. The smaller amounts of sugar and water make it slightly less fragile and just strong enough to shape as a free-form tart.

GÂTEAU ENGADINE

This is my interpretation of a classic tart from the Swiss mountain region of Engadine. I sampled it, for the first time, with my Swiss friends Rüdi and Vera Sprüngli, in a mountaintop restaurant in Klosters, when Vera gave me her piece to taste. When she noticed my reluctance to return the rest of it, I knew this was a dangerous dessert because I couldn't keep away from it.

This tart resembles a giant circle of Scottish shortbread promising something scrumptious inside. The walnut/caramel filling in the middle complements the sweet cookie crust's tender, crisp texture and buttery flavor perfectly.

OVEN TEMPERATURE: 375°F. • BAKING TIME: 35 TO 45 MINUTES   **SERVES: 8**

INGREDIENTS	MEASURE	WEIGHT	
	VOLUME	OUNCES	GRAMS
double recipe Sweet Cookie Tart Crust (page 56)		28 ounces	811 grams
sugar	1 cup	7 ounces	200 grams
corn syrup	2 tablespoons	1.5 ounces	42 grams
water	¼ liquid cup	2 ounces	59 grams
heavy cream, at room temperature or hot	⅔ liquid cup	approx. 5 ounces	153 grams
walnut halves, lightly toasted* and coarsely broken	2 cups (broken)	8 ounces	227 grams
honey	2 tablespoons	approx. 1.5 ounces	42 grams

*Toast for about 10 minutes in a preheated 350°F. oven, until golden but not brown, lest they become bitter. Rub the nuts between paper towels to remove most of the bitter skins.

EQUIPMENT
An 8- by 2-inch cake pan (optional) and a 9- by 2-inch loose-bottom cake pan or springform pan (the sides can be higher but lower sides are easier for placing the pastry), sprayed with Baker's Joy or greased and floured

Make the dough (page 56).

MAKE THE CARAMEL WALNUT FILLING
In a medium saucepan, preferably with a nonstick finish, stir together the sugar, corn syrup, and water until all of the sugar is moistened and then bring the mixture to a boil, stirring constantly. Stop stirring and continue boiling until the syrup is a deep amber (360°F.). If not using a thermometer, a porcelain spoon or high-temperature heat-resistant spatula makes it easier to see the color. Alternatively, you can use a spoon to dribble a tiny bit onto a white plate. Remove it at once from the heat, preferably to the sink, and, using a long ladle held at arm's length, carefully and slowly pour in the cream. (If the cream is cold, unless it is added slowly, it will harden the caramel and take longer to dissolve.)

When the liquid stops fizzling, return it to the range and simmer for 3 to 5 minutes over low heat, stirring constantly to dissolve any hardened pieces. Gently stir in the walnuts and simmer without stirring for 1 minute, swirling the pan occasionally. Pour the mixture into a lightly greased bowl to stop the cooking and gently stir in the honey.

Allow the bowl of filling to sit on a rack for at least 1½ hours or until completely cool. Avoid stirring to prevent graininess. To speed cooling, you can refrigerate the caramelized nut mixture, but you'll need to keep a close watch on it. Remove it as soon as it has cooled, or it will become too sticky to spread evenly.

Divide the dough in a ratio of two thirds : one third. If it has been refrigerated for several hours or more, it will need to sit for at least 40 minutes or until malleable.

If using the 8-inch cake pan (see illustration) as a mold, roll the larger piece of dough between two sheets of lightly floured plastic wrap to ¼ inch thick and just large enough to cut an 11-inch circle. Remove the upper piece of plastic wrap and set aside. Use an expandable flan ring or a cardboard template and a sharp knife to cut the 11-inch circle. Add the scraps to the remaining piece of dough. Return the plastic wrap to the rolled dough and invert it over the back of the 8-inch cake pan, centering it evenly. If any cracks develop, smooth them together (or wait until transferring the dough to the pan). If the dough softens and gets sticky, refrigerate or freeze it just until it is firm. Peel off the top sheet of plastic wrap and invert the loose-bottom or springform pan over the dough. Then simply invert both pans so that the larger pan is on the bottom and the dough is in it. Remove the cake pan and gently press the dough against the sides of the pan. If necessary, allow the dough to soften at room temperature for a few minutes so that it drapes into the pan. Press it against the sides and push it down so that it comes no higher than 1 inch up the sides. Leave the plastic wrap in place and refrigerate for at least 30 minutes and up to 24 hours.

If not using the 8-inch cake pan, use your fingers to press the dough into the pan instead of rolling it.

Roll the remaining dough between sheets of lightly floured plastic wrap to a little larger than 9 inches in diameter and about ¼ inch thick. Trim it to a circle just a hair under 9 inches across (measure the exact inner diameter of the pan). Chill it for at least 30 minutes, or freeze it for 20 minutes, so that it is firm.

Preheat the oven to 375°F. at least 20 minutes before baking. Set an oven rack at the lowest level before preheating.

Remove the plastic wrap from the pastry-lined pan. Scrape the filling into it and smooth it with a spatula to make it even. If the bottom pastry is very cold, lightly brush the edge of it with water.

Remove the top sheet of the plastic wrap from the pastry circle and use the remaining piece to invert it onto the filling. Remove the plastic. (If the dough is very firm, you can remove both pieces of plastic wrap and use your hands to lift and place it.) Use a fork, preferably a three-tined one, to press the edges together, making a design in the pastry that looks like the rays of the sun. Then prick the top all over, making a design of little holes.

Bake for 35 to 45 minutes or until the pastry is golden. Place the tart on a rack and allow it to cool for at least 30 minutes before unmolding. (After 2 hours, it will still be slightly warm.)

To unmold, if using a loose-bottom pan, see page 251. Or remove the sides of the springform pan. Serve the tart warm or at room temperature. Use a serrated knife to cut it into wedges.

STORE

Room temperature, airtight, up to 1 week.

UNDERSTANDING

Toasting the walnuts helps to remove the bitter skins, making the filling purer and the nuts extra crunchy.

A touch of corn syrup keeps the filling soft and slightly fluid, preventing it from becoming crystallized. Corn syrup lowers the caramelization point of the syrup slightly so that at 360°F. it is similar in color to a sugar syrup made without corn syrup that is cooked to 380°F. If the honey were added at the beginning, it would drop the caramelization still further, to 320°F. A dark caramel is more flavorful up to a point. If it is too dark, it will taste bitter.

Refined sugar rather than unrefined or raw sugar (see page 647) helps to prevent crystallization of the caramel from impurities.

The filling must be chilled so that the butter in the dough does not start to melt until it is baked. This ensures the crispest and finest texture of the pastry.

GÂTEAU BASQUE

When my friend Jim Poris of *Food Arts* begged me to include this recipe, I was confused, because *gâteau* in French means cake. But this is actually two layers of cookie crust with a rum pastry cream in between, and baked in the shape of a cake. Though the pastry cream bakes inside the dough, it stays creamy after baking and the pastry remains crisp. This recipe is from Fifi Arrambide, of the restaurant Les Pyrénées in Saint-Jean-Pied-de-Port in the French Basque country.

OVEN TEMPERATURE: 350°F. • BAKING TIME: 50 TO 60 MINUTES   SERVES: 8

INGREDIENTS	MEASURE	WEIGHT	
	VOLUME	OUNCES	GRAMS
Extra-Sweet Cookie Tart Crust		(16.7 to 18 ounces)	(477 to 515 grams)
blanched sliced almonds	½ cup	1.5 ounces	42 grams
sugar, preferably unrefined (see pages 645–46)	½ cup	3.5 ounces	100 grams
unsalted butter, cut into cubes and chilled	7 tablespoons	3.5 ounces	100 grams
bleached all-purpose flour	1⅓ cups + 1 table-spoon (dip and sweep method)	7 ounces	200 grams
baking powder	1 teaspoon	•	5 grams
salt	⅛ teaspoon	•	•
2 large egg yolks	2 tablespoons + 1 teaspoon	1.3 ounces	37 grams
pure vanilla extract	½ teaspoon	•	•
dark rum	1 tablespoon	0.5 ounce	14 grams
½ recipe Pastry Cream (page 560)	1¼ cups	13.25 ounces	375 grams
optional glaze: ½ large egg, lightly beaten	1½ tablespoons	0.75 ounce	25 grams
optional garnish: bing cherry preserves	about ½ cup	•	•

EQUIPMENT

An 8- by 2-inch cake pan (optional) and a 9- by 2-inch loose-bottom cake pan or springform pan (the sides can be higher but lower sides are easier for placing the pastry), sprayed with Baker's Joy or greased and floured

FOOD PROCESSOR METHOD

In a food processor with the metal blade, pulse the nuts and sugar until the nuts are ground fine. Pulse in the butter until no loose particles of nut/sugar mixture remain. Whisk together the flour, baking powder, and salt and add it to the butter mixture. Pulse about 15 times or until the butter is no larger than small peas.

In a small bowl, lightly beat the yolks and vanilla. Add them to the mixture and pulse just until incorporated, 8 to 10 times.

Dump the mixture into a plastic bag and press it together. Knead it lightly in the bag until it holds together. Divide the dough in a ratio of two thirds : one third and flatten each piece into a disc.

HAND METHOD

Finely grate the nuts. In a medium bowl, stir together the nuts, flour, sugar, baking powder, and salt. With a pastry cutter or two knives, cut in the cold butter until the mixture resembles coarse meal.

In a small bowl, lightly beat the yolks and vanilla. Mix them into the flour mixture until the dough comes together and can be formed into a large ball. Divide the dough in a ratio of two thirds : one third and flatten each piece into a disc.

FOR BOTH METHODS

Wrap each dough disc tightly and chill for at least 30 minutes.

If the dough has been refrigerated for several hours or more, it will need to sit for at least 40 minutes or until it is malleable before rolling.

If using the 8-inch cake pan (see illustration) as a mold, roll the larger piece between two sheets of lightly floured plastic wrap to ⅛ inch thick and just large enough to cut an 11-inch circle. Remove the upper piece of plastic wrap and set aside. Use an expandable flan ring or a cardboard template and a sharp knife to cut the 11-inch circle. Add the scraps to the remaining piece of dough. Return the plastic wrap to the dough and invert it over the back of the 8-inch cake pan, centering it evenly. If any cracks develop, smooth them together (or wait until transferring the dough to the pan). If the dough softens and gets sticky, refrigerate or freeze it just until it is firm. Peel off the top sheet of plastic wrap and invert the loose-bottom or springform pan over it. Then simply invert both pans so that the larger pan is on the bottom and the dough is in it. Remove the cake pan and gently press the dough against the sides of the pan. If necessary, allow the dough to soften at room temperature for a few minutes so that it drapes into the pan. Press it against the sides and push it down so that it comes no higher than 1 inch up the sides. Leave the plastic wrap in place and refrigerate for at least 30 minutes and up to 24 hours.

If not using the 8-inch cake pan, use your fingers to press the dough into the pan instead of rolling it.

Roll the remaining dough between sheets of lightly floured plastic wrap to a little larger than 9 inches in diameter and about ⅛ inch thick. Use an expandable flan ring or a cardboard template and a sharp knife to trim it to a circle just a hair under 9 inches across (measure the exact diameter of the pan). Chill it, still between the plastic wrap, for at least 30 minutes, or freeze it for at least 20 minutes, so that it is very firm.

Preheat the oven to 350°F. at least 15 minutes before baking. Set an oven rack at the lowest level.

Remove the plastic wrap from the pastry-lined pan. Whisk the rum into the pastry cream and spread it into the pastry. Press down the sides of the dough so that it is about ⅛ inch higher than the filling. Lightly brush the edge with water.

Remove the top sheet of plastic wrap from the top pastry and use the remaining piece to invert it onto the filling. Remove the plastic. (If the dough is very firm, you can remove both pieces of plastic wrap and use your hands to lift and place it.) Use a fork, preferably a three-tined one, to press the edges firmly together, making a design in the pastry that looks like the rays of the sun. If desired, paint the surface with the egg glaze. Then prick the top all over, making a design of little holes.

Bake for 50 to 60 minutes or until golden. Place the tart on a rack and allow it to cool for at least 30 minutes before unmolding. (After 2 hours, it will still be slightly warm.)

To unmold, if using a loose-bottom pan, see page 251. Or remove the sides of the springform pan. Serve the tart warm or at room temperature, garnished with the cherry preserves, if desired. Use a serrated knife to cut it into wedges. (It slices beautifully and can be sliced very thin, if desired.)

STORE

Room temperature, up to 1 day.

UNDERSTANDING

This tart is similar in concept to the Gâteau Engadine (page 291). The Engadine is made with a firmer and thicker sweet cookie tart crust and contains caramelized walnuts instead of pastry cream.

Compared to the Sweet Cookie Tart Crust (page 56), this crust has about one and a third times the sugar, about two thirds the butter, and no cream (2 tablespoons plus 2 teaspoons less liquid). The increase in sugar and decrease in liquid are what make it so much more tender; the decrease in butter and the addition of baking powder make it lighter in texture.

BROWNIE PUDDLE
(*with Caramel Variation*)

This brownie, baked in a tart pan, gets its moistness from cream cheese and its fudginess from the best-quality cocoa and chocolate. Little puddles of ganache are poured into holes made in the brownie, after it has baked, with the handle of a wooden spoon. Chocolate doesn't get better than this.

OVEN TEMPERATURE: 325°F. • BAKING TIME: 30 TO 35 MINUTES   **SERVES: 8**

INGREDIENTS	MEASURE	WEIGHT	
	VOLUME	OUNCES	GRAMS
pecan pieces or coarsely chopped pecans	1 cup	4 ounces	113 grams
unsalted butter	14 tablespoons	7 ounces	200 grams
bittersweet chocolate, preferably Lindt Excellence or Valrhona Caracque, broken into squares	one 3-ounce bar	3 ounces	85 grams
unsweetened cocoa, preferably fine-quality Dutch-processed (see page 626)	½ cup + 2 teaspoons (lightly spooned)	1.75 ounces	50 grams
sugar	1 cup + 3 tablespoons	8.3 ounces	238 grams
3 large eggs	4.5 fluid ounces	5.25 ounces (weighed without the shells)	150 grams
pure vanilla extract	2 teaspoons	•	8 grams
cream cheese, cut into pieces	one 3-ounce package	3 ounces	85 grams
all-purpose flour, preferably unbleached	½ cup (dip and sweep method)	2.5 ounces	71 grams
salt	a pinch	•	•
Ganache Puddle bittersweet chocolate (see above), coarsely chopped	⅔ of a 3-ounce bar	2 ounces	56 grams
heavy cream, at room temperature	⅓ liquid cup	2.7 ounces	77 grams

EQUIPMENT

A 9½-inch fluted tart pan with a removable bottom, bottom greased, lined with parchment,* and then lightly sprayed with Baker's Joy or nonstick vegetable spray

Preheat the oven to 325°F at least 15 minutes before baking. Set an oven rack in the middle of the oven before preheating.

Place the pecans on a cookie sheet and toast them, stirring occasionally, for about 10 minutes or just until the color deepens slightly. Cool completely.

In a double boiler over hot water or in microwave-proof bowl, melt the butter and chocolate, stirring two or three times. If using a double boiler, transfer the mixture to a bowl.

Beat the cocoa, then the sugar, into the chocolate mixture, beating until incorporated. (If you are doing this by hand, use a whisk.) Beat in the eggs and vanilla. When incorporated, beat in the cream cheese until only small bits remain. Add the flour and salt and mix only until the flour is fully moistened. Stir in the nuts.

Place the prepared tart pan on a cookie sheet to catch any possible leaks. Scrape the batter into the pan and spread it evenly. It will fill the pan almost to the top.

Bake for 30 to 35 minutes or until the batter has set. A toothpick inserted 1 inch from the side should come out clean. The mixture will puff and rise a little above the sides but sinks on cooling.

MAKE THE GANACHE PUDDLE

While the brownie is baking, prepare the puddle. Melt the chocolate in a double boiler over hot but not simmering water, stirring occasionally, or in a microwave, using 15-second bursts on high power and stirring several times. Add the cream and stir gently until the mixture is smooth and dark. If necessary (if the cream was too cold and the mixture is not entirely smooth), return it to the heat and stir until totally fluid and uniform in color.

As soon as the brownie is removed from the oven, grease the end of a wooden spoon (½-inch diameter) and insert it into the brownie at 1-inch intervals, all the way to the bottom, twisting slightly as you insert and withdraw it, to create 23 to 28 little holes. Using a small spoon or a reclosable freezer bag with a small piece cut off one corner, fill the holes with the ganache until slightly rounded on top (you will need at least ½ teaspoon for each). Place the pan on a wire rack and cool completely. The chocolate puddles will sink in as the brownie cools and more ganache can be added to fill in any depressions as long as the brownie is still warm enough to melt it. (If necessary, you can set the tart under a lamp to heat the ganache puddles and make them smooth.)

*A 9-inch parchment circle is the perfect size because the bottom of the tart pan is slightly smaller, so that the parchment goes a very little way up the sides, preventing any leaking.

Unmold the tart (see page 251). To remove the parchment, refrigerate the tart or allow it to sit at room temperature until the puddles are firm to the touch. Cover a flat plate with plastic wrap, spray it lightly with nonstick vegetable spray, and set it on top of the tart. Invert the tart, peel off the parchment, and reinvert it onto a serving plate.

To serve, use a thin sharp knife to cut wedges.

VARIATIONS

CARAMEL VARIATION Caramel blends perfectly with the chocolate and pecans and is wonderful both at room temperature and refrigerated, when it becomes more sticky and chewy. Make a half recipe of the Caramel Sauce (page 597) and use it in place of the chocolate puddle glaze. It is easiest to pipe it into the holes. The caramel will pipe well when warm or at room temperature.

MOCHA VARIATION Two tablespoons of Medaglia d'Oro instant espresso powder can be added with the cocoa to give the brownie a slightly bitter coffee edge.

STORE

Wrapped tightly in plastic wrap and stored in an airtight container, room temperature, up to 1 week; refrigerated, up to 1 month; frozen, several months. Try it frozen or chilled if you like a chewy brownie, at room temperature for a softer creamier texture.

POINTERS FOR SUCCESS

∿ Make the holes in the brownie for the puddles as soon as it is removed from the oven to prevent the crust from cracking. Fill them as soon as possible so the ganache melts and settles smoothly into the openings.

THE BOULDERS TART

Layers of caramelized macadamia nuts, sour cream custard ganache, whipped cream, and chocolate curls are set in a chocolate cookie crust lined with a fine coating of melted chocolate. Chef Louis Borachaner created this recipe when he was chef at the Boulders resort in Carefree, Arizona.

EQUIPMENT

A 10-inch fluted tart pan with a removable bottom; optional: a pastry bag or reclosable quart-size freezer bag and a large number 9 star pastry tube

SERVES: 8

INGREDIENTS	MEASURE	WEIGHT	
	VOLUME	OUNCES	GRAMS
Bittersweet Chocolate Cookie Tart Crust for a 10-inch tart (page 61), prebaked and cooled	1 generous cup	10.75 ounces	307 grams
Chocolate Coating fine-quality bittersweet chocolate, chopped	½ of a 3-ounce bar	1.5 ounces	43 grams
Caramel Nut Filling sugar	¾ cup	5.25 ounces	150 grams
light corn syrup	2 tablespoons	approx. 1.5 ounces	41 grams
unsalted butter, cut into 1-tablespoon pieces and softened	6 tablespoons	3 ounces	85 grams
heavy cream	⅓ liquid cup	2.7 ounces	77 grams
unsalted macadamia nuts, toasted and very coarsely chopped	1 cup	4.5 ounces	142 grams
Chocolate Custard Ganache heavy cream	½ liquid cup	4 ounces	113 grams
sour cream	½ cup	4.25 ounces	121 grams
1 large egg, at room temperature	3 tablespoons	1.75 ounces	50 grams (weighed without the shells)
2 large egg whites, at room temperature	¼ liquid cup	2 ounces	60 grams
cornstarch	2 teaspoons	0.2 ounce	6.5 grams
fine-quality bittersweet chocolate, finely chopped	one 3-ounce bar	3 ounces	85 grams
Whipped Cream Topping heavy cream	1¼ liquid cups	10 ounces	290 grams
sugar, preferably superfine	2 teaspoons	0.3 ounce	8.3 grams
pure vanilla extract	½ teaspoon	•	•
optional decoration: chocolate curls or shavings (page 617)	•	3 ounces	85 grams

Make the dough (page 61). Roll and shape it or press it into the pan and prebake it (see page 252). Let cool.

Chill a medium bowl and mixer beaters for the whipped cream.

MAKE THE CHOCOLATE COATING

In the top of a double boiler over hot, not simmering, water (the bottom of the upper container must not be touching the water), heat the chocolate, stirring often, until most but not all of it is melted. Remove the upper container, wipe all moisture from the outside, and continue stirring until the chocolate is completely melted. Or microwave for 10-second bursts, stirring after each one. Immediately pour it into the middle of the pastry shell. Use a small offset metal spatula or clean artist's brush to spread a very thin layer of the melted chocolate over the bottom of the pastry. Allow it to set for at least 10 minutes or until it dulls (loses its sheen).

MAKE THE CARAMEL NUT FILLING

In a heavy medium saucepan, place the sugar and corn syrup. *Without stirring,* cook over low heat until the sugar dissolves and the liquid is clear. Raise the heat to medium and continue cooking, swirling the liquid in the pan occasionally so that it cooks evenly, until it becomes deep amber (370° to 380°F.; 380°F. will give the deepest caramel flavor, but any higher will begin to have a bitter edge, so an accurate thermometer, a pot that releases the heat quickly [not ceramic or enameled iron] and the speedy addition of the butter and cream are required if you take it up that high). The whole process will take about 8 minutes. Immediately remove the caramel from the heat and whisk in the butter, 1 tablespoon at a time, until incorporated. Add the cream and whisk until evenly incorporated. With a wooden spoon, stir in the nuts.

Pour the mixture into the prepared tart shell. Refrigerate until set, a minimum of 1 hour and a maximum of 3 days. After the surface is set, cover the tart with lightly greased plastic wrap or a large inverted cake pan.

MAKE THE CHOCOLATE CUSTARD GANACHE

In the top of a double boiler set over simmering water, stir together the cream, sour cream, egg, egg whites, and cornstarch and cook for 5 to 10 minutes or until the mixture is the consistency of mayonnaise. (If you are using a thermometer, it will read 160°F.) Remove from the heat and stir in the chocolate until melted and smooth. Pour the custard evenly over the caramel filling. Chill for at least 2 hours or until firm and set.

Unmold the tart (see page 251) and slide it onto a serving plate. Cover it loosely with plastic wrap and refrigerate until ready to decorate.

MAKE THE WHIPPED CREAM TOPPING
Up to four hours ahead, in the chilled bowl, beat the cream, sugar, and vanilla until peaks form when the beater is raised. Pipe rosettes of whipped cream using a pastry bag or reclosable freezer bag fitted with a number 9 large star tube, to cover the entire surface of the tart. Or simply swirl the whipped cream all over the top using a spatula. Refrigerate until serving. Immediately before serving, decorate with chocolate curls or shavings, if desired.

STORE
Refrigerated, up to 4 hours.

POINTERS FOR SUCCESS
∾ Cream, butter, and chocolate are quick to absorb other refrigerator odors. Either place the finished tart in an airtight container or be sure to wrap other foods well to prevent the tart from absorbing odors.
∾ To make superfine sugar, whirl granulated sugar in a food processor for a few minutes.

PECAN PIE
(*Baked in a Tart Pan*)

I f you love pecan pie but find it a bit too sweet, you will appreciate this version. If you use the golden syrup instead of the traditional corn syrup, the pie will taste sweet without being cloying. Straining the filling makes it clear and shiny. A prebaked crust guarantees it will stay crisp against the sticky filling. A gorgeous lacy glaze in the form of a bittersweet chocolate drizzle balances the sweetness.

I like to bake this pie in a tart pan rather than a pie pan so that every bit (except the very edge) contains the same amount of crust, nuts, and filling. (The pie plate's sloping sides provide less filling and more crust at the outside edges.)

EQUIPMENT
A 9½-inch fluted tart pan with a removable bottom and a reclosable quart-size freezer bag

Make the dough (page 29). Roll, shape, and prebake it (see page 251).

Preheat the oven to 350°F. at least 15 minutes before baking time. Set an oven rack at the lowest level before preheating.
Arrange the pecans, top sides up, in the bottom of the baked crust.
Have ready a strainer suspended over a small bowl.

OVEN TEMPERATURE: 350°F. • BAKING TIME: 20 MINUTES   SERVES: 6

INGREDIENTS	MEASURE	WEIGHT	
	VOLUME	OUNCES	GRAMS
Flaky Cream Cheese Pie Crust for a 9½-inch tart (page 29), prebaked		11 ounces	312 grams
pecan halves	1½ cups	5.25 ounces	150 grams
4 large egg yolks	2 full fluid ounces	2.6 ounces	74 grams
Lyle's Golden Syrup (refiner's syrup)* or dark corn syrup	⅓ liquid cup, lightly greased	4 ounces	113 grams
light brown sugar, preferably unrefined (see page 645)	½ cup, packed	3.75 ounces	108 grams
unsalted butter, softened	4 tablespoons	2 ounces	57 grams
heavy cream	¼ liquid cup	2 ounces	58 grams
salt	a pinch	•	•
vanilla extract	1 teaspoon	•	4 grams
Chocolate Lace Topping bittersweet chocolate, finely chopped	⅓ of a 3 ounce bar	1 ounce	28 grams
heavy cream, cold	2 tablespoons	1 ounce	30 grams
optional: Crème Fraîche, unsweetened (page 558), or bourbon whipped cream (page 551)	1 cup	•	•

*Refiner's syrup adds a special mellow flavor.

In a medium nonreactive saucepan, combine the egg yolks, syrup, brown sugar, butter, cream, and salt. Cook over moderately low heat, stirring constantly with a wooden spoon and without letting the mixture boil, until it is uniform in color and just begins to thicken slightly (160°F. on a candy thermometer), 7 to 10 minutes. Strain at once into the small bowl and stir in the vanilla.

Slowly pour the filling over the nuts, coating their upper surface.

Place a foil ring (see page 19) on top of the crust to prevent overbrowning and bake for about 20 minutes or until the filling is puffed and golden and just beginning to bubble around the edges. The filling will shimmy slightly when moved. Allow the pie to cool completely on a rack, about 45 minutes, before unmolding from the pan (see page 251).

MAKE THE CHOCOLATE LACE TOPPING

In a small microwave-proof bowl, or the top of a double boiler set over hot, not simmering, water, place the chopped chocolate. (Do not allow the water to touch the bottom of the upper container.) Heat the chocolate, stirring often, until melted and remove it from the heat; if using a microwave, stir every 15 seconds.

Pour the cream on top of the chocolate and stir until smooth. It should drop thickly from a spoon. If it is too thick, add a little bourbon or a little more heavy cream.

Pour the mixture into a reclosable quart-size freezer bag and close it securely. Use it at once to pipe onto the cooled pie. To pipe: Cut off a very small piece from one corner of the bag and drizzle lines of chocolate back and forth over the top of the pecans, first in one direction (front to back) and then the other (side to side) to form a lacy design of chocolate webbing.

Serve with crème fraîche or bourbon whipped cream.

HOLIDAY PECAN STRIPS

For large dinner parties, such as at Thanksgiving, it is very convenient for serving to bake this recipe in two 14- by 4½-inch rectangular tart forms. (Roll each piece of dough to 18 inches by 8 inches.) The recipe for both the crust and the filling needs to be increased by one and a half. The pastry shells need to be prebaked for 20 minutes before removing the parchment and weights, then pricked and baked 7 minutes more or until golden brown. The filling takes the same amount of time.

STORE

Room temperature, up to 1 week.

POINTERS FOR SUCCESS

↝ Using refiner's syrup and unrefined light brown sugar makes a real difference in excellence of flavor.

↝ Be sure to check the pie toward the end of the baking time to prevent over-baking and keep the filling from drying.

CHOCOLATE PECAN PIE
(*Baked in a Tart Pan*)

For people who find even my less sweet Pecan Pie too sweet, or who are hopeless chocolate lovers, this is the answer. Cocoa perfectly tempers the sweetness of the filling and adds a full chocolate flavor that goes so well with pecans. If correctly baked, the filling, when cut, is soft and slightly molten.

The surface of the pie is unusually appealing. Unlike the regular pecan pie where you can see clearly the shape of each nut, this filling cloaks the nuts with a dark milk-chocolaty glisten so you can just make out their shape.

OVEN TEMPERATURE: 350°F. • BAKING TIME: 20 TO 25 MINUTES   SERVES: 8

INGREDIENTS	MEASURE	WEIGHT	
	VOLUME	OUNCES	GRAMS
Flaky Cream Cheese Pie Crust for a 9½-inch tart (page 29), prebaked		11 ounces	312 grams
pecan halves	1½ cups	5.25 ounces	150 grams
unsweetened cocoa, preferably Dutch-processed	⅓ cup (lightly spooned)	1 ounce	30 grams
4 large egg yolks	2 full fluid ounces	2.6 ounces	74 grams
Lyle's Golden Syrup (refiner's syrup)* or dark corn syrup	⅓ liquid cup, lightly greased	4 ounces	113 grams
light brown sugar	½ cup, packed	3.75 ounces	108 grams
unsalted butter, softened	4 tablespoons	2 ounces	57 grams
heavy cream	¼ liquid cup	2 ounces	58 grams
salt	a pinch	•	•
vanilla extract	1 teaspoon	•	4 grams
optional: Crème Fraîche, unsweetened (page 558) or bourbon whipped cream, unsweetened (page 551)	1 cup	•	•

*Refiner's syrup adds a special mellow flavor.

EQUIPMENT

A 9½-inch fluted tart pan with a removable bottom

Make the dough (page 29). Roll, shape, and prebake it (see page 251).

Preheat the oven to 350°F. at least 15 minutes before baking. Set an oven rack at the lowest level before prebaking.

Arrange the pecans, top sides up, in the bottom of the baked crust.

In a medium nonreactive saucepan, combine the cocoa, egg yolks, syrup, brown sugar, butter, cream, and salt. Cook over moderately low heat, stirring constantly with a wooden spoon and without letting the mixture boil, until it is smooth and uniform in color and hot to the touch (115° to 120°F. on a candy thermometer), about 5 minutes. Pour the mixture into a small bowl and stir in the vanilla.

Slowly pour the filling over the nuts, coating their upper surface.

Place a foil ring (see page 19) on top of the crust to prevent overbrowning and bake for 20 to 25 minutes or until the filling is puffed but still soft enough to shimmy like jelly when moved. Allow the pie to cool completely on a rack about 45 minutes before unmolding it from the pan (see page 251). Serve with crème fraîche or whipped cream, if desired.

STORE
Room temperature, up to 1 week.

POINTERS FOR SUCCESS
∾ Be sure to check the pie toward the end of the baking time to prevent over-baking and drying the filling.

UNDERSTANDING
The filling is brought to a lower temperature than for the nonchocolate version because the acidity of the cocoa would cause coagulation of the egg yolks at a higher temperature. Straining is difficult because of the thickening quality of the cocoa and unnecessary in any case, as the cocoa masks any slight graininess from the eggs.

MAPLE WALNUT PIE
(*Baked in a Tart Pan*)

This pie exploits the classic harmony of maple and walnut. Even if you use granulated rather than maple sugar, the filling will taste strongly of maple. Walnuts are harder than pecans and create a more crunchy/nutty filling.

EQUIPMENT
A 9½ inch tart pan with a removable bottom

Make the dough (page 29). Roll, shape, and prebake it (see page 251).

Preheat the oven to 350°F. at least 15 minutes before baking. Set an oven rack at the lowest level before preheating.

Arrange the walnuts, top sides up, in the bottom of the baked crust.

Have ready a strainer suspended over a small bowl.

In a medium nonreactive saucepan, combine the egg yolks, syrup, sugar, butter, cream, and salt. Cook over moderately low heat, stirring constantly with a wooden spoon and without letting the mixture boil, until it is uniform in color and just begins to thicken slightly (150°F. on a candy thermometer), 7 to 10 minutes. Strain it at once into the small bowl and stir in the vanilla and maple extracts. (At 160°F., little specks start to form. If this should happen, it's fine to push as much of this thicker part through the fine strainer as possible. It will not disturb the silkiness of the filling.)

OVEN TEMPERATURE: 350°F. • BAKING TIME: 20 MINUTES   SERVES: 6

INGREDIENTS	MEASURE	WEIGHT	
	VOLUME	OUNCES	GRAMS
Flaky Cream Cheese Pie Crust for a 9½-inch tart (page 29), prebaked		11 ounces	312 grams
walnut halves	1½ cups	5.25 ounces	150 grams
4 large egg yolks	2 full fluid ounces	2.6 ounces	74 grams
maple syrup	⅓ liquid cup, lightly greased	4 ounces	113 grams
maple sugar,* or granulated sugar	⅔ cup	3.75 ounces / 4.6 ounces	108 grams / 132 grams
unsalted butter, softened	4 tablespoons	2 ounces	57 grams
heavy cream	¼ liquid cup	2 ounces	58 grams
salt	a pinch	•	•
vanilla extract	1 teaspoon	•	4 grams
maple flavor*	½ teaspoon	•	•

*Maple sugar is available at specialty food stores, such as Balducci's or Dean & DeLuca (see page 675). If using granulated sugar, increase the maple flavor to 1 teaspoon.

Slowly pour the filling over the nuts, coating their upper surface.

Place a foil ring (see page 19) on top of the crust to prevent overbrowning and bake for about 20 minutes or until the pie is puffed and golden and just beginning to bubble around the edge. The filling will shimmy slightly when moved. Allow the pie to cool completely on a rack, about 45 minutes, before unmolding from the pan (see page 251).

STORE

Room temperature, up to 1 week.

UNDERSTANDING

The filling for this pie is slightly sweeter than for the pecan pie to compensate for the slight bitterness of the walnuts. The walnuts cannot be toasted to remove the skins because they will become too roasted when baked in the filling.

CHOCOLATE OBLIVION TARTLETS

This tartlet is for the pure chocolate lover. It contains a filling featuring chocolate at its most intense flavor and perfect consistency, which has been described by Susan Wyler, as editor of *Food and Wine* magazine, as the creamiest of truffles married to the purest chocolate mousse. This is an easy filling to make, consisting of only three ingredients: bittersweet chocolate, butter, and eggs.

The sweet cookie tart crust protects the filling from the oven's heat the way a water bath would protect a cake. It also provides a crisp and flavorful container for it. For an all-chocolate tart, the sweet walnut cookie tart crust can be replaced with the Bittersweet Chocolate Cookie Tart Crust (page 61). I prefer the contrast of a nonchocolate crust, as it provides a flavor accent and visual contrast.

OVEN TEMPERATURE: 350°F. •   MAKES: SEVEN 4¾-INCH TARTLETS
BAKING TIME: 10 MINUTES   OR EIGHT 4-INCH TARTLETS

INGREDIENTS	MEASURE	WEIGHT	
	VOLUME	OUNCES	GRAMS
Sweet Nut Cookie Tart Crust, made with walnuts, for eight 4-inch tartlets or seven 4¾-inch tartlets (page 59), prebaked and cooled		14 ounces	402 grams
Chocolate Filling	(2⅔ cups)	(1 pound)	(460 grams)
bittersweet chocolate, chopped	2⅔ 3-ounce bars	8 ounces	227 grams
unsalted butter, softened	8 tablespoons	4 ounces	113 grams
6 large eggs	scant 10 fluid ounces (19 tablespoons)	10.5 ounces 300 grams (weighed without the shells)	
Optional Garnishes Lightly whipped cream (pages 551–53)	1 cup	4.25 ounces	120 grams
Raspberry Sauce (page 603)	full ¾ cup	7.5 ounces	211 grams

EQUIPMENT
Eight 4- by ¾-inch flan rings or seven 4¾-inch fluted tart pans with removable bottoms

Make the dough (page 59). Roll, shape, and prebake it (see page 254). Leave the shells in the flan rings or tart pans on the baking sheet. Let cool.

Preheat the oven to 350°F. at least 15 minutes before baking the tartlets.

MAKE THE CHOCOLATE FILLING

In a large bowl set over a pan of hot, not simmering, water (the bottom of the bowl should not touch the water), combine the chocolate and butter and let them stand, stirring occasionally, until smooth and melted. (The mixture can be melted in the microwave on high power, stirring every 15 seconds. Remove it when there are still a few lumps of chocolate and stir until fully melted.) Set it aside.

In a large mixer bowl, set over the same pan of water—which should now be simmering—heat the eggs, stirring constantly to prevent curdling, until just warm to the touch. Remove the bowl from the heat and beat, using the whisk beater, until *tripled* in volume and soft peaks form when the beater is raised, about 5 minutes. (If using a hand mixer, to ensure maximum volume, beat the eggs over simmering water until they are hot to the touch, about 5 minutes. Remove the bowl from the heat and beat until cool.)

Using a large wire whisk or rubber spatula, fold half the eggs into the chocolate mixture until almost incorporated. Fold in the remaining eggs until just blended and no streaks remain. Finish by using a rubber spatula to ensure that the heavier mixture at the bottom is incorporated. Fill the pastry-lined molds, using a heaping ¼ cup (2 ounces/57 grams) for each flan ring (almost to the top), or ⅓ cup (2.25 ounces/65 grams) for each fluted tart pan (two-thirds full).

Bake the tarts for 10 minutes or until the filling is slightly puffed, the surface has dulled, and the centers wobble when tapped gently on the sides. Remove the baking sheet to a rack and cool for at least 30 minutes.

Remove the flan rings or unmold the fluted tart molds (see page 251) and serve warm or at room temperature.

If desired, garnish each tartlet with a 2-tablespoon dollop of whipped cream. To gild the lily, make a depression in the cream and fill it with a generous tablespoon of raspberry sauce.

VARIATIONS

CHOCOLATE INDULGENCE TARTLETS   Almond/hazelnut paste, with its slight caramelized edge, adds an extra flavor dimension while accentuating the chocolate flavor of the filling. Add ¼ cup (2.25 ounces/78 grams) praline paste to the chocolate before melting it. (This will give you 1½ teaspoons more filling for each tart, which is fine if using the fluted tart pans; if using the flan rings, you will have enough extra filling to make an extra tartlet.)

CHOCOLATE DEPENDENCE TARTLETS   Liqueur adds both flavor and a heightened sensation in the mouth. Add 1 tablespoon of your favorite liqueur to the melted chocolate mixture and serve with crème anglaise flavored with the same liqueur. Some of my favorites are: Grand Marnier, Frangelico, Kahlúa, Nocello, and Pistacha.

CHOCOLATE FLAME TARTLETS   Raspberry purée blends magnificently with the chocolate, brightening the flavor with its fresh fruit acidity and deepening the color. Stir ⅓ cup lightly sweetened Raspberry Sauce (page 603) into the melted chocolate mixture and add 2 tablespoons of sugar when beating the eggs. Alternatively, you can use 6 tablespoons of commercial seedless raspberry jam, but its taste will be sweeter. (This will give you about 2 teaspoons of extra filling for each tart, which is fine if you are using the fluted tart pans; if you are using flan rings, you will have enough filling left over to make an extra tart.)

If desired, brush the surface of the baked tartlets with heated and strained raspberry preserves and serve with crème anglaise flavored with Chambord (black raspberry liqueur).

OPTIONAL ALTERNATIVE DECORATION

A design of contrasting cocoa made with a stencil is easy and dramatically elegant. Center the stencil over each tartlet and use a fine strainer to sift cocoa over it, using a small spoon to tap the side of the strainer or to stir the cocoa to disperse it. Carefully lift the stencil straight off.

STORE

Uncovered, room temperature, up to 2 days; refrigerated, up to 2 weeks. (Covering the tarts makes the crust soggy.)

POINTERS FOR SUCCESS

∾ Leave the pastry in the flan rings after cooling to serve as support for the filling.

∾ Use your favorite high-quality eating chocolate, which will have about 53 percent chocolate mass. A chocolate with 70 percent chocolate mass, such as Valrhona Guanaja or Lindt's Excellence 70 percent cocoa bar, will make the texture of the filling too stiff.

UNDERSTANDING

The pastry shells serve as the buffer, like a water bath, to keep the filling equally moist and creamy throughout.

MOLTEN CHOCOLATE SOUFFLÉ TARTLETS

A fine crisp dark chocolate pastry shell makes an ideal container for this airy, creamy, intensely chocolate soufflé that oozes chocolate when it is cut into. Not only does it offer a great presentation, it also keeps the sides of the soufflés from drying, while providing crispness where it is desirable. The molten centers provide yet another textural contrast, of thickly flowing chocolate.

For a crustless version, bake the filling without the crust, for the same amount of time, in four 3¼- by 1¾-inch buttered and sugared ramekins.

OVEN TEMPERATURE: 400°F. • BAKING TIME: 8 TO 10 MINUTES   SERVES: 4

INGREDIENTS	MEASURE	WEIGHT	
	VOLUME	OUNCES	GRAMS
½ recipe Bittersweet Chocolate Walnut Cookie Tart Crust for four 4-inch tartlets (page 62)		8 ounces	227 grams
Ganache Centers	(¼ cup)	•	•
bittersweet chocolate, chopped	⅔ of a 3-ounce bar	2 ounces	60 grams
heavy cream	1 tablespoon	•	•
Soufflé			
bittersweet chocolate, preferably Lindt Excellence, chopped	13 little squares	1.33 ounces	38 grams
unsalted butter	2 tablespoons + 2 teaspoons	1.33 ounces	38 grams
unsweetened Dutch process cocoa	3 tablespoons	0.7 ounce	20 grams
Crème Fraîche (page 558) or heavy cream	2 tablespoons + 2 teaspoons	1.3 ounces	38 grams
2 large eggs, separated, + 2 large egg whites			
yolks	2 tablespoons + 1 teaspoon	1.3 ounces	37 grams
whites	½ liquid cup, divided	4.25 ounces	120 grams
cream of tartar	⅜ teaspoon		
sugar	2 tablespoons	approx. 1 ounce	25 grams

EQUIPMENT
Four 4- by 1¼-inch fluted tart pans with removable
bottoms

Make the dough (page 62).

Divide the dough into 4 pieces. It can be rolled or pressed into the tart pans. If the dough has been refrigerated for more than 30 minutes, it will be too cold to roll without cracking. It will take at least 40 minutes at room temperature to become malleable.

To roll the dough, roll each piece between lightly floured sheets of plastic wrap ¹/₁₆ inch thick and large enough to cut a 5¾-inch circle. Use a cardboard template and a sharp knife as a guide to cut the circles. Drape the dough circles into the tart pans and trim if necessary to ⅛ inch above the top of the pan.

Cover the tartlet shells with plastic wrap and freeze or refrigerate for a minimum of 1 hour and a maximum of 24 hours before baking.

Preheat the oven to 375°F. for at least 20 minutes before baking.

Line the dough with parchment and fill with rice or dried beans. Bake for 10 minutes. Lift out the parchment with the rice or beans and continue baking for 2 to 3 minutes. The dough will deepen in color but it should not start to brown, or it will take on a burnt flavor.

Use a pancake turner to slide the tart pans onto a wire rack to cool.

MAKE THE GANACHE CENTERS
In a small microwave-proof bowl, or the top of a double boiler set over hot, not simmering, water, place the chopped chocolate. (Do not allow the water to touch the bottom of the upper container.) Heat the chocolate, stirring often, until melted and remove it from the heat; if using a microwave, stir every 15 seconds.

Pour the cream on top of the chocolate and stir until smooth. Refrigerate the ganache for at least 1 hour so that it is firm enough to shape.

Preheat the oven to 400°F. at least 20 minutes before baking.

Divide the ganache in fourths and shape each into a ball with your fingers. Set them aside or refrigerate them.

MAKE THE SOUFFLÉ
In a medium microwave-proof bowl, or the top of a double boiler set over hot, not simmering, water, place the chopped chocolate, butter, and cocoa. (Do not allow the water to touch the bottom of the upper container.) Heat the mixture, stirring often, until melted and smooth and remove it from the heat; if using a microwave, stir every 15 seconds. Transfer to a bowl if using a double boiler.

In a small bowl, whisk together the crème fraîche or cream and the yolks and whisk this into the chocolate mixture.

Lightly whisk the egg whites to break them up for easier pouring. Pour 2 tablespoons of the egg whites into a small bowl and with the whisk, gently stir them into the chocolate mixture, just until incorporated.

In a large bowl, beat the remaining egg whites until foamy. Add the cream of tartar and beat at medium speed until soft peaks form when the beater is raised slowly. Add the sugar and continue beating on high speed until stiff peaks form (when the whisk is raised, the mixture will form stiff peaks that curve over slightly). Stir one fourth of the beaten whites into the chocolate mixture, then fold in the remainder.

Arrange the pastry-lined tart pans on a baking sheet. Fill the tart pans almost to the top with the chocolate filling. Drop a ganache ball into the center of each.

Bake the soufflés for 8 to 10 minutes. They will have puffed, the top surface will have dulled, and only a dimple in the center of each suggests the molten surprise. When touched gently, they should no longer wobble.

While the soufflés are baking, ready a heavy container, slightly smaller than the bottom of the opening of the tart pans, for unmolding (a tall little spice jar filled with water for stability works well) and a thin pancake turner.

UNMOLD THE SOUFFLÉS

Place each tart pan on top of the container and, with both hands protected by pot holders, press the sides firmly downward. Slip the pancake turner between the bottom of the pastry and the metal tart pan bottom, lift it, and slide the soufflé tart gently onto a serving plate. Serve immediately.

POINTERS FOR SUCCESS

➣ Soufflés should still be quite moist when baked. If overbaked, the centers will be dry and they will fall.

UNDERSTANDING

The ganache centers, made with a higher proportion of chocolate to cream than is usual, have the perfect thickly flowing consistency when hot and melted.

Stirring a small proportion of unbeaten egg white into the soufflé is a brilliant technique developed by Shirley Corriher, author of *CookWise*. Since the white is not beaten, its structure has *not* been weakened, and therefore it offers more structural strength, preventing the soufflés from falling for a significantly longer time after they have been removed from the oven.

CHOCOLATE PECAN BLASTS

These tartlets have all the intensity of a candy bar with none of the cloying sweetness. The combination of crisp bittersweet chocolate pastry, creamy dark mocha filling, crunchy pecans, and chewy caramel satisfies just about every craving for texture and flavor. The tartlets look every bit as good as they taste, with the dark chocolate glistening through lacings of amber caramel set off by the scattering of broken toasted pecans.

MAKES: SEVEN 4¾-INCH TARTLETS
OR EIGHT 4-INCH TARTLETS

INGREDIENTS	MEASURE	WEIGHT	
	VOLUME	OUNCES	GRAMS
Bittersweet Chocolate Cookie Tart Crust for eight 4-inch tartlets or eight 4¾-inch tartlets (page 61), prebaked and cooled		1 pound	455 grams
Mocha Filling	(2 cups)	(15.25 ounces)	(434 grams)
Medaglia d'Oro instant espresso powder	1 teaspoon	•	•
boiling water	2 tablespoons	•	•
heavy cream	¼ liquid cup	2 ounces	58 grams
unsalted butter, softened	6 tablespoons	3 ounces	85 grams
2 large eggs, separated yolks whites	2 tablespoons ¼ liquid cup	1.3 ounces 2 ounces	37 grams 60 grams
bittersweet chocolate, chopped	two 3-ounce bars	6 ounces	170 grams
cream of tartar	¼ teaspoon	•	•
Butterscotch Bourbon Caramel	(1 cup)	(10.5 ounces)	(300 grams)
light brown sugar	⅓ cup, packed	2.5 ounces	71 grams
sugar	3 tablespoons	1.3 ounces	37 grams
Lyle's Golden Syrup (refiner's syrup) or light corn syrup	3 fluid ounces (6 tablespoons)	approx. 4.5 ounces	127 grams
heavy cream	3 fluid ounces (6 tablespoons)	3 ounces	87 grams
unsalted butter	1 tablespoon	0.5 ounce	14 grams
bourbon	1½ tablespoons	•	•
pecan halves, broken or coarsely chopped and lightly toasted*	1 cup	3.5 ounces	100 grams
Topping bittersweet chocolate, chopped	⅓ of a 3-ounce bar	1 ounce	28 grams
heavy cream	2 tablespoons	1 ounce	29 grams

*Toast for about 7 minutes in a preheated 350°F. oven until their color deepens only slightly.

EQUIPMENT
Eight 4- by ¾-inch flan rings or eight 4¾-inch fluted tart pans with removable bottoms

Make the dough (page 61). Roll, shape, and prebake it (see page 254). Let cool.

MAKE THE MOCHA FILLING
In a small bowl, stir together the espresso powder and boiling water until the espresso is dissolved.

In a small saucepan, whisk together the espresso mixture, cream, butter, and yolks and heat, stirring constantly with the whisk, until the mixture reaches 160°F. (*not less*) on a candy thermometer and is the consistency of heavy cream. Remove it from the heat and, with the whisk, stir in the chocolate until it is melted. Pour the mixture into a bowl and set it aside until lukewarm or cool.

In a mixing bowl, beat the egg whites until foamy. Add the cream of tartar and beat at medium speed until soft peaks form when the beater is raised slowly. Continue beating on high speed until stiff peaks form when the beater is raised. With a whisk, fold the beaten whites into the chocolate mixture.

With a spatula or spoon, spread ¼ cup of the mocha filling (scant 2 ounces/54 grams) into each tartlet shell. Freeze until very firm, at least 2 hours. (Once the filling is frozen solid, wrap the tartlets airtight.)

MAKE THE BUTTERSCOTCH BOURBON CARAMEL
Remove the flan rings from the tartlets and place the tartlets close together on a sheet of parchment or waxed paper.

Have a greased 1-cup heatproof measuring cup next to the stove.

In a small heavy saucepan, preferably with a nonstick lining, combine all the ingredients for the caramel except the bourbon and cook over medium-low heat, stirring often, for 7 to 10 minutes or until it turns a deep amber; a candy thermometer will read 246°F., the firm ball stage (a dab of caramel dropped into ice water can be formed into a firm ball that does not lose its shape when removed from the water but is still malleable). Immediately pour the mixture into the measuring cup. Add the bourbon and swirl it in.

Pour 2 tablespoons of caramel on top of each tartlet, quickly tilting it to spread the caramel evenly. Immediately sprinkle 2 tablespoons of the pecans over each tartlet.

MAKE THE TOPPING
In a small microwave-proof bowl, or the top of a double boiler set over hot, not simmering, water, place the chopped chocolate. (Do not allow the water to touch the bottom of the upper container.) Heat the chocolate, stirring often, until melted and remove it from the heat; if using a microwave, stir every 15 seconds.

Pour the cream on top of the chocolate and stir until smooth.

Pour the mixture into a reclosable quart-size freezer bag and close it securely. Use it at once to pipe the topping onto the cooled tartlets. To pipe, cut off a very small piece from one corner of the bag and form lines of chocolate back and forth over the top of the pecans, first in one direction (front to back) and then the other (side to side). If the topping is too thick, add a little more heavy cream. Serve chilled.

STORE

Refrigerated, up to 3 days; frozen, up to 1 month.

NOTE

For a Big Chocolate Pecan Blast, as pictured on page 15 of the photograph insert, use a 9½- by ½-inch entremet ring and increase the filling by one and a half.

POINTERS FOR SUCCESS

∾ Leave the pastry in the flan rings after cooling to serve as support for the filling. Unmold after filling.

∾ For a silky smooth chocolate filling that does not curdle, the mixture must not be allowed to boil.

∾ For the best chewy texture, use a thermometer for testing the caramel. If it is not cooked long enough, it will be too soft; if cooked too long, it will be hard instead of sticky.

CHOCOLATE PEANUT BUTTER MOUSSE TART

This is my take on the classic American peanut butter pie. It manages to be intensely peanut buttery but light and soft, with a wonderfully chewy peanut butter cookie crust and meltingly smooth chocolate topping. Creamy/fudgy when cold, creamy/moussy when closer to room temperature, this tart is reminiscent of the much-loved Reese's peanut butter cup.

EQUIPMENT
A 9½-inch fluted tart pan with a removable bottom

Make the dough (page 63). Roll, shape, and prebake it (see page 252). Let cool.

INGREDIENTS	MEASURE	WEIGHT	
	VOLUME	OUNCES	GRAMS
Sweet Peanut Butter Cookie Tart Crust for a 9½-inch tart (page 63), prebaked and cooled		•	•
Peanut Butter Mousse	(about 2½ cups)	(15.6 ounces)	(444 grams)
cream cheese, softened	7 tablespoons	4 ounces	113 grams
peanut butter, preferably Jif, at room temperature	½ cup	4.6 ounces	133 grams
sugar	¼ cup	1.75 ounces	50 grams
pure vanilla extract	1 teaspoon	•	•
heavy cream, softly whipped	¾ liquid cup	6 ounces	174 grams
Milk Chocolate Ganache Topping	1¼ cups	7.5 ounces	212 grams
milk chocolate	one 3-ounce bar	3 ounces	85 grams
bittersweet chocolate	⅔ of a 3-ounce bar	2 ounces	57 grams
heavy cream	⅓ liquid cup	2.7 ounces	77 grams
pure vanilla extract	⅛ teaspoon	•	•

MAKE THE PEANUT BUTTER MOUSSE

In a mixer bowl, preferably with the whisk beater, beat the cream cheese, peanut butter, and sugar until uniform in color. On low speed, beat in the vanilla. Beat in ¼ cup of the whipped cream just until incorporated. With a large rubber spatula, fold in the rest of the whipped cream until blended but still airy. Scrape the mousse into the prepared tart shell and smooth the surface so that it is level. Refrigerate the tart while preparing the ganache.

MAKE THE GANACHE TOPPING

Break the chocolates into several pieces into the bowl of a food processor with the metal blades. Process until the chocolate is very finely ground.

In a heatproof glass measure, if using a microwave oven, or in a small saucepan, bring the cream to a boil. With the motor running, immediately pour it through the feed tube onto the chocolate. Process until smooth, about 15 seconds, scraping the sides of the bowl once or twice. Add the vanilla and pulse a few times to incorporate it. Pour the ganache into a liquid measure or bowl. Let cool to room temperature.

Pour the ganache over the peanut butter mousse in a circular motion, so that it does not land too heavily in any one spot and cause a depression. With a small metal spatula, start by spreading the ganache to the edges of the pastry, then spread it evenly to cover the entire surface. Make a spiral pattern by lightly pressing the spatula against the surface and running it from the outside to the center.

Refrigerate the tart for at least 2 hours to set.

Remove the tart from the refrigerator at least 15 minutes before serving. Unmold the tart (see page 251) and cut with a sharp thin blade, dipped in hot water between each slice. It is as good lightly chilled as it is at room temperature.

STORE

Room temperature, up to 1 day; refrigerated, up to 5 days; frozen, up to 3 months.

UNDERSTANDING

For the ganache, the flavor of milk chocolate seems to meld better with peanut butter than the usual bittersweet chocolate. A little bittersweet chocolate is added just to temper the sweetness. Milk chocolate is softer than bittersweet, so less cream is used than for the standard ganache. Amazingly, it stays shiny even after freezing as long as it is wrapped once it is frozen so the plastic wrap does not mar the surface.

CHOCOLATE PEANUT BUTTER MOUSSE SEVEN-TIER TART

There are many people who would be thrilled to find this exquisitely delicious tiered tart in place of the traditional wedding cake. And it is very practical to make it, as it freezes perfectly for up to 3 months. There are three luscious layers to each tier of this tart: a quarter-inch-deep peanut butter cookie crust, a five-eighths-inch deep peanut butter mousse, and a just under one-eighth-inch-thick milk chocolate ganache. It is delicious both chilled and at room temperature, making it perfect for a presentation piece. The special acrylic stand (page 670) makes it appear to be levitating in air.

The recipe here is given for all seven layers, but if you prefer not to make all the layers, the components are broken down in amounts for each individual size in the chart on page 321.

SERVES: 55 AS A DESSERT, 80 AS A WEDDING TART

INGREDIENTS	MEASURE	WEIGHT	
	VOLUME	OUNCES	GRAMS
6 recipes Sweet Peanut Butter Cookie Tart Crust (page 63), prebaked in 7 tart pans	8½ cups + 2 tablespoons (1 cup dough = 8.8 ounces/252 grams)	76.2 ounces	2 kg 178 grams
Peanut Butter Mousse	(17½ cups)	(7 pounds)	(3 kg 223 grams)
cream cheese, softened	3½ cups	2 pounds	904 grams
peanut butter (at room temperature), preferably Jif	4 cups	36.75 ounces	1 kg 64 grams
sugar	2 cups	14 ounces	400 grams
pure vanilla extract	2 tablespoons + 2 teaspoons	approx. 1 ounce	32 grams
heavy cream, softly whipped	6 liquid cups (1½ quarts)	48 ounces	1 kg 392 grams
Milk Chocolate Ganache Topping	(7½ cups)	(45 ounces)	(1 kg 272 grams)
milk chocolate	six 3-ounce bars	18 ounces	510 grams
bittersweet chocolate	four 3-ounce bars	12 ounces	342 grams
heavy cream	2 liquid cups	16.2 ounces	462 grams
pure vanilla extract	¾ teaspoon	•	•

EQUIPMENT

Seven fluted tart pans with removable bottoms (see page 664: 4¾-inch, 5½-inch, 7¾-inch, 9½-inch, 10-inch, 11-inch, and 12½-inch) and Pie in the Sky acrylic tiered stand (see page 670)

Make the dough (page 63). Roll, shape (see page 252), and prebake it, starting with the largest tart (see chart, page 321). Add scraps to the dough for each subsequent tart as you proceed, ending with the smallest. Let cool. Leftover dough can be frozen or made into cookies.

MAKE THE PEANUT BUTTER MOUSSE

In a mixer bowl, preferably with the whisk beater, beat the cream cheese, peanut butter, and sugar until uniform in color. On low speed, beat in the vanilla. Beat in 2 cups of the whipped cream just until incorporated. With a large rubber spatula, fold in the rest of the whipped cream until well blended. Scrape the mousse into the prepared shells, filling them to ⅛ to ¼ inch below the top of the crusts (for exact amounts, see page 321), and smooth the surface of each so that it is level. Refrigerate the tarts while preparing the ganache.

MAKE THE GANACHE TOPPING

Break the chocolates into small pieces into the bowl of a food processor with the metal blade. Process until the chocolate is very finely ground.

In a heatproof glass measure, if using a microwave oven, or in a small saucepan, bring the cream to a boil. With the motor running, immediately pour it through the feed tube onto the chocolate mixture. Process until smooth, about 15 seconds, scraping the sides of the bowl once or twice. Add the vanilla and pulse a few times to incorporate it. Pour it into a bowl. Let cool to room temperature.

Pour the ganache over the peanut butter mousse in each tart in a circular motion, so that it does not land too heavily in any one spot and cause a depression. (For exact amounts for each tart, see page 321.) If the ganache becomes too firm to pour, spread it instead or reheat it slightly, stirring very gently, in a microwave or double boiler. With a small metal spatula, start by spreading the ganache to the edges of the pastry. Then spread it evenly to cover the entire surface of each tart; make a thin layer, a little under ⅛ inch. Make a spiral pattern by lightly pressing the spatula against the surface and running it from the outside to the center.

Refrigerate the tarts for at least 2 hours to set.

ASSEMBLE THE TART

Unmold the tart (see page 251) and set each layer on its base. Place the center post firmly into the base of the stand. Slide the first acrylic spacer onto the post. Cut out a 1¾-inch hole in the center for the center post in all of the tiers except the top one. Slide each tier onto the post, placing an acrylic spacer in between each one.

To serve, cut with a sharp thin-bladed knife, preferably dipped in hot water between each slice.

STORE

Room temperature, up to 1 day; refrigerated, up to 5 days; frozen, up to 3 months.

NOTE

If the dough is rolled to the exact thickness specified, the filling and ganache amounts will be exact. If the dough is rolled a little thicker, there will be a little leftover filling and ganache.

TART SIZE	DOUGH CIRCLE DIAMETER	APPROXIMATE BAKING TIME AT 375°F.	FILLING	GANACHE
4¾ inches/12 cm	6 inches	8 min.	⅔ cup	3 tablespoons
5½ inches/14 cm	7¾ inches	10 min.	1 cup	¼ cup
7¾ inches/19½ cm	9½ inches	10 min.	2½ cups	¾ cup
9½ inches/24 cm	11½ inches	10 to 12 min.	3⅓ cups	1 cup
10 inches/25½ cm	12½ inches	10 to 12 min.	4½ cups	1⅓ cups
11 inches/28 cm	13 inches	12 to 14 min.	5¾ cups	1¾ cups
12½ inches/32 cm	14½ inches	14 min.	7½ cups	2 to 2¼ cups

SAVORY TARTS AND PIES—AND QUICHE

A flaky pie crust elevates even the most homey savory dish. Meat loaf (page 331), a classic American favorite, has a much more exciting visual, taste, and texture appeal when wrapped in a Cheddar cheese flaky pie crust. The recipes I have included in this section are my all-time favorites and ones I will be making for many years to come.

When it comes to quiche, though I have always enjoyed this custard tart, I have never been able to eat more than a small piece because of its richness. I love a custard filling in a sweet tart or pie, but find it easier to eat because the sweet versions are eaten cold or at room temperature. The cool creamy filling against the buttery crust seems less rich. For this reason, I prefer to serve quiche warm or at room temperature, rather than hot from the oven. This has the additional advantage of giving the flavors a chance to blend and intensify. (I find this also works well for other savory tarts. Potpies, however, which contain more liquid, or gravy, are better eaten hot.)

Another great technique for making a delicious savory custard quiche or tart is to use just enough custard to create a soft creaminess and bind the solid ingredients, such as vegetables or seafood. The basic proportion of liquid to egg for a custard that will set nicely is ⅓ cup of liquid to 1 large egg. If there is a large amount of solid ingredients, then a softer custard of ½ cup of liquid to 1 large egg also works. I find that using all cream is far too rich. Half-and-half (which is half milk, half light cream) is my usual choice for a lighter custard. All milk will work as well. I sometimes use a combination of crème fraîche or heavy cream and milk for a richer filling when the custard is the main ingredient, as for quiche Lorraine.

A pie crust filled with a creamy mixture has the best texture if it has been fully prebaked. (Most frozen crusts will develop fissures if prebaked, so this is not recommended for them.)

A **9½-inch tart pan (or 9-inch pie pan)** lined with dough requires 2½ to 3¼ cups of filling and serves 4 to 6.

A **7¾-inch tart pan (or 7- to 7¼-inch pie pan)** lined with a half recipe of dough (6 to 6½ ounces) requires 1½ to 2¼ cups of filling and serves 2 to 3. Bake for 20 to 25 minutes.

For individual quiches, use 4-inch tart pans (see page 664), lined with 2 ounces each of dough. Use a scant ⅓ cup of filling for each and bake for about 20 minutes.

DEEP-DISH CHICKEN POTPIES

This is not by any means a traditional chicken potpie. It is my dream chicken potpie, inspired by a one-star Michelin restaurant's signature dish: *poulet au vin jaune*. Several years ago, my friend Shirley Corriher and I traveled to the restaurant Hôtel de Paris in Arbois to sample this specialty of chef/owner Jeunet and ended up staying in Arbois for several days, just to eat it again and again.

The filling for the pie consists of moist chunks of dark chicken meat and morel mushrooms with just enough carrot to add a little sweetness and just enough intense gravy reduction to flavor and moisten the filling. *Vin jaune,* from the Jura region of France, has a unique sort of zingy tartness that enlivens the sauce, but a good-quality German or Alsatian Riesling offers a very similar quality. Although morels possess a flavor unlike any other mushroom, button mushrooms or a combination of the two will also yield great results.

An herbed pie dough, baked separately and then placed on top of the pie just before the final heating, maintains its flakiness even on the underside. I prefer this to a two-crust pastry, as the moistness of the filling would make the bottom crust entirely soggy.

When time allows, I soak the chicken overnight in buttermilk to cover (and then drain and discard the buttermilk). The acidity of the buttermilk acts as a tenderizer and also makes the meat more flavorful.

This is a potpie elegant enough to serve at a fancy dinner party. (Use the Emile Henry 4½-inch pie plates, page 663.) Guests seem to enjoy having individual little pies.

EQUIPMENT
Six 4-inch deep-dish pie plates

Make the dough (page 45 or 29).

Divide the dough into 6 equal pieces. Roll each one between sheets of lightly floured plastic wrap ⅛ inch thick and large enough to cut a 5½-inch circle. Use a template and a sharp knife to cut the circles. Place them on a baking sheet and refrigerate, tightly covered, for at least 1 hour to relax the dough. (If desired, reroll the scraps and use a small cutter to cut a chicken shape for each pie. You will need a dab of yolk/cream glaze [page 21] to attach them and for color contrast.)

Bake the chilled pastry rounds or freeze until ready to use.

BAKE THE PASTRY

The pastry can be baked several hours ahead. *Preheat the oven to 425°F. at least 20 minutes before baking.*

Bake for 10 to 12 minutes or until golden brown. (The rounds will shrink to about 4¾ inches.) Transfer them to wire racks to cool.

MAKE THE FILLING

In a medium bowl, place the morels and water and allow them to sit for at least 30 minutes and up to several hours. They will become soft and spongy.

In a large saucepan, place the chicken broth. Strain the liquid from the morels into the pot and bring it to a boil. Set the morels aside, covered. Add the chicken to the stock and simmer, covered, for 20 to 25 minutes or until almost cooked through (the internal temperature should be 170°F.). Remove the chicken from the stock to cool.

Raise the heat and reduce the stock to about ½ cup. It will become very syrupy and bubble thickly. Add the wine and reduce the liquid to 1 cup. Add the milk and cream, remove from the heat, and set it aside.

Meanwhile, remove and discard the bones from the chicken. Cut the chicken into 1-inch pieces and place them in a large bowl.

Preheat the oven to 425°.

Cut the morels into halves or quarters if they are very large.

In a large frying pan, melt 2 tablespoons of the butter. Add the morels, carrots, and onion, and salt lightly. Sauté the vegetables over medium-low heat, stirring often, for 10 minutes or until the carrots are tender/crisp. Transfer the mixture to a large bowl.

Add the remaining 4 tablespoons of butter to the skillet. When melted, stir in the flour and cook, stirring, for 1 minute. Stir in the stock mixture. Lower the heat and cook, stirring constantly, for about 5 minutes or until the sauce is very thick; it should just barely drip from the spoon. Add salt and pepper to taste. (There will be 2¼ cups of gravy.) Stir it gently into the chicken mixture, along with the parsley and thyme. (The filling can be refrigerated for up to 24 hours at this point.)

Spoon the mixture into the pie pans and cover each with greased foil. Bake for 10 minutes (15 if the filling was refrigerated). Place a baked pastry lid on each pot-pie and bake 5 minutes more.

OVEN TEMPERATURE: 425°F. • BAKING TIME: 15 MINUTES   SERVES: 6

INGREDIENTS	MEASURE	WEIGHT	
	VOLUME	OUNCES	GRAMS
Flaky Goose Fat Pie Crust (page 45) or Flaky Cream Cheese Pie Crust (page 29) for a 9-inch pie, made with optional 1 tablespoon (3 grams) finely chopped fresh thyme or 1 teaspoon dried (added to the flour)		11 ounces	312 grams
about 24 dried morel mushrooms*	approx. 5 cups (after soaking)	2½ ounces (dried)	70 grams
water	2 liquid cups	16.6 ounces	473 grams
3 cans (14.5 ounces each) no-salt chicken broth	about 5½ liquid cups	43.5 ounces	1 kg 233 grams
chicken thighs (about 15 to 16), skinned†		3½ pounds	1 kg 588 grams
white wine, preferably Spätlese Riesling	1½ liquid cups	12.5 ounces	354 grams
milk	1 liquid cup	8.5 ounces	242 grams
heavy cream	⅓ liquid cup	2.75 ounces	77 grams
unsalted butter	6 tablespoons, divided	3 ounces	85 grams
2 large carrots, scraped, quartered, and sliced ¼ inch thick	½ cup (sliced)	2.25 ounces (sliced)	64 grams
1 medium onion, chopped	1 cup	4.5 ounces	128 grams
salt	•	•	•
all-purpose flour	¼ cup	1.25 ounces	36 grams
freshly ground black pepper to taste	•	•	•
chopped fresh parsley, preferably Italian	1 tablespoon	•	3 grams
fresh thyme leaves	1 tablespoon	•	3 grams

*One pound of fresh morels or ordinary mushrooms, sliced, can be substituted. Sauté them until their moisture has evaporated and they begin to brown.

†Or 6 cups (2 pounds) 1-inch chunks cooked chicken, preferably dark meat.

POINTERS FOR SUCCESS

∾ After I make the dough, I like to fold it in thirds like a business letter. It strengthens it slightly and also makes it puff up a bit unevenly, which adds to the rustic charm. Since it is baked separately, it still remains very tender because it does not pick up any moisture from the filling.

UNDERSTANDING

I find dark meat infinitely preferable to white meat, as it stays moister. White meat can take on a sawdusty texture.

The chicken has some residual moisture that thins the sauce, so the sauce must be very thick before it is combined with the chicken.

Although peas add a shot of green color, I find they interfere with the purity of the chicken and mushroom flavor. If you can't eat chicken potpie without them, defrost baby frozen peas and add them after you have combined the chicken with the sauce so they cook as little as possible.

STEAK AND KIDNEY POTPIES

I love the combination of beef and kidneys, so I developed a recipe for this English classic. I chose sirloin, the most flavorful cut of beef, and cooked it medium-rare. To intensify the beefy flavor, I chose portobello mushrooms, which taste almost like meat themselves. For the kidneys, I chose veal because their flavor is more delicate than beef kidneys. A crisp, flaky herbed beef suet crust is the ideal "lid." The filling can be prepared as much as twenty-four hours ahead, which makes this excellent party fare for hearty eaters.

EQUIPMENT
Six 4-inch deep-dish pie plates

Make the dough (page 43).

Divide the dough into 6 equal pieces. Roll each one between sheets of lightly floured plastic wrap ⅛ inch thick and large enough to cut a 5½-inch circle. Use a template and a sharp knife to cut the circles. Place them on a baking sheet and refrigerate, tightly covered, for at least 1 hour to relax the dough.

Bake the chilled pastry or freeze until ready to use.

BAKE THE PASTRY
The pastry can be baked several hours ahead. *Preheat the oven to 425°F. at least 20 minutes before baking.*

OVEN TEMPERATURE: 425°F. • BAKING TIME: 15 MINUTES   SERVES: 6

| INGREDIENTS | MEASURE | WEIGHT | |
	VOLUME	OUNCES	GRAMS
1½ recipes Flaky Beef Suet Pie Crust (page 43), made with 1 tablespoon (3 grams) finely chopped fresh thyme or 1 teaspoon dried (added to the flour)		scant 12 ounces	340 grams
beef stock (low-sodium)*	4½ cups	36 ounces	1 kg 20 grams
1½ veal kidneys		13.5 ounces	383 grams
boneless sirloin steak, 1-inch thick		1½ pounds	680 grams
optional: blood sausage		4.5 ounces	127.5 grams
portobello mushrooms		1 pound	454 grams
salt	•	•	•
rendered fat from the kidneys or beef marrow (see page 44) or unsalted butter	6 tablespoons, divided	3 ounces	85 grams
chopped onions	1 cup	4.5 ounces	127.5 grams
flour	¼ cup	1.25 ounces	36 grams
Worcestershire sauce	1 tablespoon	•	•
freshly ground black pepper	•	•	•
chopped fresh parsley, preferably Italian	1 tablespoon	•	4 grams
finely chopped fresh thyme	1 tablespoon	•	3 grams

*Or veal stock.

Bake for 8 to 10 minutes or until golden brown. (The rounds will shrink to about 4¾ inches.) Transfer them to wire racks to cool.

MAKE THE FILLING

In a large saucepan, over high heat, boil the beef stock until reduced to 2¼ cups, about 15 minutes. Set it aside, covered.

Wash and skin the kidneys. With scissors, snip the membrane and fat where it is connected to the core and peel away the membrane with your fingers. Separate them into lobes. Slice them ½ inch thick. Cut the steak into 1-inch cubes. Cut the optional blood sausage into ½-inch cubes.

Run the tops of the mushrooms under cold water to remove any dirt, then rinse the gills (undersides) briefly, so they won't absorb much water. With a small sharp knife, cut off the stems and slice them ¼ inch thick. Cut the caps into wedges about 1 inch long by ½ inch wide. Set them on paper towels to drain well.

Preheat the oven to 425°.

Lightly salt the steak cubes. In a large heavy skillet, over medium-high heat, and brown the steak cubes in batches, without crowding, turning to brown on all sides, until cooked to rare (115 or to 120°F.), about 4 minutes. (They will continue cooking slightly in the pies.) Remove them to a bowl.

Reduce the heat to medium and, if using, sauté the blood sausage pieces until lightly browned, about 2 minutes. Remove them to the bowl.

Lightly salt the kidneys. Add 3 tablespoons of the rendered fat to the skillet and brown the kidneys for 2 minutes, or until barely pink inside. Remove them to the bowl.

Add the onions to the skillet and sauté them for 3 minutes or until translucent. Add the mushrooms, along with about 2 tablespoons of water if they appear dry (stored mushrooms often lose moisture), cover, and cook over low heat, stirring occasionally and adding a little water if needed, for 10 to 15 minutes or until tender when pierced with a skewer. Remove them to the bowl.

Add the remaining 3 tablespoons of fat to the skillet. Stir in the flour and cook, stirring, for 1 minute. Stir in the stock. Cook, stirring constantly, for about 5 minutes or until the sauce is very thick; it should just barely drip from the spoon. Add the Worcestershire and salt and pepper to taste. (There will be 2¼ cups of gravy.) Stir it gently into the beef mixture, along with the parsley and thyme. (The filling can be refrigerated for up to 24 hours at this point.)

Spoon the mixture into the pie pans and cover each with greased foil. Bake for 10 minutes (15 if the filling was refrigerated). Place a baked pastry lid on each pielet and bake 5 minutes more.

POINTERS FOR SUCCESS

ᶜ◦ Don't simmer the kidneys in the sauce, as this would toughen them.

SHEPHERD'S PIE

I have always been intrigued by a "pie" that had no bottom crust and mashed potatoes as a top crust. I have since learned that although it is now prepared with many sorts of leftover meats, shepherd's pie traditionally was prepared with leftover lamb, which gave it its name. My favorite dish growing up was my grandmother's succulent lamb shank stew with prunes and potato, but I had always been hesitant to serve it to company, as it was somewhat lacking in refinement, so I decided to try it as a sort of upscale shepherd's pie, with my favorite Crème-Fraîche/white-truffle-oil mashed potatoes as decorative topping. Even without the truffle oil, this pie is soul-satisfyingly fabulous.

OVEN TEMPERATURE: 425°F. • BAKING TIME: 10 MINUTES
(PLUS 3 TO 5 MINUTES BROILING)   SERVES: 6

INGREDIENTS	MEASURE	WEIGHT	
	VOLUME	OUNCES	GRAMS
all-purpose flour	1½ tablespoons	0.5 ounce	14 grams
salt	1 teaspoon	0.25 ounce	7 grams
freshly ground black pepper	⅛ teaspoon	•	•
cayenne pepper	a big pinch	•	•
lamb shanks, cut into 3-inch pieces		3 pounds	1 kg 360 grams
extra-virgin olive oil	1½ tablespoons, divided	•	•
1 medium onion, thinly sliced	1 cup	4 ounces	114 grams
1 rib celery (including leafy portion), thinly sliced	½ cup	1.5 ounces	45 grams
1 medium clove garlic, minced	1 teaspoon	•	3.5 grams
fresh thyme leaves*	1 teaspoon	•	
1 small bay leaf	•	•	•
water	¾ liquid cup†	•	•
12 pitted prunes, preferably Sunsweet premium prunes‡	1 cup, firmly packed	6 ounces	170 grams
Mashed Potatoes 2 large boiling potatoes, preferably Yukon Gold	(3 cups)	1½ pounds	680 grams
unsalted butter	2 tablespoons	1 ounce	28 grams
Crème Fraîche (page 558) or sour cream	½ cup	4 ounces	116 grams
salt	½ teaspoon	•	•
nutmeg, preferably freshly grated	a grating	•	•
freshly ground white pepper	a few grindings	•	•
optional: white truffle oil (see page 638)	1 teaspoon	•	•

*Or ¼ teaspoon dried thyme.

†2 cups if making by the traditional method.

‡These are exceptionally moist.

EQUIPMENT
Six 4-inch deep-dish pie plates; optional: a 4-quart pressure cooker

In a reclosable gallon-size freezer bag, combine the flour, salt, black pepper, and cayenne; shake to mix. Add a few pieces of lamb at a time and toss to coat with the flour. If any of the flour mixture remains, set it aside.

Heat a large heavy frying pan, preferably cast iron, until hot. Add 1 tablespoon of the oil and when a film appears over the oil, add only as much lamb as will fit in a single layer without crowding. Brown the lamb over medium-high heat, turning occasionally, for about 8 to 10 minutes or until browned on all sides. Remove the lamb to a bowl. Cook the remaining lamb in batches and set it aside.

In the same pan, heat the remaining 1½ teaspoons of oil. Sauté the onion and celery until the onions are golden brown and the celery wilted, about 5 minutes. Sprinkle on any remaining flour mixture, stir in the garlic, and cook, stirring, for about 30 seconds.

PRESSURE COOKER METHOD
Spoon the vegetable mixture into the pressure cooker. Top with the lamb. Add the thyme, bay leaf, and water. Cook at full pressure for 20 minutes. Release the pressure, stir, add the prunes, and cook at full pressure for 10 more minutes. The meat should be almost falling-off-the-bone tender.

With a skimmer, remove the lamb, vegetables, and prunes to a large platter to cool. Tilt the pot and skim off the fat from the top of the gravy. Bring the gravy to a boil over medium-high heat and boil it down to ⅔ cup, stirring often to prevent scorching, about 5 minutes. Transfer it to a medium bowl.

TRADITIONAL METHOD
Spoon the vegetable mixture into a large pot. Top with the lamb. Add the thyme, bay leaf, and 2 cups water. Bring to a boil over medium-high heat, reduce the heat, and simmer, partly covered, for 1½ hours.

Add the prunes and cook for about 30 minutes or until the meat is almost falling-off-the-bone tender. Remove the lamb, vegetables, and prunes to a large platter to cool. Tilt the pot and skim off the fat from the gravy. Over medium-high heat, boil down the gravy to ⅔ cup, stirring often to prevent scorching, about 5 minutes. Transfer it to a medium bowl.

FOR BOTH METHODS
Remove the meat from the bones and cut it into 1-inch pieces. (There will be about 3½ cups.) Add it to the bowl together with the vegetables and prunes and stir together gently. (The filling can be refrigerated for up to 24 hours at this point.)

Preheat the oven to 425°F. at least 20 minutes before baking.

MAKE THE MASHED POTATOES

Peel and quarter the potatoes. Place them in a medium saucepan and cover them with a few inches of cold water and add the salt. Boil them for 20 minutes or until just tender when pierced with a skewer or sharp knife. Drain the potatoes thoroughly and put them through a ricer, or sieve, or mash them. The secret to silky, smooth mashed potatoes is to press them through a ricer, sieve, or food mill. Using a food processor or blender will make them pasty, while mashing them with a fork or potato masher will never make them as smooth.

Stir in the butter with a wooden spoon. Heat the crème fraîche and add it gradually to the potatoes, whisking briefly. Whisk in the salt, nutmeg, pepper, and optional truffle oil. Taste to adjust the seasoning. (I add about ⅛ teaspoon of salt.)

Spoon the meat mixture into the pie pans and cover each with ½ cup of the mashed potatoes. Using a fork, make concentric circular marks in the potato topping to resemble a rose. Bake for 10 minutes (15 if the filling was refrigerated). Turn the oven to broil and place under the broiler for 3 to 5 minutes or until the mashed potatoes are golden.

POINTERS FOR SUCCESS

∿ Lamb shank is the most flavorful and succulent cut of lamb. I prefer the cooked meat to have a little bite. If it is cooked to the point where it is actually falling off the bone, it will be less moist.

MEAT LOAF IN A FLAKY CHEDDAR CRUST

I first encountered a version of this pastry-wrapped meat loaf when I worked at *Ladies' Home Journal* over twenty years ago. The Cheddar cheese crust is fantastic with the meat. It is crisp, flaky, and tender with just enough heat (from cayenne pepper) to complement the zesty filling. It's also excellent prepared with a packaged crust.* This recipe was quick to become a family favorite and a regular at our table.

EQUIPMENT

An 8½- by 4½-inch 6-cup bread pan and a cookie sheet, lined with foil

*I like the Betty Crocker packaged crust. Simply add the ¾ cup grated cheese to it and follow the package directions.

OVEN TEMPERATURE: 400°F., THEN 375°F. • BAKING TIME: 65 TO 75 MINUTES   SERVES: 6

INGREDIENTS	MEASURE	WEIGHT	
	VOLUME	OUNCES	GRAMS
Flaky Cheddar Cheese Pie Crust (page 39)		14.4 ounces	412 grams
fresh bread crumbs*	¼ cup	0.3 ounce	11 grams
1 large egg		•	•
ketchup	¼ cup	approx. 2.5 ounces	69 grams
Worcestershire sauce	1½ teaspoons	•	•
minced fresh parsley	2 tablespoons	approx. 0.25 ounce	8 grams
dry mustard	1½ teaspoons	•	3.6 grams
salt	1½ teaspoons	0.3 ounce	10 grams
freshly ground black pepper	½ teaspoon	•	•
1 small white onion, finely chopped	¼ cup	approx. 2 ounces	60 grams
ground round	•	2 pounds	907 grams

*For more even processing, allow the bread to sit uncovered to dry for about 3 hours before processing into crumbs.

Make the dough (page 39).

Preheat the oven to 400°F. at least 20 minutes before baking. Set an oven rack a little below the center of the oven before preheating.

In a large bowl, mix the bread crumbs, egg, ketchup, Worcestershire, parsley, mustard, salt, and pepper. Add the onion and meat and mix just until evenly combined.

Pack the meat gently into the pan and bake it for 25 to 30 minutes or until a thermometer inserted in the center registers 115°F. Allow the meat loaf to cool completely on a wire rack, 50 minutes to 1 hour. Unmold it onto paper towels and then invert it so that it is right side up.

WRAP THE MEAT LOAF

Roll the pastry between two sheets of lightly floured plastic wrap into a 13- by 14-inch rectangle, ⅛ inch thick. Remove the top sheet of plastic and place the meat loaf lengthwise on one 13-inch-long side of the pastry. Use the plastic wrap to lift the dough up and over the meat loaf. Do not stretch the pastry, as it will shrink slightly on baking and would tear. Remove the plastic wrap and pinch the seams to seal them. Trim, if necessary, leaving enough to tuck under about 1 inch at the bottom and a little more at the ends. Moisten the bottom side of this border with a little water. Fold the long side underneath and then fold under the ends as if you were wrapping a present.

Use a small scalloped cutter or pastry tube to cut 2 vents in the top of the pastry. If desired, cut the scraps into decorative shapes and attach them to the top of the pastry with a little water.

Place the meat loaf on the cookie sheet, cover it lightly with foil, and refrigerate it for at least 30 minutes and up to 6 hours.

Preheat the oven to 375°F. at least 20 minutes before baking. Set an oven rack at the lowest level and place a baking stone or baking sheet on it before preheating.

Bake the meat loaf for 35 to 45 minutes or until the pastry is golden and the meat juices start to bubble through the vents. (A thermometer should read 160°F.) Place the meat loaf, still on the cookie sheet, on a rack to cool for 10 to 15 minutes before serving it.

Using a serrated knife and a large pancake turner held against the cut end of the loaf for support, slice 1-inch-thick slices.

STORE

Refrigerated, 3 to 4 days.

POINTERS FOR SUCCESS

∽ For the best flavor, chop the onion just before adding it to the mixture.

∽ The meat *must not* be warm when you wrap it with the dough.

∽ The meat loaf is not adequately cooked until the juices start bubbling through the vent.

UNDERSTANDING

The dough-wrapped meat loaf is baked on the bottom oven rack on a stone or baking sheet so that the bottom gets crisp despite the juicy meat.

BAKED EMPANADAS

My editor, Maria Guarnaschelli, insisted that I include a recipe for this Latin American specialty because it is such a popular savory pastry. When she described the filling, I suspected that my Miracle Flaky Lard Pie Crust, with its crisp, flaky texture and wheaty meat flavor, would be the perfect wrapping for a spicy meat filling.

These spicy meat turnovers give definition to the word *savory*. Their subtle but tantalizing piquancy comes not only from herbs and spices but also from the occasional sweet/sour zing of raisins, accented by the mild brininess of chopped olives.

I love these empanadas so much they will now appear with great regularity at my table.

As with all spicy mixtures, these empanadas are possibly even more delicious as leftovers.

INGREDIENTS	MEASURE	WEIGHT	
	VOLUME	OUNCES	GRAMS
1½ recipes Miracle Flaky Lard Pie Crust (page 41), Flaky Cheddar Cheese Pie Crust (page 39), or Basic Whole Wheat Flaky Pie Crust (page 24)		19.5 ounces	555 grams
Savory Meat Filling *optional:* raisins	(2 full cups) 2 tablespoons	(14.75 ounces) 0.6 ounce	421 grams 18 grams
lard or olive oil	2 teaspoons	•	•
chopped onion	1 heaping cup	4.25 ounces	120 grams
sugar	a pinch	•	•
1 medium clove garlic, minced	1½ teaspoons	•	•
paprika	½ teaspoon	•	•
ground cumin	¼ teaspoon	•	•
ground round	•	12 ounces	340 grams
salt	½ teaspoon	•	•
freshly ground black pepper	¼ teaspoon	•	•
ancho chile powder (see note) or chili powder	¾ teaspoon ½ teaspoon	•	•
dried thyme	½ teaspoon	•	•
dried oregano	¼ teaspoon	•	•
optional: 7 green olives stuffed with pimientos, coarsely chopped	2 tablespoons	0.7 ounce	20 grams
whole wheat flour	approx. ½ cup	2.5 ounces	72 grams
1 large egg white, lightly beaten	2 tablespoons	1 ounce	28 grams

EQUIPMENT
A cookie sheet or inverted half-sheet pan

Make the dough (page 41 or 39 or 24).

MAKE THE FILLING

In a small bowl, place the optional raisins with 1 tablespoon of water and allow them to sit for at least 20 minutes; drain.

Heat a medium skillet over low heat until hot. Add the lard or oil and the onions, sprinkle with the sugar, and fry the onions, stirring occasionally, for about 10 minutes or until they become deep golden. Add the garlic and sprinkle with the paprika and cumin. Cook, stirring constantly, for about 2 minutes, just to bring out the flavor of the spices without burning them. Add the ground beef and sprinkle with the salt, pepper, chili powder, thyme, and oregano. Raise the heat to medium and cook, stirring often, for 3 to 5 minutes or until the meat is no longer pink.

Remove the pan from the heat and stir in the optional drained raisins and chopped olives. Allow the filling to cool to room temperature. (It must not be warm when placed on the dough, or it will soften the pastry.) To speed cooling, you can transfer it to a baking sheet or piece of aluminum foil laid on the counter.

SHAPE THE EMPANADAS

I prefer to roll the dough rounds one at a time so that there is no need to reroll the scraps.

Process the whole wheat flour for a few minutes in a food processor with the metal blade.

Divide the dough into 12 equal pieces (1.6 ounces/46 grams each). Work with one piece at a time and keep the rest refrigerated. On a counter well floured with the whole wheat flour, or between two sheets of plastic wrap well floured with the whole wheat flour, roll the piece of dough into a circle about 1/16 inch thick and large enough to cut out a 6-inch circle. Use a template and a sharp knife to cut out the circle. *Alternatively,* roll the dough into a large rectangle or, working with half the dough at a time, 2 large rectangles, and cut out 6-inch circles. Then lay the scraps side by side, slightly overlapping and in a few layers. Roll them between plastic wrap, folding the piece of dough in thirds like a business letter, and cut out more circles; you should have 12 in all. Refrigerate the dough for at least 15 minutes before you shape the empanadas.

Transfer each dough circle to the bottom end of a 9-inch-long piece of plastic wrap. Brush the bottom half of it with the egg white. Spoon 3 tablespoons of the filling onto this section, leaving a 1-inch border. Using the plastic wrap if the dough is at all sticky, fold the top part of the dough over the fruit, so that the edges are flush. With your fingers, firmly press the 1-inch border to seal it. Fold the edge up over itself, a little at a time, pleating it as you go and pressing again to seal it. (There is no need to cut vents, because the filling is precooked, so there will be no steam or bubbling juices to burst the seams of the empanadas.)

Lap the top piece of plastic wrap over the dough and lift the empanada onto the baking sheet. Repeat with the remaining empanadas and refrigerate them for at least 30 minutes.

Preheat the oven to 425°F. at least 20 minutes before baking. Set an oven rack at the middle level and place a baking stone or inverted baking sheet on it before preheating.

Unwrap the empanadas and space them evenly on the sheet. Place the sheet directly on the stone and bake for 20 to 25 minutes or until the pastry starts to turn golden. Place the empandas on serving plates and allow them to cool for 10 minutes before eating. They are also delicious at room temperature.

STORE

Unbaked, frozen, up to 3 months. (To bake from frozen, bake in a preheated 400°F. oven for 30 to 35 minutes or until golden.) Baked, refrigerated, up to 5 days. (Reheat, if desired, in a 300 °F. oven for 5 minutes.)

NOTE

To make your own ancho chile powder, on a small baking sheet, toast an ancho chile in a preheated 350°F. oven for 5 minutes or just until it puffs up and becomes crisp, turning it halfway through. (Overtoasting will make it bitter.) Remove and discard the stem and seeds. Process it in a food processor or spice blender until it turns into a fine powder. Store any leftover powder in an airtight jar.

UNDERSTANDING

Ancho chiles are dried poblano peppers. These are the chiles that give the distinctive flavor to commercial chili powder. Freshly roasted and ground, they are more aromatic than chili powder. Ancho chiles are sold in Spanish markets and by mail order from Balducci's (see page 675).

Rolling out the pie dough on whole wheat flour gives it extra texture and flavor. To prevent the coarse bran from breaking through the dough, process it first for a few minutes in a food processor with the metal blade.

QUICHE LORRAINE

This was probably everyone's first taste of quiche and is still many people's favorite. Although a classic quiche Lorraine does not contain cheese, I wouldn't dream of making one without it. I would miss not only the flavor but also the beautiful golden color cheese adds. Let's face it: With bacon, cream, and eggs, this is a cholesterol avoider's forbidden pleasure, so a small piece, on a special occasion, should be everything it can be. For me, that means the slight crunch and flavor of onion and using not only the best bacon, but also Gruyère cheese and, preferably, a lard pie crust. You could serve it with red wine, which, in what is touted as the "French paradox," is said to counteract the effects of the high-fat French diet. Or do what I would do and serve it with an Alsatian Riesling, which is from the area of the quiche's origins and, with its resonating mineral acidity, a fantastic accompaniment.

OVEN TEMPERATURE: 350°F. • BAKING TIME: 30 TO 40 MINUTES **SERVES: 4 TO 6**

INGREDIENTS	MEASURE	WEIGHT	
	VOLUME	OUNCES	GRAMS
Flaky Pastry for a 9½-inch tart, preferably lard (page 41), prebaked and still warm		13 ounces	370 grams
½ large egg white, lightly beaten	1 tablespoon	0.5 ounce	15 grams
bacon	5 strips	4 ounces	113 grams
finely chopped onion	¼ cup	approx. 1 ounce	32 grams
grated Gruyère cheese	1 cup (firmly packed), divided	3 ounces	85 grams
Crème Fraiche (page 558) or heavy cream	½ liquid cup	4 ounces	116 grams
milk	½ liquid cup	4.25 ounces	121 grams
3 large eggs	scant ⅔ liquid cup	5.25 ounces	150 grams
salt	¼ teaspoon	•	•
freshly ground black pepper	⅛ teaspoon	•	•
cayenne pepper	a pinch	•	•
nutmeg, preferably freshly grated	a pinch	•	•

EQUIPMENT

A 9½-inch fluted tart pan with a removable bottom

Make the dough (page 41). Roll, shape, and prebake it (see page 251). While it is still warm, brush it with the egg white (see page 20).

Preheat the oven to 350°F. at least 15 minutes before baking. Set an oven rack at the middle level and place a baking stone or cookie sheet on it before preheating.

In a large frying pan, fry the bacon over low heat, for about 8 minutes or until barely crisp. With a slotted skimmer, remove it to paper towels to drain.

Distribute the chopped onion evenly over the prepared crust. Crumble the bacon into small pieces and sprinkle it evenly over the crust. Sprinkle half the Gruyère over it.

In a medium bowl, whisk together the cream, milk, eggs, and seasonings just until thoroughly blended. (The custard will measure about 1⅔ cups.) Pour this mixture over the bacon and cheese. Sprinkle evenly with the remaining Gruyère and place the pan on the baking stone or sheet.

Bake for 30 to 40 minutes or until the filling is slightly puffed, the top is golden brown, and a thin knife blade inserted near the center comes out clean (165° to 170°F.). Allow it to cool on a rack for at least 10 minutes before unmolding.

Unmold the quiche (see page 251) and serve warm or at room temperature.

STORE

Refrigerated, covered, up to 2 days. To reheat, bake for 10 to 15 minutes in a preheated 350°F. oven.

POINTERS FOR SUCCESS

෴ A prebaked pie crust is desirable because a raw one will still be uncooked and pasty in the middle, even if the quiche is baked directly on the oven floor.

෴ The filling should not come up past ⅛ inch below the top of the crust.

෴ If using a two-piece tart pan, place it on a foil-lined baking sheet with low sides or a jelly-roll pan just in case the filling should leak.

෴ To prevent curdling, bake only until the knife blade comes out clean.

CARAMELIZED ONION TART

This tart is for the onion lover. (Me, me!) It is truly amazing how, when cooked very slowly, the sugar contained in the onions caramelizes and turns the onions a deep golden brown. The onions cook down to less than one third their original volume. In my opinion, this method produces onions at their most delicious. The tangy/sweet onions contrast wonderfully with the salty oil-cured olives. I borrowed them for this recipe from the *pissaladière*—an onion tart of Provençal origin.

I like to make a lard crust, rolled out in whole wheat flour, for this tart. The crisp, crunchy texture and faintly wheaty flavor go especially well with the filling. The butter flavor and firmer texture of a flaky butter crust or cream cheese crust would also be great.

As this tart, like quiche Lorraine, is an Alsatian specialty, it goes without saying that a Riesling would be a fine accompaniment. Its tart/fruity quality also balances perfectly with the tart/sweetness of the onion.

OVEN TEMPERATURE: 400°F. • BAKING TIME: 15 TO 20 MINUTES   **SERVES: 6**

INGREDIENTS	MEASURE	WEIGHT	
	VOLUME	OUNCES	GRAMS
Flaky Pastry for a 9½-inch tart, preferably lard (page 41), partially prebaked and still warm		13 ounces	370 grams
½ large egg white, lightly beaten	1 tablespoon	0.5 ounce	15 grams
extra-virgin olive oil	2 tablespoons	1 ounce	28 grams
unsalted butter	1 tablespoon	0.5 ounce	14 grams
6 medium onions, halved and sliced paper-thin	7 cups (sliced)	32 ounces (sliced)	907 grams
sugar	¼ teaspoon	•	•
salt	½ teaspoon	•	•
freshly ground black pepper	¼ teaspoon	•	•
1 large clove garlic, minced	2 teaspoons	0.25 ounce	7 grams
fresh thyme leaves or dried thyme	1 teaspoon ¼ teaspoon	• •	• •
grated Gruyère cheese	2 tablespoons, lightly packed	0.5 ounce	14 grams
9 black oil-cured olives, halved and pitted	•	0.75 ounce	21 grams

EQUIPMENT
A 9½-inch tart pan with a removable bottom

Make the dough (page 41). Roll, shape, and partially prebake it (see page 251). While the crust is still warm, brush it with the egg white (see page 20).

In a large heavy sauté pan or skillet, heat the oil and butter over low heat until bubbling. Add the onions and sprinkle with the sugar, salt, and pepper. Cover tightly and cook, without stirring, over the lowest possible heat for about 45 minutes. The onions will be soft and their liquid will have been exuded.

Meanwhile, preheat the oven to 400°F. at least 20 minutes before baking. Set an oven rack at the lowest level before preheating.

Raise the heat under the onions to medium, uncover the pan, and continue cooking, stirring often, until all liquid has evaporated and the onions are deep gold in color. Turn down the heat to low. Add the garlic and thyme and cook for 3 minutes, stirring often. Remove from the heat.

Fill the tart shell with the onion mixture. Sprinkle evenly with the Gruyère and arrange the olives decoratively on top. Bake for 15 to 20 minutes or until the cheese is melted and the top is deeply browned.

Unmold the tart (see page 251). Serve hot, warm, or at room temperature.

VARIATION

CARAMELIZED ONION TART WITH CUSTARD   The addition of a small amount of custard serves to bind together the onions and makes the overall effect somewhat more mellow. For this version, simply beat together ½ cup half-and-half and 1 large egg. Pour it over the onion mixture before sprinkling with the Gruyère. Bake at 375°F., rather than 400 °F., for 15 minutes, as the custard requires more gentle heat.

STORE
Room temperature, up to 1 day.

POINTERS FOR SUCCESS
- To slice the onions, I use a food processor with a 1-millimeter slicing blade.
- Slow cooking results in the unique sweetness and flavor of the onions.

UNDERSTANDING
The texture of the onions is dependent on the way in which the onion is cut. If chopped, they would not develop the same flavor and texture. If sliced whole (into rings), the cooked onions are difficult to cut and to eat in a neat manner.

The 7 cups of onions reduce to only 2 cups, which means an intense concentration of flavor.

The tart crust is only partially baked because there is no liquid or custard in the filling, so starting with a fully baked crust would make the tart dry.

ROASTED RED PEPPER
AND POBLANO QUICHE

This quiche has Southwestern flavors with a mild spiciness. If you do not share my love of the slightly smoky, faintly fiery poblano pepper, substitute an equal volume of sweet red peppers. For flavor and texture, I like to use a high proportion of peppers to custard. Their bright red and green colors offer an eye-catching contrast against the golden custard. Any leftover quiche is at least as tasty the following day, reheated or at room temperature.

OVEN TEMPERATURE: 350°F. • BAKING TIME: 35 TO 40 MINUTES   **SERVES: 6**

INGREDIENTS	MEASURE	WEIGHT	
	VOLUME	OUNCES	GRAMS
Flaky Pastry for a 9½-inch tart, preferably Cheddar or lard (page 39 or 41), prebaked and still warm		13 ounces	370 grams
½ large egg white, lightly beaten	1 tablespoon	0.5 ounce	15 grams
olive oil	1 tablespoon	0.5 ounce	13 grams
½ small onion, chopped	⅓ cup	1.5 ounces	43 grams
2 large roasted red peppers, chopped (see below)	2 cups	12 ounces	340 grams
2 poblano peppers, chopped	⅓ cup	2 ounces	57 grams
1 large clove garlic, minced	2 teaspoons	0.25 ounce	7 grams
half-and-half or milk	⅔ liquid cup	5.6 ounces	160 grams
2 large eggs	3 fluid ounces	3.5 ounces	100 grams (weighed without the shells)
salt	¼ teaspoon	•	•
freshly ground black pepper	⅛ teaspoon	•	•
coarsely torn fresh cilantro or chopped fresh basil	2 tablespoons 1 tablespoon	• •	10 grams 5 grams
grated Gruyère cheese	½ cup	1.5 ounces	43 grams

EQUIPMENT
A 9½-inch fluted tart pan with a removable bottom

Make the dough (page 39 or 41). Roll, shape, and prebake it (see page 251). While it is still warm, brush it with the egg white (see page 20).

Preheat the oven to 350°F. at least 15 minutes before baking. Set a rack at the lowest level and place a baking stone or cookie sheet on it before preheating.

In a medium sauté pan or skillet, heat the oil over medium heat. When hot, add the onion and sauté, stirring often, for about 3 minutes or until translucent. Add the peppers and garlic and sauté, stirring, for 1 minute. Remove the skillet from the heat and spoon the mixture into the prepared tart shell.

In a 2-cup liquid measure or a small bowl, whisk together the half-and-half, eggs, salt, and pepper just until thoroughly blended. (You will have about 1 cup.) Pour this mixture over the pepper mixture. It will come almost to the top of the crust. (The filling makes about 2¾ cups.) Sprinkle the cilantro or basil and Gruyère evenly over the top.

Place the quiche on the baking stone or sheet and bake for 35 to 40 minutes or until the filling is slightly puffed, the top is golden brown, and a thin knife blade inserted near the center comes out clean (165° to 170°F.). Allow the quiche to cool for at least 10 minutes on a rack before unmolding.

Unmold the quiche (see page 251) and serve warm or at room temperature.

STORE

Refrigerated, covered, up to 2 days. To reheat, bake for 20 minutes, uncovered, in a preheated 350°F. oven.

NOTE

To roast peppers, wash and leave them whole. Place them on a charcoal grill or gas or electric burner over medium-low heat. (If using a gas burner, line the plate underneath with heavy-duty foil; if using an electric burner, cover the coils with foil.) Roast the peppers, turning often with tongs so as not to pierce them, for about 20 minutes or until blackened all over. Place them in a bag and allow them to sit briefly to help loosen the skin.

When cool enough to handle, cut out the cores and discard the liquid (or save it to add to soup). Using your fingers, remove the skin. Cut the peppers lengthwise in half and remove and discard the seeds. For this recipe, slice them into ¼-inch strips and then cut the strips into ¼-inch cubes.

POINTERS FOR SUCCESS

If using a two-piece tart pan, place it on a baking sheet with low sides or a jelly-roll pan just in case the filling should leak.

To prevent curdling, bake only until the knife blade comes out clean.

UNDERSTANDING

The peppers must be roasted whole so that steam contained inside keeps them from drying.

CREAMY AND SPICY CRAB TARTLETS

The filling for this exciting appetizer comes from Master Chef Nobu Matsuhisa, of his restaurant, Nobu, in New York City. Nobu is renowned for his creative fusion of Japanese and Western ingredients.

These little tartlets contain fresh crabmeat napped with a spicy flavorful mayonnaise sauce. The small amount of tobanjan (hot bean paste) in the sauce adds more than a mild fire. It also has a unique slightly fermented flavor. The fish eggs contribute the perfect amount of saltiness and intriguing crunchy crackle.

Three-inch tarts are the smallest that I find convenient to make and are a perfect size for an appetizer, with this rich filling. Also, this size tart is easier to eat by hand. If desired, they can certainly be made smaller to pass with cocktails. But even at three inches, they are sturdy enough to be hand-held. The crisp whole wheat crust is a lovely taste and textural contrast.

OVEN TEMPERATURE: 350°F. • BAKING TIME: 7 TO 10 MINUTES   **SERVES: 6**

INGREDIENTS	MEASURE	WEIGHT	
	VOLUME	OUNCES	GRAMS
½ recipe Flaky Pastry, preferably whole wheat (page 24), prebaked in six 3-inch tartlet pans and still warm		4.5 ounces	128 grams
½ large egg white, lightly beaten	1 tablespoon	0.5 ounce	15 grams
mayonnaise	⅓ cup	2.5 ounces	72 grams
minced tobanjan (Szechwan hot bean paste)*	½ to 1 teaspoon	•	•
minced scallions (white part only)	2 teaspoons	0.3 ounce	9 grams
smelt eggs† or red lumpfish caviar	2 teaspoons	•	8 grams
fresh lump crabmeat	¾ cup	4.5 ounces	128 grams

*Available in Asian markets. Use the larger amount if you like things on the *hot* side.
†Available in Asian markets. If omitting these or the caviar, add salt to taste.

EQUIPMENT
Six 3-inch fluted tart pans with removable bottoms

*Make the dough (page 24). Roll, shape, and prebake it
(see page 251). While it is still warm, brush it with the egg
white (see page 20). Unmold the tart shells.*

*Preheat the oven to 350°F. at least 15 minutes before baking. Set an oven rack at the
middle level before preheating.*

MAKE THE FILLING
In a small bowl, stir together the mayonnaise, bean paste, and scallions. Gently stir
in the smelt eggs or caviar. Cover tightly and refrigerate until ready to use. (The
filling can be made ahead and refrigerated for up to 24 hours.)

Pick through the crab, removing any cartilage. Place 2 tablespoons of crab in
each tartlet shell. Spread about 1 tablespoon of the filling evenly on top of each.

Set the tartlets on a baking sheet. Bake for 7 to 10 minutes or until the topping
sets and dulls. Serve hot or warm.

POINTERS FOR SUCCESS
∿ The bean paste is minced to reduce any large pieces of bean and chili, which
would result in an uneven distribution of spiciness.
∿ To make as a 9½-inch tart, double all the ingredients and bake for about 15
minutes.

SPRING WINDFALL MOREL QUICHE

I would never have thought I could find enough morel mushrooms to make
a quiche featuring them, but May 1996 was a bumper harvest for morels. I
found a record total of eight and a quarter pounds of them within the short
two-week season at my country home in New Jersey. Two had heads larger than
a tennis ball. Normally I dry the morels, which intensifies their flavor, but with
an unexpected embarrassment of riches, I was prompted to create this recipe. It
is also delicious with the more affordable and readily available fresh shiitake
mushroom.

This quiche is mostly butter-sautéed morels, with a mere film of
flavorful custard to hold them together. The concentrated chicken
stock in the custard intensifies the backwoodsy bouquet of the mushrooms and the slightly sweet/acid Riesling elevates the taste to the
addictive category.

This quiche would make a lovely brunch dish or appetizer for a fancy dinner
party.

OVEN TEMPERATURE: 350°F. •
BAKING TIME: 20 TO 25 MINUTES

SERVES: 2 AS A MAIN COURSE,
6 AS AN APPETIZER

INGREDIENTS	MEASURE	WEIGHT	
	VOLUME	OUNCES	GRAMS
½ recipe Flaky Pastry for a 7¾-inch tart or 7-inch skillet, preferably lard (page 41), prebaked and still warm		6 ounces	170 grams
½ large egg white, lightly beaten	1 tablespoon	0.5 ounce	15 grams
1 can no-salt chicken broth	approx. 1¾ cups	approx. 14.5 ounces	411 grams
unsalted butter	1 tablespoon	0.5 ounce	14 grams
minced shallots	4 teaspoons	•	•
1 large garlic clove, smashed		0.25 ounce	7 grams
fresh morel mushrooms, halved or quartered, depending on size*	3½ cups	12 ounces	340 grams
white wine, preferably Spätlese Riesling†	¼ liquid cup	•	•
fresh thyme leaves‡	1 teaspoon	•	•
milk	¼ liquid cup	•	•
heavy cream	1 tablespoon	•	•
1 large egg	3 tablespoons	1.75 ounces (weighed without the shells)	50 grams
salt	⅛ teaspoon	•	•
freshly ground black pepper	1/16 teaspoon	•	•

*You can substitute 2 ounces of dried morels soaked in 1½ cups water for at least 30 minutes. Add the strained soaking liquid to the stock before reducing it.
†Or 1 tablespoon freshly squeezed lemon juice and a pinch of sugar.
‡Or ¼ teaspoon dried thyme.

EQUIPMENT
A 7¾-inch fluted tart pan with a removable bottom
or a 7-inch skillet

*Make the dough (page 41). Roll, shape, and prebake
it (see page 251). While it is still warm, brush it with
the egg white (see page 20).*

*Preheat the oven to 350°F. at least 15 minutes
before baking. Set an oven rack at the lowest level and
place a baking stone or cookie sheet on it before preheating.*

In a medium saucepan, place the chicken stock and, over high heat, boil it
down until it is reduced to ¼ cup, about 15 minutes. Set it aside.

In a medium sauté pan, over low heat, melt the butter and sauté the shallots
and smashed garlic until the shallots are translucent. Add the morels, raise the
heat to medium-low, and cook, covered, for 10 to 15 minutes or until tender when
pierced with a skewer. (If you are using store-bought morels and they are somewhat dry, add 2 to 4 tablespoons of water.) Uncover and cook for 5 minutes or
until all the liquid has evaporated. (The morels will have reduced in volume to
about 1 cup.) Add the wine and cook for about 3 minutes or until most of it has
evaporated. Remove and discard the garlic and stir in the thyme. Spoon the mixture into the prepared tart shell.

In a 1-cup liquid measure or a small bowl, whisk together the reduced stock,
the milk, cream, egg, salt, and pepper. (You will have about ¾ cup.) Pour this mixture over the mushroom mixture.

Place the tart pan on the baking stone or sheet. Bake for 20 to 25 minutes or
until a thin knife blade inserted near the center comes out clean. Allow the quiche
to cool at least 10 minutes before unmolding.

Unmold the quiche (see page 251) and serve warm or at room temperature.

STORE
Refrigerated, covered, up to 2 days. To reheat, bake for 15 minutes in a preheated
350°F. oven.

NOTE
To dry morels without a dehydrator, place them on wire racks in an oven with a
pilot light. Place a sheet of foil on the oven rack below or on the oven floor to capture the mushroom dust. Small morels require about 48 hours; large one (tennis
ball–size heads), 60 hours. When the morels are totally dried, snap off the stems.
(They are too tough to eat but can be pulverized in a food processor and added to
stock or grain dishes or even mixed into the flour for making pasta.) Store the

dried morels in glass canning jars, tightly capped. They will keep indefinitely. I am grateful to James Beard, who gave me my first dried morel, from his home state of Oregon.

POINTERS FOR SUCCESS

∾ If using a two-piece tart pan, place it on a baking sheet with low sides or a jelly-roll pan just in case the filling should leak.

∾ To prevent curdling, bake only until the knife blade comes out clean.

UNDERSTANDING

The custard in this mixture will not be quite as silky smooth as usual because of an enzyme in the morel that alters it slightly. For this reason also, crème fraîche is not an acceptable substitute for the heavy cream, as the enzyme would cause it to separate.

SPICY SPINACH QUICHE

The spinach filling in this quiche is novelist and cookbook writer Laurie Colwin's spinach soufflé. People who love spinach adore this recipe, but what is amazing is that dyed-in-the-wool spinach haters also seem to make an exception for the dish. The sautéed onion and garlic help, but it's no doubt the spicy, creamy cheese that makes the critical difference.

I have added optional quail egg yolks because when the quiche is cut into slices, the contrast of the deep forest green filling against the tiny, bright yellow egg yolks is stunning. The yolks also add the element of a sauce, as they are still runny. Alternatively, the pine nut garnish is an attractive and delicious toasty adjunct to the slight bitterness of the spinach.

EQUIPMENT
A 9½-inch fluted tart pan with a removable bottom

INGREDIENTS	MEASURE	WEIGHT	
	VOLUME	OUNCES	GRAMS
Flaky Pastry for a 9½-inch tart, preferably whole wheat cream cheese (page 32), prebaked and still warm		11 ounces	312 grams
½ large egg white, lightly beaten	1 tablespoon	0.5 ounce	15 grams
1 package frozen chopped spinach	1 cup	10 ounces	283 grams
unsalted butter	1 tablespoon	0.5 ounce	14 grams
½ small onion, chopped	⅓ cup	1.5 ounces	43 grams
1 large garlic clove, minced	2 teaspoons	0.25 ounce	7 grams
evaporated milk	¼ liquid cup	2 ounces	58 grams
2 large eggs	3 fluid ounces	3.5 ounces (weighed without the shells)	100 grams
celery salt	½ teaspoon	•	•
freshly ground black pepper	⅛ teaspoon	•	•
grated Monterey Jack pepper cheese or Muenster	1 cup (medium-firmly packed)	3 ounces	86 grams
Optional Garnish 6 quail egg yolks or lightly toasted pine nuts	• 3 tablespoons	• approx. 1 ounce	• 33 grams

Make the dough (page 32). Roll, shape, and prebake it (see page 251). While it is still warm, brush it with the egg white (see page 20).

Preheat the oven to 350°F. at least 15 minutes before baking. Set an oven rack at the lowest level and place a baking stone or cookie sheet on it before preheating.

Cook the spinach according to the package directions. Set it aside, covered.

In a medium sauté pan, melt the butter over medium heat. When bubbling, add the onion and sauté, stirring often, for about 3 minutes or until translucent. Add the garlic and sauté, stirring, for 1 minute. Remove from the heat and allow it to cool.

In a large bowl, beat together the evaporated milk, eggs, celery salt, and pepper. Stir in the onion mixture, then the spinach and any liquid, and the cheese. (You will have 2½ cups of filling [about 20 ounces/570 grams].) Spoon this mixture into the prepared tart shell.

Place the tart pan on the baking stone or sheet. Bake for 20 to 30 minutes or until the filling puffs slightly, the top is set to the touch, and a thin knife blade inserted near the center comes out clean.

If using the quail egg yolks, with the back of a wooden spoon, make 6 small depressions at even intervals about 1 inch from the outside edge of the quiche. Place a quail egg yolk in each. Continue baking for 5 minutes. Remove the quiche from the oven and allow it to cool for at least 10 minutes before unmolding. If using pine nuts, scatter them around the periphery of the quiche, about 1 inch from the outer edge.

Unmold the quiche (see page 251) and serve warm or at room temperature.

STORE

Refrigerated, covered, up to 2 days. To reheat, bake for 20 minutes in a preheated 350°F. oven.

POINTERS FOR SUCCESS

∽ Quail eggs are available in specialty food stores and Asian markets. If you have trouble finding them, ask your local Japanese restaurant where they get theirs; they are a popular ingredient for sushi.

∽ If using a two-piece tart pan, place it on a baking sheet with low sides or a jelly-roll pan just in case the filling should leak.

∽ To prevent curdling, bake only until the knife blade comes out clean.

BISCUITS AND SCONES

In pastry terms, the only difference between biscuits and scones is shape. Biscuits are round, scones triangular. Biscuits and scones are actually the bridge between pastry and cake. They are prepared like a flaky pie dough but they contain the same basic ingredients as cake (flour, fat, liquid, sugar, and leavening)—only less liquid. If the butter or fat is kept cold and in large pieces, biscuits and scones will be a little flaky, though never as flaky as puff or flaky pastry.

Puff pastry consists of equal weights of flour and butter (e.g., 8 ounces each) and half the weight of water (4 ounces). Basic flaky pastry has the same proportion of butter to water (8 ounces to 4 ounces) and about one and a half times more flour than puff pastry, which makes it quite similar to puff pastry, depending on how it is made.

Cream scones and biscuits, on the other hand, have the same basic ratio of flour to butter as flaky pastry but twice as much liquid. (This is taking into consideration the 36 percent butterfat contained in the cream. If buttermilk is used, they have still more liquid and less fat.) They also contain sugar and baking powder and/or baking soda, which sweeten and tenderize the dough, making it more cake-like. No wonder biscuits and scones are so popular; they are like having your cake and eating pie crust too!

TOUCH-OF-GRACE BISCUITS

There are many people who consider Shirley Corriher to be the queen of Southern biscuits. This recipe for her biscuits has appeared in articles and cookbooks, including her own *CookWise*. The secret to her fluffy biscuits is using a lot more liquid (more than double the usual amount!). Another secret is the Southern tradition of the "rising oven." This means that when the biscuits are set in the oven, the temperature is immediately turned up so that a burst of heat rises up, giving extra lift to the biscuits.

Heavy cream will make a more tender biscuit, while buttermilk will make a little lighter biscuit with a slight tang. Compared to Butter Biscuits (page 353), these biscuits have less fat and more sugar and liquid, making them very light. Because they are made with shortening, the biscuits have less flavor than biscuits made entirely with butter, but the trade-off is that they are whiter, lighter, and fluffier. Of course, they can be spread with butter after baking if you love the butter flavor. They are also tasty Southern-style, filled with ham and topped with pepper jelly.

OVEN TEMPERATURE: 475°F., THEN 500°F. •
BAKING TIME: 15 TO 20 MINUTES
INTERNAL TEMPERATURE: 160°F.   MAKES: NINE 2½- BY 2-INCH-HIGH BISCUITS

INGREDIENTS	MEASURE	WEIGHT	
	VOLUME	OUNCES	GRAMS
White Lily self-rising flour*	1½ cups (dip and sweep method)	approx. 7.5 ounces	213 grams
sugar	3 tablespoons	1.3 ounces	37.5 grams
salt	½ teaspoon	•	•
vegetable shortening, cold	3 tablespoons	1.25 ounces	36 grams
heavy cream or buttermilk (or a combination of the two)	1¼ liquid cups	10.2 ounces 10.6 ounces	290 grams 302 grams
all-purpose flour	1 cup	5 ounces	142 grams
optional: melted butter, cooled	1 tablespoon	0.5 ounce	14 grams

*Or White Lily regular flour (or 1 cup bleached all-purpose plus ½ cup cake flour) plus 2 teaspoons baking powder and an extra ¾ teaspoon salt.

EQUIPMENT

An 8-inch round cake pan (or 6-inch pan or skillet for half the recipe), lightly greased (biscuits must be snug in the pan, so make only half the recipe if you have the 6-inch pan); optional: a number 30 cookie scoop (2 tablespoon capacity)

Preheat the oven to 475°F. at least 20 minutes before baking. Set an oven rack at the middle level and place a bread pan half filled with very hot water on it before preheating.

In a medium bowl, whisk together the self-rising flour, sugar, and salt (and baking powder and extra salt if not using self-rising flour). Add the shortening in 1-teaspoon-size pieces and, with your fingertips, work the shortening into the flour until pea-size or smaller. Mix in the cream and/or buttermilk. (You can also use an electric mixer on low speed.) The mixture will be very soft, like mashed potatoes. Allow it to sit for 2 to 3 minutes; it will stiffen slightly.

Place the all-purpose flour in a small pan. Using a cookie scoop or a large spoon, scoop out a biscuit-size lump of wet dough (a heaping scoopful) and drop it onto the flour. Sprinkle the top lightly with some of the flour, then pick up the biscuit and shape it into a round, gently shaking off any excess flour. (Hold the biscuit in your left hand, with fingers partially closed so that thumb and index finger form the letter C; with your right hand, tamp down the top of the dough so that the biscuit is 1 inch high and 2 inches in diameter.) As soon as it is shaped, place the biscuit in the cake pan. Repeat with the remaining dough, placing the biscuits snugly up against each other so that the soft dough rises up instead of spreading sideways.

Brush the biscuits with the optional melted butter and place them in the oven. Raise the heat to 500°F. and bake for 5 minutes. Lower the heat to 475°F. and continue baking for 10 to 15 minutes, until the tops are lightly brown. Allow the biscuits to cool in the pan for 1 to 2 minutes before unmolding them onto a plate. Split the biscuits in half, preferably using a three-tined fork.

STORE

Room temperature, airtight, up to 2 days; frozen, up to 3 months. To reheat frozen biscuits, sprinkle with water and bake in a preheated 300°F. oven for 15 minutes. A cake tester inserted in the center and removed will feel warm and the outside of the biscuits will be crunchy.

POINTERS FOR SUCCESS

∾ Any bleached all-purpose flour will be fine for these biscuits, but White Lily (see page 634) really makes the softest, lightest ones.

∾ If the flour is measured instead of weighed, you may need to adjust the texture of the dough by adding a little more flour or a little more liquid.

∾ Do not use self-rising flour for shaping the biscuits, as the leavening it contains will give a bitter taste to the outside of the biscuits.

UNDERSTANDING

These biscuits must be baked in a pan for support because their high moisture content would otherwise cause them to lose their shape before they set.

The oven temperature can be higher than for biscuits made with butter because vegetable shortening doesn't brown as fast as butter.

Sprinkling the biscuits with water before reheating them results in a crisp top and softer inside.

BUTTER BISCUITS

These biscuits have the most extraordinary golden color, velvety texture, and haunting flavor. The ingredients responsible are butter and hard-boiled egg yolk. These are the biscuits I use for strawberry shortcake.

OVEN TEMPERATURE: 375°F., THEN 400°F. •
BAKING TIME: 15 TO 20 MINUTES
INTERNAL TEMPERATURE: 200°F.

MAKES: NINE 2½- BY 1½-INCH-HIGH
BISCUITS

INGREDIENTS	MEASURE	WEIGHT	
	VOLUME	OUNCES	GRAMS
2 large eggs	3 fluid ounces	4 ounces (weighed in the shells)	113 grams
White Lily self-rising flour*	2 cups (dip and sweep method)	10 ounces	284 grams
sugar	3 tablespoons	1.3 ounces	37.5 grams
unsalted butter, cut into small bits and chilled	6 tablespoons	3 ounces	85 grams
heavy cream or buttermilk (or a combination of the two)	¾ liquid cup	6 ounces 6.3 ounces	174 grams 182 grams
Optional Topping melted butter, cooled	1 tablespoon	0.5 ounce	14 grams
sugar	approx. 1 teaspoon	•	•

*Or White Lily regular flour (or 1⅓ cups bleached all-purpose plus ⅔ cup cake flour) plus 1 tablespoon baking powder and ¾ teaspoon salt.

EQUIPMENT

A 2½-inch scalloped round cutter and a cookie sheet or inverted half-size sheet pan, lined with parchment*

Preheat the oven to 375°F. at least 20 minutes before baking. Set an oven rack at the middle level and place a bread pan half filled with very hot water on it before preheating.

In a small nonreactive saucepan with a tight-fitting cover, place the eggs and add enough cold water to cover them. Bring the water to a boil, cover tightly, and remove the pan from the heat. Allow it to sit for 20 minutes. Drain the eggs and run under cold water. Allow them to cool completely before peeling.

In a large bowl, whisk together the flour and sugar (and baking powder and salt if not using self-rising flour). Add the butter and, with your fingertips, work the bits into small pieces resembling coarse meal. (Or use an electric mixer on low speed to blend the butter into the flour mixture.)

Press the egg yolks through a fine strainer onto the flour mixture and whisk to distribute them evenly. (Reserve the whites for another use.) Mix in the cream and/or buttermilk just until the flour is moistened, the dough starts to come together, and you can form it into a ball.

Empty the dough onto a counter lightly dusted with all-purpose flour and knead it a few times until it develops a little elasticity and feels smooth. Dust the dough lightly with more all-purpose flour if it is a little sticky, and pat or roll it ¾ inch thick.

Dip the cutter into all-purpose flour before each cut and cut cleanly through the dough, lifting out the cutter without twisting it so that the edges will be open for the maximum rise. For soft sides, place the biscuits almost touching (about ¼ inch apart) on the cookie sheet. For crisp sides, place the biscuits 1 inch apart. Knead the dough scraps again, pat or roll out, and cut out more biscuits. Brush off any excess flour from the biscuits. If a crisp top is desired, brush with the melted butter and sprinkle lightly with sugar.

Place the biscuits in the oven, raise the temperature to 400°F., and bake for 5 minutes. Lower the temperature to 375°F. and continue baking for 10 to 15 minutes or until the tops are golden. Split the biscuits in half, preferably using a three-tined fork.

VARIATION

GINGER BUTTER BISCUITS   These are great for peach shortcake. Add 2 tablespoons of finely chopped crystallized ginger (1 ounce/28 grams) to the flour mixture and 1 tablespoon (⅓ ounces/17 grams) of grated fresh ginger along with the liquid.

*Or a cushioned baking sheet or 2 baking sheets placed one on top of the other, without parchment.

STORE

Room temperature, airtight, up to 2 days; frozen, up to 3 months. To reheat frozen biscuits, sprinkle with water and bake in a preheated 300°F. oven for 15 minutes. A cake tester inserted in the center and removed will feel warm and the outside of the biscuits will be crunchy.

POINTERS FOR SUCCESS

∽ If the flour is measured instead of weighed, you may need to adjust the texture of the dough by adding a little more flour or a little more liquid.

∽ Be sure to knead the dough to develop the gluten, or the biscuits will not have the strength to rise.

∽ Do not use self-rising flour for kneading the dough or shaping the biscuits, as the leavening it contains will give a bitter taste to the outside of the biscuits.

UNDERSTANDING

Any bleached all-purpose flour will be fine for these biscuits, but White Lily (see page 634) really makes the softest, lightest ones.

Sprinkling the biscuits with water before reheating them results in a crisp top and softer inside.

ANGEL BUTTER BISCUITS

When biscuits are made with yeast instead of baking powder, they rise more and become lighter in texture, which accounts for the name *angel*. For this recipe, I have added yeast to my best butter biscuit recipe. The yeast gives the biscuits a lovely flavor and makes it possible to prepare this dough up to three days ahead. This makes them ideal to serve hot for breakfast, spread with butter and preserves.

EQUIPMENT

A 2½-inch scalloped round cutter and a cookie sheet or inverted half-size sheet pan, lined with parchment*

*Or a cushioned baking sheet or 2 baking sheets placed one on top of the other, without parchment.

OVEN TEMPERATURE: 375°F., THEN 400°F. •
BAKING TIME: 15 TO 20 MINUTES   MAKES: NINE 2½- BY
INTERNAL TEMPERATURE: 200°F.   2-INCH-HIGH BISCUITS

INGREDIENTS	MEASURE	WEIGHT	
	VOLUME	OUNCES	GRAMS
2 large eggs	3 fluid ounces	4 ounces	113 grams (weighed in the shells)
warm water	2 tablespoons + 2 teaspoons	•	•
sugar	3 tablespoons, divided	1.3 ounces	37.5 grams
SAF-Instant yeast (see page 654) or 1 package active dry yeast (not rapid rise) or compressed fresh yeast	2 teaspoons 2¼ teaspoons 1 tablespoon (packed)	0.25 ounce 0.25 ounce 0.75 ounce	7 grams 7 grams 21 grams
White Lily self-rising flour*	2 cups (dip and sweep method)	10 ounces	284 grams
unsalted butter, cut into small bits and chilled	6 tablespoons	3 ounces	85 grams
heavy cream or buttermilk (or a combination of the two)	¾ liquid cup	6 ounces 6.3 ounces	174 grams 182 grams
Optional Topping: melted butter, cooled	1 tablespoon	0.5 ounce	14 grams
sugar	approx. 1 teaspoon	•	•

*Or White Lily regular flour (or 1⅓ cups bleached all-purpose plus ⅔ cup cake flour) plus 1 tablespoon baking powder and ¾ teaspoon salt.

In a small nonreactive saucepan with a tight-fitting cover, place the eggs and add enough cold water to cover them. Bring the water to a boil, cover tightly, and remove the pan from the heat. Allow it to sit for 20 minutes. Drain the eggs and run under cold water. Allow them to cool completely before peeling.

To proof the yeast: If using active dry or fresh (do not use hot water, or the yeast will die), in a small bowl, combine the water (ideally a tepid 100°F. if using fresh yeast, a little warmer, 110°F., if using dry), ½ teaspoon of the sugar, and the yeast. If using fresh yeast, crumble it slightly as you add it. Set the mixture aside in a draft-free spot for 10 to 20 minutes. By this time, the mixture should be full of bubbles. (If not, the yeast is too old to be useful and you must start again with newer yeast.)

In a large bowl, whisk together the flour and (remaining) sugar (and the baking powder and salt if not using self-rising flour). Add the butter and, with your fingertips, work the bits into small pieces resembling coarse meal. (Or use an electric mixer on low speed to blend the butter into the flour mixture.)

Press the egg yolks through a fine strainer onto the flour mixture and whisk to distribute them evenly. (Reserve the whites for another use.) Mix in the cream and/or buttermilk and yeast mixture just until the flour is moistened, the dough starts to come together, and you can form it into a ball. The dough should be very soft and sticky. Cover it tightly with plastic wrap and allow it to rise for about 1½ hours or until it becomes puffy but doesn't quite double.

Gently pat down the dough, cover, and refrigerate for at least 4 hours and up to 3 days.

When ready to bake, lightly flour a counter with all-purpose flour. Scrape the dough onto the counter and knead it a few times until it develops a little elasticity and feels smooth. Dust the dough lightly with all-purpose flour if necessary and pat or roll it ¾ inch thick.

Dip the cutter into all-purpose flour before each cut and cut cleanly through the dough, lifting out the cutter without twisting it so that the edges will be free for the maximum rise. For soft sides, place the biscuits almost touching (about ¼ inch apart) on the cookie sheet. For crisp sides, place the biscuits 1 inch apart. Knead the dough scraps, pat or roll out, and cut out more biscuits. Cover the biscuits with plastic wrap and allow them to rise for about 1 hour or until 1 inch high.

Preheat the oven to 375°F. at least 20 minutes before baking. Set an oven rack at the middle level and place a bread pan half filled with very hot water on it before preheating.

Gently brush off any excess flour from the biscuits. If a crisp top is desired, brush with the melted butter and sprinkle lightly with the sugar.

Place the biscuits in the oven, raise the temperature to 400°F., and bake for 5 minutes. Lower the temperature to 375°F. and continue baking for 10 to 15 minutes or until the tops are golden. Split the biscuits in half, preferably using a three-tined fork.

VARIATION

GINGER ANGEL BUTTER BISCUITS   See Ginger Butter Biscuits (page 354).

STORE

Airtight, room temperature, up to 2 days; frozen, up to 3 months. To reheat frozen biscuits, sprinkle with water and bake in a preheated 300°F. oven for 15 minutes. A cake tester inserted in the center and removed will feel warm and the outside will be crunchy.

POINTERS FOR SUCCESS

〜 See page 352.

UNDERSTANDING

See page 355.

STRAWBERRY SHORTCAKE
(*With Variations*)

What could be better than tender/soft biscuits with crisp tops, filled with lightly whipped cream and fresh strawberries? For a variation, do try other berries or fruit, or a combination of the two, and the more intense passion or lemon curd whipped cream. For a less rich version, the lemon yogurt cream is lighter and very compatible with berries. And for a fabulous peach shortcake, make the ginger version of the biscuits and use the Crème Fraîche or sour cream.

Serves: 6
1 recipe Butter Biscuits (page 353), or
Angel Butter Biscuits (page 355)

Perfect Whipped Cream (page 551),
Passion Fruit Curd (page 570), or
Lemon Curd Cream (page 571), or
lightly sweetened Crème Fraîche (page 558), or
Lemon Yogurt Cream (recipe follows)

STRAWBERRY FILLING

3 pints (1½ pounds/680 grams) strawberries and 2 tablespoons sugar

Hull the strawberries, rinse, pat dry, and cut them in half, or quarter them if they are very large. Sprinkle the strawberries with the sugar and allow them to sit for at least 1 hour at room temperature and up to 6 hours refrigerated.

Drain the strawberries, reserving the syrup. You will have about ½ cup syrup. Place the syrup in a greased 4-cup heatproof glass measure and reduce it to ⅓ cup in a microwave on high power. (Or reduce in a saucepan on the stove, stirring frequently.)

MARIONBERRY FILLING

4 cups (1 pound/454 grams) frozen Marionberries (fresh blackberries or raspberries can be substituted), 2½ tablespoons sugar, and (optional) 2 tablespoons Chambord (black raspberry liqueur)

In a large bowl, place the Marionberries and sprinkle them with the sugar. Toss gently to coat evenly. Set the Marionberries aside to thaw, about 2 hours at room temperature, or refrigerate for several hours. Or, if using fresh berries, allow them to sit with the sugar for 30 minutes to 1 hour.

Drain the berries thoroughly, reserving the syrup. There should be ½ cup of syrup; if less, allow them to sit longer. Place the syrup in a greased 4-cup heatproof glass measure and reduce it in a microwave on high power to ⅓ cup. (Or reduce in a saucepan on the stove, stirring frequently.) When cool, add the optional Chambord.

PEACH FILLING

1 pound (454 grams/3 cups) peaches (about 3 peaches), 3 tablespoons sugar, and 1 teaspoon freshly squeezed lemon juice

Peel, pit, and slice the peaches into ½-inch-thick slices. Place them in a medium bowl. Sprinkle them with the sugar and lemon juice and allow them to sit for at least 30 minutes at room temperature and up to 3 hours refrigerated.

Drain the peaches, reserving the syrup. There will be about 2 tablespoons of syrup (less than for peach pie, as less sugar is used since the peaches will not be cooked).

ASSEMBLE THE SHORTCAKE

If necessary, warm the biscuits and split them open, preferably with a three-tined fork. Spoon a little syrup over each cut half. Spoon about ½ cup of berries or peaches on top of each biscuit bottom and mound about ¼ cup of the topping over them, leaving a border of berries or peaches showing through. Set the biscuit tops on top of the topping, slightly off center. Serve the extra topping on the side.

LEMON YOGURT CREAM

For 1⅔ cups: In a small bowl, whisk together 1⅓ cups of yogurt with ¼ cup of sugar and ⅓ cup Lemon or Passion Fruit Curd.

CURRANT SCONES

These scones are ample, warm, and comforting—crisp on the outside, soft, moist, and layered inside with purely butter/flour flavor and just the right touch of sweet stickiness from the currants. I've tried many other recipes and discarded them all. These are the best. They are prepared by layering butter flakes into the dough much in the style of puff pastry, which gives the dough a slightly flaky texture, but since they contain only about one third butter to flour (in contrast to puff pastry, which employs equal parts) and heavy cream instead of water, they offer a far more substantial, soul-satisfying texture. If you want each scone to be a perfect even triangle, there will be some waste. Personally, I prefer to use every scrap of the delicious dough and embrace the rustic misshapen ones along with the more even variety.

EQUIPMENT

Two cookie sheets or inverted half-size sheet pans, lined with parchment

OVEN TEMPERATURE: 400°F. •
BAKING TIME: 15 TO 20 MINUTES
INTERNAL TEMPERATURE: 200°F.   MAKES: TWELVE TO SIXTEEN 4-
                                                BY 1½-INCH-HIGH SCONES

INGREDIENTS	MEASURE	WEIGHT	
	VOLUME	OUNCES	GRAMS
unsalted butter, cold	1 cup (2 sticks)	8 ounces	227 grams
unbleached all-purpose flour, preferably Hecker's	about 4 cups (dip and sweep method)	21.25 ounces	608 grams
sugar	½ cup	3.5 ounces	100 grams
baking powder	2 teaspoons	•	9.8 grams
baking soda	½ teaspoon	•	•
salt	¼ teaspoon	•	•
heavy cream	2 liquid cups	16.3 ounces	464 grams
currants	1 cup	4.6 ounces	131 grams

Cut the butter into 1-inch cubes and refrigerate them for at least 30 minutes or freeze them for 10 minutes.

In a large bowl, whisk together the flour, sugar, baking powder, baking soda, and salt. Add the butter and, with your fingertips, press the cubes into large flakes. (Or use an electric mixer on low speed and mix until the butter is the size of small walnuts.) Mix in the cream just until the flour is moistened and the dough starts to come together in large clumps. Mix in the currants. Knead the dough in the bowl just until it holds together and turn it out onto a lightly floured board.

Lightly flour the top of the dough, or use a rolling pin with a floured pastry sleeve, and roll out the dough into a rectangle 1 inch thick and about 8 inches by 12 inches. Use a bench scraper (see page 659) to keep the edges even. Fold the dough in thirds, like a business letter. Lightly flour the board and rotate the dough so that the smooth side faces to the left. Roll it out again to an 8- by 12-inch rectangle and repeat the "turn" 3 times (for a total of 4 turns), refrigerating the dough, covered with plastic wrap, for about 15 minutes if it begins to soften and stick.

Preheat the oven to 400°F. at least 20 minutes before baking. Set an oven rack at the middle level before preheating.

Roll out the dough once more and trim off the folded edges so that it will rise evenly.* Cut it lengthwise in half so you have 2 pieces, each about 4 inches by 12 inches. Cut each piece of dough on the diagonal to form triangles with about a

---

*The scraps can be rerolled by pressing them together and giving them 2 turns, then rolling the dough into a square. Cut into 2 triangles.

3-inch-wide base and place them about 1 inch apart on the prepared cookie sheets. (The dough rises but does not expand sideways.)

Bake the scones for 15 to 20 minutes or until the edges begin to brown and the tops are golden brown and firm enough so that they barely give when pressed lightly with a finger. Check the scones after 10 minutes of baking, and if they are not baking evenly, rotate the cookie sheets from top to bottom and front to back. Do not overbake, as the scones continue baking slightly after removal from the oven and are best when slightly moist and soft inside.

Place a linen towel on each of two large racks and place the baked scones on top. Fold the towels over loosely and allow the scones to cool until warm or room temperature. (Since linen breathes, the scones will not become soggy, but they will have enough protection to keep from becoming dry and hard on the surface.)

VARIATIONS

DRIED CRANBERRY SCONES   The same amount of dried cranberries can be substituted for the currants for more tang.

LEMON POPPY SEED SCONES   Omit the currants and add 3 tablespoons (1 ounce/28 grams) poppy seeds and 2 tablespoons (0.5 ounce/12 grams) finely grated lemon zest to the flour mixture.

STORE

Airtight, room temperature, up to 2 days; frozen, up to 3 months. To reheat frozen scones, heat in a preheated 300°F. oven for 20 minutes. A cake tester inserted in the center and removed will feel warm and the outside will be crunchy .

UNDERSTANDING

Hecker's flour has a protein content somewhere between that of Gold Medal unbleached all-purpose and King Arthur all-purpose, which is slightly higher. Any of the three flours will produce excellent scones, but Hecker's is my preference because it results in the best compromise between tenderness and flakiness. A slightly stronger flour can be used for scones than for puff pastry because the sugar and baking powder tenderize the dough.

PASTRY

Fillo, strudel, puff pastry, croissant, Danish, and brioche all consist of the same basic ingredients in different proportions, handled in different manners. The three ingredients common to all are flour, liquid (water or milk), and fat (usually butter). In fillo and strudel, the melted butter is added after the dough is mixed and rolled (or stretched), and sometimes these doughs also contain egg. Danish and brioche doughs always have egg. And croissant, Danish, and brioche doughs by definition are partially raised by yeast. The only way really to perceive the difference between all these doughs, aside from actually eating them, is by comparing the percentage of the basic ingredients in each (see the chart on page 363). For purposes of comparison, the egg and liquid are combined, although eggs behave in a somewhat different way from the liquids, producing a more cake-like texture, as in the brioche. The techniques for making puff pastry, croissant, and Danish doughs are actually very similar. So it is through comparing these percentages of ingredients that one begins to comprehend why these pastries seem to be almost worlds apart.

Puff pastry, croissant, and Danish doughs are all prepared by making a dough using a small amount of the total butter and wrapping it around the remaining butter, which is mixed with a little flour to keep it from getting too soft. There are several acceptable ways to wrap the butter. I prefer the method that involves rolling the dough into a square and then rolling the four corners of the dough into thin flaps and wrapping them over the top of the butter because it is easier than trying to roll out the entire piece of dough to a rectangle large enough to wrap around the butter. When overlapped, the four flaps become the same thickness as the dough beneath the butter. The dough-wrapped butter is then rolled and folded (these folds are referred to as turns) to create the many layers of pastry.

In puff pastry, the dough depends entirely on steam from the moisture in the butter to lift it (whereas croissant and Danish both have yeast to lift it as well). Puff pastry dough is usually given a minimum of 6 turns, resulting in 729 layers; croissant dough, 4 turns, resulting in 81 layers; and Danish dough, 3 turns, resulting in 27 layers. This explains why puff pastry dough must be stronger, with more protein development, to be able to form such very thin layers without the butter breaking through, although if it is too strong, the pastry will be tough. This strength can be achieved by using a high-protein flour and/or by of mixing the dough. In addition, the dough needs to be cold when baked so that the butter does not leak out. Because croissant and Danish doughs have yeast, they require warmth, or proofing, before baking, so they cannot be as layered as puff pastry. Because Danish dough contains egg and has one less turn, it is not as light nor quite as flaky as the croissant dough, but it is richer and more tender.

All three of these doughs require enough strength in the form of a relatively high-protein flour to retain the layering. As any of us who has tried to roll out a high-gluten dough knows, it can be very elastic and resistant to rolling. Shirley Corriher encouraged me to create very wet, soft doughs to achieve maximum strength while softening the elasticity. The extra moisture converts to steam during baking, helping it rise more. The technique works brilliantly.

To sum it up: Croissant dough is essentially puff pastry with the addition of yeast and fewer turns. Danish dough is essentially croissant dough with the addition of egg and one turn less. Brioche is essentially a croissant dough with more liquid that contains a much higher percentage of egg and almost double the sugar, all of which make it more cake-like. Fillo and strudel doughs are the same as puff pastry except that only half the butter is used and it is added after baking the dough, in a melted form. This results in crisper pastry.

PERCENTAGE OF FLOUR, BUTTER, AND LIQUID BY WEIGHT*					
	PUFF PASTRY	CROISSANT	DANISH	BRIOCHE	FILLO/ STRUDEL†
flour	39.5%	40.2%	39.8%	41.3%	49.3%
butter	39.5%	35.2%	33.8%	24.2%	24.1%
water or milk	20.9%	24.5%	19.6%	7.1%	26.5%
egg	—	—	6.6%	27.3%	—
(total water and egg)	(20.9)	(24.5)	(26.2)	(34.4)	(26.5)
COMPARISON OF ALL INGREDIENT AMOUNTS					
flour	10 oz	10 oz	10.5 oz	10 oz	10 oz
butter	10 oz	9 oz	9 oz	5 oz	5 oz‡
water or milk	10.4 tbs**	¾ cup	10 tbs	3.12 tbs	10.4 tbs
egg	—	—	1	11.8 tbs	—
(total water or milk and egg)	(10.4 tbs)	(¾ cup)	(13 tbs)	(15 tbs)	(10.4 tbs)
yeast	—	½ oz	½ oz	⅔ oz	—
salt	⅔ tsp	1 tsp	½ tsp	⅔ tsp	⅜ tsp
sugar	—	2 tbs	2 tbs	3¾ tbs	—

*The figures do not add up to exactly 100 percent because of fractional amounts of certain ingredients.

†This is approximate, as some of the dough gets trimmed off before brushing with butter.

‡Includes 4 teaspoons oil (0.6 ounce).

**Includes 1½ teaspoons lemon juice.

FILLO

F illo (FEElo)—also spelled phyllo—strudel, and puff pastry are all members of the pastry leaf family. In fact, the word *fillo* means leaf in Greek. Its origins go back over two thousand years to Persia, Turkey, and Egypt. It has been speculated that the first fillo pastry was baklava, created in Topkapi Palace in Istanbul. Fillo traveled to Hungary, where it became the base for strudel. This type of pastry is considered to be the mother of French puff pastry. There is a profound relationship between these three pastries.

I once enjoyed a pastry case filled with seafood at a restaurant in New York City called Capsuto Frères, owned by three charming Egyptian brothers. The pastry seemed like the lightest puff pastry I had ever experienced. Intrigued, I asked one of the *frères* and was embarrassed to discover that it was not puff pastry at all, but fillo. I shouldn't have been so hard on myself though, because on analyzing the doughs, I realized that the light flaky layers of both doughs are, in fact, made of the same elements, but created in different ways. For puff pastry, the butter is rolled into thin sheets between layers and folds of dough; for fillo, the dough is pulled very thin and the butter, which is melted and clarified, is then brushed on each layer, together with a sprinkling of sugar and/or ground nuts or bread crumbs to keep them separate during baking. (Using unclarified butter for fillo would keep it from being as crisp. The opposite is true for puff pastry, where the water in the unclarified butter is *needed* to create steam to separate the layers.)

If the equivalent amount of flour used for puff pastry were used to make fillo, and the dough cut to the same finished size and then stacked, there would be 76 separate layers. Though mathematically (and microscopically) puff pastry given 6 turns has 729 layers, these layers are not distinct and separate as are the fillo layers, so the fillo is lighter and crisper. Layers of butter-brushed fillo can, therefore, be used in place of puff pastry in, for example, the Classic Napoleon (page 457). Use 20 layers of fillo to replace puff pastry rolled ⅛ inch thick.

The dough to which the Greek fillo has the closest kinship is the Austro/Hungarian strudel. They both consist of the same ingredients: unbleached flour, salt, water, and oil (some recipes for each include eggs or egg whites; I find the dough more tender without them). If both are handmade, the only perceptible difference comes from the type of flour used and how thin the dough is pulled (or rolled, as is the case with authentic fillo). The greater difference comes from the fact that if you want a large sheet of strudel dough, you have to make it yourself, whereas commercial machine-made fillo dough can be purchased.* Handmade strudel dough, using about 10 ounces of flour, if stretched to 48 inches and trimmed, weighs about 7 ounces. The equivalent amount of fillo, for a 16-inch roll, would be six 12- by 17-inch sheets, which weigh about 3.5 ounces—or half the weight of the strudel dough. The actual difference in surface area is that the fillo is 67.6 percent that of the strudel, not 50 percent; this means it will result in both slightly thinner and fewer layers or leaves. The reason is that commercial fillo is slightly stronger than handmade, so less can be used, but it won't be as tender. The main difference between fillo and strudel is what they are used to make. In fact, they can be used interchangeably. To make a large strudel, for example, sheets of commercial fillo can be overlapped (see page 393).

I find using thawed frozen fillo dough to be very frustrating unless I have frozen it myself from the fresh. That is because many markets allow it to thaw and then refreeze during the stocking process. This causes it to stick together and tear when one attempts to separate the sheets. The best results are achieved when the frozen fillo is allowed to defrost refrigerated overnight, but if the fillo has thawed and refrozen, even this won't help. Fortunately, excellent fresh fillo sheets, cups, and shredded fillo can be ordered by mail from The Fillo Factory in Dumont, New Jersey (see page 675). The fresh fillo keeps refrigerated for two months and can be refrozen twice. It separates readily into sheets and does not dry out while working with it nearly as quickly as the store-bought frozen. It is a joy to work with and after you have experienced it, there is no going back! I prefer using these precut sheets of fillo to pulling my own strudel for shaped pastries, as opposed to rolled ones, as it is easier to handle than cutting the enormous gossamer-thin sheet of strudel.

The finest and most fragile of all the leaf-type pastries is *warka*, or *pâte à Brique*, from Morocco. The ingredients are identical to fillo, though instead of ⅓ cup of water it requires ½ cup. The technique, however, is astoundingly different: Instead of being rolled or stretched, the sheets are formed by touching the dough briefly and repeatedly to the back of a heated lightly oiled pan to create the most gossamer-thin layer imaginable. Each small fine leaf of dough is then painstakingly peeled off the hot pan. I saw this dough demonstrated by master

---

*The Fillo Factory (see page 675) has 38-inch sheets of fillo available for food service (it comes by the case).

baker Esther McManus at a meeting of The Baker's Dozen East, and we were all awestruck. She has a school (Cuisine Ecole) in Philadelphia, so should you desire to learn this method, I heartily recommend a class with her. She is an inspired and generous baker and teacher—and it would be very difficult, if not impossible, to learn this dough from even the best instructions in a book.

POINTERS FOR SUCCESS IN WORKING WITH FILLO

∾ Fresh fillo is easiest to work with, but whether it is fresh or thawed, be sure to keep it covered with plastic wrap and a damp towel to prevent drying.

∾ If using frozen fillo, defrost it for a minimum of 8 hours, preferably 24 hours, and a maximum of 3 days in the refrigerator and then let it sit at room temperature for 2 hours.

∾ One pound of frozen fillo contains about 22 to 24 sheets about 12 inches by 16 to 17 inches (each one weighs about 0.66 ounce/18 grams). (Fresh fillo has 25 to 31 sheets to a pound, as it is slightly thinner. Each weighs about 0.57 ounce/16 grams.)

∾ Lay the stack of fillo on a dry counter. Remove the amount needed and refrigerate or freeze the rest as soon as possible, rerolled and double-wrapped in plastic wrap, preferably Saran.

∾ Use 1 to 2 teaspoons of clarified butter for each sheet of fillo. Alternatively, for savory fillings, use olive oil spray or olive oil, or a combination of olive oil and butter. Butter produces the crispest texture.

∾ Using clarified butter prevents spotting, uneven browning, and sogginess, but it's fine just to melt the butter, as the milk solids and liquid will sink to the bottom, leaving the clarified butter on the top. For true clarified butter, estimate a maximum of half the weight of the fillo in butter, but start with a little extra, as you lose one quarter of the weight when clarifying it.

∾ To brush fillo with melted butter, start around the edges, where it will dry out the most quickly, and then dapple it lightly all over.

∾ If a fillo sheet tears, patch it by brushing it with a little of the butter and overlapping the tear with a small piece of dough.

∾ To cut fillo, use a ruler and a sharp knife.

∾ After assembling a fillo pastry, brush it with butter to prevent it from drying.

∾ Filled fillo pastries can be assembled 1 day ahead and refrigerated, or frozen for longer storage.

∾ To store filled fillo refrigerated, cover it loosely with foil. To freeze it, place the pastries on baking sheets and freeze until frozen hard. Then transfer them to a freezer-weight storage bag or other container.

∾ Bake filled fillo at 375°F., in the upper part of the oven, until golden but not brown. If frozen, bake without thawing, to prevent sogginess.

PISTACHIO BAKLAVA

I s there anyone who hasn't tasted this Greek sweet, available in every Greek diner throughout the country? For many of us, these crisp pastry diamonds layered with honeyed nuts were our first introduction to fillo.

Baklava prepared with walnuts, almonds, or a combination of the two is the most commonly available, but a pure pistachio version is my preference. Don't compromise on the quality of the pistachio nuts. Use only fresh, bright green unsalted pistachio nuts.

OVEN TEMPERATURE: 300°F. •   MAKES: THIRTY-EIGHT
BAKING TIME: 30 MINUTES   2½-INCH DIAMONDS

INGREDIENTS	MEASURE	WEIGHT	
	VOLUME	OUNCES	GRAMS
unsalted butter, clarified (see page 629)	12 tablespoons (4.5 ounce)	6 ounces	200 grams
blanched pistachio nuts*	1½ generous cups	8 ounces	228 grams
sugar	¼ cup	1.75 ounces	50 grams
ground cinnamon	½ teaspoon	•	•
fillo, preferably fresh (see page 365)	12 sheets	8 ounces	227 grams
Syrup	(1⅓ cups)	•	•
sugar	1 cup	7 ounces	200 grams
water	½ liquid cup	4 ounces	118 grams
mild, light honey	6 tablespoons	4.5 ounces	128 grams
Lyle's Golden Syrup (refiner's syrup) or light corn syrup	1 tablespoon	0.75 ounce	21 grams
freshly squeezed lemon juice	1 tablespoon	0.5 ounce	16 grams

*If you cannot use the best-quality blanched pistachio nuts, such as the bright green Sicilian variety (see page 642), it is preferable to use almonds or walnuts. Blanched sliced almonds or lightly toasted walnuts, skins removed (page 641), can be substituted.

EQUIPMENT

A quarter-size sheet pan (9 inches by 12 inches, measured at the top), buttered*

Preheat the oven to 300°F. at least 15 minutes before baking. Set an oven rack at the middle level before preheating.

If the clarified butter has solidified, heat it so that it is liquid, but allow it to cool to lukewarm or room temperature.

In a food processor with the metal blade, pulse the nuts until the largest pieces are no larger than small peas and the remainder are in fine pieces (or chop by hand). Reserve 1 tablespoon for decoration. Add the sugar and cinnamon and pulse 2 or 3 times to combine them well. Empty the mixture into a bowl.

With a pastry brush or feather, lightly coat the bottom of the sheet pan with some of the clarified butter.

Place the fillo between 2 sheets of plastic wrap, preferably Saran, and cover it with a damp dish towel. Keep it well covered, re-covering it each time you remove a sheet, to prevent it from drying. Remove 1 sheet and place it on the work surface. Brush it with about 1 teaspoon of clarified butter and fold it crosswise in half so that it fits into the pan. Quickly brush it with another 1 teaspoon of clarified butter, starting at the perimeter and then dabbing it in the center. Do not attempt to coat the entire sheet evenly, as too much butter will result in a greasy texture. Lay a total of 4 folded sheets in the pan, brushing each with about 2 teaspoons of butter.

Sprinkle half the nut mixture evenly over the fillo and add 2 more folded sheets of fillo, buttering it in the same manner as before. Sprinkle the remaining nut mixture over the fillo and then add 6 more folded sheets of fillo, buttering as before.

With a sharp knife, score a diamond pattern in the fillo, going through only the upper layer so that the baklava will hold together well while baking. (Start at one corner and make a cut all the way across to the opposite corner. Continue making parallel cuts 1⅝ inches apart, 3 on either side of the first cut, for a total of 7 cuts. Then start at another corner and repeat.

Bake the baklava for about 30 minutes or until the top is golden. Remove it to a rack to cool to room temperature.

PREPARE THE SYRUP

In a medium saucepan, preferably nonstick, stir together the sugar, water, honey, and syrup until all of the sugar is moistened. Over medium heat, stirring constantly, bring it to a simmer. Lower the heat and simmer, stirring occasionally, for

---

*The pan can be slightly larger without affecting the recipe. The fillo sheets are 12 inches by 16 inches, so when folded in half they are 12 inches by 8 inches and fit perfectly into the pan. A little room around the sheets, however, will not be a detriment.

30 minutes. Remove the syrup from the heat and add the lemon juice. Cover it to keep it hot, or reheat it when the baklava has cooled.

With a sharp knife, slash all the way through to the bottom of the baklava along each scored line. Spoon the hot syrup over the cooled pastry. Allow it to stand uncovered for at least an hour to absorb the syrup, then sprinkle the baklava with the reserved pistachio nuts.

STORE

Room temperature, 3 to 7 days. (The syrup starts to crystallize after 3 days, but some people actually prefer this change in texture. I prefer it uncrystallized, as it seems more moist.)

POINTERS FOR SUCCESS

∾ Fresh fillo (see page 365) is easiest to work with, but, in either case, be sure to keep it covered to prevent drying.

∾ This recipe can be doubled or tripled and baked in a larger pan. If making larger sizes, to cut the diamonds, divide a short end of the pan by increments of approximately 2 inches and a long side by the same number of divisions and make angled cuts connecting these division marks. (A full-size professional sheet pan measuring 24 inches by 16 inches will have 8 divisions on each side.) Increase the baking time and bake until the top is golden.

UNDERSTANDING

The addition of a small amount of corn syrup to the sugar syrup prevents crystallization for 3 days, though some people enjoy the crystallized effect.

The nuts are not toasted (except walnuts, which are only roasted briefly to remove the skins) because they cook and darken during baking.

Clarifying the butter makes the fillo sheets more crisp.

In order for the baklava to absorb the syrup well, there must be a contrast in temperature. Either the baklava must be hot and the syrup cool or the baklava cool and the syrup hot for it to be absorbed evenly.

GASCON APPLE PIE

I first sampled this unusual pastry when visiting André and Joceleine Daguin at their renowned Hôtel de Paris in Auch, in the Southwest of France.

In this recipe, the fine, flaky fillo encases tart apple slices that are perfumed with Armagnac and orange flower water. A simple arrangement of the fillo scraps makes the dessert resemble a giant ethereal pastry rose that seems to float in the pie plate. It is one of the most naturally beautiful pastries I know. In Gascony, where it is called *pastis Gascon,* the dough is handmade and stretched. It is very similar to strudel, but with the addition of egg yolks for extra color and richness of flavor. Gascony's proximity to Morocco, and its large North African population, are evidenced by the popularity of couscous restaurants and Middle Eastern pastries like this magical one.

OVEN TEMPERATURE: 375°F. •
BAKING TIME: 50 TO 60 MINUTES   SERVES: 6 TO 8

| INGREDIENTS | MEASURE | WEIGHT | |
	VOLUME	OUNCES	GRAMS
1⅔ pounds apples (about 4 medium), peeled, cored, and sliced ⅛ inch thick*	6 cups (sliced)	1½ pounds (sliced)	680 grams
granulated sugar	3 tablespoons	1.3 ounces	38 grams
light brown sugar	3 tablespoons, packed	1.5 ounces	45 grams
salt	⅛ teaspoon	•	•
Armagnac or cognac	⅓ liquid cup	2.6 ounces	75 grams
orange flower water (see page 638)	1½ tablespoons	0.75 ounce	22 grams
walnuts, lightly toasted and chopped medium-fine	¾ cup	2.6 ounces	75 grams
melted butter, preferably clarified (see page 629)	7 tablespoons	3.5 ounces	100 grams
fillo, preferably fresh (see page 365)	12 sheets	8 ounces	227 grams
optional: powdered sugar	•	•	•

*To core apples, cut them in half and use a melon baller to scoop out the cores.

EQUIPMENT
A 10-inch pie plate, preferably glass

In a large bowl, gently toss the apples with the sugars, salt, and Armagnac or Cognac. Cover tightly and allow to sit at room temperature for at least 2 hours, and up to overnight, tossing once or twice. (If macerating the apples overnight, refrigerate them.)

Drain the apples, reserving the juice. You should have about ¾ cup. Place it in a greased 4-cup heatproof glass measure and reduce it in the microwave to about 3 tablespoons. (Or reduce it in a small saucepan, stirring constantly.) When cool, swirl in the orange flower water. Add it to the apples, together with the walnuts, and mix them gently together.

Preheat the oven to 375°F. at least 20 minutes before baking. Set an oven rack at the middle level before preheating.

With a pastry brush or feather, lightly coat the bottom of the pie pan with some of the clarified butter.

Place the fillo between two sheets of plastic wrap and cover it with a damp dish towel. Keep it well covered, re-covering it each time you remove a sheet, to prevent it from drying. Remove 1 sheet and place it on the work surface. Quickly brush it with about 1 teaspoon of clarified butter, starting at the perimeter and then dabbing it in the center. Do not attempt to coat the entire sheet evenly, as too much butter will result in a greasy texture. Drape the fillo sheet into the pie pan, molding it to fit the pan and allowing the excess to drape over the sides. Repeat with 7 more sheets, brushing each with butter.

Empty the apple mixture into the fillo-lined pie pan. Bring the overhanging fillo up and over the apples to enclose them partially. Brush another 2 fillo sheets with butter and fold them crosswise in half. Butter them again on both sides, place them on top of the apples, covering them completely, and tuck the ends into the sides of the pie pan. There will be a depression in the center.

Butter another sheet of fillo and cut it in half. Gather up each piece in loose ruffles and arrange it toward the center of the pie to fill the depression partially. Butter the final piece of fillo and fold it in the long way into thirds. Coil it loosely to form a rose and place it in the center of the pie.

Bake for 50 to 60 minutes or until the fillo is golden and a cake tester or skewer inserted into the apples meets with little resistance. Allow the pie to cool to room temperature, as the moistened pastry seems slightly tough when warm.

If desired, dust the pie lightly with powered sugar before serving.

STORE
Room temperature, up to 3 days. (The flavors are even more delicious the second day.)

PEARS WRAPPED IN FILLO

The translucent delicacy of pear melds beautifully with an almond cream filling and is all the more alluring encased in a fine crunchy pastry such as fillo.

EQUIPMENT
Kitchen twine and a 17- by 12-inch baking sheet or jelly-roll pan (or 2 smaller sheets)

POACH THE PEARS
Peel the pears just before you poach them so that they do not darken.

In a nonreactive skillet just large enough to hold the pears in a single layer, combine the water, lemon juice, eau-de-vie, sugar, and vanilla bean and stir to dissolve the sugar. Add the pears and bring the liquid to a boil. Place a round of parchment on top of the pears. Simmer over low heat, tightly covered, for 8 to 10 minutes (turn the pears after 5 minutes if the liquid does not cover them completely) or until a cake tester inserted in thickest part of a pear enters easily. The pears should still be slightly firm. Remove the pan from the heat and cool, covered only by the parchment, for at least 1 hour.

Remove the vanilla bean, rinse, and dry it (for future use or to use as decorative stems for the pears). Transfer the pears and their liquid to a bowl and refrigerate tightly covered, until ready to use.

MAKE THE ALMOND CREAM FILLING
In a food processor with the metal blade, process the almonds, sugar, and flour until the almonds are very fine. Empty the mixture into a bowl and set aside.

In a medium mixing bowl, beat the butter until creamy. Beat in about ½ cup of the nut mixture until incorporated. Beat in 1 egg along with another ½ cup of the nut mixture. Then beat in the second egg along with the remaining nut mixture until incorporated. Beat in the vanilla. Refrigerate until about 10 minutes before assembling the pears.

Preheat the oven to 375°F. at least 20 minutes before baking. Set an oven rack at the lowest level before preheating.

WRAP THE PEARS
Drain the pears and place on paper towels to drain thoroughly.* Core, starting at the base but not going all the way through to the stem end. Pipe or spoon about 2 tablespoons of the almond cream into the hollow of each pear to fill it. Set the rest aside.

---

*If desired, the syrup can be refrigerated for several weeks or frozen for months and used to brush on sponge cakes.

OVEN TEMPERATURE: 375°F. •
BAKING TIME: 45 TO 50 MINUTES   SERVES: 4

INGREDIENTS	MEASURE	WEIGHT	
	VOLUME	OUNCES	GRAMS
Poached Pears 4 large ripe but firm pears, such as Bartlett or Bosc		2⅓ pounds	1 kg 58 grams
water	6 liquid cups	49.6 ounces	1 kg 418 grams
freshly squeezed lemon juice	4 teaspoons	0.7 ounce	21 grams
Poire William eau-de-vie	¼ liquid cup	2 ounces	56 grams
sugar	1 cup	7 ounces	200 grams
vanilla bean, split lengthwise	2-inch piece	•	•
Almond Cream	(1¾ cups)	(14 ounces)	(400 grams)
sliced blanched almonds	1 cup	3.5 ounces	100 grams
sugar	½ cup	3.5 ounces	100 grams
bleached all-purpose flour	2 tablespoons	0.63 ounce	18 grams
unsalted butter, softened	7 tablespoons	3.5 ounces	100 grams
2 large eggs, at room temperature	3 fluid ounces	3.5 ounces	100 grams
pure vanilla extract	½ teaspoon	•	•
fillo, preferably fresh (see page 365)	8 sheets	5.25 ounces	150 grams
melted butter, preferably clarified (see page 629)	8 tablespoons	4 ounces approx. 3.5 ounces (clarified)	114 grams 97.5 grams
sugar	3 tablespoons	1.3 ounces	37 grams
optional: Vanilla Custard Sauce (page 606) and Raspberry Sauce (page 603)	½ cup approx. 2 tablespoons	• •	• •

Lay the stack of fillo on the counter and keep it well covered with plastic wrap to prevent drying. Lay a piece of fillo on the counter and brush it with about 2 teaspoons of melted butter. Sprinkle it with ½ teaspoon of the sugar. Fold it in thirds, like a business letter. Repeat with a second fillo sheet. Lay this sheet on top of the first sheet to form a cross. Brush the edges with melted butter and spread 4 to 5 tablespoons of the almond cream filling evenly over the rest of the dough. Set a pear upright in the center of the fillo cross. Bring the four arms of the cross over the top of the pear, smoothing the sides against the pear, and tie the top of the fillo loosely together with twine. Repeat with the remaining pears and fillo.*

Set each fillo package on a square of aluminum foil large enough to come up to the top of the pear. Bring up the foil to encase the fillo, pressing it against the bottom of the pear but leaving it loose and wide open at the top. Set the pears, evenly spaced, on the baking sheet(s) and bake for 45 to 50 minutes or until golden brown. After the first 20 minutes, open the foil completely, crimping it if necessary to expose the fillo, but make a small foil cap for each top so that it doesn't burn. Remove the pan(s) to a wire rack to cool for 20 to 30 minutes, then remove and discard the twine.

If desired, place a small piece of vanilla bean, reserved from the poaching, at the top of each pear as a stem. Serve warm, accompanied, if desired, by vanilla custard sauce (made with pear liqueur, or vanilla ice cream made with pear liqueur instead of vodka) and decorative drizzles of raspberry sauce. Use a pancake turner to lift the pear dumplings to the serving plates.

POINTERS FOR SUCCESS

∾ To prevent separation while mixing, the butter and eggs for the almond cream must not be cold.

UNDERSTANDING

During poaching and cooling, the parchment keeps the tops of the pears moistened, as they tend to bob up to the surface, and prevents browning by oxidation (exposure to air).

The poaching syrup has double the water and sugar of that for poached pear halves baked in almond cream (see page 260). More water is needed to cover the pears and more sugar is needed because, unlike almond cream, the fillo has very little added sugar.

Although the filling gets baked and set, the pears do not become mushy because they are insulated by the fillo.

The foil prevents the almond filling from leaking through the fillo before it has set. Once it is removed, the fillo browns perfectly. As the pears are baked standing up, the upper part tends to brown more, making it desirable to bake them in the lower part of the oven.

*Any leftover almond cream can be frozen for up to a month.

SYRIAN KONAFA

T he pastry component of this layered Syrian dessert is shredded fillo, called *konafa* (thin wiry strands of fillo dough, called *kadaif* by Greek and Turkish cooks). The shredded fillo on top stays crunchy, the bottom becomes chewy and moist with the rose-scented syrup. In between, there is a ricotta filling.

Unlike most layered desserts, this one is very simple and uncomplicated to prepare. The only effort is to find the konafa and the rose water. (To order konafa by mail, see page 675.) The dough keeps for 2 months, refrigerated.

OVEN TEMPERATURE: 350°F. •
BAKING TIME: 25 TO 30 MINUTES   **MAKES: SIXTEEN 2-INCH SQUARES**

INGREDIENTS	MEASURE	WEIGHT	
	VOLUME	OUNCES	GRAMS
Fragrant Rose Syrup	(1½ cups)	(14.7 ounces)	(420 grams)
sugar	1½ cups	10.5 ounces	300 grams
water	½ liquid cup	4 ounces	118 grams
Lyle's Golden Syrup (refiner's syrup) or light corn syrup	1½ teaspoons	0.3 ounce	10 grams
freshly squeezed lemon juice	½ teaspoon	•	•
rose water (see page 638)	½ teaspoon	•	•
konafa	•	8 ounces	227 grams
milk	⅓ liquid cup	approx. 2.75 ounces	80 grams
heavy cream	½ liquid cup	4 ounces	116 grams
sugar	1 tablespoon	approx. 0.5 ounce	12.5 grams
cornstarch	1 tablespoon	0.33 ounce	9.5 grams
ricotta cheese	1 container*	approx. 1 pound	454 grams
rose water or orange flower water	½ teaspoon	•	•
unsalted butter	12 tablespoons	6 ounces	170 grams

*Most containers are only 15 ounces, rather than 16, but this is fine.

EQUIPMENT

An 8-inch square glass baking pan or a 10- by 2-inch round cake pan

MAKE THE FRAGRANT ROSE SYRUP

In a medium saucepan, stir together all of the syrup ingredients except the rose water. Cook over medium heat, stirring constantly, until the mixtures comes to a boil. Stop stirring, reduce the heat, and boil the mixture for 5 minutes. (The temperature will be 225°F.) Pour the syrup into a 2-cup heatproof glass measure or bowl and refrigerate it.

When the syrup is cool, add the rose water, stirring it in very gently. Cover tightly with plastic wrap and keep the syrup refrigerated.

In a large bowl, using your fingers, gently pry apart the strands of konafa. Set the bowl aside.

In a medium saucepan, stir together the milk, cream, sugar, and cornstarch until very well mixed. Over medium heat, stirring constantly, bring the mixture to a boil. Reduce the heat to low and boil, stirring, for 2 minutes. Remove the pan from the heat, cover the surface of the mixture with greased plastic wrap to prevent a skin, and cool it completely.

When the mixture is cool, stir in the ricotta and rose water or orange flower water until well blended.

Preheat the oven to 350°F. at least 15 minutes before baking. Set one oven rack at the bottom and one at the top of the oven before preheating.

In a small saucepan over low heat, or in a heatproof glass container in the microwave, heat the butter just until melted fully. Pour the butter over the konafa and, with your fingers, mix until all the strands of the konafa are well coated.

Spread half the konafa evenly in the baking pan, flattening it with your hand. Spread the ricotta mixture over the konafa, leaving a ½-inch border all around. Top with the remaining konafa mixture.

Place the pan on the bottom oven rack and bake for 15 to 20 minutes or until the bottom is golden. (If you are using a metal pan, transfer it to the top rack after 15 minutes.) Transfer the pan to the top rack and continue baking for about 10 minutes or until the top is golden, a cake tester inserted in the center comes out clean, and the filling shakes like firm jelly when moved.

Remove the pan to a rack and immediately pour the cold syrup on top. Allow it to cool completely, about 2½ hours.

Cut the konafa into squares. The texture is most perfect (the top most crunchy and the filling soft and creamy) the day it is made.

STORE

Room temperature, up to 6 hours; refrigerated, up to 3 days. If it is refrigerated, it is best reheated in a 300°F. oven for 7 to 10 minutes or until a skewer inserted in the center no longer feels cold and the top is crisp.

UNDERSTANDING

The refiner's syrup prevents crystallization of the rose water syrup, which would interfere with the smooth creamy texture of the dessert.

Leaving a border when spreading the cheese mixture keeps it from browning and drying at the edges.

Either the konafa must be hot and the syrup cool or the konafa cool and the syrup hot for it to absorb evenly.

PANNA COTTA FILLO FLOWERS

With this recipe, I have arranged a marriage between an Italian and a Middle Eastern dessert. Panna cotta, similar to the custard crème caramel, translates from the Italian as "cooked cream." It replaces the usual eggs contained in a custard with gelatin, which results in a lighter, cleaner taste and intriguingly resilient texture. It is a dessert of such astonishing purity and simplicity I was inspired to use delicate, crisp fillo dough as an enchanting container for it. Strips of fillo are molded in custard cups, so, when baked, they resemble flowers.

Both the fillo shells and the filling have to be made ahead, but for maximum crispness of the shells, the flowers should be assembled shortly before serving. As this takes only moments, it does not present a problem. If desired, the panna cotta can be served without the pastry, simply by unmolding it onto the plates. A four-inch scalloped tart mold, which holds one-third cup of filling, works nicely and the scalloped edges of the unmolded cream and the tiny grains of vanilla that sink to the bottom make for a charming presentation. The panna cotta is also very attractive unmolded into the fillo cups, but it is somewhat free-form, as the custard is larger than the cup and will fold and curve.

Drizzled with Clear Caramel or topped with fresh seasonal berries, this dessert makes a spectacular presentation. I am also offering a savory version, using Brie cheese, that makes an excellent first course for a dinner party.

EQUIPMENT

Six 6-ounce custard cups (3½ inches by 2 inches) and six 10-ounce custard cups or ramekins (4½ inches by 2 inches), buttered

OVEN TEMPERATURE: 325°F. • BAKING TIME: 8 TO 10 MINUTES   SERVES: 6

INGREDIENTS	MEASURE	WEIGHT	
	VOLUME	OUNCES	GRAMS
fillo, preferably fresh (see page 365)	5 sheets	3.3 ounces	94 grams
melted butter, preferably clarified (see page 629)	4 tablespoons	2 ounces	28 grams
sugar	approx. 1 teaspoon	•	•
Panna Cotta Filling heavy cream, preferably not ultrapasteurized	(2⅓ cups) 2 liquid cups	16.25 ounces	464 grams
sweetened condensed milk	¼ liquid cup	2.75 ounces	78 grams
vanilla bean, split lengthwise	3-inch piece*	•	•
gelatin	2 teaspoons	0.25 ounce	7 grams
optional: Clear Caramel Sauce (page 599) or fresh berries, lightly sugared	•	•	•

*If using a Tahitian vanilla bean, use 1½ inches.

Advance preparation: At least 3 hours.

Preheat the oven to 325°F. at least 15 minutes before baking. Set an oven rack at the middle level before preheating.

MAKE THE FILLO SHELLS

Lay the stack of fillo sheets on the counter and cut it into quarters, to make 6-inch squares. (If the fillo is under 12 inches wide, the squares will be slightly under 6 inches.) There will be 20 squares; only 18 are needed. Keep the fillo well covered with plastic wrap and a damp towel to prevent drying.

Remove 1 square of fillo and brush it lightly with the butter, using about ½ teaspoon, starting around the edges where it will dry out the most quickly and then dappling it lightly all over. Sprinkle it lightly with a pinch of sugar. Place a second square of fillo over the first and repeat the butter and sugar. Place a third square on top, placing it so that the corners do not line up evenly and 8 points or corners are visible, and butter and sugar it. (Figure 1) Press the fillo into a buttered 10-ounce custard cup so that it forms a cup. (Figure 2) Repeat to make a total of 6 fillo shells. Place a 6-ounce custard cup inside each one to maintain the shape during baking.

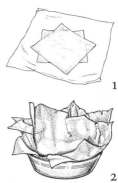

1

2

Bake the shells for 6 minutes. With tongs, carefully remove the 6-ounce custard cups and with a skewer, pierce the bottom of each cup. Continue baking for 2 to 4 minutes or until golden brown. Allow the shells to cool for at least 5 minutes before unmolding them onto racks to cool completely

MAKE THE FILLING

Lightly spray the 6-ounce custard cups with vegetable oil spray or grease them. In a 2-cup heatproof measure, if using the microwave, or a saucepan, stir together the cream and condensed milk. Scrape the vanilla bean seeds into the cream and add the pod. Sprinkle the gelatin on top and stir it in. Allow to sit for at least 5 minutes to soften the gelatin.

Scald* the cream mixture, stirring often. Strain it into a 2-cup measure. Pour the mixture into the custard cups, using 6 tablespoons (3 fluid ounces) for each. Cover them tightly with plastic wrap and refrigerate them for at least 3 hours and up to 3 days.

ASSEMBLE THE PANNA COTTA FLOWERS

The panna cotta must be unmolded onto a greased nonstick surface, such as the bottom of a two-piece tart pan or a flat plate covered with greased plastic wrap, and then reinverted onto a similar surface. Unmold each custard by running a small metal spatula around the edges, then holding it upside down over the non-stick surface and inserting the metal spatula into the side between the panna cotta and the ramekin to create an air pocket. Reinvert it onto the second nonstick surface and slide it into a fillo shell. Refrigerate for up to 6 hours.

Allow the panna cotta to sit for 30 minutes at room temperature before serving to soften slightly. If desired, drizzle the top lightly with caramel or spoon lightly sugared berries on top.

VARIATION

SAVORY BRIE FILLO FLOWERS   Cut the fillo to the same size but shape it into 6-ounce custard cups. Replace the sugar with an equal volume of ground almonds; replace the panna cotta with 2 cups of room-temperature Brie with the rind removed. (Purchase at least 1¼ pounds/567 grams.) Shape the Brie into ⅓-cup balls. Place 2 squares of fillo in each cup, brushing them with butter and sprinkling lightly with ground almonds, and angling the second squares as above. Wrap each Brie ball in a third layer of fillo, bunching it together like a pouch, and press each wrapped ball, bunched side down, into the center of an unbaked fillo flower. Brush the tops with melted butter and bake as above until the shells are golden brown. Serve warm.

Camembert or soft goat cheese also makes delicious fillings.

---

*Small bubbles will form around the perimeter.

SPANAKOPITA TRIANGLES (OR PIE)

This Greek specialty of spinach and cheese filling in little triangles of crisp fillo has long served as a favorite appetizer. I also like it as an accompaniment to lamb chops or leg of lamb. If you would prefer to make it as a pie, follow the directions for the Gascon Apple Pie (page 370), substituting the spinach filling for the apple filling.

If desired, to keep the fillo lighter, the butter can be replaced by olive oil spray, but butter is best for brushing the top layer, as it gives it the most golden brown color.

OVEN TEMPERATURE: 375°F. •
BAKING TIME: 15 TO 20 MINUTES   **MAKES: ABOUT 28 TRIANGLES (OR ONE 10-INCH PIE)**

INGREDIENTS	MEASURE	WEIGHT	
	VOLUME	OUNCES	GRAMS
2 large eggs, beaten	3 fluid ounces	3.5 ounces (weighed with the shells)	100 grams
whole milk ricotta cheese	1 container*	approx. 1 pound	454 grams
olive oil	1½ teaspoons	•	•
minced scallions (including 3 inches of green)	⅓ cup	1 ounce	31 grams
frozen chopped spinach, cooked and drained well†	1 package	10 ounces	284 grams
crumbled feta cheese	⅔ cup	2.6 ounces	74 grams
shredded mozzarella cheese	½ cup	1.5 ounces	43 grams
minced fresh dill	3 tablespoons	approx 0.5 ounce	12 grams
salt	½ teaspoon	•	•
freshly ground black pepper	a few grindings	•	•
fillo, preferably fresh (see page 365)	14 to 16 sheets	approx. 12 ounces	approx. 340 grams
melted butter, preferably clarified (see page 629), or olive oil spray	7 tablespoons	3.5 ounces	100 grams

*Most containers are only 15 ounces, rather than 16, but 1 ounce more or less will make no perceptible difference.

†Place the cooked spinach in a strainer and press and squeeze it well to get rid of as much liquid as possible.

EQUIPMENT

Two large cookie sheets or inverted baking sheets, lightly buttered or sprayed with olive oil

In a medium mixing bowl, whisk together the eggs and ricotta cheese until smooth.

Heat a small skillet over medium heat. Add the olive oil and scallions and sauté the scallions for about 3 minutes or until softened. Add this to the ricotta mixture. Add the drained cooked spinach, the cheeses, dill, salt, and pepper. Whisk until well combined. Taste to adjust the seasoning. (There will be about 3⅓ cups/ 28 ounces/794 grams of filling.)

Preheat the oven to 375°F. at least 20 minutes before baking. Set an oven rack at the top level before preheating.

ASSEMBLE THE TRIANGLES

Lay the stack of fillo on the counter and keep it well covered with plastic wrap and a damp towel to prevent drying. Remove 1 sheet of fillo and place it on the work surface. Brush it lightly with the butter, using about 1 teaspoon, starting around the edges where it will dry out the most quickly and then dappling it lightly all over (or spray it lightly with olive oil). Place a second sheet of fillo over the first. Brush it lightly with butter (or spray it lightly with olive oil). With a sharp knife and a long ruler, cut it lengthwise into 4 strips. Place a rounded tablespoon of the spinach/cheese mixture near the bottom of each strip. To shape each triangle, fold the bottom of the dough over by lifting the right cor- 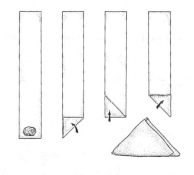 ner and bringing it to the left edge so that it partially covers the filling (the next fold will cover the filling completely). Continue folding the strip, as though folding a flag, and always maintaining the triangle. Tuck under or trim the end. Place the finished triangle seam side down on a greased cookie sheet and brush the tops lightly with butter. Repeat with the remaining filling and fillo, placing the triangles about ½ inch apart.

Bake the spanakopita for 15 to 20 minutes or until golden brown and the filling sizzles. Serve hot or warm. (Reheat baked spanakopita in a preheated 300°F. oven for 7 minutes.)

STORE

Unbaked, refrigerated, up to 24 hours; frozen, up to 3 months. To freeze, wrap each cookie sheet with plastic wrap and then foil, or freeze the triangles on the baking sheets until hard, then transfer to a container.

MOROCCAN BISTEEYA TRIANGLES

I adore the classic Moroccan pie of pigeon and cinnamon-scented custard in fillo, but I prefer this appetizer-size version because the crisp fillo is a better balance to the filling than when it is prepared as one large pie. It is neater to serve and you get a bite of crisp fillo with every bite of filling.

Pigeon, or squab, offers a richer flavor, but using all dark chicken meat is almost as delicious. Most recipes for bisteeya call for almonds, but my research revealed that peanuts, which grow in Africa, are also traditional. I find their flavor even more compatible and interesting in the dish.

Although wrapping three dozen triangles can be a little time-consuming, using olive oil spray and fresh fillo, which does not stick together, makes them a snap to prepare.

EQUIPMENT
Two large cookie sheets or inverted baking sheets, lightly buttered or sprayed with olive oil

Rinse and dry the squab and chicken; rub them all over with the garlic and 1 teaspoon of the oil. Cover tightly and refrigerate for at least 2 and up to 24 hours.

Heat a medium Dutch oven or pot over medium heat. Add the remaining 1 teaspoon of oil. Remove and reserve the garlic from the squab and chicken, and season them with the salt and black pepper. Place the squab and chicken in the pot and cook, turning to brown, until the fat is rendered and the fowl has a light golden color. Add the reserved garlic and sauté it for 30 seconds. Add the onion, spices, and parsley, then add the broth and water, adding more water if necessary to cover. Bring the liquid to a boil, then lower the heat to maintain a simmer. Cook for about 1 hour or until the meat falls from the bones.

Remove the squab and chicken from the pot and allow them to cool. Add the currants to the braising liquid and reduce to 1 to 1⅓ cups, about 20 minutes. It will be very thick. Remove and discard the cinnamon stick, bay leaf, and parsley.

Remove all meat from the chicken and squab and chop it into ¼-inch pieces. (You may include or discard the skin, according to your preference.) (There will be about 2½ cups/10.5 ounces/298 grams.)

Whisk the eggs until frothy and add them to the broth. Turn the heat to low and whisk until it forms a curdy consistency, about 1 minute. Stir all the meat into the pot and adjust the seasonings. Spoon the mixture into a bowl to cool to room temperature, or refrigerate it for up to 12 hours. (There will be about 3⅓ cups of filling.) When cool, chop and stir in the cilantro.

Preheat the oven to 375°F. at least 20 minutes before the baking. Set an oven rack at the top level before preheating.

OVEN TEMPERATURE: 375°F. •
BAKING TIME: 15 TO 20 MINUTES   MAKES: ABOUT 3 DOZEN TRIANGLES

INGREDIENTS	MEASURE	WEIGHT	
	VOLUME	OUNCES	GRAMS
1 squab		14 ounces	397 grams
1 chicken leg and thigh		9.25 ounces	262 grams
1 clove garlic, chopped fine		•	•
olive oil	2 teaspoons, divided	•	•
salt	approx. ½ teaspoon	•	•
freshly ground black pepper	⅜ teaspoon	•	•
coarsely grated white onion	½ cup	2.5 ounces	71 grams
cinnamon stick	⅔ stick	•	•
bay leaf	1 small	•	•
saffron	¹⁄₁₆ teaspoon	•	•
turmeric	⅜ teaspoon	•	•
cayenne pepper	a pinch	•	•
paprika	⅛ teaspoon	•	•
parsley, preferably flat-leaf	approx. 6 sprigs		7 grams
chicken broth, preferably no salt added	one 15-ounce can	15 ounces	425 grams
water	1 liquid cup	8.3 ounces	236 grams
currants	¼ cup	approx. 1 ounce	33 grams
2 large eggs	3 fluid ounces	3.5 ounces (weighed without the shells)	100 grams
cilantro	approx. 6 sprigs	approx. 0.25 ounce	8 grams
fillo, preferably fresh (see page 365)	18 to 20 sheets	approx. 1 pound	approx. 454 grams
melted butter, preferably clarified (see page 629), or olive oil spray	8 tablespoons	4 ounces	114 grams
unsalted peanuts or sliced almonds, toasted and finely chopped	⅓ cup	1.5 ounces	40 grams
powdered sugar	1 teaspoon	•	•
ground cinnamon	1 teaspoon	•	•

ASSEMBLE THE BISTEEYA

Lay the stack of fillo on the counter and keep it well covered with plastic wrap and a damp towel to prevent drying. Remove 1 sheet of fillo and place it on the work surface. Brush it lightly with the butter, using about 1 teaspoon, starting around the edges where it will dry out the most quickly and then dappling it lightly all over (or spray it lightly with olive oil). Sprinkle the fillo with 2 teaspoons of the finely chopped nuts and lay another sheet of fillo over it. Brush it lightly with butter (or spray it lightly with olive oil). With a sharp knife and a long ruler, cut it lengthwise into 4 strips. Place a rounded tablespoon of the bisteeya mixture near the bottom of each strip. To shape each triangle, fold the bottom of the dough over by lifting the right corner and bringing it to the left edge so that it partially covers the filling. (The next fold will cover the filling completely.) Continue, folding the strip as though folding a flag, always maintaining the triangle. Tuck under or trim the end. Place the finished triangle, seam side down, on a greased cookie sheet and brush the top lightly with butter. Repeat with the remaining filling and fillo, placing the triangles about ½ inch apart.

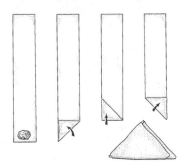

    Bake the bisteeya for 15 to 20 minutes or until golden brown. Serve hot, warm, or room temperature, sprinkled with the remaining nuts and the sugar and cinnamon. (Reheat in a preheated oven to 300°F. for 7 minutes.)

VARIATION

LARGER BISTEEYA (FOR A FIRST COURSE)   Butter eight 5- to 6-ounce ramekins (about 3 by 1½ inches) and line each with 2 sheets of fillo, letting the overhang drape over the sides. Fill each mold to the top and fold the fillo over the filling. Brush the top with melted butter. Bake for 20 minutes or until golden. After baking, sprinkle with the powdered sugar, cinnamon, and nuts.

STORE

Unbaked, refrigerated, up to 24 hours; frozen, up to 3 months. To freeze, wrap the cookie sheets with plastic wrap and then foil, or freeze the triangles on the baking sheets until hard, then transfer to a container.

STRUDEL

S trudel. What an evocative word! In German, it means whirlpool. In pastry, it means heaven—the thinnest leaves of flaky pastry wrapped around warm, cinnamon-laced slices of apple, served with whipped cream (*schlag* in German). The very word seems to elicit sighs of nostalgia from people who have eaten the real thing. And anyone who has will never be content to substitute commercially produced fillo, which lacks both the tenderness and finesse.

Because strudel always seemed like a magical dough to me, I was terrified of it. It took a trip to Austria to overcome my strudel phobia. My friends Sissi Pizutelli and Gabriele Wolf from the Austrian tourist office in New York City assured me that since my paternal grandmother was Austro/Hungarian, I had strudel-making skills in my blood! Bolstered by their confidence in my ancestry, I made strudel in restaurants and bakeries from Innsbruck to Vienna, with some of Austria's finest chefs and pastry chefs. In Innsbruck, I had my first lesson with pastry chef Klaus Huber, who, in true pastry tradition, had everything written out and weighed. Then on to the head chef, Elmar Steinberger, to learn many varieties of delicious savory strudels. In Bad Ischl, at Zauner (the finest bakery I have every encountered, where I had the privilege of being the first outsider to work in their kitchen), pastry chef Alfred Schachner had me make a strudel by hand and without weighing or measuring anything just to see how easy it is to do by feel. In Vienna, at the Hilton, which produces some of the best strudel anywhere, pastry chef Andreas Eckstein made me throw the dough up in the air the way you would pizza (it landed on my chest—much to the amusement of all the chefs, but it sure broke the ice). In the kitchen at Hotel Sacher, I watched two bakers stretch strudel dough over an eight-foot table. But it really wasn't until I made strudel entirely on my own in my own kitchen that I was convinced that strudel making, once learned, is both easy and delightful. Stretching a 3-inch ball of silken dough into a gossamer four-foot-long translucent sheet gives one a sense of accomplishment unequal to any other in baking. And strudel dough actually benefits from heat and humidity, making it the ideal pastry for summer.

Though making and rolling out strudel is practically child's play, the secret to success is, once again and here more than ever, the *type of flour*. In order for the dough to stretch without breaking and forming many holes, it needs to contain not merely gluten-forming protein but a specific kind of protein that has extensibility, i.e., the ability to stretch. This quality changes slightly with each harvest of wheat. In bleached flour, most of this protein has been completely destroyed, which will result in a dough that is not as smooth, is very difficult to stretch, and is full of holes. (Equal weights of both bleached and unbleached Gold Medal flour required the same amount of water, indicating that the gluten-forming protein content was the same.)

King Arthur regular flour is the easiest flour to work with, resulting in a dough that can be stretched so thin, and virtually without holes, as to become indistinguishable to the touch from the soft cotton sheet beneath it, but its higher protein content makes it slightly less fragile and dissolving when eaten. Doughs made with national brands of bread flour, which have only a slightly higher protein count than King Arthur, did not stretch as far or with as few holes.

Gold Medal unbleached flour has a lower protein content than these but even greater extensibility. I was able to stretch a dough made with it to fifty-four inches, but it dried out so quickly it almost disintegrated as I brushed it with butter. (I, therefore, do not recommend stretching the dough beyond forty-eight inches.) Dough made from Gold Medal Flour will have a tendency to tear (I did stretch a dough to forty-nine inches without a single hole on a rainy day), but a few holes really don't matter because since rolled strudel has so many layers, there aren't enough holes once it's rolled for the filling to leak through. Moreover, the baked strudel will be as crisp and flaky as one made with King Arthur flour, the most gossamer and dissolving of all, making it my personal first choice. Using this flour, I felt that my strudel was as good as any I had made or tasted in Austria—and more tender. For first-time strudel makers, I recommend using King Arthur flour, the results of which seemed identical to the Austrian strudel. Some bakers will even prefer the slightly firmer bite. Also, when you start out, it's important to have successful results to build confidence.

STRUDEL DOUGH
(*Master Recipe*)

Strudel dough takes less time to make than pie dough. It takes only minutes to mix and knead and then about ten minutes to stretch. Wrapping it around the filling and shaping it into a roll is the easiest part of all. Making strudel dough is fun, but *only* if you use the recommended flour! With this recipe, you can make just about any strudel and the pastry will be crisp, flaky, and dissolving. A series of step-by-step drawings follows the instructions. But if you are willing to forgo the pleasure of making your own dough, the simple technique for using commercial fillo dough in its place is on page 393.

MAKES: 8.7 OUNCES/248 GRAMS OF DOUGH,
ENOUGH FOR ONE 16- TO 18-INCH-LONG STRUDEL

INGREDIENTS	MEASURE	WEIGHT	
	VOLUME	OUNCES	GRAMS
unbleached all-purpose national-brand flour, such as King Arthur's regular flour or Gold Medal	approx. 1 cup (dip and sweep method)	5 ounces	142 grams
salt	⅜ teaspoon	•	•
warm water	⅓ liquid cup + approx. 1 teaspoon	2.75 ounces	78 grams
vegetable oil	4 teaspoons*	•	•
To Brush on the Dough melted butter, preferably clarified,† warm or room temperature	6 tablespoons	3 ounces	85 grams

*You will also need a little oil to coat the finished dough and plate.

†See page 629; you will need to start with 8 tablespoons (4 ounces/113 grams). There will usually be about 1 tablespoon left over.

EQUIPMENT
A 36- to 48-inch-wide table, preferably round, covered with a clean sheet or table-cloth rubbed with a little flour, and a 17- by 12-inch cookie sheet or half-size sheet pan, buttered

ELECTRIC MIXER METHOD
In the bowl of a heavy-duty stand mixer, preferably with the dough hook attachment, place the flour and salt and whisk them together by hand. Make a well in the

center and pour in the ⅓ cup of water and the oil. On medium speed, mix until the dough cleans the sides of the bowl. If the dough does not come together after 1 minute, add more water, ½ teaspoon at a time. Don't worry if it becomes sticky; adding more flour to make it smooth will not affect the strudel's texture. Remove the dough to a counter and knead it lightly for 1 to 2 minutes or until smooth and satiny. It will be a round ball that flattens on relaxing.

Pour 1 teaspoon of oil onto a small plate and turn the dough so that the oil coats it all over. Cover it with plastic wrap and allow it to sit at room temperature for at least 30 minutes, or refrigerate it overnight.

HAND METHOD

On a counter, mound the flour and sprinkle it evenly with the salt. Make a well in the center and add the oil. Gradually add the ⅓ cup water in 3 or 4 parts, using your fingers and a bench scraper or spatula to work the flour into the liquid until you can form a ball. If necessary, add up to 1 teaspoon more water. Knead the dough until it is very smooth and elastic and feels like satin, about 5 minutes, adding extra flour only if it is still very sticky after kneading for a few minutes. Oil and allow it to rest as above.

STRUDEL FILLING

This basic strudel recipe can be used to wrap any firm filling, sweet or savory. The recipes I offer in this chapter are the classics and, of course, my personal take on them. But you will easily be able to make many variations and combinations to your taste. Any of the fresh fruit pie fillings in Fruit Pies can be used for strudel. Apple, pear, nectarine, peach, apricot, and plum all make fabulous strudel fillings; you will need only 1 pound of prepared fruit and you will need to cut strong spices such as cinnamon by half to two thirds to balance the delicacy of the dough when you prepare the fillings. (Omit the cornstarch and substitute the brusel [see below].)

The more intense fillings, such as cherry or any of the berries, are too concentrated in flavor to balance well with the finesse of strudel dough. To my taste, they require a more substantial dough, such as flaky pastry. They do, however, work well in a strudel dough if mixed with a cream cheese filling, as in the Cherry Cheese Strudel (page 399). To use a berry filling, be sure to cook the berries with the sugar and thickener and cool it before filling the dough, or it will not thicken evenly and will dampen the pastry before thickening takes place.

THICKENER FOR THE FILLING

In classic fruit strudels, the filling is thickened with a mixture called, in German, *brusel*, bread crumbs, sometimes with ground nuts added, sprinkled with sugar and sautéed in butter. (Some bakers in America have been known to use cake crumbs instead of bread crumbs, but Austrians consider this to be heresy.) Too much brusel, like too much of any thickener in a filling, takes away from the clarity of the fruit flavor and makes the texture sludgy and less juicy. I use the same technique for strudel fillings that I do for fresh fruit pie fillings: tossing the fruit with sugar and allowing it to sit until the fruit releases as much of its liquid as possible, then concentrating this liquid and returning it to the fruit to intensify the fruit flavor. This technique makes it possible to use a minimum of brusel. As a gauge for the amount of brusel needed, replace 2 teaspoons of the cornstarch in the filling with ½ cup (1 ounce/28 grams) of medium-fine fresh bread crumbs sautéed in 1½ teaspoons of butter with ½ teaspoon of sugar. Ground nuts can be added to the brusel to taste, as they hardly absorb any of the liquid. To determine how much sugar is needed, refer to the chart on page 77.

To make the crumbs for brusel, grate or process stale French bread, with crusts removed. Or slice fresh bread and bake it in a single layer on a baking sheet, at 200°F. for about 1 hour or until completely dry, turning once or twice; then process or chop it until medium-fine crumbs are formed.

ROLL AND STRETCH THE DOUGH (BOTH METHODS)

Brush the center of the baking sheet with a little of the melted butter; set aside.

Work carefully but as quickly as possible to keep the dough from drying and becoming brittle.

The easiest and most effective way to stretch dough is on a round table, 36 to 48 inches or so, that you can walk around as you pull and stretch the dough evenly. A 48-inch round folding card-table top works well. But you can also make strudel on a square or rectangular surface, using three sides if it is too large. I use an old white sheet on top of the table, but some strudel makers prefer a tablecloth with a pattern so they can see how sheer and translucent their strudel is becoming.

In winter, the dry air will cause the dough to lose moisture very quickly, particularly around the edges. When this happens, I spray the edges with nonstick vegetable shortening. For savory strudels, I sometimes use olive oil spray instead of butter, though butter produces the crispest texture.

Clarified butter is best for brushing on the dough because moisture makes the dough less tender, and the water in clarified butter has been evaporated. Also, the milk solids in unclarified butter will result in brown spots in the dough. If you don't want to go to the trouble of clarifying butter, use the top portion only of the melted butter for brushing on the dough, avoiding the liquid and solids that settle on the bottom.

On a lightly floured counter, roll the dough into a 10-inch round. Brush it with a little of the melted butter to keep the surface from drying.

Slip your hands, palms down, underneath the dough and lift it so that it lies on your knuckles. Partially close your hands and move the dough over your knuckles

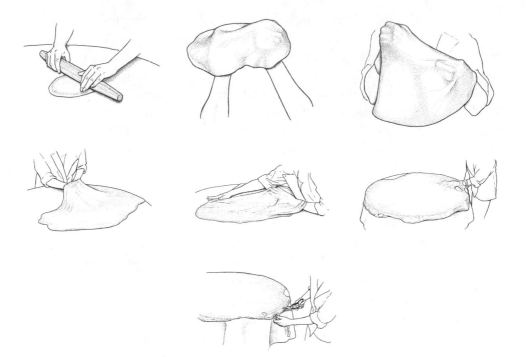

in a circle, allowing it to droop, to stretch it slightly all around. Lay the dough on the cloth. Slip your hands, palms down, under the dough, curving them slightly. Starting at the edges, gently move your hands toward the edges, stretching the dough evenly so as not to tear it and working all around the dough in a circle. Then concentrate on the middle. Ideally, the dough should stretch to 48 inches. It helps to allow the edge of the dough to hang over the sides of the table by an inch or so.

With scissors, trim off the thicker outer border and discard it or reserve it, well wrapped and refrigerated, for future use. The scraps can be refrigerated for a day or rekneaded the same day and stretched again after relaxing for about 30 minutes without any decrease in quality.

At this point, the dough sheet's surface should not be sticky to the touch. If it is a very humid day and the dough still feels tacky, allow it to dry for a few minutes. Dapple it all over with the butter, reserving about 2 tablespoons for brushing the outside while rolling it.

WRAP AND ROLL THE STRUDEL

If using brusel, starting about 6 inches from the bottom edge of the dough, sprinkle half the brusel across the dough in a 9- by 14-inch rectangle. Spread the filling mixture on top, leaving behind any liquid. Sprinkle the remaining brusel over it. If not using brusel, make a rectangle of filling about 9 by 12 to 14 inches.

Use the sheet or cloth or your fingers to lift the bottom edge of the dough and flip it over the filling. It doesn't have to cover the entire filling at this point. Use the sides of the cloth to flip the sides of the dough over the filling, leaving a 3-inch border on either side of the filling to tuck under at the end. (The dough will be about 20 inches wide at this point.) Brush the top of the dough and the side borders with some of the butter and use the cloth to roll it, brushing it with butter - every other turn. If necessary, brush off any flour clinging to the dough before brushing it with butter. Use the cloth to flip the roll onto the prepared baking sheet, seam side down. Turn under the ends. The strudel will be about 16 inches long; the exact length depends on how much the filling spreads while you rolled it. Brush the top with the remaining butter and use a sharp knife to cut a few horizontal steam vents in the dough. At this point, the strudel can be covered with plastic wrap and refrigerated overnight without harm to the dough (unless indicated otherwise in the recipe) or baked immediately.

BAKE THE STRUDEL

I bake most strudels at 400°F. for 35 minutes in the upper part of the oven so that the dough browns. If the filling is cooked and the dough is still pale, I turn up the oven to 425°F. for the last 5 minutes. If the outer edges of the strudel brown faster than the middle, I cover them loosely with aluminum foil. I also like to set a baking

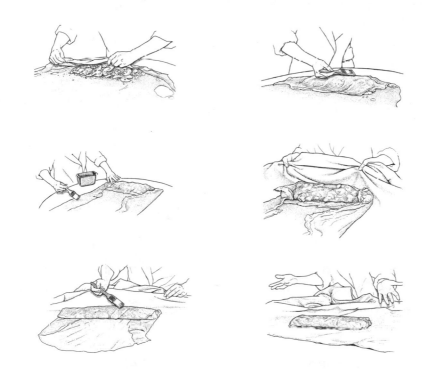

stone or cookie sheet on the upper rack in the oven before preheating. I set the baking sheet with the strudel directly on it to help crisp the bottom of the strudel. Strudels with cheese or custard, however, should be baked at no higher than 375°F.

A baked strudel can be reheated in a 300°F. oven for 5 minutes if it is at room temperature, 10 to 15 minutes if refrigerated.

SERVE THE STRUDEL

Use two flat cookie sheets or two heavy-duty long pancake turners to lift the strudel onto a serving plate or inverted carving board. Use a serrated or sharp knife to cut 1- to 2-inch-thick diagonal slices.

Dessert strudel is most transporting either warm or at room temperature, lightly dusted with powdered sugar just before it is served. To reheat strudel, place it, uncovered, on a baking sheet in a preheated 350°F. oven for about 10 minutes. I love a dollop of unsweetened crème fraîche on the plate as well, but lightly sweetened whipped cream (*schlag*) is also wonderful and traditional in the Austro-Hungarian part of the world.

STORE

Unstretched dough, refrigerated, wrapped airtight, up to 24 hours.

POINTERS FOR SUCCESS

∿ Use a national brand of *unbleached* all-purpose flour, such as King Arthur's regular or Gold Medal.

∿ Let the dough rest before stretching to allow it to absorb the liquid evenly and to relax the gluten.

∿ Work quickly and evenly when stretching the dough to keep it from drying. If any holes or tears develop, they will be covered by the many layers of untorn dough.

COMMERCIAL FILLO AS A STRUDEL SUBSTITUTE

If you prefer to use commercial fillo, simply overlap the sheets to form a larger rectangle. It is easy to do, but the results will not be quite as tender as making your own strudel.

EQUIPMENT

A 17- by 12-inch cookie sheet or half-size sheet pan, buttered

INGREDIENTS	MEASURE	WEIGHT	
	VOLUME	OUNCES	GRAMS
6 fillo sheets, 17 inches by 12 inches, preferably fresh (see page 365)		approx. 3.5 ounces	100 grams

Lay the stack of fillo on the counter and keep it well covered with plastic wrap and a damp towel to prevent drying.

Remove 1 sheet of fillo and place it on the prepared cloth with a 17-inch-long edge toward you. (Figure 1) Brush it lightly with the butter (using about 2 teaspoons), starting around the edges where it will dry out the most quickly and then dappling it lightly all over. Overlap a second sheet on top of it, starting 3 to 4 inches in from the left edge so the fillo rectangle is 20 inches wide when finished. (Figure 2) Butter as before. Continue with the remaining sheets of fillo, building the rectangle downward, toward you, by overlapping about 2 inches of the fillo at the bottom edge, buttering each sheet as before. (Figures 3, 4, 5, 6) If each sheet is 12 inches high, three overlapped sheets will result in a length of 32 inches. The final dimensions of the sheet will thus be approximately 32 inches long by 20 inches wide. The exact length is unimportant.

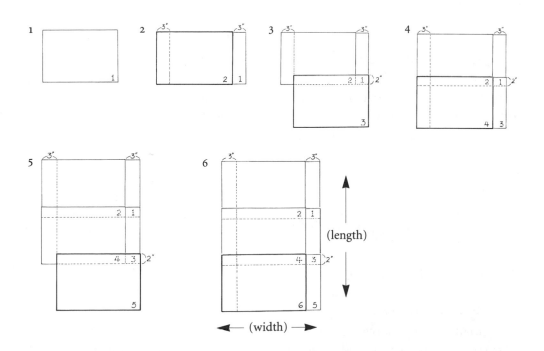

Starting about 6 inches from the bottom edge of the dough, make a rectangle of filling about 9 inches by 12 to 14 inches across the dough. Fold over the sides so that the edges just reach the filling, leaving a 1½-inch border on either side of it. (The dough will be about 17 inches wide at this point.) Use the sheet or cloth or your finger to lift the bottom edge of dough and flip it over the filling. It doesn't have to cover the entire filling at this point. Brush the top of the dough and the side borders with some of the butter and use the cloth to roll it, brushing it with butter every other roll. If necessary, brush off any flour clinging to the dough before brushing it with butter. Use the cloth to flip the roll onto the prepared baking sheet, seam side down. Tuck under the ends. The strudel will be about 16 inches long. Brush the top with butter and use a sharp knife to cut a few horizontal steam vents in the dough. At this point, the strudel can be covered with plastic wrap and refrigerated overnight or baked immediately.

All strudel, except those with a cheese or milk filling, should be baked at 400°F. for about 35 minutes. It is best to bake strudel in the upper part of the oven on a preheated oven stone or baking sheet, so the bottom crisps and the top browns. The outer edges of the strudel tend to brown faster than the middle, so, halfway through the baking, cover them loosely with aluminum foil.

A baked strudel can be reheated in a 300°F. oven for 5 minutes if it is at room temperature, 10 to 15 minutes if refrigerated.

APPLE STRUDEL

I was in my twenties when I tasted my first apple strudel at Kleine Konditorei, a café in Yorkville, the old German section of New York City. It was unlike any pastry I had ever experienced, juicy slices of warm apple enfolded in a crisp leafed pastry. It transported me to another world, of Old Vienna and a baking tradition I had only dreamed about. I never would have dreamed that someday I would be turning out fabulous strudel myself. If you follow this recipe, it will be a reality for you too.

EQUIPMENT
A 36- to 48-inch-wide table, preferably round, covered with a clean sheet or tablecloth rubbed with a little flour, and a 17- by 12-inch cookie sheet or half-size sheet pan, buttered

Make the dough (page 387).

MAKE THE BRUSEL
In a small frying pan, over medium heat, melt the butter. Add the bread crumbs, sprinkle with the sugar, and sauté for a few minutes until golden, stirring constantly. Empty the crumbs into a small bowl and set aside.

INGREDIENTS	MEASURE	WEIGHT	
	VOLUME	OUNCES	GRAMS
1 recipe Strudel Dough (page 387)		8.5 ounces	245 grams
melted unsalted butter, preferably clarified (see page 629)	8 tablespoons	4 ounces	114 grams
Brusel unsalted butter	1½ teaspoons	0.25 ounce	7 grams
fresh bread crumbs	½ cup	1 ounce	28 grams
sugar	¼ teaspoon	•	•
Filling 1¼ pounds apples (about 3 medium), peeled, cored, and sliced ⅜ inch thick	4 cups (sliced)	1 pound	454 grams (sliced)
freshly squeezed lemon juice	1½ teaspoons	0.25 ounce	8 grams
sugar	¼ cup	1.75 ounces	50 grams
ground cinnamon	½ teaspoon	•	•
nutmeg, preferably freshly grated	⅛ teaspoon	•	•
salt	⅛ teaspoon	•	•
walnuts, toasted and coarsely chopped	⅓ cup	approx 1 ounce	33 grams
optional: powdered sugar for dusting	approx. 1 tablespoon	•	•
optional: Crème Fraîche (page 558) or lightly sweetened whipped cream (pages 551–53)	1 cup	approx. 8 ounces	232 grams

MAKE THE FILLING

In a large bowl, combine the apples, lemon juice, sugar, cinnamon, nutmeg, and salt and toss to mix. Allow the apples to macerate for a minimum of 30 minutes and a maximum of 3 hours.

Transfer the apples to a colander suspended over a bowl to capture the liquid. The mixture will release at least ¼ cup of liquid. In a small saucepan (preferably with a nonstick surface), reduce this liquid to 1½ tablespoons (a little more if you started with more than ¼ cup of liquid), until syrupy and lightly caramelized. Swirl but do not stir the liquid. (Or spray a 2-cup heatproof measure with non-stick vegetable spray, add the liquid, and reduce it in the microwave, about 4 minutes on high.) Add the nuts and liquid to the apple mixture; toss to blend. (Do not worry if the liquid hardens on contact with the apples; it will dissolve during baking.)

Roll and stretch the dough (see page 389).

FILL AND ROLL THE STRUDEL

Starting about 6 inches from the bottom edge, sprinkle half the brusel across the dough in a 9- by 14-inch rectangle. Spread the apple mixture on top, leaving behind any liquid. Sprinkle it with the remaining brusel. Use the sheet or cloth or your fingers to lift the bottom of the dough and flip it over the apples. It does not have to cover them completely at this point. Use the sides of the cloth to flip the sides of the dough over the filling, leaving a 3-inch border on either side of the filling to tuck under at the end. (The strudel dough will be about 20 inches wide at this point.) Brush the top of the dough and the side borders with some of the melted butter and use the cloth to roll it, brushing it with butter every other roll. If necessary, brush off any flour clinging to the dough before brushing it with butter. Use the cloth to flip the roll onto the prepared sheet, seam side down. Tuck under the ends. The strudel will be about 16 inches long. Brush the top with some of the remaining melted butter and use a sharp knife to cut a few horizontal steam vents in the dough. (At this point, the strudel can be covered with plastic wrap and refrigerated overnight if desired.)

Preheat the oven to 400°F. at least 20 minutes before baking. Set an oven rack at the highest level and place a baking stone or baking sheet on it before preheating.

Bake for 35 minutes or until the filling bubbles through the vents. If the outer edges brown faster than the middle, cover them loosely with foil. If the filling is bubbling and the top is still pale, turn up the oven to 425°F. and bake for about 5 minutes. Remove the pan to a wire rack and allow the strudel to cool until warm.

If desired, sprinkle the strudel lightly with powdered sugar. Cut into 1¾- to 2-inch pieces on the bias. Discard the end pieces or cut up and serve in pieces for those who enjoy extra pastry without the filling. Serve with whipped cream.

STORE

Room temperature, up to 2 days. (This is best eaten the day of baking.)

APPLE STREUSEL STRUDEL

This variation of classic apple strudel is thickened with streusel, a crumb topping like the one adorning the top of an apple crumb pie. Streusel, an Eastern European topping, especially popular for cakes, consists of butter, flour, walnuts, sugar, and cinnamon. It adds a wonderful cinnamon/butter flavor and absorbs any juices from the apple slices as they bake.

OVEN TEMPERATURE: 400°F. • BAKING TIME: 35 MINUTES   SERVES: 6

INGREDIENTS	MEASURE	WEIGHT	
	VOLUME	OUNCES	GRAMS
1 recipe Strudel Dough (page 387)		8.5 ounces	245 grams
melted unsalted butter, preferably clarified (see page 629)	8 tablespoons	4 ounces	114 grams
Filling 1¼ pounds apples (see page 635; about 3 medium), peeled, cored, and sliced ⅜ inch thick	4 cups (sliced)	1 pound	454 grams (sliced)
raisins or dried cranberries	⅓ cup	1.7 ounces	48 grams
freshly squeezed lemon juice	1½ teaspoons	0.25 ounce	8 grams
sugar	2 tablespoons	0.75 ounce	25 grams
ground cinnamon	¼ teaspoon	•	•
nutmeg, freshly grated	⅛ teaspoon	•	•
salt	⅛ teaspoon	•	•
walnuts, toasted and finely chopped	⅓ cup	1 ounce	33 grams
Streusel (page 592)	1 cup	5.5 ounces	157 grams
optional: powdered sugar for dusting	about 1 tablespoon	•	•

EQUIPMENT

A 36- to 48-inch-wide table, preferably round, covered with a clean sheet or tablecloth rubbed with a little flour, and a 17- by 12-inch cookie sheet or half-size sheet pan, buttered

Make the dough, page 387.

MAKE THE FILLING

In a large bowl, combine the apples, raisins or cranberries, lemon juice, sugar, cinnamon, nutmeg, and salt and toss to mix. Allow the apples to macerate for a minimum of 30 minutes and a maximum of 3 hours.

Transfer the apples to a colander suspended over a bowl to capture the liquid. The mixture will exude a scant ¼ cup of liquid. In a small saucepan (preferably lined with a nonstick surface), reduce this liquid to 1 tablespoon. (Or spray a 2-cup heatproof measure with nonstick vegetable spray, add the liquid, and reduce in the microwave, about 4 minutes on high.) Add the liquid to the apple mixture and toss to blend.

Roll and stretch the strudel dough (see page 389).

FILL AND ROLL THE STRUDEL

Starting about 6 inches from the bottom edge of the dough, sprinkle the ground nuts evenly across the dough in a 14-inch-long column. Spread the apple mixture on top in a 14- by 4-inch rectangle, leaving behind any liquid. Sprinkle it with the streusel. Use the sheet or cloth or your fingers to lift the bottom edge of the dough and flip it over the apples. Use the sides of the cloth to flip the sides of the dough over the filling, leaving a 3-inch border on either side of the filling to tuck under at the end. (The strudel dough will be about 20 inches wide at this point.) Brush the top of the dough and the side borders with some of the butter and use the cloth to roll it, brushing it with butter every other turn. If necessary, brush off any flour clinging to the dough before brushing it with butter. Use the cloth to flip the roll onto the prepared sheet, seam side down. Tuck under the ends. The strudel will be about 16 inches long. Brush the top with the remaining butter and use a sharp knife to cut a few steam vents in the dough. (At this point, the strudel can be covered with plastic wrap and refrigerated overnight, if desired.)

Preheat the oven to 400°F. at least 20 minutes before baking. Set an oven rack at the highest level and place a baking stone or cookie sheet on it before preheating.

Bake for 35 minutes or until the filling bubbles through the vents. If the outer edges of the strudel brown faster than the middle, cover them loosely with aluminum foil. If the filling is bubbling and the top of the strudel is still pale, turn up the oven to 425°F. and bake for 5 minutes. Remove the pan to a wire rack and allow the strudel to cool until warm.

Sprinkle it lightly with powdered sugar, if desired. Cut into 2-inch pieces on the bias. Discard the end pieces or cut and serve in pieces for those who enjoy extra pastry without the filling.

STORE

Room temperature, up to 2 days. (This is best eaten the day of baking.)

CHERRY CHEESE STRUDEL

In this recipe, a creamy cheesecake-like layer topped with a layer of sour cherries is encased in strudel dough. I support the strudel with two bread pans placed on either side to prevent the filling from breaking through during baking. If it seems like a lot of trouble, it's because you haven't yet tasted this strudel!

OVEN TEMPERATURE: 350°F. • BAKING TIME: 40 TO 50 MINUTES   **SERVES: 10 TO 12**

INGREDIENTS	MEASURE	WEIGHT	
	VOLUME	OUNCES	GRAMS
1 recipe Strudel Dough (page 387)		8.5 ounces	245 grams
melted unsalted butter, preferably clarified (page 629)	8 tablespoons	4 ounces	114 grams
Sour Cherry Filling sugar*	7 tablespoons	3 ounces	88 grams
cornstarch	1 tablespoon	0.3 ounce	9.5 grams
salt	a pinch	•	•
12 ounces fresh sour cherries	1¾ cups (pitted† and juices reserved)	10 ounces (pitted)	284 grams
pure almond extract	⅛ teaspoon	•	•
Creamy Cheese Filling cream cheese, softened	(2½ cups) 1½ large packages or 4 small	(19.25 ounces) 12 ounces	(550 grams) 340 grams
sugar	¼ cup + 2 tablespoons	2.6 ounces	75 grams
2 large egg yolks	2 tablespoons + 1 teaspoon	1.3 ounces	37 grams
salt	a pinch	•	•
finely grated lemon zest	2 teaspoons	•	4 grams
freshly squeezed lemon juice	2 teaspoons	0.3 ounce	10.5 grams
pure vanilla extract	1 teaspoon	•	4 grams
sour cream	½ cup	4 ounces	116 grams
cornstarch	2 teaspoons	0.2 ounce	6 grams
Optional: powdered sugar for dusting	about 1 tablespoon	•	•

*If the fruit is particularly tart, add up to ½ cup.

EQUIPMENT

A 36- to 48-inch-wide table, preferably round, covered with a clean sheet or table-cloth rubbed with a little flour; a 17- by 12-inch cookie sheet or half-size sheet pan; heavy-duty aluminum foil; and 2 narrow bread pans (for support)

Make the dough, page 387.

MAKE THE CHERRY FILLING

In a small saucepan, stir together the sugar, cornstarch, and salt. Stir in the cherries, along with any reserve juices. Allow the mixture to sit for at least 10 minutes for the cherries to start exuding some of their juices.

Over low heat, bring the mixture to a boil, stirring constantly. The juice will thicken and become translucent. Allow it to simmer for 1 minute. Empty it into a bowl and very gently stir in the almond extract. Allow it to cool completely.

MAKE THE CHEESE FILLING

In a large mixer bowl, preferably with a whisk beater, beat the cream cheese and sugar until very smooth, about 3 minutes. Add the egg yolks, beating until smooth and scraping down the sides once or twice. Add the salt, lemon zest, lemon juice, and vanilla and beat until incorporated. Beat in the sour cream and cornstarch just until blended. Refrigerate while stretching the strudel dough.

Make a foil collar: Tear off a 22-inch-long piece of heavy-duty aluminum foil. Brush some of the butter the entire length in a 12-inch-wide strip down the middle. Lay it on the baking sheet.

Roll and stretch the dough (see page 389).

Preheat the oven to 350°F. at least 15 minutes before baking. Set an oven rack at the highest level and place a baking stone or cookie sheet on it before preheating.

FILL AND ROLL THE STRUDEL

Starting about 6 inches from the bottom edge of the dough, spread the cheese filling across the dough in a 3- by 14-inch rectangle (it will spread to about 16 inches during rolling). Gently spoon the cherry topping over it. Use the sheet or cloth or your fingers to lift the bottom edge of the dough and flip it over the filling. Use the sides of the cloth to flip the sides of the dough over the filling, leaving a 3- to 4-inch border on either side of the filling to tuck under at the end. The strudel dough will be about 20 inches wide at this point. Brush the top of the dough and the side borders with some of the butter and use the cloth to roll it, brushing it with butter every other roll. To allow for expansion, do not wrap the dough too tightly. If necessary, brush off any flour clinging to the dough before brushing it with butter. Use the cloth to flip the roll onto the foil band on the baking sheet, seam side down. Tuck under the ends of the dough. The strudel will be about 16 inches long. Brush the top with the remaining melted butter and use a sharp knife to cut a few horizontal steam vents in the dough.

Bring up the foil all around the strudel roll to support it, first folding over the long sides so that they are 3 inches high (the strudel will rise) and then turning up the short ends. Place a bread pan right up against each long side of the roll, in the center, for additional support. (It is best to bake this strudel shortly after making it.)

Bake the strudel for 40 to 50 minutes or until the pastry is golden and the filling is set. A thermometer inserted in the center will read 165°F. (It should be no higher than 185°F. in order to keep the filling smooth and creamy; the filling will jiggle slightly when the pan is moved.) Remove the pan to a wire rack and allow the strudel to cool for 30 minutes.

Sprinkle the strudel lightly with powdered sugar, if desired. Cut into 1¼- to 1½-inch pieces on the bias. Discard the end pieces or cut up and serve in pieces for those who enjoy extra pastry without the filling. Serve at once.

VARIATIONS

"FRUIT PERFECT"™ CHERRY/CHEESE STRUDEL Place 1 jar of Fruit Perfect Cherries (see Sources, page 639; 13.5 ounces/400 grams) in a strainer suspended over a bowl and stir them gently to drain out all the slightly thickened juices. Place the juices in a small saucepan.

In a small bowl, stir together 2 tablespoons of sugar (omit this if you like very tart cherry filling), 1½ teaspoons of cornstarch, and 1½ teaspoons of water until the cornstarch is dissolved. Add this to the cherry juice. Over low heat, stirring constantly, bring to a boil. Simmer, stirring gently, for 1 minute or until very thick. Empty it into a small bowl, add the cherries, and allow to cool completely.

FLUFFY CREAMY CHEESE FILLING Folding in a small amount of meringue produces an airier filling that is particularly compatible with the crisp delicate pastry, but it is a little trickier to roll the pastry because the filling is softer before baking. If you have a gentle touch, however, you should have no problem.

In a mixing bowl, beat 1 egg white until foamy. Add ⅛ teaspoon of cream of tartar and beat at medium speed, gradually adding 1½ teaspoons of sugar, until stiff peaks form when the beater is raised. Fold this meringue into the cream cheese mixture.

STORE

Refrigerated, up to 3 days.

HUNGARIAN POPPY SEED STRUDEL
(*Mákos Kalácz*)

This strudel is dense with a ground black poppy seed filling through which the thinnest possible crust is spiraled. In Hungary, this poppy seed filling is used both in a strudel and in this easy-to-make pastry that is like a pie crust with yeast. I learned the strudel version from the pastry chefs at Gundel's Restaurant in

Budapest. This recipe comes from my friend and former student Jan Kish, whose mother makes it every Christmas Eve. Jan remembers as a child sneaking downstairs in the middle of the night to taste some fresh from the oven. If you love poppy seeds, as do I, you will have to try this recipe.

**OVEN TEMPERATURE: 375°F. •
BAKING TIME: 30 TO 35 MINUTES**

**MAKES: A 16-INCH-LONG BY 4-INCH-WIDE BY
2-INCH-HIGH STRUDEL SERVES: 6 TO 8**

INGREDIENTS	MEASURE	WEIGHT	
	VOLUME	OUNCES	GRAMS
Dough		(9.25 ounces)	(261 grams)
unsalted butter	2 tablespoons	1 ounce	28 grams
bleached all-purpose flour	1 cup (dip and sweep method)	5 ounces	142 grams
warm water	scant ¼ liquid cup	•	•
sugar	½ teaspoon	•	•
compressed fresh yeast,*	1½ tablespoons, packed	0.75 ounce	21 grams
active dry yeast (not rapid-rise) or	2¼ teaspoons	0.25 ounce	7 grams
SAF-Instant yeast (page 654)	2 teaspoons	0.25 ounce	7 grams
salt	¼ teaspoon	•	•
½ large egg yolk	1½ teaspoons	0.3 ounce	9 grams
Poppy Seed Filling			
milk	½ liquid cup	4.25 ounces	121 grams
poppy seeds, ground†	approx. 2⅔ cups‡	8 ounces	227 grams
sugar	⅔ cup	4.6 ounces	132 grams
finely grated lemon zest	½ teaspoon	•	•
freshly squeezed lemon juice	2½ tablespoons	1.3 ounces	39 grams
golden raisins, plumped in warm water**	½ cup	2.5 ounces	72 grams
Egg Glaze			
lightly beaten egg	1 tablespoon	•	•

*Fresh yeast causes dough to rise faster.

†Grind in a poppy seed grinder or a blender.

‡1⅓ cups whole seeds.

**In a small bowl, place the raisins and ¼ cup of water, heated until hot. Cover with plastic wrap and allow to sit, stirring once, until softened, about 30 minutes. Drain, reserving the water to use as part of the water for the dough.

EQUIPMENT
A heavy cookie sheet, lightly buttered

MAKE THE DOUGH
Cut the butter into ½-inch cubes, wrap them in plastic wrap, and freeze them for at least 30 minutes. Place the flour in a reclosable gallon-size freezer bag (or covered bowl) and freeze it for at least 15 minutes.

Proof the yeast, if using active dry or fresh (do not use hot water, or the yeast will die): In a small bowl, combine the water (ideally a tepid 100°F. if using fresh yeast, a little warmer, 110°F., if using dry), 1 teaspoon of the sugar, and the yeast. If using fresh yeast, crumble it slightly as you add it. Set the mixture aside in a draft-free spot for 10 to 20 minutes. By this time, the mixture should be full of bubbles. (If not, the yeast is too old to be useful and you must start again with newer yeast.)

Place the flour and salt in a food processor with the metal blade* and process for a few seconds to combine them. Add the frozen butter cubes and pulse until the butter is the size of peas. Add the egg yolk and pulse 6 times just to incorporate it. Remove the cover and add the yeast mixture. Pulse about 15 times or until most of the butter is the size of small peas. (Toss with a fork to assess the texture.) The mixture will be in particles and will not hold together.

Empty it out onto a large piece of plastic wrap and, using the wrap and your knuckles, knead and press the mixture until it holds together in one piece. Transfer the dough to a work surface and knead it for about 10 minutes or until satiny smooth, adding flour if necessary. Cover the dough with plastic wrap and allow it to rise until doubled in bulk, 45 minutes to 1 hour.

MAKE THE POPPY SEED FILLING
In a small saucepan, heat the milk. Add the poppy seeds, stirring until the milk is absorbed (a few seconds). Remove the pan from the heat and stir in the remaining ingredients, except the raisins, until incorporated. Cool the filling to room temperature.

On a lightly floured sheet of plastic wrap, roll the dough to a rectangle about 15 inches long by 11 inches wide and as thin as possible. Spread small dollops of the poppy seed filling evenly over the dough. Then gently spread it evenly over the dough, out to the edges. Strew the raisins evenly on top. Starting at a long side, roll up the dough jelly-roll fashion, gently tucking under the ends. The roll will be about 14 inches by 3 inches wide.

Place the roll on the buttered cookie sheet. Brush it with the egg glaze and cover it lightly with greased waxed paper. Cover and refrigerate the remaining glaze. Allow the roll to rise until doubled in bulk, about 45 minutes.

Preheat the oven to 375°F. at least 20 minutes before baking. Set an oven rack at the middle level and place a baking stone or cookie sheet on it before preheating.

---

*The dough can also be made by hand (see the procedure for Basic Flaky Pie Crust, page 22).

Brush the roll again with the glaze and place it in the oven on the stone. Bake for 30 to 35 minutes or until golden brown. Using two large pancake turners, lift the roll to a rack to cool. Cut into 2-inch pieces on the bias. Discard the end pieces or cut up and serve in pieces for those who enjoy extra pastry without the filling.

VARIATION

STRUDEL DOUGH OR FILLO POPPY SEED ROLL   Replace the dough with 1 recipe of strudel dough (page 387) or 6 sheets of fillo (see page 393). Mix the raisins into the poppy seeds. Spread the mixture in a 14- by 3-inch rectangle across the bottom of the dough. Roll as directed for strudel or fillo and cut 3 steam vents (see page 391). Bake in the upper part of the oven at 375°F. for 30 to 35 minutes or until golden. Cool for at least 15 minutes before cutting with a thin sharp knife. (Serrated works well for the dough but not for the filling.) This variation keeps at room temperature for up to 3 days but, after the first day, needs to be covered with plastic wrap, or the dough becomes too dry (as there is very little moisture in the filling).

STORE
Room temperature, up to 2 days; frozen, up to 6 months.

POINTERS FOR SUCCESS
∽ Use fresh poppy seeds. When stale, they become rancid and very bitter. Do not grind them too fine or the oil will start to exude. (Poppy seeds can be stored in the refrigerator for several months or frozen for about a year.)

MILK RUM STRUDEL ROYALE

This is an amazing strudel, unlike any other. It has straight as opposed to rounded sides, because it is baked in a long loaf pan instead of free-form on a baking sheet. The purpose of the loaf pan is to contain a vanilla-and-rum-flavored custard that is poured over the almond-and-buttery-bread-filled strudel. During baking, the filling absorbs the custard, expanding and taking on the moist and creamy texture of a bread pudding soufflé, encased in a golden, crunchy pastry. The contrast of textures is at its best when the strudel is still warm, but it is also absolutely delicious at room temperature. This recipe requires a special pan called a Pullman loaf pan, but it is well worth the investment because you will want to make this strudel many times for special occasions.

OVEN TEMPERATURE: 375°F. •   MAKES: A 15-INCH BY 3½-INCH BY
BAKING TIME: 45 MINUTES   1½-INCH-HIGH STRUDEL   SERVES: 10 TO 12

INGREDIENTS	MEASURE	WEIGHT	
	VOLUME	OUNCES	GRAMS
1 recipe Strudel Dough (page 387)		8.5 ounces	245 grams
melted, unsalted butter, preferably clarified (page 629)	8 tablespoons	4 ounces	114 grams
Brusel			
unsalted butter	1 teaspoon	•	5 grams
fresh bread crumbs*	⅓ cup	approx. 1 ounce	33 grams
sugar	¼ teaspoon	•	•
sliced blanched almonds, chopped medium-fine	full ⅓ cup	approx. 1 ounce	33 grams
Bread Filling			
crustless fresh bread or rolls, loosely torn	1 cup	2 ounces	58 grams
milk	½ liquid cup	4.25 ounces	121 grams
unsalted butter	4½ tablespoons	2.25 ounces	64 grams
powdered sugar	¼ cup (lightly spooned)	1 ounce	28 grams
3 large eggs, separated yolks whites	scant 2 fluid ounces 3 fluid ounces	2 ounces approx. 3 ounces	56 grams 90 grams
finely grated lemon zest	1½ teaspoons	•	3 grams
pure vanilla extract	1 teaspoon	•	4 grams
Crème Fraîche (page 558) or sour cream	½ cup	4 ounces	116 grams
cream of tartar	⅜ teaspoon	•	•
granulated sugar	3 tablespoons	1.3 ounces	38 grams

*Use stale French bread, sliced with crusts removed, or leave sliced bread exposed to the air for several hours to dry. Process it or chop it with a sharp knife until medium-fine crumbs are formed. It's okay to use commercial bread crumbs in this strudel, but, as they are finer, use only 3 tablespoons.

EQUIPMENT

A 36- to 48-inch-wide table, preferably round, covered with a clean sheet or tablecloth, rubbed with a little flour, and a Pullman loaf pan (15¾ inches by 3¾ inches, measured at the bottom), buttered

Make the dough (page 387).

MAKE THE BRUSEL

In a small frying pan, over medium heat, melt the butter. Add the bread crumbs, sprinkle with the sugar, and sauté for a few minutes until golden, stirring constantly. Empty the crumbs into a small bowl, add the almonds, and set aside.

MAKE THE BREAD FILLING

In a medium bowl, soak the bread in the milk for at least 10 minutes or until the milk is absorbed. The bread will soften but not fall apart easily or be mushy; there will still be some dry parts.

In a mixer bowl, preferably with the paddle beater, combine the butter, powdered sugar, egg yolks, and lemon zest and beat on medium speed for 3 to 5 minutes, scraping the sides of the bowl as necessary, until smooth and creamy. On low speed, beat in the vanilla. Add the soaked bread and the brusel and beat on medium speed until the bread breaks up, about 30 seconds. Whisk in the crème fraîche or sour cream by hand.

In a large mixer bowl, beat the egg whites until foamy. Add the cream of tartar and beat at medium speed, gradually adding 1 tablespoon of the sugar, until soft peaks form when the beater is raised slowly. Gradually beat in the remaining 2 tablespoons of sugar and continue beating on high speed until stiff peaks form when the beater is raised.

Using a large rubber spatula, fold this meringue into the bread mixture; it will be soft. (The filling will measure about 4 cups/22.25 ounces/363 grams.) Refrigerate it, tightly covered, while stretching the strudel dough.

Roll and stretch the dough (see page 389).

Preheat the oven to 375°F. at least 20 minutes before baking. Set the oven rack in the middle position before preheating.

FILL AND ROLL THE STRUDEL

Starting about 6 inches from the bottom edge of the dough, spread the bread filling across the dough in a 9- by 12-inch rectangle (it will spread to 15 inches during rolling). Use the cloth or your fingers to lift the bottom edge of the dough and flip it over the filling. It doesn't have to cover all the filling at this point. Use the sides of the cloth to flip the sides of the dough over the filling, leaving a 3- to 4-inch border on either side of the filling to tuck under at the end. Brush the top of the dough and the side borders with some of the butter and use the cloth to roll it, brushing it with butter every other turn. If necessary, brush off any flour clinging to the dough before brushing it with butter. With the seam on the top, fold the ends up over the top of the strudel. The strudel should be no more than 15 inches long; if it is longer, push in the ends so it will fit into the pan. Use the cloth to flip the roll seam side down into the prepared pan. Brush the top with the remaining melted butter. There is no need to cut steam vents, as the top splits naturally as the filling swells.

MAKE THE ROYALE CUSTARD

INGREDIENTS	MEASURE	WEIGHT	
	VOLUME	OUNCES	GRAMS
Royale Custard milk	½ liquid cup	4.25 ounces	121 grams
1 large egg yolk	1 generous tablespoon	0.6 ounce	18 grams
sugar	1¾ teaspoons	0.25 ounce	7.3 grams
freshly squeezed lemon juice	1 teaspoon	•	•
rum	1 tablespoon	0.5 ounce	14 grams
pure vanilla extract	1 teaspoon	•	4 grams
optional: powdered sugar for dusting	approx. 1 tablespoon	•	•

In a medium bowl, combine the milk, egg yolk, sugar, lemon juice, rum, and vanilla and whisk to blend well. Strain the mixture into a 1-cup or larger measuring cup with a spout.

Bake the strudel for 20 minutes. Pour the royale around the sides of the strudel (not on the top). It will come about halfway up the sides. Bake for 25 minutes longer or until the pastry is golden and the filling is set. (A thermometer inserted in the center will read 210°F. and the filling where the split develops will spring back when lightly pressed.) Remove the pan to a wire rack and allow the strudel to cool for 30 minutes.

Run a small metal spatula or knife between the sides of the strudel and the pan and invert it into a large cookie sheet. Reinvert it onto the top of the Pullman loaf pan cover (it makes an attractive and perfect-sized serving plate). Sprinkle the strudel lightly with powdered sugar, if desired. Cut into 1¼- to 1½-inch pieces on the bias. Discard the end pieces or cut up and serve in pieces for those who enjoy extra pastry without the filling. Serve at once.

STORE

Room temperature, up to 1 day; refrigerated, up to 2 days. (This is best eaten the day of baking, still warm.)

CABBAGE AND BACON STRUDEL

The smokiness of bacon combined with the buttery sweet/savory flavors of sautéed cabbage and onion makes for a fantastic strudel filling. The filling can be made up to three days ahead and the flavors only benefit from the prolonged intermingling. When you cut into the golden crisp strudel roll, the savory aromas make your nostrils tingle with anticipation.

EQUIPMENT

A 36- to 48-inch-wide table, preferably round, covered with a clean sheet or table-cloth rubbed with a little flour; a 12-inch frying pan or Dutch oven; and a 17- by 12-inch cookie sheet or half-size sheet pan, buttered

Make the dough (page 387).

MAKE THE BRUSEL

In a small frying pan, over medium heat, melt the butter. Add the bread crumbs, sprinkle with the sugar, and sauté until golden, stirring constantly. Empty the crumbs into a small bowl and set it aside.

MAKE THE FILLING

Quarter the cabbage vertically and remove and discard any tough outer leaves and the center core. Slice the cabbage into thin vertical strips. Set it aside.

Slice the bacon into ¼-inch strips. In the large frying pan, on low heat, fry the bacon for about 10 minutes or until crisp and golden. With a slotted skimmer, remove it to paper towels to drain. Pour off and discard all but 1 tablespoon of the bacon fat. Add the cabbage, onion, sugar, salt, and pepper to the pan. Cook for about 20 minutes, stirring occasionally, until the cabbage is tender but not browned. Stir in the dill, parsley, and bacon and taste to adjust the seasoning. Set aside to cool to room temperature.

Roll and stretch the dough (see page 389).

Preheat the oven to 400°F. at least 20 minutes before baking. Set an oven rack at the top level and place a baking stone or cookie sheet on it before preheating.

FILL AND ROLL THE STRUDEL

Starting about 6 inches from the bottom edge of the dough, sprinkle the brusel across the dough in a 4- by 14-inch rectangle. Spread the cabbage mixture on top. Use the sheet or cloth or your fingers to lift the bottom edge of the dough and flip it over the filling. Use the sides of the cloth to flip the sides of the dough over the filing, leaving a 3-inch border on either side of the filling to tuck under the roll at the end. (The dough will be about 20 inches wide at this point.) Brush the top of the dough and the side borders with some of the butter and use the cloth to roll it,

INGREDIENTS	MEASURE	WEIGHT	
	VOLUME	OUNCES	GRAMS
1 recipe Strudel Dough (page 387)		8.5 ounces	245 grams
melted unsalted butter, preferably clarified (see page 629)	8 tablespoons	4 ounces	114 grams
Brusel			
unsalted butter	1 teaspoon	•	•
fresh bread crumbs*	¼ cup	0.5 ounce	14 grams
sugar	¼ teaspoon	•	•
Cabbage and Bacon Filling	(4 cups)		
cabbage		1¼ pounds	567 grams
bacon†	4 strips	3.5 ounces	100 grams
1 medium onion, cut in half and sliced	1 cup (sliced)	4.5 ounces	128 grams (sliced)
sugar	1 teaspoon	•	•
salt	½ teaspoon	•	•
freshly ground black pepper	to taste	•	•
chopped fresh dill	2 tablespoons	0.25 ounce	7 grams
minced fresh parsley, preferably flat-leaf	2 tablespoons		8 grams
optional: Crème Fraîche (page 558) or sour cream, plus sprigs of dill	1 cup	approx. 8 ounces	232 grams

*Use stale bread with crusts removed or leave sliced bread exposed to the air for several hours to dry or bake it in a single layer on a baking sheet at 200°F. for about 1 hour or until completely dry, turning once or twice. Process it or chop it with a sharp knife until medium-fine crumbs are formed. If using commercial bread crumbs, which are fine, use only 2 tablespoons.

†I use Harrington bacon from Vermont, which is smoked over corncobs. (See Sources, page 675.)

brushing it with butter every other turn. If necessary, brush off any flour clinging to the dough before brushing it with butter. Use the cloth to flip the roll onto the prepared sheet, seam side down. Tuck under the ends. The strudel will be about 16 inches long. Brush the top with the remaining butter and use a sharp knife to cut a few horizontal steam vents into the dough. (At this point, the strudel can be covered with plastic wrap and refrigerated overnight, if desired.)

Bake for 30 to 40 minutes or until the strudel is golden brown. (A thermometer inserted in the middle will read 175°F.) After the first 15 minutes of baking, cover the edges of the strudel loosely with aluminum foil. Remove the pan to a wire rack and allow the strudel to cool until warm, about 20 minutes.

Cut into 1¾- to 2-inch pieces on the bias. Discard the end pieces or cut up and serve in pieces for those who enjoy extra pastry without the filling. If desired, garnish each plate with a dollop of crème fraîche or sour cream and a few sprigs of dill.

STORE

Refrigerated, up to 3 days.

PUFF PASTRY
AND CROISSANT

Puff pastry is the king of pastries—crisp, buttery, flaky, and incomparably light. In French it is called *pâte feuilletée*, or leafed pastry, because of its many layers, or leaves. These layers of dough and fat are created by folding the dough, a technique referred to as giving the dough "turns." Classic puff pastry is given a minimum of 6 turns, which form 729 layers. Gluten-forming protein, found in greater quantities in unbleached hard wheat than bleached or softer flour, plays an important role in the pastry's ability to puff. Gluten is made up of one part protein and two parts water. On heating, the water turns to steam, thus creating a great deal of pressure within the gluten structure, causing it to rise. Puff pastry, when baked, rises to about eight times its original height.

Puff pastry works best in cool, dry weather, because if the fat becomes too warm, it melts and breaks through the dough layers. The best-*tasting* puff pastry is made with butter. However, the best-*textured* puff pastry is achieved with vegetable shortening. Butter with a low water content, such as Plugrá, is highly desirable, because too much water will toughen the gluten. (An excess of water may appear as spots on the surface of the final pastry.)

Unbleached all-purpose flour (use a national brand, as some Southern flours are much lower in protein), which has more gluten-forming proteins than bleached, is necessary to provide the extra support for the thin, fragile layers of butter and dough. Bread flour is too high in protein and results in tough pastry. The acidity of the added lemon juice relaxes the dough by breaking down the proteins just enough to make rolling easier.

I am indebted to Bernard Clayton (*The Complete Book of Breads*) for coming up with the most significant secret to making successful puff pastry: that is, the ideal temperature, 60°F., for the butter. It is quite easy to achieve because when the butter, direct from the refrigerator, is pounded and flattened into a square, provided one works fairly quickly, the temperature will be exactly correct. If I want to hold the butter at that temperature, my wine cellar, which is 58°F., is ideal. If the butter is too hard, it will break through the dough; if too soft, it will be absorbed into the dough. Either way, the layers will be destroyed.

Puff pastry has innumerable uses. It can be sprinkled with cheese and paprika and twisted into straws. It can be baked in rectangular sheets and layered with pastry cream to make a Napoleon, baked as a round disc to serve as the base for a Gâteau St.-Honoré, or baked in a tart pan to serve as crust for fruit or cream pies and tarts. One of its most appealing forms is the small patty shell known as *bouchée*, in which a tiny cap of pastry is perched atop a filling of chilled pastry cream and fresh fruit. Any leftover pastry scraps can be made into savory pastries, hors d'oeuvres, or cheese straws. Traditionally, puff pastry is served hot only in its savory forms.

ROLLING OUT THE DOUGH

Marble is the preferred surface for working with puff pastry, because it maintains a cool temperature, but oilcloth, Formica, or wood is fine. If the pastry starts to soften, quickly slide it onto a flat baking sheet, cover it with plastic wrap, and refrigerate it for about 30 minutes or until it is firm and cool again.

The work surface should be lightly dusted with flour to prevent sticking, and a small amount of flour rubbed lightly into the surface of the pastry. Always roll puff pastry into a square or rectangular shape, regardless of the final shape desired. Decrease the pressure as you roll toward the edges to avoid flattening the edges and compressing the layers. Evenness of rolling is essential for even rising. A heavy rolling pin is an asset.

A *tutove* rolling pin is specially designed for rolling puff pastry. Its surface is covered with rounded ridges, which help to distribute the butter evenly without breaking through the dough. A long heavy rolling pin is also a great help, because it alleviates the need to press too hard when rolling out the pastry.

During the final turns, the dough becomes more difficult to roll, as more gluten is developed through repeated rolling. If the dough is very elastic and hard to roll, a method that my friend Shirley Corriher swears by in her book *CookWise* to relax the gluten in the dough is to roll it out as large as possible and then to brush it heavily with ice water before continuing to roll.

For most purposes, the pastry is rolled ⅛ inch thick. For tartlets, I prefer 1/16 inch thick, and for larger pastries, such as the Gâteau St.-Honoré, 3/16 inch thick.

With puff pastry there will always be some degree of shrinkage, except when it is baked blind in a tart pan. Before cutting, lift it slightly and allow it to fall back on the counter so that it will shrink *before* cutting, and cut a circle ½ to 1 inch larger than the desired baked size or transfer it to the baking sheet before cutting.

RESTING AND RELAXATION (OF PASTRY!)

The gluten in pastry causes it to shrink or spring back when rolled. It is therefore important to rest puff pastry after shaping it. The ideal is to refrigerate it (covered to avoid drying, because moisture is important to its rise) 6 hours to overnight, and up to 2 days, before baking. Next best would be to bake it from a thoroughly frozen state, or partially frozen for 30 minutes to 1 hour in the freezer (wrapped airtight), but be sure to let it relax before freezing. At the very least, it should be refrigerated for 30 minutes to 1 hour.

SHAPING

When cutting the pastry, the object is to create edges that leave the layers of pastry open and able to rise freely, as opposed to edges that are stuck together or sealed. To accomplish this, always use a sharp knife and an up-and-down motion as opposed to a dragging motion, or use an unfloured biscuit cutter pressed firmly down, straight through the pastry. Do not twist the cutter, and be sure to wipe it clean after each cut. Never use puff pastry with an uncut edge, because the layers will be sealed.

To attach one piece of puff pastry to another, use an egg wash made from one egg yolk lightly beaten with one teaspoon water. This acts as glue, so it is important that it be applied carefully and not allowed to drip onto the sides, sealing them shut. *Never* pinch the edges together. Only press lightly from the top. The same egg wash can be used as a glaze. It should be applied just before baking. A second coat can be applied after a minute.

SCRAPS

Puff pastry trimmings will not puff quite as high as the original dough but will still be amazingly flaky. They will distort less if they are laid on top of each other as much as possible in the same direction as the original sheet. Dust them lightly with flour or cover them with plastic wrap and roll over them so that they adhere to each other. Do a "turn" before wrapping and refrigerating (or freezing) them to relax and firm before reuse.

BAKING SHEETS

Avoid nonstick and black-bottomed baking sheets when baking puff pastry. When used in gas nonconvection ovens, the nonstick surface does not provide the necessary traction to enable the puff pastry to keep its shape as it rises, and the black-bottomed baking sheets cause the bottoms of the pastries to brown too quickly. A heavy baking sheet lined with parchment or brushed with water is best. Pastries should be placed about 1 inch apart.

STORAGE

Puff pastry can be kept frozen for up to 1 year in a good freezer (one that maintains close to 0°F.). It can also be refrozen twice after its initial freezing without any significant loss in rising ability. This is particularly useful for make-ahead hors d'oeuvres—the frozen dough can be rolled, stuffed, shaped, and refrozen until shortly before serving time. In fact, puff pastry bakes best from the frozen state, because the contrast from very cold to very hot gives it an added shock, or boost, on its way up! It also tends to bake more evenly and with less shrinkage.

Once the pastry is defrosted, it should not remain in the refrigerator for more than 2 days. If you cannot use it before then, it is better to refreeze it.

DEFROSTING

Frozen puff pastry will defrost in 4 hours to overnight in the refrigerator or 1 to 2 hours at room temperature. It should still be cool but malleable enough to roll smoothly. Do not roll it if it is still stiff, partly frozen, or too hard.

To defrost only part of a piece of frozen pastry, use a serrated knife and make a ¼-inch-deep cut across the dough, marking the size you want. Then strike the pastry sharply on the edge of a tabletop or counter, along the underneath side of the cut, and the piece will break off cleanly. If the defrosted pastry is very sticky, dust it well with flour and brush off the excess before rolling.

BAKING

Convection ovens are marvelous for puff pastry, enabling them to rise to their fullest height and evenly browning them with no excess browning of the base. In a conventional oven, it is best to place the pastry in the upper third of the oven to avoid overbrowning the bottom. I like to start the baking at 425° to 450°F. for the first 10 minutes and then finish baking at 350°F. to ensure that the inside gets baked. In a convection oven, however, I usually bake at 400°F. for the entire time. Some convection oven manufacturers recommend 375°F. for their pastry, especially if it is a thick piece, so that the top does not overbrown before the center is fully baked.

Underbaked puff pastry is unappealingly doughy; overbaked pastry is dry. One way to tell if the center of the pastry is baked is to use the tip of a sharp knife to dig out a little piece. You can also *hear* when the pastry is not yet cooked through, because as long as there is water still remaining in the crust, you can hear it bubbling. When the water boils, at 212°F., it will evaporate, so using an instant-read thermometer is an excellent test. For large pastry cases, if there is still a little doughy pastry remaining in the center when the rest is baked, it is best to dig it out and discard it.

SERVING

Puff pastry cuts best with a serrated knife.

MAKING A VOL-AU-VENT

A vol-au-vent is a large patty shell. Its name is French for "fly in the wind." Roll 1¼ pounds of puff pastry into a square a little larger than 12 inches. It will be about ¼ inch thick. Transfer it to a parchment-lined baking sheet (or brush the baking sheet with water) at this point because, once it is cut, it will be very difficult to transfer it

1   2   3

without deforming it and even the slightest irregularity becomes magnified after baking.

Using a lid, cake pan, or similar guide, cut a 12-inch circle. (Figure 1) Reserve the cutaway edges for another use. To form the rim, cut a ¾-inch ring from the edge of the circle. (Figure 2) Brush a ¾-inch band of egg wash around the border of the circle. Cut through the ring to open it and place it on top of the egg-washed border so that the edges of the strip and circle are even. Cut off the excess from the ends of the ring so that they overlap only slightly and attach the overlap with egg wash. (Figure 3) Press gently all along the top of the ring. With a sharp knife, make a shallow cut all around the inside of the ring to form a lid. Cut a diagonal lattice design into it by cutting evenly spaced lines first in one direction and then the other all around. With the back of a knife, held at a slight angle against the side of the pastry, score vertical marks all around the outside. Cover it with plastic wrap and chill it for at least 1 hour. Before baking, apply an egg wash glaze, if desired, or brush the pastry lightly with cold water. (The water will create steam, which also helps it to rise.)

MAKING BOUCHÉES

These individual patty shells are the perfect-size little pastry cases for individual sweet or savory fillings. Roll 1¼ pounds of puff pastry into a square a little larger than 12 inches. It will be about ¼ inch thick. (It can even be a little larger and only ³/₁₆ inch thick.) With a 4-inch fluted or plain round cutter, cut 8 circles. Using a 3½-inch round cutter, cut out the centers of 4 of these circles. Using egg wash to make them adhere, place the resulting rims on the remaining 4 circles. (Use the cut centers as covers, if desired.) Prick the centers up to the rims (and prick the covers if using) to prevent shrinkage. Transfer them to a parchment-lined baking sheet, using a wide spatula and being careful not to alter their shape. To ensure that they hold their shape, you can transfer the rolled sheet of dough to a parchment-lined baking sheet before cutting them and cover and chill the dough before cutting and shaping them.

BAKING VOL-AU-VENTS AND BOUCHÉES

In a convection oven preheated to 400°F., vol-au-vents take about 20 to 30 minutes, bouchées about 15 minutes. In a conventional oven, bake at a preheated 450°F. for 10 minutes, then reduce the temperature to 350°F. and bake bouchées for 10 to 15 minutes more, vol-au-vents 15 to 20 minutes more, or until they are golden brown. To make beautifully even vol-au-vents, check them after 4 minutes of baking (8 minutes if baked from the frozen state). They will just be beginning to puff up—no dramatic rise will have taken place yet, but you will be able to see which part (or parts) is rising higher than the rest. Using a small sharp knife, insert it quickly about half an inch into the edge of the rim where it meets the center—not the rim itself—in front of the higher part. This will release the steam and cause the higher part to level off. The pastry will continue to rise evenly. (Do this as quickly as possible so that heat from the oven does not escape.)

Another technique used to make a perfectly even vol-au-vent is to suspend a rack about 2 inches over the vol-au-vent, using Pyrex cups or other 2-inch-high supports (Figure 4). If one side of the vol-au-vent rises faster than the rest, it hits the rack and levels out instead of continuing to rise and toppling over.

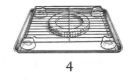

4

The bouchées can be shaped ahead and frozen. If the shells are brushed with apricot or chocolate glaze, they can be filled with pastry cream several hours in advance, as the glaze keeps them from getting soggy.

GALETTES, TARTS, AND TARTLETS

For a small flat galette, roll the pastry ⅛ inch thick and cut it into a 5½-inch round. (You will need about 2.25 ounces/64 grams of dough.) It will shrink about ½ inch during baking.

Puff pastry makes a fabulous tart shell, not only because of its delicious flavor and flaky texture but also because of its dramatically irregular shape. For tarts and tartlets, roll the pastry ⅟₁₆ to ⅛ inch thick; the smaller the tart, the thinner the pastry should be. Lift it slightly and allow it to fall back on the counter so that it will shrink before cutting. Measure the inside of the pan with a tape measure, starting at one top edge and going down the side, across the bottom, and up the other side. Cut the pastry ¼ to ½ inch larger than this measure for tartlets, 1 inch larger for tarts. The dough should come at least ¼ inch above the sides of the pan. It will rise during baking. After shaping, cover the tart or tartlet shells with plastic wrap and refrigerate for at least 1 hour to relax the dough. Freeze them, if desired (but refrigerate for 1 hour first).

FAVORITE SIZES FOR TARTLETS

For a 4- by 1¼-inch-high tartlet: Cut the pastry into a 5-inch circle. (You will need about 1½ ounces/44 grams of dough.) It will be large enough to hold a generous ¼ cup of filling.

For a 4¾- by ¾-inch-high tartlet: Cut the pastry into a 6-inch circle. (You will need 2½ ounces/72 grams of dough.) It will be large enough to hold ¼ to ⅓ cup of filling.

BAKING BLIND

Puff pastry lining a tart pan needs to be weighted with serious weights to hold it down. I like to use copper pennies because they are less expensive than scrap metal pie weights and are also the best conductor of heat. To my knowledge, there is no law against baking your money as long as it's coins!

Line the pastry with parchment or a cup-shaped coffee filter, pleating it as necessary. Place the tart pan (or pans) on a baking sheet and fill with the pennies. Bake in a preheated 400°F. convection oven (425°F. in a conventional oven) for 15 to 20 minutes or until set. Remove the parchment or filter with the weights. Prick the bottom and sides of the shell(s) and continue baking for about 5 minutes or until golden. Turn off the oven and leave the tart(s) in it with the door ajar for 5 minutes. Remove the tart pan(s) to racks and allow to cool completely. Puff pastry unmolds easily. Unmold tart shells before filling them.

CLASSIC PUFF PASTRY

T he average puff pastry, which is given 6 "turns," or folds, has 729 layers. I like to give the pastry a total of 7 turns, forming 2187 layers, because the resulting pastry is incredibly light and flaky.

Single turns (folding the dough like a business letter) as opposed to the newer double turns (bringing the two ends of the dough to meet in the center and then folding the dough in half) make it easier to control the shaping and layering of the pastry, so it will rise more evenly when baked. Although the actual working time is short, you will need to be around for a four-hour period to complete the turns.

The finished pastry must be allowed to rest refrigerated for at least two hours. If it will not be used by the next day, it can be frozen for months.

INGREDIENTS	MEASURE	WEIGHT	
	VOLUME	OUNCES	GRAMS
unsalted butter, ideally Plugrá or French butter	1 cup	8 ounces	227 grams
unbleached all-purpose flour	1½ cups (dip and sweep method)	8 ounces	227 grams
salt	½ teaspoon	•	3.5 grams
water	½ liquid cup	4 ounces	118 grams
freshly squeezed lemon juice	1 teaspoon	•	5 grams

INGREDIENTS	MEASURE	WEIGHT	
	VOLUME	OUNCES	GRAMS
unsalted butter, ideally Plugrá or French butter	2 cups	1 pound	454 grams
unbleached all-purpose flour	3 cups (dip and sweep method)	1 pound	454 grams
salt	1 teaspoon	•	7 grams
water	1 liquid cup	8.3 ounces	236 grams
freshly squeezed lemon juice	2 teaspoons	0.3 ounces	10.5 grams

THE DÉTREMPE (DOUGH)
(AMOUNTS FOR THE LARGER QUANTITY ARE IN BRACKETS)

Place 2 tablespoons (1 ounce) [4 tablespoons/2 ounces] of the butter in a mixing bowl and refrigerate the remainder. Add 1⅓ cups (7 ounces) [2⅔ cups/14 ounces] of the flour and the salt. Rub this mixture between your fingers until it is very fine and grainy and no lumps of butter are discernible, about 5 minutes. Add 6 tablespoons [¾ cup] of the water and the lemon juice and stir gently with a fork to incorporate. The dough should be soft and clumpy. If necessary, add some of the remaining water by droplets.

Dump the dough out onto a floured surface and gently knead only until the dough holds together and looks fairly smooth. It should not become too elastic, or it will be difficult to roll. Cover the dough and allow it to rest for 20 minutes at room temperature or up to 24 hours well wrapped and refrigerated.

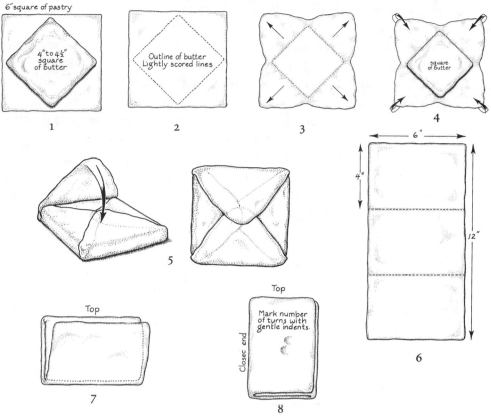

THE BUTTER SQUARE

Place the remaining 3 tablespoons (1 ounce) [6 tablespoons/2 ounces] of flour on a sheet of plastic wrap and place the reserved butter on top. Sprinkle a little of the flour on top of the butter and cover with the plastic wrap. Pound the butter lightly with a rolling pin to flatten and soften it, then knead the butter and flour together, using the plastic wrap and your knuckles to avoid touching the butter directly. Work quickly and, as soon as the flour is incorporated, shape it into a 4 - to 4½-inch [6-inch] square, no thicker than ¾ inch. At this point, the butter should be cool but workable, 60°F. Use it at once, or keep it cool. The butter must not be colder than 60°F. when rolled into the pastry, or it will break through the dough and not be evenly distributed.

THE DOUGH PACKAGE

Roll out the dough on a well-floured surface to a 6-inch [8-inch] square. (Figure 1) Place the butter square diagonally in the center of the dough square and, with the dull side of a knife, lightly mark the dough along the edges of the butter. (Figure 2) Remove the butter and roll each marked corner of the dough into a thin flap. (Figure 3) The dough will be slightly elastic. Moisten these flaps lightly with water, replace the butter on the dough, and wrap it securely, stretching the flaps slightly to reach across the dough package. (Figures 4 and 5) On a well-floured surface, keeping the dough seam side up and lightly floured, gently roll the dough package into a 6- by 12-inch [7- by 15-inch] rectangle. (Figure 6) Brush off all the flour from the surface of the dough and fold it into thirds as you would fold a business letter. (Figure 7) This is the first "turn." Before each subsequent turn, position the dough so that the closed side is facing to your left.

Clean the work surface, reflour it, and press down on the edges of the dough with the rolling pin to help keep them straight. (The upper part tends to lengthen faster than the bottom.) As you roll, turn the dough over occasionally to keep the seams and edges even. Be sure to roll into all four corners of the dough and use a pastry scraper to even the edges. Mark the dough with two fingertips (or knuckles if you have long nails) to indicate that two turns have been completed. (Figure 8) Wrap it with plastic wrap and then foil and refrigerate for 30 to 40 minutes. *The dough must not chill for longer than 40 minutes or the butter will never be evenly distributed.*

Continue to roll and turn the dough, marking the turns with fingertips and resting the dough for 30 minutes between turns, for a total of 7 turns. It is best to do only one turn at a time now as the dough will become elastic and best results are obtained when the dough is not forced and the layers not pressed together.

STORE
Refrigerated, up to 2 days; frozen, up to 1 year.

QUICK PUFF PASTRY

This speedy way to make puff pastry is not a copout; in fact, it is sometimes preferable to classic puff pastry because though slightly less flaky, it also distorts less and is more tender. The secret to success is that not only is it quick to make, but you have to work quickly to keep the butter from softening. Don't let it throw you that the dough is messy until it goes through several "turns." We have Julia Child to thank for presenting this clever technique.

Cut the butter into ½-inch cubes. Refrigerate the butter for at least 30 minutes or freeze it for 10 minutes.

In a large mixer bowl, place both flours and the salt and mix on low speed to blend them well. Add the cold butter and mix only until the butter forms lumps about the size of lima beans. (If mixing by hand, rub the butter and flour between your fingers until large flakes, about 1 inch in size, form.) Add the water, beating on low speed only until the dough roughly masses together; the butter pieces should remain about the same size. (If the dough does not come together, add more ice water by the teaspoon.)

MAKES: 1¼ POUNDS/567 GRAMS

INGREDIENTS	MEASURE	WEIGHT	
	VOLUME	OUNCES	GRAMS
unsalted butter, ideally Plugrá or French butter	18 tablespoons (2 sticks + 2 tablespoons)	9 ounces	255 grams
unbleached all-purpose flour	1¼ cups (dip and sweep method)	6.5 ounces	185 grams
cake flour (not self-rising)	¼ cup (dip and sweep method)	1.25 ounces	35 grams
salt	¾ teaspoon (1 teaspoon for savory)	•	•
ice water	⅓ liquid cup	2.75 ounces	79 grams

Turn the dough out onto a lightly floured surface and, with your hands, quickly push and pat it into a rectangle about 10 inches by 8 inches. Lightly flour the surface of the dough. Using a flat cookie sheet or dough scraper to flip over the dough, fold it into thirds as you would fold a business letter. Clean the work surface, flour it lightly, and position the dough so that the closed side is toward your left. Lightly flour the surface of the dough and, with a rolling pin, roll the dough into a rectangle about the same size as before. Fold the dough into thirds as before, clean and reflour the work surface, and place the dough so that once again the top flap is to your right. Repeat these steps two more times and mark the 4 turns (folds) by lightly pressing your fingertips (or knuckles if you have long nails) into the smooth surface of the dough to create 4 shallow indentations. Cover the dough with plastic wrap and refrigerate it for at a minimum of 40 minutes and a maximum of 1 day before completing the last 2 turns.

STORE
Refrigerated, up to 2 days; frozen, up to 1 year.

POINTERS FOR SUCCESS
∾ If at any point the dough starts to soften and stick, slip it onto a cookie sheet, cover it with plastic wrap, and refrigerate it until firm (but no longer than 30 minutes, to keep the butter from getting too hard, as it will not soften evenly at room temperature until at least 4 turns have been accomplished).
∾ Baking the pastry directly on a moistened baking sheet helps the dough adhere to the sheet, keeping it from sliding and distorting during baking. Using parchment or a nonstick sheet usually results in some distortion. Do not use a black baking sheet, as it would overbrown the bottom crust.

UNDERSTANDING

Plugrá butter or French butters have less water than other butters, so they stay pliant even when cold.

The combination of unbleached flour and cake flour results in just the right amount of protein to support the layers without making the dough too elastic to roll.

Compared to classic puff pastry, which uses equal weights of butter and flour, quick puff pastry starts off using 9 ounces of butter to 7.75 ounces of flour, but since the butter is not contained within a dough package, more flour gets worked in during the rolling and turning.

STRAWBERRY STRIP

A fresh strawberry tart made with puff pastry and pastry cream is a true French classic and a perfection of flavors and textures.

This tart should be put together no more than two to three hours in advance. Too much time in the refrigerator will toughen the pastry.

OVEN TEMPERATURE: 425°F. • BAKING TIME: 20 MINUTES   **SERVES: 8**

INGREDIENTS	MEASURE	WEIGHT	
	VOLUME	OUNCES	GRAMS
puff pastry (page 417 or 420) (see Note, page 424)		12 ounces	340 grams
Egg Glaze 1 large egg yolk	approx. 1 tablespoon	0.6 ounce	18 grams
heavy cream	1 teaspoon	•	•
Pastry Cream, preferably whipped cream variation (page 560)	1 cup	•	•
strawberries, preferably small and nicely shaped, rinsed, hulled, and dried	6 cups	24 ounces	680 grams
Berry Glaze currant jelly, raspberry jelly, or half of each	⅓ cup	3.7 ounces	106 grams

EQUIPMENT

A cookie sheet at least 16 inches long or inverted half-size sheet

Make the dough (page 417 or 420).

On a floured surface, roll the dough into a 9- by 16-inch rectangle, ¹⁄₁₆ to ⅛ inch thick. Brush off the excess flour.

Spray the cookie sheet with water and invert the dough onto it. Brush off the excess flour and, with a sharp knife, trim the edges of the dough to form an even rectangle. (Make clean cuts so as not to compress the layers of the dough.) Brush about a 1-inch border along each long edge with water and fold the edges over to form a 1¼-inch-wide rim. Trim a very narrow slice from the two rolled edges so that the edges of the pastry are open and will be able to rise. Using the back of the knife, press slanted vertical notches about ½ inch apart into each long side. Prick the center section of the dough all over with a fork.

Freeze the pastry for 20 minutes, or, if time allows, refrigerate it for 1 hour to relax and chill it.

Preheat the oven to 425°F. at least 20 minutes before baking. Set an oven rack at the middle level before preheating.

Stir together the egg yolk and cream and brush the top of the dough rim with it, being careful not to let any drip onto the sides, or it will seal the edges.

Bake for 20 minutes or until the pastry is puffed and lightly browned and the center is fully baked (use the tip of a sharp knife to lift out a little dough from the center to check; an instant-read thermometer will register 212°F.). If the top is perfectly browned and the center still not done, turn off the oven and leave the pastry in the oven with the door propped open with a wooden spoon for 15 minutes. Place the cookie sheet on a rack to cool the pastry completely. If not using the pastry right away, store it airtight at room temperature up to 24 hours.

ASSEMBLE THE STRIP

Use a small offset spatula or rubber spatula to spread the pastry cream evenly over the center of the strip. Arrange the berries evenly on top.

MAKE THE BERRY GLAZE

In a small saucepan or a microwave oven, heat the jelly until melted and bubbling; strain into a small cup. Cool until lukewarm.

Using a pastry brush or small clean artist's brush, brush the glaze onto the berries.

STORE

Cool room temperature or refrigerated, up to 3 hours. This is best eaten within 2 hours of assembling it.

NOTE

If using a Pepperidge Farm frozen puff pastry sheet, roll it, to press out the creases, to 12 inches in length. Trim it to 8 inches wide. Use three quarters the amount of pastry cream, strawberries, and glaze.

UNDERSTANDING

Purchased puff pastry may require a lower oven temperature (375° to 400°F.).

The technique for shaping the borders of pastry case is slightly different from that for the apricot strip (below). The two methods can be used interchangeably, depending on which works best for you.

APRICOT STRIP

This is a classic French apricot tart strip: a rectangular case of puff pastry filled with fresh apricot halves baked in a layer of pastry cream, glazed with apricot preserves, and garnished with bright green pistachio nuts.

This is an elegant but practical company dish; it's especially speedy if you use store-bought puff pastry and canned apricots.

OVEN TEMPERATURE: 400°F., THEN 350°F. •
BAKING TIME: 50 MINUTES   SERVES: 8

INGREDIENTS	MEASURE	WEIGHT	
	VOLUME	OUNCES	GRAMS
puff pastry (page 417 or 420) (see Note, page 426)		12 ounces	340 grams
8 apricots,* rinsed	3 cups (halved and pitted)	1 pound	454 grams (pitted)
Egg Glaze			
1 large egg yolk	approx. 1 tablespoon	0.6 ounce	18 grams
milk	1 teaspoon	•	•
Pastry Cream (page 560)	1 cup	9 ounces	260 grams
Apricot Glaze			
apricot preserves	½ cup	6 ounces	170 grams
optional: pistachio nuts, blanched† and cut in half	1 cup	5 ounces	142 grams

*Well-drained canned apricot halves in heavy syrup work very well.

†Place the nuts in boiling water for 1 minute; drain, rinse, and pinch each nut to slip off the skins.

EQUIPMENT

A 17-inch cookie sheet, preferably insulated, or inverted half-size sheet pan

Make the dough (page 417 or 420).

On a floured surface, roll the puff pastry into a rectangle a little over 16 inches by 8 inches and $\frac{1}{16}$ to $\frac{1}{8}$ inch thick. Brush off the excess flour.

Spray the cookie sheet with water and invert the pastry on it. Brush off excess flour, cover with plastic wrap, and refrigerate for 20 to 30 minutes, until firm.

Meanwhile, with a small, sharp knife, cut the apricots in half, remove the pits, and sprinkle them with the lemon juice.

Using a ruler and a sharp knife, trim the pastry to 8 inches wide by 16 inches long. Carefully cut off two 1- by 16-inch strips. Lightly brush a 1-inch-wide border along one long side of the pastry rectangle with water. Place a pastry strip on top of it, lining up the edge of the strip precisely with the edge of the rectangle. Be careful not to stretch the strip. Press along the top of the strip to help it adhere. Repeat with the second strip on the opposite side. With the back of a knife held perpendicular to the edge and at a slight angle, make $\frac{1}{4}$-inch notches about $\frac{1}{2}$ inch apart along each long edge. (This helps the strips adhere to the base and makes an attractive edge.) Use a skewer or sharp three-tined fork to make holes all over the pastry, including the strips. With a sharp knife, carefully make a shallow cut down the length of the pastry on either side where the strip meets the base, being careful not to cut through to the bottom. This helps the sides to rise freely.

ASSEMBLE THE STRIP

Stir together the egg yolk and milk. With a small clean artist's paint brush or pastry feather, apply a coat of egg glaze to the top of the strips, being careful not to allow it to drip onto the sides. Cover and refrigerate the remaining glaze. Pipe or spread the pastry cream evenly over the center, starting 1 inch from either end and keeping it about $\frac{1}{2}$ inch from the side bands. Starting close to the edge, place 2 apricots, cut sides up and as close together as possible, at the top of the strip. Continue with the remaining apricots, placing them so that each row touches the one before. Refrigerate the tart while preheating the oven.

Preheat the oven to 400°F at least 20 minutes before baking. Set an oven rack at the bottom level before preheating.

Apply a second coat of egg glaze to the border and bake for 20 minutes or until the top of the pastry browns. Lower the heat to 350°F. and continue baking for 30 minutes more or until the apricots are tender when pierced with a skewer and the bottom of the pastry is golden brown. (Use a pancake turner to lift an edge to check for doneness.) Remove the baking sheet to a rack to cool.

When the pastry is cool, slip a long metal spatula or pancake turner under the strip to dislodge it and transfer it to a serving plate, cutting board, or inverted carving board. It can sit at room temperature, uncovered, for a day, but do not apply the apricot glaze more than 4 hours before serving, or it will become runny.

MAKE THE APRICOT GLAZE

Place the preserves in a 1-cup heatproof glass measure and microwave until bubbling. (Or heat them in a small saucepan.) Strain them into a small bowl. Using a clean artist's brush or the back of a spoon, coat the apricots and then the pastry cream with the glaze. Scatter the optional pistachio nuts along the center of the tart, where the apricots have separated.

STORE

Room temperature, up to 1 day. This is best eaten the same day.

NOTE

If using a Pepperidge Farm frozen puff pastry sheet, roll it, to press out the creases, to 12 inches in length. Trim it to 8 inches wide. Use three quarters the amount of pastry cream, apricots, pistachios, and glaze.

POINTERS FOR SUCCESS

∼ Glazing the tart more than 4 hours ahead will cause the glaze to thin because of the moisture in the apricots.

PEACH TARTE TATIN
(*Upside-Down Peach Tart*)

The first time I made peach tarte Tatin, I discovered that the fragile flesh of peaches makes it impossible to bake them beneath a top crust of regular pie pastry. By the time the pastry is cooked through, the peaches are mush. The solution was to bake the peaches separately and place them on baked puff pastry.

EQUIPMENT

A heavy pizza pan or a rectangular baking sheet at least 11 inches wide; a 13- by 9-inch baking pan; and aluminum foil

Make the dough (page 417 or 420).

On a well-floured surface, roll the puff pastry into a 10½-inch square ⅛ inch to ³⁄₁₆ inch thick, rolling evenly from the center in all directions; move the pastry occasionally to be sure it is not sticking and reflour the surface if necessary. Push in the corners of the pastry and roll it into an 11½- to 12-inch circle.

Spray or brush the baking sheet with water and transfer the dough to it. Cover it with plastic wrap and refrigerate until firm, at least 30 minutes.

Preheat the oven to 400°F. at least 20 minutes before baking. Set an oven rack in the middle level before preheating.

OVEN TEMPERATURE: 400°F. • BAKING TIME: 30 MINUTES
(PLUS 15 MINUTES IN THE TURNED-OFF OVEN)   SERVES: 8

INGREDIENTS	MEASURE	WEIGHT	
	VOLUME	OUNCES	GRAMS
Classic Puff Pastry (page 417) made with only 4 turns or Quick Puff Pastry (page 420)		1¼ pounds	567 grams
3 pounds peaches (about 9 medium), peeled, pitted, and sliced into eighths (1-inch-thick slices)	8 cups (sliced)	2 pounds 5 ounces to 2½ pounds (sliced)	1 kg 50 grams to 1 kg 134 grams
freshly squeezed lemon juice	1 tablespoon	0.5 ounce	16 grams
sugar	⅔ cup	4.6 ounces	133 grams
unsalted butter	4 tablespoons	2 ounces	56 grams
apricot preserves	¼ cup	3 ounces	85 grams
optional: Crème Fraîche (page 558)	1 cup	approx. 8 ounces	232 grams

Remove the plastic wrap and, using a cardboard template and a sharp knife, cut an 11-inch circle from the dough. Prick the dough all over with a fork. For even rising, grease the bottom of a cake pan at least 10 inches in diameter and place it on top of the pastry. (If using commercial puff pastry, evenly distribute some metal pie weights or beans in the pan as additional weight—not too many! The object is not to keep the pastry from rising completely, but to keep it from rising excessively while remaining tender and very flaky.)

Bake for 20 minutes. Remove the cake pan and continue baking for 10 more minutes or until the pastry is golden brown. Prop open the oven door with a wooden spoon and bake for another 5 minutes. Then turn off the oven, leaving the door propped open, and leave the dough in the oven for 15 minutes to dry the center layers. Remove the baking sheet to a wire rack to cool the pastry completely. (It will have shrunk by ½ to 1 inch and be about ¾ inches high at the outside edge.) If not using the pastry right away, store it airtight at room temperature up to 24 hours.

BAKE AND CARAMELIZE THE PEACHES

While the pastry is baking and cooling, in a large bowl, combine the peaches, lemon juice, and sugar and toss gently to mix them. Allow them to sit for 30 minutes to 1 hour.

Preheat the oven to 400°F. at least 20 minutes before baking. Set an oven rack in the middle level before preheating.

Transfer the peaches to a colander suspended over a bowl to capture the liquid. The mixture will exude about 1 cup of liquid. Place this and the butter in a saucepan and heat over medium heat, stirring often, until bubbling. Continue cooking, stirring often, until the liquid caramelizes and turns a medium amber, about 5 minutes. (Or microwave in a greased 4-cup heatproof measure for about 15 minutes.) The syrup will be reduced to ½ cup and an accurate thermometer will register 220°F. Immediately remove the caramel from the heat and pour it into the baking pan.

Arrange the peaches, in a single layer, over the caramel. (Be careful not to touch the caramel, as it is very hot.) Cover tightly with foil and bake for 15 to 20 minutes or until just tender but still firm when pierced with a skewer. Cool completely, uncovered. Remove the peaches to a large plate or bowl, reserving all the liquid (there will be about ¾ cup). If you are not ready to assemble the tart, set aside, covered, at room temperature.

ASSEMBLE THE TART

Up to 4 hours before serving, in a small saucepan or microwave oven, heat the apricot preserves until melted and bubbling and strain into a small cup.

Brush the preserves evenly over the baked pastry. Arrange the drained peach slices in slightly overlapping circles on top.

Shortly before serving, boil down the caramel peach juice to ½ cup or until dark brown and syrupy (the temperature will be 196°F.). Spoon it evenly over the peaches. (If using a microwave, place the juice in a 2-cup greased heatproof measure. It will take about 6 minutes to reduce in the microwave.)

Serve accompanied by the crème fraîche, if desired.

STORE

Room temperature, up to 1 day. The tart is still good on the second day but the peaches will be less firm and less glossy in appearance.

POINTERS FOR SUCCESS

∾ To prevent a burnt flavor, do not exceed the recommended temperature for the caramel.

∾ Use a white porcelain spoon or drop a small amount of caramel onto a white plate to check the color, as it will look darker in the pan.

UNDERSTANDING

The temperature for the caramel is much lower than the usual temperature, because the peach juices lower the caramelization point.

APRICOT TARTLETS WITH ALMOND CREAM

These tartlets look as fantastic as they taste. If puff pastry is used, it rises in a delightfully irregular fashion, giving the finished tarts dramatic visual appeal. The almond cream filling rises during baking, turning golden and surrounding the deeper golden fanned apricot halves. The apricot glaze topping gives a shiny burnt orange hue to the apricot and the almond cream, and it keeps them moist and fresh for as long as three days. It also adds a wonderful bright sweet/tart sticky quality.

OVEN TEMPERATURE: 350°F. • BAKING TIME: 20 MINUTES   **SERVES: 10**

INGREDIENTS	MEASURE	WEIGHT	
	VOLUME	OUNCES	GRAMS
puff pastry (page 417 or 420) or Deluxe Flaky Pie Crust (page 26) for ten 4-inch tartlets, prebaked and cooled	1 small-quantity recipe	1¼ pounds	567 grams
Almond Pastry Cream	(2½ cups)	(21 ounces)	(600 grams)
sliced blanched almonds	1 generous cup	3.5 ounces	100 grams
sugar	½ cup	3.5 ounces	100 grams
bleached all-purpose flour	2 tablespoons	0.6 ounce	18 grams
unsalted butter, softened	7 tablespoons	3.5 ounces	100 grams
2 large eggs, at room temperature	3 fluid ounces	3.5 ounces (weighed without the shells)	100 grams
pure vanilla extract	½ teaspoon	•	•
Pastry Cream (page 560)	¾ cup	7 ounces	200 grams
10 poached apricot halves (page 587) or canned apricot halves in heavy syrup (one 15¼-ounce/432-gram can)	2 cups	8.75 ounces	250 grams
apricot preserves	2 tablespoons	1.5 ounces	42 grams

EQUIPMENT
Ten 4-inch fluted tartlet pans with removable bottoms

Make the dough (page 417 or 420 or 26). Cut and pre-bake it or roll and prebake it (see pages 416 and 417 or pages 9, 13, and 18). Let cool.

Preheat the oven to 350°F. at least 15 minutes before baking. Set an oven rack at the middle level before preheating.

MAKE THE ALMOND PASTRY CREAM

In a food processor fitted with the metal blade, process the almonds, sugar, and flour until the almonds are very fine. Empty the mixture into a bowl and set it aside.

In a medium mixing bowl, beat the butter until soft. Beat in about ½ cup of the nut mixture until incorporated. Beat in 1 egg with another ½ cup of the nut mixture, then beat in the second egg with the remaining nut mixture until incorporated. Beat in the vanilla and pastry cream. (If not using immediately, cover and refrigerate. Remove from the refrigerator about 10 minutes before assembling the tartlets. The filling can be made up to 1 week ahead.)

ASSEMBLE THE TARTLETS

In a colander, drain the poached or canned apricots well. Pat them dry with paper towels. Using a thin sharp blade, slice each apricot half crosswise into thin slices without slicing all the way through to the bottom. Press gently on top of each apricot to fan the slices slightly.

Place the tartlet shells on a large baking sheet. Spoon ¼ cup (approx. 2 ounces/60 grams) of the almond pastry cream into each shell. (It will be soft and creamy.) Place a fanned apricot half, rounded side up, on top of each.

Bake for 20 minutes or until the filling is set. When pressed very lightly with a fingertip, the almond cream will spring back. Cool the tartlets on a wire rack.

MAKE THE GLAZE

In a small saucepan, or a 1-cup heatproof glass measure in the microwave, heat the apricot preserves until bubbling and strain. Using a clean artist's brush or the back of a spoon, coat the apricots and almond pastry cream with glaze. Allow it to set for at least 30 minutes before serving.

VARIATION

THE CRUST   Sweet Cookie Tart Crust (page 56) or Sweet Nut Cookie Tart Crust (page 58) can be used in place of the puff pastry or flaky pastry. For 4-inch tartlets, you will need only 3 tablespoons (1.6 ounces/45 grams) of almond cream filling for each. For 3-inch tartlets, you will need 1 tablespoon (0.5 ounce/15 grams) of almond cream for each; reduce the baking time to 15 minutes.

STORE

Room temperature, up to 12 hours; refrigerated, covered, up to 3 days. (Allow the chilled tarts to come to room temperature before serving.)

POINTERS FOR SUCCESS

∾ The prebaked pastry shells must be fully baked to ensure that even the bottoms stay crisp after the almond cream is added. An instant-read thermometer inserted into the center of the pastry will be 212°F. when completely baked. Alternatively, lift a small amount of the pastry with the tip of a sharp knife to ensure that there is no uncooked dough in the center.

∾ To prevent separation while mixing, the butter and eggs for the almond cream must not be cold. If the butter is not soft, it will not mix smoothly with the eggs.

UNDERSTANDING

This almond cream has double the egg, more butter, and some flour, all of which make it softer than the frangipane (almond cream) used in a galette (page 446). Since it is contained in pastry shells, it can be softer, and it becomes firmer after baking. Almond cream freezes well for about a month.

The pastry cream is half the weight of the almond cream. A higher proportion of pastry cream would make the filling brown less and be more creamy.

RED CURRANT TARTLETS
WITH ALMOND CREAM

Red currants are one of the most intensely flavorful fruits. For a long while they were in scarce supply, but happily they are now more widely available, though their season is an all too short few weeks in July. One of loveliest ways to enjoy this fruit is uncooked, as a topping. Not only are these tartlets exquisite in appearance, the flavor and textural contrasts are fantastic. Imagine a buttery crisp puff pastry, the creamy perfume of almond filling, and bright, tart, juicy bursts of fresh plump currants. Because currants have such a short season, I also use small wild blueberries. Tiny purple champagne grapes, though less tangy, also work well.

INGREDIENTS	MEASURE	WEIGHT	
	VOLUME	OUNCES	GRAMS
puff pastry (page 417 or 420) or Deluxe Flaky Pie Crust (page 26) for ten 4-inch tartlets, prebaked and cooled		1¼ pounds	567 grams
fresh red currants, stemmed	2 full cups	11.5 ounces	330 grams
Almond Pastry Cream	(scant 3 cups)	(24.5 ounces)	(700 grams)
sliced blanched almonds	1 generous cup	3.5 ounces	100 grams
sugar	½ cup	3.5 ounces	100 grams
bleached all-purpose flour	2 tablespoons	0.6 ounce	18 grams
unsalted butter, softened	7 tablespoons	3.5 ounces	100 grams
2 large eggs, at room temperature	3 fluid ounces	3.5 ounces	100 grams (weighed without the shells)
pure vanilla extract	½ teaspoon	•	•
Pastry Cream (page 560)	1 full cup	10.5 ounces	300 grams
Jelly Glaze red currant jelly	approx. ¼ cup	3 ounces	85 grams

EQUIPMENT
Ten 4-inch fluted tartlet pans with removable bottoms

Make the dough (page 417 or 420 or 26). Cut and pre-bake it or roll and prebake it (see pages 416 and 417 or pages 9, 13, and 18). Let cool.

Preheat the oven to 350°F. at least 15 minutes before baking. Rinse the currants and dry them thoroughly on paper towels. Set an oven rack at the middle level before preheating.

MAKE THE ALMOND PASTRY CREAM
In a food processor fitted with the metal blade, process the almonds, sugar, and flour until the almonds are very fine. Empty the mixture into a bowl and set it aside.

In a medium mixing bowl, beat the butter until soft. Beat in about ½ cup of the nut mixture until incorporated. Beat in 1 egg with another ½ cup of the nut mixture, then beat in the second egg with the remaining nut mixture until incorporated. Beat in the vanilla and pastry cream. (If not using at once, cover and refrigerate. Remove from the refrigerator about 10 minutes before assembling the tartlets. The filling can be made up to 1 week ahead.)

ASSEMBLE THE TARTLETS

Place the tartlet shells on a baking sheet. Spoon ¼ cup (2 ounces/60 grams) of the almond pastry cream into each shell. (It will be soft and creamy.) (You will have a scant ½ cup left over, which can be frozen for up to 1 month.)

Bake the tartlets for 20 minutes or until set. When pressed very lightly with a fingertip, the almond cream will spring back. Cool the tartlets on a wire rack.

MAKE THE JELLY GLAZE

Place the currant jelly in a 1-cup heatproof glass measure and microwave until bubbling; strain. (Or heat it in a small saucepan.) Use a clean artist's brush or the back of a spoon to brush a thin layer (about ½ teaspoon) of jelly onto the pastry cream in each tartlet. Place a single layer of currants (a scant ¼ cup) on top of each and coat the currants with the remaining hot glaze. (If the glaze becomes too thick, stir in a very small amount of cassis [black currant liqueur], Chambord [black raspberry liqueur], or water, or reheat.) Allow the glaze to set for at least 30 minutes before serving.

VARIATIONS

THE CRUST   Sweet Cookie Tart Crust (page 56) or Sweet Nut Cookie Tart Crust (page 58) can be used in place of the puff pastry or flaky pastry for a completely different effect. For the same size tartlets, you will need only 3 tablespoons (1.6 ounces/45 grams) of almond cream filling for each. For 3-inch tartlets, you will need 1 tablespoon (0.50 ounce/15 grams) of almond cream for each; reduce the baking time to 15 minutes.

BLUEBERRY OR CHAMPAGNE GRAPE TARTLETS WITH ALMOND CREAM   Small wild blueberries, available in August, and tiny purple champagne grapes, which appear from midsummer to Thanksgiving, make lovely variations. The blueberries will approach the currants in tartness, but the grapes will be milder. You will need 1¼ cups (7 ounces/200 grams) of stemmed champagne grapes or 1¼ cups (5.3 ounces/150 grams) of blueberries (2 tablespoons for each tartlet). Replace the currant jelly with apple jelly.

STORE

Room temperature, up to 24 hours; refrigerated, covered, up to 3 days. (Allow the tartlets to come to room temperature before serving.)

POINTERS FOR SUCCESS

∾ See page 431.

UNDERSTANDING

More pastry cream is used in the almond cream filling than for a tart where the fruit is baked into it, to make it slightly softer and more creamy.

TWO MINIATURE GOLDEN APPLE GALETTES

*G*alette is a French word that refers to an open-faced tart or tartlet that is baked flat or free-form, without a tart pan or flan ring. In both these versions, the lightly sugared juices from the apples form a caramel layer on the bottom of the pastry during baking.

The basic version of this tart is from my friend David Shamah, who created it for his Brooklyn, New York, restaurant, Back to Nature. It consists of a round of buttery, flaky puff pastry topped with substantially chunky slices of apple that are only very lightly sugared so that they remain pleasantly tart despite the addition of a caramel sauce.

The almond upper crust version is from one of my favorite pastry chefs, Stacie Pierce, at New York City's Union Square Café. In this version, an almond-butter top crust is added, which melds into the apples during baking, leaving a delicate sugary crisp coating with a hint of cinnamon.

Both versions can be prepared ahead and frozen for unexpected company. They will be ready to be eaten an hour from inspiration. They are most delicious while still warm with a scoop of slowly melting caramel or vanilla ice cream on the side.

EQUIPMENT
Two cookie sheets or inverted baking sheets, lined with parchment

Preheat the oven to 400°F. at least 20 minutes before baking. Set an oven rack at the lowest level before preheating.

Make the dough (page 417 or 420).

MAKE THE BASIC GALETTES
On a lightly floured counter, roll out the dough ⅛ inch thick. Using a sharp knife, cut six 6- to 6½-inch squares. Place them at least ½ inch apart on the parchment-lined sheets. (If you have only one cookie sheet, place 3 of the galettes on a sheet of parchment. Cover and chill until the first batch is baked. When the second batch is ready to bake, quickly slip the remaining galettes, still on the parchment, onto the cookie sheet, and immediately place it in the hot oven to bake.)

Using a cardboard template and a sharp knife, cut out a 5½-inch round from each pastry square, and remove the excess dough. Starting ½ inch from the outer edge, arrange 4 apple slices on each round, cored sides facing toward the center, and then arrange 2 more slices in the middle. Brush the apples with the softened butter, using 1 teaspoon for each galette, and sprinkle each one with ½ teaspoon of sugar.

Bake the galettes for 30 to 35 minutes or until the apples are tender when pierced with a skewer, and the dough is risen and golden. (If frozen, they will need an additional 10 minutes. Halfway through the baking time, move the tartlets on

OVEN TEMPERATURE: 400°F. • BAKING TIME: 30 [TO 35] MINUTES   SERVES: 6 [OR 12]

INGREDIENTS	MEASURE	WEIGHT	
	VOLUME	OUNCES	GRAMS
puff pastry (page 417 or 420)		1¼ pounds (1½ pounds for the variation)	567 grams
3 Golden Delicious apples (about 22 ounces), peeled, cored, and cut into 12 slices each*	approx. 5 cups (sliced)	19 ounces	538 grams (sliced)
unsalted butter, softened	2 tablespoons	1 ounce	28 grams
sugar	2 tablespoons	1 ounce	25 grams
1 double recipe basic version Caramel Sauce (page 597)	1 full liquid cup	10.75 ounces	308 grams
optional: ice cream (Caramel or Triple Vanilla, page 243 or 232)	6 scoops	•	•
optional: Almond Upper Crust blanched sliced almonds, finely grated (see page 641)	(1 cup + 2 tablespoons) ¾ generous cup	(11 ounces) 2.3 ounces	(315 grams) 66 grams
sugar	¾ cup	5.25 ounces	150 grams
ground cinnamon	1/16 teaspoon	•	•
unsalted butter, softened	7½ tablespoons	3.75 ounces	106 grams
½ large egg white, lightly beaten	1 tablespoon	0.5 ounce	15 grams

*For attractive slices, cut the apples lengthwise in half and use a melon baller to scoop out the cores. Slice each apple first into quarters, then cut each quarter into 3 slices.

the parchment to prevent steaming from any condensation from the thawing pastry or leaking juices.)

Remove the galettes to racks and allow them to cool until warm, about 10 minutes. Set them on serving plates and drizzle each with the caramel sauce (about 1½ tablespoons for each one). Place a scoop of ice cream on the side of each and pass the remaining caramel sauce.

MAKE THE ALMOND UPPER CRUST VARIATION
These galettes are slightly larger and richer, so each tart will serve two.

MAKE THE UPPER CRUST

In a food processor with the steel blade, process the almonds, sugar, and cinnamon until the almonds are as fine as powder. Add the butter and process, scraping the sides of the bowl as necessary, until smooth. Scrape the dough into a bowl and refrigerate it for at least 30 minutes or until firm. (To prepare it with a mixer, finely grate the almonds, or use ¾ cup almond flour, which is finely grated almonds. Combine all the ingredients in a mixer bowl and mix until smooth.)

For each tartlet, remove 3 tablespoons (1.75 ounces/50 grams) of the dough from the refrigerator, leaving the remaining dough refrigerated. Place the dough on a piece of plastic wrap and knead it lightly a few times to make it malleable. Top it with a second sheet of plastic wrap and roll it into a 4-inch circle. Work quickly to keep it from softening, or return it briefly to the refrigerator or freezer. When all the dough has been rolled, freeze the discs until firm.

Preheat the oven as above.

On a lightly floured counter, roll out the puff pastry ⅛ inch thick. (You need a scant 3.5 ounces/96 grams of puff pastry for each, so start with at least 1½ pounds of puff pastry.) Cut six 7-inch squares. Place them at least ½ inch apart on the parchment-lined sheets. Using a cardboard template and a sharp knife, cut a 6½-inch round from each square. Brush a ½-inch band of egg white around the edge of each round and turn the dough over itself to make a ½-inch border, pressing firmly on the dough. (This border will hold just until the topping has set and then will open out.) Brush the border with a little of the egg white and dust it lightly with sugar. Place the apples on the tart as above, but omit the butter and sugar.

Peel off the top piece of plastic wrap from each frozen disc of almond dough and invert the almond dough over the apples. Peel off the other piece of plastic wrap.

Bake the galettes for 20 minutes. Lower the heat to 375°F. and continue baking for 15 minutes or until the pastry and upper crust are golden and the apples are tender when pierced with a skewer or fork. Let cool briefly and serve as above, without the caramel sauce.

STORE

Unbaked, frozen, up to 3 months; baked, up to 2 days. (These are best eaten warm.)

PARIS RITZ PASTRY CRISPS

I had known Gregory Usher for many years before he started the famed pastry school at the Ritz Hotel in Paris. He was a man of quiet dignity, who glowed with passion for his profession and warmth for his friends. Every time I made a trip to Paris, I visited him.

I have only stayed at the Ritz once, and it remains the most exquisite hotel I have ever stayed in, rich with beauty, charm, history, and comforts. It was during that stay that Gregory gave me a pastry recipe for this book to represent the hotel and school. I had no idea at the time that it would also be a commemoration to him, as my dear friend Gregory died that year.

The recipe is a sandwich of two discs of crisp, caramelized puff pastry that are especially crunchy because they are sprinkled with crumbled nougatine before baking. After baking, they are filled with satiny-smooth pastry cream, lightened with whipped cream, and fresh juicy berries. They are further enhanced by an intensely tart berry sauce. All the components can be made well ahead and the crisps composed four hours ahead of serving, making this the ideal dessert for your most elegant dinner or holiday party.

OVEN TEMPERATURE: 475°F. • BAKING TIME: 8 TO 10 MINUTES   **SERVES: 8**

INGREDIENTS	MEASURE	WEIGHT	
	VOLUME	OUNCES	GRAMS
½ recipe Quick Puff Pastry (page 420)		10 ounces	284 grams
Nougatine Crumble	(scant ½ cup)	(2.6 ounces)	(76 grams)
granulated sugar	2 tablespoons + 2 teaspoons	1.2 ounces	33 grams
light corn syrup	4 teaspoons	1 ounce	27 grams
unsalted butter	1 tablespoon	0.5 ounce	14 grams
toasted sliced almonds, coarsely chopped	¼ cup	0.75 ounce	21 grams
powdered sugar	•	•	•
Cream Filling			
optional: kirsch	2 teaspoons	•	•
Pastry Cream (page 561)	1¼ cups	11.3 ounces	325 grams
heavy cream	½ liquid cup	4 ounces	116 grams
fresh fruit, such as raspberries (or other berries), fraises des bois, or currants	1 cup (plus extra for optional garnish)	4 to 5 ounces	113 to 142 grams
Raspberry Sauce (page 603) or Strawberry Sauce (page 605)	full ¾ cup 1 cup	7.5 ounces 9.25 ounces	211 grams 263 grams
optional: powdered sugar	•	•	•

EQUIPMENT
Two or more cookie sheets or inverted half-size sheet pans

Make the dough (page 420).

MAKE THE NOUGATINE CRUMBLE

Lightly oil a marble counter or baking sheet and two spatulas or triangular turners.

In a small heavy pan, combine the sugar and corn syrup and bring to a boil, stirring constantly. Stop stirring and allow the syrup to boil undisturbed until medium golden brown (360°F.). Remove it from the heat, immediately add the butter, and stir in the almonds.

Scrape the mixture onto the lightly oiled marble surface or baking sheet. Using the oiled spatulas or triangular scrapers, turn the nougatine over itself, folding in the corners to ensure even cooling.

As soon as the nougatine is cool enough to handle, use a lightly oiled heavy rolling pin to roll it as thin as possible. Work quickly before the nougatine hardens. (If necessary, it can be softened in a 300°F. oven for a few minutes.) When the nougatine is cool, place it on a cutting board and coarsely chop it. (Stored in an airtight container at room temperature, and low humidity, the nougatine will keep for about 6 weeks.)

MAKE THE CRISPS

On a lightly floured counter, roll the puff pastry into a ⅛-inch-thick rectangle about 8 inches by 18 inches. Starting at an 8-inch side, roll up the pastry, brushing off any excess flour as you go. Brush the very edge with water and press gently so that it will adhere to the pastry. Cover the pastry roll with plastic wrap, place seam side down on a baking sheet, and refrigerate it for at least 30 minutes or until very firm.

Preheat the oven to 475°F. at least 20 minutes before baking. Set an oven rack at the middle level and place a baking stone or cookie sheet on it before preheating.

With a sharp or serrated knife, cut sixteen ¼-inch-thick rounds from the pastry roll. (You will only need about half the roll. The remainder can be frozen, tightly wrapped, for up to 3 months.) Sprinkle the counter with powdered sugar, roll each round into a very thin circle, 4 to 4½ inches in diameter and about 1/16 inch thick, and place the rounds about 1 inch apart on the cookie sheets. (You will need to bake the rounds in three to four batches. Chill them covered until ready to bake. Be sure that the cookie or baking sheets are no longer warm before placing the dough on them.) Sprinkle each with about 1 teaspoon of the nougatine crumble. Place a second cookie sheet directly on top of the pastry to keep the pastry from losing its shape.

Bake for 8 to 10 minutes, until the tops are golden and caramelized, checking carefully a few times after the first 5 minutes of baking by lifting off the top baking sheet. The pastry discs will shrink to about 3½ inches in diameter and rise to about ⅜ inch high. If you would like the discs to be exact in shape, as soon as they come out of the oven, lift them, one at a time so that they remain hot, from the cookie sheet onto a cutting board and use a cutter just slightly smaller than the diameter of the discs to cut them into even rounds. (A rubber mallet to strike the cutter is helpful.) Transfer the pastry rounds to racks to cool completely. (They will keep in an airtight container at room temperature for up to 3 days.)

MAKE THE CREAM FILLING

Chill a small bowl along with the beaters for whipping the cream.

In a medium bowl, whisk the optional kirsch into the cold pastry cream until smooth.

Whip the heavy cream until stiff peaks form when the beater is lifted. Using a large whisk or rubber spatula, fold it into the pastry cream. Use it at once, or cover and chill it for up to 8 hours.

ASSEMBLE THE PASTRY CRISPS

Place 8 of the crisps, nougatine side up, on individual serving plates. Pipe or spread about ¼ cup of the filling onto each crisp. (It will be about ½ inch thick.) Place an even layer of berries on top (about 2 tablespoons). Top with a second crisp, nougatine side up.

Just before serving, spoon some sauce onto each plate (1½ tablespoons raspberry sauce, or 2 tablespoons strawberry sauce, as it is less intense) and dust the pastry very lightly with powdered sugar, if desired. It is also attractive to place a few whole or sliced and fanned berries on top of the sauce.

STORE

Cool to room temperature, up to 4 hours.

POINTERS FOR SUCCESS

∾ If it is necessary to assemble the pastries more than 4 hours ahead, it will be necessary to refrigerate them. In this case, they will stay crisper if you have both the nougatine side of the crisps facing the cream filling. Alternatively, you can add the top crisps just before serving.

UNDERSTANDING

Quick puff pastry is preferable to classic for this recipe because it is far easier to roll as thin as is required.

Nougatine is an opaque caramel with nuts. The opaqueness is created by the controlled crystallization of the sugar. Butter is added to prevent the nuts from crystallizing the sugar prematurely. The mixture is turned and folded to promote the formation of fine, even sugar crystals for the best texture.

CRÈME BRÛLÉE TARTLETS

Traveling around the country over the last decade, I have sampled so many versions of this tartlet, I cannot guess who originated the concept, but whoever did should be congratulated, because it is an inspired combination of crisp puff pastry, vanilla-infused custard, and a caramel crust. The puff pastry renders the custard impeccably creamy from stem to stern, the way a water bath would.

Dean Fearing of the Inn at Turtle Creek in Dallas makes a perfect rendition of this recipe, and whenever I visit I order one. Nancy Silverton makes a delightful variation by brushing the bottom of the baked puff pastry with a fine layer of ganache and then adding a layer of griottes (cherries in brandy) before pouring in the custard mixture. Gary Danko, when he was at the Ritz in San Francisco, made a fabulous chocolate crème brûlée. My version keeps the pastry crisp and the cream silky but firm enough to hold up in the pastry when cut. The secret is cooking the custard and cooling it before pouring it into the prebaked pastry shells and then baking it to give the custard a chance to thicken more.

OVEN TEMPERATURE: 400°F., THEN 325°F. •
BAKING TIME: 50 TO 64 MINUTES   SERVES: 6

INGREDIENTS	MEASURE	WEIGHT	
	VOLUME	OUNCES	GRAMS
puff pastry (page 417 or 420)	•	1¼ pounds	567 grams
1 large egg white, lightly beaten	2 tablespoons	1 ounce	30 grams
Custard Filling	(2 cups)	•	•
½ Tahitian vanilla bean,* split lengthwise	•	•	•
½ Madagascar vanilla bean, split lengthwise	•	•	•
sugar	¼ cup	1.75 ounces	50 grams
6 large egg yolks	3½ fluid ounces	4 ounces	112 grams
heavy cream	1½ liquid cups	12.2 ounces	348 grams
milk	¾ liquid cup	approx. 6.3 ounces	182 grams
pure vanilla extract	1 teaspoon	•	4 grams
Caramel Topping light brown sugar	¼ cup, packed	approx. 1.75 ounces	54 grams

*Or use a total of 1 Madagascar vanilla bean. If vanilla beans are unavailable, increase the vanilla extract to 1½ teaspoons.

EQUIPMENT
Six 4¾-inch fluted tartlet pans or 4- by ¾-inch flan rings with removable bottoms and a large cookie sheet or inverted half-size sheet pan

Make the dough (page 417 or 420).

MAKE THE PASTRY SHELLS
On a lightly floured counter, roll the puff pastry into a rectangle at least 13 by 19 inches in size and about ⅛ inch thick. Using a cardboard template and a sharp knife, cut six 6-inch circles. Set the tart pans or flan rings about 1 inch apart on the cookie sheet. Line them with the pastry (it will extend ¼ inch above the edge). Cover with plastic wrap and chill for at least 30 minutes.

Preheat the oven to 400°F at least 20 minutes before baking. Set an oven rack at the lowest level before preheating.

Line each pastry shell with parchment and fill it with pennies or pie weights. Bake the pastry for 15 to 20 minutes or until set. Remove the parchment and pennies or weights and prick the pastry all over with a fork. Continue baking for 5 to 7 minutes or until the pastry begins to brown lightly. Turn off the oven and leave the pastry shells in the oven with the door open for 5 minutes. Brush the pastry shells with the egg white, turn the oven heat to 325°F., and bake for 7 minutes longer. Remove the baking sheet to a rack to cool the pastry shells completely.

MAKE THE CUSTARD FILLING
Have a fine strainer suspended over a 4-cup glass measure with a spout or a small mixing bowl ready near the range.

In a heavy nonreactive saucepan, place the vanilla beans and sugar and, using your fingers, rub the seeds into the sugar. Remove and reserve the pods. Using a wooden spoon, stir the yolks into the sugar until well blended.

In a saucepan (or a heatproof glass measure if using a microwave on high power), combine the cream, milk, and vanilla pods and heat to the boiling point. Stir a few tablespoons into the yolk mixture, then gradually add the remaining mixture, stirring constantly. Heat the mixture to just below the boiling point (180°F.). Steam will begin to appear and the mixture will be slightly thicker than heavy cream. If a finger is run across the back of the spoon, it will leave a well-defined track. Immediately remove the pan from the heat and pour into the strainer, scraping up the thickened cream that has settled on the bottom of the pan. Remove the vanilla pods (and rinse and dry for future use). Cool the mixture completely, then stir in the vanilla extract. (At this point, the custard can be used immediately or refrigerated for up to 24 hours.)

Preheat the oven to 325°F. at least 15 minutes before baking. Set an oven rack in the middle position before preheating.

Pour the custard into the pastry shells (still on the cookie sheet). Bake for 20 to 30 minutes until the crème shimmies like jelly when shaken and a knife inserted into the center comes out almost clean. (The temperature will be 175°F.) Place the cookie sheet on a rack and allow the tarts to cool completely, a minimum of 30 minutes and a maximum of 3 hours.

**FIFTEEN TO 30 MINUTES BEFORE SERVING,
MAKE THE CARAMEL TOPPING***

Sift 2 firmly packed teaspoons of brown sugar onto each tart. Use a mini propane torch (see page 670) to caramelize the topping, or place the tartlets under a pre-heated broiler, 4 inches from the heat source, and broil for 1 to 3 minutes, watching carefully to prevent burning, just until the sugar melts and turns a deep brown. Serve immediately.

VARIATION

CHOCOLATE CRÈME BRÛLÉE TARTLETS Stir 3 ounces of bittersweet chocolate, coarsely chopped, into the hot custard before straining it. When filling the pastry shells, there will be about 1 tablespoon more filling. (See above for the caramel topping.)

STORE

Although best eaten right after caramelizing the topping, the finished tartlets can be refrigerated overnight and allowed to come to room temperature for about 30 minutes. In some refrigerators the caramel will retain its hard texture, but in a high-humidity refrigerator, it will liquefy.

UNDERSTANDING

I prefer the combination of milk and cream, as it is a little lighter in texture than all cream.

The only reason to heat the cream and milk is to steep the vanilla beans, to extract the maximum flavor from them. If not using the vanilla beans, you can add the milk and cream without heating them.

Preparing the custard and cooling it before pouring it into the pastry keeps the pastry shells crisp. Rebaking it allows the egg yolk molecules to reconnect and thicken so that the custard is still soft and creamy but does not flow out of the crust when cut.

---

*If it is necessary to make the topping ahead, to ensure that it will be crunchy, refrigerate the finished tartlets for up to 4 hours before serving. The chocolate crème will become firmer, so use 1 less egg yolk in the custard to compensate.

DANISH WAFFLE CREAMS

I n this pastry from Denmark, two ovals of the flakiest, lightest, melt-in-the-mouth quick puff pastry sandwich fluffy whipped cream buttercream. On a trip to Copenhagen, I discovered that they sell a special plate on which to roll this dough that gives it the slightly waffled texture.

This is an exciting party dessert because it is unlike anything most people have ever experienced. Also, the components are easy to make and are quick to assemble up to four hours ahead of serving.

OVEN TEMPERATURE: 425°F. • BAKING TIME: 12 TO 15 MINUTES   SERVES: 4

INGREDIENTS	MEASURE	WEIGHT	
	VOLUME	OUNCES	GRAMS
Danish Waffle Dough	•	(11 ounces)	(311 grams)
unsalted butter	8 tablespoons	4 ounces	113 grams
bleached all-purpose flour	1 cup (dip and sweep method)	5 ounces	142 grams
salt	⅜ teaspoon	•	•
heavy cream	3½ tablespoons	1.75 ounces	50 grams
sugar for rolling	•	•	•
Rich Whipped Cream Filling	(2 cups)	(10.5 ounces)	(300 grams)
2 large egg yolks	approx. 2 tablespoons	1.25 ounces	37 grams
sugar	3 tablespoons	1.3 ounces	37 grams
water	½ tablespoon	•	•
unsalted butter, softened	6 tablespoons	3 ounces	85 grams
heavy cream	⅔ liquid cup	5.3 ounces	153 grams
pure vanilla extract	½ teaspoon	•	•
powdered sugar	•	•	•
optional: fresh berries	•	•	•

EQUIPMENT
Two cookie sheets or inverted half-size sheet pans, lined with parchment, and a 3-inch round cookie cutter

Cut the butter into ½-inch cubes and refrigerate for at least 30 minutes. Place the flour and salt in a reclosable freezer bag and freeze for at least 15 minutes.

FOOD PROCESSOR METHOD

Place the flour and salt in a food processor with the metal blade and process for a few seconds to combine them. Add the butter cubes and pulse until the butter is the size of small lima beans. Add the cream and pulse until the butter is the size of large peas.

Empty the mixture onto a large piece of plastic wrap and, using the wrap and your knuckles, knead and press the mixture until it holds together. If you find it easier, you can use a reclosable gallon-size freezer bag instead; holding both ends of the bag opening with your fingers, alternate using the heels of your hands and your knuckles to knead the mixture from the outside of the bag until it holds together. Remove the dough to a work surface and knead it briefly until you can form a smooth ball. If the dough starts to soften and become sticky, wrap it with plastic wrap, flatten it into a disc, and chill it for 20 minutes.

On a well-floured counter, place the dough and dust it well with flour. Roll it into a rectangle (the exact size is unimportant). Using a flat cookie sheet or dough scraper to flip over the bottom and top of the dough, fold it as you would fold a business letter, brushing off any excess flour. Lift up the dough, clean the work surface, lightly reflour it, and position the dough so that the closed side is toward your left. Lightly flour the top of the dough and roll the dough into a rectangle about the same size as before. Fold the dough as before, clean the surface, reflour it, and position the dough so that the closed side is to your left. Repeat these steps one more time, then divide the dough into 2 pieces. Wrap each and chill them for at least 45 minutes and up to 2 days. (The dough can be frozen for up to 3 months.)

HAND METHOD

In a bowl, combine the flour and salt and whisk to combine them. Add the butter and rub the mixture between your fingertips until large flakes form. Add the cream and stir the mixture until it holds together.

Empty the dough onto a work surface and *fraisez* it (smear it in front of you with the palm of your hand two or three times—but don't overwork it). The dough should feel slightly elastic and large flakes of butter still be visible. Roll and chill the dough as above.

Preheat the oven to 425°F at least 20 minutes before baking. Set an oven rack at the middle level before preheating.

ROLL, SHAPE, AND BAKE THE WAFFLES

Work with one piece of dough at a time, leaving the remaining dough in the refrigerator. On a lightly floured surface, roll the dough into a square about 7 inches across and ¼ inch thick. Use the cookie cutter to cut out four 3-inch rounds. Sprinkle a clean work surface and the rounds of dough with sugar. Gently roll each round to make a 5- by 3-inch oval. Using a small flexible pancake turner or offset metal spatula, transfer the ovals to the cookie sheets, spacing them at least 1 inch apart. (If you have only 1 cookie sheet, place the second 4 waffles on a sheet of parchment. Cover and chill until the first batch is baked. Quickly slip the remaining waffles, still on the parchment, onto the cookie sheet and immediately place in the hot oven to bake.)

Bake the waffles until they are puffed and lightly browned, about 12 to 15 minutes. Remove the cookie sheets to racks and allow the waffles to cool slightly, then remove them to racks to cool completely.

MAKE THE RICH WHIPPED CREAM FILLING

Chill a medium bowl for the whipped cream. Have ready a greased 1-cup heat-proof glass measure near the range.

In a medium bowl, beat the yolks with an electric mixer until light in color.

Combine the sugar and water in a small saucepan (preferably with a nonstick lining) and heat, stirring constantly, until the sugar dissolves and the syrup comes to a boil. Continue cooking, without stirring, until to 238°F. (the soft ball stage). Immediately transfer the syrup to the glass measure to stop the cooking.

If using an electric hand-held mixer, beat the syrup into the yolks in a steady stream. Don't allow the syrup to fall directly on the beaters, or it will spin it onto the sides of the bowl. If using a stand mixer, turn it off, very briefly, while adding the syrup in 3 parts. Use a rubber scraper to remove the syrup clinging to the glass measure. Continue beating until completely cool.

Gradually beat in the butter. The buttercream will not thicken until almost all of the butter has been added. (The filling can be stored at this point, refrigerated, for up to 5 days, but it must be softened to room temperature for about 1 hour before adding the whipped cream.)

Beat the heavy cream in the chilled bowl until soft peaks form when the beater is lifted. With a large whisk, fold the whipped cream and vanilla extract into the buttercream. This filling will be very fluffy. If you're not ready to use it shortly, it can be refrigerated for up to 8 hours, but it must be allowed to soften to room temperature before filling the waffles.

ASSEMBLE THE WAFFLE SANDWICHES

Up to 4 hours before serving, place 4 waffles on a counter, flat side up. Spread ½ cup of the filling evenly on top of each waffle (it will be about ¼ inch thick). Top each with a waffle, flat side down. Dust lightly with powdered sugar. Use a pancake turner to lift the filled waffles onto serving plates (they are very fragile). If desired, place a few fresh berries on each plate.

STORE

Room temperature, uncovered, up to 4 hours.

POINTERS FOR SUCCESS

∾ The egg yolk and sugar syrup mixture for the filling must be completely cool before adding the butter.

∾ This pastry is too fragile to line a pie or tart pan.

UNDERSTANDING

This dough has almost equal weights of butter and flour, a ratio that approaches that of puff pastry. It has ⅓ cup (1¾ ounces/50 grams) less flour than the basic flaky pie crust, half the water (3.5 tablespoons of cream contains about 2 tablespoons of water), and about 1¾ ounces/50 grams more butterfat, from the cream—this is why it is so much more tender.

TWELFTH NIGHT GALETTE
(*Galette des Rois*)

This flower-like disc of the flakiest, most decorative puff pastry is filled with a thin layer of frangipane for the added flavor of almonds and sweetness. In France, it is traditionally baked to celebrate Twelfth Night and a *fève* (fava bean) or tiny ceramic figure is baked into the pastry. The person who discovers it in his or her portion is considered to be lucky for the whole year. (Without the bean, it is called Pithiviers.)

This is an ideal make-ahead dessert because the pastry and the filling actually benefit from being frozen before baking. Individual galettes (see the variation) also make charming presentations. I love this dessert because of its beauty and its delicious taste.

EQUIPMENT

A heavy pizza pan or inverted half-size sheet pan

Make the dough (page 417 or 420), or defrost it according to the package directions.

MAKE THE FRANGIPANE

In a food processor, pulse the nuts until finely chopped. Add the remaining ingredients and process only until mixed. Chill, tightly covered, for at least 1 hour or as long as 1 week. (Alternatively, you can combine all the ingredients in a small bowl, stirring by hand. In this case, the mixture may be firm enough to use without chilling.)

MAKE THE GLAZE

Beat together the egg yolk and cream just to mix.

OVEN TEMPERATURE: 400°F., THEN 375°F •
BAKING TIME: 75 [60] MINUTES, (PLUS 15
MINUTES INTO TURNED-OFF OVEN)   SERVES: 10 TO 12 [OR 8 TO 10]

INGREDIENTS	MEASURE	WEIGHT	
	VOLUME	OUNCES	GRAMS
2½ pounds puff pastry (pages 417 or 420) or two 1-pound packages frozen puff pastry, defrosted (see page 414)*		2.5 pounds	1 kg 134 grams
Frangipane	(1 cup + 2 tablespoons)	(11 ounces)	(313 grams)
sliced almonds	1 generous cup	3.5 ounces	100 grams
sugar	½ cup	3.5 ounces	100 grams
unsalted butter, softened	4 tablespoons	2 ounces	57 grams
1 large egg	3 tablespoons	1.75 ounces (weighed without the shell)	50 grams
dark rum	1 tablespoon	•	•
finely grated lemon zest	1 teaspoon	•	•
pure almond extract	¼ teaspoon	•	•
pure vanilla extract	¼ teaspoon	•	•
salt	a pinch	•	•
Egg Glaze 1 large egg yolk	approx. 1 tablespoon	0.6 ounce	18 grams
heavy cream	1½ teaspoons	•	•
optional: powdered sugar	•	•	•

*Pepperidge Farm frozen puff pastry comes in prerolled 9½-inch sheets, which limits the size of the galette to 9 inches (without having to patch it). Use the amounts in brackets for the smaller-size galette.

ASSEMBLE THE GALETTE

You will need to roll out two 11-inch rounds [or two 9-inch rounds] of puff pastry, the bottom layer ⅛ inch thick and the top ³⁄₁₆ inch thick, so when cutting the dough, make one piece slightly larger than the other. To roll, push in the corners of the dough and roll from the center to the edge, trying to keep the dough as round as possible.

Roll out the smaller piece of dough and transfer it to a pizza pan that has been moistened with water. Using a 10-inch [9-inch] inverted cake pan, gently mark a ring in the dough. Spread the frangipane [use only ¾ cup] in the center of the dough, making the outer edge higher than the center and leaving a 1-inch border. Paint the border with the egg glaze.

Roll out the second piece of puff pastry and place it over the first piece, pressing down firmly on the border to make the two pieces adhere. With a 10-inch [9-inch] inverted cake pan, gently mark a ring in the dough. Cover the pastry with plastic wrap and freeze it until firm enough to cut without compressing the pastry layers at the edge, about 30 minutes. (They must be left open to allow the pastry full flight when it rises.)

Use the tip of a sharp knife to cut the pastry into a 10-inch (9-inch) circle. Brush the top of the pastry with egg glaze, being careful not to allow it to drip onto the sides (and thus sealing them closed). Freeze for 20 minutes.

Brush the pastry again with egg glaze. Using the tip of a sharp knife, cut a leaf pattern (Figures 1 and 2) into the top of the dough, going about ¹⁄₁₆ inch deep, or one third of the way through.* Cut a steam vent into the center of the pastry or into a few of the decor lines, going through to the filling. Using a sharp blade, make ¼-inch-long vertical slashes about ¼ inch deep† at even intervals into the border of the dough. For an alternative design, see Figure 3. Using the tip of a sharp knife, starting at the center of the galette and continuing to the slash marks, make curved lines in the top of the dough, going about ¹⁄₁₆ inch deep, or one third of the way through. Cut small steam vents into 3 of these lines, piercing the upper layer of the dough. Cover the pastry with an inverted bowl or cake pan and allow it to rest, refrigerated for 2 hours, to relax the dough and prevent distortion.

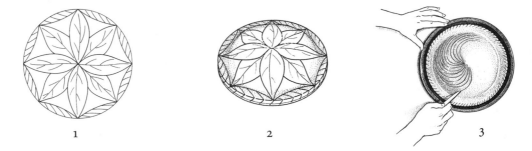

1   2   3

Place the pastry, still covered, in the freezer for at least 4 hours, preferably overnight. (At this point it can stay frozen for up to 3 months, but wrap it tightly in plastic wrap [Saran is the most airtight] and then place it in a freezer weight bag.)

Preheat the oven to 400°F. at least 20 minutes before baking. Set an oven rack at the lowest level and place a baking stone or cookie sheet on it before preheating.

Bake the galette for 20 minutes. Cover it loosely with foil if it is browning too fast and bake for an additional 10 minutes. Lower the heat to 375°F. and bake for 45

---

*If using frozen dough that is only ⅛ inch thick, make the cuts slightly less than ¹⁄₁₆ inch deep.
†If using frozen dough that is only ⅛ inch thick, make the cuts almost to the bottom of the dough—not quite ¼ inch deep.

minutes [30 minutes] longer. Turn off the oven, prop the door open with a wooden spoon, and allow the galette to cool in the oven for 15 minutes.

The egg glaze produces a rich golden crust, but for a shiny effect you can sprinkle the surface lightly with powdered sugar and place it under the broiler for a few seconds or in a 500°F. oven for about 5 minutes. Watch carefully to prevent burning! The galette is most delicious when served slightly warm.

VARIATION

INDIVIDUAL GALETTES   These four smaller gallettes have double the frangipane filling to puff pastry, and each will serve 2. The baked galettes will be about 1½ inches high all over and 4 inches wide. You will need 4½ ounces of cut pastry for each, so start with at least 1¾ pounds of dough to make four 4½-inch pastry rounds that are ⅛ inch thick for the bottoms and four 4½-inch pastry rounds that are 3⁄16 inch thick for the tops. Divide the dough in half, with one piece slightly larger. For the best shape, roll out the pastry and cut squares about 5 to 5½ inches in size. Place the 4 bottom pieces on a cookie sheet lined with parchment or lightly sprayed with water. Gently mark each one with a 4½-inch round cutter or template. Spread ¼ cup of frangipane on each one, leaving a ½-inch border. Brush this border with the egg glaze and cover each with a top pastry square, pressing firmly all around the border. Cover with plastic wrap and freeze until firm enough to cut without compressing the layers of pastry at the edges, about 30 minutes. (They must be left open to allow the pastry full flight when it rises.)

Use the cutter or template and a sharp knife tip to cut out the 4½-inch pastries; discard the scraps. Press firmly around the border from the top only, so as not to compress the layers of pastry at the edge. Using a small sharp blade, make ¼-inch-long angled slashes about ¼ inch deep* at even intervals into the border of the dough. Brush the top of each galette with the egg glaze, being careful not to allow it to drip onto the sides (and thus sealing them closed). Freeze the pastries for 20 minutes.

Brush the galettes again with the egg glaze. Cut a design into the dough as illustrated in Figure 3 above.† Cover the galettes with inverted bowls or cake pans and allow them to rest, refrigerated, for 2 hours to relax the dough and prevent distortion, then place them, still covered, in the freezer for at least 4 hours, preferably overnight. (At this point, they can stay frozen for up to 3 months, but wrap each one tightly in plastic wrap [Saran is the most airtight] and then place them in freezer-weight bags.)

Bake the galettes in a preheated 400°F. oven for 20 minutes, then lower the heat to 375°F. and continue baking for 25 minutes. (If the pastry is browning too fast, cover it loosely with foil.) Turn off the oven and leave the galettes in it (uncovered), propping the door open with a wooden spoon, for 5 minutes.

---

*If using frozen dough that is only ⅛ inch thick, make the cuts slightly less than 1⁄16 inch deep.
†If using frozen dough that is only ⅛ inch thick, make the cuts almost to the bottom of the dough—not quite ¼ inch deep.

STORE

As with all puff pastry, the galette is best eaten the same day it is baked, although it is still delicious the following 2 days. Do not refrigerate, as the pastry will toughen to cardboard.

POINTERS FOR SUCCESS

↷ The oven must be very hot, or butter will leak from the pastry and it will not rise as high. The two pieces of dough must be joined securely to prevent the filling from leaking. If a little leaks, however, it is firm enough to self-seal once set, which will keep the rest from oozing out.

↷ In some convection ovens, the pastry stays a beautiful golden brown without needing to be covered. To prevent overbrowning, a whole egg glaze in place of the yolk/cream one works perfectly, but it will produce a slightly less shiny surface.

INDIVIDUAL TWELFTH NIGHT CHOCOLATE GALETTES

This Twelfth Night galette contains a filling of chocolate walnut frangipane. Walnut's synergy with chocolate makes the chocolate taste more chocolaty. Hazelnuts also make a fine variation and impart their own more distinctive flavor. When I worked out this variation, I was hoping for a flow of chocolate filling when the pastry was cut, but with puff pastry there is *always* a little leak where the top and bottom crusts join and if it flows after baking, it is sure to flow during baking and create a mess. If you love the consistency of a chocolate flow, serve the galettes with hot fudge sauce (page 596)!

EQUIPMENT

A large cookie sheet or inverted half-size sheet pan, preferably lined with parchment

Make the dough (page 417 or 420), or defrost it according to the package directions.

MAKE THE CHOCOLATE FRANGIPANE

In a food processor, finely grate the chocolate. Add the nuts and sugar and process until the nuts are finely chopped. Add the remaining ingredients and process only until mixed. Chill for at least 1 hour. (Alternatively, you can combine all the ingredients in a small bowl, stirring by hand. In this case, the mixture may be firm enough to use without chilling.)

MAKE THE GLAZE

Beat together the egg yolk and cream just to mix.

OVEN TEMPERATURE: 400°F., THEN 375°F •   SERVES: 6; THE GALETTES WILL BE
BAKING TIME: 45 MINUTES   ABOUT 1½ INCHES HIGH AND 4 INCHES WIDE

INGREDIENTS	MEASURE	WEIGHT	
	VOLUME	OUNCES	GRAMS
2½ pounds puff pastry (page 417 or 420) or two 1-pound packages frozen puff pastry, defrosted (see page 414)		2½ pounds	1 kg 134 grams
Chocolate Frangipane	(scant 1½ cups)	(13.75 ounces*)	(392 grams)
bittersweet chocolate	one 3-ounce bar	3 ounces	85 grams
walnut halves, lightly toasted, or hazelnuts, lightly toasted, hulled (see page 642), and coarsely grated†	1 cup 1 cup	3.5 ounces 5 ounces	100 grams 142 grams
sugar	½ cup	3.5 ounces	100 grams
unsalted butter, softened	4 tablespoons	2 ounces	57 grams
1 large egg	3 tablespoons	1.75 ounces	50 grams
nut liqueur, preferably Nocello for the walnut version or Frangelico for the hazelnut version	1 tablespoon	•	•
pure vanilla extract	½ teaspoon	•	•
salt	a pinch	•	•
Egg Glaze 1 large egg yolk	approx. 1 tablespoon	0.6 ounce	18 grams
heavy cream	1½ teaspoons	•	•
optional: powdered sugar	•	•	•

*About 15 ounces (430 grams) if using hazelnuts.
†The coarse grating disc of a food processor works well. Adding the hazelnuts whole to the food processor risks making them pasty.

ASSEMBLE THE GALETTES

Remove the chocolate frangipane from the refrigerator to soften to a spreadable consistency.

You will need six 4½-inch pastry rounds that are ⅛ inch thick for the bottoms and six 4½-inch pastry rounds that are 3⁄16 inch thick for the tops. Divide the dough in half, with one piece slightly larger. For the best shape, roll out the pastry and cut squares about 5 to 5½ inches in size. Place the 6 bottom pieces about 1 inch apart on a cookie sheet lined with parchment or lightly sprayed with water. Gently mark each one with a 4½-inch cutter or template. Spread a scant ¼ cup of chocolate frangi-pane (stir it first, if necessary, to soften it enough for spreading) on each one, leaving a ½-inch border. Brush this border with the egg glaze and cover each with a top pastry square, pressing firmly all around the border. Cover with plastic wrap and freeze until firm enough to cut without compressing the layers of pastry at the edges, about 30 minutes. (They must be left open to allow the pastry full flight in rising.)

Use the cutter or template and a sharp knife tip to cut out the 4½-inch pastries. Discard the scraps. Press firmly around the border from the top only so as not to compress the layers of pastry at the edges. Using a small sharp blade, make ¼-inch-long vertical slashes about ¼ inch deep* at even intervals into the border of the dough. Brush the top of each galette with the egg glaze, being careful not to allow it to drip onto the sides (and thus sealing them closed). Freeze them for 20 minutes.

Brush the galettes again with egg glaze. Using the tip of a sharp knife, starting at the center of each galette and continuing to the slash marks, make curved lines in the top of the dough, going about 1/16 inch deep, or one third of the way through.† Cut small steam vents into 3 of these lines, completely piercing the upper layer of the dough. Cover the galettes with inverted bowls or cake pans and allow to rest, refrigerated, for 2 hours. Then place them, still covered, in the freezer for at least 4 hours, preferably overnight. (At this point, they can stay frozen for up to 3 months.)

Preheat the oven to 400°F. at least 20 minutes before baking. Set an oven rack at the lowest level and place a baking stone or cookie sheet on it before preheating.

Place the galettes about 1 inch apart on the cookie sheet or sheet pan. Bake for 20 minutes, then lower the heat to 375°F. and continue baking for 25 minutes. (If the pastry is browning too fast, cover it loosely with foil.) Turn off the oven and leave the galettes in it (uncovered), with the door slightly propped open with a wooden spoon, for 5 minutes. The galettes are most delicious when served slightly warm.

STORE

Room temperature, up to 3 days. As with all puff pastry, these are best eaten the same day they are baked, although they will still taste good the following 2 days. Do not refrigerate, as the pastry will toughen to cardboard.

POINTERS FOR SUCCESS

∿ See page 450.

---

* If using frozen dough that is only ⅛ inch thick, make the cuts almost to the bottom—not quite ¼ inch deep.

† If using frozen dough that is only ⅛ inch thick, make cuts slightly less than 1/16 inch deep.

CLASSIC NAPOLEON

S ay the word *pastry,* and for many people a Napoleon is what comes to mind. A classic Napoleon is made up of layers of puff pastry filled with pastry cream and topped with a layer of chocolate-decorated shiny poured fondant. In addition to classic Napoleons, I offer recipes for several different Napoleons.

Jeff Tomcheck, whom I met when he was chef at the Old Angler's Inn in Potomac, uses the more delicate and crisp fillo instead of puff pastry and a fabulous chocolate mousse filling in his Napoleon of Chocolate Mousse. As a variation to this filling, I also adore the airy, creamy bittersweet chocolate eggless mousse of Bill Yosses, pastry chef at Bouley Restaurant and Bakery in New York City.

Two fruit variations are Strawberry Chiboust Napoleon and Marionberry and Passion Cream, or Raspberry and Lemon Cream, Napoleon. Yet another delicious and fun variation comes from Patrick Lemblé, pastry chef of the Four Seasons Restaurant in New York City: Bite-Size Peanut Butter Napoleons, which are filled with peanut butter pastry cream.

The most outrageously different variation comes from my friend and fellow cookbook author Faith Willinger, who lives in Tuscany. She reported to me that at Ristorante Antonello Colonna, in Florence, they make a casual Napoleon by breaking up the puff pastry into bits and tossing it with the pastry cream. They call it *millefoglie con panna e crema chantilly.* I call it La Smithereen.

OVEN TEMPERATURE: 400°F • BAKING TIME: 30 MINUTES, OR 29
MINUTES PLUS 15 MINUTES IN THE TURNED-OFF OVEN   SERVES: 8

INGREDIENTS	MEASURE	WEIGHT	
	VOLUME	OUNCES	GRAMS
Quick Puff Pastry (page 420) or Classic Puff Pastry (page 417), made with only 4 turns		1¼ pounds	567 grams
Chocolate Drizzle Glaze bittersweet chocolate, chopped	⅓ of a 3-ounce bar	1 ounce	28 grams
heavy cream, cold	2 tablespoons	1 ounce	29 grams
1 recipe Poured Fondant (page 581)	1¾ cups	•	•
1 recipe Pastry Cream (page 560)	2½ cups	22.75 ounces	650 grams

EQUIPMENT

Two inverted half-size sheet pans or large baking sheets, lined with parchment, and a reclosable quart-size freezer bag

Make the dough (page 417 or 420).

If using quick puff pastry, divide the pastry dough in half and keep the second piece chilled while you work with the first one. Roll the dough into a ¹⁄₁₆-inch-thick rectangle about 16 inches by 10 inches. If using classic puff pastry, you will probably only be able to roll it ⅛ inch thick. Make only one 16- by 10-inch sheet. (On baking, it will rise to about ¾ inch; you can cut it into 2 layers after baking.) Transfer the dough to the back of an inverted sheet pan or cookie sheet. As the dough shrinks slightly when moved, roll it again to the correct size. Cover it with plastic wrap and freeze it for at least 30 minutes or until very firm. If using quick puff pastry, repeat with the second piece of dough.

Preheat the oven to 400°F. at least 20 minutes before baking. Set an oven rack at the middle level before preheating.

Using a ruler and sharp knife, trim the edges of the pastry so they are even. With a fork, prick the dough all over so that it will rise evenly. If using classic puff pastry, place a second sheet pan or cookie sheet directly on top of the pastry. Place the pastry in the oven and, if using quick puff pastry, bake for 30 minutes or until puffed and golden. For classic puff pastry, remove the second pan after 20 minutes; open the oven door and bake for another 5 minutes with the oven door propped open with a wooden spoon, then turn off the oven, leaving the door propped open, and leave the pastry for 15 minutes to dry the center layers. Remove the sheet pan(s) to a wire rack to cool. (If not using right away, store the pastry airtight at room temperature up to 24 hours.)

CUT THE PASTRY

Using a serrated knife, trim the pastry to even the edges. With quick puff pastry, each rectangle will be about 14 inches by 10 inches, or a little larger. Cut each one lengthwise in half, to make 4 rectangles about 14 inches by 5 inches. For classic puff pastry, cut the rectangle horizontally into 2 layers, then cut each layer lengthwise in half.

MAKE THE CHOCOLATE DRIZZLE GLAZE

In a small microwave-proof bowl, or the top of a double boiler set over hot, not simmering, water (do not allow the water to touch the bottom of the upper container), melt the chocolate, stirring often (if using a microwave, stir every 15 seconds). Remove it from the heat.

Pour the cream on top of the chocolate and stir until smooth. It should form soft peaks when a spoon is dipped into it and lifted out. If it is too thick, add a little more heavy cream. Pour the glaze into a reclosable quart-size freezer bag and close it securely. Set it aside briefly while you glaze the pastry with the fondant.

DECORATE THE TOP PASTRY LAYER

Place 1 pastry rectangle on a rack set over a sheet pan to catch the excess fondant. Pour the fondant over the pastry to coat it evenly (Figure 1). Before the fondant starts to set and crust, pipe the chocolate: Cut off a very small corner from the bag. Pipe lines of chocolate spaced about 1 inch apart across the pastry (Figure 2). With the back of a knife, create a chevron pattern by drawing the blade three times down the length of the surface of the fondant, alternating directions and spacing the lines evenly (start with the center line). (Figure 3)

ASSEMBLE THE NAPOLEON

Sandwich each pastry layer with a generous ¾ cup of pastry cream. Use an offset spatula to spread it evenly. Set the glazed pastry on top of the third layer of pastry cream. Refrigerate for a minimum of 1 hour and a maximum of 3 hours before cutting.

Use a serrated knife to cut the napoleon into 1¾-inch pieces.

VARIATION

STRAWBERRY AND CHIBOUST NAPOLEON

Omit the fondant and drizzle glaze.

INGREDIENTS	MEASURE	WEIGHT	
	VOLUME	OUNCES	GRAMS
strawberries, rinsed, hulled, and halved (or quartered if large)	1½ pints	12 ounces	340 grams
sugar	1 tablespoon	approx. 0.5 ounce	12.5 grams
½ recipe Chiboust Cream (page 565)	2¾ cups	14.75 ounces	420 grams
optional: powdered sugar	approx. ¼ cup	•	•

OPTIONAL EQUIPMENT

A pastry bag or reclosable quart-size freezer bag and a number 9 large star tube

In a bowl, toss the strawberries with the sugar and allow them to sit for at least 1 hour at room temperature and up to 6 hours refrigerated. Drain the strawberries, discarding the syrup, and place them on paper towels. (You will have about 1½ cups of berries.)

Pipe or spread a generous ¾ cup of the Chiboust between each pastry layer, topping each layer of Chiboust with ½ cup of the strawberries. Dust the final pastry layer with the optional powdered sugar. If desired, make a crosshatch design in the sugar by heating a metal skewer in a gas flame or on an electric burner until very hot and setting it on the powdered sugar at about 1-inch diagonal intervals until it caramelizes. Wipe the skewer each time and reheat it when it cools.

VARIATION

MARIONBERRY AND PASSION CREAM (OR RASPBERRY AND LEMON CREAM) NAPOLEON

Omit the fondant and drizzle glaze.

INGREDIENTS	MEASURE	WEIGHT	
	VOLUME	OUNCES	GRAMS
frozen Marionberries (or fresh raspberries)	2 cups 1½ cups	8 ounces	227 grams
sugar (omit if using raspberries)	1 tablespoon + 1 teaspoon	approx. 0.5 ounce	16.6 grams
1½ recipes Passion Fruit Curd Cream (page 571) or Classic Lemon Curd Cream (page 571)	approx. 3 cups	•	•
optional: powdered sugar	approx. ¼ cup	1 ounce	28 grams

If using Marionberries, in a large bowl gently toss them with the sugar. Set the Marionberries aside to thaw (about 2 hours at room temperature, or refrigerate for up to 8 hours). Drain them thoroughly, discarding the syrup, and place them on paper towels.

Spread about ¾ cup of the passion curd cream (or lemon cream) between each pastry layer, topping each layer of pastry cream with ½ cup of the Marionberries (or raspberries). Dust the final pastry layer with the optional powdered sugar; if desired, make a crosshatch design by heating a metal skewer in a gas flame or on an electric burner until very hot and setting it on the powdered sugar at about 1-inch diagonal intervals until it caramelizes. Wipe the skewer each time and reheat it when it cools.

LA SMITHEREEN   Leave the puff pastry uncut after baking. Just before serving, crumble the pastry into about 1-inch pieces and gently stir it together with the pastry cream. Scoop it onto serving plates and, if desired, garnish it with fresh fruit.

CHOCOLATE MOUSSE NAPOLEON

Jeff Tomcheck, chef/owner of Indigo Restaurant in Great Falls, Virginia, created this Napoleon when he was chef at the Old Angler's Inn in Potomac. Instead of puff pastry, he uses three layers of delicate, crisp fillo, coated with a thin layer of melted bittersweet chocolate. The chocolate serves to moisture-proof the baked pastry, keeping it from coming in direct contact with the two layers of rich chocolate mousse filling.

For a lighter, eggless chocolate mousse filling, try the variation from Bill Yosses, pastry chef at Bouley Restaurant and Bakery in New York City. It's actually a light ganache, made with a chocolate that contains 70 percent cocoa solids, which makes it smooth as silk, and nearly three times the cream to milk, making it very light. (Bill reminds me occasionally that I was his first teacher! Hard to believe; he has risen to such stellar heights of baking excellence, refinement, and imagination.)

OVEN TEMPERATURE: 375°F. • BAKING TIME: 7 TO 10 MINUTES   **SERVES: 6**

INGREDIENTS	MEASURE	WEIGHT	
	VOLUME	OUNCES	GRAMS
fillo, preferably fresh (see page 365)	4 sheets	approx. 3 ounces	approx. 82 grams
melted unsalted butter, preferably clarified (see page 629)	2 tablespoons (clarified)	approx. 1 ounce	24 grams
sugar	1 tablespoon + 1½ tablespoons	scant 0.75 ounce	19 grams
unsweetened cocoa	2 tablespoons	scant 0.5 ounce	12 grams
couverture or fine-quality bittersweet chocolate, quick-tempered (see page 616)	•	2 ounces	57 grams

EQUIPMENT

Two half-size sheet pans or large baking sheets, lined with parchment; a small offset spatula or small (number 9) clean artist's brush; and a pastry bag and number 7 large star pastry tube

Preheat the oven to 375°F. at least 20 minutes before baking. Set an oven rack at the middle level and place a baking stone or cookie sheet on it before preheating.

MAKE THE LAYERS

Lay the stack of fillo on the counter. Cut it crosswise in half so that there are two 8-by 12-inch pieces. Keep the fillo well covered with plastic wrap and a damp towel as you work to prevent drying.

Remove 1 sheet of fillo, place it on the work surface, and brush it lightly with the butter (using about ¾ teaspoon), starting around the edges where it will dry out the most quickly and then dappling it lightly all over. Sprinkle the fillo with ½ teaspoon of the sugar and ¾ teaspoon of the cocoa and lay another sheet of fillo over it. Brush it lightly with butter and sprinkle it with sugar and cocoa. Continue this way with the remaining sheets of fillo, brushing the top with butter and sprinkling it with the remaining 1 teaspoon of sugar, but no cocoa (reserve the remaining cocoa).

With a sharp knife and long ruler, cut the fillo stack lengthwise in half into two 4- by 12-inch stacks. Cut each stack into nine 1¼- by 4-inch rectangles. (You have ¾ inch extra in length, which will allow for a little imprecision.) Place the fillo rectangles on the parchment-lined sheet, top with the second sheet of parchment, and place the second baking sheet on top of it.

Bake the pastries for 7 to 10 minutes or until the fillo is golden. Remove the top sheet and parchment and allow the fillo to cool to room temperature.

COAT THE FILLO WITH CHOCOLATE

Use a small offset metal spatula or small artist's brush to apply a very thin coating of chocolate to all the fillo rectangles. Six of the rectangles need to be coated on both sides. Allow the coating to set before applying the chocolate to the second side. Set the coated layers on a baking sheet in the refrigerator for about 5 minutes, or leave at room temperature if it is cool, to set.

MAKE THE CHOCOLATE MOUSSE FILLING

In a large mixer bowl, place the cream and refrigerate for at least 15 minutes. Chill the whisk beater alongside the bowl.

Beat the cream until soft peaks form when the beater is raised. Cover and refrigerate.

Have ready near the range a 1-cup heatproof glass measure.

In a small heavy saucepan (preferably with a nonstick lining), stir together the sugar and water. Heat, stirring constantly, until the sugar dissolves and the syrup is bubbling. Stop stirring and turn down the heat to the lowest setting. (If using an electric range, remove the pan from the heat.)

In a mixer bowl, preferably with the whisk beater, on high speed, beat the egg and yolks until very thick and pale yellow.

Increase the heat under the syrup and boil it until a thermometer registers 236°F. (soft ball stage). Immediately pour the syrup into the glass measure to stop

INGREDIENTS	MEASURE	WEIGHT	
	VOLUME	OUNCES	GRAMS
Chocolate Mousse Filling	(4 cups)	(18.5 ounces)	(530 grams)
heavy cream	1 liquid cup	8 ounces	232 grams
sugar	¼ cup	1.75 ounces	50 grams
water	1 tablespoon	•	•
1 large egg	approx. 3 tablespoons	1.75 ounces (weighed without the shell)	50 grams
approx. 4 large egg yolks (stir before measuring)	¼ liquid cup	2.25 ounces	65 grams
bittersweet chocolate, preferably Lindt's 70% Excellence or Valrhona's Guanaja, quick-tempered (see page 616)	•	6 ounces	170 grams
optional accompaniment: Pistachio Custard Sauce (page 610) and 18 griottes (brandied tart cherries; see page 594 or 639)	¾ cup	13 ounces	approx. 370 grams

the cooking. If using an electric hand-held mixer, beat the syrup into the yolks in a steady stream. To keep syrup from spinning onto the sides of the bowl, do not allow it to fall directly on the beaters. If using a stand mixer, pour a small amount of syrup over the eggs with the mixer off. Immediately beat at high speed for 5 seconds. Stop the mixer and add a larger amount of syrup. Beat at high speed for 5 seconds. Continue with the remaining syrup. With the last addition, use a rubber scraper to remove the syrup clinging to the measure. Scrape the chocolate into the egg mixture and beat until uniform. Immediately, so that the chocolate does not start to become firm, beat in a few spoonfuls of the whipped cream. Remove the mixer from the stand, if using, and use the whisk beater or a large whisk to fold in the remaining cream in three parts. Cover and chill for at least 1 hour and up to 3 hours before piping.

ASSEMBLE THE NAPOLEONS

Fill the pastry bag, fitted with the star tube, with the chocolate mousse. Pipe a small star of the mixture onto each serving plate to affix the pastry. (I like to set the Napoleon toward one side and place the sauce and griottes on the other.) For each Napoleon, set a fillo rectangle (one coated only on one side) on top of the chocolate star, chocolate side up. Pipe two rows of shells (see page 621) side by side down each rectangle. Place the fillo rectangle coated on both sides with the chocolate on top and pipe a second layer of shells onto each. Dust the plain side of the remaining fillo rectangles lightly with the reserved cocoa and place, chocolate side down, on top of the napoleons. If desired, spoon 2 tablespoons of the pistachio sauce onto one side of each napoleon and place 3 griottes on top.

VARIATION

NAPOLEONS WITH EGGLESS CHOCOLATE MOUSSE (4 CUPS/28 OUNCES/ 800 GRAMS)   Substitute this mousse for the chocolate mousse filling.

Break 8 ounces (226 grams) Valrhona Guanaja (or other 70 percent chocolate cocoa solids) or fine-quality bittersweet chocolate into pieces and process it in a food processor with the metal blade until it is very fine. Heat 2⅔ liquid cups (21.6 ounces/612 grams) heavy cream to the boiling point and, with the motor running, pour it through the feed tube in a steady stream. Process for a few seconds or until smooth. Transfer the mixture to a large mixer bowl and refrigerate it for at least 6 hours.

Beat the mousse *only* until very soft peaks form when the beater is raised. It will continue to thicken after a few minutes at room temperature.

STORE

Fillo rectangles, room temperature, airtight, up to 3 days.

Chocolate mousse: The basic version can be refrigerated for 2 to 3 hours, but it is best piped before it becomes too stiff; the eggless mousse can be refrigerated for up to 1 week. The finished Napoleons are best held at room temperature for no longer than 6 hours. (The chocolate filling is most delicious when not refrigerator-hard.)

UNDERSTANDING

Couverture chocolate is best for coating the baked pastry because the high amount of cocoa butter makes it more fluid when melted, so it forms the thinnest coating. Its purpose is to moisture-proof the fillo (though the fillo will stay crunchy for at least 3 hours without it), and it also adds splendid flavor.

BITE-SIZE PEANUT BUTTER NAPOLEONS

Thiese whimsical two-bite-size Napoleons are modeled after the bicorne hat the general wore. They are composed of triangles of puff pastry topped with a thin layer of royal icing. When baked, the royal icing becomes crisp on top, though its middle remains pleasantly sticky. Before serving, the pastries are filled with smooth peanut butter pastry cream.

These Napoleons were created by Patrick Lemblé, pastry chef of the Four Seasons Restaurant in New York City, for a peanut promotion party. Chef Lemblé may come from Alsace, but he sure has a feel for American peanuts.

OVEN TEMPERATURE: 425°F. • BAKING TIME: 12 MINUTES   MAKES: ABOUT 30 NAPOLEONS

INGREDIENTS	MEASURE	WEIGHT	
	VOLUME	OUNCES	GRAMS
puff pastry (page 417 or 420)		10 ounces	283 grams
Royal Icing		(6 ounces)	(172 grams)
1 large egg white	2 tablespoons	1 ounce	30 grams
powdered sugar	1⅓ cups (lightly spooned)	5.3 ounces	150 grams
blanched and unsalted peanuts, separated into halves	approx. ⅓ cup	1.6 ounces	45 grams
Pastry Cream (page 560)	½ cup	4.5 ounces	130 grams
smooth peanut butter, preferably Jif, at room temperature	2 tablespoons	approx. 1 ounce	33 grams

EQUIPMENT
Two large cookie sheets or half-size sheet pans, lined with parchment

Make the dough (page 417 or 420).

Roll the dough about ⅛ inch thick and a little over 10 inches by about 10 inches. Transfer it to a piece of parchment. As it shrinks slightly when moved, reroll it to the correct size. Slip the parchment with the puff pastry onto a cookie sheet or an inverted half-size sheet pan. Cover it with plastic wrap and freeze it for at least 30 minutes or until very firm.

MAKE THE ROYAL ICING

In a large mixer bowl, beat the egg white and powdered sugar, preferably with the whisk beater, at low speed until the sugar is moistened. Beat at high speed until the icing is very glossy and stiff peaks form when the beater is lifted, 5 to 7 minutes. The tips of the peaks should curve slightly; if the mixture is too soft, a bit more powdered sugar can be added. If it is too stiff, add water by the ¼ teaspoon. If not using the icing immediately, keep the bowl covered with a damp cloth and plastic wrap. (Or transfer it to a tightly covered container and store at room temperature for up to 3 days. Rebeat lightly before using it.)

ICE AND CUT THE PUFF PASTRY

Slip the puff pastry, still on the parchment, onto a counter. Return the baking sheet to the freezer, along with the second baking sheet. With a sharp knife, trim the edges so that the pastry is 10 inches wide. Work quickly so that the pastry stays firm. With a long metal spatula, coat it with a thin, even layer (about ⅛ inch thick) of the royal icing. With a wet sharp knife, cut the puff pastry, the long way, into five 2-inch-wide strips. Cut each strip into 6 triangles with 3-inch bases (Figure 1); each strip will yield 6 triangles and 2 small scraps that can be baked or discarded.

Imbed 3 peanut halves in the center of each iced triangle, radiating them out from the center to resemble a flower. Remove the baking sheets from the freezer, line them with the parchment, and place the triangles about 1 inch apart on the baking sheets. Set the sheets in the freezer for 10 minutes or in the refrigerator for 30 minutes to chill.

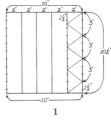

1

Whisk the peanut butter into the ½ cup hot pastry cream. Let cool at room temperature, then refrigerate for 1 hour.

Preheat the oven to 425°F. at least 20 minutes before baking. Set an oven rack at the middle level before preheating.

Bake the triangles, 1 sheet at a time, keeping the remaining sheet chilled, for about 12 minutes or until the pastry has puffed and turned golden and the royal icing has turned a pale brown. (Do not cover the triangles with parchment during baking, as this would cause the royal icing to steam and crack.) The pastry will rise to between 1 and 1½ inches. If the pastry rises unevenly and the royal icing slides to the side, you can simply reposition it after baking, because the bottom will still be sticky. (A trick for keeping them perfectly even as they bake is to suspend a lightly greased rack about 1 inch above each baking sheet; two inverted tartlet tins work well to suspend the rack.) Remove the pans to racks to cool completely.

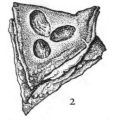

2

With a serrated knife, cut each pastry triangle horizontally in half. Fill each one with about 1 teaspoon of peanut pastry cream. (Figure 2)

STORE
Cool room temperature, 4 to 6 hours.

POINTERS FOR SUCCESS
〜 Work quickly when icing and cutting the pastry. If it stays cold, it cuts cleanly, enabling it to rise more evenly. If it softens after you apply the royal icing, return it to the freezer for 10 to 15 minutes before cutting it.

CHEESE STRAWS

This is a perfect appetizer to serve with champagne or before-dinner drinks. It can be made with puff pastry scraps or quick puff pastry. The deep rust color of the paprika makes a lovely contrast to the gold of the pastry.

OVEN TEMPERATURE: 425°F., THEN 400°F. •
BAKING TIME: 10 TO 12 MINUTES

MAKES: ABOUT 12 DOZEN
4-INCH CHEESE STRAWS

INGREDIENTS	MEASURE	WEIGHT	
	VOLUME	OUNCES	GRAMS
Quick Puff Pastry (page 420), made with 1 teaspoon of salt and only 4 turns		1¼ pounds	567 grams
grated Parmesan or Asiago cheese	⅓ cup	0.5 ounce	14 grams
paprika	2 tablespoons	0.5 ounce	14 grams
1 large egg, lightly beaten	approx. 3 tablespoons	1.75 ounces (weighed without the shell)	50 grams

EQUIPMENT
A cookie sheet, lined with parchment or sprayed with water

Make the dough (page 420).

In a small bowl, mix together the grated cheese and paprika.

On a floured counter, roll the dough into a large rectangle 14 inches by 20 inches and about ⅛ inch thick. Brush the pastry well with the beaten egg and dust it evenly with half the cheese mixture, rubbing it into the surface. Turn the dough over and brush off any flour. Brush it well with the beaten egg and dust it evenly with the remaining cheese mixture. Fold the dough crosswise in half and slip it onto a cookie sheet. (Figure 1) Cover it with plastic wrap and freeze for 20 minutes or refrigerate it for a minimum of 1 hour and a maximum of 8 hours.

Cut the dough crosswise into ⅜-inch strips. (Figure 2) Unfold each piece and, holding it by the ends, give it three and a half twists. (Figure 3) Place it on the prepared cookie sheet, pressing the ends down firmly to hold the twist. (Figure 4) Cover the twists with plastic wrap and refrigerate for at least 30 minutes.

Preheat the oven to 425°F. at least 20 minutes before baking. Set an oven rack at the middle level before preheating.

Place the cheese straws in the oven, lower the heat to 400°F., and bake for 10 to 12 minutes or until brown and crisp. Trim off the ends and cut the cheese straws into 4-inch lengths while still warm.

STORE
Room temperature, airtight, up to 5 days.

UNDERSTANDING
The cheese straws are rolled thin so that they bake extra crisp without burning the temperature-sensitive cheese and paprika.

COULIBIAC

The traditional version of this dish, of Russian origin, ranks as one of the world's top pastries. I have adapted it to suit modern tastes. The salmon is poached lightly in broth so that it remains succulent, then is spread with a mushroom velouté sauce and layered with couscous (I find the lightness of texture and sweet nuttiness preferable to the traditional rice). This is first encased in dill crêpes and then in puff pastry. The crêpes keep the pastry from becoming soggy and add a delicate texture and flavor.

The entire dish can be made as far as three weeks ahead since the coulibiac benefits from being cooked frozen.

OVEN TEMPERATURE: 425°F., THEN 400°F.,
THEN 375°F. • BAKING TIME: 60 TO 70 MINUTES   SERVES: 10; FINISHED SIZE IS
(PLUS 30 TO 60 MINUTES STANDING TIME)   11 INCHES BY 8 INCHES

INGREDIENTS	MEASURE	WEIGHT	
	VOLUME	OUNCES	GRAMS
puff pastry (page 417 or 420) or 2 sheets (about 11 inches by 14 inches) frozen puff pastry, defrosted (see page 414)		2½ pounds	1 kg 134 grams
Salmon and Mushrooms 2 salmon fillets (preferably center-cut), skinned and any bones removed	•	2 pounds	907 grams
unsalted butter, softened	1 tablespoon + 1 teaspoon, divided	0.6 ounce	19 grams
finely chopped onion	2 tablespoons	0.5 ounce	16 grams
finely chopped shallots	1 tablespoon	0.33 ounce	9 grams
salt	¾ teaspoon	•	5 grams
freshly ground black pepper	¼ teaspoon	•	•
thinly sliced fresh mushrooms	2½ cups	8 ounces	227 grams
chopped fresh dill	2½ tablespoons, packed	0.33 ounce	9 grams
dry white wine*	⅔ liquid cup	•	•
chicken broth	⅔ liquid cup	•	•

*Or use ⅓ cup vermouth and increase the broth to 1 cup.

EQUIPMENT

A baking dish or roasting pan about 14- by 9- by 2 inches; a baking sheet with very low or no sides; a dark steel baking sheet or baking stone; a 6-inch crêpe pan

Make the dough (page 417 or 420), or defrost according to package directions. Divide it into 2 pieces, about 14 ounces (one third) and 26 ounces (two thirds).

Advance preparation: The salmon and mushrooms can be prepared a day ahead of final assembly; the crêpes can be prepared up to 2 days ahead and refrigerated, or frozen for up to 3 months; the filling can be prepared up to 2 days ahead.

PREPARE THE SALMON AND MUSHROOMS

Preheat the oven to 400°F. at least 20 minutes before baking. Set an oven rack at the lowest level before preheating.

Butter the baking dish with the 1 tablespoon of butter. Cut each salmon fillet on the bias into slices about ½ inch thick. (Hold the knife at a slight angle and slice across the fish.)

In a small sauté pan, over medium-low heat, melt the remaining 1 teaspoon of butter and sauté the onion and shallots until softened and translucent, about 3 minutes. Spoon the onion and shallots into the baking dish, staying within a 9-inch square in the center, and sprinkle with half the salt and pepper. Arrange two parallel, slightly overlapping rows of the salmon slices on top. Sprinkle with the remaining salt and pepper. Scatter the mushrooms over the salmon and sprinkle with the dill.

Heat the wine and chicken broth until hot and pour it over the salmon. Cover the dish with aluminum foil and bake for 15 minutes. The salmon should be barely opaque around the edges and still quite rare in the center. (It will continue cooking when baked in the pastry.)

Pour the accumulated liquid around the salmon into a medium saucepan (or a 2-cup heatproof glass measure). Remove the mushrooms to a small bowl and set them aside. Allow the salmon to cool, draining the liquid that accumulates into the saucepan or glass measure. (There will be about 1 cup.)

MAKE THE VELOUTÉ

INGREDIENTS	MEASURE	WEIGHT	
	VOLUME	OUNCES	GRAMS
Velouté			
unsalted butter	4 teaspoons	0.6 ounce	19 grams
all-purpose flour	2 tablespoons	0.6 ounce	18 grams
cayenne pepper	scant ⅛ teaspoon	•	•
freshly squeezed lemon juice	2 tablespoons	approx. 1 ounce	32 grams
3 large egg yolks, lightly beaten	3 tablespoons + 1½ teaspoons	2 ounces	56 grams
freshly ground white pepper	a few grindings	•	•

*Or use ⅓ cup vermouth and increase the broth to 1 cup.

Over high heat, bring the liquid in the saucepan to a full boil; reduce the heat to low. (Or use a microwave if using a glass measure.)

In a second medium saucepan, over medium-low heat, melt the butter. Reduce the heat to low, add the flour, and cook for 1 minute, whisking constantly. Add the hot liquid all at once, whisking rapidly. Add the reserved mushrooms and simmer over very low heat, stirring often, for 20 minutes.

Whisk in the cayenne pepper and lemon juice and then the egg yolks. Continue cooking for 30 seconds, whisking rapidly. The sauce will be very thick but pourable. Remove it from the heat and add the white pepper. Spoon the sauce over the salmon and spread it evenly to cover it all. Allow it to cool, then press a piece of plastic wrap, lightly sprayed with nonstick vegetable spray, on top and refrigerate until cold, at least 1 hour, preferably overnight.

MAKE THE DILL CRÊPES

INGREDIENTS	MEASURE	WEIGHT	
	VOLUME	OUNCES	GRAMS
Dill Crêpes	(8 to 9 crêpes)		
1 large egg	3 tablespoons	1.75 ounces (weighed without the shell)	50 grams
milk	⅓ liquid cup	approx. 2.75 ounces	80 grams
unsalted butter, melted	1 tablespoon	0.5 ounce	14 grams
cornstarch	⅓ cup	1.33 ounces	40 grams
salt	1/16 teaspoon	•	•
minced fresh dill	1 teaspoon	•	•
minced fresh parsley	1 teaspoon	•	•
clarified butter*	1½ teaspoons	0.2 ounce	6 grams

*If you do not have clarified butter on hand, you will need to clarify 3 tablespoons (1.5 ounces/43 grams) of unsalted butter (see page 629).

In a blender container, place all the ingredients for the crêpes except the clarified butter and blend at high speed for 10 seconds. Alternatively, in a large bowl, combine the cornstarch and salt. Slowly stir in the milk. Use a hand-held electric or rotary beater to beat in the eggs one at a time, beating for about 1 minute after each addition. Beat until the batter is smooth. Beat in the dill, parsley, and the 1 tablespoon melted butter.

Heat the crêpe pan over medium high heat until hot enough to sizzle a drop of water. Brush it lightly with some of the clarified butter and pour a scant 2 tablespoons of batter into the center. Immediately tilt the pan to the left and then down and around to the right so that the batter covers the entire pan. Cook until the top starts to dull and the edges begin to brown, 15 to 20 seconds. Use a small metal spatula to lift an edge and check to see if the crêpe is golden brown on the bottom. Then, grasping the edge of the crêpe with your fingers, flip it over and cook for 10 seconds, or just until lightly browned. Invert the pan over the counter and the crêpe will release. Repeat with the remaining batter.

It is fine to stack the crêpes if using them the same day. If refrigerating or freezing the crêpes, however, separate them with pieces of waxed paper, or they may stick to each other.

MAKE THE COUSCOUS AND EGG FILLING

INGREDIENTS	MEASURE	WEIGHT	
	VOLUME	OUNCES	GRAMS
Couscous and Egg Filling			
water	⅔ cup	5.5 ounces	156 grams
unsalted butter	2 teaspoons	0.33 ounce	9 grams
salt	¼ teaspoon	•	•
freshly ground black pepper	1/16 teaspoon	•	•
couscous	½ cup	2.75 ounces	80 grams
2 large eggs, hard-cooked, shelled, and finely chopped	•	4 ounces	112 grams
minced fresh parsley, preferably flat-leaf	3 tablespoons	1.5 ounces	42 grams
minced fresh dill	2 teaspoons	•	•
Egg Glaze 2 large egg yolks	2 tablespoons	1.25 ounces	37 grams
heavy cream	1 tablespoon	0.5 ounce	15 grams

In a small covered saucepan, bring the water and butter to a boil. Add the salt and pepper and slowly stir in the couscous, making sure the water boils continuously. Simmer over low heat, stirring constantly, until almost all of the water is absorbed. Remove from the heat, cover, and allow to sit for 5 minutes. Fluff the couscous with a fork and cool uncovered.

Use a fork or wet fingers to separate the grains of couscous. Combine them with the chopped egg, parsley, and dill, mixing lightly with a fork. (If preparing ahead, cover and refrigerate.)

ASSEMBLE THE COULIBIAC

At least 8 hours ahead, remove the salmon from the refrigerator and divide it in half down the center, where the two columns of salmon meet.

On a lightly floured counter, roll out one piece of puff pastry (about 14 ounces) into an 11- by 8-inch rectangle about ⅛ inch thick. (If using prerolled purchased puff pastry, after thawing, dust it well with flour and roll it to the proper length.) Transfer it to the flat baking sheet, trim off the excess, and reserve the trimmings, covered and chilled.

Arrange 3 overlapping crêpes over the center of the rectangle, leaving a 1-inch border on all sides. Sprinkle the crêpes with about one third of the couscous mixture, maintaining the 1-inch border. Place half of the chilled salmon, mushroom side down, on top of the couscous mixture. Sprinkle the top of the salmon with another one third of the couscous mixture and pat it in place. Place the remaining salmon on top, mushroom side up, and sprinkle with the remaining couscous mixture. Pat the couscous in place. Cover with the remaining crêpes, overlapping them and making sure all the salmon is covered.

Roll out the second piece of puff pastry into a 16- by 11-inch rectangle, sprinkling with flour as necessary to keep it from sticking. (The top piece of pastry has to be wider and longer than the bottom piece because it needs to cover the sides as well as the top.) Stir together the egg yolks and cream and brush the 1-inch border with this egg glaze. Brush off any excess flour and, starting at a short side, roll the top piece of pastry loosely around the rolling pin. Position it over the salmon and, starting at the bottom, unroll it evenly over it, tugging it gently to stretch it forward. Smooth the sides in place over the salmon and filling and press down firmly on the border so the top pastry adheres to the bottom one, leaving an opening at each end to expel any air pockets if necessary before pressing and sealing the ends. The pastry should rest snugly against the crêpe-wrapped salmon. Cover the coulibiac with plastic wrap and freeze it for about 20 minutes. Cover and refrigerate the remaining egg glaze.

With a very sharp knife, trim the excess pastry so that only the 1-inch border remains. Wrap and chill the scraps. Brush the entire pastry with the egg glaze, taking care to avoid the sides, as the glaze would seal them and prevent rising. Freeze the coulibiac again, uncovered, for 20 minutes.

MEANWHILE, MAKE THE DECORATIONS

Roll the pastry scraps about ⅟₁₆ inch thick. Using a sharp knife, cut out at least twelve 2½-inch rose leaves. Use the knife to make shallow vein lines. Or, if you have a metal rose-petal mold, simply invert it, veined side down, on the pastry and press firmly, then use the tip of a sharp knife to cut around the mold, lift the mold away, and lift up the leaf. Place the leaves on a flat surface, such as a cookie sheet. Cover with plastic wrap and refrigerate until just before ready to use.

Remove the coulibiac from the freezer and, using a small cutter, about ¾ inch and preferably scalloped, cut a steam vent in the center of the pastry. Use a second larger cutter (about 1½ inches) to cut a circle from a pastry scrap. Cut out the center with the smaller cutter, brush the bottom with egg glaze, and fit it around the steam vent. Place the leaves, overlapping slightly, as they will spread apart during baking, radiating from the center, brushing the bottoms with egg glaze to attach them. Give the pastry a second egg wash, covering the pastry leaves as well. Return it to the freezer for 30 minutes.

Cover the pastry with a large piece of plastic wrap, lightly sprayed with non-stick vegetable spray or buttered. Freeze the coulibiac for at least 5 hours. (The coulibiac can be frozen for up to 3 weeks. If planning to freeze it longer than 1 day, wrap it with heavy-duty foil after it is frozen solid.)

Preheat the oven to 425°F. at least 30 minutes before baking. Set an oven rack at the lowest level and place a baking stone or dark steel sheet on it before preheating.

Bake the coulibiac for 10 minutes, then lower the heat to 400°F. and bake for another 10 minutes. Cover it *loosely* with a piece of aluminum foil (do not crimp it tightly, or the pastry will steam) and bake for another 10 minutes. Lower the heat to 375°F. and bake for 30 minutes. Remove the coulibiac from the oven and insert an instant-read thermometer into the steam vent to check the temperature. It will read 115°F. when done; if it is not yet done, return it to the oven, turning it around for more even baking, and continue baking for 10 to 15 minutes, uncovered, until it tests done. Allow it to sit on the baking sheet for at least 30 minutes and up to 1 hour before cutting it. (The temperature will rise at least 5 degrees.)

When ready to serve, slip a large rimless baking sheet (at least 12 inches long) under the coulibiac and transfer it to a serving platter or an inverted cutting board. Using a serrated knife, cut the coulibiac into 1-inch slices. (Use a wide pancake turner or spatula pressed up against the cut end to support the coulibiac and then a second one to lift the pieces to the plates, laying them on their sides.)

NOTE

Leftover coulibiac is, quite possibly, even more delicious than the first time around because the pastry becomes crisper than it was initially. After slicing the leftover coulibiac, carefully remove the pastry, with the crêpe layer attached to it, from each slice and place on a baking sheet. Bake in a preheated 425°F. oven for about 10 minutes. If desired, warm the insides by placing each slice on its plate in the microwave for 1 minute on medium. Rearrange the pastry around each slice of filling. This "recomposition" is easy to accomplish, looks great, and tastes fantastic. For a simpler method that is also delicious but results in less crisp pastry, reheat whole leftover coulibiac from frozen in a preheated 350°F. oven for about 30 minutes or until a skewer inserted in the center feels warm.

UNDERSTANDING

The salmon is poached first both for flavor and to release some of its liquid before wrapping it in the filling, crêpes, and pastry.

For the crêpes, cornstarch is used in place of flour because it absorbs liquid more readily, making it possible to use the batter without resting, and results in more tender crêpes.

The pastry is frozen before trimming so that it cuts cleanly and the edges do not seal. Freezing the entire coulibiac and baking it on a hot baking stone or sheet serves to create as crisp a pastry as possible. The pastry has a chance to cook and start to rise before the filling defrosts and releases its moisture.

BEEF WELLINGTON

This timeless classic is one of the most elegant and delicious dishes, perfect for a gala event such as New Year's Eve dinner. It is practical as well, because all the components except for the beef can be made two days in advance. The puff pastry can be made months ahead and frozen (or purchased frozen). Cooked properly, the filet mignon is rare throughout and the pastry flaky and buttery. Because the meat is rare, any leftover reheats magnificently. The secret to keep it from becoming soggy at the bottom is borrowed from the classic coulibiac of salmon: the layer of crêpes lining the puff pastry. Thyme replaces the dill for a more compatible flavor.

I find the traditional foie gras spread too heavy and not the flavor that best complements the beef. Duxelles, particularly made with part morel mushrooms, is a fabulously flavorful and compatible stand-in. I first learned about duxelles at James Beard's cooking school more than twenty-five years ago and placed it at once in that special category of culinary jewels that work magic to enhance other ingredients. This enrichment of finely minced mushrooms, slowly sautéed in butter until they turn almost black with concentration, is wonderful to have on hand in the freezer for any number of dishes. Preprocessor days, it was necessary to use the largest chef's knife available for the laborious task of mincing the mushrooms. Now the task is reduced to a matter of seconds. My friend Andreas Holder, food and beverage manager at the Kitano Hotel in New York City, suggested the morels, saying that in Switzerland duxelles is usually prepared that way.

Although this full-flavored dish stands on its own just as it is, it deserves a fine sauce, served on the side. It also merits your best Bordeaux or cabernet.

OVEN TEMPERATURE: 425°F., THEN 400°F.,
THEN 375°F. • BAKING TIME: 55 TO 60 MINUTES   SERVES: 8 TO 10; FINISHED
(PLUS 20 TO 30 MINUTES STANDING TIME)   SIZE IS 13 INCHES BY 8 INCHES

INGREDIENTS	MEASURE	WEIGHT	
	VOLUME	OUNCES	GRAMS
puff pastry (page 417 or 420) or 2 sheets (about 11 inches by 14 inches) frozen puff pastry (see page 414)		2½ pounds	1 kg 134 grams
Thyme Crêpes 1 large egg	(8 to 9 crêpes) 3 tablespoons	1.75 ounces (weighed without the shell)	50 grams
milk	⅓ liquid cup	2.75 ounces	80 grams
unsalted butter, melted	1 tablespoon	0.5 ounce	14 grams
cornstarch	⅓ cup	1.33 ounces	40 grams
salt	1/16 teaspoon	•	•
minced fresh thyme	1 teaspoon	•	•
minced fresh parsley, preferably flat-leaf	1 teaspoon	•	•
clarified butter*	1½ teaspoons	0.2 ounce	6 grams
Duxelles dried morels†	heaping ⅓ cup	1.33 ounces	38 grams
water	1 liquid cup	8.3 ounces	236 grams
fresh mushrooms	approx. 8 cups	24 ounces	680 grams
unsalted butter	8 tablespoons	4 ounces	113 grams
1 medium clove garlic, lightly smashed	•	•	•
salt	½ teaspoon	•	•
freshly ground black pepper	¼ teaspoon	•	•

*If you do not have clarified butter on hand, you will need to clarify 3 tablespoons (1.5 ounces/43 grams) of unsalted butter (see page 629).

†Or 8 ounces fresh morels or white mushrooms chopped with the other mushrooms.

EQUIPMENT

A 17-inch baking sheet with very low or no sides; a dark steel baking sheet or baking stone; and a 6-inch crêpe pan

INGREDIENTS	MEASURE	WEIGHT	
	VOLUME	OUNCES	GRAMS
Beef Fillet 1 beef tenderloin, trimmed		5 pounds	2 kg 268 grams
1 medium clove garlic, cut in half	•	•	•
freshly ground black pepper	½ teaspoon	•	•
fresh thyme, coarsely chopped	1 bunch	0.75 ounce	22 grams
melted unsalted butter	2 tablespoons	1 ounce	28 grams
salt	1 teaspoon	•	•
Egg Glaze 1 large egg white, lightly beaten	2 tablespoons	1 ounce	30 grams
2 large egg yolks	2 tablespoons	1.3 ounces	37 grams
heavy cream	1 tablespoon	0.5 ounce	15 grams
Optional: Périgueux Sauce demi-glace (see page 653)*	(2 cups) 6 tablespoons	• •	• •
Port or Madeira	2 cups	•	•
unsalted butter	4 tablespoons	2 ounces	56 grams
optional: 1 black truffle, cut into small pieces	•	•	•

*Or 2 cups unsalted beef stock, reduced to 6 tablespoons.

Advance preparation: The crêpes can be prepared up to 2 days ahead and refrigerated, or frozen for up to 3 months; the duxelles can be prepared a day ahead of the final assembly.

Make the dough (page 417 or 420), or defrost according to package directions. Divide it into 2 pieces, about 14 ounces (one third) and 26 ounces (two thirds).

MAKE THE THYME CRÊPES

In a blender container, place all the ingredients for the crêpes except the clarified butter and blend at high speed for 10 seconds. Alternatively, in a large bowl, combine the cornstarch and salt. Slowly stir in the milk. Use a hand-held electric or rotary beater to beat in the eggs one at a time, beating for about 1 minute after each addition. Beat until the batter is smooth. Beat in the thyme, parsley, and the 1 tablespoon melted butter.

Heat the crêpe pan over medium-high heat until hot enough to sizzle a drop of water dropped on it. Brush it lightly with some of the clarified butter and pour a scant 2 tablespoons of batter into the center. Immediately tilt the pan to the left and then down and around to the right so that the batter covers the entire pan. Cook until the top starts to dull and the edges begin to brown, 15 to 20 seconds. Use a small metal spatula to lift an edge and check to see if the crêpe is golden brown on the bottom. Then, grasping the edge of the crêpe with your fingers, flip it over and cook for 10 seconds, or just until lightly browned. Invert the pan over the counter and the crêpe will release. Repeat with the remaining batter.

It is fine to stack the crêpes if using them the same day. If refrigerating or freezing the crêpes, however, separate them with pieces of waxed paper, or they may stick to each other.

MAKE THE DUXELLES

In a medium bowl, soak the dried morels in the water for at least 30 minutes. Drain them in a cheesecloth-lined strainer, to catch any residual sand, gently squeezing out the liquid. Reserve the liquid. (There will be about ½ cup.)

Clean the fresh mushrooms by brushing off any dirt with a damp paper towel and cutting off the tough stem ends. Cut any large mushrooms into quarters.

In a food processor with the medium shredding blade, shred the fresh mushrooms. Empty the mushrooms into a bowl and insert the metal blade in the processor. Pulse the fresh mushrooms and the morels in 3 batches until finely chopped.

In a large (12-inch) skillet, over medium heat, melt the butter. Add the garlic and sauté it for a minute. Add the reserved mushroom soaking water, bring to a boil, and reduce it for 3 to 4 minutes or until the butter and juices are sizzling. Add the mushrooms, salt, and pepper, and simmer, covered, over low heat, for 5 minutes. They will release a lot of liquid. Uncover and simmer for 50 to 60 minutes, stirring occasionally, until all the liquid has evaporated and the mushrooms have turned dark brown. Discard the garlic and allow the duxelles to cool completely.

FLAVOR THE FILLET

Two hours before wrapping the fillet in the pastry, place it in a pan and rub it all over with the cut clove of garlic. Sprinkle it with the pepper and thyme. Allow it to sit at room temperature for 1 to 2 hours.

Preheat the broiler.

Discard the thyme and brush the fillet all over with the melted butter. Sprinkle it with the salt and broil, close to the heat, for 4 to 5 minutes on each side or until browned. Remove it to a rack to cool completely.

ASSEMBLE THE BEEF WELLINGTON

On a lightly floured counter, roll out one piece of puff pastry (about 14 ounces) into a 16½- by 7-inch rectangle about ⅛ inch thick. (If using prerolled purchased puff pastry, after thawing, dust it well with flour and roll it to the proper length.) Transfer it to the flat baking sheet and brush lightly with some of the egg white.

Arrange 3 overlapping crêpes, trimmed to the width of the fillet, over the center of the rectangle, leaving a 1-inch border on all sides. Spread a thin layer (about one third of it) of the duxelles mixture over the crêpes, maintaining the 1-inch border. Place the fillet on top of the duxelles. Spread and pat the rest of the duxelles over the top and sides of the fillet. Cover with 4 overlapping crêpes, making sure the entire fillet is covered and pressing the overhanging sides of the crêpes against the sides of it.

Roll out the second piece of puff pastry into a 20- by 11-inch rectangle, sprinkling with flour as necessary to keep it from sticking. (The top piece of pastry has to be wider and longer than the bottom piece because it needs to cover the sides as well as the top.)

Brush the crepes and the 1-inch border with egg white. Brush off any excess flour from the pastry and, starting at a short side, roll it loosely around the rolling pin. Position it over the fillet and starting at the bottom, unroll it evenly over it, tugging it gently to stretch it forward. Smooth the sides in place over the fillet and filling and press down firmly on the border so the top pastry adheres to the bottom one, leaving an opening at each end to expel any air pockets if necessary before pressing and sealing the ends. The pastry should rest snugly against the crêpe-wrapped fillet. Cover the pastry with plastic wrap and freeze it for about 20 minutes or until firm.

With a very sharp knife, trim the excess pastry so that only a 1-inch border remains. Wrap and chill the scraps. Stir together the egg yolk and heavy cream and brush the entire pastry with this glaze, taking care to avoid the sides, as the glaze would seal them and prevent rising. Freeze the beef again, uncovered, for 20 minutes.

Preheat the oven to 425°F. Set an oven rack at the lowest level and place the baking stone or steel sheet on it before preheating.

MAKE THE DECORATIONS

Roll the pastry scraps about ¹⁄₁₆ inch thick. Using a sharp knife, cut out at least twelve 2½-inch rose leaves; use the knife to make shallow vein lines. Or, if you have a metal rose-petal mold, simply invert it, veined side down, on the pastry and press firmly, then use the tip of a sharp knife to cut around the mold, lift the mold away, and lift up the leaf.

Remove the fillet in pastry from the freezer and, using a small cutter, about ¾ inch and preferably scalloped, cut a steam vent in the center of the pastry. Use a second larger cutter (about 1½ inches) to cut a circle from a pastry scrap. Cut out the center with the smaller cutter, brush the bottom with egg wash, and fit it around the steam vent. Place the leaves, overlapping slightly, as they will spread apart during baking, radiating from the center, brushing the bottoms with egg wash to attach them. Give the pastry a second egg wash, covering the pastry leaves as well.

Bake the Wellington for 10 minutes, then lower the heat to 400°F. and bake for another 10 minutes. Cover it *loosely* with a piece of aluminum foil (do not crimp it tightly, or the pastry will steam) and bake for another 10 minutes. Lower the heat to 375°F. and bake for 25 to 30 minutes. Remove the Wellington from the oven and insert an instant-read thermometer into the steam vent to check the temperature. It will read 115°F. when done. Allow it to sit on the baking sheet for 20 to 30 minutes before cutting it. (The temperature will rise about 5 degrees.)

When ready to serve, slip a large rimless baking sheet (at least 12 inches long) under the Wellington and transfer it to a serving platter or an inverted cutting board. Using a serrated knife, cut the Wellington into 1¼- to 1½-inch slices. (Use a wide pancake turner or spatula pressed up against the cut end to support the coulibiac and then a second one to lift the pieces to the plates, laying them flat on their sides.)

MAKE THE PÉRIGUEUX SAUCE

If omitting the périgueux sauce, pour the meat juices into a gravy pitcher to serve with the beef. To make the sauce, pour them into a small saucepan, add the demi-glace, bring to a boil, and reduce to about ⅓ cup. Add the port or Madeira and reduce it to about 1¾ cups. Remove the sauce from the heat and whisk in the butter 1 tablespoon at a time. Add the optional black truffle.

NOTE

Leftover Beef Wellington is quite possibly even more delicious than the first time around because the pastry becomes crisper than it was initially. After slicing the leftover Wellington, carefully remove the pastry, with the crêpe layer attached to it, from each slice and place on a baking sheet. Bake it in a preheated 425°F. oven for about 10 minutes. If desired, warm the insides by placing each slice on its plate in the microwave for 1 minute on medium. Rearrange the pastry around each slice of filling. This "recomposition" is easy to accomplish, looks great, and tastes fantastic. For a simpler method that is also delicious but results in less crisp pastry, reheat the whole leftover Wellington from frozen in a preheated 350°F. oven for about 30 minutes or until a skewer inserted in the center feels warm.

UNDERSTANDING

Broiling the meat is the most effective way to seal in the juices. Cooling the meat on a rack results in even and rapid cooling.

WHOLE WHEAT CROISSANTS

I tasted my first croissant in Paris when I was sixteen, on the way to Italy for The Experiment in International Living. (The Experiment, which originated in Putney, Vermont, was created to give young Americans the opportunity to live with a family in another country for the summer.) This first croissant was not from a fine bakery and nothing to rave about, but one of my fellow "experimenters" had a delightfully elegant Russian émigré aunt who insisted we taste a *real* croissant. She gave us each one to eat on the train to Italy, and it is no exaggeration to say that I was transported. The softness and crispness and buttery perfume filled my entire mouth with such repletion, it might well have been the beginning of my lifelong pursuit of such culinary moments.

Years later, I tasted an even better croissant in Montreal, Canada. The croissants were part whole wheat. Prior to this, I had only experienced the heaviness that whole wheat produced in pastry, but the texture of these croissants was uncompromised, while the flavor added a new dimension of wheatiness. It became my goal to reproduce this croissant, but I did not think that it would be possible to do at home without commercial equipment. To my surprise, I had to eat my words. These croissants are crisp, light, tender, and delicious. The secret ingredient is reduced-bran whole wheat flour. It offers a sweet, slightly nutty flavor and beautiful golden color without the bitterness or heaviness of texture of regular whole wheat flour. If you prefer a traditional croissant, it's a simple matter to replace the whole wheat flour with an equal volume of unbleached flour.

Croissant dough is essentially puff pastry with a little extra liquid and the addition of yeast. A croissant, for me, remains the most delicious way to enjoy the pure flavor of butter I know. Put *nothing* on these but your mouth!

EQUIPMENT
Two large baking sheets or half-size sheet pans, lined with parchment*

---

*Plus, if possible, two 18- by 2-inch-deep sheet pans, to be used as a proofing box.

OVEN TEMPERATURE: 425°F., THEN 400°F. •   MAKES: ABOUT 27 OUNCES/765 GRAMS)
BAKING TIME: 25 MINUTES   DOUGH; SIXTEEN TO EIGHTEEN 5- BY 3- BY
                                1½-INCH-HIGH CROISSANTS

INGREDIENTS	MEASURE	WEIGHT	
	VOLUME	OUNCES	GRAMS
milk, lukewarm	¾ liquid cup	approx. 6.5 ounces	182 grams
sugar	2 tablespoons	approx. 0.75 ounce	25 grams
SAF-Instant yeast (see page 653) or compressed fresh yeast or active dry yeast (not rapid-rise)	1½ teaspoons 2 teaspoons, packed ½ tablespoon	• 0.5 ounce •	5.3 grams 11 grams 4.5 grams
King Arthur Green Mountain Gold (reduced-bran) flour or an extra ½ cup of unbleached all-purpose flour (a total of 9.3 ounces/266 grams)	½ cup + extra for rolling	3.2 ounces	91 grams
King Arthur unbleached all-purpose flour or national-brand bread flour	1½ cups	7 ounces	200 grams
salt	1 teaspoon	scant 0.25 ounces	6 grams
unsalted butter, preferably Plugrá or French butter	18 tablespoons	9 ounces	255 grams
Glaze 1 large egg beaten with 1 tablespoon of water*	•	•	•

*This makes ¼ cup; you will actually need only 1 tablespoon. The remainder can be refrigerated for a few days or frozen for up to 3 months.

To proof the yeast (if using fresh or active dry), in a small bowl, combine 2 tablespoons of the milk (ideally, a tepid 100°F. if using fresh yeast, a little warmer, 110°F., if using dry), ½ teaspoon of the sugar, and the yeast. If using fresh yeast, crumble it slightly as you add it. Set the mixture aside in a draft-free spot for 10 to 20 minutes. By this time the mixture should be full of bubbles. (If not, the yeast is too old to be useful and you must start again with newer yeast.)

In a food processor with the metal blade, process the whole wheat flour for about 5 minutes to break up the bran and germ. Add the unbleached flour and pulse to blend. Remove 1 tablespoon and set aside. Add the remaining sugar, salt, and yeast mixture to the flour and pulse to blend.

Transfer this mixture to the bowl of a heavy-duty mixer with the dough hook. Add the remaining milk and mix, starting on low speed, until the dry ingredients are moistened. Raise the speed to medium and beat for 4 minutes. The dough will be silky smooth and have cleaned the sides of the bowl, but it will stick to the bottom. Lightly oil a medium bowl and, with an oiled spatula, scrape the dough into it. Turn it over to oil the top, cover it with plastic wrap, and allow it to sit at room temperature for 30 minutes.

Using the oiled spatula, gently fold the dough over itself to deflate it slightly and refrigerate it for a minimum of 2 hours and a maximum of overnight.

Place the reserved 1 tablespoon of the flour mixture on a sheet of plastic wrap and put the butter on top of it. Wrap the plastic wrap loosely around it. Pound the butter lightly with a rolling pin to flatten and soften it, then knead it together with the flour, using the plastic wrap and your knuckles to avoid touching the butter directly. Work quickly and, as soon as flour is incorporated, shape it into a 5-inch square (no thicker than ¾ inch). At this point, the butter should be cool but workable, 60°F. Use it at once or keep it cool. The butter must not be colder than 60°F. when rolled into the pastry, or it will break through the dough and not be evenly distributed. (A cool cellar, particularly a wine cellar, is an ideal place to maintain this temperature. Alternatively, refrigerate it but allow it to soften slightly before using it. The butter should be cool but malleable.)

On a well-floured surface, roll out the dough to an 8-inch square. Place the butter square diagonally in the center of the dough square and, with the dull side of a knife, lightly mark the dough at the edges of the butter. Remove the butter and roll each marked corner of the dough into a flap. The dough will be slightly elastic. Moisten these flaps lightly with water, replace the butter on the dough, and wrap it securely, stretching the flaps slightly to reach across the dough package. Refrigerate it for 30 minutes (not longer).

On a well-floured surface, keeping the dough seam side up and lightly floured, gently roll the dough package into a long rectangle 7 inches by 16 inches. Brush off all the flour from the surface of the dough and fold it into thirds as you would fold a business letter. This is the first "turn." Cover the dough with plastic wrap and refrigerate it for at least 20 and up to 40 minutes. (Mark the turns on a slip of paper or parchment, as the fingertip impressions in the dough used for puff pastry would disappear in this dough as it rises.)

Before each subsequent turn, position the dough so that the closed side is facing to your left. Clean the work surface, reflour it, and press down on the edges of the dough with the rolling pin to help keep them straight. (The upper part tends to lengthen faster than the bottom.) Roll and fold the dough a second time exactly the same way, but turn it over occasionally to keep the seams and edges even. Be sure to roll into all four corners of the dough and use a pastry scraper to even the edges. Do a total of 4 turns, resting the dough in the refrigerator for 20 to 40 minutes between each. Refrigerate the dough for at least 2 hours before rolling it.

SHAPE THE CROISSANTS

Remove the dough from the refrigerator. Allow it to sit for 15 minutes.

On a floured counter, roll the dough to a rectangle 12 to 14 inches by 22 to 24 inches. Brush off all the flour. Fold over the dough lengthwise so that it is 6 to 7 inches by 20 to 22 inches. Using a pizza wheel or sharp knife, trim one end on an angle, cutting through the two layers, and then cut the dough into 8 or 9 triangles with 4-inch bases. (Figure 1) Reserve the trimmings from either end. Make a ½-inch notch at the center of each base. Open up the two layers of dough of each folded triangle and cut each piece in half at the base to form 2 triangles. (Figure 2) Shape the croissants one at a time, keeping the rest of the triangles covered with plastic wrap. Use the scraps to make 16 to 18 balls the size of green grapes (about 4 grams each); scissors work best to cut the dough for the balls.* Keep the balls covered with plastic wrap too. Gently stretch a triangle of dough to about 9 inches long—first stretch the base gently, but firmly to widen it, then, holding the base in your left hand, use your thumb and first two fingers of your right hand to work down the length, elongating it). (Figure 3)

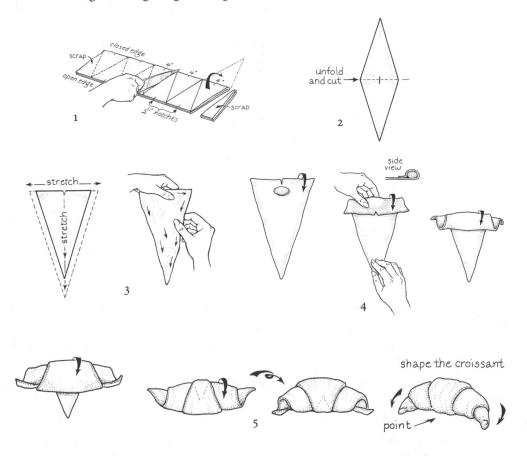

*If desired, a tablespoon of Remonce (page 510) per croissant can be substituted for the dough balls for moistness and flavor.

Place the triangle on the counter with the point toward you. Shape one of the round scraps into a 1¼-inch-long football and place it at the base of the triangle. Roll the base over the scrap of dough to cover it by about ½ inch and continue rolling the dough with your left hand while keeping the triangle stretched with your right hand. (Figure 4) Place it point side down on a lined baking sheet and curve the ends so that they turn in on the side of the croissant opposite the point. (Figure 5) Keep the finished croissants covered with plastic wrap while you shape the remainder, placing 8 or 9 evenly spaced on each pan so there will be room for them to expand to the finished size of 5 inches by 3 inches.

When all the croissants are formed, brush them with the egg glaze. If you have two 2-inch-deep by 18-inch sheet pans, invert them over the croissants.* Alternatively, cover them lightly with plastic wrap that has been sprayed with nonstick vegetable spray and set the sheet pans aside in a warm spot. Allow the croissants to rise for about 2 hours.† They should double in size and be very light to the touch.

Preheat the oven to 425°F. at least 20 minutes before baking. Set an oven rack on the lowest level before preheating.

Five minutes ahead, place a pan with about 1 inch of boiling water on a rack toward the bottom of the oven. (To prevent a ring from forming if using a metal pan, add a pinch of cream of tartar to the water.)

Place the croissants in the oven and turn the temperature down to 400°F. Bake for 25 minutes or until golden brown (210°F.). After the first 10 minutes, turn around and reverse the position of the two sheets. The texture will still be slightly doughy inside but while cooling, the croissants will continue to cook through perfectly.

Remove the croissants to a rack and cool for 20 to 30 minutes. They are best eaten warm, when the outside is crisp and light and the center is soft and tender, or within 3 hours of baking.

STORE

Unbaked croissant dough, refrigerated, up to 2 days; frozen, up to 3 months. Use 25 percent more yeast if planning to freeze the dough, as some yeast will die during freezing. Baked croissants, room temperature, up to 1 day; frozen, several months. Reheat them in a preheated 300°F. oven for 5 minutes (8 minutes if frozen).

---

*To create an ideal environment similar to a proofing box, place one or two small custard cups, filled with very hot water, on the baking sheet, not too close to the dough. Cover with the inverted pan and lay a heating pad set to low or medium on top of it. (My heating pad on medium produces a temperature of 82° to 86°F. inside the pan.) If you have a proofing box, set it to 88° to 90°F.

†At 70°F., they will take 3 to 4 hours.

POINTERS FOR SUCCESS

∾ A *tutove* (ridged) rolling pin can be used for added ease in rolling up until the last 2 turns, after which the dough layer becomes too thin and the butter could break through.

∾ Do the turns after 20 minutes but no more than 40 minutes of refrigerating; if chilled further, the outside of the dough will soften while the center remains firm, so the layering is not as even. Once all the turns have been completed, the butter is evenly dispersed in thin sheets, so the dough stays evenly pliant.

∾ Brush off all flour when rolling and keep the unused dough covered to avoid crusting, which would cause separation of the rolled layers during baking. The inside of the baked croissant should be numerous little open cells with no visible striations.

∾ If the room is cool (68°F. or under), it is desirable to leave the rolled dough covered on the counter for 15 to 30 minutes to relax before the final shaping.

∾ Although a tightly rolled croissant with seven distinct sections is attractive, I find that the texture is lighter and better they are if not rolled too tightly, especially when using part whole wheat flour in the dough.

∾ To get a more pronounced curve, after proofing and gently egg glazing again, so your fingers won't stick to the dough, very gently recurve the two ends inward.

UNDERSTANDING

My friend Shirley Corriher is a passionate defender of the moist dough technique. She assured me that making this dough exceptionally moist would render it less resistant to rolling and would produce lighter croissants because of the steam released in the oven. I am now a believer! She also made the excellent suggestion of processing the whole wheat flour to reduce further the size of the bran and germ so that it would not cut through the gluten strands of the dough.

I am also indebted to Dorie Greenspan and Esther McManus for the brilliant idea of using the dough scraps to create the higher center for a lovely shape.

Plugrá butter or French butters have less water than other butters, so they stay pliant even when cold.

King Arthur's unbleached flour and supermarket bread flours have a similar protein content, just enough to provide enough gluten to support a high rise yet make a tender dough. Flour with higher protein would result in a dough with a chewy texture; with less protein, it would be less light and airy.

Notching the base of the triangle helps it to spread sideways and over the extra little ball of dough, which also adds to its attractive shape.

Although it may seem as if a lot of extra flour is added during rolling out the dough, actually, it is only about ½ ounce more.

CHOCOLATE CROISSANTS
(Pain au Chocolat)

One of the great joys of working with the Bernachons in Lyon, France, when I was translating their book *A Passion for Chocolate,* was the pleasure of eating freshly baked *pain au chocolat* every day for breakfast. These rectangles of croissant dough wrapped around small rectangles of bittersweet chocolate are most delicious when eaten still warm from the oven, because the chocolate inside is still slightly melted. Of course they can be reheated to achieve this same effect.

OVEN TEMPERATURE: 425°F., THEN 400°F. •
BAKING TIME: 25 MINUTES

MAKES: TWELVE 4- BY 3-INCH
PAINS AU CHOCOLAT

INGREDIENTS	MEASURE	WEIGHT	
	VOLUME	OUNCES	GRAMS
Croissant Dough (page 477), prepared with all unbleached all-purpose flour, preferably King Arthur		27 ounces	765 grams
bittersweet chocolate	two 3-ounce bars	6 ounces	170 grams
Glaze 1 large egg beaten with 1 tablespoon water*	•	•	•

*This makes ¼ cup; you will only actually need 1 tablespoon. The remainder can be refrigerated for a few days or frozen for up to 3 months.

EQUIPMENT
Two large baking sheets or half-size sheet pans, lined with parchment*

Make the dough (page 477).

SHAPE THE PAIN AU CHOCOLAT
Remove the dough from the refrigerator. Let sit for 15 minutes. Meanwhile, with a sharp knife, cut the chocolate bars along each vertical seam so that each bar yields 6 little bars. (3-ounce European chocolate bars are the ideal size and shape.)

On a floured counter, roll the dough to a 6- by 24-inch rectangle. Using a pizza wheel or sharp knife, cut the dough lengthwise in half to make 2 rectangles 24 inches long by 3 inches wide. Cut each rectangle crosswise into 4-inch pieces. You will now have twelve 4- by 3-inch rectangles of dough. Brush off all the flour.

*Plus, if possible, two 18- by 2-inch-deep sheet pans, to be used as a proofing box.

Shape the *pains* one at a time, keeping the rest of the dough covered with plastic wrap. Lay a piece of chocolate on a piece of dough so that the length of the chocolate is parallel to a long side of the dough and, starting from that long side, roll up the dough so that it encloses the chocolate. Moisten the end of the dough with a bit of water to seal, and place the *pain* seam side down on a lined baking sheet. As you form the remaining *pains*, place them at least 2 inches apart on the baking sheets (6 on each sheet).

When all the *pains* are formed, brush them with the egg glaze. If you have 2-inch-deep by 18-inch sheet pans, invert them over the dough.* Alternatively, cover them lightly with plastic wrap that has been sprayed with nonstick vegetable shortening and set the sheet pan(s) aside in a warm spot. Allow the *pains* to rise for about 2 hours.† The *pains* should double in size and be very light in texture.

Preheat the oven to 425°F. at least 20 minutes before baking. Set an oven rack on the lowest level before preheating.

Five minutes ahead, place a pan with about 1 inch of boiling water in on a rack toward the bottom of the oven. (To prevent a ring from forming if using a metal pan, add a pinch of cream of tartar to the water.)

Place the *pains* in the oven and turn the temperature down to 400°F. Bake for 25 minutes or until golden brown (210°F.). After the first 10 minutes, turn around and reverse the position of the two sheets.

Remove the *pains* to a rack and cool for 20 to 30 minutes. They are best eaten warm, when the outside is crisp and light, the center is soft and tender, and the chocolate still soft, or within 3 hours after baking.

STORE

Unbaked *pains*, refrigerated, up to 2 days; frozen, up to 3 months. Use 25 percent more yeast if planning to freeze them, as some yeast will die during freezing. Baked *pains*, room temperature, up to 1 day; frozen, several months. Reheat them in a preheated 300°F. oven for 5 minutes (8 minutes if frozen).

---

*To create an ideal environment similar to a proofing box, place one or two small custard cups, filled with very hot water, on the baking sheet, not too close to the dough. Cover with the inverted pan and lay a heating pad set to low or medium on top of it. (My heating pad on medium produces a temperature of 82° to 86°F. inside the pan.) If you have a proofing box, set it to 88° to 90°F.

†At 70°F., they will take 3 to 4 hours.

DANISH PASTRY

uthentic Danish pastry is crisp, tender, and slightly flaky. American-style Danish is far more sweet and cakey in texture.

Danish pastry is truly one of the world's greatest pastries, but chances are you'll never know just how extraordinary it can be if you don't make it yourself. Even in Denmark, where it is known as *Wienerbrod* (Viennese bread), because of the city of its origin, it is rare to encounter Danish pastry that has been made with butter rather than margarine, and, of course, that makes an enormous difference in flavor. Danish is a true pastry, falling somewhere between croissant and brioche. The dough is spread with Remonce (page 510), made of almond paste, sugar, butter, and vanilla. The fillings and toppings consist of fruit jams such as apricot or prune, preserves such as sour cherry or blueberry, brandied raisins, lightly sweetened cream cheese, nuts, and sugar glazes. But it is the different shapes, from pretzel to bear claw, that give them drama.

My skills with Danish pastry making come from having studied with two masters who got their training in two different countries: Denmark and Switzerland. I spent several days in the kitchen of the renowned Konditerei La Glace in Copenhagen, working with chef Arne Plough-Jacobsen, who has been in charge of Danish production there for over forty years. I have also incorporated many valuable techniques learned from Dieter Schorner, chairman of Pastry Art at the French Culinary Institute.

Danish dough is easy to make and keeps well in the freezer for several weeks. When it's defrosted, it is a quick and enjoyable process to fill, shape, and bake it. This makes it practical as a special treat around the holidays. The dough can be made several weeks ahead and defrosted the night before. Children can participate in the shaping and decorating, and everyone can enjoy the pastries for a memorable holiday breakfast.

I also like to freeze some of the baked Danish for future breakfasts. They take only about eight minutes in a 300°F. oven to become warm and crisp.

AUTHENTIC DANISH PASTRY DOUGH
(*Master Recipe*)

This is the dough that is used for every Danish variation. It produces a baked Danish that has a crisp outer crust and a tender slightly layered interior.

The most important factor for making perfect Danish is the same as for any dough, such as puff pastry and croissant, into which the butter is layered. The butter must be cold but malleable: too cold, and it breaks through the dough; too soft, and it melts into the flour, destroying the carefully achieved layering. I made my first Danish dough, however, in a fairly warm room (73°F.) and it still had wonderful layering. If you work quickly and have everything cold, it's fine to try this dough at any time of year; but if you prefer to work at a more relaxed pace, wait until cool weather!

The sugar glaze, which is simply powdered sugar, water, and lemon juice or vanilla, is brushed on the baked Danish, hot from the oven, to form a very fine coating on the surface. It requires no heating, does not get absorbed by the dough, and remains transparent and shiny.

OVEN TEMPERATURE: 400°F., THEN 375°F. •
BAKING TIME: 18 MINUTES   **MAKES: 26.7 OUNCES/762 GRAMS DOUGH**

INGREDIENTS	MEASURE	WEIGHT	
	VOLUME	OUNCES	GRAMS
milk	⅔ liquid cup	5.6 ounces	160 grams
sugar	2 tablespoons	1 ounce	25 grams
SAF-Instant yeast (page 653) or compressed fresh yeast or active dry yeast (not rapid-rise)	1½ teaspoons 2 teaspoons, packed 1½ teaspoons	• 0.5 ounce •	5.3 grams 11 grams 4.5 grams
King Arthur unbleached flour or national-brand bread flour	2¼ cups, divided	10.5 ounces	300 grams
salt	½ teaspoon	•	•
ground cardamom*	⅛ teaspoon	•	•
1 large egg	approx. 3 tablespoons	1.75 ounces (weighed without the shell)	50 grams
unsalted butter, preferably Plugrá or French butter	18 tablespoons (soften 1 tablespoon)	9 ounces	255 grams

*Cardamom is most aromatic when freshly ground. I use a mortar and pestle; a spice or coffee mill also works well.

EQUIPMENT

Two half-size sheet pans, lined with parchment*

To proof the yeast, if using fresh or active dry, in a small bowl, combine 2 table-spoons of the milk (ideally a tepid 100°F. if using fresh yeast, a little warmer, 110°F., if using dry), ½ teaspoon of the sugar, and the yeast. If using fresh yeast, crumble it slightly as you add it. Set the mixture aside in a draft-free spot for 10 to 20 minutes. By this time, the mixture should be full of bubbles. (If not, the yeast is too old to be useful and you must start again with newer yeast.)

In the bowl of a heavy-duty mixer, place all but 1 tablespoon of the flour, the remaining sugar, salt, yeast (or yeast mixture), and cardamom. Add the remaining milk, the egg, and the 1 tablespoon of softened butter and, with the dough hook, mix, starting on low speed, until the dry ingredients are moistened. Continuing on low speed, beat for 4 minutes. The dough will be silky smooth and have cleaned the sides of the bowl, but it will stick to the bottom and be very soft. Lightly oil a medium bowl and, with an oiled spatula, scrape the dough into it. Turn it over to oil the top; cover it with plastic wrap and allow it to sit at room temperature for 30 minutes.

Using the oiled spatula, gently fold the dough to deflate it slightly and refrigerate it for at least 2 and up to 8 hours.

Place the remaining 1 tablespoon of flour on a large sheet of plastic wrap and place the remaining 17 tablespoons of butter on top. Wrap it loosely with the plastic wrap. Pound the butter lightly with the rolling pin to flatten and soften it, then knead it together with the flour, using the plastic wrap and your knuckles to avoid touching the butter directly. Work quickly and, as soon as flour is incorporated, shape it into a 5-inch square (no thicker than ¾ inch). At this point, the butter should be cool but workable, 60°F. Use it at once, or keep it cool. The butter must not be colder than 60°F. when rolled into pastry, or it will break through the dough and not distribute evenly.†

On a well-floured surface, roll out the dough to an 8-inch square. Place the butter square diagonally in the center of the dough square and lightly mark the dough at the edges of the butter with the dull side of a knife. Remove the butter and roll each marked corner of the dough into a flap. The dough will be slightly elastic. Moisten these flaps lightly with water, replace the butter on the dough, and wrap it securely, stretching the flaps slightly to reach across the dough package. Refrigerate it for 30 minutes (not longer).

On a well-floured surface, keeping the dough seam side up and lightly floured, gently roll the dough package into a long rectangle 7 inches by 16 inches. Brush off all the flour from the surface of the dough and fold it into thirds as you would fold a business letter. This is the first "turn." Cover the dough with plastic wrap and

---

*Plus, if possible, two 18- by 2-inch-deep sheet pans to be used as a proofing box.

†A cool cellar, particularly a wine cellar, is an ideal place to maintain this temperature. Alternatively, refrigerate it but allow it to soften slightly before using it. The butter should be cool but malleable.

refrigerate it for at least 20 minutes and up to 40 minutes between each turn. (Mark the turns on a slip of paper or parchment, as the fingertip impressions in the dough used for puff pastry would disappear in this dough as it rises.)

Before each subsequent turn, position the dough so that the closed side faces your left. Clean the work surface, reflour it, and then press down the edges of the dough with the rolling pin to help keep them straight. (The upper part tends to slide more than the bottom.) Roll and fold the dough a second time exactly the same way, but turn the dough over occasionally to keep the seams and edges even. Be sure to roll into all four corners of the dough and use a pastry scraper to even the edges. Do a total of 3 turns, resting the dough for 20 to 40 minutes between each. Refrigerate the dough for at least 2 hours before rolling it. (See illustrations, page 419.)

SHAPE THE DANISH

Remove the dough from the refrigerator and cut it in half. Work with half the dough at a time, refrigerating the other half. Allow the dough to sit for 15 minutes before rolling it. On a floured counter, roll the dough to a rectangle about 10 inches by 12 inches. Slip it onto a cookie sheet, cover it lightly, and refrigerate it for 30 minutes to relax the dough.

Return the rolled-out dough to the floured counter, flour the top, and roll it to about 12 inches wide and 12 to 13 inches long. It will be about ⅛ inch thick. Use a bench scraper or ruler to keep the sides straight; if necessary, use a pizza cutter or sharp knife to trim it so that the sides are even. Brush off all excess flour. Spread the dough with a thin layer of filling, then proceed as for the specific recipe, shaping it before allowing it to rise.

Repeat this process with the remaining dough (or store the second piece of dough in the refrigerator for up to 2 days or freeze for up to 3 months).

PROOF THE DANISH

If you have 2-inch-deep 18-inch sheet pans, invert them over the dough. To create an ideal environment similar to a proofing box, place one or two small custard cups, filled with very hot water, on each baking sheet, not too close to the dough, cover with the inverted pan, and lay a heating pad set to low or medium on top of it. (My heating pad on medium produces a temperature of 82° to 86°F. inside the pan.) If you have a proofing box, set it to 88° to 90°F. Alternatively, place the dough on the sheet pans, cover lightly with plastic wrap that has been sprayed with nonstick vegetable spray, and set the sheet pans aside in a warm spot. Allow the Danish to rise for about 2 hours. The dough should double in size and be very light to the touch. (If using a proof box with moisture, the dough will be tacky enough to stick to your fingers.)

Preheat the oven to 400°F. at least 20 minutes before baking. Set an oven rack at the middle level before preheating.

BAKE THE DANISH

Five minutes ahead, place a pan with about 1 inch of boiling water in the lower part of the oven. (To prevent a ring from forming if using a metal pan, add a pinch of cream of tartar to the water.) Place the Danish in the oven, lower the temperature to 375°F., and bake for 18 to 20 minutes (after 10 minutes, turn and reverse the positions of the two sheets) or until golden brown (210°F.). The texture will still be slightly doughy inside but while cooling will continue to cook through perfectly.

EGG GLAZE OR SUGAR GLAZE

When topping Danish with nuts or seeds, a thin egg-and-water glaze is brushed on before baking to make them adhere. Otherwise, a sugar glaze made of powdered sugar, water and lemon juice is applied immediately after baking for a beautiful classic sheen.

If using the sugar glaze, prepare it while the Danish bake, as it needs to be applied while the Danish are very hot. The glaze should be the consistency of egg white. If necessary, add a bit more sugar or water.

When the Danish are baked, remove them to a rack and brush them immediately with the sugar glaze, if using. Cool for 20 to 30 minutes. Danish are best eaten warm, when the outside is crisp and light and the center soft and tender, or within 3 hours of baking. Baked Danish can be reheated in a preheated 300°F. oven for 5 minutes (8 minutes if frozen). Most people do not recommend freezing baked Danish, but I find that though not as perfect reheated, they are still far more delicious than any commercial product.

STORE

Unbaked Danish dough, either plain or filled, refrigerated, up to 2 days; frozen, up to 3 months. Use 25 percent more yeast if planning to freeze it, as some will die during freezing. If the dough is filled, it is best to thaw it refrigerated, so it thaws evenly before the final rise. Unfilled, it can be thawed either refrigerated (8 to 12 hours) or at room temperature until malleable enough to roll. Once thawed, it should be used within 12 hours.

POINTERS FOR SUCCESS

∿ Make the turns after 20 minutes but no more than 40 minutes of refrigerating. If chilled further, the outside of the dough will soften while the center remains firm, so layering is not as even. Once all the turns have been completed, the butter is evenly dispersed in thin sheets so the dough stays evenly pliant.

∿ Brush off all flour when rolling and keep unused dough covered to avoid crusting. This prevents separation of the rolled layers during baking.

∿ Leftover scraps of pastry can be placed on top of each other and rerolled.

∿ When adding coarsely chopped nuts, use walnuts, pecans, or hazelnuts—but not almonds, as they are sharp and would pierce the dough.

∽ If the room is cool (68°F. or under), it is desirable to leave the rolled-out dough covered on the counter for 15 to 30 minutes to relax before the final shaping.

∽ It is best to cover the dough with the inverted 2-inch-deep pans so that nothing touches the surface. (When my friend Angelica Pulvirenti had a small restaurant and needed to utilize every available space, she used the salamander [broiler]over her range as a proof box by putting a tray of hot water in the drip pan and setting the sheet of Danish on the rack above it. The partially enclosed space trapped the rising moisture and heat.)

∽ It is important to allow the dough a full proofing as described above. If it has not risen enough, some of the butter will leak out during baking. If it has risen too much, the layers will collapse and be heavier and more cakey.

UNDERSTANDING

Plugrá butter or French-style butters have less water then other butters, so they stay pliant even when cold.

King Arthur's unbleached flour and supermarket bread flours have a similar protein content, sufficient to provide enough gluten to support a high rise yet produce tender dough. Flour with higher protein would result in a dough with chewy texture; with less protein, it would be less light and airy.

An egg wash is usually unnecessary on Danish pastries because the transparent glaze after baking gives them a beautiful shiny surface.

THE DANISH BRAID

This filled and braided strip of Danish dough is as stunningly beautiful to behold as it is delicious to taste. The filling, a combination of bittersweet chocolate, tart raspberry, and almonds, is an eternal favorite. Encased in Danish dough, it is nothing short of fantastic. The strip can also be filled with remonce (almond filling), or a combination of remonce and pastry cream, or cream cheese filling and preserves. If made double in size, it can be formed into an impressive wreath.

EQUIPMENT

A 10- by 15-inch cookie sheet or half-size sheet pan, lined with parchment*

Make the dough (see page 486).

---

*Plus, if possible, an 18- by 2-inch deep sheet pan, to be used as a proofing box.

OVEN TEMPERATURE: 400°F., THEN 375°F. •   MAKES: A 14- BY 6½- BY
BAKING TIME: 25 TO 30 MINUTES   1½-INCH-HIGH PASTRY; SERVES: 12

INGREDIENTS	MEASURE	WEIGHT	
	VOLUME	OUNCES	GRAMS
½ recipe Danish Pastry Dough (page 486)		13.3 ounces	381 grams
Raspberry Filling frozen raspberries, with no added sugar	(1 full cup) 3 cups (a 12-ounce bag)	• 12 ounces	• 340 grams
sugar	½ cup, divided	3.5 ounces	100 grams
sliced blanched almonds	1 cup	3 ounces	85 grams
Chocolate Butter Filling bittersweet chocolate	⅔ of a 3-ounce bar	2 ounces	56 grams
unsalted butter, softened	2 teaspoons	0.3 ounce	10 grams
egg wash: 1 large egg beaten with 2 tablespoons of water	approx. 3 tablespoons (only about 1 teaspoon is needed)	2.7 ounces	79 grams
sliced unblanched almonds	¼ cup	0.75 ounce	21 grams

MAKE THE RASPBERRY FILLING

At least 4 hours before making the filling, in a strainer suspended over a deep bowl, thaw the raspberries completely. This will take several hours. (To speed thawing, place in an oven with a pilot light.)

Press on the berries to force out all the juice. There should be about ½ cup of juice. In a small saucepan (or a greased 2-cup heatproof glass measure or bowl if using a microwave on high power, about 8 minutes), boil the juice until it is reduced to 2 tablespoons. Pour it into a lightly oiled heatproof cup.

Purée the raspberries and strain them through a food mill fitted with a fine disc; or use a fine strainer to remove all the seeds. You should have ½ liquid cup of purée. Stir in the reduced raspberry syrup. There should be a scant ⅔ cup of raspberry purée (4.3 ounces/123 grams). (If you have less, simply add less sugar; if more, then add more sugar. The correct amount of sugar is three quarters the volume of the purée—or to taste.) Reserve 2 tablespoons of the sugar and stir the remainder into the purée until it dissolves.

In a food processor with the metal blade, process the almonds and the reserved sugar until the almonds are very finely ground. Stir this mixture into the raspberry purée until well blended and refrigerate for at least 1 hour and as long as overnight. (It spreads more easily when thickened slightly from chilling.)

MAKE THE CHOCOLATE BUTTER FILLING

In the microwave, stirring every 20 seconds, or a double boiler set over very hot, not simmering, water, stirring often, melt the chocolate and butter together. Remove from the heat and allow to cool to room temperature.

SHAPE THE BRAID

Remove the dough from the refrigerator and allow it to sit for 15 minutes. Flour it lightly and set it on a floured piece of parchment at least 16 inches long by 12 inches wide. Roll the dough to a rectangle 14 inches by 10 inches. It will be about ⅛ inch thick. Brush off all the excess flour and slip the dough on the parchment onto a baking sheet.

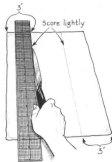

With the back of a knife, mark a 4-inch-wide rectangle in the dough by running the knife lightly from the top to bottom of the dough 3 inches in from either 14-inch side. Starting 1 inch from the top and going to 1 inch from the bottom, spread the cooled chocolate mixture evenly over this 4-inch-wide rectangle. Set it in the freezer for 5 to 15 minutes to set the chocolate.

Spread the reserved raspberry mixture evenly on top of the chocolate.

With a sharp knife, cut through the 3-inch side margins of dough on the diagonal at 1-inch intervals. Cut off the excess dough from the top and bottom (see illustrations). Turn the 1-inch-top and bottom borders over the filling. Fold the 1-inch strips of dough over the filling at an angle, alternating from right to left and sealing them where they overlap in the middle by brushing the ends of the dough with a little water and pressing it gently. Don't be concerned if some of the raspberry filling shows through, as all the slits will open a little during baking.

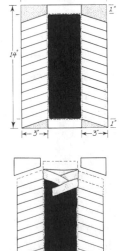

Brush the braid with the egg wash, reserving any leftover, and scatter the sliced almonds down the center. (The braid will now measure 5 inches by 12 inches by 1 inch high.) If you have a 2-inch-deep 18-inch sheet pan, invert it over the dough. Or, cover the dough lightly with plastic wrap that has been sprayed with nonstick vegetable spray and set the sheet pan aside in a warm spot. Allow it to rise for about 2 hours. The braid should be about 1½ inches high and very light to the touch.

Preheat the oven to 400°F. at least 20 minutes before baking. Set an oven rack at the middle level before preheating.

Five minutes ahead, place a pan with about 1 inch of boiling water in the lower part of the oven. (To prevent a ring from forming if using a metal pan, add a pinch of cream of tartar to the water.) Place the braid in the oven, lower the temperature to 375°F., and bake for 25 to 30 minutes or until golden brown (200° to 210°F.). After 20 minutes, brush any paler areas in the center with the reserved egg wash. Remove the baking sheet to a rack and cool for 20 to 30 minutes.

Using a serrated or sharp knife, cut into 1-inch-wide strips. The braid is best eaten warm, while the outside is crisp and light and the center soft and tender, or within 3 hours of baking.

STORE

Room temperature, up to 2 days; frozen, up to 3 months. The baked braid can be reheated in a preheated 300°F. oven for 5 minutes (10 minutes if frozen).

POINTERS FOR SUCCESS

∿ It is best to cover the dough with the inverted 2-inch-deep pan so that nothing touches the surface.

UNDERSTANDING

The water in the 2 teaspoons of butter added to the chocolate makes it just firm enough to spread perfectly onto the dough.

DANISH ENVELOPES
(*Spandau*)

Spandau is the Danish word for envelope. The word serves as a good description for these pastries, because the dough is folded like an envelope over the filling. There are several ways to fold the dough in addition to the familiar two corners meeting in the center with filling showing at either end. Some of the shapes look elaborate, but they are all very easy to create.

I find these four-corner envelopes to be the prettiest of all. They start off as square packages with four little oval openings containing preserves at each corner, and during baking, they blossom open like flowers to reveal more of the filling.

Each envelope shape creates a different texture in the dough.

EQUIPMENT

A large baking sheet or half-size sheet pan, lined with parchment*; 2 pastry bags or reclosable freezer bags; a number 6 (½-inch) plain round pastry tube; and a number 5 (⅛-inch) plain round decorating tube and coupler

---

* Plus, if possible, an 18- by 2-inch-deep sheet pan to be used as a proofing box.

OVEN TEMPERATURE: 400°F., THEN 375°F. •
BAKING TIME: 18 TO 20 MINUTES   MAKES: NINE 4-INCH-SQUARE ENVELOPES

INGREDIENTS	MEASURE	WEIGHT	
	VOLUME	OUNCES	GRAMS
½ recipe Danish Pastry Dough (page 486)		13.3 ounces	381 grams
Filling 1 recipe Remonce (page 510)	14 tablespoons	8 ounces	227 grams
egg wash: 1 large egg beaten with 2 tablespoons of water	approx. 3 tablespoons (only about 2 teaspoons are needed)	2.75 ounces	79 grams
sliced unblanched almonds	3 tablespoons	0.5 ounce	16 grams
Transparent Sugar Glaze powdered sugar	(approx. 2 tablespoons) ¼ cup	 1 ounce	 30 grams
water	1½ teaspoons	•	•
freshly squeezed lemon juice	1 teaspoon	•	•
optional: 1 recipe Sugar Glaze for Danish (page 509)	•	•	•

Make the dough (see page 486).

SHAPE THE ENVELOPES

Remove the dough from the refrigerator and allow it to sit for 15 minutes. On a floured counter, roll the dough to a rectangle 12 inches by 9 to 10 inches. It will be ¼ inch thick. Slip it onto a cookie sheet, cover it lightly, and refrigerate it for 30 minutes to relax the gluten.

Return the dough to the floured counter, flour the top, and roll it to a rough 12-inch square. It will be about ⅛ inch thick. Brush off all the excess flour.

Using a ruler and a sharp knife or pizza cutter, cut the dough into nine 4-inch squares. With the ½-inch pastry tube (or use a spoon), pipe a walnut-size dollop (about 1½ tablespoons) of the remonce into the center of each. (Figure 1) Bring the corners to the center so that they meet, brush each with egg wash, and press down well to make them adhere. (Figure 2) Brush the center of each

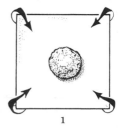

envelope with egg wash and place a few almonds on top of it. Arrange the envelopes on the baking sheet, leaving at least 1½ inches between them. (Only 8 will fit on a sheet, so the ninth one needs to bake separately on a small cookie sheet or an inverted cake pan. The envelopes can be frozen for up to 3 weeks, thawed, proofed, and baked.)

If you have a 2-inch-deep 18-inch sheet pan, invert it over the dough (see page 488). Alternatively, cover the dough lightly with plastic wrap that has been sprayed with nonstick vegetable spray and set the envelopes aside in a warm spot. Allow them to rise for about 2 hours. They should almost double and be very light to the touch.

Preheat the oven to 400°F. at least 20 minutes before baking. Set an oven rack at the middle level before preheating.

Five minutes ahead, place a pan with about 1 inch of boiling water in the lower part of the oven. (To prevent a ring from forming if using a metal pan, add a pinch of cream of tartar to the water.) Press the center of each envelope to help it adhere during baking. Place the envelopes in the oven, lower the temperature to 375°F., and bake for 18 to 20 minutes or until golden brown (200° to 210°F.).

While the envelopes are baking, prepare the sugar glaze: In a small bowl, place the powdered sugar. Whisk in the water and lemon juice. The glaze should be the consistency of egg white. If necessary, add a bit more sugar or water.

When the spandau are done, remove the baking sheet to a rack and immediately brush them with the glaze. Cool for 5 to 10 minutes.

If desired, pipe the drizzle glaze around the edges of the spandau. Danish are best eaten warm, while the outside is crisp and light and the center soft and tender, or within 3 hours of baking.

VARIATIONS

TRIANGLE TWISTS   To make this intriguing shape, fold over each dough square. (Figure 1) Starting ¾ inch from either point at the base of the triangle, cut a second smaller triangle through both layers of dough. (Figure 2) Open up the triangle to return to the square shape. (Figure 3) Two opposite corners of dough will still be attached to the outer frame of dough. Turn the dough over and brush off any excess

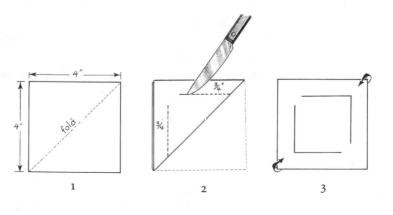

flour. Reinvert and brush the border with the egg wash. With your fingers, lift each of the two unattached edges of the dough and slip one under the other, crossing them over and pulling them out to the edge. This will cause the attached edges to cross over each other to form triangular shapes with two twisted corners. (Figure 4)

Pipe two fillings, such as remonce and pastry cream or remonce and preserves, into the center of each triangle, side by side, using about ½ teaspoon of each, and sprinkle each with about 2 teaspoons of nuts. Proceed as for the spandau. The baked triangles will be 5 inches by 4 inches by 1 inch high. (Figure 5) For very puffy triangles, roll double the amount of dough to a ¼-inch thickness.

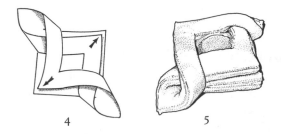

The finished pastries will be 6 inches by 4½ inches by 1½ inches high. Baking times for both will be 20 to 30 minutes.

BALLOONS   Spreading the spandau with a thin layer of remonce and baking them upside down causes them to blow up like hot air balloons, lending the dough a wonderfully soft, light texture with the denser almond filling in the center. I adore this shape. You will need only about ⅓ cup of remonce and the egg wash to seal the spandau; omit the almonds. Brush the egg wash over all four edges of each square. Spread a very thin layer of remonce (a scant 2 teaspoons) over the pastry, almost up to the egg-washed edges. Bring up the four corners to the center and pinch the seams closed. Place the spandau seam side down on the prepared baking sheet. Proceed as above, brushing them with the transparent glaze after baking. The baked balloons will be about 4 inches square by 1½ inches high.

PRUNE OR APRICOT TRIANGLES   This is the classic Danish shape you see in delis and bakeries. The luscious fillings are very easy to make. Spread about 2 tablespoons of Prune or Apricot Lekvar (page 513 or 512) to within ½ inch from the edges of each dough square (Figure 1, page 497). Dab the overlap with a little egg yolk to secure it. (Figure 2) Bring two opposite corners to the center (Figure 3), overlapping them by about ½ inch. (Figure 4) After the triangles have risen, press the centers firmly with your finger to keep them from opening during baking. (Figure 5)

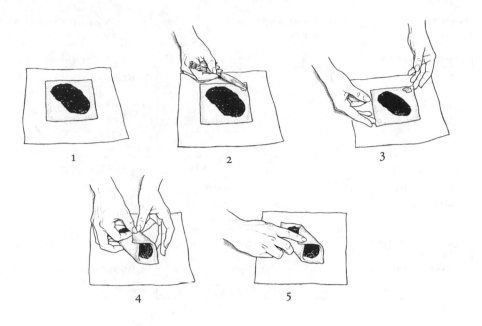

1   2   3

4   5

STORE

Room temperature, up to 2 days; frozen, up to 3 months. The baked Danish can be reheated in a preheated 300°F. oven for 5 minutes (8 minutes if frozen).

POINTERS FOR SUCCESS

∽ It is best to cover the dough with the inverted 2-inch-deep pan, so that nothing touches the surface.

BEAR CLAWS (OR COCKSCOMBS)

In Denmark, this is the most popular of all Danish pastry shapes, especially with children. The upper part of the dough is filled with the traditional remonce (almond filling) and sealed so that the lower part can be slashed and spread apart to form the claws without any of the filling leaking. Should a little leak, however, the filling puddles next to the Danish and bakes into a delicious crisp disc that can be eaten like a cookie along with the bear claw—a special treat. The tops of these Danish glisten with coarse granulated sugar and are further adorned by a sprinkling of golden sliced almonds.

OVEN TEMPERATURE: 400°F., THEN 375°F. •   MAKES: NINE 5- BY 3- BY
BAKING TIME: 18 TO 20 MINUTES   1¼-INCH-HIGH PASTRIES

INGREDIENTS	MEASURE	WEIGHT	
	VOLUME	OUNCES	GRAMS
½ recipe Danish Pastry Dough (page 486)		13.3 ounces	381 grams
½ recipe Remonce (page 510)	7 tablespoons	4 ounces	113 grams
egg wash: 1 large egg beaten with 2 tablespoons of water	approx. 3 tablespoons (only about 2 teaspoons are needed)	2.75 ounces	79 grams
pearl sugar (see page 647)	2½ tablespoons	1 ounce	30 grams
sliced unblanched almonds	½ cup	1.5 ounces	43 grams

EQUIPMENT

Two half-size sheet pans, lined with parchment*; optional: a pastry bag or freezer-weight reclosable bag and a number 6 (½-inch) plain round pastry tube

Make the dough (see page 486).

Remove the dough from the refrigerator and allow it to sit for 15 minutes. Flour it lightly. On a floured counter, roll the dough to a rectangle about 10 inches by 12 inches. Slip it onto a cookie sheet, cover it lightly, and refrigerate it for 30 minutes to relax the dough.

Return the dough to the floured counter, flour the top, and roll it into a 12-inch square. It will be about ⅛ inch thick. Cut the dough lengthwise into 3 long strips, each one 4 inches wide. Then cut each strip crosswise into 3 pieces so you have nine 4-inch squares. (Figure 1) Brush off all the excess flour.

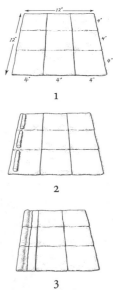

1

2

3

Starting ½ inch from the top and ½ inch from the left side of each square, pipe or spread a column of remonce, ending ½ inch from the bottom edge. (Figure 2) Brush egg wash over the right side of each strip from the edge up to the filling. Bring the left side of each dough square up and over the filling so the entire ½-inch border rests on the egg-washed dough. Press it down onto the dough so that it will adhere. (Figure 3) Fold over the right side of each dough square so that it comes just to the edge of

*Plus, if possible, two 18- by 2-inch-deep sheet pans to be used as a proofing box.

the column of filling. (It will overlap the other edge by ½ inch.) Press firmly on this overlap and on the bottom and top edges of the dough so the dough adheres and the filling is sealed. (Figure 4) The pastries will now be about 4 inches long by about 1¾ inches wide.

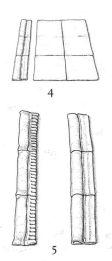

4

Use a small sharp knife to cut slashes about ½ inch long and ¼ inch apart along the right side of the dough, where there is no filling. (Be sure not to cut up to the filling, or it will leak.) (Figure 5)

Turn each pastry seam side down and arrange them so that they are close together on the counter. Brush them with egg wash and sprinkle them with the pearl sugar and sliced almonds. Pick up each bear claw, shaking off any nuts that do not adhere, arch it into a cres-

5

cent, so that the cuts open, and set the pastries at least 2 inches apart on the prepared baking sheets, maintaining the open cuts and arch. Press any fallen nuts onto the dough. (The nuts can be quite close together, as the expanding dough during rising and baking will move them farther apart.) (Figure 6)

If you have two 2-inch-deep 18-inch sheet pans, invert them over the bear claws (see page 488). Alternatively, cover them lightly with plastic wrap that has been sprayed with nonstick vegetable spray and set the sheet pans aside in a warm spot. Allow the bear claws to rise for 1½ to 2 hours. (As they take about a half hour to shape, the dough gets a head start rising.) They should almost double in size and be very light to the touch.

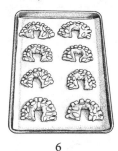

6

Preheat the oven to 400°F. at least 20 minutes before baking. Set an oven rack at the middle level before preheating.

Five minutes ahead, place a pan with about 1 inch of boiling water in the lower part of the oven. (To prevent a ring from forming if using a metal pan, add a pinch of cream of tartar to the water.) Place the bear claws in the oven, lower the tempera-

7

ture to 375°F., and bake for 18 to 20 minutes or until golden brown (200° to 210°F.). Remove the bear claws to a rack and cool for 5 to 10 minutes.

The bear claws are best eaten warm or within 3 hours of baking. (Figure 7)

STORE

Room temperature, up to 2 days; frozen, up to 3 months. The baked bear claws can be reheated in a preheated 300°F. oven for 5 minutes (8 minutes if frozen).

POINTERS FOR SUCCESS

∾ It is best to cover the dough with the inverted 2-inch-deep pans so that nothing touches the surface.

APRICOT DANISH SLIPS

I learned this lovely Danish shape and recipe twenty years ago from master baker and teacher John Clancy. It was the first Danish I ever made and I was surprised by how easy it was to create the complicated-looking shape. A slip is two layers of rectangular dough sandwiched with a thin layer of preserves. It is called a "slip" because a slit is cut in the middle through which one or both ends of the dough are slipped and then pulled through.

OVEN TEMPERATURE: 400°F., THEN 375°F. •
BAKING TIME: 15 TO 18 MINUTES

MAKES: EIGHT 5½- BY 2½- BY
1-INCH-HIGH SLIPS

INGREDIENTS	MEASURE	WEIGHT	
	VOLUME	OUNCES	GRAMS
½ recipe Danish Pastry Dough (page 486)		13.3 ounces	381 grams
Apricot Lekvar (page 512) or apricot preserves + finely grated lemon zest	½ cup full ¾ cup ½ teaspoon	6.5 ounces approx. 8.75 ounces	186 grams 254 grams
Transparent Sugar Glaze powdered sugar	(2 tablespoons) ¼ cup	• 1 ounce	• 30 grams
water	1½ teaspoons	•	•
freshly squeezed lemon juice	1 teaspoon	•	•

EQUIPMENT
Two large baking sheets or half-size sheet pans, lined with parchment*

Make the dough (see page 486).

If using apricot preserves, place them in a small saucepan over medium heat (or in a heatproof glass measure in the microwave on high power) and heat them, stirring often, until bubbling. Pass them through a strainer into a bowl. Stir in the lemon zest and set aside to cool completely.

SHAPE THE SLIPS
Remove the dough from the refrigerator and allow it to sit for 15 minutes. On a floured counter, roll the dough into a rectangle 12 inches by 9 to 10 inches. It will be ¼ inch thick. Slip it onto a cookie sheet, cover it lightly, and refrigerate it for 30 minutes to relax the gluten.

Return the dough to the floured counter, flour the top, and roll it out 16 inches long by 10 inches wide. It will be about ⅛ inch thick. Brush off all the excess flour.

*Plus, if possible, two 18- by 2-inch-deep sheet pans to be used as a proofing box.

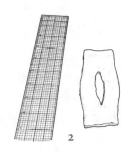

1

2

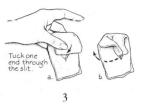

3

Spread the apricot filling lengthwise evenly over half the dough. Starting from one long side, fold the dough in half so that the edges meet. You will now have a 16- by 5-inch rectangle of dough. Gently pat the dough so it adheres to the filling. With a pizza cutter or sharp knife, cut the dough crosswise into 2- by 5-inch rectangles. (Figure 1) Cut a 3-inch-long slit down the center of each rectangle. (There will be 1 inch of uncut dough at either end.) (Figure 2) Lift each rectangle, spread the slit to open it, and pull one uncut end of the pastry down through the slit and up and over to form a bow shape. (Figures 3 and 4) (For a double slip, repeat with the other end.) Place the slips at least 1½ inches apart on the prepared baking sheets.

4

If you have two 2-inch-deep 18-inch-long sheet pans, invert them over the dough (see page 488). Alternatively, cover the dough lightly with plastic wrap that has been sprayed with nonstick vegetable spray and set the sheet pans aside in a warm spot. Allow to rise for about 2 hours. The slips should almost double and be very light to the touch.

Preheat the oven to 400°F. at least 20 minutes before baking. Set an oven rack at the middle level before preheating.

Five minutes ahead of baking, place a pan with about 1 inch of boiling water in the lower part of the oven. (To prevent a ring from forming if using a metal pan, add a pinch of cream of tartar to the water.) Place the slips in the oven, lower the temperature to 375°F., and bake for 15 to 18 minutes or until golden brown (200° to 210°F.).

While the slips are baking, prepare the sugar glaze: In a small bowl, place the powdered sugar. Whisk in the water and lemon juice. The glaze should be the consistency of egg white. If necessary, add a little more sugar or water.

When the slips are done, remove the baking sheet to a rack and immediately brush the slips with the glaze. Cool for 5 to 10 minutes.

These are best eaten warm or within 3 hours of baking.

STORE

Room temperature, up to 2 days; frozen, up to 3 months. The baked Danish can be reheated in a preheated 300°F. oven for 5 minutes (8 minutes if frozen).

POINTERS FOR SUCCESS

➤ It is best to cover the dough with the inverted 2-inch-deep pans so that nothing touches the surface.

DANISH SNAIL BUNS

These classic Danish pastries are spread with just enough almond filling to keep them moist, sprinkled with brandy-plumped raisins, walnuts, and cinnamon sugar, and finally rolled and cut to resemble snails.

OVEN TEMPERATURE: 400°F., THEN 375°F. •   MAKES: TWENTY-FOUR 3¼- TO 3½
BAKING TIME: 18 TO 20 MINUTES   BY 1-INCH-HIGH BUNS

INGREDIENTS	MEASURE	WEIGHT	
	VOLUME	OUNCES	GRAMS
1 recipe Danish Pastry Dough (page 486)		26.7 ounces	762 grams
Filling Brandied Raisins (page 514)	¾ cup	4.75 ounces	135 grams
Remonce (page 510)	⅔ cup	6 ounces	170 grams
Cinnamon Sugar and Walnut Sprinkle sugar	1 tablespoon	approx. 0.5 ounce	12.5 grams
ground cinnamon	⅛ teaspoon	•	•
toasted walnuts, chopped medium-fine	¾ cup	2.6 ounces	75 grams
Transparent Sugar Glaze powdered sugar	(2 tablespoons) ¼ cup	• 1 ounce	• 30 grams
water	1½ teaspoons	•	•
freshly squeezed lemon juice	1 teaspoon	•	•

EQUIPMENT
Two large baking sheets or half-size sheet pans, lined with parchment*

Make the dough (see page 486).

Advance preparation: The brandied raisins must be made at least 24 hours ahead.

SHAPE THE SNAILS
Remove the dough from the refrigerator and cut it in half. Work with half the dough at a time, refrigerating the other half. Allow the dough to sit for 15 minutes.

*Plus, if possible, two 18- by 2-inch-deep sheet pans to be used as a proofing box.

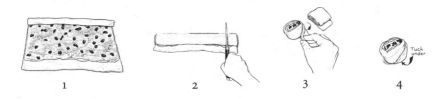

1   2   3   4

On a floured counter, roll it out to a rectangle about 10 inches by 12 inches. Slip it onto a baking sheet, cover it lightly, and refrigerate it for 30 minutes to relax the gluten.

Return the dough to the floured counter, flour the top, and roll it to about 12 inches wide by 13 inches long. It will be about ⅛ inch thick. Brush off all the excess flour.

Combine the sugar and cinnamon. Spread half the almond filling evenly over the dough in a thin layer, leaving a 1-inch-wide strip of dough bare at the bottom of the rectangle. Sprinkle half the cinnamon sugar, chopped nuts, and raisins evenly over the almond filling. Starting at the top of the dough, and brushing off the excess flour as you go, tightly roll the dough just up to the 1-inch strip at the bottom, leaving it free for tucking under each snail. (Figure 1)

With a sharp knife, cut the roll into 1-inch slices. (Figure 2) Tucking the 1-inch free strip of dough underneath each one (this keeps it from unrolling), place the slices 2 inches apart on a prepared baking sheet. (Figures 3 and 4)

If you have two 2-inch-deep 18-inch sheet pans, invert them over the dough (see page 488). Or, cover the snails lightly with plastic wrap that has been sprayed with nonstick vegetable spray and set the sheet pans aside in a warm spot. Repeat this process with the remaining dough (or store the dough refrigerated for up to 2 days).

Allow the Danish to rise for about 2 hours. They should almost double in size and be very light to the touch.

Preheat the oven to 400°F. at least 20 minutes before baking. Set an oven rack at the middle level before preheating.

Five minutes ahead of baking, place a pan with about 1 inch of boiling water in the lower part of the oven. (To prevent a ring from forming if using a metal pan, add a pinch of cream of tartar to the water.) Place the Danish in the oven, lower the temperature to 375°F., and bake for 18 to 20 minutes (after 10 minutes, turn around and reverse the positions of the two sheets) or until golden brown (210°F.).

While the Danish are baking, prepare the sugar glaze: In a small bowl, place the powdered sugar. Whisk in the water and lemon juice. The glaze should be the consistency of egg white. If necessary, add a bit more sugar or water.

When the snails are done, remove the baking sheets to racks and immediately brush the snails with the glaze. Cool for 20 to 30 minutes.

The snails are best eaten warm or within 3 hours of baking.

STORE

Room temperature, up to 2 days; frozen, up to 3 months. The baked Danish can be reheated in a preheated 300°F. oven for 5 minutes (8 minutes if frozen).

POINTERS FOR SUCCESS

∽ See page 489.

DANISH PASTRY TWISTS

The dough for this Danish is cut into strips, twisted, and then coiled to form a bun shape. A depression is made in the center, which can be filled with cream cheese filling and/or preserves. My preference is cream cheese filling and sour cherry or blueberry preserves.

These pastry twists are double the size of the Snail Buns (page 502). The optional layer of remonce adds a touch of moistness and lovely flavor, but it makes it a little trickier to cut the dough into strips.

OVEN TEMPERATURE: 400°F., THEN 375°F. •
BAKING TIME: 18 TO 20 MINUTES   MAKES: TWELVE 4½- BY 1-INCH-HIGH TWISTS

INGREDIENTS	MEASURE	WEIGHT	
	VOLUME	OUNCES	GRAMS
1 recipe Danish Pastry Dough (page 486)		26.7 ounces	762 grams
optional: 1 recipe Remonce (page 510)	14 tablespoons	8 ounces	227 grams
Filling Honey-Stung Cream Cheese Filling (page 511) or Pastry Cream (page 560)	1 cup	9 ounces	255 grams
sour cherry or other jam	¾ cup	9 ounces	255 grams
Transparent Sugar Glaze powdered sugar	(3 tablespoons) ¼ cup + 2 tablespoons	• 1.5 ounces	• 43 grams
water	1 tablespoon + ¼ teaspoon	•	•
freshly squeezed lemon juice	1½ teaspoons	0.3 ounce	8 grams
Sugar Glaze (page 509)	scant 3 tablespoons	approx. 2 ounces	60 grams

EQUIPMENT

Two half-size sheet pans, lined with parchment*; 2 pastry bags or reclosable freezer bags; a number 4 (⅜-inch) plain round pastry tube; and a number 5 (⅛-inch) plain round decorating tube (number 5) and coupler

SHAPE THE TWISTS

Remove the dough from the refrigerator. Allow it to sit for 15 minutes. On a floured counter, roll the dough to a rectangle 6 inches by 14 inches. It will be about ½ inch thick. Brush off all the excess flour.

If using the optional remonce filling, cut the dough lengthwise into 2 strips, each 3 inches wide. Spread one with the remonce and carefully place the second strip on top, lining up the edges. Roll the rectangle back to 6 inches wide.

With a sharp knife, cut the dough lengthwise into ½-inch-wide strips. (Figure 1) (The strips will stretch and lengthen on handling to about 20 inches.) To twist a strip, press the end closest to you against the counter. Hold it in place with your left hand, place your right hand palm down on the opposite end of the strip, and move your hand back and forth, rolling the strip from right to left, until it is tightly twisted. (Figure 2) Brush off any excess flour to ensure that the dough will not separate after baking. Keeping the end of the strip against the counter with your left hand, lift the strip so that the rest of it is raised off the counter and coil the strip around the end, maintaining the twist as you spiral around and allowing the rest of the strip to fall on the counter as you go. (Figures 3 and 4) Tuck under the last 1 inch of dough to keep the coil from unrolling and lift it onto a prepared baking sheet. (Figures 5 and 6) Continue making twists, placing them at least 2 inches apart. They will now be about 3 inches in diameter.

If you have two 2-inch-deep 18-inch sheet pans, invert them over the twists (see page 488). Alternatively, cover them lightly with plastic wrap that has been sprayed with nonstick vegetable spray and set the sheet pans aside in a warm spot. Allow the twists to rise for about 2 hours. They should almost double in size and be very light to the touch.

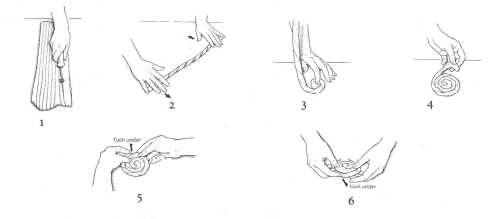

*Plus, if possible, two 18- by 7-inch-deep pans to be used as a proofing box.

Preheat the oven to 400°F. at least 20 minutes before bak-
ing. Set an oven rack at the middle level before preheating.

With lightly greased fingers, gently make about a 2-inch depression in the center of each twist. (Figure 7) Pipe or spoon about 1 tablespoon of the cream cheese filling or pastry cream around the outer edge of the depression and spoon about 1 tablespoon of the jam into the center. (Figures 8 and 9)

Five minutes ahead of baking, place a pan with about 1 inch of boiling water in the lower part of the oven. (To prevent a ring from forming if using a metal pan, add a pinch of cream of tartar to the water.) Place the twists in the oven, lower the temperature to 375°F., and bake for 18 to 20 minutes (after 10 minutes, turn and reverse the positions of the two sheets) or until golden brown (200° to 210°F.).

While the twists are baking, prepare the transparent sugar glaze: In a small bowl, place the powdered sugar. Whisk in the water and lemon juice. The glaze should be the consistency of egg white. If necessary, add a bit more sugar or water.

When the twists are done, remove the baking sheets to racks and brush immediately the twists with the glaze. (Figure 10) Cool for 20 to 30 minutes.

Pipe or use a spoon to drizzle lines of the second sugar glaze over the top. (Figure 11) These are best eaten warm, while the outside is crisp and light and the center soft and tender, or within 3 hours of baking.

7

8

9

10

11

VARIATION

MINI TWISTS   This is a great quick, easy, and delicious use for scraps of dough. Place the dough scraps on top of each other and roll them into a 4-inch-wide strip. If the dough becomes sticky, refrigerate it until firm. Cut about 6-inch-long by ½-inch-wide strips and coil them as above. After they have risen, make depressions in the centers and fill each one with a dab of cream cheese and/or preserves. They will be 2½ inches in diameter and grow to 3 inches after baking. Bake them for 15 minutes or until golden brown.

STORE

Room temperature, up to 2 days; frozen, up to 3 months. The baked Danish can be reheated in a preheated 300°F. oven for 5 minutes (8 minutes if frozen).

THE ALLIGATOR

My friend David Shamah has been telling me about this unique Danish pastry for years. In fact, he brings it up every time he goes to Los Angeles, because it is practically an institution there. Baker Viktor Benes created "The Alligator," so named because the large rectangle of filled pastry is topped with rows of pecans on top that resemble the roughly grooved hide of an alligator. (Or perhaps it's because of what is written on the package: "One Bite and We Gotcha.")

My curiosity was so aroused I asked Gelson's Bakery, where Benes worked, to FedEx me one. I created this version based on it. This is a fun shape for Danish pastry, but it is also exceptionally mouthwatering because the variation on the classic remonce filling contains pecans and a touch of honey, which blend mellifluously with the rich buttery dough.

OVEN TEMPERATURE: 400°F., THEN 375°F. • MAKES: 15- BY 6½- BY 1-INCH-HIGH
BAKING TIME: 18 TO 20 MINUTES PASTRY; SERVES: ABOUT 15

INGREDIENTS	MEASURE	WEIGHT	
	VOLUME	OUNCES	GRAMS
½ recipe Danish Pastry Dough (page 486)		13.3 ounces	381 grams
⅓ cup pecan halves	full ⅓ cup, ground	approx. 1 ounce	33 grams
sugar	2½ tablespoons	1 ounce	31 grams
all-purpose flour	1 tablespoon	0.3 ounce	9 grams
Almond/Pecan Remonce Filling	(¾ cup)	(7 ounces)	(200 grams)
almond paste, room temperature	approx. 3 tablespoons	1.75 ounces	50 grams
unsalted butter, softened	3½ tablespoons	1.75 ounces	50 grams
honey	1 tablespoon	0.75 ounce	21 grams
egg wash: 1 large egg beaten with 2 tablespoons of water	approx. 3 tablespoons	2.7 ounces	79 grams
40 pecan halves	⅔ cup	2.3 ounces	66 grams
½ recipe Sugar Glaze (page 509), made with maple flavoring	•	•	•

EQUIPMENT

A large baking sheet or half-size sheet pan, lined with parchment*

Make the dough (see page 486).

FOOD PROCESSOR METHOD

In a food processor with the metal blade, pulse together the pecans, sugar, and flour until the pecans are finely ground. Add the almond paste, butter, and honey and pulse until smooth and creamy, scraping the sides of the bowl as necessary.

MIXER METHOD

Finely grind the pecans. In a large mixer bowl, on low speed, mix the almond paste and sugar. Add the butter and continue mixing on low speed until incorporated. Add the honey, flour, and ground pecans and mix just until incorporated.

SHAPE THE ALLIGATOR

Remove the dough from the refrigerator and allow it to sit for 15 minutes. On a floured counter, roll the dough to a rectangle 12 inches by 9 to 10 inches. It will be ¼ inch thick. Slip it onto a cookie sheet, cover it lightly, and refrigerate it for 30 minutes to relax the gluten.

Return the dough to the floured counter, flour the top, and roll it to about 12 inches wide by 13 inches long. It will be about ⅛ inch thick. Brush off all the excess flour. Spread the almond/pecan filling evenly over the dough in a thin layer by placing dabs of it all over the dough, leaving a 1-inch plain border on both short ends, then covering it with plastic wrap and rolling it with a rolling pin. As you roll the dough, it will grow to about 16 inches in length. Remove the plastic wrap and brush the 1-inch borders with a little of the egg wash. Starting from a long side, fold the dough in thirds like a business letter. The length will shrink from 16 to about 14 inches and the width will be 4 inches. The pastry will be almost 1 inch high. Firmly press the open ends that were brushed with the egg wash to seal them.

Slip the alligator onto the prepared baking sheet. Brush with the egg wash and place the pecan halves, top sides up, lengthwise in 4 rows, about ½ inch apart, on top.

If you have a 2-inch-deep 18-inch sheet pan, invert it over the dough (see page 488). Alternatively, cover it lightly with plastic wrap that has been sprayed with nonstick vegetable spray and set the sheet pan aside in a warm spot. Allow it to rise for about 2 hours. The alligator should be about 1½ inches high and be very light to the touch.

Preheat the oven to 400°F. at least 20 minutes before baking. Set an oven rack at the middle level before preheating.

Five minutes ahead of baking, place a pan with about 1 inch of boiling water in the lower part of oven. (To prevent a ring from forming if using a metal pan, add a

---

* Plus, if possible, an 18- by 2-inch deep sheet pan to be used as a proofing box.

pinch of cream of tartar to the water.) Place the alligator in the oven, lower the temperature to 375°F., and bake for 18 to 20 minutes or until golden brown (210°F.). Remove the baking sheet to a rack and cool for 20 to 30 minutes.

Drizzle the maple sugar glaze over the top of the alligator. Using a serrated or sharp knife, cut it into 1-inch-wide strips. The alligator is best eaten warm, while the outside is crisp and light and the center soft and tender, or within 3 hours of baking.

STORE

Room temperature, up to 2 days; frozen, up to 3 months. The baked alligator can be reheated in a preheated 300°F. oven for 5 minutes (10 minutes if frozen).

POINTERS FOR SUCCESS

∿ Pinch the ends well, or some of the filling will flow out before it sets.
∿ It is best to cover the dough with the inverted 2-inch-high pan so that nothing touches the surface.

UNDERSTANDING

The Pecan Remonce filling has the same basic proportions as the standard Remonce (page 510), equal weights of almond paste, sweetener, and butter.

SUGAR GLAZE FOR DANISH
(AND OTHER PASTRY)

This shiny but opaque glaze is the traditional decoration for many pastries.

MAKES: SCANT ¼ CUP

INGREDIENTS	MEASURE	WEIGHT	
	VOLUME	OUNCES	GRAMS
powdered sugar	½ cup (dip and sweep method)	2 ounces	58 grams
heavy cream	2 tablespoons	1 ounce	29 grams
dark rum or pure vanilla extract or maple flavoring	⅛ teaspoon	•	•

OPTIONAL EQUIPMENT
A reclosable pint- or quart-size freezer bag

In a small bowl, whisk or stir together the powdered sugar, most of the cream, and the rum or vanilla until smoothly incorporated. The mixture will thin on whisking. To use as a drizzle glaze, the glaze should run thickly when the whisk is lifted; to pipe raised lines, it should form soft peaks. If necessary, whisk in the remaining cream or additional powdered sugar.

Pipe or drizzle the glaze over the cooled pastry. (Empty the glaze into the reclosable bag, seal it, and cut a small piece from one of the corners to serve as a piping bag; or use a spoon to drizzle the glaze.)

NOTE

If desired, a small amount of egg white (about 1 teaspoon) can be whisked into the mixture to strengthen it for smoother piping. You will have to whisk the egg white lightly first to break it up in order to measure such a small amount.

REMONCE
(Almond Cream Filling)

This is the classic filling for Danish pastry. A very thin layer spread on the dough before filling and shaping it adds a lovely flavor and moisture to the dough without adding excess sweetness. The egg adds flavor and also sets the filling so that it doesn't spread and leak. If it is spread in a thin layer, the remonce disappears into the dough before baking.

MAKES: 14 TABLESPOONS/8 OUNCES/227 GRAMS

INGREDIENTS	MEASURE	WEIGHT	
	VOLUME	OUNCES	GRAMS
almond paste (see page 642)	3 tablespoons + ½ teaspoon	2 ounces	56 grams
sugar	¼ cup + 1½ teaspoons	2 ounces	56 grams
unsalted butter, cut into 3 pieces and softened	4 tablespoons	2 ounces	56 grams
1 large egg, at room temperature, lightly beaten	3 tablespoons	1.7 ounces (weighed without the shell)	50 grams
pure vanilla extract	½ teaspoon	•	•
bleached all-purpose flour	1 tablespoon + 1½ teaspoons	0.5 ounce	14 grams

FOOD PROCESSOR METHOD

In a food processor with the metal blade, pulse together the almond paste and sugar until the almond paste is in fine particles. Add the butter and pulse 3 or 4 times until incorporated. Scrape the sides of the bowl. Add the egg, vanilla, and flour and pulse just until incorporated. It will be a soft cream.

ELECTRIC MIXER METHOD

In a large mixer bowl, on low speed, mix the almond paste and sugar. Add the butter and continue mixing on low speed until incorporated. Add the egg, vanilla, and flour and mix just until incorporated.

STORE

Refrigerated, up to 1 week; frozen, up to 1 month.

POINTERS FOR SUCCESS

∼ To prevent separation while mixing, the butter and eggs must be not be cold.

HONEY-STUNG CREAM CHEESE FILLING

Lightly sweetened cream cheese filling is a perfect foil for Danish pastry. The filling has a slightly lemony flavor and the creaminess is especially pleasing against the backdrop of crisp, yeasty dough. It blends nicely with preserves such as sour cherry, orange marmalade, or lemon curd.

MAKES: 1 CUP/9.25 OUNCES/262 GRAMS

INGREDIENTS	MEASURE	WEIGHT	
	VOLUME	OUNCES	GRAMS
cream cheese, softened	1 large package	8 ounces	227 grams
honey	2 tablespoons	1.5 ounces	43 grams

In a small bowl, whisk together the cream cheese and honey until smooth and creamy. Place in an airtight container.

STORE

Refrigerated, up to 5 days; frozen, up to 6 months.

APRICOT LEKVAR

This lilting apricot filling is thicker and more flavorful than strained preserves. It is especially useful for Danish and Un-Rugelach (page 138), as it
does not leak out of the dough during baking.

For many years, H. Roth (Lekvar by the Barrel) and Paprikas Weiss supplied
New Yorkers with incomparable Hungarian apricot lekvar, whose intensity came
from both the quality of the apricots and the process of preserving them with the
flavorful skins. Now, sadly, both have closed.

This homemade version, adapted from beloved baking teacher John Clancy,
uses dried apricots, and its intensity is close to the original.

MAKES: 2¾ CUPS/APPROXIMATELY 29.5 OUNCES/840 GRAMS

INGREDIENTS	MEASURE	WEIGHT	
	VOLUME	OUNCES	GRAMS
dried apricots	2⅔ cups	1 pound	454 grams
water	2 liquid cups	16.6 ounces	472 grams
sugar	1 cup + 3 tablespoons	8 ounces	227 grams
finely grated lemon zest	2 teaspoons	•	4 grams

In a medium saucepan with a tight-fitting lid, combine the dried apricots with
the water and allow them to sit for 2 hours to soften.

Bring the water to a boil, cover the pan tightly, and simmer over the lowest
possible heat for 20 to 30 minutes or until the apricots are very soft when pierced
with a skewer.

In a food processor with the metal blade, place the apricots and any liquid, the
sugar, and lemon zest and process until smooth.

Scrape the apricot mixture back into the saucepan and simmer, stirring constantly to prevent scorching, for 10 to 15 minutes or until deep orange in color and
very thick. A tablespoon of the mixture when lifted will take about 3 seconds to
fall from the spoon. Empty it into a bowl and cool completely.

STORE
Refrigerated, in an airtight container, about 1 year.

PRUNE LEKVAR

This was my favorite Danish filling as a child. Those of you who adore prune will want to use the lower amount of lemon zest and omit the cardamom for a pure prune flavor. Those of you who love it less may learn to appreciate it with the higher amount of lemon zest, which cuts through the pruniness, and the addition of cardamom, which accentuates the cardamom in the Danish dough.

MAKES: 2 CUPS/22 OUNCES/624 GRAMS

INGREDIENTS	MEASURE	WEIGHT	
	VOLUME	OUNCES	GRAMS
pitted prunes	4 cups, tightly packed	1 pound	454 grams
water	2 liquid cups	16.6 ounces	472 grams
sugar	¼ cup	1.75 ounces	50 grams
salt	a pinch	•	•
finely grated lemon zest	1 to 2 teaspoons	•	2 to 4 grams
optional: ground cardamom*	⅛ teaspoon	•	•

*Cardamom is most aromatic when freshly ground. I use a mortar and pestle. A spice or coffee mill also works.

In a medium saucepan with a tight-fitting lid, combine the prunes with the water and allow them to sit for 2 hours to soften.

Bring the water to a boil, cover the pan tightly, and simmer over the lowest possible heat for 20 to 30 minutes or until the prunes are very soft when pierced with a skewer.

In a food processor with the metal blade, place the prunes and any liquid, the sugar, salt, and lemon zest and process until smooth.

Scrape the prune mixture back into the saucepan and simmer, stirring constantly to prevent scorching, for 10 to 15 minutes or until dark brown in color and very thick. A tablespoon of the mixture when lifted will take about 3 seconds to fall from the spoon. Empty into a bowl and stir in the optional cardamom. Cool completely.

STORE

Refrigerated, in an airtight container, about 1 year.

BRANDIED RAISINS

These incredible aromatic raisins are simple to make and indispensable in Danish pastry. They could find their way into an apple pie as well. (To store, mark them "for baking only" and hope no one understands why and eats them anyway!)

MAKES: 2 SCANT CUPS 11.7 OUNCES/334 GRAMS;
1 CUP DRAINED = 6.3 OUNCES/180 GRAMS

INGREDIENTS	MEASURE	WEIGHT	
	VOLUME	OUNCES	GRAMS
sugar	½ cup	3.5 ounces	100 grams
water	½ liquid cup	approx. 4 ounces	118 grams
dark raisins	about 2 cups (1 box)	9 ounces	255 grams
1 vanilla bean, split lengthwise	•	•	•
cognac	1 liquid cup	4 ounces	112 grams

EQUIPMENT
A 1-quart canning jar

Advance preparation: 3 days.

In a small saucepan, stir together the sugar and water and bring to a full boil, stirring constantly. Remove from the heat and add the raisins and vanilla bean. Cover tightly and allow to cool to room temperature.

Transfer the raisins and liquid to the 1-quart jar and add the Cognac. Cover the jar tightly and swirl to mix well. Let stand for at least 3 days before using.

STORE
In a cool dark cellar or refrigerated, indefinitely.

BRIOCHE

Brioche belongs in the pastry repertoire, yet it doesn't have the crispness of what we usually think of as pastry. It seems more like a bread or a cake. This is because brioche has more liquid, more egg, and more sugar than any other dough. Actually, it is very similar to Danish pastry, and the doughs can be used interchangeably.

Brioche comes in many shapes and varieties beyond the classic breakfast bun with topknot. It makes the softest, most buttery sticky buns. In Austria, shaped into little buns and set atop a vanilla cream sauce, they are called *buchteln* and are served for dinner. And for lovers of escargots, the snail buns, which are a savory version of sticky buns, will be a unique treat.

BRIOCHE
(Master Recipe)

This is my basic buttery brioche recipe, used for both sweet and savory recipes. For those who desire even more butter, it can be increased to 6 ounces, which will also make the crumb finer and more dense.

OVEN TEMPERATURE: 425°F. •
BAKING TIME: 10 TO 15 MINUTES   **MAKES: 19 OUNCES/538 GRAMS**
INTERNAL TEMPERATURE: 180°F.   **DOUGH; 16 BRIOCHE**

INGREDIENTS	MEASURE	WEIGHT	
	VOLUME	OUNCES	GRAMS
water	2½ tablespoons	1.3 ounces	36 grams
sugar	3 tablespoons, divided	1.3 ounces	38 grams
compressed fresh yeast or active dry yeast (not rapid-rise) or SAF-Instant yeast (see page 654)	2 packed teaspoons 1½ teaspoons scant 1½ teaspoons	0.5 ounce • •	11 grams 4.5 grams 5 grams
bread flour or unbleached all-purpose flour flour	approx. 1½ cups (dip and sweep method), divided	8 ounces	227 grams
3 large eggs, at room temperature	generous ½ liquid cup	5.25 ounces (weighed without the shells)	150 grams
salt	½ teaspoon	•	3.5 grams
unsalted butter, very soft	8 tablespoons*	4 ounces	113 grams
Egg Glaze 1 large egg yolk	1 tablespoon	0.6 ounce	18 grams
cream or milk	1 teaspoon	•	•

*For an extra-rich, delicious flavor, melt and brown about 2 tablespoons of the butter.

EQUIPMENT

A heavy-duty mixer with the flat beater and dough hook attachments and sixteen 2¾-inch brioche molds, well buttered or sprayed with nonstick vegetable spray

Advance preparation: at least one day ahead.

To proof the yeast (if using fresh or active dry yeast), in a small bowl combine the water (ideally a tepid 100°F. if using fresh yeast, a little warmer, 110°F., if using dry; do not use hot water, or the yeast will die), ½ teaspoon of the sugar, and the yeast. If using fresh yeast, crumble it slightly while adding it. Set the mixture aside in a draft-free spot for 10 to 20 minutes. By this time, the mixture should be full of bubbles. (If not, the yeast is too old to be useful and you must start again with newer yeast.)

MAKE THE SPONGE

Place ⅓ cup of the flour and 1 of the eggs in the large mixer bowl and whisk until mixed. Add the yeast or yeast mixture and whisk until smooth. Sprinkle the remaining flour (for a total of 1½ cups) over the mixture but do not mix it in. Cover tightly with plastic wrap and let it stand for 1½ to 2 hours.

MAKE THE DOUGH

In a small bowl, whisk together the remaining sugar and the salt until well combined. Add this mixture, together with the remaining 2 eggs, to the sponge and beat on medium speed with the flat beater. (If the dough starts to climb up the beater, change to the dough hook.) You will need to beat for about 5 minutes or until the dough is smooth, shiny, and very elastic and it begins to clean the bowl. If it does not, add more flour by the tablespoonful. Increase the speed to medium-high and add the butter by the tablespoon, beating until it is incorporated.

FIRST RISE

Scrape the dough into a lightly buttered bowl. It will be very soft and elastic. Sprinkle it lightly with flour to prevent a crust from forming. Cover the bowl tightly with plastic wrap (preferably Saran brand) and let it rise in a warm place (80° to 85°F., but not above, or the yeast will develop a sour taste) until doubled in bulk, 1½ to 2 hours.

Refrigerate the dough for 1 hour to firm it so the butter will not separate. Gently deflate the dough by stirring it with a rubber scraper and return it to the refrigerator for another hour so that it will be less sticky to handle.

REDISTRIBUTING THE YEAST AND FINAL RISE

Turn the dough out onto a floured surface and gently press it into a rectangle, flouring the surface and dough as needed to keep the dough from sticking to your hands. Fold the dough into thirds (as you would a business letter), brushing off any excess flour, and again press it out into a rectangle. Fold it again into thirds and dust it lightly on all sides with flour. Wrap it loosely but securely in plastic wrap and place it in a large reclosable bag or wrap it in foil. Refrigerate for at least 6 hours and up to 2 days to allow the dough to ripen and become firm.

SHAPE THE BRIOCHE

Gently knead the dough a few times to deflate it. Divide it into 16 pieces (scant 1¼ ounces/33 grams). If not using a scale, the easiest way to divide the dough evenly is to lightly flour your hands and roll it into a long cylinder; cut it in half, then continue cutting each piece in half until there are 16 pieces.

Pinch off a little less than one quarter of each piece to make the topknot. Roll each larger piece of dough into a ball and press it into a brioche mold. With lightly floured hands, shape each piece of reserved dough into an elongated pear form. Using your index finger, make a hole in the center of each brioche, going almost to the bottom of the mold, and insert the elongated part of a topknot deeply into this hole. Place the molds on a large baking sheet, cover the molds loosely with greased plastic wrap, and set aside in a warm spot away from drafts for about 1 hour or until the dough reaches the top of the molds.

Preheat the oven to 425°F. (400°F. if using a dark pan) at least 30 minutes before baking. Set an oven rack at the lower level and place a baking stone or cookie sheet on it before preheating.

Lightly beat together the egg yolk and cream or milk for the glaze. Brush the top of each brioche with the egg glaze, being careful not to drip any on the side of the pan, or it will impede rising. Allow the glaze to dry for 5 minutes and then brush the brioche a second time. Use greased scissors or a small sharp knife to make a ¼-inch-deep cut all around each topknot where it joins the rest of the brioche so it will rise to an attractive shape.

Place the pan of brioche on the hot stone or sheet and bake for 10 to 15 minutes or until a skewer inserted under the topknot of a brioche comes out clean. An instant-read thermometer will register 190°F.

Unmold the brioche onto a rack. They are delicious eaten warm. They can be reheated in a 350°F. oven for 5 minutes.

VARIATION

SWEET POTATO BRIOCHE   Sweet potato, or the more orangy yam, gives the brioche a beautiful golden color and moister texture, without adding an eggy flavor. The flavor of the sweet potato, however, is so subtle as to be unnoticeable. This was the inspiration of Julia Carter, who was Susan Spicer's pastry chef at Bayonna in New Orleans.

Simply add ½ cup (about 4.5 ounces/126 grams) of strained baked yam or sweet potato to the dough when adding the final eggs. The overall sugar can be decreased by 1 tablespoon to compensate for the sweetness of the potato.

STORE

Airtight, room temperature, up to 2 days; frozen, up to 3 months.

POINTERS FOR SUCCESS

෴ Use King Arthur's all-purpose flour or a national-brand supermarket bread flour. King Arthur's will result in a brioche that is a little more tender.

෴ Fresh yeast causes the dough to rise faster. *Do not,* however, use rapid-rise yeast.

෴ Be sure the yeast is active.

෴ Do not allow the dough to rise in an area over 80° to 85°F.

∾ Do not allow the dough to rise more than recommended amounts, or it will weaken the structure.

∾ Do not deflate the dough before chilling, or the butter will leak out. (If this should happen, chill the dough for 1 hour and knead the butter back into the dough.)

∾ Unbaked dough can be frozen for up to 3 months. It is best to add 25 percent more yeast if you are planning to freeze it, since some of it will die.

UNDERSTANDING

Unlike a cake, which is primarily a starch structure, bread depends on protein in the form of gluten to create its framework. The higher the protein content of the flour, the stronger the structure will be and the finer the grain of the bread (directly the opposite of cake). Too high a protein content, however, will result in a less soft and more chewy crumb, so if using bread flour, use a national-brand supermarket bread flour.

This dough is exceptionally wet. Just enough extra flour is added to handle it for shaping, resulting in a very light, soft brioche.

I do not use rapid-rise yeast, because the flavor development and texture are superior with slower rising.

Compared to Danish dough, brioche has less liquid, much more egg, and double the sugar. Also, the butter is not layered in, so it is more cake-like. The hot baking stone or cookie sheet will boost the "oven spring" (the amount it rises from the heat of the oven) of the brioche.

STICKY BUNS

This is essentially the same recipe I included in *The Cake Bible,* with a few refinements. I have since found that King Arthur's all-purpose flour makes an equally light but slightly more tender dough than bread flour, and that refiner's or corn syrup added to the sugar topping makes a perfect caramel topping that never crystallizes. I also apply the pecans directly to each bun instead of leaving where they land to chance. For a variation, Danish pastry (page 486) can be substituted for the brioche dough for this recipe. It will be less soft inside but crisper outside.

EQUIPMENT
An 8- by 2-inch square pan or a 10-inch round pan, lightly greased*

---

*My favorite pan for these is a 10-inch (bottom measurement) by 2-inch-high round copper tarte Tatin pan (see page 281). For half the dough, use a 7- by 2-inch pan or an 8- by 2-inch tarte Tatin or cake pan with a ball of crumpled foil in the center.

OVEN TEMPERATURE: 425°F. • BAKING TIME: 25 MINUTES
INTERNAL TEMPERATURE: 180°F.   MAKES: 12 BUNS

INGREDIENTS	MEASURE	WEIGHT	
	VOLUME	OUNCES	GRAMS
1 recipe Brioche Dough (page 516)		19 ounces	538 grams
Sticky Bun Filling raisins	½ cup	2.5 ounces	72 grams
dark rum	2 tablespoons	1 ounce	28 grams
boiling water	¼ liquid cup	2 ounces	60 grams
coarsely chopped pecans, toasted	¼ cup	1 ounce	28 grams
light brown sugar	¼ cup, packed	2 ounces	54 grams
granulated sugar	1 tablespoon	0.5 ounce	12.5 grams
ground cinnamon	2 teaspoons	•	•
Sticky Bun Topping unsalted butter, softened	¼ cup	2 ounces	56 grams
light brown sugar	½ cup, packed	4 ounces	108 grams
Lyle's Golden Syrup (refiner's syrup) or light corn syrup	1 tablespoon	0.75 ounce	21 grams
lightly beaten egg	2 tablespoons	approx. 1 ounce	32 grams
pecan halves	½ cup	1.75 ounces	50 grams
Sticky Bun Glaze reserved raisin soaking liquid	•	•	•
unsalted butter	1 tablespoon	0.5 ounce	14 grams

Make the dough (page 516) at least 1 day ahead.

MAKE THE STICKY BUN FILLING

In a small heatproof bowl, place the raisins and rum. Add the boiling water, cover, and let stand for at least 1 hour. When ready to fill the dough, drain the raisins, reserving the soaking liquid for the glaze.

In another bowl, combine the chopped nuts, sugars, and cinnamon.

MAKE THE STICKY BUN TOPPING

In a small bowl, stir together the butter, brown sugar, and syrup until well mixed. Spread the mixture evenly into the prepared pan with a small offset spatula or rubber scraper.

FILL THE DOUGH

On a well-floured surface, roll out the dough into a 14- by 12-inch rectangle. Brush it with the lightly beaten egg and sprinkle it with the sugar mixture and raisins. Roll it up from a short end, brushing off excess flour as you go.

Using a sharp knife, cut the roll into 4 pieces, then cut each piece into thirds. Place 3 pecan halves on one cut end of each roll and place it, pecan side down, in the prepared pan. Press the tops down so that the sides touch. Cover the buns with plastic wrap that has been sprayed with nonstick vegetable spray or buttered. Let the buns rise in a warm place for 1 to 2 hours or until they reach the top of the pan.

Preheat the oven to 425°F. (400°F. if using a dark pan) at least 30 minutes before baking. Set an oven rack at the lower level and place a baking stone or baking sheet (lined with foil to catch any bubbling caramel) on it.

MAKE THE STICKY BUN GLAZE

In a small saucepan over high heat, or in a 2-cup heatproof measuring cup in a microwave oven on high power, reduce the raisin soaking syrup to 1 tablespoon. Add the butter and stir until melted. The glaze should be lukewarm when brushed onto the buns.

Brush the buns with the glaze. Place the pan on the hot stone or baking sheet and bake for 10 minutes. Lower the heat to 375°F. and bake for 15 minutes or until a skewer inserted in the center comes out clean. To keep the buns from becoming too brown, cover them loosely with foil after the first 7 minutes.

Let the buns cool in the pan for 3 minutes before unmolding them onto a serving plate or foil-lined counter. They can be eaten at once, or reheated later in a 350°F. oven for 15 minutes, loosely wrapped in foil, or in a microwave oven on high power for 30 seconds, wrapped in a damp paper towel.

STORE

Airtight, room temperature, up to 2 days; frozen, up to 3 months.

POINTERS FOR SUCCESS

∾ See page 518.

AUSTRIAN BUCHTELN
(BUCHtel)

These ethereal, sweet, yeasty little rolls contain the same ingredients as brioche but are lighter because they have less egg and butter and more tender because they use a softer bleached flour. Proof that Austrians adore their sweet pastry is that *buchteln,* fresh and warm from the oven, are sometimes served as dinner.

Buchteln have a long history. In the old days, they were called "lottery" because lottery tickets were baked into the centers. Nowadays, some people tuck in a tiny dollop of prune or apricot preserves before baking instead. My favorite way to enjoy *buchteln,* however, is plain uninterrupted fluff, floating on a pool of vanilla-imbued cream sauce. The warm buns soak it up like little sponges, becoming even more tender.

I discovered *buchteln* at Hawelka, the oldest student café in Vienna, where they are the house specialty. They only make *buchteln* between 9:30 in the evening and midnight. There is such a great demand for them one feels privileged to be served, despite what is always a very long wait. I was told at first with utter conviction by the waiter that it would be forty-five minutes, then I was told ten minutes more, then just a few more minutes, and then, "I have no idea!" Finally I confronted the owner and pleaded. She handed over the plate she held, obviously intended for someone else. They were so wonderful I didn't care.

EQUIPMENT
A 9- by 2-inch round cake pan, well buttered*

To proof the yeast, in a small bowl, combine 2 tablespoons of the milk (ideally a tepid 100°F. if using fresh yeast, a little warmer, 110°F., if using dry; do not use hot milk, or the yeast will die), the powdered sugar, and yeast. If using fresh yeast, crumble it slightly while adding it. Set the mixture aside in a draft-free spot for 10 to 20 minutes. By this time, the mixture should be full of bubbles. (If not, the yeast is too old to be useful and you must start again with newer yeast.)

In a medium heavy saucepan, over medium heat, melt 2 tablespoons (1 ounce/ 30 grams) of the butter. Set it aside in a warm spot so that it stays liquid but is no hotter than tepid.

MAKE THE DOUGH
In a large bowl, using your hand or a wooden spoon, stir together the sugar and eggs. Warm the remaining ½ cup plus 2 tablespoons of milk so that it is no hotter than tepid and stir it in. Stir in the yeast mixture and then about ¼ cup of the flour, stirring until smooth. Set it aside briefly.

In a medium bowl, whisk together the remaining 1¾ cups of flour and the salt until well combined. Stir it into the dough until incorporated. Continue stirring

*A half recipe can be prepared in a 7-inch pan.

INGREDIENTS	MEASURE	WEIGHT	
	VOLUME	OUNCES	GRAMS
milk	¾ liquid cup, divided	6.3 ounces	181 grams
powdered sugar	1 tablespoon	0.25 ounce	7 grams
compressed fresh yeast* or active dry yeast (not rapid-rise)	2 packed teaspoons 1½ teaspoons	0.5 ounce •	11 grams 4.5 grams
unsalted butter	6 tablespoons, divided	3 ounces	85 grams
granulated sugar	¼ cup	1.75 ounces	50 grams
1½ large eggs, at room temperature (beat lightly before measuring)	5 tablespoons	2.6 ounces (weighed without the shells)	75 grams
bleached all-purpose flour, such as Gold Medal†	approx. 2 cups (dip and sweep method), divided	10.5 ounces	300 grams
salt	¼ teaspoon	•	•
Vanilla Custard Sauce (page 606)	2 cups	•	•
powdered sugar for dusting	approx. 1 tablespoon	0.25 ounce	7 grams

*Fresh yeast causes dough to rise faster.

†It is preferable to use Gold Medal or Pillsbury, as regional brands may vary in strength. If the flour is too low in protein, it will be too weak and the dough will not rise well.

for about 5 minutes or until the dough is smooth, shiny, elastic, and cool to the touch. It will be very sticky. Add the melted butter and stir it into the dough for about 5 minutes, until it becomes very smooth, soft, and elastic. It will still stick slightly to your hands.

FIRST RISE

Place the dough into a lightly buttered 4-cup bowl. Cover the bowl tightly with plastic wrap and let it rise in a warm place (80° to 85°F. but not above, or the yeast will develop a sour taste) until doubled in bulk, 1½ to 2 hours. (The dough will rise to fill about three quarters of the bowl.)

Gently deflate the dough by kneading it a few times. It now can be shaped and baked, although it is preferable to refrigerate it for at least 1 hour to firm the dough and make it easier to handle; or cover tightly with plastic wrap and refrigerate for up to 2 days. If it has been refrigerated, gently knead it to deflate it before shaping.

SHAPE THE BUCHTELN

Melt the remaining 4 tablespoons of butter and strain it into a small bowl. (A small custard cup works well.) Allow it to cool until no hotter than tepid.

Empty the dough onto a floured counter. It will still be slightly sticky. Flour your hands lightly if necessary. Divide the dough into 28 pieces; the dough weighs about 21 ounces (604 grams), so each roll should be about 0.75 ounce (21 grams), or a rounded tablespoon. A 1½-inch biscuit cutter works well to cut the dough into pieces. Roll each piece between the palms of your hands into a ball. (They will be 1¼ inches in diameter.) Dip each dough ball into the melted butter, turning it to coat it all over, and place it in the cake pan. There will be a few spaces, which will fill in during rising.

Cover the dough lightly with buttered plastic wrap and allow it to rise in a warm place until the top of the dough comes to ½ inch from the top of the pan, about 1½ hours.

Preheat the oven to 425°F. (400°F. if using a dark pan) at least 30 minutes before baking. Set an oven rack at the lower level and place a baking stone or cookie sheet on it before preheating.

Place the pan on the stone or sheet and bake for 5 minutes. Lower the heat to 375°F. and continue baking for 15 to 20 minutes or until a skewer inserted in the center comes out clean.

Pour about ¼ cup of the sauce onto each serving plate. Unmold the *buchteln* onto a wire rack and reinvert onto a serving plate or cookie sheet. Gently pull apart the rolls and place about 4, right side up, on the sauce on each serving plate. Sprinkle lightly with powdered sugar and serve at once.

NOTE

At Bagolyvar (Owl's Castle) in Budapest, George Lang's sister restaurant to Gundel, I discovered something very similar to this recipe called Golden Dumplings. It consisted of two layers of torpedo-shaped dough, made with only half the butter. In between the layers was a sprinkling of chopped toasted nuts and sugar.

POINTERS FOR SUCCESS

‿ Use bleached all-purpose flour.
‿ Make sure the yeast is active by proofing it.
‿ Do not allow the dough to rise more than recommended amounts, or it will weaken the structure.

UNDERSTANDING

This dough is exceptionally wet. Just enough extra flour is added to handle it for shaping, resulting in a very light, tender roll.

SNAIL BUNS

This recipe, dedicated to much-beloved chef André Soltner, formerly of Lutèce, in New York City, is the savory version of sticky buns. Instead of caramel and pecans, it is spiraled with snails and herbed garlic butter. The buns not only look like coiled snails in their shells, they are also far more convenient than eating escargots, where the tradition is to dip the bread in the snail butter. Here the butter is already in the bread! Chef Soltner once offered me a little brioche timbale with snails nestled in it as an appetizer for my birthday dinner. He said it was a specialty of Alsace. I found the combination of succulent garlicky snails and buttery soft brioche to be so memorable I longed to taste it again. So I created this version in his honor. Snail buns make a great brunch dish. These are rich, so offer one per person and serve with a mixed green salad.

OVEN TEMPERATURE: 425°F., THEN 375°F. •
INTERNAL TEMPERATURE: 180°F. •
BAKING TIME: 25 MINUTES

MAKES: 6 BUNS

INGREDIENTS	MEASURE	WEIGHT	
	VOLUME	OUNCES	GRAMS
½ recipe Brioche Dough (page 516)		9.5 ounces	269 grams
Garlic Butter Filling unsalted butter, softened	3 tablespoons	1.5 ounces	43 grams
1 clove garlic, minced	1½ teaspoons	•	5 grams
1 small shallot, minced	1½ teaspoons	•	5.5 grams
salt	¹⁄₁₆ teaspoon	•	•
optional: Pernod	1 teaspoon	•	•

EQUIPMENT
An 8- by 2-inch square pan or a 10-inch round pan*

Make the dough (page 516) at least 1 day ahead.

MAKE THE GARLIC BUTTER FILLING
In a small bowl, with a rubber spatula or wooden spoon, stir together all the ingredients for the garlic butter filling until evenly mixed.

On a well-floured surface, roll out the dough into a 14- by 6-inch rectangle. Place dabs of the garlic butter evenly over the surface. Fold the dough in thirds (as

*My favorite pan for these is a 10-inch (bottom measurement) by 2-inch-high round copper tarte Tatin pan (see page 281).

you would a business letter), brushing off excess flour from the bottom of the dough before overlapping it. Wrap well and refrigerate for at least 30 minutes and up to 8 hours.

MAKE THE SNAIL FILLING

INGREDIENTS	MEASURE	WEIGHT	
	VOLUME	OUNCES	GRAMS
Snail Filling			
1 can Helix large snails	12	4.3 ounces	125 grams
chicken stock or canned no-salt chicken broth	2 tablespoons ¼ liquid cup	•	•
Alsatian Riesling, pinot blanc, or other dry white wine	2 tablespoons	•	•
fresh thyme	1 small sprig	•	
bay leaf	1 small	•	
salt	a pinch	•	
black peppercorns	2	•	
lightly beaten egg	1 tablespoon	approx. 0.5 ounce	16 grams
minced fresh parsley, preferably flat-leaf	¼ cup	0.3 ounce	10 grams
unsalted butter, softened	1 tablespoon	0.5 ounce	14 grams

Drain the snails and rinse them under cold running water.

In a small saucepan, combine the snails, stock, wine, herbs, salt, and peppercorns and bring to a boil. Lower the heat and simmer for 5 minutes. Remove the pan from the heat and allow the snails to cool in the broth. Strain the broth, reserving the liquid, and cut each snail crosswise in half.

With a piece of plastic wrap, coat the bottom and sides of the pan with the softened butter.

FILL THE DOUGH

On a well-floured surface, roll out the dough again into a 14- by 6-inch rectangle. Brush with the lightly beaten egg and sprinkle evenly with the parsley. Roll it up from a short end, brushing off excess flour as you go.

Using a sharp knife, cut the roll into 3 pieces, then cut each piece in half. Place cut side down in the prepared pan. Press the tops down so that the sides touch. Use a greased wooden spoon handle or small knife to make holes and insert 4 pieces of snail into the top of each bun, pressing them in deeply. (Place 1 in the center and the other 3 evenly around it.) Cover the buns with plastic wrap that has been sprayed with nonstick vegetable shortening or buttered. Let the buns rise in a warm place for 1 to 2 hours or until they reach the top of the pan.

Preheat the oven to 425°F. at least 30 minutes before baking. Set a baking sheet lined with foil (to catch any juices) on the lowest oven rack before preheating.

MAKE THE SNAIL BUN GLAZE

INGREDIENTS	MEASURE	WEIGHT	
	VOLUME	OUNCES	GRAMS
Snail Bun Glaze reserved snail poaching broth	¼ liquid cup to 6 tablespoons	•	•

In a small saucepan over high heat, or in a 1-cup heatproof measuring cup in a microwave oven on high power, reduce the strained snail poaching broth to 2 tablespoons. The glaze should be lukewarm when brushed onto the buns.

Brush the buns with the glaze. Place the pan on the hot baking sheet and bake for 10 minutes. Lower the heat to 375°F. and bake for 15 minutes or until a skewer inserted in the center comes out clean. To keep the buns from becoming too brown, cover them loosely with foil after the first 7 minutes.

Let the buns cool in the pan for 3 minutes before unmolding them onto a serving plate or foil-lined counter. They can be eaten at once, or reheated later in a 350°F. oven for 15 minutes, loosely wrapped in foil, or in a microwave oven on high power for 30 seconds, wrapped in a damp paper towel.

STORE
Airtight, room temperature, up to 2 days; frozen, up to 3 months.

POINTERS FOR SUCCESS
∿ See page 518.

UNDERSTANDING
The hot baking sheet will boost the "oven spring" (the amount it rises from the oven heat) of the brioche.

CREAM PUFF PASTRY

(Pâte à Choux)

In French, *choux* means cabbage. The French name for this pastry (pronounced pat ah shoe) derives from its shape when the dough is piped and baked into cream puffs.

If ever there was a foolproof pastry, this is it. Crisp, light, and eggy, this versatile pastry dough can be used to make a host of recipes, sweet and savory, simple and complex. They include cream puffs (profiteroles), gougère, éclairs, and the most glamorous of all pastries, Gâteau St.-Honoré.

Years ago, before the Cuisinart became my first official kitchen assistant, Carl Sontheimer (its producer) telephoned just as I was in the middle of making a batch of cream puff pastry with the wooden-spoon-and-elbow-grease technique. Beating the eggs into the thickened flour/water/butter mixture was always tiring, but I had never realized there was an alternative. I could hear the astonishment in Carl's voice when I told him I wasn't using a food processor. He assured me that not only did it make blending in the eggs effortless, it also produced the lightest cream puffs imaginable. Although I am offering the "by hand" version in addition to the food processor one, I have never gone back to it.

Although my cream puffs were vastly improved, I still wasn't totally satisfied. The goal in making perfect cream puff pastry is to have the finest crisp crust, the lightest interior, and the roundest and/or most attractive shape. I increased the eggs to the maximum possible but still felt the puffs weren't as light as they could be. I discussed this with my friend and colleague Shirley Corriher, complaining that increasing the liquid is what makes the puffs puffier, but it also makes them lose their shape. Her immediate response was, "Add egg whites; and while you're at it, why don't you try bread flour as well? They both will increase the strength of the dough and the egg white will make it more crisp when baked, the way it does in a meringue." The result was the Cordon Rose Cream Puff Pastry (page 534). It is excellent for cream puffs and éclairs, but for larger shapes, such as the spiral used for Gâteau St.-Honoré, or delicate shapes such as the heads and necks of pastry swans, the less delicate Classic Cream Puff Pastry recipe (page 530) is preferable.

POINTERS FOR SUCCESS FOR CREAM PUFF PASTRY

∽ Though it is not absolutely necessary, if you sift the flour after measuring or weighing it, it will be incorporated more easily into the liquid mixture.

∽ Water makes a lighter puff than milk because milk causes the eggs to coagulate sooner.

∽ The proper amount of liquid in the dough is maintained by not allowing the water to boil off and by using a liquid measure or scale to ensure using the full quantity of eggs.

∽ Spraying or brushing the baking sheets with water to create steam during baking will help the puffs rise.

∽ After piping puffs, if not ready to bake them, cover them with plastic wrap sprayed with nonstick vegetable shortening so the surface will not dry and crack during baking, and refrigerate them for up to 2 hours.

∽ To prevent cracking, don't open the oven door during the early part of baking, but do open it toward the end to dry the center. (If the puff is not dried adequately, it will collapse.)

∽ To gauge the size of a cream puff and the yield of a specific recipe, follow this guide: A puff piped 1½ inches in diameter by ½ to ¾ inch high, weighing about ½ ounce (13 grams) before baking, will measure 2 inches by 1½ to 1¾ inches after baking.

CLASSIC CREAM PUFF PASTRY

This is the basic recipe for cream puff pastry but with a slightly higher amount of egg than usual to ensure lightness. It makes a sturdy enough dough, however, to use for piping a spiraled dough ring for making Gâteau St.-Honoré (page 538) or for piping figures such as swans (page 532). It can be used to make profiteroles or éclairs, though I prefer the Cordon Rose version on page 534.

OVEN TEMPERATURE: 400°F. • BAKING TIME: 30 MINUTES (PLUS 1 HOUR 40 MINUTES IN THE TURNED-OFF OVEN)

MAKES: ABOUT 23.25 OUNCES/666 GRAMS DOUGH; ABOUT 4 DOZEN 2- BY 1½-INCH-HIGH PUFFS, ABOUT SIXTEEN 5- BY 1¾-INCH-HIGH ÉCLAIRS, OR ABOUT 20 SWANS

INGREDIENTS	MEASURE	WEIGHT	
	VOLUME	OUNCES	GRAMS
water	1 liquid cup	8.3 ounces	236 grams
unsalted butter	8 tablespoons	4 ounces	113 grams
sugar	1 teaspoon	•	4 grams
salt	½ teaspoon	•	3 grams
bleached all-purpose flour	1 cup (dip and sweep method)	5 ounces	142 grams
5 large eggs	1 liquid cup	8.75 ounces (weighed without the shells)	250 grams

EQUIPMENT
Cookie sheet(s) or inverted half-size sheet pan(s); for puffs or éclairs, a pastry bag and a number 6 (½-inch) plain round tube plus a second pastry bag and a Bismarck tube for puffs; for swans, 2 pastry bags, number 8 (⅝-inch) and 9 (¾-inch) plain round tubes, and number 2D or closed star decorating tip

In a medium saucepan, combine the water, butter, sugar, and salt and bring to a full rolling boil. Immediately remove the saucepan from the heat and add the flour all at once. Stir with a wooden spoon until the mixture forms a ball, leaves the sides of the pan, and clings slightly to the spoon. Return the pan to low heat and cook, stirring and mashing continuously, for about 3 minutes to cook the flour.

FOOD PROCESSOR METHOD

Without scraping the pan, transfer the mixture to the bowl of a food processor fitted with the metal blade. With the feed tube open to allow steam to escape, process for 15 seconds. With the motor running, pour in the eggs all at once and continue processing for 30 seconds.

HAND METHOD

Without scraping the pan, empty the mixture into a bowl. Add the eggs one at a time, beating vigorously with a wooden spoon after reach addition.

FOR BOTH METHODS

The mixture will be smooth and shiny and it should be too soft to hold peaks when lifted with a spoon. If it is too stiff, add a little extra water. (The dough can be stored in an airtight container and refrigerated overnight. Beat it lightly with a wooden spoon before piping.)

SHAPE THE PUFFS

Dab a small dot of the dough in each corner of the baking sheet and line the sheet with parchment or a Teflon-type liner, pressing lightly to make it adhere; or use foil. Alternatively, you can grease and flour the baking sheet. (Do not use Baker's Joy, as it makes piping the puffs too slippery.)

Preheat the oven to 400°F. at least 20 minutes before baking. Set an oven rack in the middle level before preheating.

For cream puffs and éclairs: Fill a pastry bag fitted with a ½-inch diameter tube with the dough.

For cream puffs: Pipe puffs about 1½ inches in diameter and ½ inch to ¾ inch high about 1 inch apart onto the prepared sheet. (By hand, you can use two greased teaspoons instead of piping. Use one to scoop out the dough and the other, or your fingertip, to push it off onto the baking sheet. If necessary, use your fingertip, dipped first in a little water, to smooth the shape.)

For éclairs: Pipe 4- by 1½-inch lengths, ½ inch to ¾ inch high, about 3 inches apart onto the sheet. (If you are using a spoon, use a damp metal spatula to spread them into shape, making the ends slightly wider than the centers.) Run the tines of a fork down the length of the tops to encourage the éclairs to crack evenly when they bake.

For swans: About 1 ounce (30 grams) of dough is needed for each body and only about 3 grams for each head and neck. Use the number 9 tube to pipe teardrop-shaped puffs about 3 inches long, ½ inch to ¾ inch high, 2 inches apart onto the prepared sheet. (Figure 1) On a separate sheet, use the number 8 tube to pipe the heads and necks. (Figure 2) Use a moistened toothpick to draw out a little beak, and, if desired, place a black sesame seed (available in Eastern markets) on each head as an eye.

Bake for 30 minutes (20 minutes for the swan heads). Remove the puffs (including swan bodies) or éclairs to racks. (Do not turn off the oven.) Holding each puff or éclair (not the swan heads) gently on either side, invert it and use the tip of a knife to make a ¼-inch slit in the bottom to release steam. (Alternatively, a decorating tube, preferably the Bismarck filling tube, can be used to make a small hole that will later be used for filling the puffs. Twisting it as you push it into the puff helps to cut the hole.) Return the puffs or swan bodies, still on the racks, and heads to the oven. Turn off the oven and use a wooden spoon or wedge to prop the oven door slightly ajar and let the pastry dry for 10 minutes. At this point, you can close the door and leave the puffs or éclairs in the turned-off oven for 1½ hours to dry out completely, or continue baking them for 45 minutes at 200°F.

Test a pastry by cutting it open. The dough inside (except for the swan bodies or éclairs) should not be soft to the touch. Remove the puffs, on the racks, and allow them to cool completely.

TO FILL THE PUFFS

For cream puffs: Use a pastry bag fitted with a Bismarck tube to pipe the filling through the slit or hole into the hollow center of each cream puff. Then dip the tops of the puffs into chocolate glaze. **For profiteroles:** Use a serrated knife to split them horizontally in half. Fill with small scoops of ice cream and pour hot glaze on top.

For éclairs: Use a serrated knife to split them horizontally in half. Remove some of the soft dough from the inside. Use a pastry bag fitted with a number 6 (½-inch) round tube (or a teaspoon) to fill each one with a scant ¼ cup of filling.

To assemble swans: Use a serrated knife to split the bodies horizontally at an angle, starting higher at the pointed end. (Figure 3) Remove and discard the soft dough from the inside. Carefully cut the top part of the puff lengthwise in half to form the wings. (Figure 4)

Fill the pastry bag, fitted with the number 2D decorating tip with whipped cream. Starting at the rounded lower end of the base, using a back-and-forth motion, ruffle the whipped cream into it, allowing it to mound slightly—32 grams for each, a total of 3 cups of cream, whipped. (Figure 5) Place a wing on either side, leaning it up against the cream. (Figure 6) Insert the neck into the cream at the rounded front.

STORE

Unfilled puffs, in reclosable freezer bags or airtight containers, refrigerated, up to 1 week; frozen, up to 6 months.

UNDERSTANDING

The small amount of sugar in the dough adds flavor and helps in browning.

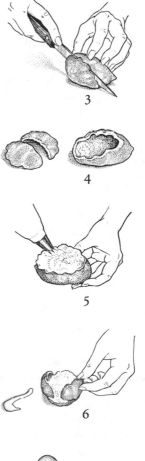

CORDON ROSE CREAM PUFF PASTRY

R ound, light, crisp, and delicate, these puffs are perfect for profiteroles. The dough also makes light and crispy éclairs (page 536). It is too delicate, however, for larger pastries such as the Gâteau St.-Honoré (page 538).

(page 536)
(page 538)

OVEN TEMPERATURE: 425°F. •
BAKING TIME: 25 TO 35 MINUTES (PLUS 1 HOUR
40 MINUTES IN THE TURNED-OFF OVEN)

MAKES: ABOUT 4 DOZEN
2- BY 1¾-INCH-HIGH PUFFS OR ABOUT
SIXTEEN 5- BY 1¾-INCH-HIGH ÉCLAIRS

INGREDIENTS	MEASURE	WEIGHT	
	VOLUME	OUNCES	GRAMS
water	1 liquid cup	8.3 ounces	236 grams
unsalted butter	8 tablespoons	4 ounces	113 grams
sugar	1 teaspoon	•	4 grams
salt	½ teaspoon	•	3.3 grams
bread flour or unbleached all-purpose flour	1 cup minus 1½ tablespoons 1 cup (dip and sweep method)	5 ounces •	142 grams •
3 large eggs + 3 large egg whites	1 liquid cup (total)	8.5 ounces	240 grams

EQUIPMENT
Cookie sheet(s) or inverted half-size sheet pan(s); for the puffs or éclairs, a pastry bag and a number 6 (½-inch) plain round tube, plus a second pastry bag and a Bismarck tube for filling the puffs

In a medium saucepan, combine the water, butter, sugar, and salt and bring to a full rolling boil. Immediately remove the saucepan from the heat and add the flour all at once. Stir with a wooden spoon until the mixture forms a ball, leaves the sides of the pan, and clings slightly to the spoon. Return the pan to low heat and cook, stirring and mashing continuously, for about 3 minutes to cook the flour.

FOOD PROCESSOR METHOD
Without scraping the pan, transfer the mixture to the bowl of food processor fitted with the metal blade. With the feed tube open to allow steam to escape,

process for 15 seconds. With the motor running, pour in the eggs and whites all at once and continue processing for 30 seconds.

FOR HAND METHOD

Without scraping the pan, empty the mixture into a bowl and add the eggs one at a time, and then the egg whites, beating vigorously with a wooden spoon after each addition.

FOR BOTH METHODS

The mixture will be smooth and shiny and it should be too soft to hold peaks when lifted with a spoon. If it is too stiff, add a little extra water. (The dough can be stored in an airtight container and refrigerated overnight. Beat it lightly with a wooden spoon before piping.)

Preheat the oven to 425°F. at least 20 minutes before baking. Set an oven rack in the middle level before preheating.

SHAPE THE PUFFS

Dab a small dot of the dough in each corner of the baking sheet and line the sheet with a Teflon-type liner, pressing lightly to make it adhere; or use foil, or grease and flour the pan. (Do not use parchment, as these puffs will stick. Also, do not use Baker's Joy, as it makes piping the puffs too slippery.) Fill a pastry bag fitted with the number 6 (½-inch) tube with the mixture.

For cream puffs: Pipe puffs about 1½ inches in diameter and ½ inch to ¾ inch high about 1 inch apart onto the sheet. (By hand, you can use two greased teaspoons instead of piping. Use one to scoop out the dough and the other, or your fingertip, to push it off onto the baking sheet. If necessary, use your fingertip, dipped first in a little water, to smooth the shape.)

For éclairs: Pipe 4- by 1½-inch lengths, ½ inch to ¾ inch high, about 3 inches apart onto the sheet. (If you are using a spoon, use a damp metal spatula to spread them into shape, making the ends slightly wider than the centers.) Run the tines of a fork down the length of the tops to encourage the éclairs to crack evenly when they bake.

Bake for 10 minutes, then lower the temperature to 350°F. and bake for 15 to 20 minutes or until golden brown. Remove the puffs or éclairs to racks. (Do not turn off the oven.) Holding each puff gently on either side, invert it and use the tip of a knife to make a ¼-inch slit in the bottom to release steam. (Alternatively, a decorating tube, preferably the Bismarck filling tube, can be used to make a small hole that will be used later for filling the puffs. Twisting it as you push it into the puff helps to cut the hole.) Or, for the éclairs, make 2 or 3 slits in the sides of each. Return the puffs or éclairs to the oven, still on the racks, turn off the oven, and use a wooden spoon or wedge to prop the oven door slightly ajar. Allow the puffs to dry for 10 minutes. Close the door and leave them in the oven for 1½ hours to dry out completely (or continue baking them for 45 minutes at 200°F.).

Test a puff by cutting it open. The dough inside the puffs should not be soft to the touch. If it is, return it to the oven for a little longer. Allow the puffs or éclairs to cool completely on the racks.

TO FILL THE PUFFS

For cream puffs: Use a pastry bag fitted with a Bismarck tube to pipe filling through the slit or hole into the hollow center of each cream puff. Then dip the tops of the puffs into chocolate glaze. **For profiteroles:** Use a serrated knife to split them horizontally in half. Use a small scoop or spoon to fill them with ice cream. Drizzle hot glaze on top.

For éclairs: Use a serrated knife to split them in half horizontally. Remove some of the soft dough from the inside. Use a pastry bag fitted with a number 6 (½-inch) round tube (or a teaspoon) to fill each one with a scant ¼ cup of filling.

STORE

Unfilled puffs, in reclosable freezer bags or airtight containers, refrigerated, up to 1 week; frozen, up to 6 months.

ÉCLAIRS AND CREAM PUFFS (PROFITEROLES)

*É*clair, a French word that means lightning bolt, is also the name, both in French and English, for one of the world's great pastries. I wonder if it was named for its long straight shape or for the speed with which one consumes it. The only meaning most Americans know, however, is that it is an enduring favorite consisting of an elongated golden cream puff filled with whipped cream or pastry cream, or a combination of the two, and most often glazed with chocolate.

When you take a bite of an éclair, the squish of the airy/creamy filling against the crunchy/soft dough and melding of comforting and tantalizing flavors is unforgettable. It was the only dessert my mother bought. She would have to walk one mile to the famous Eclair Bakery on West 72nd Street in New York City, so it was an occasional treat.

Profiteroles are cream puffs filled with whipped cream or, most often, with ice cream and then sauced with hot fudge or caramel sauce (page 596 or 597). They make an incredible easy dessert. Try it with some of the ice creams starting on page 243. Peanut butter or pistachio ice cream is delicious with chocolate sauce. Caramel ice cream with caramel sauce is over the top.

MAKES: ABOUT SIXTEEN 5- BY 1¾-INCH-HIGH ÉCLAIRS
OR ABOUT 4 DOZEN 2- BY 1½-INCH-HIGH PUFFS

INGREDIENTS	MEASURE	WEIGHT	
	VOLUME	OUNCES	GRAMS
1 recipe Cream Puff Pastry (page 530 or 534), shaped into puffs or éclairs		•	•
Chocolate Glaze or Sauce fine-quality bittersweet chocolate, grated	(approx. 2 cups) four 3-ounce bars	12 ounces	340 grams
heavy cream	1¼ liquid cups, divided	approx. 10.2 ounces	290 grams
optional: Cognac or other liqueur	1 tablespoon	•	•
Filling 1 recipe perfect Whipped Cream (page 551), Pastry Cream (page 560), Light Whipped Ganache (page 559), or Triple Vanilla Lover's Ice Cream (page 232)	2½ to 3 cups, (a scant tablespoon for each puff; 3 to 4 tablespoons for each éclair)	•	•

EQUIPMENT

For puffs, a pastry bag and a number 12 (¼-inch) plain round tube or a Bismarck tube; for éclairs, a pastry bag and a number 6 (½-inch) plain round tube

Make the dough (page 530 or 534). Pipe, shape, and bake the puffs (see page 535).

PREPARE THE CHOCOLATE GLAZE OR SAUCE

Place the chocolate in a small heavy saucepan with a lid. Place 1 cup of the cream in a small saucepan, or a heatproof glass measure if using a microwave, and bring it to the boiling point. Pour it over the chocolate, cover it tightly, and allow it to sit for 5 minutes to melt the chocolate. Gently stir the mixture together until uniform in color, trying not to create air bubbles. Pass it through a fine strainer and stir in the optional liqueur. Allow the glaze to cool until just tepid.

    To check the consistency: When it is tepid, a small amount of glaze should mound a bit on the surface when dropped from a spoon before smoothly disappearing. If the glaze is too thick and the mound remains on the surface, or if the glaze seems curdled, warm the remaining ¼ cup of cream and add it by the tablespoon.

FILL AND GLAZE THE PUFFS

Preferably no more than 3 hours ahead, use a pastry bag fitted with a long Bismarck or number 12 (¼-inch) round tube to pipe filling through the slit or hole into the hollow center of each cream puff. Then dip the tops of puffs into the chocolate glaze. They can be eaten immediately, or after the glaze sets (about 1 hour). Refrigeration dulls the glaze slightly.

FILL AND GLAZE THE ÉCLAIRS

Use a pastry bag fitted with a number 6 (½-inch) tube (or a teaspoon) to fill each one with a scant ¼ cup of filling. Place the filled éclairs on a rack over a sheet pan and pour the tepid glaze over them. They can be eaten immediately, or after the glaze sets (about 1 hour). Refrigeration dulls the glaze slightly.

FILL AND GLAZE THE PROFITEROLES

Use a serrated knife to split them horizontally in half. Use a small scoop or spoon to fill them with the ice cream. Place in bowls and drizzle the hot glaze on top.

STORE

If filled with pastry cream or ganache, room temperature, up to 3 hours; refrigerated, up to 2 days. Both éclairs and profiteroles are the crispest within 3 hours of being made, but they are still delicious even after the pastry softens.

NOTE

For profiteroles filled with ice cream, it's preferable to use the full amount of cream and pour the sauce over the filled puffs while it is still hot.

GÂTEAU ST.-HONORÉ

This triumph of French classic pastry consists of a disc of puff pastry topped with a ring of caramel-glazed cream puffs that have been filled with Chiboust pastry cream. This was the grand finale of my baking classes—the perfect lesson, because it teaches so many of the basic pastry components: puff pastry, cream puff pastry, pastry cream perfumed with Grand Marnier, caramel, and spun sugar. The contrast of textures—flaky, crunchy, soft, and creamy—

makes this the most thrillingly complex of any pastry. The piped spiral of cream puff pastry, set on top of the puff pastry disc in the center of the cream puff halo, is an idea I learned from a course in France at LeNôtre's pastry school in Plaisir. It is a lovely architectural addition to the gâteau, appreciated only when it is served and the round open cross sections of the spiral coil, surrounded by pastry cream, become apparent.

This is the dessert to make for your grandest, most elegant dinner party. The puff pastry, cream puff pastry, and pastry cream can all be prepared well ahead, but the final assembly of filling the puffs, dipping them in caramel, shaping the gâteau, and making the optional spun sugar, which takes about thirty minutes, is best performed no more than two to three hours before serving. This makes it ideal for couples who cook together. One can attend to the appetizer and main course while the other completes the dessert.

The optional spun sugar is pure fantasy, but don't make it unless the weather is dry, as heat and humidity cause it to evaporate.

OVEN TEMPERATURE: 400°F. •
BAKING TIME: 35 MINUTES
(PLUS 15 MINUTES IN THE TURNED-OFF OVEN)   SERVES: 8 TO 10

INGREDIENTS	MEASURE	WEIGHT	
	VOLUME	OUNCES	GRAMS
Classic Puff Pastry(page 417), made with only 4 turns, or Quick Puff Pastry (page 420)		1¼ pounds	567 grams
1 recipe Classic Cream Puff Pastry (page 530)		23.25 ounces	666 grams
Chiboust Cream (page 565)	5½ cups	29.5 ounces	840 grams
1 recipe Caramel for Dipping (page 600)		•	•
optional: spun sugar (page 602)		•	•

EQUIPMENT
A heavy pizza pan or a rectangular baking sheet at least 10 inches wide; a 10-inch cake pan; a second large baking sheet for the puffs, lined with parchment or greased and floured; and a pastry bag, a number 6 (½-inch) plain round pastry tube, a Bismarck tube or a number 12 (¼-inch) round tube, and a number 7 large star pastry tube

Make the puff pastry dough (page 417 or 420) and the cream puff dough (page 530).

ROLL AND BAKE THE PUFF PASTRY BASE

On a well-floured surface, roll the puff pastry into a 9½-inch square about ³⁄₁₆ inch thick, rolling evenly from the center out in all directions. Move the pastry occasionally to be sure it is not sticking and flour the surface if necessary. Push in the corners and roll the pastry into a 10-inch circle.

Spray or brush the pizza pan or heavy baking sheet with water to prevent distortion and transfer the dough to it. Cover it with plastic wrap and refrigerate it until firm, at least 30 minutes.

Preheat the oven to 400°F. at least 20 minutes before baking. Set an oven rack at the lowest level before preheating.

Remove the plastic wrap and prick the dough all over with a fork. For even rising, grease the bottom of a cake pan or sheet pan at least 10 inches in diameter and place it on top of the pastry. If using classic puff pastry, evenly distribute some metal pie weights or beans in the pan as additional weight. (Don't use too many, as the object is not to keep the pastry from rising completely but just to keep it from rising excessively yet allowing it to remain tender and very flaky.)

Bake for 20 minutes. Remove the cake pan and continue baking for 10 minutes or until golden brown. Open the oven door and bake for another 5 minutes with the oven door propped open with a wooden spoon. Then turn off the oven, leaving the door propped open, and leave the pastry in it for 15 minutes to dry the center layers. Remove it to a wire rack to cool, then wrap airtight until ready to use.

FORM AND BAKE THE CREAM PUFF PASTRY HALO, SPIRAL, AND PUFFS

Preheat the oven to 425°F. at least 20 minutes before baking. Set an oven rack at the middle level before preheating.

Measure the baked puff pastry round and cut a piece of parchment the same diameter. Using a few dabs of the cream puff pastry as adhesive, attach the parchment round to the baking sheet.

Have a glass of water and small metal spatula or knife nearby. Fill the pastry bag fitted with the ½-inch tube with cream puff pastry and pipe a circle just inside the edge of the parchment for the halo. Dip the spatula in water, cut off the end of the pastry, and smooth together the break where it begins and ends.

Pipe a spiraled coil of pastry inside the halo, at least ½ inch away, so that during baking the expanding dough will not connect.

Use the remaining cream puff pastry to pipe puffs about 1½ inches in diameter ½ to ¾ inch high about 1 inch apart onto a second baking sheet. (You can use two greased teaspoons instead of piping. Use one to scoop out the dough and the other, or your fingertip, to push it off onto the baking sheets. If necessary, use your fingertip, dipped first in a little water or oil, to smooth the shape.) (You will have about 28 puffs, but only 16 are needed for this recipe.)

Spray or brush the halo, spiral, and puffs lightly with water. Bake for 10 minutes, then lower the heat to 350°F. and continue baking for 15 to 20 minutes or until the halo and spiral are golden and firm enough to lift without collapsing. Remove the halo, spiral, and puffs to racks (leave the oven on). Make a small slit in the bottom of each puff to release steam. (Or use a decorating tube, preferably the Bismarck filling tube, to make a small hole that will be used later for filling the puffs, twisting it as you push it into the puffs to help cut the hole.) Return the puffs, halo, and spiral to the oven, still on the racks. Turn off the oven, use a wooden spoon to prop the oven door slightly ajar, and let the pastry dry for 10 minutes. Close the door and leave the pastry in the oven for 1½ hours to dry out completely (or continue baking for 45 minutes at 200°F.). Test a puff by cutting it open. The dough inside should not be soft to the touch; if it is, return them to the oven. Allow all the pastry to cool completely. Store it airtight in a plastic bag or container until ready to use.

ASSEMBLE THE GÂTEAU

Fill the puffs: Fill a pastry bag, fitted with the Bismarck tube, with a small amount of the pastry cream and fill the hollow centers of 16 cream puffs.

Prepare the caramel: If you have a microwave oven, pour the caramel into a 2-cup heatproof glass measure. This will enable you to remelt it easily if it hardens. Alternatively, it can be reheated over low heat in the pan, but try not to drip any of the caramel onto the outside of the pot.

Allow the hot caramel to sit for about 5 minutes to thicken slightly for coating the puffs. Meanwhile, spoon a few drops of it onto the puff pastry round and affix the halo and spiral to it.

Holding a filled puff at the bottom with tongs or fingertips, carefully dip the top into the caramel and then allow the excess to drip off onto the halo. Quickly attach the bottom of the puff to the halo before the caramel hardens. Continue with the remaining filled puffs until the circle is completed, placing each puff snugly against the one before it.

When the gâteau is no longer hot from the caramel, pipe or spoon the remaining pastry cream into the center.

MAKE THE OPTIONAL SPUN SUGAR

If the weather is very dry, the spun sugar can be made a day ahead, but it must be shaped immediately after preparation, while it is still flexible. Use an inverted cake pan the size of the finished gâteau, well sprayed with nonstick vegetable spray, to shape the spun sugar. Leave it on this mold until ready to transfer it to the gâteau. I find it preferable to make the spun sugar after the rest of the dessert has been assembled and wrap the golden strands directly around the outside of the gâteau.

To serve, use sharp shears to cut through the spun sugar and a serrated or sharp thin-bladed knife to cut through the pastry. Be sure to do this in front of your guests, as the wonderful variety of crunchy sound effects is part of the joyful anticipation! Serve 1½ to 2 puffs per person.

STORE

Unfilled halo, spiral, and puffs, room temperature, up to 1 day; refrigerated, up to 1 week; frozen, up to 3 months. (To recrisp, place them in a 350°F. oven for 10 to 15 minutes. Cool completely before filling them.) Gâteau, cool room temperature, 4 to 6 hours.

NOTE

For a larger gâteau to serve 12 to 14, you will need 1⅓ pounds of puff pastry rolled into a 12-inch circle and 1½ times the pastry cream (made with 3½ to 5 teaspoons gelatin). (There will be more than enough extra puffs for this larger size.)

POINTERS FOR SUCCESS

∾ If you wish to assemble the gâteau the day before, it can be done up to the point of filling the puffs and gâteau with the pastry cream and making the spun sugar, providing the humidity is low to prevent the caramel from becoming sticky. ∾ If piping the pastry cream, do not fill the bag too full, or the heat of your hand will soften the cream.

UNDERSTANDING

Classic puff pastry made with only 4 turns, and 2 days old, or quick puff pastry is best for the least distortion.

The puff pastry needs to be very flat on top so you can attach the halo and spiral to it .

SAVORY CREAM PUFFS

These delectable puffs are as round as golf balls, fine and crisp on the outside, and with an open but soft, herbal-flavored interior. The use of herb-infused oil or truffle oil in place of butter offers more flavor and a lighter texture compared to sweet classic cream puffs. Unlike the classic cream puffs, these puffs do not have an eggy taste. The flavorful oil, herbs, and garlic render them perfect containers for escargots (see page 547).

The puffs can be filled with a variety of savory fillings, using a pastry bag or cut in half and stuffed with lobster or chicken salad, but they are also delicious on their own with cocktails from champagne to martinis.

Instructions for this recipe and the two variations that follow begin on page 545.

OVEN TEMPERATURE: 400°F. •
BAKING TIME: 30 MINUTES
(PLUS 10 MINUTES IN THE TURNED-OFF OVEN)

MAKES: ABOUT 4 DOZEN
2- BY 1¾-INCH-HIGH PUFFS

INGREDIENTS	MEASURE	WEIGHT	
	VOLUME	OUNCES	GRAMS
water	1 liquid cup	8.3 ounces	236 grams
infused extra-virgin olive oil of your choice	½ liquid cup minus 1 tablespoon	3.3 ounces	94 grams
sugar	½ teaspoon	•	2 grams
bread flour or unbleached all-purpose flour	1 cup minus 1½ tablespoons 1 cup (dip and sweep method)	5 ounces	142 grams
3 large eggs + 3 large egg whites	1 liquid cup (total)	8.5 ounces	240 grams
3 large cloves garlic	•	•	•
salt	½ teaspoon	•	3 grams

WHITE TRUFFLE OIL VARIATION

I f you adore the flavor of white truffle, as I do, these puffs will be special treat. The amount of white truffle oil used makes the fragrance not overly intense; rather, it perfumes the puffs with a mysterious but unmistakable taste. White truffle oil is available in tiny bottles, by mail order, from Balducci's (see page 676). This smaller-quantity recipe makes just the right amount for a batch of escargot puffs (page 547).

MAKES: FOURTEEN TO SIXTEEN 2- BY 1¾-INCH-HIGH PUFFS;
SERVES 4 AS AN APPETIZER

INGREDIENTS	MEASURE	WEIGHT	
	VOLUME	OUNCES	GRAMS
water	⅓ liquid cup	2.7 ounces	78 grams
safflower oil	2 tablespoons	•	•
white truffle oil	2 teaspoons		
sugar	⅛ + ¹⁄₁₆ teaspoon	•	2 grams
bread flour or unbleached all-purpose flour	5 tablespoons ⅓ cup (dip and sweep method)	• 1.66 ounces	• 47.3 grams
1 large egg + 1 large egg white	⅓ liquid cup (total)	approx. 2.75 ounces	80 grams
1 large clove garlic	•	•	•
salt	⅛ + ¹⁄₁₆ teaspoon	•	3 grams
minced fresh thyme or ⅛ teaspoon dried thyme	½ teaspoon	•	•
minced fresh parsley, preferably flat-leaf	½ teaspoon	•	•

SPICY CHEESE PUFF VARIATION
(Gougères) (gooJAIR)

I n Burgundy, these cream puffs are made with Gruyère cheese and baked in the form of a large ring. It is cut into slices and served cold to visitors in wine-tasting cellars, to accompany the wine. I usually form them as individual puffs and replace the Gruyère with Cheddar cheese. I also add chopped ham, a whisper of cayenne pepper, and fresh garlic for extra flavor.

These crisp, moist, and spicy puffs are delightful with cocktails from beer to red wine. The addition of ham and cheese to these puffs makes them more dense than usual cream puff pastry, but using the extra egg whites and oil instead of butter gives them a smoother shape, finer crust, and less eggy, more delicious flavor.

MAKES: ABOUT FORTY-SIX 1½- BY 1¼-INCH-HIGH PUFFS

INGREDIENTS	MEASURE	WEIGHT	
	VOLUME	OUNCES	GRAMS
water	1 liquid cup	8.3 ounces	236 grams
extra-virgin olive oil	⅓ liquid cup	2.5 ounces	72 grams
sugar	½ teaspoon	•	6 grams
bread flour or unbleached all-purpose flour	1 cup minus 1 tablespoon 1 cup (dip and sweep method)	• 5 ounces	• 142 grams
3 large eggs + 3 large egg whites	1 liquid cup (total)	8.5 ounces	240 grams
2 large cloves garlic	•	0.5 ounce	14 grams
salt	½ teaspoon	•	3.3 grams
optional: ham, finely chopped	•	2 ounces	57 grams
sharp Cheddar cheese, finely grated	½ cup	2 ounces	57 grams
cayenne pepper	¼ teaspoon	•	•

EQUIPMENT (FOR ALL SAVORY PUFFS)
A cookie sheet or inverted half-size sheet pan and pastry bag and number 6 (½-inch) plain round tube

In a medium saucepan, combine the water, oil(s), and sugar and bring to a full rolling boil. Immediately remove the saucepan from the heat and add the flour all at once. Stir with a wooden spoon until the mixture forms a ball, leaves the sides of the pan, and clings slightly to the spoon. Return the pan to low heat and cook, stirring and mashing continuously, for about 3 minutes to cook the flour.

FOOD PROCESSOR METHOD
Without scraping the pan, transfer the mixture to the bowl of a food processor fitted with the metal blade. With the feed tube open to allow steam to escape, process for 15 seconds. With the motor running, pour in the eggs all at once and continue processing for 30 seconds. The mixture will be smooth and shiny and it

should be too soft to hold peaks when lifted with a spoon. If it is too stiff, add a little extra water. On a cutting board, smash the garlic with the flat side of a large knife, sprinkle it with the salt to soften it, and chop until very fine. Add the garlic mixture and the thyme and parsley for white truffle puffs or the optional ham, the cheese, and cayenne pepper for gougères to the dough mixture and pulse a few times until evenly incorporated.

HAND METHOD

Without scraping the pan, empty the mixture into a bowl and add the egg(s), one at a time, and then the egg white(s), beating vigorously with a wooden spoon after each addition.

Chop the garlic with the salt as above. Beat the garlic mixture and the thyme and parsley for white truffle puffs or the optional ham, the cheese, and cayenne pepper for gougères until evenly incorporated. The mixture can be stored in an airtight container and refrigerated overnight. Beat it lightly with a wooden spoon before piping.

Preheat the oven to 400°F. at least 20 minutes before baking. Set an oven rack in the middle level before preheating.

SHAPE THE PUFFS

Dab a small dot of the mixture in each corner of the baking sheet and line the sheet with a Teflon-type liner, pressing lightly to make it adhere; or use foil or grease and flour the pan. (Do not use parchment, as these puffs will stick. Also, do not use Baker's Joy, as it makes piping the puffs too slippery.) Fill the pastry bag fitted with a ½- to ¾-inch pastry tube with dough and pipe puffs about 1½ inches in diameter and ½ to ¾ inch high at least 1 inch apart onto the sheet. (By hand, you can use two greased teaspoons instead of piping. Use one to scoop out the dough and the other, or your fingertip, to push it off onto the baking sheets. If necessary, use your fingertip, dipped first in a little water, to smooth the shape.)

Bake for 30 minutes or until the puffs are golden brown and firm enough to lift without collapsing. Remove them to racks. (Do not turn off the oven.) Holding each puff gently on either side, invert it and use the tip of a knife to make a ¼-inch slit in the bottom to release steam. Return them to the oven, still on the racks. Turn off the oven, use a wooden spoon or wedge to prop the oven door slightly ajar, and let the puffs dry for 10 minutes. Serve warm or at room temperature.

FILL THE PUFFS

Use a serrated knife to slice off the top quarter of each puff, reserving the tops. Pipe or spoon about 2 teaspoons of filling into each bottom. Cover with the tops.

STORE

Unfilled puffs, in heavy-duty freezer bags or airtight containers, refrigerated, up to 1 week; frozen, up to 6 months. Reheat in a 350°F. oven for 10 minutes before serving.

UNDERSTANDING

This pastry replaces the 8 tablespoons of butter in the classic recipe with 7 table-spoons of oil, because butter contains only 81 percent fat (compared to the oil's 100 percent) and 15.5 percent water. For the gougères, 1 tablespoon less oil is used than for the basic savory cream puffs to offset the fat contained in the Cheddar cheese.

ESCARGOT PUFFS

For me, these puffs are the world's best appetizer and a perfect party dish. Quick and easy to make, the recipe can be increased to make dozens, and they can be prepared two days ahead, refrigerated, and reheated in five minutes. The crisp and airy garlic-and-herb-imbued cream puffs have a moist interior that makes a perfect edible "shell" in which to nestle the snails, cloaked with a dab of classic garlic/herb butter. When they are heated, the garlic butter melts into the puff. Every bite is something delectable. Escargots never get as good as these.

OVEN TEMPERATURE: 450°F. •
BAKING TIME: 3 TO 5 MINUTES

MAKES: 1 DOZEN;
SERVES 4 AS AN APPETIZER

INGREDIENTS	MEASURE	WEIGHT	
	VOLUME	OUNCES	GRAMS
1 recipe White Truffle Cream Puff Pastry (page 544) or Savory Cream Puffs (page 543), shaped and baked	12 puffs	7.3 ounces	210 grams
unsalted butter, softened	4 tablespoons	2 ounces	56 grams
1 small shallot	•	0.3 ounce	10 grams
1 large clove garlic	•	0.25 ounce	7 grams
salt	¹⁄₁₆ teaspoon, or to taste	•	•
parsley leaves, preferably flat-leaf	¼ cup, firmly packed	0.3 ounce	10 grams
hot sauce or cayenne pepper	5 drops or a pinch	•	•
nutmeg, preferably freshly grated	a tiny pinch	•	•
freshly ground white pepper	to taste	•	•
1 can Helix large snails	12 snails	4.3 ounces	125 grams

EQUIPMENT

A cookie sheet or half-size sheet pan, lined with foil

Make the dough (page 543 or 544). Pipe, shape, and bake the puffs (see page 546).

In a small bowl, place the butter. On a chopping block, smash the shallot and garlic with the flat side of the blade of a sharp chopping knife. Sprinkle them with the salt and mince them fine. Add the parsley and mince it together with the shallot and garlic mixture until finely chopped. Stir this mixture into the butter along with the hot sauce or cayenne pepper, nutmeg, and white pepper. Add salt to taste. Cover and refrigerate until ready to use.

ASSEMBLE THE ESCARGOT PUFFS

Allow the garlic/herb butter to soften until spreadable (at least 1 hour at room temperature).

Use a serrated knife to slice off the top quarter of each puff and reserve each top next to its bottom. Place the puffs on the foil-lined sheet. Place a snail inside each puff and spread about 1 teaspoon of the garlic/herb butter on top. Cover with the reserved tops. Set aside at room temperature for up to 1 hour or refrigerate, tightly covered, for up to 2 days.

Preheat the oven to 450°F. at least 20 minutes before baking.

Uncover the puffs and bake them for 3 to 5 minutes or until the puffs are crisp and the butter is bubbling.

STORE

Garlic/herb butter, refrigerated, up to 5 days.

UNDERSTANDING

Mincing the garlic by hand gives a better flavor than the processor. The salt releases some of their moisture and softens the garlic and shallots, making them easier to chop.

When baking the puffs, make the steam release hole near the top so the butter won't leak out.

FILLINGS AND TOPPINGS

The texture of cakes lends itself to being decorated with buttercream, but pies and tarts are far more compatible with pastry cream or fruit curd or accompanied by whipped cream or ice cream. Heavy cream is actually a superior medium for blending flavors because it has a much lighter texture and less pronounced flavor than buttercream, allowing other flavors to come through more clearly. Fruit purées lightened with whipped cream have the intense, fresh flavor of the fruit and make heavenly fillings and piped toppings. Chocolate blended with heavy cream to become the most divine of all chocolate fillings, ganache, can be whipped full of air or left alone to become dense and creamy. Plain lightly sweetened whipped cream complements any pie or tart because of its soft, cloud-like texture and rich, faintly flowery flavor. It is particularly suited to open-faced pies and tarts.

When used to accompany a slice of pie or tart, whipped cream is loveliest if beaten only until it softly mounds when dropped from a spoon—not until stiff peaks form when the beater is lifted. To avoid overbeating, I usually finish beating it by hand with the detached whisk beater from the machine. When I raise the whisk and small but straight peaks form, the cream is the perfect consistency. When beaten conventionally, heavy cream at least doubles in volume. The food processor, however, produces a whipped cream that does not increase in volume. Its dense and velvety texture makes it ideal for piping decorative borders.

I like to sweeten whipped cream with one tablespoon of granulated sugar per cup of cream. Powdered sugar adds an undesirable slightly powdery texture because of the cornstarch it contains to keep it from lumping. (I use powdered sugar only when it is dissolved in liquid and heated to boiling to swell the starch and make its presence undetectable.)

Whipped cream must be refrigerated to preserve its texture. Therefore, unless the pie requires refrigeration anyway, such as a chiffon pie, it is best to add the whipped cream shortly before serving if you are not using a stabilizer.

The high heat required for ultrapasteurizing destroys some of the butterfat in cream, and many areas of the country have cream with a low butterfat content to begin with. The combination of ultrapasteurization and low butterfat content makes whipping the cream more difficult and causes the finished cream to lack stability without the addition of certain stabilizers, losing two or more table-spoons of water per cup of cream if allowed to sit, even in the refrigerator. Consequently, ultrapasteurized cream has many other stabilizers added to it to enable it to whip. I have worked out a simple method for increasing the butterfat content of cream (see page 552) and another easy method using cornstarch that locks in the moisture without increasing the butterfat. Both result in a more stable cream that holds up beautifully when piped. I have recently seen a "gourmet whipping cream," with a higher butterfat content, in the supermarket, standing shoulder to shoulder with all the low-fat, no-fat permutations, and rejoice in its appearance. Very little whipped cream goes a long way to enhancing a slice of pie or tart, and it should be all that it can be.

Chilling the mixing bowl, beater, heavy cream, and even the sugar before beat-ing helps to make the most of what butterfat the cream does contain. Whipped creams flavored with firm ingredients such as chocolate, cocoa, or fruit jams do not require any additional stabilizer. Except for chocolate or chestnut whipped cream, however, these will not hold for prolonged periods at room temperature.

To make plain whipped cream ahead without stabilizers, place the whipped cream in a cheesecloth-lined sieve to allow the excess liquid to drain off and then refrigerate, lightly covered with plastic wrap. Or refrigerate the whipped cream and when ready to use whip it lightly to reincorporate the liquid.

For topping a pie or making decorations, it is best to use whipped cream as soon as it is made, when its texture is smoothest. Decorated pies can be kept one or two days in the refrigerator. Because cream absorbs other odors, it is important to cover tightly any other more odiferous ingredients in the refrigerator, as storing the pie or tart airtight will cause the crust to become soggy.

The best cream stabilizer I know of is Cobasan, from Germany (see page 644), available to the industry, and a reasonably small quantity can also be purchased by the consumer. It is one of the staples in my baking kitchen and I consider it to be sheer magic. Just a few drops of this colorless, flavorless liquid added to the cream before whipping produces a whipped cream that is exceptionally light and soft, yet with a seemingly magical, invisible, totally undetectable veil that maintains its form for as long as six hours at room temperature. Cobasan doesn't do a thing for ultrapasteurized cream (which is the soul of mediocrity and should be banned). If cream is ultrapasteurized, it will be indicated on the container.

Another excellent stabilizer for whipped cream, available in some supermar-kets and specialty stores, is Whipit by Oetker of Ontario, Canada. It is a powder undetectable in the cream and gives a slightly ivory color and slight sweetness, with no added flavor, to the whipped cream. The sweetness can be counteracted by using less sugar than usual. Whipit will work with ultrapasterurized cream and is slightly more stable than Cobasan but produces a slightly less light textured whipped cream.

PERFECT WHIPPED CREAM

A dollop of softly whipped fresh cream alongside a piece of pie is one of life's perfect things. If you want the cream to hold up for hours, the optional Cobasan will make it possible, with no compromise of flavor or texture. If you prefer an unsweetened counterpoint to a sweeter pastry, leave out the sugar.

MAKES: 2 CUPS

INGREDIENTS	MEASURE	WEIGHT	
	VOLUME	OUNCES	GRAMS
heavy cream, cold	1 liquid cup	8 ounces	232 grams
sugar	1 tablespoon	0.5 ounce	12.5 grams
pure vanilla extract	½ teaspoon	•	•
optional: Cobasan (only if cream is not ultrapasteurized)	full ½ teaspoon	•	•

In a large mixer bowl, place all the ingredients and refrigerate for at least 15 minutes. (Chill the whisk beater alongside the bowl.)

Beat the mixture until soft peaks form when the beater is raised or the cream mounds softly when dropped from a spoon. Do not overbeat.

VARIATIONS

MOCHA WHIPPED CREAM   Increase the sugar to 2 tablespoons and add 1 tablespoon of cocoa (preferably Dutch-processed) and 1 teaspoon of Medaglia d'Oro instant espresso powder. Refrigerate for at least 1 hour to dissolve the cocoa before beating.

COCOA WHIPPED CREAM   Increase the sugar to 2½ tablespoons and add 2 tablespoons of cocoa (preferably Dutch-processed). Refrigerate for at least 1 hour to dissolve the cocoa before beating.

BOURBON WHIPPED CREAM   Decrease the sugar to ½ teaspoon, decrease the vanilla extract to ¼ teaspoon, and add 1 tablespoon of bourbon.

STORE

Refrigerated, 2 to 3 days.

552   THE PIE AND PASTRY BIBLE

REAL OLD-FASHIONED WHIPPED CREAM

Aﬆer years of groaning about the deterioration of the quality of heavy cream (ultrapasteurization and a decrease in butterfat are the culprits) and envying those with access to 40 percent butterfat cream, I finally found a way to get the butterfat back into the cream that is the very soul of simplicity. If the cream is very low in butterfat (20 percent), this method will bring it to exactly 40 percent. If the cream is higher in butterfat (36 percent—it whips readily), use only 3 tablespoons butter, and the cream will end up with 52.5 percent butterfat and greatly increased stability.

This cream has the stability to use as a filling, yet it has an extraordinarily light texture.

MAKES: 2 CUPS

INGREDIENTS	MEASURE	WEIGHT	
	VOLUME	OUNCES	GRAMS
heavy cream, cold	1 liquid cup	8 ounces	232 grams
unsalted butter, softened	4 tablespoons	2 ounces	56 grams
pure vanilla extract	½ teaspoon	•	•
sugar	1 tablespoon	0.5 ounce	12.5 grams

Refrigerate the mixer bowl and whisk beater for at least 15 minutes.

In a small saucepan, melt the butter with ¼ cup of the cream, stirring constantly until the butter is fully melted. Pour it into a small heatproof measuring cup and cool to room temperature. Add the vanilla.

In the chilled bowl, beat the remaining ¾ cup of cream and the sugar just until traces of beater marks begin to show distinctly. On low speed, add the butter mixture in a steady stream, beating constantly. Beat just until stiff peaks form when the beater is raised.

STORE

Refrigerated, 2 to 3 days.

POINTERS FOR SUCCESS

ᗕ The whipped cream is smoothest when the butter mixture is added gradually.
ᗕ If the finished pastry will have to sit at room temperature for more than 30 minutes, use whipped cream stabilized with gelatin (page 557), as Real Old-Fashioned Whipped Cream will begin to soften.

UNDERSTANDING

According to the law of the land, heavy cream must be 20 to 40 percent butterfat. The average fat content is 37.5 percent, but, alas, to date no law requires that the fat content be listed. You will know if the cream your area of the country offers is the 20 percent variety because you will encounter difficulty whipping it stiffly and, once whipped, it will separate or seem to curdle slightly at the edges if a fruit sauce is spooned onto it.

Butter contains 81 percent butterfat. The rest is milk solids and water. Using the method in the above recipe rehomogenizes the butterfat into the cream.

STABILIZED WHIPPED CREAM

Cornstarch and powdered sugar (which contains 2 percent cornstarch) are cooked with a little heavy cream until the starch swells and thickens it. The mixture is then beaten into the softly whipped cream. This whipped cream will not water out for up to twenty-four hours. While using this method does not affect the consistency, it will not stabilize the cream enough to keep at room temperature. It is excellent for garnishing a pie that will remain refrigerated until serving time or for making whipped cream several hours ahead to serve on the side.

MAKES: 2 CUPS

INGREDIENTS	MEASURE	WEIGHT	
	VOLUME	OUNCES	GRAMS
powdered sugar	2 tablespoons	0.5 ounce	14 grams
cornstarch*	1 teaspoon	•	•
heavy cream, cold	1 liquid cup	8 ounces	232 grams
pure vanilla extract	½ teaspoon	•	•

*If your cream is very low in butterfat (see page 552), use 1¼ teaspoons cornstarch.

Refrigerate the mixer bowl and beater for at least 15 minutes.

In a small saucepan, place the powdered sugar and cornstarch and gradually stir in ¼ cup of the cream. Bring the mixture to a boil, stirring constantly, and simmer for just a few seconds, until the liquid is thickened. Scrape it into a small bowl and cool to room temperature. Add the vanilla.

Beat the remaining ¾ cup of cream just until traces of the beater marks begin to show distinctly. Add the cream and cornstarch mixture in a steady stream, beating constantly. Beat just until soft peaks form when the beater is raised. Do not overbeat.

STORE
Refrigerated, up to 24 hours.

CHOCOLATE CHIP WHIPPED CREAM

This whipped cream is amazingly delicious—good enough, in fact, to eat by itself. It also makes a sensational filling for cream puffs and éclairs, and a topping for or accompaniment to the Chocolate Oblivion Tartlets (page 308).

MAKES: 3 CUPS

INGREDIENTS	MEASURE	WEIGHT	
	VOLUME	OUNCES	GRAMS
gelatin*	1 teaspoon	•	3.5 grams
water*	1½ tablespoons	0.75 ounce	22 grams
heavy cream, cold	1 liquid cup	8 ounces	232 grams
sugar	1 tablespoon	0.5 ounce	12.5 grams
pure vanilla extract	½ teaspoon	•	•
finely grated bittersweet chocolate, chilled	½ cup	2.5 ounces	71 grams
finely ground almonds	¼ cup	1 ounce	27 grams

*To use as a topping, omit the gelatin and water.

Refrigerate the mixer bowl and whisk beater for at least 15 minutes.

In a small heatproof glass measuring cup, place the gelatin and water. Allow the gelatin to soften for 5 minutes. Set the cup in a pan of simmering water and stir occasionally until the gelatin is dissolved. (This can also be done in a microwave on high power, stirring once or twice.) Remove the cup and cool to room temperature, about 7 minutes. (The gelatin must be liquid but not warm when added to the cream, or it will lump.)

In the chilled bowl, beat the cream and sugar just until traces of beater marks begin to show distinctly. Add the gelatin mixture in a steady stream, beating constantly. Add the vanilla and beat just until soft peaks form when beater is raised. In a small bowl, stir together the chocolate and nuts and fold them into the whipped cream until evenly incorporated. Cover with plastic wrap and refrigerate.

STORE
Refrigerated, up to 3 days.

POINTERS FOR SUCCESS
 Do not overbeat the cream, as the whipped cream will continue to stiffen after folding in the chocolate and nuts.

∾ If the grated chocolate is not cold when it is folded into the whipped cream, it will turn the whipped cream a light brown instead of white.

CARAMEL WHIPPED CREAM

A small amount of this light caramel-imbued whipped cream goes a long way in enhancing an apple or pear tart or crisp, or a chocolate or coffee tart. Saving a little of the powdered caramel to add shortly before serving offers a lovely textural delight. The powdered caramel keeps for several weeks.

MAKES: 2 CUPS

INGREDIENTS	MEASURE	WEIGHT	
	VOLUME	OUNCES	GRAMS
sugar	½ cup	3.5 ounces	100 grams
water	2 tablespoons	1 ounce	30 grams
heavy cream, cold	1 liquid cup	8 ounces	232 grams
pure vanilla extract	1 teaspoon	•	•

EQUIPMENT
A heavy saucepan, at least 5-cup capacity, ideally with a nonstick lining, and a baking sheet, covered with aluminum foil and lightly greased

In the saucepan, stir together the sugar and water until the sugar is completely moistened. Heat, stirring constantly, until the sugar dissolves and the syrup is bubbling. Stop stirring completely and allow it to boil undisturbed until it turns a deep amber (380° to 385°F. on a candy thermometer). Immediately remove it from the heat and pour it onto the prepared baking sheet.

When the caramel is completely cool, break it into pieces and process in a food processor until it becomes a powder. You will have about ½ cup.

In a medium mixing bowl, place 3 tablespoons of the caramel powder and the cream. Cover it tightly (to prevent absorption of other odors) and refrigerate for at least 2 hours or until the caramel has softened and dissolved.

Within 30 minutes of serving, beat the cream until it starts to thicken and the beater marks become visible. Add another tablespoon of the caramel powder and the vanilla and beat until it mounds softly when dropped from a spoon. Do not overbeat.

STORE

Leftover caramel powder: room temperature (low humidity), tightly covered, up to 3 weeks; frozen, up to 2 months. Whipped cream: refrigerated, tightly covered, 2 to 3 days.

POINTERS FOR SUCCESS

∾ To prevent crystallization, do not allow any sugar crystals to get on the sides of the pan and be sure to moisten all the sugar with the water. Stop stirring entirely as soon as the mixture comes to a boil. If using a thermometer, be sure to rinse it and dry it if you remove it and then reinsert it in the syrup. If any sugar remains on the thermometer, it will cause crystallization.

∾ One quarter of the caramel powder is added shortly before serving to maintain the crunch. If you prefer a totally smooth cream, you can add all the caramel in the beginning.

UNDERSTANDING

I adore the flavor of caramel, so I like to have as much depth of flavor as possible without any burnt flavor. I bring it up to 380°F. for maximum flavor. The darker you make the caramel, the less sweet it will seem, but you risk burning it if you don't have an absolutely accurate thermometer (see page 673).

WHIPPED CREAM FOR PIPING

Using a food processor to "whip" the cream means that it will not be as light and airy as beaten whipped cream because it does not increase in volume. The added density makes this velvety whipped cream pipe like a dream.

MAKES: 2 CUPS

INGREDIENTS	MEASURE	WEIGHT	
	VOLUME	OUNCES	GRAMS
heavy cream, cold	2 liquid cups	16.25 ounces	464 grams
sugar	2 tablespoons	1 ounce	25 grams
pure vanilla extract	1 teaspoon	•	•
optional: Cobasan (only if cream is not ultrapasteurized)	full ½ teaspoon	•	•

Place all the ingredients in the bowl of food processor fitted with the metal blade. Process, checking every few seconds by lifting a small amount of cream with a small metal spatula or spoon, until the mixture looks thick and creamy and forms a slight peak when lifted. It will not be fluffy. Use it at once.

STORE

Refrigerated, up to 24 hours once piped onto the pastry (the cream will not water out).

POINTERS FOR SUCCESS

∾ Do not overprocess. Even a few seconds past the peaking stage and the consistency will no longer be smooth.

∾ For stability at prolonged room temperature, use the Cobasan (see page 644).

SUPERSTABILIZED WHIPPED CREAM

This whipped cream has the most firm texture, making it ideal for adding to pastry creams. If heavy fruit, such as slices of mango, papaya, or large strawberries, is used for the topping, use the larger amount of gelatin. For smaller fruit, such as blackberries or raspberries, use the smaller amount.

MAKES: 1 CUP

INGREDIENTS	MEASURE	WEIGHT	
	VOLUME	OUNCES	GRAMS
gelatin	½ to 1 teaspoon	•	•
water	1 tablespoon	0.5 ounce	15 grams
heavy cream, cold	½ liquid cup	4 ounces	116 grams
sugar	1 teaspoon	•	•

Refrigerate the mixing bowl and beater for at least 15 minutes.

In a small heatproof measuring cup, place the gelatin and water and allow it to sit for 5 minutes. Set the cup in a pan of simmering water for a few minutes, stirring occasionally until the gelatin is dissolved (or microwave on high power for a few seconds, stirring once or twice). Set it aside briefly. (The mixture must still be warm, or it will lump when added to the cold cream.)

In the chilled mixing bowl, beat the cream and sugar until the cream begins to thicken. Gradually beat in the warm gelatin mixture and beat just until stiff peaks form when the beater is raised.

STORE

Refrigerated, up to 3 days.

POINTERS FOR SUCCESS

∾ Do not overbeat. Even a few seconds past stiff peaks, and the consistency will no longer be velvety smooth.

UNDERSTANDING

The gelatin makes the texture seem fuller and slightly spongy.

CRÈME FRAÎCHE
(krem fresh)

This recipe produces a crème fraîche reminiscent of the enchanting varieties found in France. Crème fraîche is wonderful just as it is to adorn a pie or pastry, but it can also be lightly sweetened and whipped while still maintaining its mild tang. Any left over is great for finishing savory sauces because, unlike sour cream, it does not curdle with heat.

MAKES: ABOUT 2 CUPS (ABOUT 3⅔ CUPS WHIPPED)

INGREDIENTS	MEASURE	WEIGHT	
	VOLUME	OUNCES	GRAMS
heavy cream, preferably not ultrapasteurized*	2 liquid cups	16 ounces	464 grams
buttermilk	2 tablespoons	approx. 1 ounce	30 grams
optional: 1 Tahitian vanilla bean,† split lengthwise	•	•	•

*Ultrapasteurized cream may take as long as 36 hours to thicken and will not have as full a flavor.
†Or use 2 regular (Madagascar) vanilla beans.

Combine the ingredients in a jar with a tight-fitting lid and place it in a warm spot, such as the top of the refrigerator or near the stove. Allow it to sit undisturbed for at least 12 hours or until thickened but still pourable.

Refrigerate. Crème fraîche will continue to thicken on chilling.

If using the vanilla bean, remove it just before using the crème fraîche and scrape the seeds from the bean into the cream.

TO MAKE LIGHTLY SWEETENED WHIPPED CRÈME FRAÎCHE   Add 1 tablespoon of sugar and whisk the cream lightly until soft peaks form when the whisk is raised.

STORE

Refrigerated, up to 3 weeks.

LIGHT WHIPPED GANACHE

This chocolate whipped cream is denser and more chocolaty than the chocolate chip whipped cream because it has a little more than three times the chocolate, yet it is so light and airy it seems to disappear in the mouth. It makes a dreamy filling and can be used in the same way as the chocolate chip version. It also pipes beautifully at room temperature.

MAKES: 3 CUPS

INGREDIENTS	MEASURE	WEIGHT	
	VOLUME	OUNCES	GRAMS
bittersweet chocolate*	two 3-ounce bars	6 ounces	170 grams
heavy cream	1½ liquid cups	12 ounces	348 grams
pure vanilla extract	½ teaspoon	•	•

*My favorite sweetness balance is either 6 ounces of 56 percent cocoa mass chocolate such as Valrhona Caracque, or a combination of 4 ounces of Lindt's Excellence, which is about 50 percent cocoa mass, and 2 ounces of Lindt's Excellence 70 percent cocoa mass chocolate. Either way, the total will be around 56 percent cocoa mass.

Break the chocolate into pieces and process it in a food processor with the metal blade until very fine.

Heat the cream to the boiling point and, with the motor running, pour it through the feed tube in a steady stream. Process for a few seconds or until smooth. Pour the mixture into the large bowl of an electric mixer and refrigerate until cold, stirring once or twice, about 2 hours. You can speed chilling by setting the bowl in an ice water bath and stirring frequently. Do not allow the mixture to get too cold, or it will be too stiff to incorporate air.

Add the vanilla and beat the mixture just until very soft peaks form when the beater is raised. It will continue to thicken after a few minutes at room temperature. The safest way not to overbeat is to use an electric mixer until the ganache starts to thicken and then continue with a hand-held whisk. If the mixture gets overbeaten and grainy, the texture can be restored by remelting, chilling, and rebeating the ganache.

VARIATION

QUICK LIGHT WHIPPED GANACHE If you need the whipped ganache sooner and cannot wait for the mixture to chill, the following method will yield equal results but involves a little more work.

Refrigerate the mixer bowl and beaters.

In a double boiler or a microwave oven on high power (stirring every 10 seconds if using a microwave), melt the chocolate pieces with ½ cup of the cream.

Remove from the heat source before the chocolate is melted fully and finish melting by stirring it constantly. Set the mixture aside until no longer warm.

In the chilled bowl, beat the remaining 1 cup of cream until traces of the beater marks just begin to show distinctly. Add the chocolate mixture and beat just until soft peaks form when the beater is raised.

STORE

In a pastry: room temperature, up to 1 day; refrigerated, up to 1 week; frozen, up to 3 months. By itself: remelt, chill, and reheat.

POINTERS FOR SUCCESS

✣ The temperature of the mixture is critical when beating. If not cold, it will not stiffen; if too cold, it will not aerate well.

✣ Overbeating causes curdling.

PASTRY CREAM
Crème Pâtissière

This classic custard laced with specks of vanilla bean is the traditional filling for Napoleons, éclairs, and a variety of fruit tarts. Combined with whipped cream and a touch of gelatin, both of which lighten it, it becomes the filling for the famous Gâteau St.-Honoré. Although it is sometimes prepared with all egg yolks and heavy cream, this lighter version uses whole eggs and half-and-half.

MAKES: 2½ CUPS/22¾ OUNCES/650 GRAMS; 1 CUP = 9 OUNCES/260 GRAMS

INGREDIENTS	MEASURE	WEIGHT	
	VOLUME	OUNCES	GRAMS
2 large eggs	3 fluid ounces	3.5 ounces (weighed without the shells)	100 grams
cornstarch	3 tablespoons	1 ounce	28 grams
half-and-half	2 liquid cups	8.5 ounces	242 grams
sugar	½ cup	3.5 ounces	100 grams
vanilla bean, split lengthwise*	2-inch piece	•	•
salt	a pinch	•	•
unsalted butter	1 tablespoon	0.5 ounce	14 grams

*Or 1 teaspoon pure vanilla extract.

EQUIPMENT
A piano wire whisk (one with 10 loops of wire)

Have a strainer set over a small bowl near the range.

In a small bowl, whisk together the eggs and cornstarch. Gradually add ¼ cup of the half-and-half, whisking until the mixture is smooth and the cornstarch is dissolved.

In a medium heavy nonreactive saucepan, place the sugar and vanilla bean and, using your fingers, rub the seeds into the sugar. Stir in the remaining 1¾ cups of half-and-half and the salt. Over medium heat, bring the mixture to a full boil, stirring occasionally. Whisk 2 tablespoons of this hot mixture into the egg mixture. Pass the egg mixture through a strainer into a small bowl.

Bring the half-and-half mixture back to a boil over medium heat. Remove the vanilla pod (rinse and dry it for future use). Quickly add all of the egg mixture, whisking rapidly. Continue whisking rapidly for about 20 to 30 seconds, being sure to go into the bottom edge of the pan. The mixture will become very thick. Remove the mixture from the heat and whisk in the butter. (If not using the vanilla bean, whisk in the vanilla extract at this point.) Immediately pour the mixture into a bowl and place a piece of greased plastic wrap directly on top of the cream to prevent a skin from forming. Allow it to cool to room temperature, about 1 hour, then refrigerate until cold.

VARIATIONS

CHEF ARTHUR OBERHOLZER'S MERINGUE PASTRY CREAM This produces a lighter texture without the addition of whipped cream, but it must be used right after preparing and consumed the same day, as it will water out slightly on sitting longer. Just before cooking the pastry cream, beat 4 large egg whites (½ cup) until foamy. Beat in ½ teaspoon of cream of tarter. Continue to beat until soft peaks form when the beater is raised slowly. Beat in 2 tablespoons of superfine sugar and beat until stiff peaks form when the beater is raised. Set it aside.

Use a large pan to prepare the pastry cream, as the addition of the egg whites will result in double the volume. As soon as the pastry cream has thickened, add the meringue and continue cooking over low heat, beating with the piano wire whisk as vigorously as possible, for about 30 seconds.

This pastry cream spreads and sets up best if used while still hot or warm. Spread it on baked pastry (see Classic Napoleon, page 453). Refrigerate for at least 1 hour or up to 3 hours.

LIQUEUR PASTRY CREAM Whisk up to 2 tablespoons of liqueur, such as kirsch, cognac, or Grand Marnier, into the hot or cooled pastry cream.

BUTTERSCOTCH PASTRY CREAM Replace the sugar with light brown sugar, preferably unrefined (see page 646).

CARAMEL PASTRY CREAM   More sugar is needed because caramelization decreases sweetness; more liquid is needed because it gets reduced with the caramelized sugar. Because of this concentration, it is preferable to use milk instead of half-and-half. Increase the sugar to ⅔ cup (4.6 ounces/132 grams). Stir ¼ cup of milk into the cornstarch and egg mixture and heat 2⅓ cups of milk with the vanilla bean.

In a medium heavy saucepan, preferably nonstick, stir together the sugar and 2 tablespoons of water until the sugar is completely moistened. Bring it to a boil, stirring constantly. Cook without stirring until deep amber (380°F.). Remove it from the heat and slowly pour in the hot milk, reserving the vanilla bean. It will bubble up furiously for about a minute. Return it to low heat and cook, stirring, until the caramel is totally dissolved and the mixture is reduced to 1¾ cups. Proceed as above.

CHOCOLATE PASTRY CREAM   Add from 1½ ounces to 4 ounces of fine-quality bittersweet chocolate, finely chopped, to the hot pastry cream. Stir until melted. If adding more than 3 ounces, decrease the cornstarch to 2 tablespoons, as on chilling the chocolate will harden and cause the pastry cream to firm.

COFFEE PASTRY CREAM   Add 4 teaspoons of instant espresso powder (Medaglia d'Oro) or powdered instant coffee to the half-and-half/sugar mixture and, if desired, up to 2 tablespoons of Kahlúa to the hot pastry cream.

PRALINE CRUNCH PASTRY CREAM   Decrease the sugar by 2 tablespoons and gently stir ½ cup of Praline Powder (page 564) into the chilled plain or chocolate or coffee pastry cream.

PRALINE PASTE PASTRY CREAM   Decrease the sugar to ¼ cup. Beat ½ cup (5.5 ounces/154 grams) of praline paste (see page 643) into the yolk mixture after the hot half-and-half has been added. (There is no need to strain the yolk mixture.) If desired, add up to 2 tablespoons of Frangelico or cognac.

PEANUT BUTTER PASTRY CREAM   Whisk ½ cup plus 1 tablespoon (5.3 ounces/150 grams) of smooth peanut butter (preferably Jif) into the hot pastry cream.

ORANGE PASTRY CREAM   Add 1 tablespoon (about 0.25 ounce/6 grams) of finely grated orange zest (the orange portion only of the orange peel) to the half-and-half/sugar mixture. If desired, add up to 2 tablespoons of Cointreau or Grand Marnier to the hot pastry cream, or ¼ teaspoon of orange oil (see page 638).

WHIPPED CREAM PASTRY CREAM   Fold whipped cream into the plain pastry cream or any of the above variations; use from ½ cup to 1¼ cups heavy cream, whipped. To prevent thinning, it is preferable to use gelatin-stabilized whipped cream (page 557). The gelatin also provides a lighter, airy texture.

WHITE CHOCOLATE PASTRY CREAM   Adding white chocolate will sweeten the pastry cream, which is already perfectly balanced, but in an emergency, if the pastry cream requires speedy thickening, a half ounce to an ounce of white chocolate, melted, will do the trick.

STORE

Refrigerated, up to 3 days; frozen, up to 1 month.

NOTE

Frozen pastry cream will thin on defrosting, so it is not suitable for holding its shape for a large tart unless gelatin is added. For every cup of pastry cream (9 ounces/260 grams), use 1 teaspoon of gelatin. Place it in a small heatproof cup and add 1 tablespoon of water. Allow it to sit for at least 3 minutes. Then heat it in a microwave for a few seconds, or in a pan set in simmering water, until the mixture is transparent. Whisking constantly, pour the hot liquid into the cooled room temperature pastry cream. (If the pastry cream is cold, the gelatin may lump.) Refrigerate it for 45 minutes to 1 hour or until the pastry cream is firm. Then whisk briefly for a few seconds until it is smooth.

To make a crème St.-Honoré (Chiboust), for every ½ cup of pastry cream, after the gelatin has set, whisk in ½ to 1 teaspoon of Grand Marnier and fold in ¼ cup of heavy cream, whipped to stiff peaks. Starting with ½ cup of pastry cream will yield 1 cup of crème St.-Honoré.

POINTERS FOR SUCCESS

∽ A heavy well-insulated pan is essential to keep the pastry cream from scorching.
∽ A 10-loop piano wire (fine) whisk is practically indispensable to prevent lumps from forming in the finished pastry cream.
∽ It is possible to make half this recipe if you have a small piano wire whisk.
∽ Do not beat vigorously after cooling or the pastry cream will break down.

UNDERSTANDING

The eggs and milk do not curdle even though brought to a boil because the protein is stabilized by the cornstarch.

A small amount of scalding hot half-and-half is beaten into the egg to coagulate the chalaza attached to the yolk. It is then strained to remove this ropy textured element.

The butter is added at the end to maximize its fresh flavor.

PRALINE POWDER

This crunchy hazelnut and caramel powder is a delicious addition to plain or chocolate pastry cream.

MAKES: ABOUT 2 CUPS

INGREDIENTS	MEASURE	WEIGHT	
	VOLUME	OUNCES	GRAMS
hazelnuts, peeled (see page 642)	1 cup	5 ounces	142 grams
sugar	generous ⅔ cup	5 ounces	142 grams
water	¼ liquid cup	2 ounces	60 grams

EQUIPMENT

A heavy saucepan, at least 5-cup capacity, ideally with a nonstick lining, and a nonstick baking sheet or baking sheet, covered with aluminum foil and lightly greased

Preheat the oven to 350°F.

Place the hazelnuts on a second baking sheet and toast in the oven until lightly browned, about 20 minutes. Place them, close together, on the nonstick or prepared baking sheet.

In the saucepan, stir together the sugar and water until the sugar is completely moistened. Heat, stirring constantly, until the sugar dissolves and the syrup is bubbling. Stop stirring completely and allow it to boil undisturbed until it turns a deep amber (380°F. on a candy thermometer). *Immediately* pour the caramel over the nuts.

When the caramel is completely cool, about 15 to 20 minutes, remove it from the sheet and break it into a few pieces. Process it in a food processor until it becomes a powder.

STORE

Room temperature (low humidity), tightly covered, up to 3 weeks; frozen, up to 2 months.

POINTERS FOR SUCCESS

∿ To prevent crystallization, do not allow any sugar crystals to get on the sides of the pan and be sure to moisten all the sugar with the water. Stop stirring entirely as soon as it comes to a boil. If using a thermometer, be sure to rinse it and dry it if you remove it and reinsert it in the syrup. If any sugar remains on the thermometer, it will cause crystallization.

UNDERSTANDING

I adore the flavor of caramel, so I like to have as much depth of flavor as possible without any burnt flavor. I like to bring it up to 380°F. for maximum flavor. The darker you make the caramel, the less sweet it will seem, but you risk burning it if you don't have an absolutely accurate thermometer (see page 673).

This praline powder has 50 percent hazelnuts, just like the finest-quality praline paste, but it has a crunchier texture.

CHIBOUST CREAM

Chiboust was the pastry chef who created the Gâteau St.-Honoré, which he filled with this whipped cream–lightened pastry cream. The Grand Marnier in this version perfumes the custard, lending to the illusion of lightness. The gelatin makes it possible to pipe magnificent swirls on a pastry.

MAKES: 5½ CUPS/APPROXIMATELY 29.5 OUNCES/840 GRAMS

INGREDIENTS	MEASURE	WEIGHT	
	VOLUME	OUNCES	GRAMS
heavy cream	1½ liquid cups	12 ounces	348 grams
milk	1½ liquid cups	12 ounces	363 grams
sugar	½ cup	3.5 ounces	100 grams
½ Tahitian* vanilla bean, split lengthwise	•	•	•
½ Madagascar vanilla bean, split lengthwise	•	•	•
4 large egg yolks	2¼ fluid ounces	2.6 ounces	74 grams
cornstarch	2 tablespoons	0.6 ounce	19 grams
gelatin	2 teaspoons	•	6.3 grams
pure vanilla extract	½ teaspoon	•	•
Grand Marnier	2 tablespoons	1 ounce	30 grams

*If Tahitian vanilla beans are unavailable, use a total of 1½ ordinary (Madagascar) vanilla beans or increase the vanilla extract to 1½ teaspoons. In place of vanilla beans, you can use a total of 1 tablespoon of vanilla extract.

Pour the cream into a mixing bowl; cover and refrigerate it.

In a medium heavy saucepan, scald* the milk, cover, and keep it hot over very low heat. In a mixer bowl, place the sugar and vanilla beans and, using your fingers, rub the seeds into the sugar. Add the vanilla pods to the cream. Add the yolks to the sugar and, preferably with the whisk beater, beat the yolks and sugar until well blended. Add the cornstarch and gelatin and beat until well blended. Gradually beat in the hot milk.

Return the yolk mixture to the saucepan and bring it to a boil, stirring constantly with a whisk, reaching well into the bottom edges of the pan. As soon as the mixture comes to a boil, it will become very thick. Reduce the heat and simmer for 1 minute, stirring constantly with the whisk. Remove the pan from the heat, whisk in the vanilla extract and Grand Marnier, and pour the mixture into a bowl. Press a piece of greased plastic wrap directly onto the surface of the mixture to prevent a skin from forming. Allow it to cool completely at room temperature or refrigerated. (You can speed cooling by placing the bowl in the freezer for about 30 minutes, but to prevent stiffening around the sides, transfer to a glass or plastic bowl if necessary, and stir gently 2 or 3 times.) When the pastry cream is cool, set it aside briefly at room temperature while whipping the cream.

Remove the vanilla pods from the cream (rinse and dry and save for another use). Whip the cream until stiff peaks form when the beater is raised. Using a large whisk or rubber spatula, fold it into the cooled pastry cream. Use it at once or cover and chill.

STORE
Refrigerated, up to 3 days.

POINTERS FOR SUCCESS
∾ If time does not allow for chilling the completed pastry cream and you are planning to serve the dessert immediately, increase the gelatin to 1 tablespoon plus a scant ½ teaspoon (1½ envelopes /10 grams).

∾ The completed pastry cream is most easy to pipe either immediately after completion or after 30 minutes of chilling, while it is still very smooth and soft and the gelatin has not yet had a chance to set completely. If it has been held longer and is no longer smooth and soft enough to pipe, it can be softened by placing it briefly over a pot of hot water, folding it gently with a large whisk or rubber spatula. Care must be taken, however, not to overheat the mixture, as the whipped cream will lose some of its aeration if warmed. Alternatively, if you are planning to make the pastry cream ahead, wait until shortly before using it to add the whipped cream. Soften the pastry cream over the hot water and be sure it is not warm before adding the whipped cream.

---

*Heat until small bubbles form around the perimeter.

UNDERSTANDING

Cornstarch protects the yolks from curdling when boiled. The mixture must be boiled to activate the cornstarch's thickening ability.

This recipe is similar to classic pastry cream, but instead of 2 cups of half-and-half, it uses 1½ cups of milk, and instead of 3 tablespoons of cornstarch, it uses only 2 tablespoons, because the 2 teaspoons of gelatin, which aerates it, also thickens it enough to accommodate the 1½ cups of heavy cream, whipped to add further lightness.

FRUIT CURDS AND CURD CREAMS
(*Lime, Juice Orange, Blood Orange, Bitter Seville Orange, and Passion Fruit*)

Fruit curd is actually a custard that depends on the high acidity of the fruit, in combination with egg yolks and butter, to achieve its gloriously silken texture without the addition of a starch thickener. This results in an utterly uncompromised purity of liltingly bright flavor.

Fruit curd is one of the most delightful and useful components in the dessert kingdom. Lemon has always been the queen of curds, described as capturing sunshine in a jar. But I've discovered that passion fruit takes curd to new heights, difficult to describe other than to say it brings to mind words like *tropical* and *tantalizing* and *addicting*. The lime and orange curds are like pure concentrations of these often illusive flavors. They taste the way one hopes for the best variety of this fruit to be at its peak of ripeness and freshness.

Fold whipped cream or meringue into curd and you have a lighter and more mellow filling or topping that is an unrivaled partner for fresh fruit. A little curd folded into plain yogurt does wonders to enliven it. Curd also serves as the base for the most creamy, flavorful chiffon pie and ice creams (see Lemon-Luscious Ice Cream, page 235, and Pure Passion Ice Cream, page 237).

Different citrus fruits vary in flavor intensity and acidity, thereby requiring differing amounts of sugar. The stronger the acid and the less sugar used, the sooner the curd thickens (the lower the finished temperature). Each one of these fruit variations has been worked out carefully, taking these factors into consideration and resulting in the most intensely pure flavor of each fruit.

It is rare that I would recommend a commercial product to replace a homemade one, but, when time is a factor, it's helpful to know that Tiptree makes an exceptionally high quality lemon curd (very close to homemade) with no additives (and the same yield as this recipe), and it can be used in any recipe calling for lemon curd.

CLASSIC LEMON CURD

MAKES: 1 CUP + 2½ TABLESPOONS/11 OUNCES/312 GRAMS

INGREDIENTS	MEASURE	WEIGHT	
	VOLUME	OUNCES	GRAMS
finely grated lemon zest	2 teaspoons	•	4 grams
4 large egg yolks	¼ liquid cup	2.6 ounces	74 grams
sugar	¾ cup*	6 ounces	150 grams
lemon juice, freshly squeezed and strained (about 2½ large lemons)	3 fluid ounces (6 tablespoons)	3.3 ounces	94 grams
unsalted butter, cut into pieces or softened	4 tablespoons	2 ounces	57 grams
salt	a pinch	•	•

*Use 10 tablespoons (4.3 ounces/125 grams) if pairing the curd with something very sweet, such as meringue.

Have ready near the range a strainer suspended over a medium bowl that contains the lemon zest.

In a heavy nonreactive saucepan, beat the yolks and sugar until well blended. Stir in the lemon juice, butter, and salt. Cook over medium-low heat, stirring constantly (be sure to scrape the sides of the pan), until the mixture is thickened and resembles hollandaise sauce; it should thickly coat a wooden spoon but still be liquid enough to pour. The mixture will change from translucent to opaque and begin to take on a yellow color on the back of the spoon; it must not be allowed to boil, or it will curdle. Whenever steam appears, remove the pan briefly from the heat, stirring constantly to keep the mixture from boiling. When the mixture has thickened (196°F. on an accurate thermometer), pour it at once into the strainer. Press with the back of a spoon until only the coarse residue remains. Discard the residue (or enjoy it as a treat—it tastes great). Gently stir in the zest and allow it to cool.

VARIATIONS

For all variations, the amount of fruit juice and sugar varies but the yolks, butter, and salt remain constant.

LIME CURD   Lime is one of the most difficult flavors to describe and yet it has a strong and irreplaceable hold on flavor memory. It has a fresh sour tartness that is just right. Though often thought of as a less interesting cousin to lemon, in a drink and in certain flavor combinations, lemon would overpower instead of blend and is simply not its equal. Though lime juice is really pale yellow, it somehow tastes as if it is green. This curd captures lime's essence. It blends perfectly with both blueberry and kiwi—it serves as the cream base for the kiwi tart (page 271) and can be used to replace the lemon curd in the blueberry tart (page 258).

Replace the lemon zest with an equal amount of lime zest and the lemon juice with an equal amount of freshly squeezed lime juice (from about 3 small limes). Decrease the sugar to ½ cup (3.5 ounces/100 grams). The finished temperature is 185°F. If desired, for a pale green color, gently stir 2 drops of liquid green food color into the finished curd. (Makes 1 cup/9¼ ounces/262 grams.)

BITTER SEVILLE ORANGE CURD   Orange juice always seems to lose its flavor when combined with other ingredients, except when it's from a Seville variety. This is the orange used to make marmalade. It makes an orange curd with the truest orange flavor, sweet-sour like a sour ball. In fact, the flavor seems to bounce around in your mouth, it is so alive and vibrant. Seville oranges are very thick skinned and the zest would produce a horrid taste in the curd, so be sure to use navel orange zest. The curd is a beautiful bright gold flecked with orange zest. Seville oranges have a short season, but the juice freezes perfectly for several months.

Replace the lemon zest with 4 teaspoons (8 grams) navel orange zest and the lemon juice with an equal amount of bitter Seville orange juice (from about 1½ oranges). Use the same amount of sugar for a more tart curd or decrease it to ⅔ cup (4.6 ounces/132 grams). The finished temperature is 185°F. (Makes 1 cup plus almost 2 tablespoons/approx. 10.5 ounces/296 grams.)

BLOOD ORANGE CURD   Blood oranges are delicious, but they are not as intensely flavored, or acidic, as Seville oranges. Reducing the juice by half concentrates the flavor and intensifies the color. This curd can vary in color from deep rose to purple. The darker the blood orange skin, the deeper the color of the flesh. Blood oranges from Sicily have the most delicious flavor. Balducci's (see page 676) has frozen blood orange juice available all year around.

Use the same amount of zest as for lemon curd, but start with 1 cup of juice (from about 4 oranges) and reduce it to ½ cup (see Pointers below). Decrease the sugar to ½ cup (3.5 ounces/100 grams). The finished temperature is 185°F. (Makes 1 cup plus 2 tablespoons/approx. 11 ounces/311 grams.)

JUICE ORANGE CURD   This orange has a lovely flavor but is far less intense than blood or bitter oranges, so the juice must be reduced by three quarters and the curd requires more orange zest. A touch (about ¼ teaspoon) of fine-quality orange oil (see page 638) does wonders to intensify the flavor.

Use navel orange zest and increase the zest to ¼ cup (scant 1 ounce/24 grams). Start with 2 cups of juice (from about 8 juice oranges) and reduce it (in two batches if using the microwave) to ½ cup (see Pointers below). Decrease the sugar to ⅔ cup (4.6 ounces/132 grams). Add the zest before cooking the curd and do not strain it. If desired, gently stir in ½ teaspoon of fine-quality orange oil at the end. The finished temperature is 180°F. (Makes a scant 1½ cups/14 ounces/400 grams.)

PASSION FRUIT CURD   Passion fruit has an aromatic, tropical, and near-addictive aroma and flavor. The king of all curds, passion fruit curd is wonderful in a tart and beyond sublime in ice cream (page 237), particularly served with peach pie (page 124).

Replace the lemon juice with 5 fluid ounces (10 tablespoons/4.75 ounces/136 grams) of passion fruit juice* (from 6 to 7 passion fruit). Add 6 tablespoons with the yolk mixture and gently stir the remaining 4 tablespoons into the strained curd. (Uncooked, it offers more aromatic vibrancy.) Decrease the sugar to ⅔ cup (4.6 ounces/132 grams). The finished temperature is 190°F. (Makes 1 cup + 6 table-spoons/12.5 ounces/355 grams, or 1 cup + 2 tablespoons/approx. 11.5 ounces/323 grams, if using the concentrate.)

STORE

Refrigerated in an airtight container, up to 3 weeks. (Longer storage dulls the fresh citrus flavor.)

POINTERS FOR SUCCESS

∾ For finely grated zest, use a zester (page 661), a vegetable peeler, or a fine grater to remove the colored portion only of the peel. The white pith beneath is bitter. If using the zester or peeler, finish by chopping the zest with a sharp knife.

∾ If you heat a citrus fruit (about 10 seconds in a microwave oven on high power) and roll it around on the counter while pressing on it lightly, it will release a significantly greater quantity of juice.

∾ When reducing juices in a microwave, be sure to grease the cup to keep the juices from bubbling over. Use no more than 1¼ cups of juice in a 4-cup heatproof liquid measuring cup. It will take 10 to 15 minutes to reduce it by one half to three quarters in the microwave. Watch carefully toward the end so that it does not overconcentrate and start to caramelize.

∾ To prevent curdling, be sure to mix the sugar with the yolks before adding the fruit juice. Use a heavy nonreactive pan that conducts heat evenly or a double boiler. Also to prevent curdling, do not allow the mixture to boil. Remove the curd immediately from the heat when thickened and strain it at once, as the residual heat in the pan will continue to raise the temperature. (If you are working with an accurate thermometer,[†] you can refer to the specified finished temperature.)

---

*Commercial passion fruit purée can be substituted. Use 8½ tablespoons (136 grams) if using Albert Uster's (see page 677), ⅓ cup when preparing the curd and stir in the remaining approximately 3 table-spoons after straining.

[†]For availability of the Cordon Rose candy thermometer, see page 673.

UNDERSTANDING

An (unlined) aluminum pan should not be used, because it reacts with the egg yolks, turning them chartreuse.

Sugar raises the coagulation point of the egg yolks. It also protects them from premature coagulation during the addition of the acidic fruit juice. If the juice were added directly to the unprotected yolks, the yolks would partially coagulate and, when strained, a large percentage of them would be left behind in the strainer.

Straining the curd after cooking produces the silkiest texture because it removes any coagulated bits of egg. The zest is therefore added after straining, except for the juice orange curd. In order to maximize the elusive orange flavor, the zest must be heated with the yolk mixture and left in after cooking.

Except for bitter Seville oranges, oranges require concentration of their juices for adequate flavor impact. Reducing fruit juices in a microwave results in the purest fruit flavor without any of the slight browning, or caramelization, of the fruit sugars that often takes place using the cooktop.

CURD CREAM FILLING AND TOPPING

Fruit curd combined with lightly stabilized whipped cream makes a wonderful filling for fresh fruit tarts. In this recipe, just enough gelatin is added to firm the filling enough to slice well. For a topping or a garnish for pies or tarts, omit the gelatin and double, or as much as quadruple, the heavy cream. The more cream in proportion to the curd, the lighter and airier the texture and the more subtle the fruit flavor.

MAKES: SCANT 2 CUPS

INGREDIENTS	MEASURE	WEIGHT	
	VOLUME	OUNCES	GRAMS
gelatin	1 teaspoon	•	3 grams
water	1 tablespoon	0.5 ounce	15 grams
heavy cream	½ liquid cup	approx. 4 ounces	116 grams
sugar	1 teaspoon	•	•
1 recipe Fruit Curd (page 568)	approx. 1 cup + 2 tablespoons	•	•

Chill a medium bowl for the cream.

In a small heatproof measuring cup, place the gelatin and water and allow it to sit for 5 minutes. Set the cup in a pan of simmering water for a few minutes, stirring occasionally until the gelatin is dissolved (or microwave on high power for a few seconds, stirring once or twice). Set it aside briefly. (The mixture must still be warm when added to the cold cream, or it will lump.)

In the chilled mixing bowl, beat the cream and sugar until it begins to thicken. Gradually beat in the warm gelatin mixture and beat just until stiff peaks form when the beater is raised. With a large wire whisk, fold the whipped cream into the fruit curd until uniform in color. Pour it immediately into the prebaked pastry crust and chill for at least 1 hour.

STORE

Refrigerated, up to 2 days.

POINTERS FOR SUCCESS

∾ The thickness of the curd will vary depending on the acidity of the fruit juice. If it is very thick, whisk a small amount (about 1 tablespoon) of the whipped cream into it to soften it before folding in the rest.

MERINGUE FILLINGS AND TOPPINGS

Meringue, in its many forms, always contains two ingredients: egg whites and sugar. Since the finished texture is dependent on the proper beating of egg whites, it is important to understand a few basic facts about egg whites. First let's try to settle the age-old controversy: Which beat better, fresh egg whites or older ones? The answer is six of one, half a dozen of the other. When beaten, egg whites will increase six to eight times in volume. Fresh whites are thicker, so they take longer to beat. The resulting foam has less volume but more stability and loses less volume when folded into other ingredients. Older whites are thinner, so they beat more quickly and yield greater but less stable volume. When folded into other ingredients, they lose the extra volume.

The flavor of fresh egg whites is slightly superior to that of older whites, so I tend to prefer them for recipes like mousses, where the egg white does not get cooked.

The following is a simple demystification from research biochemist and cookbook author Shirley Corriher:

Egg white is made up of water and protein. When exposed to air, heat, or acid, the proteins in the egg whites change (denature) from their original form. For the perfect egg white foam, the egg whites should be beaten so that the egg white proteins denature (change) just the right amount. They must remain moist and flexible and not dry out and become rigid. When the beaten egg white, filled with air bubbles, goes into a hot oven or is subjected to hot syrup, it should be soft, moist, flexible, and able to expand until it reaches the temperature that coagulates (sets) it. Overbeating produces dried-out, rigid egg white foam that will not expand properly in the oven. The cook has several secret weapons to produce the perfect degree of egg white denaturization to result in beaten egg whites with the greatest volume and stability. These are the copper bowl, cream of tartar, and sugar. The copper bowl produces stable egg whites by combining with conalbumin, the protein in the egg white that lines each air bubble, to form a totally new protein, copper conalbumin. This copper conalbumin remains moist and flexible even when slightly overbeaten and provides a more stable foam.

Cream of tartar, an acid salt (by-product of the wine industry), provides an even more stable foam in another way. The acid serves to denature the protein just enough to produce a moist stable foam. I have performed several experiments with cream of tartar and find that when the correct amount (1 teaspoon cream of tartar per cup of egg whites—⅛ teaspoon per large egg white) is used, there is no danger at all of overbeating. Because of this, I recommend always using cream of tartar for egg whites that will be cooked. If the egg whites will remain uncooked, I prefer using the copper bowl because it offers the least possibility of extraneous flavor.

Sugar is effective, with either the copper bowl or cream of tartar, to keep the proteins moist and flexible, because sugar itself holds moisture. Superfine sugar is preferable because it dissolves faster. (Undissolved sugar will appear as teardrops on the surface of the meringue.) Sugar can be added at any time while beating the egg whites; however, if it is added early, the whites will require much longer beating and may not reach as great a volume. If sugar is added very late in the beating process, drying may already have started to occur. Most recipes specify to start adding the sugar after the soft peak stage but before the stiff peak stage.

Salt not only increases beating time, it decreases the egg white foam's stability by drawing out water from the egg whites. I prefer adding salt to the other ingredients in the recipe.

Any fat substance or egg yolk is a foam inhibitor and even one drop will keep the egg whites from becoming stiff.

For the most stable foam, start beating the egg whites slowly, gradually increasing speed. Never decrease speed or the volume will permanently decrease. When it is necessary to stop the beater to check consistency, turn it off only very briefly and then bring up the speed quickly to prevent deflation.

Because sugar is hygroscopic (readily absorbs water), avoid making royal icing, meringue, or dacquoise on humid days, as they will be soft and sticky and will not set well.

The recipes in this chapter appear as components throughout the book in many interesting and varied ways. The crisp meringue shell is juxtaposed against creamy lemon chiffon in the Lemon Angel Chiffon Pie (page 157) and the crisp cocoa version becomes boulders atop the Grand Canyon Pie (page 190). Soft meringue topping and extra-light Italian meringue lend their incomparable sweet airiness to Lemon Meringue and Key Lime pies. Italian meringue adds its billowy texture to mixtures such as chiffon pies. And, of course, the various meringues, from chocolate to speckled, are great to eat by themselves when baked until crisp.

I have experimented with many possibilities for stabilizing soft meringue toppings to keep them from shrinking and deflating, or breaking down and watering out on sitting. The shrinking problem is the easier of the two, as this can be prevented by being careful to attach the meringue to the crust before baking and cooling it away from drafts. The watering problem was more of a challenge. Ideal was the late Michael Field's idea of adding ¼ teaspoon of bone meal to every 3 egg whites. I have no idea how he ever came up with this concept, but it works wonderfully *except* that there is a perceptible, slightly sandy crunch that I don't enjoy. I have tried, so far without luck, to interest industry in producing a bone meal for bakers that would be reduced to a micron so that the tongue could not perceive it. A traditional slurry of cornstarch, which I found so successful in whipped cream, compromises the ethereal lightness of the meringue. Making a hot sugar syrup and beating it into the egg whites (Italian meringue) or spreading meringue on hot filling to set the meringue on the bottom turned out to be the best solutions.

I have also experimented with different flavors in meringue and ruled out both coffee and brown sugar. The coffee, instead of tempering the sweetness, gave it an overriding bitter, off flavor. The moisture and weight of the brown sugar (I replaced half the granulated sugar with it) resulted in a heavier meringue, the volume of which was 5 cups instead of the usual 6, with the proportions in the basic 4-egg-white recipe. The addition of cocoa or bitter chocolate, however, not only is delicious, it also serves to temper the sweetness of the meringue.

CRISP MERINGUE PIE SHELL OR TOPPING
(*White, Cocoa, and Bitter Chocolate–Speckled*)

This recipe, when used to make a pie shell, provides an excellent fat-free container for fillings. This meringue has double the sugar of soft meringue to give it more density and stability. Replacing half the granulated sugar, by weight, with powdered sugar that is folded into the meringue produces the lightest possible crisp meringue.

The cocoa and bitter chocolate–speckled variations are less sweet, so they are also excellent to eat plain when baked only briefly so that they remain soft inside.

OVEN TEMPERATURE: 200°F. •
BAKING TIME: 2 TO 2½ HOURS

MAKES: ONE 10-INCH PIE SHELL;
ABOUT 4 CUPS/11.7 OUNCES/331 GRAMS

INGREDIENTS	MEASURE	WEIGHT	
	VOLUME	OUNCES	GRAMS
4 large egg whites, at room temperature	½ liquid cup	4.25 ounces	120 grams
cream of tartar	½ teaspoon	•	•
superfine sugar*	½ cup + 1 tablespoon	4 ounces	115 grams
powdered sugar	1 cup (lightly spooned)	4 ounces	115 grams

*To make your own superfine sugar, simply place granulated sugar in a food processor with the metal blade and process for a few minutes or until fine.

EQUIPMENT

A 10-inch pie plate, lightly greased or sprayed with nonstick vegetable spray; optional: a number 6 (½-inch) plain round pastry tube, a number 7 large pastry star tube, and 2 reclosable quart-size freezer bags or 2 pastry bags

Preheat the oven to 200°F.

In a large mixer bowl, beat the egg whites until foamy. Add the cream of tartar and beat at medium speed, gradually adding 2 tablespoons of the superfine sugar, until soft peaks form when the beater is raised slowly. Gradually beat in the remaining 7 tablespoons of superfine sugar and continue beating on high speed until very stiff and glossy. Sift the powdered sugar over the meringue and, using a slotted skimmer or large rubber spatula, fold it in.

If using the freezer or pastry bags, insert the star tube into one bag and fill it with a cup of the meringue. Insert the plain round tube into the second bag and fill the bag with the remaining meringue. Starting at the center of the pie plate, using the larger amount of meringue, pipe a spiral coil (see page 621) to cover the bottom and sides of the pan. Use a small metal spatula and any leftover meringue to fill in any gaps. Using the meringue in the bag with the star tube, pipe a border of shells or stars (see page 621).

Alternatively, use a large spoon to spread a ½-inch-thick layer of meringue over the bottom and sides of the pie pan.

Place the meringue in the oven and bake without opening the oven door for 2 hours. The meringue should not begin to brown. To check for doneness, without removing it from the oven, use the tip of a small sharp knife to dig out a little from the center. It can still be a tiny bit sticky, as it will continue to dry while cooling. If it is stickier, leave it in the oven for another 30 minutes or until done.

To prevent cracking, turn off the oven and prop the oven door open with a wooden spoon handle. Allow the meringue to sit for 10 minutes. Then open the oven door completely and allow the meringue to sit for another 10 minutes before removing it from the oven.

Alternatively, if your oven has a pilot light, and time allows, the most even way to dry the meringue is to bake it for 1 hour, then turn off the heat and allow it to sit undisturbed for 8 hours.

VARIATIONS

Adding unsweetened cocoa or chocolate to the meringue does wonders for tempering the sweetness. The chocolate version, however, is too soft to make a well-articulated raised border.

COCOA MERINGUE Whisk 2 tablespoons (scant 0.9 ounce/12 grams) of unsweetened cocoa (preferably Dutch-processed) into the powdered sugar until evenly blended before folding it into the meringue. A few drops of liquid red food color, added to the egg whites, will give the meringue a nicer shade of brown. (Do not use paste food color, as it would break down the egg white foam.) (Makes about 4 cups/12 ounces/343 grams.)

BITTER CHOCOLATE–SPECKLED MERINGUE In a food processor with the metal blade, place the powdered sugar and 2 ounces of unsweetened chocolate, broken into pieces, and process until the chocolate is powdery. Refrigerate the mixture for about 30 minutes before folding it into the meringue. (If the chocolate is cold and hard, the meringue will stay white; otherwise, it will become pale tan.) (Makes about 4 cups/13.5 ounces/382 grams.)

STORE

Airtight, room temperature (low humidity), at least 6 months.

NOTE

For a 9-inch pie shell (but without a raised decorative border), make three quarters of the recipe, using 3 whites.

POINTERS FOR SUCCESS

∽ The egg whites and all utensils must be entirely grease-free in order for the whites to beat to stiff peaks.

SOFT MERINGUE TOPPING

(Meringue for Piping)

This is the meringue to make for topping a pie if the pie will not sit very long after preparation. It is light and billowy and not overpoweringly sweet.

OVEN TEMPERATURE: 350°F. •
BAKING TIME: 10 TO 15 MINUTES

MAKES: ABOUT 4.5 CUPS/5.7 TO 7
OUNCES/165 TO 200 GRAMS

INGREDIENTS	MEASURE	WEIGHT	
	VOLUME	OUNCES	GRAMS
3 large egg whites, at room temperature	3 fluid ounces (6 tablespoons)	approx. 3 ounces	90 grams
cream of tartar	⅜ teaspoon	•	•
superfine sugar*	6 to 9 tablespoons†	2.6 to 4 ounces	75 to 112 grams

MAKES: ABOUT 6 CUPS/7.7 TO 9.3 OUNCES/220 TO 265 GRAMS

INGREDIENTS	MEASURE	WEIGHT	
	VOLUME	OUNCES	GRAMS
4 large egg whites, at room temperature	½ liquid cup	4.25 ounces	120 grams
cream of tartar	½ teaspoon	•	•
superfine sugar*	½ cup to ¾ cup†	3.5 to 5.25 ounces	100 to 150 grams

*To make your own superfine sugar, simply place granulated sugar in a food processor with the metal blade and process for a few minutes or until fine.
†Use the larger amount if planning to pipe the meringue.

In a large mixer bowl, beat the egg whites until foamy. Add the cream of tartar and beat at medium speed, gradually adding 2 tablespoons of the sugar, until soft peaks form when the beater is raised slowly. Gradually beat in the remaining sugar and continue beating on high speed until stiff peaks form when the beater is raised.

Spread the meringue topping onto the pie in decorative swirls, making sure that it touches the edges of the pie so that it will not shrink.

To bake: For a 3-egg-white meringue, bake in a preheated 350°F. oven for 10 to 12 minutes, or until golden; for a 4-egg-white meringue, bake for 12 to 15 minutes. (The temperature will be 115°F.)

POINTERS FOR SUCCESS

∾ The egg whites and all utensils must be entirely grease-free in order for the whites to beat to stiff peaks.

∾ Cool the baked meringue away from drafts to prevent deflating. A cupboard is ideal.

LIGHT ITALIAN MERINGUE

Classic Italian meringue contains double the weight of sugar to egg whites. This recipe has only a little more than one and a half times the sugar, giving it just enough body and sweetness to lighten chiffon pies.

MAKES: 5 CUPS

INGREDIENTS	MEASURE	WEIGHT	
	VOLUME	OUNCES	GRAMS
sugar	¾ cup + 2 tablespoons, divided	approx. 6 ounces	175 grams
water	¼ liquid cup	2 ounces	60 grams
4 large egg whites, at room temperature	½ liquid cup	4.25 ounces	120 grams
cream of tartar	½ teaspoon	•	•

Have ready near the range a 1-cup heatproof glass measure.

In a small heavy saucepan (preferably with a nonstick lining), stir together ¾ cup of the sugar and the water until all the sugar is moistened. Heat, stirring constantly, until the sugar dissolves and the syrup is bubbling. Stop stirring and turn down the heat to the lowest setting. (If using an electric range, remove the pan from the heat.)

In a mixing bowl, beat the egg whites until foamy. Add the cream of tartar and beat until soft peaks form when the beater is raised slowly. Gradually beat in the remaining 2 tablespoons of sugar until stiff peaks form when the beater is raised slowly.

Increase the heat under the sugar syrup and boil the syrup until a thermometer registers 248° to 250°F. (the firm ball stage). Immediately pour it into the glass measure to stop the cooking.

If using an electric hand-held mixer, beat the syrup into the whites in a steady stream. To keep syrup from spinning onto the sides of the bowl, do not allow it to fall directly on the beaters. If using a stand mixer, pour a small amount of syrup over the whites with the mixer off. Immediately beat at high speed for 5 seconds. Stop the mixer and add a larger amount of syrup. Beat at high speed for 5 seconds. Continue with the remaining syrup. With the last addition, use a rubber scraper to remove the syrup clinging to the measure. Beat at medium speed until cool, about 2 minutes. Use at once for maximum volume.

STORE

Room temperature, up to 2 hours; refrigerated, up to 2 days. Rebeat the chilled meringue briefly before using; the meringue will still be smooth and creamy but will decrease in volume by half.

POINTERS FOR SUCCESS

꽈 For maximum stability, the syrup must reach 248°F. but not exceed 270°F., as higher temperatures will break down the whites.

꽈 The whites must be free of any grease or trace of yolk.

꽈 Do not overbeat the meringue after cooling.

EXTRA-LIGHT ITALIAN MERINGUE

This meringue has equal volume sugar and egg white, which means even less sugar than in the light Italian meringue. This gives it a greater volume and, of course, it is therefore lighter in texture. It is less stable, and therefore not as suited to folding into other ingredients, but it is my first choice to use as a pie topping because it is exceptionally light and moist but will not deflate, form teardrops, or become watery at the bottom.

MAKES: 6½ CUPS

INGREDIENTS	MEASURE	WEIGHT	
	VOLUME	OUNCES	GRAMS
sugar	½ cup	3.5 ounces	100 grams
water	2 tablespoons	1 ounce	30 grams
4 large egg whites, at room temperature	½ liquid cup	4.25 ounces	120 grams
cream of tartar	½ teaspoon	•	•

Have ready near the range a 1-cup heatproof glass measure.

In a small heavy saucepan (preferably with a nonstick lining), stir together the sugar and water. Heat, stirring constantly, until the sugar dissolves and the syrup is bubbling. Stop stirring and turn down the heat to the lowest setting. (If using an electric range, remove the pan from the heat.)

In a mixing bowl, beat the egg whites until foamy. Add the cream of tartar and beat until stiff peaks form when the beater is raised slowly.

Increase the heat under the syrup and boil the syrup until a thermometer registers 236°F. (soft ball stage). Immediately pour it into the glass measure to stop the cooking.

If using an electric hand-held mixer, beat the syrup into the whites in a steady stream, avoiding the beaters to keep syrup from spinning onto sides of bowl. If using a stand mixer, pour a small amount of syrup over the whites with the mixer off. Immediately beat at high speed for 5 seconds. Stop the mixer and add a larger amount of syrup. Beat at high speed for 5 seconds. Continue with the remaining syrup. With the last addition, use a rubber scraper to remove the syrup clinging to the measure. Beat at medium speed until cool, about 2 minutes. Use at once for maximum volume.

Spread the meringue topping onto the pie in decorative swirls, making sure that it touches the edges of the pie crust so that it will not shrink. Broil it for 20 seconds to a minute, watching carefully to prevent burning, until the meringue is golden.

If you prefer a less moist meringue, bake it in a preheated 350°F. oven for 5 minutes before browning it under the broiler. Do not bake it for more than 5 minutes, or it risks collapse.

STORE

Room temperature, up to 2 hours; refrigerated, up to 2 days. Rebeat briefly before using; the meringue will still be smooth and creamy but will decrease in volume by half.

POINTERS FOR SUCCESS

∾ For maximum stability without compromising volume, the syrup should reach but not exceed 236°F.

∾ Do not overbeat the meringue after cooling.

∾ The egg whites and all utensils must be entirely grease-free in order for the whites to beat to stiff peaks.

∾ Cool the baked meringue away from drafts to prevent deflating. A cupboard is ideal.

UNDERSTANDING

Classic Italian meringue has double the weight of sugar to egg whites. This recipe has less sugar than egg (equal volume but less weight) and is brought to a lower temperature. It, therefore, is not only less sweet but also lighter, and it has more volume since it is not weighed down by the sugar. Classic Italian meringue is cooked to 248°F., which makes it more stable but also less soft.

FOOD-PROCESSOR POURED FONDANT

This shiny fondant is the traditional topping for Classic Napoleon (page 453). Using the food processor makes what used to be a painstaking process extraordinarily easy.

MAKES: 1¾ CUPS

INGREDIENTS	MEASURE	WEIGHT	
	VOLUME	OUNCES	GRAMS
sugar	2½ cups	17.5 ounces	500 grams
water	½ liquid cup	4 ounces	118 grams
corn syrup	¼ liquid cup, lightly greased	3 ounces	82 grams
pure vanilla extract	1 teaspoon	•	4 grams
Stock Syrup sugar	2 tablespoons	scant 1 ounce	25 grams
water	¼ liquid cup	2 ounces	60 grams

EQUIPMENT
An accurate candy thermometer

Advance preparation: 24 hours.

Have ready near the range a food processor fitted with the steel blade.

In a medium heavy saucepan (preferably with nonstick lining), combine the sugar, water, and corn syrup and bring it to a boil, stirring constantly. Stop stirring and allow the syrup to cook to 238°F. (the soft ball stage). Immediately pour it into the food processor.

Wash the thermometer and reinsert it into the syrup. Allow it to cool, uncovered, to exactly 140°F.; this will take 25 to 35 minutes.

Add the vanilla and process for 2 to 3 minutes or until the fondant becomes opaque. (The fondant starts as a transparent syrup. As crystallization of the sugar starts, it becomes translucent and finally opaque or white.)

Pour the fondant into a container, such as a 2-cup glass measure, lined with a reclosable quart-size freezer bag. Close the bag without sealing it. When the fondant is completely cool and firm, expel the air, seal the bag, and lift it out of the container. Store it at room temperature for at least 24 hours.

MAKE THE STOCK SYRUP

In a small saucepan, stir together the sugar and water and bring it to a full boil, stirring constantly. Remove it from the heat and allow it to cool until warm before using it to thin the fondant. (The syrup will keep for months in an airtight container, refrigerated.)

PREPARE THE FONDANT FOR POURING

Heat the fondant in the top of a double boiler set over hot water, stirring gently, until warm. To maintain its sheen, the fondant must not exceed 105°F. Stir in enough warm syrup to make the fondant pourable; start with 1 tablespoon.

STORE

Room temperature, up to 1 week; refrigerated, up to 6 months.

POINTERS FOR SUCCESS

∾ See Sugar Syrups (page 648). To prevent premature crystallization, do not stir after the syrup comes to a boil.

∾ To keep the temperature from rising too high, remove the pan from the heat slightly before the syrup reaches 238°F. and then pour it into the processor as soon as it reaches 238°F.

∾ It is essential to use an accurate thermometer (see page 673). To prevent crystallization, the thermometer must be clean before you reinsert it into the syrup.

∾ When reheating the fondant, do not use an aluminum pan, as it would cause discoloration. The fondant must not be overheated, or it will lose its shine.

∾ Avoid vigorous stirring to prevent air bubbles.

LIGHT SPONGE CAKE LAYERS

This indispensable cake takes about five minutes to mix and less than ten minutes to bake. It is a slender, airy yet velvety cake layer containing no fat other than what is in the egg yolks, making it sturdy enough to absorb moisture from fruit or other components. Instead of falling apart, it becomes only more tender. It also unites a filling and meringue, keeping them from separating or slipping when cut. The cake layer is barely perceptible, yet its presence makes a great difference to the success of many tarts.

Use the tart pans to bake the cake, and you will have four cake layers (extras freeze perfectly). Or, use the sheet pan and you will have two slightly smaller layers and scraps that can be cut and sprinkled on the tart.

OVEN TEMPERATURE: 450°F. •
BAKING TIME: 7 TO 10 MINUTES

MAKES: TWO 8½- BY ¼-INCH-THICK LAYERS AND
CRUMBS OR FOUR 9- BY ¼-INCH-THICK LAYERS

INGREDIENTS	MEASURE	WEIGHT	
	VOLUME	OUNCES	GRAMS
sifted cake flour	⅓ cup (sifted and leveled off)	approx. 1.2 ounces	33 grams
unsifted cornstarch	2½ tablespoons	0.75 ounce	23 grams
4 large eggs, at room temperature	¾ liquid cup	7 ounces (weighed without the shells)	200 grams
1 large egg yolk, at room temperature	approx. 1 tablespoon	0.6 ounce	18 grams
sugar, preferably superfine	½ cup + 1 tablespoon, divided	4 ounces	113 grams
pure vanilla extract	¾ teaspoon	•	3 grams
cream of tartar	¼ teaspoon	•	•

EQUIPMENT

Two 9½- by 1-inch fluted tart pans or one 17- by 12-inch baking pan (half-size sheet pan), greased bottom lined with a nonstick liner or parchment, and then greased again and floured (or sprayed with Baker's Joy)

Preheat the oven to 450°F. at least 20 minutes before baking. Set the oven rack at the lower level before preheating.

In a small bowl, whisk the cake flour and cornstarch to combine them well.

Separate 2 of the eggs, placing the yolks in one large mixer bowl and the whites in another. To the yolks, add the 2 remaining eggs, the additional yolk, and ½ cup of the sugar. Beat, preferably with the whisk attachment on high speed, until thick, fluffy, and tripled in volume, about 5 minutes. Lower the speed and beat in the vanilla.

Sift half the flour mixture over the egg mixture and, using a large balloon whisk, slotted skimmer, or rubber spatula, fold it in gently but rapidly until the flour has disappeared. Repeat with the remaining flour mixture.

Beat the egg whites until foamy. Add the cream of tartar and beat until soft peaks form when the beater is raised slowly. Beat in the remaining 1 tablespoon of sugar and continue beating until stiff peaks form when the beater is raised. Fold the whites into the batter and pour it into the prepared pans (or pan), using a spatula to level it. If you are using the tart pans, the batter will come halfway up the sides.

Bake for 7 minutes if using the sheet pan, 10 minutes if using the tart pans, or until the cake is golden brown and springs back when lightly pressed in the center with a fingertip.

If necessary, loosen the sides of the cake with the tip of a sharp knife, and unmold at once: If using a sheet pan, grasp a long edge of the liner or parchment overhang and gently slide the cake from the pan onto a flat surface. If using the tart pans, place each pan over a heatproof container that is smaller than the opening of the pan bottom and gently push down on the rim, causing the rim to release and leaving the cake sitting on the tart pan bottom. (If the tart pans do not have removable bottoms, simply invert each layer onto a greased wire rack, lift off the pan, peel away the parchment, and reinvert onto another greased wire rack to cool top side up for maximum height.) Allow the cake to cool.

If desired, use a serrated knife to remove the top crust. For the sheet pan layer, use scissors and a cardboard circle slightly less than 8½ inches in diameter as a template to cut the 2 layers. As the finished size of the sheet is 16¾ inches, you will have almost 8½-inch rounds. Allow the scraps to dry for a few hours and then chop them with a sharp knife or in the food processor to make cake crumbs.

The layers baked in the tart pans will each be a little over ½ inch high. To split each in half, use a long serrated knife held horizontally to make a shallow cut in the middle of each layer, going all the way around. Using this cut as a track for the knife, with a sawing motion, slice from one side all the way through to the other. As you proceed, be sure to check that the far end of the blade stays in the groove.

Wrap each layer in plastic wrap.

STORE

Room temperature, up to 3 days; refrigerated, up to 5 days; frozen, up to 2 months. Do not stack the layers unless they are frozen; once frozen, they can be stacked and placed in reclosable freezer bags.

POINTERS FOR SUCCESS

∾ Use superfine sugar for the finest texture. (You can make it by processing granulated sugar in the food processor for a few minutes until fine.)

∾ Use cake flour without leavening.

∾ To measure the cake flour, use a ⅓-cup measure and sift directly into it until the flour mounds above the rim. Run a metal spatula or knife blade across the rim of the cup, getting rid of the excess flour.

∾ The bowl, beater, and egg whites must be absolutely free of grease (including even a speck of egg yolk) for the egg whites to beat to stiff peaks.

∾ The egg mixture and the egg whites must be beaten very stiffly. There is no danger of overbeating.

∾ Work quickly once the eggs are beaten so that they do not deflate. Fold the flour gently but thoroughly into the batter. Bake immediately after mixing.

∾ Use the correct pan size.

∾ If using syrup, for one 9- by ½-inch layer, use about ½ cup if topping it with fruit, which will moisten it further. If topping it with a custard filling, as in the Tiramisù Tart (page 212), you can use up to ⅔ cup syrup.

UNDERSTANDING

Using ⅛ teaspoon of cream of tartar per egg white (2 tablespoons) prevents the possibility of overbeating them, which would cause them to lose moisture and not hold air. This batter has very little flour and depends on the eggs for structure. Since it is a thin layer, it does not require as much structure as would a higher cake.

LIGHT CHOCOLATE SPONGE CAKE LAYERS

This chocolate sponge cake works well with many fruits, particularly cherries and oranges.

EQUIPMENT

Two 9½- by 1-inch fluted tart pans or one 17- by 12-inch half-size sheet pan, greased, bottom lined with a nonstick liner or parchment, and then greased again and floured (or sprayed with Baker's Joy)

INGREDIENTS	MEASURE	WEIGHT	
	VOLUME	OUNCES	GRAMS
unsweetened cocoa, preferably Dutch-processed	¼ cup (lightly spooned)	0.75 ounce	23 grams
boiling water	¼ liquid cup	2 ounces	60 grams
pure vanilla extract	¾ teaspoon	•	3 grams
4 large eggs, at room temperature	¾ liquid cup	7 ounces (weighed without the shells)	200 grams
1 large egg yolk, at room temperature	approx 1 tablespoon	0.6 ounce	18 grams
sugar, preferably superfine	⅔ cup + 1 tablespoon, divided	5 ounces	145 grams
sifted cake flour	⅓ cup (sifted and leveled off)	approx. 1.2 ounces	33 grams
cream of tartar	¼ teaspoon	•	•

Preheat the oven to 450°F at least 20 minutes before baking. Set the oven rack at the lowest level before prebaking.

In a small bowl, with a rubber spatula, stir together the cocoa and boiling water until smooth. Stir in the vanilla and cover tightly with plastic wrap.

Separate 2 of the eggs, placing the yolks in one large mixing bowl and the whites in another. To the yolks, add the 2 remaining eggs, the additional yolk, and ⅔ cup of the sugar. Beat, preferably with the whisk attachment, on high speed until thick, fluffy, and tripled in volume, about 5 minutes. Add the cocoa mixture, beating a few seconds until incorporated. Sift the flour mixture over the egg mixture and set it aside.

Beat the egg whites until foamy. Add the cream of tartar and beat until soft peaks form when the beater is raised. Beat in the remaining 1 tablespoon of sugar and beat until stiff peaks form when the beater is raised slowly. With a large rubber spatula, fold one third of the whites into the batter until all of the flour is incorporated. Gently fold in the remaining whites. Pour the batter into the prepared pans (or pan), using a spatula to level it. If you are using the tart pans, the batter will come halfway up the sides.

Bake for 7 minutes if using the sheet pan, 10 minutes if using the tart pans, or until the cake is golden brown and springs back when lightly pressed in the center with a fingertip.

If necessary, loosen the sides of the cake with the tip of a sharp knife, and unmold at once: If using a baking pan, grasp a long edge of the liner or parchment overhang and gently slide the cake from the pan onto a flat surface. If using the tart pans, place each pan over a heatproof container that is smaller than the opening of the pan bottom and gently push down on the rim, causing the rim to release and leaving the cake sitting on the tart pan bottom. (If the tart pans do not have removable bottoms, simply invert each layer onto a greased wire rack, lift off the pan, peel away the parchment, and reinvert onto another greased wire rack to cool top side up for maximum height.) Allow the cake to cool.

For the sheet pan layer, use scissors and a cardboard circle slightly less than 8½ inches in diameter as a template to cut the 2 layers. As the finished size of the sheet is 16¾ inches, you will have almost 8½-inch rounds. Allow the scraps to dry for a few hours and then chop them with a sharp knife or in the food processor to make cake crumbs.

The layers baked in the tart pans will each be a little over ½ inch high. To split each in half, use a long serrated knife held horizontally to make a shallow cut in the middle of each layer, going all the way around. Using this cut as a track for the knife, with a sawing motion, slice from one side all the way through to the other. As you proceed, be sure to check that the far end of the blade stays in the groove.

Wrap each layer in plastic wrap.

STORE

Room temperature, up to 3 days; refrigerated, up to 5 days; frozen, up to 2 months. Do not stack the layers unless frozen; once frozen, they can be stacked and placed in reclosable freezer bags.

POINTERS FOR SUCCESS

❧ See Light Sponge Cake Layers, page 583.

❧ If you forget to cover the cocoa and water mixture and it dries, add water, a few droplets at a time, until it is soft enough to form soft peaks when lifted with the spatula.

POACHED APRICOTS

Ripe, deep golden apricots with a faint pink blush are one of the world's most glorious fruits. In Austria, they are so revered an entire region, the Wachau, between Vienna and Salzburg, is devoted to growing them.

In this country, the apricot season starts in June and continues until August. When shopping for apricots to use for tarts, choose firmer ones, as they hold their shape better. The skin should be left intact after poaching. If using softer apricots, they will lose their skin after poaching.

Poaching does wonders to bring out the hidden flavor and perfect the texture of apricots that are picked slightly underripe. It's as though the cooking completed the ripening.

MAKES: APPROXIMATELY 3 CUPS

INGREDIENTS	MEASURE	WEIGHT	
	VOLUME	OUNCES	GRAMS
1½ pounds fresh apricots (12 to 15, depending on size)	4 cups (halved and pitted)	22 ounces (pitted)	624 grams
freshly squeezed lemon juice	2 teaspoons	•	10 grams
water	4 liquid cups	2 pounds	944 grams
sugar	1 cup	7 ounces	200 grams
corn syrup	1 tablespoon	0.7 ounce	20 grams

With a small sharp knife, cut the apricots in half and remove and discard the pits. Place the apricots in a bowl and sprinkle them with the lemon juice.

In a large saucepan, over high heat, stir together the water and sugar until the sugar is dissolved. Add the corn syrup and heat until simmering.

Meanwhile, prepare a large bowl of ice water.

Add the apricots to the sugar syrup and simmer over low heat for 4 to 5 minutes or until just barely tender. (A skewer inserted into an apricot should meet with a little resistance.) With a slotted skimmer or spoon, immediately transfer the apricots from the syrup to the ice water. Allow the syrup to cool completely.

Drain the apricots and place them in a bowl. Pour the cooled syrup over the apricots. Cover them tightly with plastic wrap and allow them to sit at room temperature for at least 8 hours, or refrigerate them for up to 3 days.

VARIATION

For a solution to apricots that look beautiful but turn out to have no flavor, I am indebted to David Karp for the following technique, which gives them a lovely flavor.

Prepare a large bowl of cold tap water with ice cubes in it.

In a medium saucepan, combine 2 cups (23.75 ounces/672 grams) of honey, the zest of 1 lemon (removed in strips), 3 tablespoons of freshly squeezed lemon juice, and ½ cup of water. Bring the mixture to a boil, stirring constantly. Lower the heat. Add the apricots, in batches, so that they are covered by the mixture, and simmer each batch of apricots for 4 to 5 minutes or until just barely tender. (A skewer inserted into an apricot should meet with little resistance.) With a slotted skimmer or spoon, immediately remove the apricots from the syrup to the ice water to stop the cooking. Allow the syrup to cool completely.

When the apricots are cool, drain them in a colander and place them in a bowl. Pour the cooled syrup over the apricots. Cover them tightly with plastic wrap and allow them to sit at room temperature for at least 8 hours, or refrigerate them for up to 3 days.

UNDERSTANDING

Corn syrup is added to the poaching liquid to make it smoother and give it more body. The lemon juice prevents browning after the apricots are removed from the syrup. The apricots will not take on the sweetness of the poaching liquid unless they have been cut in half and are allowed to sit in the syrup for at least 8 hours. As the apricots continue cooking from residual heat even after being removed from the syrup, to retain a firm texture, they should be poached only until barely tender, removed from the syrup, and then returned to the cooled syrup.

RASPBERRY CONSERVE

This conserve is worth every bit of the effort involved, because a product tasting of this much raspberry simply cannot be bought. (It would take a jar of commercially made jam two and a third times the size to equal the amount of fruit used in one jar of this recipe). This unique method of preparing jam triples the concentration of the fruit so that it gels without having to add pectin or the usual high amount of sugar (in excess of two thirds more). The conserve is tart and full of fruit flavor, with a deep garnet hue. It will make the best Linzertorte (page 283) you have ever eaten.

MAKES: ABOUT 1 QUART/4 HALF-PINT JARS + ½ CUP/2.5 POUNDS/1 KILOGRAM 157 GRAMS

INGREDIENTS	MEASURE	WEIGHT	
	VOLUME	OUNCES	GRAMS
sugar	2 cups + 2 tablespoons	15 ounces	425 grams
water	1 liquid cup + 2 tablespoons	9.3 ounces	266 grams
raspberries	3 quarts	3 pounds	1 kg 361 grams

Have ready near the range a colander suspended over a bowl.

In a wide pot (about 9 inches), combine the sugar and water and bring to a boil, stirring constantly. Boil for 1 minute. Add 3 to 4 cups of berries (so that they are in a single layer) and boil for 1 minute. Remove them with a slotted spoon or skimmer to the colander. Over high heat, boil down the syrup in the pot to 2 cups. Add another 3 to 4 cups of berries and boil for 1 minute. Add them to the berries sitting in the colander. Again boil down the syrup in the pot to 2 cups. Continue with the remaining berries, cooking 3 to 4 cups at a time. When you are boiling down the syrup, add the syrup that has drained from the cooked berries to the pot. Skim the white foam from the surface.

When the last batch of raspberries is cooked, again boil the syrup down to 2 cups (the temperature will be 210°F.). Set the pot aside.

Press the berries through a sieve to remove most of the seeds. (When condensing raspberries to this degree, leaving all the seeds would be excessive; however, some seeds lend a nice texture to the conserve. I use the colander/sieve attachment on my KitchenAid, which has large enough holes to allow a few seeds to pass through. You can also use a food mill fitted with the finest disc.) You should have at least 2 cups raspberry pulp.

Add the sieved berries to the reserved syrup and simmer for 10 minutes or until reduced to 4 cups. Fill four ½-pint canning jars that have been rinsed in boiling water, leaving a ⅜-inch head space (see Note, page 591). Screw on the caps and process them in a water bath, covered, for 10 minutes after the water comes to a boil. The jars must be sitting on a rack in the water bath to allow the water to flow all around them, and the water must be high enough to cover them by 1 inch. They must be upright to expel any air inside the jars, producing a vacuum that seals the jars. Remove the jars and allow them to cool before checking the seal.

If the water bath process is eliminated, be sure to store the conserve in a cool dry area away from light, as there are no preservatives in it to prevent mold from forming. (If mold does form, scrape it off and reboil the conserve.) The conserve takes 2 days in the jar to thicken.

TIP

The conserve can be prepared using frozen raspberries without added sugar. Allow them to defrost in a colander, reserving the juice. Add the juice to the sugar syrup and proceed as with fresh berries. The flavor will be indistinguishable from conserve prepared with fresh berries.

STORE

This conserve can be stored for as long as 4 years. The flavor does not deteriorate, but after 2 years the color deepens and is less bright. A cool area such as a wine cellar is ideal.

NOTES

Half-pint jars can hold only 7 fluid ounces because of the ⅜-inch head space required on top. You will have a bonus of about ½ cup conserve left. Refrigerated, it will keep for 2 weeks.

For an excellent-quality *seedless* raspberry preserve from Columbia Empire Farms, see page 676.

UNDERSTANDING

Formula: 1 pound berries/5 ounces sugar/3 ounces water

A large unlined copper pot is traditional for jam making because the faster the berries and syrup cook, the better the flavor and jelling. Be sure to use a pot with a large diameter to speed evaporation of the syrup.

Raspberries are very fragile and washing them causes them to break down faster.

FRESHLY GRATED COCONUT

Freshly grated coconut is a fabulous topping for pies, worlds apart from the sweetened canned or packaged varieties. A medium coconut, weighing about 1½ pounds/680 grams, will yield about 4 cups (10.5 ounces/300 grams) of finely grated coconut.

To open the coconut, with an ice pick or nail and hammer, pierce the three holes at one end of the coconut. Drain the liquid and reserve it, if desired, for another use. Wrap the coconut with a towel to keep the shell from flying about and use a hammer to crack open the shell. Separate the coconut meat from the shell and use a vegetable parer to remove the brown skin. With the fine shredding disc of a food processor or grater, grate the coconut meat. (Or use the special coconut grater described on page 661.)

To toast coconut: Spread the grated meat on a baking sheet in a single layer and bake in a preheated 350°F. oven for about 10 minutes or until light brown.

STORE

Airtight, refrigerated, up to 1 week; frozen, up to 1 year.

STREUSEL TOPPING
(*STROIsel*)

This sweet pastry is a crumb topping. Because it does not require rolling, it needs no liquid and can support a higher amount of butter and sugar than the standard sweet pastry. These qualities conspire to make it exceptionally tender.

MAKES: 3 CUPS/16.5 OUNCES/471 GRAMS

INGREDIENTS	MEASURE	WEIGHT	
	VOLUME	OUNCES	GRAMS
light brown sugar	⅓ cup, packed	2.5 ounces	72 grams
granulated sugar	2 tablespoons	1 ounce	25 grams
walnut or pecan halves	1 cup	3.5 ounces	100 grams
ground cinnamon	1½ teaspoons	•	•
bleached all-purpose flour	1 cup (dip and sweep method)	5 ounces	142 grams
unsalted butter, softened	8 tablespoons	4 ounces	113 grams
pure vanilla extract	1½ teaspoons	•	6 grams
salt	⅛ teaspoon	•	•

FOR A 9-INCH PIE   MAKES: 1 CUP/5.6 OUNCES/160 GRAMS

INGREDIENTS	MEASURE	WEIGHT	
	VOLUME	OUNCES	GRAMS
light brown sugar	1½ tablespoons, packed	0.75 ounce	20 grams
granulated sugar	1 tablespoon	0.5 ounce	12.5 grams
walnut or pecan halves	⅓ cup	approx. 1.25 ounces	33 grams
ground cinnamon	½ teaspoon	•	•
bleached all-purpose flour	⅓ cup (dip and sweep method)	1.6 ounces	47 grams
unsalted butter, softened	3 tablespoons	1.5 ounces	42 grams
pure vanilla extract	½ teaspoon	•	•
salt	a pinch	•	•

In a food processor fitted with the metal blade, pulse together the sugars, nuts, and cinnamon until the nuts are coarsely chopped (about 20 times). Add the flour, butter, vanilla, and salt and pulse until the mixture is coarse and crumbly. Empty it into a small bowl and, with your fingertips, lightly pinch it together to form clumps about ½ inch in size.

STORE

Room temperature, up to 1 day; refrigerated, up to 1 week; frozen, up to 3 months. Allow it to come to room temperature before using.

UNDERSTANDING

A high oven temperature (400°F.) is desirable to set the streusel and keep it from being greasy. The streusel bakes in 15 to 20 minutes, at which point it is golden brown; longer, and it will become bitter. It is, therefore, best to apply it during the last 15 to 20 minutes of baking.

SUGAR-GLAZED NUTS

This simple technique for crisping nuts also adds a slight touch of sweetness. It makes them ideal for use as a garnish.

OVEN TEMPERATURE: 350°F. •
BAKING TIME: 25 TO 30 MINUTES

MAKES: ABOUT 2 CUPS

INGREDIENTS	MEASURE	WEIGHT	
	VOLUME	OUNCES	GRAMS
sugar	⅓ cup	2.3 ounces	66 grams
water	½ liquid cup	approx. 4 ounces	118 grams
corn syrup	2 tablespoons	approx. 1.5 ounces	41 grams
nuts without skin, such as pecans, walnuts, macadamias, or hazelnuts*	approx. 2 cups	8 ounces	227 grams
unsalted butter, softened	1 tablespoon	0.5 ounce	14 grams

*To remove the skins from hazelnuts, see page 642.

EQUIPMENT

A heavy saucepan, about 4-cup capacity, ideally with a nonstick lining, and a baking sheet

Preheat the oven to 350°F.

In the saucepan, stir together the sugar, water, and corn syrup until the sugar is completely moistened. Heat, stirring constantly, until the sugar dissolves and the syrup is bubbling all over the surface. Add the nuts and stir to coat them well. Spoon the nuts onto the baking sheet, leaving behind any excess syrup.

Bake the nuts, stirring several times, for 25 to 30 minutes or until the sugar caramelizes. It will turn a dark brown and start bubbling on the surface of the nuts, creating a fine glaze. Empty the nuts into a bowl, add the butter, and toss to coat them with the butter. Allow them to cool completely, then store them airtight. To use the nuts as a garnish, leave them whole or break them into pieces.

STORE

Room temperature, airtight, up to 3 weeks.

UNDERSTANDING

The corn syrup prevents crystallization of the sugar. The butter helps to keep the nuts separate and adds flavor.

BRANDIED BURGUNDY CHERRIES

MAKES: 1 QUART (2 FULL CUPS OF CHERRIES)

INGREDIENTS	MEASURE	WEIGHT	
	VOLUME	OUNCES	GRAMS
dark sweet cherries, individually quick frozen	12-ounce bag	1½ pounds	680 grams
sugar	½ cup	3.5 ounces	100 grams
kirsch or cognac	½ cup	4 ounces	112 grams

EQUIPMENT
1-quart canning jar

The night before, refrigerated, or several hours ahead, room temperature, thaw the cherries fully in a colander suspended over a deep bowl. Pour the juice (about 10 tablespoons) into a 2-cup liquid measure and add enough water to equal 1½ cups.

In a medium saucepan, combine the cherry liquid and sugar and bring to a boil; simmer for 1 minute. Remove the pan from the heat. With a slotted spoon, transfer the cherries to the quart jar. Pour in the kirsch or cognac and cover.

In a large pan, boil the cherry syrup (it bubbles up, so stir often) until reduced to 1 cup. Pour it over the cherries. Cover tightly and swirl to mix. If storing for more than 3 months, add enough liqueur to reach nearly the top. Cool, then refrigerate.

SAUCES AND GLAZES

DESSERT SAUCES AND GLAZES

There are some tarts and pastries and even pies that rise to another dimension when lightly napped with a complementary sauce or glaze. Chiffon pie, for example, looks beautiful and tastes great with a fruit sauce—such as Lemon Angel Chiffon Pie (page 157) with raspberry sauce. Apple tartlets are at their finest with a little caramel sauce. Raspberry Chiffon Pie (page 149) looks terrific and tastes equally wonderful with pistachio cream sauce. Few people will turn down a hot fudge sauce. And a glistening glaze lightly coating fresh fruit atop a pie, such as strawberries, makes them come alive while preserving their moisture and freshness. A caramel glaze can be an exciting contrast to a cold or frozen pastry such as profiteroles. A cold raspberry sauce or cream sauce can elevate a warm pastry to the sublime.

For a really quick custard sauce, melt a custard-based ice cream. After all, that's what ice cream is—a frozen custard sauce! (It is usually a little sweeter, however, because freezing suppresses the perception of sweetness.) If using a commercial variety of ice cream, and it seems a little thicker than desired, simply thin it with cream, half-and-half, milk, or a little liqueur.

Without a sauce to add texture, flavor, and beauty to the plate, many a pastry would seem unfinished and incomplete.

HOT FUDGE SAUCE

This sticky, intense hot fudge is my favorite version of all that I have tried over the years. The addition of cocoa provides a deep chocolate flavor and rich, dark color.

MAKES: ¾ CUP

INGREDIENTS	MEASURE	WEIGHT	
	VOLUME	OUNCES	GRAMS
bittersweet chocolate, preferably Lindt Excellence or Valrhona	½ of a 3-ounce bar	1.5 ounces	43 grams
Dutch-processed unsweetened cocoa	2 tablespoons	approx. 0.5 ounce	12 grams
water	⅓ liquid cup	2.75 ounces	78 grams
unsalted butter	3 tablespoons	1.5 ounces	42 grams
sugar	⅓ cup	2.3 ounces	66 grams
corn syrup	2 tablespoons	1.5 ounces	41 grams
salt	a pinch	•	•
pure vanilla extract	½ teaspoon	•	•

In a small heavy saucepan (ideally with a nonstick lining), melt the chocolate with the cocoa and water, stirring constantly. Add the butter, sugar, corn syrup, and salt. Simmer, stirring until the sugar has completely dissolved. Stop stirring and cook at a moderate boil for 5 to 10 minutes or until the mixture thickens and reduces to about ¾ cup (use a greased heatproof glass cup for measuring). Swirl the mixture in the pan occasionally but do not stir. Toward the end of cooking, reduce the heat to low to prevent scorching.

Cool slightly and add the vanilla. Keep warm or reheat in a water bath or microwave, stirring gently.

STORE
Refrigerated, up to 1 month.

NOTE
The microwave is great for making hot fudge because the chocolate does not come into contact with direct heat, so there is less risk of scorching. Use a greased 4-cup heatproof glass measure or bowl, as the fudge will bubble up while reducing.

CARAMEL SAUCE

This sauce is for the caramel lover. It's equally wonderful over ice cream, cake, or apple pie. It is just thick enough when hot, but not clumpy or sticky as it cools on the plate. Don't be afraid of making caramel. If you follow the simple but important Pointers for Success on page 601, it will be easy. Do be sure when making it not to have any small children about and give it your undivided attention. Caramel burns are extremely painful.

MAKES: 1 FULL CUP/APPROXIMATELY 10.75 OUNCES/308 GRAMS

INGREDIENTS	MEASURE	WEIGHT	
	VOLUME	OUNCES	GRAMS
sugar	1 cup	7 ounces	200 grams
Lyle's Golden Syrup (refiner's syrup) or corn syrup	1 tablespoon	0.75 ounce	21 grams
water	¼ liquid cup	2 ounces	60 grams
heavy cream, heated	½ liquid cup	4 ounces	116 grams
unsalted butter, softened	2 tablespoons	1 ounce	28 grams
pure vanilla extract	1 teaspoon	•	•

EQUIPMENT
A heavy saucepan, at least 5-cup capacity, ideally with a nonstick lining

In the saucepan, stir together the sugar, syrup, and water until the sugar is completely moistened. Heat, stirring constantly, until the sugar dissolves and the syrup is bubbling. Stop stirring completely and allow it to boil undisturbed until it turns a deep amber (380°F.). Immediately remove it from the heat and slowly and carefully pour the hot cream into the caramel. It will bubble up furiously.

Use a high-temperature heat-resistant rubber spatula, or a porcelain or wooden spoon to stir the mixture until smooth, scraping up the thicker part that settles on the bottom. If any lumps develop, return the pan to the heat and stir until they dissolve. Stir in the butter. The mixture will be streaky but become uniform after cooling slightly and stirring.

Allow the sauce to cool for 3 minutes. Gently stir in the vanilla extract.

For a decorative lacing effect, this caramel pours perfectly at room temperature. For the greatest precision, use a pastry bag with a small decorating tube or a reclosable bag with a small piece cut from one corner.

VARIATIONS

BURNT ORANGE CARAMEL SAUCE   The fructose in the orange juice causes the sugar to caramelize at a much lower temperature. Replace the water with 1 cup of freshly squeezed orange juice. The mixture will caramelize to the correct degree at 310°F.

RUBY PORT CARAMEL SAUCE   Great color and flavor contrast with chocolate. Substitute 3 tablespoons of ruby port for an equal amount of the cream. Add it together with the vanilla extract.

BOURBON BUTTERSCOTCH CARAMEL SAUCE   A sauce with a mellow butterscotchy effect that is superb with bananas or chocolate. Substitute 2 tablespoons of bourbon for an equal amount of the cream. Add it together with the vanilla extract.

STORE

Room temperature, up to 3 days; refrigerated, at least 3 months. To reheat: If the caramel is in a microwave-safe container at room temperature, microwave it on high power for 1 minute, stirring twice. If cold, it will take a few seconds more. Alternatively, place it in a bowl in a pan of simmering water and heat, stirring occasionally, until warm, about 7 minutes.

POINTERS FOR SUCCESS

See page 601.

UNDERSTANDING

Refiner's or corn syrup helps to prevent the caramel sauce from crystallizing when stirred. It also lowers the caramelization temperature.

I adore the flavor of caramel, so I like to have as much depth of flavor as possible without any burnt flavor. I bring this caramel up to at least 380°F. for maximum flavor. The darker you make the caramel, the less sweet it will seem, but you risk burning it if you don't have an absolutely accurate thermometer (see page 673).

It's best to have the cream hot and the butter at room temperature to avoid splattering when they are added to the hot caramel. Cold cream, however, speeds the cooling and is practical if you're pressed for time—but it must be added very slowly.

I do not recommend using crème fraîche in place of heavy cream, as it does not decrease sweetness to any significant degree nor does it add interest of flavor.

Unrefined sugar, which contains a small amount of natural molasses—which caramelizes at a slightly lower temperature—provides a flavor that is deliciously reminiscent of butterscotch. The "impurities" in unrefined sugar can cause crystallization so if you use it, care must be taken not to stir the caramel too much.

CLEAR CARAMEL SAUCE

This caramel sauce, from the incomparable baker and cookbook author Maida Heatter, is the purest possible version of caramel because it contains nothing but sugar and water and optional liquor for an edge of heightened flavor. Because there are no added dairy products, in the form of butter or cream, it is sparkling clear and has an indefinite shelf life. It is the perfect garnish to complement a light creamy dessert such as Panna Cotta (page 377).

MAKES: ¾ CUP

INGREDIENTS	MEASURE	WEIGHT	
	VOLUME	OUNCES	GRAMS
sugar	1 cup	7 ounces	200 grams
water	1⅓ liquid cups, divided	11 ounces	313 grams
optional: dark rum or bourbon	1 tablespoon	0.5 ounce	14 grams

EQUIPMENT
A heavy saucepan, at least 5-cup capacity, ideally with a nonstick lining

In the saucepan, stir together the sugar and ⅓ cup of the water until the sugar is completely moistened. In a small saucepan, heat the remaining water until very hot and set it aside.

Heat the sugar syrup, stirring constantly, until the sugar dissolves and the syrup is bubbling. Stop stirring completely and allow it to boil undisturbed until it turns a deep amber (380°F.). Immediately remove it from the heat and slowly and carefully pour the remaining hot water into the caramel. It will bubble up furiously.

Return the caramel to low heat and use a high-temperature heat-resistant rubber spatula or a porcelain or wooden spoon to stir the mixture until smooth, scraping up the thicker part that settles on the bottom. Simmer it for 5 to 10 minutes, or until reduced to ¾ cup. Pour it into a heatproof glass measure and set it aside until cool. Stir in the optional liqueur.

Use a spoon to pour the caramel onto the dessert plates or drizzle it on top of a tart.

STORE
Room temperature, indefinitely.

POINTERS FOR SUCCESS

∽ See page 601.

UNDERSTANDING

I adore the flavor of caramel, so I like to have as much depth of flavor as possible without any burnt flavor. I like to bring it up to 380°F. for maximum flavor. The darker you make the caramel, the less sweet it will seem, but you risk burning it if you don't have an absolutely accurate thermometer (see page 673).

It's best to have the water hot to avoid splattering when added to the hot caramel. Cold water, however, speeds the cooling and is practical if you're pressured for time, but it must be added very slowly.

If unrefined sugar is used, the flavor will be more delicious, but over a period of weeks the sauce may crystallize because of impurities in the sugar.

CARAMEL FOR DIPPING

This is a transparent hard caramel that graces the tops of the cream puffs for the Gâteau St.-Honoré (page 538).

MAKES: ½ CUP

INGREDIENTS	MEASURE	WEIGHT	
	VOLUME	OUNCES	GRAMS
sugar	1 cup	7 ounces	200 grams
water	⅓ liquid cup	2.7 ounces	78 grams
cream of tartar	⅛ teaspoon	•	•

EQUIPMENT
A heavy saucepan, at least 5-cup capacity, ideally with a nonstick lining

In the saucepan, stir together the sugar, water, and cream of tartar until the sugar is completely moistened. Heat, stirring constantly, until the sugar dissolves and the syrup is bubbling. Stop stirring completely and allow it to boil undisturbed until it turns a pale amber (350° to 360°F.). Immediately remove it from the heat and pour the caramel into a heatproof 1-cup glass measure. (This retains the heat, keeping the caramel fluid, and it can be placed in the microwave to reheat if necessary. If you don't have a microwave, leave it in the pan.)

NOTE

Caramel can be made with no water by constantly stirring the sugar to prevent uneven browning. If the caramel will be used for dipping, just a few drops of lemon juice can be added to prevent crystallization. I find it far easier to add a little water to dissolve the sugar before allowing it to caramelize. The resulting caramel seems just as hard. Adding a large quantity of water, on the other hand, slows down caramelization, which results in a softer, stickier caramel.

POINTERS FOR SUCCESS

∾ Most important: When making caramel, be careful to concentrate every moment. Sugar burns are extremely painful.

∾ Do not make any form of caramel other than caramel sauce in humid weather—it will be sticky.

∾ Use refined sugar that is absolutely free of impurities, to prevent crystallization.

∾ To further prevent crystallization, do not allow any sugar crystals to get on the sides of the pan, and be sure to moisten all the sugar with the water. Stop stirring entirely as soon as it comes to a boil. If using a thermometer, be sure to rinse it and dry it if removing and reinserting in the syrup. If any sugar remains on the thermometer, it will cause crystallization.

∾ Use a pan that conducts heat well (such as unlined copper, aluminum, or anodized aluminum) so that cooking stops soon after it is removed from the heat. Alternatively, have ready a larger pan or sink partly filled with cold water to immerse the bottom of the pan. Do not use a pan with a tin or nonstick lining, as its melting point is below that of caramel.*

∾ To determine the color of the caramel, use an accurate thermometer or drop a bit of caramel on a white surface such as a porcelain spoon or a plate. When making spun sugar, too light a caramel produces a ghostly effect, too dark produces a brassy color when spun.

∾ To prevent breakage, never put a thermometer used for caramel into water until completely cool.

∾ Soaking utensils in hot water will remove hardened caramel.

∾ After the caramel is prepared, do not stir it too much, as this may eventually cause crystallization.

UNDERSTANDING

The cream of tartar is a disturbing agent that prevents the caramel from crystallizing during the repeated dipping of the cream puffs.

---

*There are some special pans, such as the Scanpan, from Denmark (see page 667), with nonstick properties that can withstand the heat of caramel.

CARAMEL FOR SPUN SUGAR
(*Angel's Hair*)

The addition of corn syrup and beeswax makes this the ideal caramel for spinning into the gold strands called angel's hair that transform any dessert into a festive creation.

MAKES: ENOUGH FOR A GÂTEAU ST.-HONORÉ (PAGE 00)

INGREDIENTS	MEASURE	WEIGHT	
	VOLUME	OUNCES	GRAMS
sugar	½ cup	3.5 ounces	100 grams
corn syrup	⅓ liquid cup	3.75 ounces	108 grams
optional: grated beeswax	1 teaspoon		

EQUIPMENT
A cut whisk (see page 672) or 2 forks

Cover the floor near your table or countertop with newspaper. Oil the handles of two long wooden spoons or broomsticks and tape them to the table or countertop 12 inches apart so that the handles extend well beyond the edge of the table or counter. Have ready near the range a 2-cup or larger heatproof glass measure.

In a small heavy saucepan, stir together the sugar and corn syrup and bring to a boil over medium heat, stirring constantly. Increase the heat and boil until the caramel is amber and a thermometer registers 360°F. The residual heat will raise it about 10°F. If the temperature is below 360°F., the caramel will be pale and the spun sugar white instead of gold; over 370°F., it will have a brassy color. I find 370°F. produces the perfect color.

Immediately transfer the caramel to the heatproof glass measure to stop the cooking. Allow to cool for a few minutes.

Add the optional beeswax and wait until the smoking stops. Check the caramel by lifting it with a fork to see if it will fall in strings rather than droplets. Allow to cool a little longer if droplets form.

Stand on a stool so your arms are above the wooden handles. Dip a cut whisk or two forks held side by side into the caramel and vigorously wave back and forth, allowing it to fall in long, fine threads over the handles. Waving must be continuous, or small droplets will form. (It is normal to have a few of these droplets, known poetically as angel's tears.) If the caramel starts to get too thick, return it briefly to the heat, but be careful not to darken or burn it.

Wrap the stands around the base and sides of a tart or oiled form, as they will not stay flexible for too long, especially if the beeswax was omitted. Any leftover strands can be shaped into little nests by pressing them into lightly oiled custard cups and freezing them in an airtight container. They can be filled with small colorful ovals of different flavors of ice cream or sorbet.

STORE

Spun sugar: Several hours at room temperature, if the weather is very dry; if it's humid, the sugar becomes sticky and tends to settle or mat instead of maintaining light, separate strands. The nests: stored in an airtight container at room temperature with low humidity, 2 to 3 weeks; frozen, they will keep for months.

POINTERS FOR SUCCESS

∾ See page 601.
∾ Oil the counter and all utensils to prevent sticking.

UNDERSTANDING

Corn syrup is an invert sugar that inhibits crystallization. It is added with beeswax to caramel for spun sugar because it helps keep the strands flexible. Beeswax is preferable to paraffin because it has a higher smoking point.

RASPBERRY SAUCE

Raspberries are the crown jewels of the baking world. Raspberry sauce complements and enhances all manner of pastries. For many people, this velvety sauce was one of the most important recipes in *The Cake Bible*, because it is the pure essence of raspberry without any bitterness. The secret is that the juices are concentrated by 4 times their original volume, but the pulp is not cooked at all.

MAKES: 1 FULL ¾ CUP/7.5 ounces/211 GRAMS

INGREDIENTS	MEASURE	WEIGHT	
	VOLUME	OUNCES	GRAMS
frozen raspberries,* with no added sugar (12-ounce bag)	3 cups	12 ounces	340 grams
freshly squeezed lemon juice	1 teaspoon	•	5 grams
sugar	⅓ cup	2.3 ounces	66 grams

* If using fresh berries, you will need 12 ounces or about 3 pints. In order to make them exude their juices, they must be frozen and thawed to break down the cell membranes.

In a strainer suspended over a deep bowl, thaw the raspberries completely. This will take several hours. (To speed thawing, place in an oven with a pilot light.)

Press the berries to force out all the juice. There should be about ½ cup of juice. In a small saucepan (or in a greased 2-cup heatproof glass measure or bowl in a microwave on high power), boil the juice until it is reduced to 2 tablespoons. Pour it into a lightly oiled heatproof glass measure.

In a processor, purée the raspberries and strain them through a food mill fitted with the fine disc. Or use a fine strainer to remove all the seeds. You should have ½ (liquid) cup of purée. Stir in the reduced raspberry syrup and the lemon juice. There should be about ⅔ cup of raspberry sauce (5 ounces/145 grams). If you have less, simply add less sugar. (The correct amount of sugar is half the volume of the purée.) Stir the sugar into the sauce until it dissolves.

STORE

Refrigerated, up to 10 days; frozen, up to 1 year. (The sauce can be thawed and refrozen at least three times without flavor loss.)

POINTERS FOR SUCCESS

∾   The berries must have been frozen in order to release some of their liquid. Be sure to use frozen berries with no added sugar. The juices from berries in syrup cannot be reduced as much, because the sugar starts to caramelize.

∾   Raspberry seeds are tiny and can pass through most food mills. Only the finest strainer or the puréeing attachment to the Cuisinart will remove all the seeds.

UNDERSTANDING

Raspberry pulp clings tenaciously to the seeds. The Cuisinart puréeing attachment was well worth the price because not only does it reduce this chore to a few effortless minutes, it also yields a higher amount of purée and because it is plastic as opposed to metal, results in the purest flavor. (Rubbing the seeds against metal can release some bitterness.) Unfortunately, this invaluable attachment is not being produced at the present time, so if you have one, guard it carefully; if not, look for one in a garage sale.

The microwave method of reducing the raspberry juice gives the purest flavor because it does not come into contact with direct heat, preventing any slight browning or caramel flavor.

STRAWBERRY SAUCE

I t is amazing how this sauce captures the flavor of sun-warmed strawberries at their peak—more so than fresh strawberries themselves when eaten out of season! This is partly because strawberries for freezing are picked at their prime and also because this method of concentrating the juices without cooking the fruit results in a purée of double the concentration and a much fresher flavor than conventional ones. (This is a technique I have discovered to make the berries surrender all their flavor while maintaining their brilliant color.)

This sauce can be used in place of raspberry sauce when a lighter, more subtle touch is desired.

MAKES: 1⅓ CUPS/12.25 ounces/350 GRAMS

INGREDIENTS	MEASURE	WEIGHT	
	VOLUME	OUNCES	GRAMS
frozen strawberries,* with no added sugar (20-ounce bag)	5 cups	20 ounces	567 grams
freshly squeezed lemon juice	2 teaspoons	0.3 ounce	10 grams
sugar	¼ cup	1.75 ounces	50 grams

* Fresh berries are fine to use only in season when they are full of flavor. If using fresh berries, you will need 20 ounces (5 cups). In order to make them exude their juices, they must be frozen and thawed to break down the cell membranes. A few drops of French essence of wild strawberry (see page 638) will add flavor intensity.

In a colander suspended over a deep bowl, thaw the strawberries completely. This will take several hours. (To speed thawing, place in an oven with a pilot light.)

Press the berries, if necessary, to force out the juice. There should be close to 1¼ cups of juice.

In a small saucepan (or in a 4-cup heatproof glass measure or bowl in a microwave on high power), boil the juice until reduced to ¼ cup. Pour it into a lightly oiled heatproof glass measure.

In a food processor, purée the strawberries. You should have 1 full (liquid) cup of purée. Stir in the reduced strawberry syrup and the lemon juice. There should be 1¼ cups. If you have less, add less sugar. (The correct amount of sugar is one fifth the volume of the purée; e.g., for 10 tablespoons purée, add 2 tablespoons sugar.) Stir until the sugar dissolves.

STORE

Refrigerated, up to 10 days; frozen, up to 1 year. (The purée can be thawed briefly and refrozen several times with no ill effect.)

UNDERSTANDING

The little seeds in strawberries create a lovely textural effect.

The microwave method of reducing the strawberry juice gives the purest flavor because it does not come into contact with direct heat, preventing any slight browning or caramel flavor.

VANILLA CUSTARD SAUCE
(*Crème Anglaise*)

The silken smoothness of this sauce creates a lovely contrast with tangy fruit pies.

Although it is fine to serve this sauce immediately once it's chilled, its vanilla flavor deepens and the texture thickens after about eight hours of chilling.

MAKES: 1¼ CUPS

INGREDIENTS	MEASURE	WEIGHT	
	VOLUME	OUNCES	GRAMS
sugar	2 tablespoons	1 ounce	25 grams
½ vanilla bean,* split lengthwise	•	•	•
salt	a pinch		
4 large egg yolks	¼ liquid cup	2.5 ounces	74 grams
milk	1 liquid cup	8.5 ounces	242 grams
optional: liqueur or eau-de-vie	2 to 3 tablespoons	0.75 to 1.25 ounces	21 to 35 grams

* You may substitute 1 teaspoon vanilla extract for the vanilla bean, but the bean offers a fuller, more aromatic flavor. If using extract, add it after the sauce is cool. If using a Tahitian bean, use only one quarter of the bean.

Have a fine strainer suspended over a small mixing bowl ready near the range.

In a small heavy nonreactive saucepan, place the sugar and the vanilla bean and, using your fingers, rub the seeds into the sugar. Add the salt and yolks and, using a wooden spoon, stir until well blended.

In another small saucepan (or heatproof glass measure if using a microwave on high power), scald* the milk. Stir a few tablespoons into the yoke mixture, then gradually add the remaining milk, stirring constantly. Heat the mixture to just below the boiling point (170° to 180°F.), stirring constantly. Steam will begin to appear and the mixture will be slightly thicker than heavy cream. A finger run across the back of the spoon will leave a well-defined track. Immediately remove it from the heat and pour it into the strainer, scraping up the thickened cream that has settled on the bottom of the pan. Return the vanilla pod to the sauce until serving time.

Cool the sauce in an ice-water bath or the refrigerator. Stir in the optional liqueur.

STORE

Refrigerated, up to 5 days; frozen, up to 3 months. (The sauce thickens slightly overnight in the refrigerator.)

POINTERS FOR SUCCESS

ᦄ See Ice Cream Pies and Ice Cream (page 223).

UNDERSTANDING

Vanilla cream sauce is actually very similar to unfrozen New York–style (custard-based) vanilla ice cream, but with half the liquid and one third the sugar. Unlike ice cream, which requires a high fat content to keep ice crystals from forming, this sauce can be kept lighter by using only milk and no cream or a smaller proportion of cream. For a richer, thicker sauce, use ⅔ cup of milk and ⅓ cup of cream or ½ cup of milk and ½ cup of cream.

COFFEE CUSTARD SAUCE
(*Crème Anglaise au Café*)

This classic French method of extracting coffee essence by steeping ground coffee beans in hot milk provides intense flavor. Fresh-roasted high-quality beans provide the most flavor. Extra sugar is often used to offset the bitterness of the coffee. This sauce is lovely served with tarts that have a chocolate crust, such as Chocolate Oblivion Tartlets (page 308) and the Chocolate Burnt Almond Ice Cream Tartlets (page 230).

---

* Heat until small bubbles form around the perimeter.

MAKES: 1⅓ CUPS

INGREDIENTS	MEASURE	WEIGHT	
	VOLUME	OUNCES	GRAMS
sugar	¼ cup*	1.75 ounces	50 grams
½ vanilla bean, split lengthwise†	•	•	•
salt	a pinch	•	•
4 large egg yolks	¼ liquid cup	2.5 ounces	74 grams
milk	1 liquid cup	8.5 ounces	242 grams
finely ground coffee beans	2½ tablespoons	0.3 ounce	10 grams
optional: Kahlúa	2 tablespoons	1 ounce	25 grams

*Use only 3 tablespoons sugar if adding Kahlúa.

†If using a Tahitian bean, use only one quarter bean. You can substitute 1 teaspoon vanilla extract for the vanilla bean, but the bean offers a fuller, more aromatic flavor. If using extract, add it after the sauce is cool.

Have ready near the range a fine strainer, lined with cheesecloth, suspended over a small mixing bowl.

In a small heavy nonreactive saucepan, place the sugar and the vanilla bean and, using your fingers, rub the seeds into the sugar. Add the salt and yolks and, using a wooden spoon, stir until well blended.

In another small saucepan (or heatproof glass measure if using a microwave on high power), scald* the milk and coffee. Stir a few tablespoons of the milk mixture into the yolk mixture, then gradually add the remaining milk, stirring constantly. Heat the mixture to just below the boiling point (170° to 180°F.), stirring constantly. Steam will begin to appear and the mixture will be slightly thicker than heavy cream. A finger run across the back of the spoon will leave a well-defined track. Immediately remove it from the heat and pour it into the strainer, scraping up the thickened cream that has settled on the bottom of the pan. Return the vanilla pod to the sauce until serving time.

Cool the sauce in an ice-water bath or refrigerate. Stir in the optional Kahlúa and cover tightly.

STORE

Refrigerated, up to 5 days; frozen, up to 3 months. (The sauce will thicken slightly after 8 hours.)

POINTERS FOR SUCCESS

∾ See Ice Cream Pies and Ice Cream (page 223).

*Heat until small bubbles form around the perimeter.

PRALINE CUSTARD SAUCE
(*Crème Anglaise Pralinée*)

Praline paste consists of hazelnuts and caramelized sugar pulverized to a smooth consistency. It adds incomparable nutty flavor and body, so only half the usual amount of egg yolks is needed in a sauce based in it. It also adds sweetness, making it unnecessary to add any sugar. Dark rum and Cognac both highlight the nutty flavor and cut the richness. This sauce is especially delicious beneath the Chocolate Oblivion Tartlets (page 308).

MAKES: 1⅓ FULL CUPS

INGREDIENTS	MEASURE	WEIGHT	
	VOLUME	OUNCES	GRAMS
praline paste (see page 643)	¼ cup	2.7 ounces	77 grams
milk	1 liquid cup	8.5 ounces	242 grams
salt	a speck	•	•
2 large egg yolks	2 tablespoons	1.3 ounces	37 grams
pure vanilla extract	1 teaspoon	•	4 grams
optional: rum or cognac	1½ tablespoons	0.75 ounce	21 grams

In a food processor, place the praline paste and, with the motor running, gradually add the milk. Process until smooth.

In a small heavy nonreactive saucepan, using a wooden spoon, stir together the salt and yolks until well blended.

In another small saucepan (or heatproof glass measure if using a microwave on high power), heat the praline mixture to the boiling point. Stir a few tablespoons into the yolk mixture, then gradually add the remainder of the praline mixture and the vanilla extract, stirring constantly. Heat the mixture to just below the boiling point (170° to 180°F.), stirring constantly. Steam will begin to appear and the mixture will be slightly thicker than heavy cream. A finger run across the back of the spoon will leave a well-defined track. Immediately remove it from the heat and pour it into the strainer, scraping up the thickened cream that has settled on the bottom of the pan.

Cool the sauce in an ice-water bath or the refrigerator. Stir in the optional liquor and cover tightly.

STORE

Refrigerated, up to 5 days; frozen, up to 3 months. (The sauce will thicken slightly after 8 hours.)

POINTERS FOR SUCCESS

∾ See Ice Cream Pies and Ice Cream (page 223).

PISTACHIO CUSTARD SAUCE
(*Crème Anglaise aux Pistaches*)

T his sauce is the palest of greens and beautifully perfumed by the pistachio nuts. Pistasha liqueur intensifies the pistachio flavor and slightly deepens the color. This sauce contrasts beautifully with the dark chocolate of the Chocolate Oblivion Tartlets (page 308). Since I always have difficulty deciding whether I prefer pistachio or raspberry sauce with chocolate, I sometimes drop little pools of raspberry on top of the pistachio (using a squeeze bottle) and intermingle them.

MAKES: 1 FULL CUP

INGREDIENTS	MEASURE	WEIGHT	
	VOLUME	OUNCES	GRAMS
pistachio paste (see page 643) or finely ground blanched unsalted pistachio nuts (see page 642)	2 tablespoons*	1 ounce	28 grams
milk	1 liquid cup	8.5 ounces	242 grams
sugar	3 tablespoons	1.3 ounces	38 grams
salt	a pinch	•	•
4 large egg yolks	¼ liquid cup	2.5 ounces	74 grams
optional: Pistasha (pistachio liqueur) or kirsch	2 tablespoons	0.75 ounce	25 grams

*¼ cup whole nuts (1.25 ounces/38 grams).

In a small saucepan (or heatproof glass measure if using a microwave on high power), place the nuts and milk and scald* the milk. Remove it from the heat; cover tightly and allow it to steep for at least 30 minutes up to 3 hours at room temperature.

Strain the milk through a sieve lined with several layers of cheesecloth. Press to remove all the milk, then discard the nuts. Return the milk to the saucepan or the heatproof glass measure.

Have a fine strainer suspended over a small bowl ready near the range.

In a heavy nonreactive saucepan, using a wooden spoon, stir together the sugar, salt, and yolks until well blended.

Scald the milk again and stir a few tablespoons into the yolk mixture. Then gradually add the remaining milk, stirring constantly. Heat the mixture to just

*Heat until small bubbles form around the perimeter.

below the boiling point (170° to 180°F.), stirring constantly. Steam will begin to appear and the mixture will be slightly thicker than heavy cream. A finger run across the back of the spoon will leave a well-defined track. Immediately remove the pan from the heat and pour the mixture into the strainer, scraping up the thickened cream that has settled on the bottom of the pan.

Cool the sauce in an ice-water bath or in the refrigerator. Stir in the optional liqueur and cover tightly.

STORE

Refrigerated, up to 5 days; frozen, up to 3 months. (The sauce will thicken slightly after 8 hours.)

POINTERS FOR SUCCESS

∿ See Ice Cream Pies and Ice Cream (page 223).

UNDERSTANDING

The nuts must be blanched because if the skin remains, the color will be slightly brown instead of green.

FRUIT GLAZES

Fresh fruit, particularly when sliced, requires a glaze to keep the moisture and freshness in and to add a decorative glow. I'm very proud of this recipe because it presented one of the greatest challenges in this book: how to create a glaze for cut fruit on tarts that will hold up at room temperature for several hours and not merge with the fruit's juices and slide off into little puddles as does gelatin or preserves glazes, nor be rubbery, as are some of the commercial glazes.

The ideal glaze turned out to be fruit syrup (resulting from poaching fruit) or fruit juice thickened with starch. The ideal starch is cassava (tapioca flour, see page 650). It is the clearest, with no rubbery quality, and is the least affected by acidity. Both arrowroot and cornstarch work well too, but an arrowroot glaze is slightly yellow and a cornstarch glaze slightly cloudy. A cassava glaze holds up on the fruit for eight hours at room temperature and four days in the refrigerator! A cornstarch glaze holds up for two days in the refrigerator before becoming dull and cracked. An arrowroot glaze only holds up for one day. I tested it on two difficult, watery sliced fruits: fresh strawberries and fresh figs. It does not work, however, on fresh mango or papaya, probably because of an enzyme similar to that contained in papaya. In these cases, strained preserves work best (see Apricoture, page 638). If using regular preserves, which are usually thinner, it is best to simmer the preserves first with a little refiner's or corn syrup. This thickens them by evaporating some of the liquid while the syrup keeps them fluid enough to apply to the fruit.

A gelatin-based glaze is clear, shiny, and holds up well on poached fruit if refrigerated. This glaze is a little thicker than a starch-thickened glaze in order for it to adhere well to the fruit.

TO MAKE A GELATIN GLAZE   Use the syrup from poaching the fruit (do not concentrate it). Sprinkle ¾ teaspoon of gelatin over ¾ cup of syrup and allow it to sit and soften for 5 minutes. Use a 1-cup heatproof liquid measure if using a microwave on high power, or a small heatproof cup surrounded by boiling water. Heat until the gelatin is dissolved, stirring once or twice. Stir the glaze over ice water until syrupy and use it at once.

TO MAKE A FRUIT SYRUP OR FRUIT JUICE STARCH GLAZE   In a 1-cup heatproof liquid measure if using a microwave on high power, or in a small saucepan, stir 1 teaspoon of cassava, arrowroot, or cornstarch into ¼ cup of fruit syrup or fruit juice, preferably concentrated. Heat, stirring once or twice (constantly if using the range), until thickened. (With arrowroot, this will happen before it comes to a boil; with cassava, a few seconds after it comes to a boil; and with cornstarch, it must come to a boil and simmer for 20 to 30 seconds.) Use immediately, or cover and store at room temperature for up to 12 hours. If it has been stored, reheat the glaze, using a microwave or very low heat, until just beginning to bubble. If it is no longer fluid even after heating, stir in a few drops of water to restore it to a workable consistency.

TO MAKE A LEMON STARCH GLAZE   In a 1-cup heatproof liquid measure if using a microwave on high power, or a small saucepan, stir together 2 tablespoons of strained freshly squeezed lemon juice, 2 tablespoons of water, ¼ cup of sugar, and 1½ teaspoons of cassava, arrowroot, or cornstarch. Heat, stirring once or twice (constantly if using the range), until thickened. (With arrowroot, this will happen before it comes to a boil; with cassava it must come to a boil and simmer for 20 to 30 seconds; with cornstarch it must reach a full boil and simmer for 30 seconds.) Use immediately, or cover and store at room temperature for up to 12 hours. If it has been stored, reheat the glaze, using a microwave or very low heat, until just beginning to bubble. If it is no longer fluid even after heating, stir in a few drops of water to restore it to a workable consistency.

TO GLAZE THE FRUIT   Use a clean artist's brush or pastry feather to coat the fruit with glaze.

POINTERS FOR SUCCESS

෴ Freeze some of the liquid whenever you poach fruit and you will always have a good source of flavorful syrup on hand for fruit glazes. Defrosted but undiluted frozen concentrated fruit juice such as cran/raspberry also works well.

෴ Always stir cool liquid into the starch to dissolve it before heating. Adding dry starch to hot liquid would cause it to start swelling and lump.

෴ Always dilute lemon juice with water, or it will be too acidic to thicken, even using cassava.

TECHNIQUES

CHOCOLATE

All chocolate that we buy has been tempered during production to perfect its consistency and glossy appearance. Tempering controls the crystalline structure of the cocoa butter. It also inhibits the formation of large crystals with lower melting points, which result in "bloom" (gray streaks on the surface) and a coarse, crumbly texture.

Chocolate that does not contain cocoa butter, such as compound chocolate or summer coating (see page 627), can be melted and used for decorations without tempering. Real chocolate, however, which contains cocoa butter, must be retempered if it is melted for decorations or if it loses its temper and grays due to improper temperature during storage.

Tempering chocolate consists of controlling the temperature at which the chocolate melts and sets. The classic method of tempering involves using a marble slab and an accurate thermometer. This produces the glossiest sheen for the longest period of time. Quicker methods that don't require any special equipment will still tame the chocolate into submission for any of the decorative techniques offered in this chapter. If you prefer not to temper chocolate, use compound chocolate, as real chocolate melted without tempering will be an unending source of frustration.

Tempering is unnecessary when the chocolate will not be used in its pure state—for example, when it is mixed with heavy cream for a ganache glaze.

MELTING CHOCOLATE FOR DECORATIONS

There are two important rules for melting chocolate:

1. Chocolate must never exceed 120°F., or there will be a loss of flavor.
2. Water—even a drop in the form of steam—must never touch the chocolate.

When a droplet of water enters melted chocolate, the chocolate becomes lumpy (a process called seizing). Shirley Corriher's "sugar bowl theory" explains this process: If you place a wet spoon in a sugar bowl, hard, irregular crystals form. If you pour a cup of water in the bowl, the sugar merely dissolves. Chocolate behaves the same way because it also contains sugar crystals (even unsweetened "bitter" chocolate has natural sugar). When adding liquid to chocolate, there must be a minimum of 1 tablespoon water per ounce of chocolate to keep this from happening. If seizing does occur, the addition of fat such as vegetable shortening, clarified butter, or cocoa butter will somewhat restore the chocolate to a workable condition.

For melting chocolate, unlined copper is the traditional "chocolate pot" because it is so responsive to changes in temperature. Aluminum, preferably lined with a nonstick surface, or heatproof glass also works well. Enameled cast iron, however, is unsuitable because the residual heat will overheat the chocolate. Ideally, chocolate should be heated to 120°F., the point at which all the different fat components (fractions) in the cocoa butter are melted. When melting chocolate or cocoa butter, temperatures exceeding 120°F. adversely affect the flavor. There are many acceptable methods for melting dark chocolate (or cocoa butter). If the heat source does not exceed 120°F. (the pilot light of the oven or the lowest setting on an electric griddle, hot tray, or heating pad), it is fine to add the dark chocolate to the container in large pieces and leave it to melt unmonitored. When the heat source has the potential of bringing the chocolate to over 120°F., however, the chocolate should be finely chopped or grated to ensure uniformity of melting. The chocolate must be carefully watched and stirred to avoid overheating. If using a microwave oven on high power, for example, the chocolate must be stirred every 15 seconds without fail. If using a double boiler, the water in the lower container should not exceed 140°F. and the upper container should not touch the water. The chocolate should be stirred constantly.

Milk and white chocolate must always be stirred frequently while melting because they contain milk solids that seed (lump) it left undisturbed.

Remove the chocolate from the heat source when it reaches 115°F., as the temperature may continue to rise, and stir vigorously to prevent overheating and to distribute the cocoa butter evenly.

Always melt chocolate uncovered, as moisture could condense on the lid, drop back in the chocolate, and cause seizing.

GRATING CHOCOLATE

If chocolate has been stored in a cool area (not refrigerated, where it could absorb moisture), it grates more finely and evenly. The grating disc on a food processor works well for large chunks. Thin bars can be broken up and grated in the container of the food processor fitted with the stainless steel blade.

TEMPERING CHOCOLATE

The ideal situation for working with chocolate is a cool dry draft-free area at 65° to 70°F. At temperatures above 74°F., the chocolate will not behave properly. For all methods of tempering, chocolate should be heated initially to 120°F. and the final temperature of the specific kind should be:

Dark chocolate	88° to 91°F.
Milk chocolate	84° to 87°F.
White chocolate	84° to 87°F.

Compound chocolate does not contain cocoa butter, as mentioned above, so tempering is not required. Compound chocolate should be placed in a bowl and heated over hot tap water (about 115°F.) only to a temperature of 100°F. and used at this temperature. A dab placed just below your lower lip will feel barely warm.

To hold tempered chocolate at its ideal temperature during use, place the container with the chocolate on a foil-covered heating pad turned to its lowest setting. Or return the container to the heat source very briefly, stirring constantly.

Because the formation of cocoa butter crystals continues as long as the chocolate is in a melted state, tempered chocolate will eventually thicken too much to produce a smooth coating. When this happens, melted untempered chocolate can be stirred in until the chocolate reaches the proper consistency without exceeding its ideal temperature. (This is known as drip feeding.)

If chocolate is allowed to exceed its ideal temperature, the fat crystals will start to melt, allowing cocoa particles to drop out and leaving cocoa butter crystals on the surface as unattractive streaks and spots.

If tempered chocolate gets too cold, it will be thick and dull.

Chocolate-covered bonbons or decorations are sometimes refrigerated for a few minutes after dipping in tempered chocolate. This produces a crisper coating, referred to as "snap." Chocolate can also be allowed to harden at cool room temperature. Any leftover chocolate can be spread thin on foil, allowed to harden, and retempered many times, as long as a small percentage of new chocolate is added.

CLASSIC METHOD   This method, which is dependent upon a highly accurate thermometer or tempering machine, results in the most glossy, crisp chocolate which will set with the most reliability, but it is the most painstaking and usually reserved for the most demanding chocolate techniques of decoration and candy making. It is not necessary for any of the items in this book.

QUICK-TEMPERING METHOD   There are several comparable methods for quick-tempering chocolate. All involve reserving some already tempered unmelted chocolate to serve as the pattern of cocoa butter crystal formation for the melted chocolate. (All chocolate you buy has already been tempered.) The unmelted chocolate is added to the melted chocolate and stirred until the temperature descends to the ideal temperature. This can be tested either with an accurate thermometer (see page 673) or by placing a dab of chocolate just below your lower lip. At the point when it just begins to feel cool, it is about 91°F. (the ideal temperature for dark chocolate). Use one of these methods for simple techniques and small decorative shapes such as pine cone petals, cigarettes, and leaves.

1. The simplest of all methods to remove the melting chocolate from the heat source before it has fully melted and stir until fully melted and cool.
2. It is equally simple to add clarified butter, vegetable shortening, or oil to the chocolate, preferably before melting. This serves two purposes. It results in a thinner coating of chocolate, and the addition of extra fat keeps the existing cocoa butter in suspension. Because the added fat is a different type of fat, it retards formation of large cocoa butter crystals. For dark chocolate, use 1 tablespoon fat for every 3 ounces chocolate. For milk and white chocolate, use only 1 teaspoon fat for 3 ounces of chocolate. (Note: The chocolate will be softer than if using the other methods so do not use for cigarettes or petals.)
3. Melt the chocolate, reserving a large (2- to 3-inch) piece. Heat the chocolate to 115° to 120°F., remove from the heat, and add the reserved chocolate. Stir until the correct temperature has been reached and remove any unmelted chocolate. (Wrap this in plastic wrap. It can be used for future tempering or melting.)
4. Chop or grate the chocolate, and reserve about one third. Heat the larger amount to 115° to 120°F. and remove from the heat. Stir in the reserved chocolate, 1 tablespoon at a time, stirring until it cooled to the proper temperature.

DECORATIVE TECHNIQUES

CHOCOLATE FLURRIES   I call these flurries because they should be so thin that they melt instantly on the tongue. This is an easy garnish to make, as there is no need to melt or temper the chocolate. Use white chocolate for white snowflakes. Dark chocolate makes pale brown flakes.

The chocolate needs to be as hard as possible to make thin flakes, so don't leave it in a warm kitchen. A large piece of chocolate is easiest to work with, but a flat bar will also work.

Use a melon baller to scrape the chocolate, making short, light strokes that do not cut too deeply into the chocolate. A good-quality melon baller, produced by a knife manufacturer such as Wüsthof, has sharpened edges and works best to cut thin flurries of chocolate. (Figure 1)

1

Allow the flakes to fall onto a small cool baking sheet. Place the sheet inside a large plastic bag and shake the flakes into the bag. (Avoid touching them, because they melt very easily.) Store refrigerated or at cool room temperature. Use a large spoon or bench scraper to lift the flakes and scatter them onto the pie or tart.

CHOCOLATE CURLS   Another simple decorative technique that doesn't require tempering, curls are easy to make providing the correct chocolate is used and that it is at the right temperature and has not absorbed moisture from humidity. (I tried to make these once during a New Orleans summer, and, although the room was air-conditioned, I could not get the chocolate to curl.) Couverture chocolate (see page 627), which comes in large blocks, makes the most attractive, shiny curls.

If the chocolate has been left in an 80°F. room for several hours, it is usually at a good working temperature. Alternatively, a small block of chocolate can be softened to perfect consistency by placing it under a lamp (from the heat of the light bulb) or in a microwave oven using 3-second bursts of high power. It takes a few tries to get the chocolate soft enough without oversoftening it, but once this point is reached, it will stay perfect for at least 10 minutes, during which time many curls can be formed. Chocolate can be curled with a melon baller, but my favorite utensil is a sharp potato peeler.

Hold the chocolate block in one hand, against a wad of paper toweling so that heat of your hand doesn't melt the chocolate. Hold the peeler against the upper edge and, digging in one edge of the cutter, bring the blade toward you. (Figure 2) Greater pressure forms thicker, more open curls. Lighter pressure makes tighter curls. If the chocolate is not warm enough, it will splinter. If too warm, it will come off in soft strips that will not curl. If not extremely soft, these strips can be rolled into curls with cool fingertips. Lift the curls with a wooden skewer to place on the pie or tart.

2

CHOCOLATE LEAVES   This simple decoration makes a dramatic decoration for a chocolate pie or tart. They are especially appropriate as a seasonal decoration for Halloween or Thanksgiving. Use a variety of leaves and types of chocolate for the most interesting effect. If only a few chocolate leaves are needed, summer coating is the best choice because it doesn't require tempering. Couverture (see page 627) makes the most glossy, elegant leaves. Rose, lemon, maple, and geranium leaves are some of my favorite shapes. Select well-shaped leaves with no holes. Make sure they are unsprayed. Wash the leaves and dry them thoroughly. Each leaf can be used several times, until it tears.

Holding a leaf by its stem and supporting it underneath with a finger or the palm of your hand, use a small metal spatula or artist's brush to smooth an even layer of chocolate on the underside of the leaf. (Figure 3) (Be sure to use the veiny underside so all the delicate lines will be

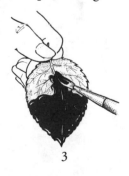

3

imprinted on the chocolate.) Don't allow any chocolate to get on the other side of the leaf, or it may break when peeling off the leaf.

Carefully place each chocolate leaf on a baking sheet lined with foil, parchment, or waxed paper and refrigerate or freeze for 3 minutes, until set and no longer shiny. If using large leaves, add a second coat of chocolate for stability and let set. White chocolate and couverture also require second coats, as the chocolate is thinner when melted and the light would shine through in spots.

To remove the chocolate from the leaf, peel back the stem end, touching the chocolate as little as possible. (Figure 4) If chocolate adheres to the leaf, it has not set long enough.

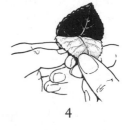

4

PIPED DECORATIONS, CREAM AND MERINGUE

The two most important criteria for success when piping decorations with a pastry tube (in addition to icing consistency) are the position of the bag and the amount and type of pressure applied.

FILLING THE PASTRY BAG

TO FILL BAG   Fold down the top to form a generous cuff and hold it beneath the cuff. Use a long spatula to fill the bag half full. Filling it more risks melting and softening the icing from the heat of your hand. (Figure 1)

To remove the icing from the spatula, hold the bag on the outside between your thumb and fingers and pull the spatula out of the bag, pinching the icing. (Figure 2) Unfold the cuff and, using the side of your hand, force icing toward the top. (Figure 3) Twist the bag closed. To be sure that no air is trapped in the bag, squeeze a small amount of icing into a bowl. It is a good idea to do this when

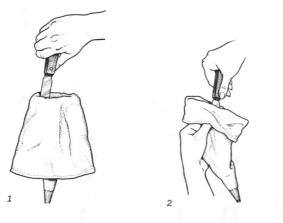

1   2   3

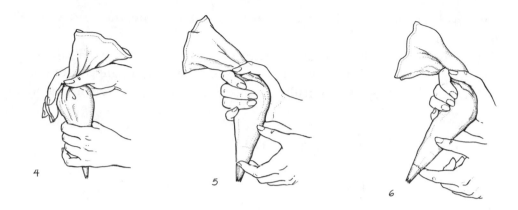

refilling the bag, or the little explosion of air when old icing meets new can disrupt the piped decoration.

TO HOLD BAG   Place the twisted part of the bag in the V between your thumb and forefinger. Lock your thumb over your forefinger to keep the icing in the lower part of the bag. (Figure 4) Press your remaining fingers against the side of the bag so that when you squeeze out the icing, you squeeze from the side while your thumb presses from the top. (Figure 5)

Steady the front end of the bag with the fingers of the other hand to support the weight of the bag and to establish the direction of the tip. (Figure 6)

POSITION OF THE BAG   The position in which the bag is held must be precise to produce a specific design. Position refers both to the *angle* of the bag relative to the work surface and the *direction* in which it points. The two basic angles at which the bag is positioned are: 90 degrees (perpendicular) and 45 degrees (halfway between vertical and horizontal).

When decorating, one hand is used to squeeze the bag and the other to help establish and steady the angle. If stars come out asymmetrical, chances are the bag is not being held at a 90-degree angle to the decorating surface.

DIRECTION OF THE BAG   This refers to the direction the end of the bag, farthest from the tip, is pointing. It is most easily described by using the position of numbers on a clock face. To better visualize this, try holding the bag at an angle to the surface and, keeping the tip in place, make a circle with the back end of the bag by rolling your wrist. Imagine that the circle is a clock face.

DIRECTION OF MOVEMENT WHEN PIPING   A right-handed person should always decorate from left to right; a left-handed person from right to left, except when writing.

PRESSURE CONTROL   The size and uniformity of icing decorations are determined by the amount and type of pressure exerted on the bag. Some decorations require a steady, even pressure, while others require a gradual tapering off as each is finished. The more rhythmic and controlled the pressure, the more exact the decoration.

It is also particularly important to release all the pressure before lifting off the tube to prevent little "tails" of icing from forming. Try wiggling your fingers slightly to be sure they are not inadvertently exerting pressure before lifting off the tube.

PIPED BORDERS AND SIDE DECORATIONS

STAR OR KISS

This is the easiest of all piped decorations and a great way to practice piping. If a round tube is used, the stars become kisses (as for the Chocolate Bisou, page 193). If piping with meringue, place the stars close enough together so that the points interlock and fill in all gaps.

Tube   A star tube or round tube.

Position of Bag   90-degree upright angle, tube ¼ inch above surface.

Method   Squeeze the bag firmly without moving it until the star or kiss is as wide as you desire. Push the tube down slightly and stop squeezing. Slowly and precisely lift the tube straight up and away.

Note: You can change the size of the star or kiss by increasing the length of time you squeeze or by the amount of pressure. If piping stars, however, if too much icing is squeezed, the lines will start to waver.

Two of the most common problems in piping show up when piping stars and kisses: continuing to squeeze while lifting off the tube, and not holding the tube upright for a symmetrical decoration.

ROSETTE

Rosettes are often used as continuous borders or, when piped with a large tube and widely spaced, as a decorative demarcation for portion size.

Tube   A star tube.

Position of Bag   90-degree upright angle, tube ¼ inch above surface.

Method   As you squeeze out the icing, move the tube in a tight arc from the 9:00 position around to the 6:00 position. (Figure 1) Release the pressure, but do not lift the tube until you have followed the circular motion all the way around to the 9:00 position at which you started. (Figure 2) This will give the rosette a wrap-around look.

SHELL AND SHELL BORDER

This is the most graceful of all piped decorations. When piped in a large size, it is also the most opulent.

Tube   A star tube.

Position of Bag   45- to 90-degree angle with end of bag at 6:00, tube slightly above surface. (I prefer the flatter, wider shell you get from the higher angle.)

3

4

5

Method Squeeze firmly, allowing the icing to fan out generously as you lift up the tube slightly. (Figure 3) (Do not move the tube forward; the force of the icing will push the shell slightly forward on its own.) Gradually relax the pressure as you lower the tube to the surface. This gradual tapering off forms a graceful tail. Stop the pressure and pull away the tube without lifting it off the surface to draw the tail to a point. (Figure 4) To make a second shell for a border, line up the tube at the top of the first shell's tail. The slight forward thrust of the icing will just cover the tail of the preceding shell. When viewed from the side, the shells should be gently rounded, not humped. If they are humped, you are lifting the tube too high above the work surface. (Figure 5)

6

7

SIDEWAYS SHELL AND BORDER

For an interesting variation, the sideways shell border produces shells that angle appealingly in one direction.

Tube A star tube.

Position of Bag 45- to 90-degree angle with end of bag at 6:00, tube slightly above surface. (I prefer the flatter, wider shell you get from the higher angle.)

Method Squeeze firmly, allowing the icing to fan out as for a regular shell. Then move the tube to the left, up and around, in a question-mark shape. (Figures 6 and 7). Gradually relax the pressure as you pull the tube down to the center, forming a straight tail. Continue as above.

MERINGUE SPIRAL DISCS

Tube A number 6 large plain round pastry tube (½ inch in diameter).

Hold the bag in a vertical position (straight up and down) with the tube at least 1½ inches above the pan. To achieve full height and a rounded shape, the batter must be allowed to fall from the tube, not be pressed against the pan. Start in the center, moving the tip with your entire arm in smooth circles. To prevent gaps, allow the spirals of batter to fall against the side of—almost on top of—previous spirals. The weight of the mixture will cause them to fall exactly in place. To correct errors, use a small clean artist's brush dipped in water.

CRYSTALLIZED FLOWERS AND LEAVES

Small edible flowers (see page 634), such as roses, lilacs, and wild violets (*not* African), and leaves such as the rose geranium (Figure 1) and mint, can be made into beautifully shimmering decorations to garnish pies or tarts. When you make them yourself, each petal remains separate and sparkling. Firm-petaled flowers such as roses are the easiest to work with. Sugared rose petals of varying hues are stunning scattered around the base of a serving plate. All that's needed is a little egg white, superfine sugar, and petal dust or powdered food color and a small unused artist's brush. Petal dust, available from cake decorating supply stores such as the New York Cake and Decorating Distributors (see page 677), comes in many subtle hues. Paste food color also works well. Wilton, for example, makes a grape paste color the perfect hue for lilacs and a violet paste color the perfect hue for violets. For red roses, it's exciting to use powdered or paste red food color, as it intensifies and preserves the flower's natural color. Most flowers will last for years after drying, with the exception of lilacs, which tend to brown around the edges after a few months.

CRYSTALLIZE THE FLOWERS AND LEAVES

Place the sugar in a small bowl and stir in the food color, starting with a small amount.

Place the egg white in another small bowl and beat it lightly.

If using roses, peel off any outer petals that are not in perfect shape. If the roses are too tightly closed, tease open the petals by blowing on them and probing them gently with the blunt end of a wooden skewer.

Dip the flowers facedown into the egg white. Use the artist's brush to remove all but a thin coating, making sure that the underside of the petals is coated too. Hold the flower over the sugar bowl and with a small spoon, spoon the sugar over the flower's petals to coat it evenly on both sides.

DRY THE CRYSTALLIZED FLOWERS AND LEAVES

Large multipetaled flowers such as roses can take up to 4 days to dry, while mint leaves can dry in just a few hours. Most flowers with softer petals, such as violets, keep their shape best when suspended upside down until partially dry and set. This works well for rose geranium leaves too. Use a clamp type of paper clip to grasp each stem and hang it by the looped end. When partially dry, transfer it to a lightly greased rack to dry completely.

For roses, the method that works best is to cover a bowl tightly with a piece of foil, preferably heavy-duty, and punch small holes in the foil to hold the flowers upright. When the petals are dry enough to hold their shape on their own, transfer them to lightly greased racks to dry completely. Cut off all but about 2 inches of each stem, which can be used to insert the flower into the pie.

STORE

Airtight, at room temperature (low humidity), away from direct sunlight.

POINTERS FOR SUCCESS

∾ Superfine sugar (available in 1-pound boxes in supermarkets), also referred to as bar sugar, coats the most evenly. Processing granulated sugar dulls the sugar crystals, resulting in less sparkle.

∾ If you've added too much food color, simply add more sugar to tone it down.

∾ It's best to sprinkle the sugar on the flowers or leaves, as dipping them into the sugar might cause it to clump both in the sugar bowl and on the flowers.

MEASURING DRY INGREDIENTS

Dry ingredients, such as flour, sugar, baking powder, baking soda, cornstarch, and salt, should be measured in solid measuring cups, i.e., ones with level unbroken rims (see page 658). As flour tends to settle on sitting, it should be stirred very lightly with a whisk or fork before measuring. The dip and sweep method means to dip the cup or measuring spoon into the dry ingredient and, without disturbing it (NO shaking or tapping, or you'll get more than desired), sweep off the excess with a metal spatula or knife.

MEASURING LIQUID INGREDIENTS

Liquid ingredients, such as water, milk, sour cream, corn syrup, and juices, should be measured in a liquid measure, i.e., one with a spout. To get an accurate measure, set the cup on a solid surface (NOT in your hand, as it is easy to tilt) at eye level. The reading should be taken from below the meniscus (the slightly curved surface of the water).

INGREDIENTS

S ugar, flour, butter, nuts, vanilla—these are the kingpins of pastry making. From these few ingredients come a world of delights, so it is important that each be of the best possible quality and the variety suited to the recipe. These days, it is easy in the supermarket, when reaching for sour cream or cream cheese, to inadvertently pick up one of the prevalent reduced-fat or fat-free versions. I find these substitutes odious, with synthetic flavor. My philosophy is to reduce portion size, or quantity—not the quality.

I have listed a few specific products because of their incomparable quality, available only through food service distributors, most of which can be purchased in reasonably small quantities.

BAKER'S JOY This is a combination of flour and oil for spraying on pans. It is faster and neater than greasing and flouring. If you can't find it in your local supermarket, get in touch with the manufacturer (see Sources) for the nearest distributor. This is a fabulous product.

BAKING POWDER Baking powders are mixtures of dry acid or acid salts and baking soda with starch or flour added to standardize and help stabilize the mixture. "Double-acting" means that they will react, or liberate carbon dioxide, first when exposed to moisture during the mixing stage and then again when exposed to heat during the baking stage. It is, therefore, important to store baking powder in an airtight container to avoid humidity. There is also a substantial loss of strength in baking powder after 1 year. Date the bottom of the can when you buy it, or write an expiration date on the lid with a felt-tip marker. To test if it is still active, sprinkle a little over hot water. If it fizzes actively, it's still okay.

I use Rumford baking powder, an all-phosphate product containing calcium acid phosphate. It lacks the bitter aftertaste associated with SAS baking powders, which also contain sodium aluminum sulfate. (The supposed advantage of SAS powders is that they release a little more carbon dioxide during the baking stage than during the mixing stage, but I find I can interchange equal volume and weight of either type of baking powder.) Rumford baking powder is usually available in health food stores (probably because aluminum compounds are considered dangerous by many health-conscious people).

BAKING SODA   Sodium bicarbonate has an indefinite shelf life if not exposed to humidity. In Canada, I once discovered a wonderful variety called Cow Brand. It contained a harmless chemical ingredient that prevented it from clumping. Unless you can obtain this type of baking soda, it is best to sift it before measuring.

BEESWAX   Used for making spun sugar (page 602) because of its high melting point, beeswax helps keep the strands flexible. It is available at sculptors' supply stores, some sewing supply stores, and, of course, through apiaries.

CHOCOLATE

Working with chocolate over the past twenty years, I have found there is an enormous difference in both texture and flavor among brands and have developed my own personal preferences. I highly recommend that you do a blind tasting to determine your own.

One of my favorite dark chocolates is Lindt Excellence. I also love Valrhona's Bittersweet and Guanaja, which have a delicious, winy undertone. When it comes to milk chocolate, I adore Lindt for its creamy smoothness and lovely caramel flavor notes. For white chocolate, I like the Lindt confectionery bar and the Valrhona.

Some fine chocolates may be produced under kashruth supervision. Write to the manufacturer or distributor for a letter of certification if you want to use a chocolate in kosher cooking.

Brands of chocolate differ partly because of the special formulas unique to each company, which determine the blend of the beans, the type and amount of flavorings, and the proportions of chocolate liquor and cocoa butter. Taste and texture are also greatly affected by the roasting, grinding, and conching, the processes that turn cocoa beans into chocolate. Grinding reduces the particle size and conching, a wave-like motion, releases volatile oils, develops flavor, and coats the sugar and cocoa particles with cocoa butter, which makes the chocolate smooth. More than 96 hours of conching can result in an oily texture. European, particularly Swiss, chocolate is usually conched for up to 96 hours, which produces the characteristic velvety-smooth texture. American chocolate may be conched for only 4 to 5 hours, if at all, though some brands claim as long as 74 hours of conching.

Lecithin, an emulsifier made from soybeans, is used to stabilize chocolate. Its presence reduces the amount of cocoa butter required to cover the cocoa particles. It frees the cocoa butter to act as a liquid medium for the particles. It also reduces viscosity, making it less thick. Only a very small quantity is necessary; for example, 1 gram lecithin per kilogram (2.2 pounds) for white chocolate, slightly more for dark chocolate. Lecithin is used even in finest-quality chocolate. It is not "Kosher for Passover," but a Swiss company, Maestrani, exports an excellent bittersweet chocolate containing no lecithin. Their dark chocolate is pareve (containing no dairy products). See Taam-Tov Food, Inc. (page 677).

The U.S. government legislates restrictions and classifications for chocolate that dictate the type of fat and percentage of chocolate liquor used. To be classified as real chocolate, it must contain no fat other than cocoa butter (with the exception of 5 percent dairy butter to aid emulsification, which does not have to appear on the label).

PURE CHOCOLATE   Pure chocolate, also referred to as bitter, baking, or unsweetened chocolate, contains only chocolate liquor (cocoa solids and cocoa butter) and flavorings. Depending on the variety of the cocoa bean used, 50 to 58 percent of the chocolate liquor is cocoa butter, averaging 53 percent. The bulk of the remainder, the cocoa solids, contains 10.7 percent protein and 28.9 percent starch. (This is the same amount present in the nibs—the term for the cocoa beans after removal of the pod—before processing.) No lecithin may be added, but a great variety of flavorings is permissible, such as vanilla or vanillin (synthesized vanilla), ground nuts, coffee, salt, and various extracts.

COCOA   Cocoa is the pure chocolate liquor with three quarters of the cocoa butter removed. The remaining cocoa is then pulverized. Most European cocoa is Dutch-processed, which means that the cocoa has been treated with a mild alkali to mellow the flavor and make it more soluble. There is no need to sift cocoa for a recipe when it will be dissolved in water. In recipes such as Cocoa Meringue (page 575), it is advisable to process or sift the cocoa if it is lumpy so it will incorporate more evenly.

My favorite Dutch-processed cocoa is Lindt's, from Switzerland, which, unfortunately, is not currently available in this country. It comes in dark and light (I prefer the dark). Valrhona cocoa (New York Cake and Baking Distributors, page 677) is another top favorite, with rich chocolate flavor and relatively higher cocoa butter content. Pernigotti from Italy (available through Williams-Sonoma, page 677), DeZann (Albert Uster, page 675), and Van Houten are also excellent Dutch-processed cocoas, though not as intense as Valrhona. Smelling the cocoa will tell you a lot about its flavor potential, but the best test is baking with it. The flavor is a result both of the type of cocoa beans used and the degree of roasting.

BITTERSWEET OR SEMISWEET AND EXTRA-BITTERSWEET CHOCOLATE   Bittersweet or semisweet, and extra-bittersweet (for which there is no U.S. government standard), are pure chocolate liquor with sugar, vanilla or vanillin, extra cocoa butter, and lecithin added. Semisweet morsels have to be more viscous to maintain their shape during baking. Every manufacturer has his oven terminology or formula for this category of chocolate. Bittersweet, semisweet, and extra-bittersweet can be used interchangeably in recipes, but their sweetness levels will vary. The higher the amount of cocoa mass (cocoa solids and cocoa butter), the lower the amount of sugar. Several manufacturers are producing a very bitter chocolate with 70 percent cocoa mass, including Lindt's 70% Excellence and Valrhona's Guanaja. These chocolates are very useful for adding to sweetened mixtures that benefit from the "tempering" of a low-sugar chocolate. Valrhonas's Extra Bitter has 67 percent cocoa mass and is perfect for any recipe, such as ganache or pastry cream, for those who appreciate an intense but bittersweet flavor. Valrhona's Caracque has 56 percent cocoa mass, which is very similar to that of Lindt's regular Excellence bar.

COUVERTURE   Used for candy dipping and some decorative work, in Europe, couverture is made from the highest-quality real chocolate, which has a high percentage of cocoa butter, resulting in low viscosity and subsequently a thin coating and a glossy sheen when used for dipping or decorations. There is no U.S. standard for couverture, but in Europe, couverture must have a minimum of 36 percent cocoa butter and may have as much as 40 percent. Japanese couverture may have as much as 42 percent.

MILK CHOCOLATE   Milk chocolate contains pure chocolate liquor, milk solids, butter, vanilla or vanillin, extra cocoa butter, and lecithin. Milk chocolate does not have as long a shelf life as dark chocolate because the milk solids can become rancid (though not as quickly as in white chocolate, due to the protective presence of cocoa solids).

WHITE CHOCOLATE   White chocolate is not considered to be "real chocolate" by the United States Department of Agriculture because it contains no cocoa solids. Better-quality white chocolates are, however, made with cocoa butter and have a delicious flavor. White chocolate contains about 30 percent fat, 30 percent milk solids, and 30 percent sugar. It also contains vanilla or vanillin and lecithin. When melted, it sets faster than dark chocolate, but it is softer at room temperature. Its shelf life is much shorter than dark chocolate because of the milk solids.

A small amount of melted white chocolate is great in an emergency to thicken pastry cream. This small amount of white chocolate adds firmness without significantly altering the character of the mixture.

COMPOUND CHOCOLATE   In the United States, compound chocolate is classified as chocolate "flavor" because, instead of cocoa butter, it contains vegetable shortening such as soya, palm kernel, or coconut oil. This type of fat is more stable than cocoa butter and does not require tempering to prevent bloom (discoloration). It also gives the chocolate a higher melting point, which means it will remain unmelted at warmer temperatures. For this reason, it is sometimes referred to as "summer coating." Its taste is acceptable and some people find it delicious (they can't have tasted the real thing!), but it lacks the complexity and fullness of fine-quality chocolate. Still, for small decorative touches, such as chocolate leaves, when you don't have the time to temper chocolate, it is a joy to have on hand.

Compound chocolate is produced in many colors. It is available at candy supply houses and by mail through New York Cake and Baking Distributors (page 677). Albert Uster Imports (page 675) carries my favorite dark compound chocolate, called Carma Glaze. It is very dark and lustrous and comes in 13.25-pound blocks.

AVERAGE CHOCOLATE MASS AND COCOA BUTTER CONTENT

Chocolate mass refers to the total amount of cocoa solids and cocoa butter.

cocoa (breakfast cocoa, usually Dutch-processed): 22 to 25 percent cocoa butter

cocoa (regular, usually nonalkalized): 10 to 21 percent cocoa butter

bitter or unsweetened baking chocolate (pure chocolate liquor): 50 to 58 percent cocoa butter, averaging 53 percent

couverture chocolate: 60 to 78 percent chocolate mass, of which 36 to 40 percent is cocoa butter

extra bittersweet chocolate: 60 percent chocolate mass, of which 30 percent is cocoa butter

semisweet or bittersweet chocolate: 49.5 to 53 percent chocolate mass, of which 27 percent is cocoa butter; U.S. government standards require a minimum of 35 percent chocolate liquor

semisweet bits: 42.5 percent chocolate mass, of which 29 percent is cocoa butter

sweet chocolate: 34 percent chocolate mass, of which 27 percent is cocoa butter; U.S. government standards require a minimum of 29 percent chocolate liquor

milk chocolate: 34 to 38 percent chocolate mass, of which 29 to 33 percent is cocoa butter, plus 12 percent whole milk solids; U.S. government standards require a minimum of 10 percent chocolate liquor

STORING CHOCOLATE   The best way to store chocolate or cocoa is to keep it well wrapped in an airtight container (chocolate is quick to absorb odors and must not be exposed to dampness) at a temperature of 60° to 75°F., with less than 50 percent relative humidity. Under these conditions, dark chocolate should keep well for at least 2 years. I have tasted chocolate stored at ideal conditions for several years and it seems to age like a fine wine, becoming more mellow and subtle. Milk chocolate keeps, even at optimum conditions, for only a little over 1 year, and white chocolate about 1 year.

CREAM OF TARTAR   Cream of tartar, or potassium acid tartrate, is a by-product of the wine industry. Its shelf life is indefinite. I have found that adding 1 teaspoon cream of tartar per 1 cup egg whites (⅛ teaspoon per egg white), stabilizes them so that it becomes virtually impossible to dry them out by overbeating. Cream of tartar is also used as an "interfering agent" in sugar syrups for making caramel, to inhibit crystallization.

CINNAMON   I have Richard Sax to thank for introducing me to Penzeys, Ltd. (page 677), purveyors of over two hundred fifty spices, herbs, and seasonings. They carry seven different varieties of cinnamon, including the subtle but complex Ceylon cinnamon and the finest stronger and sweeter cassia cinnamon from Vietnam. All their cinnamon is aromatically fresh.

DAIRY AND EGGS

BUTTER   Butter is one of my favorite flavors. The best fresh, unsalted butter has the flowery, grassy smell of a summer meadow. One of the most enjoyable ways to experience butter is in a pastry or pie crust.

Salted butter does not have the glorious flavor of fresh unsalted butter. If only salted butter is available, remove 1 teaspoon of salt from the recipe per pound of butter used.

It is possible to make your own butter from cream, but if only ultrapasteurized cream is available, it may not be worth the trouble. Commercial butter is made from cream with a very high butterfat content and is churned immediately after flash pasteurization. This ensures the best flavor and longest shelf life. If you make your own butter, it will stay fresh for only 1 week.

To make butter: Place heavy cream in a food processor and process until it begins to thicken. For every cup of cream, add 2 tablespoons cold water. Process until the cream separates into solids. Strain out the liquid (this unsoured buttermilk is delicious to drink) and dry the resulting butter thoroughly with paper towels. One cup of cream yields about 3 ounces of butter.

When buying commercial butter, keep in mind that grade A or AA contains about 81 percent fat, 15.5 percent water, and 0.6 percent protein. Lower grades contain more water, which will have a detrimental effect when making dough. Plugrá butter or French butter has less water, so it stays pliant even when cold, making it ideal for pastries where the butter is rolled into the dough in layers, such as croissant and Danish pastry. Two indications that the water content is high are that the refrigerated butter remains fairly soft and that, when the butter is cut, small droplets of water appear. Excess water can be removed by kneading the butter in ice water for several minutes and then drying it thoroughly with paper towels.

Store butter airtight, as it absorbs odors very readily. Avoid wrapping directly in foil, as the butter may absorb a metallic taste. Butter freezes well for several months. Be sure to let it defrost completely before clarifying it, or it may burn instead of brown.

CLARIFIED BUTTER   Some recipes in this book call for clarified *beurre noisette.* This refers to clarified butter that has browned to the color of *noisettes* (French for hazelnuts). Beurre noisette offers a richer, more delicious flavor.

When butter is clarified, the water evaporates and most of the milk solids drop to the bottom of the pan. The milk solids cannot begin to brown until all the water has evaporated. When adding clarified butter to chocolate, it is important that no water remain, so the milk solids in the butter should have started to turn golden brown before the liquid butter is strained. Plugrá butter, or butter that has a lower water content, is great for clarifying because it spatters less. Using very low heat also helps to prevent spattering.

To clarify butter: Melt the butter in a heavy saucepan over medium heat, partially covered to prevent spattering. Do not stir. When the butter looks clear, lower the heat to low and cook, uncovered, watching carefully, until the solids drop and begin to brown, about 20 minutes for 1 pound of butter. When the bubbling noise quiets, all the water has evaporated and the butter can burn easily. To make beurre noisette, allow the solids to turn dark brown. Occasionally, some solids remain on top. They will deepen in color toward the end of cooking, but to see the color of the solids at the bottom, you will need to tilt the pan. Strain the butter immediately through a fine strainer or cheesecloth-lined strainer. Clarified butter will keep for months refrigerated, or just about indefinitely frozen, as it is the milk solids that cause butter to become rancid quickly. I always make extra to have on hand. (The browned solids are excellent for adding flavor to bread dough.) Clarified butter will only be 75 percent the volume or weight of whole butter. For example, if you need 3 tablespoons of clarified butter, start with 4 tablespoons of butter. If using cheesecloth, start with about 1 tablespoon more as the cheesecloth absorbs some of the butter.

Clarified butter weighs a little less than whole butter because whole butter still contains water, which, per volume, weighs more than fat. One cup of whole butter weighs 8 ounces/227 grams; 1 cup of clarified butter weighs 6.8 ounces/195 grams.

COW'S MILK   Milk contains 87.4 percent water, 3.5 percent protein, and 3.5 to 3.7 percent fat.

Nature's most perfect milk, in my opinion, is goat's milk. Goat's milk is lower in cholesterol than cow's milk, with more finely emulsified butterfat, and the flavor is slightly sweeter and seems purer. If you are lucky enough to have access to goat's milk, feel free to use it in any recipe calling for milk.

CULTURED BUTTERMILK   Buttermilk contains 90.5 percent water, 3.6 percent protein, and 1.5 to 2 percent butterfat. It is a soured product obtained by treating skim or part-skim milk with a culture of lactic acid bacteria.

HALF-AND-HALF   Half-and-half is half light cream and half milk. It contains 79.7 percent water, 3.2 percent protein, and 11.7 percent fat. If you ever run out of milk and have half-and-half, it's easy to substitute for milk required in a recipe (see page 655).

LIGHT CREAM   Light cream contains 71.5 percent water, 3 percent protein, and 20.6 percent fat. It is increasingly difficult to find.

HEAVY CREAM   Heavy cream contains 56.6 percent water, 2.2 percent protein, and 36 to 40 percent fat (averaging 36 percent). If the heavy cream in your area seems low in butterfat (it is difficult to beat and separates easily), it is easy to increase the butterfat content (see page 552).

"Whipping cream" or "gourmet cream" usually has higher butterfat than regular heavy cream. Often the fat content is listed on the side of the container.

Heavy cream can be frozen for several months, defrosted, and used for making ganache. Freezing, however, alters the fat structure, making the cream impossible to whip and unsuitable for making emulsifications such as cream sauce or ice cream; the texture will not be smooth.

SWEETENED CONDENSED MILK   This product was developed by Gail Borden in 1856. The delicious, thick concentrate is made by evaporating 60 percent of the water in whole milk and adding 44 to 45 percent sugar to act as a preservative. It can be stored in a cool dry place for up to 15 months. (If stored for long periods near heat, the milk may be thick and caramel colored, but the quality will not be affected. Simply stir it briskly before pouring.) After opening, it can be stored in its original container, in the refrigerator, for up to 10 days.

EVAPORATED MILK   This product is made by evaporating enough water from whole or skim milk, under vacuum, to reduce the volume by half. No sugar is added. After opening, it should be stored, refrigerated, for no more than 5 days.

SOUR CREAM   Sour cream contains 71.5 percent water, 3 percent protein, and 18 to 20 percent fat. It is made from light cream, soured by the addition of lactic acid culture.

CREAM CHEESE   Cream cheese contains 37.7 percent fat and 51 percent water. It can be frozen for months.

MASCARPONE   Mascarpone contains about 55 percent fat. This rich, creamy, slightly tangy cream cheese is mildly acidulated by lactic fermentation and then whipped to a thickened consistency. It was originally produced only in the fall and winter in the Lombardy region of Italy. I find the flavor of the imported mascarpone the most delicious. Any left over can be frozen for months.

CHEDDAR CHEESE   Cheddar cheese contains 32.2 grams fat and 37 percent water.

EGGS   All my recipes use USDA grade large eggs. As a rule of thumb, 5 extra-large eggs equal about 6 large eggs. Since values for recipes in this book are given for weight and volume, it's fine to use any size eggs if you weigh or measure them. As the weight of the eggs and thickness of the shell can vary a great deal even within a given grade (from 1.75 ounces to 2.5 ounces for large eggs), I find it safer to weigh or measure even when using large eggs.

Duck eggs have a richer, more delicious flavor than chicken eggs. The whites do not increase in volume nearly as much as chicken eggs, so they are not suitable for meringues, and the whole eggs will produce a coarser-textured cake. However, in pastry creams, curds, ice creams, and batters they reign supreme.

Pasteurized eggs, used in food service to avoid salmonella in preparations calling for uncooked or lightly cooked eggs, hopefully will eventually become available to the consumer. Pasteurized powdered egg whites, which can be reconstituted with water or even fruit juice, are available at gourmet markets, some supermarkets, and through catalogues such as King Arthur (page 676) and New York Cake and Baking Distributors (page 677). Pasteurized egg whites are available from Eggology by mail order (page 676). They keep 4 months refrigerated and more than a year if frozen.

Egg whites contain 87.6 percent water and 10.9 percent protein. Egg yolks contain 51.1 percent water, 16 percent protein, and 30.6 percent fat.

Refrigerate eggs in a covered container, bottom (larger) sides up, for maximum freshness. Egg whites keep, refrigerated, for 10 days. Unbroken yolks, covered with water, or sprayed with nonstick vegetable spray to prevent drying, will keep refrigerated for up to 3 days. Egg whites freeze perfectly for at least 1 year. It is also possible to freeze yolks. Stir in ½ teaspoon of sugar per yolk to keep them from becoming sticky after they are defrosted. (Remember to subtract this amount of sugar from the recipe.)

DOUGH (PREPARED, STORE-BOUGHT)

CRUMB CRUST   If using a prepared crumb crust, for recipes calling for a 9-inch pie crust, be sure to use one that measures 9 inches by 1½ inches deep. (On the package it will say 10-inch size/9 ounces/255 grams.) I encourage you to make your own, however, because the flavor and texture of homemade crumb crusts is significantly superior to the commercial product.

PIE CRUST   I have tried many commercial frozen and packaged crusts over the years and have found them all to be lacking. Most were too salty for sweet pies. The greater problem with frozen crusts, however, is that when baked blind (without filling), they tend to develop fissures that allow liquid ingredients to leak through them during baking, sticking to the pan at best and messing up the oven at worst. If I had to choose the lesser of all evils, it would be the Betty Crocker crust in a box. It also is a bit salty, though it has a good neutral flavor (unfortunately, not from butter), but the texture is good and it is very quick, foolproof, and easy to mix and roll. Of all the frozen crusts, I find Pillsbury to have the best flavor (it's made with lard), but don't try prebaking it, or you will wind up with cracks.

FILLO (PHYLLO)   Excellent fresh fillo sheets, can be ordered by mail from the Fillo-Factory (page 676). The fresh fillo keeps refrigerated for 2 months. It can be frozen for 3 months, and thawed and refrozen twice during this period. It separates much more readily into sheets and does not dry out while working with it nearly as quickly as the store-bought frozen. If freezing the fresh fillo, defrost it for 24 hours in the refrigerator and allow it to sit at room temperature for about an hour before using it. If it sticks slightly around the edges, trim the edges or carefully pry them loose. Each 1-pound package contains between 25 and 31 sheets (averaging 28) measuring 12 inches by 16 to 17 inches. The Fillo Factory also has 38-inch sheets sold in large quantities for food service; shredded fillo, called *konafa* or *kadaif* (shredded, wiry strands of fillo dough); and prebaked 2- and 4-ounce fillo shells.

PUFF PASTRY   Be sure to follow the recommended baking temperatures when using commercially prepared puff pastry, as they are often different from those for homemade pastry.

Pepperidge Farm puff pastry sheets are available in the freezer section of most supermarkets. They are made with shortening rather than butter so they lack the wonderful butter flavor, but they have an excellent texture and work well in recipes where the flavor comes from other components. They come in 17¼-ounce packages, containing two pieces of pastry about 9½ by 9 inches and ⅛ to ³⁄₁₆ inch thick.

Dufour puff pastry is an excellent product prepared with butter. It comes in 14-ounce packages of one 11- by 14-inch sheet each, ³⁄₁₆ inch thick. For food service, Dufour also makes 10-pound cases of 11¼-inch squares, ¼ inch thick, and 11- to 12-inch by 16-inch sheets, ⅛ inch thick. (They will give you the nearest distributor or ship direct; see page 676.)

Voilà puff pastry is a fabulous all-butter product that is easy to roll thin, but it is available only by the case. The firm also produces excellent Danish and croissant doughs (page 677).

Hug, a Swiss company, produces excellent flaky pastry tart shells (1½-inch, 2¾-inch, and 3½-inch) and vol-au-vent shells in varying sizes and shapes, designed for food service and available from Albert Uster Imports (page 677).

ESCARGOTS   Canned snails are available in specialty food shops such as Balducci's (page 676) or in quantity from Gourmand (page 677).

FLOUR

Flour is the single most important ingredient in baking. The type of flour used— particularly the protein content and whether it is bleached or unbleached—is critical to the outcome of all pie crusts and pastry and has been addressed in the individual chapter introductions. (A thorough discussion of flour and the directions for making your own pastry flour, for example, are in the introduction to pie crust.)

Regional all-purpose flours vary widely in protein content, from 8 grams per 4 ounces, which is close to that of cake flour, to 14 grams per 4 ounces, which is close to bread flour. National brands of all-purpose flour are usually around 11 grams per 4 ounces. Even a fraction of a percent can make a significant difference. A high-protein flour will require a lot more moisture than one with low protein and will result in the development of gluten. While a high-protein flour is desirable for making a light, airy bread or brioche, it will result in a tough, chewy pie crust. I therefore recommend using national brands such as Gold Medal, Pillsbury, or King Arthur. Though the protein content will vary slightly from harvest to harvest, the companies keep the range within acceptable limits. Should you find that your results are very different from mine—for example, your pie crust is dry and crumbly using the amount of water indicated—chances are that you are using a much higher protein flour.

Although the bleached and unbleached all-purpose flour from the same national brand have essentially the same protein content, the flours will not behave in an identical manner. Bleaching destroys the extensibility, or stretching quality, of the flour, so using bleached flour would result in a strudel dough full of holes. Bleaching also diminishes the strength of the gluten formed, so using an unbleached flour for a pie crust would make a tougher crust.

APPROXIMATE PERCENTAGE OF
PROTEIN CONTAINED IN DIFFERENT FLOURS

King Arthur stone-ground whole wheat flour: 14 percent
King Arthur reduced-bran flour (Green Mountain Gold): 12.7 percent
King Arthur special bread flour: 12.7 percent
King Arthur unbleached all-purpose: 11.7 percent
Heckers flour: 11.3 percent
Pillsbury and Gold Medal bleached and unbleached all-purpose flour:
    approximately 11 percent
Wondra flour: 9.8 percent
King Arthur whole wheat pastry flour: 9.5 percent
King Arthur pastry flour: 9.2 percent
White Lily bleached all-purpose flour: 9 percent
King Arthur bleached cake flour (Guinevere): 8. 5 percent
Swans Down or Softassilk bleached cake flour: 8 percent

SELF-RISING CAKE FLOUR AND WHITE LILY BLEACHED ALL-PURPOSE SELF-RISING FLOUR
Contain 1½ teaspoons of baking powder and ½ teaspoon of salt per cup of flour.
REDUCED-BRAN WHOLE WHEAT FLOUR   In whole wheat flour, the rough bran, which is the outer covering of the flour grain, interferes with the formation of gluten by cutting through it. Removing some of this bran makes it possible to retain the wheaty flavor but have a better texture, as in the croissants (page 477). King Arthur's reduced-bran whole wheat flour is called Green Mountain Gold.
WHOLE WHEAT FLOUR   King Arthur's whole wheat flour contains a high percentage of protein but is much less "strong" than all-purpose flour because of the bran, which reduces its gluten formation to just a little more than that of cake flour. Their whole wheat pastry flour is only 9.5 percent protein, making it possible to replace one third the volume of all-purpose flour in the Basic Flaky Pie Crust (page 22) with this flour, resulting in a flakiness and tenderness equal to that of using all pastry flour but with the added flavor of wheat.
STORAGE   Flour should be stored away from heat so that it doesn't dry out. Flour with the bran removed does not become rancid or attract bugs as readily as whole grain flour. King Arthur recommends storing whole grain flours for no longer than 3 months at room temperature, 6 months refrigerated (at 40°F.), and 1 year frozen. I have found that whole grain flours can be kept for as long as 6 months in a cool room. The best test for rancidity is simply to smell the flour. The nose knows!

FLOWERS

Some fresh flowers and leaves make beautiful and sometimes even flavorful additions to pies and tarts, but great care must be taken to ensure that they are not a poisonous variety and that they have not been sprayed—i.e., that they were grown for human consumption. Some edible flowers are apple blossoms, borage flowers, citrus blossoms (orange and lemon), day lilies (not tiger lilies, which have spots), English daisies, funcia, hibiscus, hollyhocks, honeysuckle, lilacs, nasturtiums, pansies, petunias, roses, tulips, and violets. Rose geranium leaves and mint leaves also make lovely garnishes, especially when sugared (see page 622).

FRUIT

Mature fruit picked at the height of the season is always the most flavorful. Smell is an excellent indication of ripeness and flavor potential. Sugar and baking, however, do wonders to bring out the flavor in slightly underripe fruits such as strawberries and apricots. Tasting will tell you how tart the fruit is. Some years or certain harvests will yield sweeter fruit than others and a little more or less sugar will be desirable. The most intense flavor in a fruit is in the peel, so if it is not tough, such as the peel of a Bartlett pear, it can be beneficial to leave it on. Alternatively, if poaching the fruit, the peel can be added to the liquid to extract the flavor.

APPLES   For my fall apple pies, I buy local apples like Macoun (tart and crisp), Stayman-Winesap (winey and tart but less so than regular Winesaps), Cortland (deep red, strong, and fruity), or Jonathan. Other great baking apples I've discovered that are available around the country are Baldwin; Golden Delicious (resists browning and holds its shape the best); Idared (mildly tart); Pink Lady (tart sweet, spicy, and holds its shape); Red Stayman (a sweeter apple that requires less sugar); Rhode Island Greening; Winesap (tart wine-like flavor with good storage capability, so it's available October to August); York Imperial; Northern Spy; and Newtown Pippin (sweet/tart, firm, and holds its shape; available October through June). I like to combine or blend three or four varieties of apples. In the winter, I use tart and tangy Granny Smith apples from the supermarket, which also make a marvelous pie. Rome are the best apple for baked apples or apple dumplings (page 141) because they are the roundest in shape. They are also tart and have good storage capabilities.

BERRIES   There is no doubt about it: Summer brings special culinary rewards of a quality that simply does not exist other times of the year, sweet corn, alive with flavor, tomatoes, and, my favorite of all, the berries. First come the strawberries, then blueberries, quickly followed by red raspberries, currants, black raspberries, wine berries (red caps), gooseberries, and finally blackberries. Thankfully, all berries freeze wonderfully for at least a year and can be enjoyed year-round. If storing berries for a day or two in the refrigerator, don't wash them until shortly before using them to prevent deterioration. To freeze berries, first wash them briefly in a colander under cold running water. Set them on paper towels to dry. To keep them from sticking together, it is best to spread them first in a single layer on baking sheets and freeze them for about 2 hours, then place them in heavy-duty freezer bags or canning jars. (If using bags, expel as much air as possible. If using canning jars, fill them almost to the top or add crumpled plastic wrap.)

BLUEBERRIES   Available June through August, these berries have a pleasing balance of sweetness to tartness, requiring very little, if any, sugar when eaten raw but more than most berries when cooked, as they tend to become bitter.

MARIONBERRIES   For me, discovering a new berry is as exciting as discovering a new star. And this year I discovered the miracle of all berries: the Marionberry. It is actually a hybrid from Marion County, Oregon, a happy marriage of the red raspberry and the blackberry, a velvety, intensely flavorful berry that resembles the long variety of blackberry in shape, with a reddish purple hue. The Marionberry is far less bitter than the raspberry and far less seedy than the blackberry, with a perfect balance of sweet/tart reminiscent of an earthy cabernet. I guess it was inevitable that I should adore these berries, as both of their ancestors, the blackberry and the raspberry, are members of the rose family *(Rubus)*.

The most remarkably distinctive characteristic of the Marionberry is that if frozen and defrosted, it is the only berry that maintains its texture, softening only very slightly as it releases some of its purple juices. This makes it possible to have a taste of the joy of fresh summer berries all year round.

Cooked berries in general become jammy and seedy in texture and lose much of their sweetness, necessitating as much as six times more sugar than uncooked berries. Stacey Pierce, the pastry chef at Union Square Café in New York City, has come up with a lovely solution: When she makes a tart, she cooks some of the frozen Marionberries and when cool, folds in some defrosted uncooked berries. This is possible because they hold their shape so well.

RASPBERRIES   These are my favorite berry because of their luscious velvety texture and tart intense flavor. I love them best uncooked in a tart but also adore them as a purée or sauce. The best raspberries come from the Pacific Northwest and are available June through mid-September.

STRAWBERRIES   There is no fruit more glorious than a strawberry at the height of the season (April through early July). Day Neutrals, so named because they were developed by a fortuitous cross between wild strawberries and June strawberries, are constantly blossoming despite the day's length. This makes them available from June through October. But even less than perfectly ripened strawberries come alive if sprinkled with sugar and allowed to sit for about 30 minutes.

GOOSEBERRIES   Gooseberries are related to currants. They are pale green, sometimes tinged with pink or purple, an indication that they are slightly sweeter. They have a globe-like shape and papery thin husk and are a little more tart than sour cherries, with which they blend magnificently. They keep, refrigerated, for about 2 weeks, and freeze well. California gooseberries are available November through December and April through July (Frieda's Inc., page 676).

CRANBERRIES   This beloved tart berry, indigenous to America, is usually associated with sauce for turkey, but cranberries also make a fantastically flavorful and juicy pie (page 129) and a delectable cranberry walnut galette (page 286). Available fresh in the fall and winter, they freeze perfectly for at least a year. If planning to freeze them, rinse and pick over them, discarding any stems or shriveled berries. Dry thoroughly on paper towels before placing them in reclosable freezer bags or canning jars. Dried cranberries, resembling ruby red raisins, are deliciously tart/sweet and are perfect for a cranberry walnut crostata (page 288). They are available at gourmet stores and from American Spoon Foods (page 676).

CITRUS FRUIT

ZEST   Zest refers to the colored portion of the citrus peel. The white portion, or pith, should be avoided, as it is quite bitter. The fruit is easier to zest before squeezing. (See Zester, page 661.)

APPROXIMATE YIELD OF JUICE
   1 large lemon = 3 tablespoons
   1 small lime = 2 tablespoons
   1 orange = ¼ cup

MEYER LEMONS   from California have the most delicious flavor. My cousin Joan Wager, who lives just up the hill from Chez Panisse, has a Meyer lemon tree and when I visit in season, I always come home with a bagful. Meyer lemons are available mid-January through February.

BLOOD ORANGES   are more intense in flavor than the ordinary juice or navel oranges. They boast a vivid color that can vary from deep rose to purple. The grated zest is a stunning mélange of orange and crimson and can be frozen. Usually, the more crimson the skin of the blood orange, the deeper the color of the fruit within. Blood oranges are available January through March. The best I have ever tasted were imported from Sicily. Flash-frozen blood orange juice from Sicily is now available year-round from Balducci's (page 676).

BITTER SEVILLE ORANGES   have the most acidity and intensity of all oranges. They are ideal for making a true orange curd, but the peel, which has a horribly bitter taste unless heavily sugared as for marmalade, should be discarded. These oranges are very thick skinned but also very juicy. The juice freezes well. They are available January through March.

MANGOES   This lush tropical fruit is available all year round and the quality is always excellent. Florida mangoes are available June and July.

PASSION FRUIT   is available year-round from Florida, California, and New Zealand. Store the fruit at room temperature until it is slightly dimpled, then store refrigerated in a moist area or frozen (in the skin) in reclosable freezer bags for up to a year. Although no one would question the appropriateness of the name once having indulged in the fruit, it actually came from Catholic missionaries in Brazil who, upon seeing passion fruit vines in flower around Easter, found the flower symbolic of different parts of the crucifixion, or Passion of Christ. One fresh passion fruit yields 1½ tablespoons purée. An excellent frozen purée is carried by Albert Uster Imports (page 675).

PEARS   The two great baking pears are Bartlett, available August and September, and Bosc, available October through February. The Bartlett's peel is tender so it does not have to be removed, but the Bosc's peel is bitter and tough. The flesh, however, is firm and holds up best when poached.

Pears do not ripen properly on the tree, so they are picked mature but hard. They should be refrigerated until 2 or 3 days before using and then removed to room temperature to complete ripening. They are ready when they yield to slight pressure near the stem end. If allowed to soften all over, they will be overripe and fall apart when poached or baked. Barletts turn from green to yellow when ripe and become very fragrant. Boscs maintain their russet brown color.

PERSIMMON   This beautiful vermilion fruit has a unique and seductive flavor (see page 217). Ripe Hachiya persimmons puréed in a food processor will keep frozen for over a year. An excellent persimmon purée is available frozen from Dillman Farms (page 676).

PINEAPPLE   The relatively new variety of pineapple called Golden Pineapple is so sweet and flavorful I wouldn't even consider purchasing any other.

FRUIT FRESH   Juicy fruits, such as peaches, nectarines, and apricots, lend themselves well to freezing. To prevent discoloration, I like to toss them first in ¼ cup of sugar mixed with 1 tablespoon of Fruit Fresh for each 4 cups of sliced fruit. The sugar draws out some of the fruit's juices and creates a syrup that coats the fruit. Fruit Fresh, which is ascorbic acid (vitamin C), prevents darkening and discoloration.

FRUIT AND FLAVORED OILS AND ESSENCES

Boyajian orange, lemon, and lime oils, squeezed from the rind of the fresh fruit, have a perfectly pure flavor and are great for adding extra intensity. Rule of thumb: ½ teaspoon of the citrus oil = 1 tablespoon grated zest. These oils are available at gourmet stores and catalogues such as the King Arthur catalogue (page 676), Dean & DeLuca (page 676), and Williams-Sonoma (page 677). Exquisite steam-distilled French fruit essences and flower waters, such as wild strawberry, passion fruit, and apricot, and rose and orange water, are available in tiny bottles from La Cuisine (page 676). They are expensive but well worth the price. A few drops go a long way.

White truffle oil, an intensely aromatic addition to savory cream puffs and the mashed potato topping for a shepherd's pie, is available from specialty food stores and the Balducci catalogue (page 676).

ELDERBERRY FLOWER CONCENTRATE   This extraordinary flavoring tastes like a combination of very ripe peach with the freshness of lychee. It is available from Ambassador Fine Foods (page 677).

FRUIT PURÉES AND PROCESSED FRUIT

APRICOTURE This wonderful apricot glaze, which does not require straining, contains citric acid, corn syrup, sugars, pectin, and apricot pulp. Since it has less moisture than apricot preserves, it works perfectly to seal crusts and pastry and to glaze fresh fruit tarts. (It's available from Albert Uster Imports, page 677.) *To thicken supermarket apricot preserves for brushing on pie crust:* See page 20. *To thicken other supermarket preserves for brushing on fruit:* Simmer the preserves with a little refiner's or corn syrup, stirring constantly. Simmering thickens them by evaporating some of the liquid, while the syrup keeps them fluid enough to apply to the fruit.

DRIED APRICOTS   Turkish apricots, which have a pure tart flavor, are available in specialty food stores and by mail order from Sultan's Delight (page 677).

LEMON CURD   Commercial lemon curd varies widely in quality. Tiptree brand, however, is very close to homemade because it is prepared by hand in small batches. Its exceptional flavor is also due to the lemons used in its preparation, which are from Spain. Coincidentally, the jar contains the same volume and weight as one recipe of my lemon curd (page 568).

PLUM BUTTER   Sultan's Delight (page 677) carries an excellent "plum butter" from Poland, perfect as a filling for Danish.

PERSIMMON PURÉE   See page 638.

FRUIT PERFECT™ CHERRIES   To my profound astonishment, the wonders of modern technology have conspired to produce a processed food that tastes more purely delicious than the unadulterated natural fruit. Justin Rachid, of American Spoon Foods in Michigan (capital of sour cherries), revealed their secret. First, they use individual quick-frozen sour cherries picked at the height of ripeness. But the special ingredient that elevates the clarity of their flavor is the cherries' own juices, concentrated by 65 percent to a ruby red, intensely bright-flavored syrup. Rachid explained that it took two years to "develop and perfect the vision." One of the challenges was to achieve consistency in the ratio of fruit to syrup in each jar. A special cornstarch was formulated that is thick when hot, suspending the cherries evenly in the syrup, and thins to the desired consistency on cooling.

Once opened, the cherries will keep for several weeks refrigerated, but perhaps only if hidden from view, as they are hard to resist. Although they are intended to eat right out of the jar, two jars of the cherries, with the addition of a touch more cornstarch and sugar, make an easy and perfect pie (page 95). Also worth checking out are the Fruit Perfect™ blueberries, Marionberries, and peaches. (All are available from American Spoon Foods, page 676.)

GRIOTTES   These small sour cherries in brandy make a lovely accompaniment to pastries such as Napoleons. They are available in specialty stores and in larger quantities from Gourmand (page 677).

GELATIN

Gelatin is made from ground-up animal by-products, including hooves and bones. According to Knox, one 7-gram/¼-ounce package of their gelatin will gel 2 cups liquid. One package measures 2¼ teaspoons, so 1⅛ teaspoons are needed per cup of liquid. If, however, a significant part of this liquid is a fruit purée that is very concentrated, such as a raspberry or strawberry purée for a chiffon pie, then I use only about 1 teaspoon per cup of liquid (including the egg white) instead of 1⅛ teaspoons.

Leaf gelatin, which comes in sheets, can be substituted for powdered gelatin using the same weight. One package of powdered gelatin is equal to 5 sheets of leaf gelatin measuring 2⅞ inches by 8½ inches. The problem is that gelatin leaves vary in size. If using 6- by 3-inch leaves, for example, you will need 5½ instead of 5 to equal the same amount.

Leaf gelatin should be soaked for at least 30 minutes in cold water until it becomes soft like plastic wrap. As long as the water is cool, the gelatin will not start to dissolve. The excess water should then be squeezed out and the gelatin soaked in hot liquid from the recipe until dissolved.

Some people prefer leaf gelatin to powder because it imparts less flavor. I do not find the difference significant and use the powder because it is more practical. Powdered gelatin should be softened in cool water for at least 5 minutes before being heated to dissolve it. According to the Lipton Research Department, "While it is true that extensive boiling will denature unflavored gelatin, . . . normal use in recipes, including boiling, will not adversely affect the product."

Gelatin requires a minimum of 4 hours to thicken a mixture and will continue to thicken it over a 24-hour period. Once the mixture has reached its maximum thickness, it will not thicken any further, even on freezing. Freezing does not affect thickening power. A mixture containing gelatin can be frozen, thawed, remelted, and refrozen several times before losing its strength.

I use Grayslake powdered gelatin, available at cake decorating supply places such as New York Cake and Baking Distributors (page 677), because it comes in a canister, making it easy to measure out the amount needed. New York Cake also carries leaf gelatin.

A kosher gelatin, made of vegetable gum, tapioca dextrin, and acids, is produced by Kojel Food Company (page 676).

AGAR-AGAR   is an alternative jelling agent used in Japan and by vegetarians. Made from seaweed, it is available in powder and stick form. Four teaspoons (2 ounces/56 grams) of the powder will jell 2 cups of liquid. A 3-ounce/84-gram stick will jell 3 cups of liquid. It's available at Katagiri (page 675).

GOLD   Twenty-two-karat gold leaf and silver leaf are available in sign-painting supply stores and from Albert Uster Imports (page 675). Small flecks of gold make dramatic decorations for tarts. "Gold" and "silver" powders are available from New York Cake and Baking Distributors (page 675).

LARD   Leaf lard, the fat around the kidney, also has excellent flavor. A butcher will sometimes be willing to special-order it. The Yorkville Packing House, Inc., has an excellent-quality lard they will ship (page 677).

Caul fat is stored in brine, so rinse it well, or soak it for a few hours in cold water, and dry it. It still will be slightly saltier than leaf lard.

Lard or caul fat will render a little less than two thirds its weight. (If you start with a pound of caul fat or leaf lard you will have about 10 ounces lard.) The rest will be "cracklings," which are great for adding to bread dough.

To render leaf lard, chop it fine or process it until well broken up. For caul fat, there is no need to chop it, as it is lacy and thin, except for the edges. Place the fat in a small heavy pan. Cook the fat on the lowest possible heat—just barely simmering (to avoid browning)—for 5 minutes, covered. Then cook for 40 minutes to an hour, uncovered, until only little golden brown bits remain in the pan. Strain it into a jar. It will keep refrigerated for months and frozen for about 2 years.

A half cup of rendered lard weighs about 4 ounces/113 grams, varying slightly according to the type used. If you are measuring rather than weighing the rendered lard, for ½ cup: If using leaf lard, use ½ cup; if using commercial lard, use ½ cup plus 2 teaspoons; if using rendered caul fat, use ½ cup plus 1 tablespoon.

MINCEMEAT   I don't make my own mincemeat quite simply because the most fabulous mincemeat I've ever tasted, Vintage Mincemeat, is made by Postilion in Wisconsin and is available from La Cuisine (page 676). I use it in my Brandied Mincemeat Ice Cream Pie (page 228) and also as an alternative stuffing for baked apple dumplings (page 141).

MORELS   Dried golden morel mushrooms from France are carried by India Tree (page 676) and Gourmand (page 677) and dried black morel mushrooms from Washington by American Spoon Foods (page 676). The golden morels are more subtle in flavor, the black morels more intense and slightly smoky.

NUTS   Freshly shelled nuts have the best flavor, but the canned shelled varieties are excellent and a lot more convenient. *Lightly* toasting most nuts, at 350°F. for about 10 minutes, greatly enhances their flavor. It is particularly desirable to toast walnuts, because the skins are very bitter and toasting loosens most of them. If you toast 7 ounces/200 grams of walnuts, about 0.3 ounce/9 grams of skin will come off if you rub them lightly in paper towels or while you are breaking or chopping them (pick out the nut pieces and discard the skin).

Most nuts have a fat content of about 70 percent. All nuts are prone to rancidity, but higher-fat nuts such as pecans, walnuts, and macadamia nuts are more prone to it than others. Always taste nuts before using them, as rancidity will ruin the flavor of a dessert. Nuts keep well for several years if stored airtight in the freezer. I use either reclosable freezer bags, expelling all the excess air, or glass canning jars, filling the empty head space with wadded-up plastic wrap.

Nuts should always be at room temperature before grinding them to prevent them from exuding too much oil. When grating or grinding almonds, starting with sliced nuts results in more even and less oily ground nuts. For every cup of ground almonds needed, start with 1¼ cups of sliced almonds.

If only whole nuts are available, use a generous ½ cup and start by using the grating disc of the food processor. Then switch to the metal blade and pulse until the nuts are finely chopped. A tablespoon or so of cornstarch, flour, or powdered or granulated sugar—borrowed from the rest of the recipe—will help absorb oil and prevent the ground nuts from clumping.

A small food processor works best for grinding nuts evenly. The Mouli hand grinder also does a fine job.

ALMONDS   Almonds are the first-ranking nut crop in America and are grown in California. They were introduced there in the middle of the nineteenth century by Spanish missionaries.

PECANS   These are a native American nut, ranking third in harvest after almonds and walnuts. The majority of pecans are grown in Georgia and Texas. They were named *pakans* by the Algonquin Indians from the word for hard shell. Pecans have a high fat content (about 73 percent) and are therefore prone to rancidity. They should be stored frozen. If using fresh pecans, 1½ pound in the shell will yield 13½ ounces shelled. Good mail-order sources for fresh pecans, both shelled and unshelled are: San Saba, in Texas (page 677), and Sunnyland Farms, in Albany, Georgia (page 677).

WALNUTS   Our second-ranking nut crop, walnuts are grown in California, and also grown and appreciated all over the world. They have a high fat content and are quite prone to rancidity if not stored frozen.

HAZELNUTS OR FILBERTS   These nuts are grown in Washington and Oregon, from cultivated stock brought over from Europe, and can be ordered from Hazy Grove Nuts, (page 676). They have a lower fat content than walnuts and pecans. The skin on hazelnuts is very bitter and difficult to remove. An easy method, taught to me many years ago by Carl Sontheimer, of Cuisinarts fame, uses baking soda. For ½ cup of nuts, bring 1½ cups of water to a boil. Add 2 tablespoons of baking soda and the nuts and boil them for 3 minutes. The water will turn black from the color of the skins. Test a nut by running it under cold water. The skin should slip off easily. If not, boil a few minutes longer. Rinse the nuts well under cold running water, use your fingers or fingernails to remove the skins, then crisp or brown them in a 350°F. oven.

PISTACHIOS   Pistachios are a beautiful and delicious nut, but the salted variety, which is most prevalent, should not be used for dessert recipes. Wonderfully flavorful bright green pistachios from Sicily can be ordered shelled and unsalted from Gourmand (page 677) or Keenan Farms (page 676). Blanch the nuts in boiling water for about 1 minute. Drain the nuts and remove and discard the peels by pinching each one gently.

MACADAMIA NUTS   With their slightly waxy, crunchy texture and unique mellow flavor, macadamias are particularly prone to rancidity. (If unsalted macadamia nuts are difficult to find, they can be ordered directly from Hawaii from the Mauna Loa Macadamia Nut Corporation, page 677.)

NUT PASTES   Nut paste terminology is among the most confusing in the baking industry. Diamond brand almond paste, for example, claims to be 100 percent pure almonds. This actually means that it contains no other nut substance, not that it doesn't contain any sugar! (In the industry, peach kernel pits are sometimes substituted for almonds to make a less expensive "almond" paste.) Imported almond pastes may contain as much as 50 percent sugar. Distributors such as Albert Uster Imports (page 675), have this information about the products they carry.

Almond pastes manufactured in America usually consist of 25 to 35 percent sugar (some of which is invert) and sweet and bitter almonds. (The bitter almonds are much more intense in flavor than the sweet ones.) Almond paste is used to make marzipan by adding additional sugar. All of the recipes in this book calling for almond paste require the domestic, or 25 to 35 percent sugar, variety.

Diamond brand almond paste is available at some supermarkets and through New York Cake and Baking Distributors (page 677). Albert Uster Imports also carries almond paste in larger quantities.

Pure 100 percent pistachio paste with no sugar added is available in small containers from Albert Uster Imports. This is an excellent product made from the most flavorful pistachio nuts.

Pure 100 percent hazelnut paste with no sugar added is available in small containers from Albert Uster. It is impossible to make a hazelnut paste of this smoothness without highly specialized equipment.

Praline paste consists of hazelnuts or a combination of almonds, hazelnuts, and 50 percent caramelized sugar. (Lesser qualities have a higher percentage of sugar.) I prefer the 100 percent hazelnut and caramelized sugar variety. This can be purchased in small, expensive quantities from Maison Glass (page 677). A small amount goes a long way and it is worth every penny. I have experimented endlessly only to find that homemade praline paste always has a slightly gritty consistency. Nut pastes keep 1 year refrigerated and indefinitely frozen. On storage, some of the oil separates and floats to the top. This can be stirred back into the praline paste.

COCONUT   One average-size coconut weighs about 1½ pounds/680 grams and yields about 4 cups approximately 10.5 ounces/310 grams of finely shredded coconut. One cup of shredded coconut weighs about 2.6 ounces/75 grams.

To prepare a fresh coconut: With a skewer or screwdriver, pierce two of the eyes. Drain the milky liquid. If desired, strain it and use it for cooking or drinking. With a hammer or the back of a cleaver, sharply tap the coconut about one third of the way from the opposite end of the eyes. Continue tapping in a circle around the coconut until it breaks open. Use a knife to divide the coconut meat into portions that can be lifted easily from the shell. Lift out each section. Cut off the brown skin and grate the white flesh into fine flakes. If using a special coconut grater (see page 661), there is no need to remove the shell: Simply insert the head of the grater into the hollow coconut half and turn the crank.

Unsweetened flaked coconut, softer and fresher tasting than most commercially prepared coconut, is available from the King Arthur catalogue (page 676). Excellent-quality coconut in many textures and degrees of fineness is available in some Asian markets and Indian food stores.

PAM   I prefer PAM to other nonstick vegetable spray products because it has virtually no odor. It is composed of lecithin, a natural emulsifying agent derived from soybeans, and a tiny amount of soybean oil.

POPPY SEEDS   These tiny gray-blue seeds are incomparably delicious when fresh but bitter and rancid if held too long at room temperature. Poppy seeds should be stored refrigerated or frozen. They are more perishable when ground, so it's best to grind them just before using them for the freshest flavor. Penzeys, Ltd. (page 677), carries a top "A-" quality called Holland Blue.

SALT   For savory recipes, I find that people's taste for salt varies widely and that mine seems to be in the mid-range. Since salt flavors the food more evenly when it is added early in the cooking process rather than all at the very end, I like to give a suggested amount rather than indicating to "season to taste." After trying one of my recipes, you will have a reference point as to how my taste compares with yours and you can, if necessary, adjust the other recipes accordingly.

I prefer to use unsalted ingredients, such as broth, because it enables me to use as much of the ingredient as I want without adding more salt than I desire with it. A cup of salted broth contains almost a teaspoon of salt.

There is no difference in flavor between kosher and table salt because both come from the same source. The only difference in flavor will occur in instances where the salt does not dissolve fully, as, for example, in salads. Kosher salt, which is coarser, will still be in granules and therefore has a different flavor perception. If you would like to use kosher salt for the savory recipes, if using Morton brand, use it interchangeably. If using Diamond brand, you will need 1¾ times the volume amount but the same amount if weighing it.

I often use kosher or coarse sea salt to sprinkle on roasts because it distributes more evenly. There is, however, a difference in flavor with sea salt. Although, weight for weight, it is equally salty, it has a "sweeter," more pure flavor. Different varieties actually have different flavors. I use fine sea salt for all my sweet and savory recipes. Some of the best brands, such as Fleur de sel de Guérande, are available from the King Arthur catalogue (page 676) and La Cuisine (page 676).

STABILIZERS

COBASAN   This is a miracle product from Germany for stabilizing whipped cream and ice cream. It consists of sorbitol and glucose. A minute quantity added before whipping cream, or before freezing ice cream, emulsifies the fat, enabling the whipped cream to hold up for as long as 6 hours at room temperature and making the ice cream smooth and creamy. It does not work, however, with ultra-pasturized cream, because the fat molecules have been altered because of the higher temperatures at which this cream is pasteurized. Cobasan is available from Albert Uster Imports (page 675). The plastic bottle contains 1 quart, which will probably last a lifetime unless you open a bakeshop!

SANIFAX   Available from Patisfrance (page 677). This is another excellent stabilizer from Germany that also works with ultrapasteurized cream.

WHIPIT   From Oetker of Ontario, Canada, is an excellent stabilizer more readily available to consumers, as it is available in some supermarkets and specialty stores. It also works with ultrapasteurized cream. Whipit is a powder consisting of dextrose, modified food starch, and tricalcium phosphate. It makes the cream a little less airy and adds a slightly ivory color and a slight sweetness, so the sugar should be decreased accordingly.

SUGAR AND OTHER SWEETENERS

I had long regarded sugar as the one reliably standard ingredient with which it is impossible to go wrong. The only time, in fact, that sugar even nudged my attention was when I emptied a 100-pound sack of granulated sugar into the bin and noticed how odd it was that a substance that contributes the lovely quality of sweetness has such an unappealing undertone of bitterness when smelled in bulk. I assumed that this quality somehow dissipated when mixed with other ingredients, but only recently discovered the fascinating truth behind my intuition. Apparently, something in the refining and bleaching process does indeed produce an undesirable element of bitterness not present in unrefined sugar. When it comes to light brown and dark brown sugar, however, refining results in flavor differences that are even more significant. Unrefined brown sugar still contains its natural molasses, which offers bright, clear color and rich taste with delicious underlying spice, butter, and caramel flavor components. Refined brown sugar, however, has all the molasses removed and then added back, at the expense of considerable depth of flavor. It is sometimes even darkened with food color to recreate its original brown color.

Unrefined sugar from the tropical island Mauritius in the Indian Ocean off the coast of Africa is the finest quality. The special flavor of the sugar is said to be derived from the sugarcane grown on the volcanic ash. Billington's is one brand that is imported from England and available in fine groceries, gourmet markets, and health food stores, sometimes packaged under the name Simpson and Vail; it's also available in larger quantities by mail order directly from Simpson and Vail (page 677). It is available in four varieties: golden castor (fine granulated), light muscovado (light brown), dark muscovado (dark brown), and amber crystal (coarse granulated). India Tree (page 676) carries the sugar under the names *Golden Baker's* (equivalent to superfine) and *Dark Muscovado* (equivalent to dark brown). They also carry the most exquisite array of sparkling colored sugar for use as decoration. Over the past several years, I have been using all of these sugars in baking, replacing refined light and dark brown sugars with their unrefined counterparts and refined granulated sugar with the unrefined castor sugar. The only time I use refined sugar now is for meringues, where I want the pure white color, or caramel, where I want to prevent crystallization caused by "impurities."

HOW SUGAR IS MADE   Sucrose, the primary sugar used in pastry making, is a sugar obtained from sugar beets or sugarcane. There is absolutely no difference between these two sources in the final product if the sugar is refined to 99.9 percent sucrose. A molecule of sucrose is composed of one fructose and one glucose molecule joined together to form a simple carbohydrate, easy to digest and full of energy. Other plants are capable of making sugar, but both cane and beets make it in quantities large enough to support refining. Sugar from the plants is dissolved in water and the resulting syrup is boiled in large steam evaporators. The substance that remains is crystallized in heated vacuum pans and the liquid, now called molasses, is separated from the crystals by spinning it in a centrifuge. At this stage, the sugar is known as raw sugar and contains 3 percent impurities or extraneous matter. The raw sugar crystals are washed with steam and become what is called turbinado sugar, which is 99 percent pure sucrose. Although it closely resembles refined white sugar in sweetening ability and composition, it cannot always be substituted in recipes. Its moisture content varies considerably, a factor that, coupled with its molasses flavor and coarse granulation, can affect a recipe without careful adjustment.

Refined white sugar is processed from turbinado sugar. The turbinado sugar is heated again to a liquid state, centrifuged, clarified with lime or phosphoric acid, and then percolated through a column of beef-bone char or mixed in a solution of activated carbon. Either of these last processes whitens the sugar and removes all calcium and magnesium salts. Finally, the sugar is pumped back into vacuum pans, where it is heated until it crystallizes. The resulting sugar is 99.9 percent sucrose. Sugar that is less refined may be somewhat gray in color and the protein impurities may cause foaming when the sugar is added to the liquid in a given recipe.

BROWN SUGAR   Most brown sugar is ordinary refined sucrose with some of the molasses returned to it (3.5 percent for light brown sugar, 6.5 percent for dark brown). As mentioned above, I prefer to use muscovado natural raw sugar, such as Billington's and India Tree. Because muscovado natural raw sugar doesn't have its natural molasses removed, its flavor seems more pure and subtle.

An equal volume of either type of brown sugar compared to white sugar has the same sweetening power, but brown sugar must be measured by packing it into the cup. Dark brown sugar weighs the most because of the added molasses. Molasses also adds moisture to the sugar. Brown sugar contains 2.1 percent water, while plain white sucrose contains only 0.5 percent. Store brown sugar in an airtight container, such as a canning jar, to keep it from losing moisture and solidifying. If this should happen, place a slice of apple on a small piece of waxed paper on top of the sugar and cover the container tightly. After about 24 hours, the sugar will have absorbed enough moisture from the apple to soften.

If you run out of brown sugar and have white sugar and molasses on hand, it's easy to make your own (see Substitutions, page 655).

MOLASSES   Containing 24 percent water, unsulfured molasses such as Grandma's has the best flavor because it is refined from the concentrated juice of sugarcane. The sulfured variety is usually a by-product of sugar making and tastes of the residues of sulfur dioxide introduced during the sugar-making process.

REFINER'S SYRUP   Containing 15 to 18 percent water, this is a delicious by-product of sugar refining. When the sugar syrup, after many boilings, ceases to yield crystals, it is filtered and concentrated into this golden-colored syrup. Lyle's, a British company, packages it as Lyle's Golden Syrup. It can be used interchangeably with light corn syrup. Refiner's syrup is carried by supermarkets and specialty stores such as Dean & DeLuca (page 676).

CORN SYRUP   Containing about 24 percent water, corn syrup consists of glucose (from corn sugar) with fructose added to prevent crystallization. It is susceptible to fermentation if contaminated, so be sure not to return any unused portion to the bottle. Fermented corn syrup has a sour taste and should be discarded. If used in low concentration, corn syrup has, by volume, half the sweetening power of sucrose, but in high concentration it is about equal. It can be used interchangeably with refiner's syrup.

GRANULATIONS AND FORMS OF REFINED SUGAR   All 99.9 percent refined sucrose has equal sweetening power despite the degree of granulation. The only difference in content between granulated and powdered sugar is that powdered sugar has 3 percent cornstarch added to prevent lumping.

Regular granulated or fine granulated: This is the all-purpose sugar found in most sugar bowls and available in all supermarkets. This granulation is suitable for making syrups, but for most baking, a finer granulation is preferable. Using a food processor, it is possible to make a more finely granulated sugar, but the crystals will not be as uniform in size as in commercially produced finer-grain sugar. Don't confuse the term *fine granulated* with *superfine,* which is much finer.

Extra-fine: Available to the trade, this sugar is also known as fruit sugar because it is used in the preservation of fruits. Most professional bakers use this granulation as their all-purpose sugar if they can't find baker's special. Finer sugar dissolves more easily and makes lighter, more delicate meringues.

Baker's special: Available to the trade, this sugar is slightly finer than extra-fine and almost as fine as superfine. This is the perfect granulation for all baking. A close approximation can easily be made in the food processor using a coarser granulation and processing for a few minutes.

Castor sugar: This is a term that appears in British cookbooks. The sugar, commonplace in England, is slightly finer than baker's special. If you are converting a British recipe, substitute baker's special or the more widely available superfine sugar.

Superfine or ultrafine: This is the finest granulation of sugar and comes only in 1-pound boxes. It is sometimes called *bar sugar* because it is used in bars to make drinks that require fast-dissolving sugar. For the same reason, it is ideal for making meringues and fillings.

Loaf or cube sugar: This is merely granulated sugar that has been pressed into molds when moist and then allowed to dry so it maintains the shape. Some recipes, particularly in the confectionery area, specify loaf sugar because at one time it was more refined. Today, this is not the case. In fact, because of modern methods of manufacturing, the cubes have traces of oil from the molds, which makes them less desirable for sugar boiling.

Medium coarse and coarse pearl sugar, or *sanding sugar:* These are the first crystals that form in the refining process and are therefore the purest. It is also known as "strong" sugar because it resists color changes and inversion at high temperatures, which will result in stickiness. Because of the absence of impurities, this type of sugar is ideal for confections and cordials and also for preparing caramel, because impurities in other types of sugar can cause crystallization. These large granules are sometimes used to sprinkle on cookies and pastries.

Powdered, confectioners', or icing sugar: While it is possible to achieve a very fine granulation in the food processor, it is not possible to make true powdered sugar.

This can only be done commercially. At one time, powdered sugar was stone-ground, but now it is ground in steel magnesium rotaries that turn against screens of varying degrees of finess, each one determining a different fineness of the grind. The coarser the granulation of the initial sugar, the more even will be the final grind. As might be expected, the finer the granulation, the greater the tendency of the sugar to lump, which explains why 3 percent cornstarch is added to absorb any moisture from the air before the sugar can. The cornstarch also adds what is perceived as a raw taste and makes powdered sugar less suitable than granulated sugar for use with ingredients that are not cooked.

Powdered sugar comes in three degrees of fineness: 10X, the finest (available in supermarkets), and 6X and 4X, both of which are available to the trade.

DEXTROSE   Dextrose is powdered corn sugar. Its sweetening power is much lower than sucrose and it does not dissolve as readily when sprinkled on whole berries or the surface of a pie, making it ideal to use for stenciling designs and other garnishes.

SUGAR SYRUPS   When making a sugar syrup for Italian meringue or classic buttercream, for example, the sugar is concentrated to produce a supersaturated solution from a saturated one. A saturated sugar solution contains the maximum amount of sugar possible at room temperature without precipitating out into crystals. A supersaturated sugar solution contains more sugar than the water can dissolve at room temperature. Heating the solution enables the sugar to dissolve. Cold water is capable of holding double its weight in sugar, but if it is heated, more sugar can dissolve in the same amount of water. A sugar solution begins with sugar partially dissolved in at least one third its weight of cold water. It is stirred continuously until boiling, at which time all the sugar is dissolved. If sugar crystals remain on the sides of the pan, they should be washed down with a wet pastry brush. The solution is now considered supersaturated and, to avoid crystallization, must no longer be stirred.

As the water evaporates, the temperature of the solution rises and the density increases. Concentration of the syrup is dependent on the amount of water left after evaporation. The temperature of the syrup indicates the concentration. As long as there is a lot of water in the syrup, the temperature does not rise much above the boiling point of the water. But when most of the water has boiled away, the temperature can rise dramatically, passing through various stages (see page 649) and eventually rising to the temperature of melted sugar (320°F.) when all the water is gone.

Concentration can also be measured by density, using a saccharometer or Baumé sugar weight scale. A Baumé scale is graduated from 0° to 44° and corresponds in a direct relationship to degrees Fahrenheit or Centigrade. The degree of evaporation can also be measured by consistency by dropping a small amount of the syrup into ice water.

Supersaturated solutions are highly unstable and recrystallization can occur from agitation or even just on standing unless the solution was properly heated in the first place. The use of an "interfering agent," such as invert sugar (a little more than one quarter of the weight of the granulated sugar), butter, cream of tartar, or citric acid, helps keep the solution stable by interfering with the crystalline structure formation. This is useful when the solution will be used in a way that will involve repeatedly dipping into it, such as making spun sugar.

As melted sugar reaches higher temperatures, many chemical changes begin to occur. The sugar cannot start to caramelize until all the water has evaporated. As it starts to caramelize, its sweetening power decreases. At this point, when all the water has evaporated, stirring will no longer cause the sugar to crystallize. The addition of a significant amount of an ingredient, such as nuts, however, can lower the temperature considerably and this will cause crystallization to occur instantly if no interfering agent has been used.

Caramel is extremely difficult to make in humid weather because sugar is highly hygroscopic (attracts water). The moisture in the air will make the caramel sticky. *A ½ cup of sugar makes ¼ cup of caramel (plus the residue that clings to the pot).* If cooled, set, and pulverized, it returns to its original volume.

When a sugar syrup has been prepared in advance, it is sometimes necessary to check the exact quantity of sugar and water it contains. It is important to know that the Baumé reading of a cold solution will measure slightly higher than the same solution when hot.

Another variant that affects density reading is altitude. Because water boils at a lower temperature as altitude increases (there is less air pressure weighing on top of the water to prevent it from changing from liquid into vapor), there will be a different temperature for the same concentration of sugar syrup at different altitudes. For each increase of 500 feet in elevation, sugar syrup should be cooked to a temperature 1°F. lower than the temperature called for at sea level. If readings are

TEMPERATURES AND TESTS FOR SUGAR SYRUP USED FOR RECIPES IN THIS BOOK	
220° to 222°F.	Pearl: The thread formed by pulling the liquid sugar between your fingertips can be stretched. When a cool metal spoon is dipped into the syrup and then raised, the syrup runs off in drops that merge to form a sheet. This is used for making jelly.
234° to 240°F.	Soft ball: Syrup dropped into ice water can be formed into a ball that flattens on removal from the water. This is used for extra-light Italian meringue.
244° to 250°F.	Firm ball: Syrup dropped into ice water can be formed into a firm ball that does not flatten on removal from the water. This is used for light Italian meringue.
270° to 290°F.	Soft crack: Syrup dropped into ice water separates into threads that are hard but not brittle. This is used for Italian meringue used for piping elaborate designs.
320°F.	Clear liquid: The sugar has liquefied (all the moisture is removed) and can start browning.
338°F.	Brown liquid: The liquefied sugar turns brown. This is used for light carmel.
356°F.	Medium brown liquid: The liquefied sugar darkens. This is used for praline, spun sugar, caramel cages, and nougatine.
374 to 380°F.	Dark brown liquid: The liquefied sugar darkens further. This is used for intensely flavored caramel cream sauce.

taken in Celsius, for each 900 feet of elevation, cook the syrup to a temperature 1°C. lower than called for at sea level. These adjustments should be made up to 320°F., the melting point of sugar; altitude does not change this.

HONEY   This golden syrup is the only sweetener that needs no additional refining or processing to be used. There are about 300 different varieties of honeys, ranging in flavor from mild to bold, depending on the type of flowers from which the bees gathered the nectar (the National Honey Board likes to say, "The flavor of honey is determined by where the bees buzzed."). In baking, it's fun to experiment with different varieties, but I find that the milder flavors blend best with other flavors. My favorite honey is thyme, which has a delicate, floral sweetness, multidimensional flavor, and purity. Tupelo, which is also mild, has a heavy body and distinctive taste. I brought back a lavender honey from Provence that truly has the background echo of lavender. I also love avocado and eucalyptus honeys and certain wildflower honeys, particularly the Hellas brand (page 676).

Honey is composed of 32 to 42 percent fructose, glucose, sucrose, and other sugars and water. It is the high percentage of fructose, which is more hygroscopic than other sugars, that makes baked goods made with honey stay moist longer, become soft on standing, and feel chewier in the mouth. Honey has a higher sweetening power and caramelization properties than sugar, causing baked goods to brown more quickly. Because of honey's water content, a rule of thumb for replacing part of the sugar in a recipe with honey is to decrease the liquid in the recipe by ¼ cup for each cup used.

Because honey is essentially a supersaturated solution (water that holds an extra amount of sugar), it crystallizes over time. It is best stored at room temperature or in the freezer. Crystallized honey can be reliquefied easily by placing the container in warm water until the crystals dissolve or microwaving it, stirring every 30 seconds. (One cup will take 2 to 3 minutes on high power.) When I use it in a filling, such as in the Gâteau Engadine (page 291), to prevent crystallization after baking, I add a little corn syrup to the honey.

THICKENERS

The most popular starches used to thicken pie fillings are cornstarch and tapioca.

CORNSTARCH   Cornstarch is made from corn.

TAPIOCA   From a Portuguese word that means pudding, tapioca is made from the cassava root. Cassava powder is tapioca before it is subjected to the "beading" process, which gives it a pebbly texture desirable in puddings. As silky smoothness is the goal in a filling or glaze, cassava is more suitable than tapioca for these purposes. Tapioca is particularly unsuitable for a lattice pie or one made without a crust, because the grains on the surface become dry and hard. Cassava is available in Asian food stores and from the King Arthur catalogue (page 676).

ARROWROOT   Made from a tropical rhizome (underground stem), arrowroot derives its name from its use in the seventeenth century to treat arrow wounds. Arrowroot has a slight sparkle, which makes it popular for glazes to top fruit.

Because it starts to thicken long before the boiling point, it is not suitable for fruit pies that require longer baking to soften the fruit.

All three starches have twice the thickening power of flour.

HOW STARCHES WORK TO THICKEN LIQUID   Starches accomplish thickening by the absorption of liquid. As the starch granules absorb the liquid, they swell and become fragile. It is, therefore, very important when making a glaze not to stir vigorously after thickening has occurred, because you will break down these fragile, swollen granules, releasing the fluid they contain.

THICKENING POINTS   Prolonged cooking past the thickening point will also break down the starch and thin the glaze. Cornstarch does not thicken until it has reached a full boil (212°F.), cassava thickens as soon as it begins to boil; and arrowroot thickens before the boiling point, at only 158° to 176°F.

THICKENERS FOR PIE FILLINGS   The starch thickener for a pie filling is one of the most important ingredients in pie making. A pie with a watery filling resulting from not enough thickener and a pie with a pasty or rubbery filling resulting from too much thickener are equally undesirable.

Cornstarch and cassava have different qualities and I have thought long and hard and performed countless tests and combinations to determine which is superior. Hands down, cornstarch is my favorite for both flavor and texture. Some people feel that cassava masks the flavor of the fruit less than cornstarch does, but to my taste the cornstarch actually enhances the fruit, making it seem sweeter, though not in a cloying or sugary sense, more flavorful and harmonious, and brighter in color. Also, cornstarch, if used in the correct proportions, when set still has a little flow, which cassava does not. And while cassava never becomes rubbery, or bouncy, when used in a filling it has a stretchy quality, almost seeming to sheet in the mouth. Another advantage to cornstarch is that, unlike cassava, it does not thin on reheating, should you decide to reheat a slice of pie.

The one minor advantage cassava offers over cornstarch is that it is not as affected by acid. However, once cornstarch is cooked, acid will not affect it either, which is why when you are making a lemon meringue pie, the lemon juice is added after the cornstarch has thickened the filling.

AMOUNT OF THICKENER   If you are using more sugar in a pie filling than the recipe calls for, more thickener will be needed because sugar contains moisture and when cooked, it will contribute more syrup.

The same amount of thickener is needed for a pie that is baked freshly made versus one that has been frozen because the fruit contains the same amount of liquid, which is released during heating.

If making a pie to eat shortly after baking (i.e., time does not allow for the recommended cooling period), I replace half the cornstarch with 1⅓ times its volume of cassava, in order to make the filling firm enough to slice well. (For example, replace 2 tablespoons of cornstarch with 1 tablespoon of cornstarch and 1 tablespoon plus 1 teaspoon of cassava.)

If making a pie to eat the following day, however, I will use a little less cornstarch, as it will continue to thicken over a 24-hour period. (If the recipe calls for 1 table-spoon, for example, I use 2½ teaspoons.) Also, for a lattice or open-faced pie, I use a little less cornstarch than for a two-crust pie, because more liquid can evaporate.

The average amount of cornstarch for 4 ounces of fruit is 1 to 2 teaspoons; the average amount for 1 cup of fruit is 1½ to 2½ teaspoons (see charts on page 77). Should you want to experiment with tapioca or cassava, they are equal to corn-starch by weight but not by volume: *1 tablespoon of cornstarch or fine tapioca = 4 teaspoons of cassava; 1 tablespoon of cassava = 2 teaspoons plus a scant ½ teaspoon of cornstarch or fine tapioca.*

THICKENER FOR A TOPPING GLAZE FOR FRESH FRUIT PIES OR TARTS   Cornstarch, cassava, and arrowroot all produce clear glazes, but cassava is the most transpar-ent. A cornstarch glaze is slightly cloudy and an arrowroot glaze is slightly yellow.

Cassava is my favorite choice for a glaze not only because of its clarity but also because it sets as soon as it is cool, with no flow, but does not form a rigid jell, thus remaining softer. (Cornstarch takes about 2 hours to set.) Another important advantage to cassava is that it is the starch that is the least affected by acidity of the fruit and holds up the longest. A cassava glaze remains soft and shiny on most fruit for 8 hours at room temperature and 4 days in the refrigerator, whereas a cornstarch glaze holds up for only 2 days in the refrigerator and then becomes dull and cracked. An arrowroot glaze holds up for only 1 day. A cornstarch glaze on pineapple, which has high acidity, will last for about 2 hours before thinning, whereas a cassava glaze on pineapple will still be fine the next day. I have also tried a cassava glaze on two of the most watery sliced fruits, which usually will not hold a glaze at all—fresh strawberries and fresh figs—and it was perfect. None of the glazes, however, works on fresh mango, probably because of an enzyme similar to one contained in papaya that keeps gelatin from thickening.

SHELF LIFE   If stored in an airtight, moisture-proof container, cornstarch has an indefinite shelf life. Manufacturers of tapioca or cassava give it at least a 2-year shelf life, but I have found that 10-year-old cassava lost only a little of its thicken-ing power. Arrowroot has a more limited shelf life. After about 2 years, it will lose its thickening power to a significant extent.

VANILLA   Vanilla beans vary enormously in quality. The best beans come from Tahiti, Madagascar, and Mexico. The Tahitian beans are larger than the others and all three types are about twice the size and more highly perfumed with a floral quality than other vanilla beans. This makes it difficult to give equivalencies for distilled vanilla (extract), which also varies enormously in concentration (referred to commercially as "folds"). A general rule of thumb is: *A 2-inch piece of bean = 1 teaspoon of extract.* The Tahitian beans are so aromatic, I use only half a bean in a recipe specifying one bean.

Sometimes you will notice a white substance coating the vanilla beans. This is usually not mold, but rather flavorful vanillin crystals, which migrate to the sur-face. To determine which it is, simply touch your finger to the bean. If it is mold, it will not disappear, but if it is vanillin crystals, they will vanish after a few seconds.

Vanilla accentuates other flavors. The bean adds a subtle depth of flavor and unique sweet quality. The extract, though easier to use, lacks the sweet roundness and if used in excess will even impart a bitter edge.

My favorite vanilla extract is produced by Méro and comes from Grasse, the perfume region of France. It is available from La Cuisine (page 676). I like to transfer the vanilla to a plastic squeeze bottle dispenser with a pointed tip and add a Tahitian vanilla bean. This is a great use for used vanilla beans, which still have lots of flavor even after the seeds have been removed. Be sure to rinse the bean if it has been used to flavor another liquid and dry it in a low oven or with the heat of the oven's pilot light.

The recipes in this book that call for vanilla extract refer to the regular pure vanilla extract, not the concentrated variety, for purposes of standardization. When I use Méro or a concentrated vanilla extract, I use a little less than one half the amount specified in these recipes.

Another of my favorite vanillas is Nielsen-Massey vanilla, which is carried by many specialty stores and can be ordered directly from Nielsen-Massey (page 677). Recently, Nielsen-Massey introduced an excellent Tahitian vanilla extract. They also carry magnificent Tahitian vanilla beans, but these must be purchased in large quantities. Neilsen-Massey recommends storing extract and beans at room temperature, away from direct heat. They say that refrigeration is fine for extract, but since the flavoring material precipitates out when chilled, it must be shaken before use. They caution against refrigerating the beans, because they can mold, though I find that if stored in an airtight container in the refrigerator, they keep perfectly for several years.

VEAL AND CHICKEN STOCK Glace and demi-glace, the super-concentrated veal and chicken stocks made without salt or preservatives, are available from Master Chef More than Gourmet in small containers. They need no refrigeration until opened and then will keep for over a year. They are available in gourmet grocery stores such as Balducci's (page 676) and can be mail-ordered directly from Master Chef (page 677).

YEAST I prefer using fresh yeast to dry. I like its lively reaction and forthright, earthy smell. But if the yeast isn't fresh, the final baked product will have a slightly sour taste. The best way to determine freshness is by smell, as the color may not have changed even when the yeast is slightly past its prime. Fresh yeast freezes indefinitely, at 0°F. or below (above 0°F., not all activity will be arrested), but certain precautions must be taken in defrosting. Yeast is a live organism and must be "awakened" gradually from the frozen state. To defrost, place it in a refrigerator for a minimum of 48 hours. Since a few yeast cells will have been destroyed in the process, use one quarter more than the amount specified in the recipe.

It's fine to use dry yeast (see Substitutions, page 655), but the quick- or rapid-rise yeasts need a different procedure. For one thing, they cannot be proofed. In the 10 minutes of proofing time, they will have thoroughly exhausted all their energy and leavening power. Dry yeast requires warm water (about 110°F.) to activate it by enabling it to absorb water and swell. Cold water will kill it. Most strains of yeast, whether fresh or dry, die at 125°F., though some can live at temperatures up to 150°F.

My favorite dry yeast is SAF-Instant (not to be confused with rapid). It is called instant because, unlike other dry yeasts, it does not require warm water to wake it up; in fact, it can be added to the dry ingredients without proofing. It should be stored in the freezer, where it will keep for about 1 year, but it should be proofed once in a while just to make sure that it is still active. (You can simply add a pinch of it to warm water, and within 5 minutes it should start to bubble.) To substitute for regular dry yeast, see Substitutions (page 655). SAF-Instant is available at specialty food stores and from the King Arthur catalogue (page 676).

WEIGHTS

The weight for all ingredients in the recipes in this book is given in both the metric and avoirdupois system. The grams mostly have been rounded off to the nearest whole number without decimal points (except for leavening and other ingredients that need to be more precise and should be measured rather than weighed, unless using commercial-quality scales), the ounces to the nearest quarter ounce. Either system works, but do not expect the mathematics to correlate exactly.

There is no doubt about it: Weighing is faster, easier, and more accurate than measuring. Most bakers, including myself, prefer the metric system for its precision in small quantities. There isn't any adjustment necessary if you have a metric scale and the recipes give metric amounts! If you do not have a scale with a digital readout, round off the grams to the nearest convenient number. The amount will still be quite accurate, as, after all, one gram is only about one twenty-eighth of an ounce.

The way I have presented the solid volume measures is the way in which I would measure them. Instead of writing 6 tablespoons sugar, for example, I express it as ¼ cup + 2 tablespoons, because that is the more convenient approach. Also, the fewer measures used, the less room for error.

For those who measure instead of weigh, the *dip and sweep method* of measuring means dipping the measuring cup into the bin containing the ingredient and sweeping off the excess with a long flat spatula or knife. Flour should be stirred lightly before measuring.

Lightly spooned refers to spooning the ingredient into the cup and then sweeping off the excess with a long flat spatula or blade. This method yields less of the ingredient than the dip and sweep method.

Dry ingredients should be measured in a cup designed for solids. Liquid ingredients, including honey and other syrups, should be measured in a liquid measure with a spout. There is a difference in volume between liquid and solid measuring cups.

SUBSTITUTIONS: APPROXIMATE EQUIVALENCIES AND SUBSTITUTIONS

Making one thing into another is never 100 percent, but in a pinch it's nice to know how to come close to the original.

Most substitution charts indicate how to sour milk with vinegar to replace buttermilk. While the acidity level seems the same, the sour flavor is nowhere near the rich, full tanginess of buttermilk. Substituting an item such as granulated sugar and molasses for brown sugar is closer to the original because that is often the way it is done in the industry, though I prefer the unrefined brown sugar that has the original molasses in it (see page 646).

It is not possible to give a substitution for molasses, however, because in order to have enough molasses from sugar, too much sugar would need to be added.

Exchanging one type of semisweet or bittersweet chocolate for another will work but will often yield surprisingly different flavor and texture results. Even if the percentages of cocoa solids, cocoa butter, and sugar are the same, the type of bean and degree of roasting is responsible for significant variations. The best way to determine which semisweet or bittersweet chocolate to use is to taste the different types.

FOR	SUBSTITUTE
1 pound unsalted butter	1 pound lightly salted butter; remove 1 teaspoon of salt from the recipe
1 cup whole milk	1 cup minus 1 tablespoon half-and-half; remove 1 tablespoon of butter from the recipe and add 2 tablespoons water
1 cup half-and-half	¾ cup whole milk and ¼ cup heavy cream or ½ cup whole milk and ½ cup light cream
1 cup sifted cake flour	¾ cup sifted bleached all-purpose flour + 2 tablespoons cornstarch (this results in 15 percent cornstarch)
1 cup bleached all-purpose flour	1 cup + 1 tablespoon pastry flour or Wondra flour (rapid dissolve)
1 cup packed light brown sugar	1 cup granulated sugar + ¼ cup unsulfured light molasses
1 cup packed dark brown sugar	1 cup granulated sugar + ½ cup unsulfured light molasses
0.25-ounce package	1 packed tablespoon (0.75 ounce) compressed fresh yeast or (2¼ teaspoons) active dry yeast 2 teaspoons SAF-Instant yeast
1 packed tablespoon (0.75 ounce)	1 packed tablespoon + 1 packed teaspoon (1 ounce) thawed compressed fresh yeast frozen compressed yeast

These yeast equivalencies are approximate and work well. If you have a scale accurate for small amounts, you may want the more precise conversion:

1 package active dry yeast = 2¼ teaspoons = 0.25 ounce = 7 grams

1 package compressed fresh yeast = 0.6 ounce = 17 grams

SAF-Instant yeast: 1 tablespoon = 0.38 ounce/11 grams

By weight, if a recipe calls for dry or SAF-Instant yeast, $\times$ 2.42 is the amount of fresh needed.

By weight, if a recipe calls for fresh yeast, $\times$ 0.41 is the amount of dry yeast needed.

Using volume, you need 1.4 $\times$ the volume of packed fresh yeast to replace dry, 1.5 $\times$ the volume of packed fresh yeast to replace SAF-Instant.

Cornstarch, tapioca, and cassava have equal thickening power by weight but not by volume:

1 teaspoon tapioca = 3.5 grams; 1 teaspoon cornstarch = 3.16 grams; 1 teaspoon cassava = 2.6 grams

1 tablespoon tapioca = 10.5 grams; 1 tablespoon cornstarch = 9.5 grams; 1 tablespoon cassava = 8 grams

1 teaspoon cornstarch = 1¼ teaspoons cassava (tapioca powder) = scant 1 teaspoon tapioca

1 tablespoon cornstarch = 1 tablespoon + ¾ teaspoon cassava

1 teaspoon tapioca = 1⅜ teaspoon cassava

1 teaspoon tapioca = 1¼ teaspoons cornstarch

1 teaspoon cassava = ¾ teaspoon + ⅛ teaspoon cornstarch

EQUIPMENT

NOTE: *When distributors are exclusive or the item is hard to find, sources are listed. However, sources can change. Some places will special-order or direct you to the distributor if they no longer carry a given item.*

When it comes to pie and pastry making, very little equipment is needed. One could make a first-rate pie in a skillet or a free-form tart on a baking sheet with a wine bottle as a rolling pin as long as there was a decent oven, and, of course, a scale or measuring cups. But special equipment makes the pleasure of baking that much more joyful. My great-uncle Nathan George Horwit, designer of the Movado Museum watch, was an industrial designer. It was from him that I learned to appreciate the Bauhaus principle of form following function. There is little that excites me more than a tool that makes a job easier and the results more perfect. For me, a well-designed tool is a work of art and deserves to be on permanent display.

WEIGHING AND MEASURING

Of all the sweet things in life, few are as sweet as second chances. But when it comes to baking, you don't get any. When you bake a pie or tart, you cannot taste it partway through the baking process and decide what else to add. And if you measured the flour with cavalier indifference or a heavy hand, you cannot undo the effects of dryness and heavy texture. A cook must constantly taste, prod, evaluate, and adapt to the variation of ingredients. A baker, however, is working with ingredients such as flour, sugar, baking powder, water, and butter, which are far more consistent. The variance in baking results comes from the manner in which the baker measures the ingredients, even more than from the mixing technique. Using scales to weigh the ingredients totally eliminates this problem.

Any lover of baking ultimately will adore using a scale once past the fear of what sometimes, at first, is perceived as a laboratory object. Weighing ingredients is not only reassuring, it is much faster than measuring and results in far less cleanup. Consider how much easier it is to scoop cocoa or powdered sugar, with the inevitable lumps, into a bowl for weighing, rather than to try to measure out a level cup, lightly spooned. And I wouldn't dream of trying to pack brown sugar into a cup when I can weigh it in a flash. Also think how much more pleasant it is to weigh a greasy substance like vegetable shortening rather than to smear it into a measuring cup, or to weigh sticky corn syrup or honey. Scales that have the ability to eliminate (the professional term is *tare*) the weight of the bowl also make it possible for the baker to add dry ingredients to the mixing bowl one after the other, rather than having to use separate bowls for each. They can then all be mixed together, eliminating the need either to sift the flour or to sift the dry ingredients together.

Another benefit of weighing is the ease of cutting or multiplying a recipe. And once in a great while, I have completed a filling or dough and suddenly wondered if I remembered to add an ingredient. When in doubt, all I need to do is weigh the final unbaked product. If it is less than the total weight of the recipe ingredients, my suspicions are confirmed and I can add what I left out.

Pendulum scale

Of course, an inaccurate scale is worse than no scale at all. The old-fashioned beam-balance scale (the food goes on one pedestal and is balanced by weights set on the other one) is accurate but slower than pendulum or electronic scales. I avoid scales made with springs, as over time and with use they may rust or wear out and become less accurate. The best electronic scales can and should be calibrated regularly, using weights. Less expensive electronic models may not be as reliable. As an alternative to a good-quality electronic scale, I prefer a simple inexpensive pendulum scale, such as the Cuisinarts one retailing for about $35. It weighs only up to 10 ounces/300 grams and is accurate to plus or minus 2 grams.

Digital scale

The two electronic scales that I have worked with for several years and which I can swear by are the Mettler laboratory scale, Model #SB16001, retailing for about $2200; and the Edlund Model #E80, available through local food service equipment dealers for about $260. Both readily switch back and forth between ounces and grams. The Mettler's accuracy to within 0.2 gram is sufficient to weigh a teaspoon of baking powder and its range of 35 pounds/16,000 grams makes it possible to weigh ingredients in one bowl for a large wedding cake. The Edlund's capacity is only 5 pounds/2268 grams, with an accuracy of 0.1 ounce/1 gram.

If you have never baked by weight, borrow a scale and try it just once. I guarantee you will be an instant convert.

Measuring cups

*Heatproof
measuring cup*

Measuring spoons

MEASURING CUPS AND SPOONS   Foley stainless steel cups are the most attractive and among the most accurate (except for the 2-cup one, which measures slightly under). Tupperware's cups are also excellent and include practical ⅔-cup and ¾-cup sizes. Solid measures must have unbroken, smooth rims, making it possible to level off excess ingredients.

The most accurate and well-marked heatproof measuring cups I have found are made by Oven Basics, available in some supermarkets. When shopping for liquid measuring cups, look for ones that are level, not slanted. A cup of water, read below the meniscus (the curved upper surface), should weigh close to 8 ounces to be acceptable. In addition to measuring liquid, these cups are ideal for pouring hot sugar syrups and caramel. The handles remain cool to the touch and the spouts control the way the liquid pours. I use my 1-cup measures the most, but the 2-cup and 4-cup ones are often useful as well.

Foley stainless steel measuring spoons (not the oval ones) and Tupperware heavy-duty plastic are my favorites. I especially like the Tupperware spoons, because they include odd sizes such as ⅛ teaspoon, 4 teaspoons, and ½ tablespoon (1½ teaspoons). I have found other brands of measuring spoons to be somewhat smaller than these two types.

BRUSHES

LARGE SILK BRUSH   These large soft brushes, made in France, are unequaled for dusting excess flour from dough, such as puff pastry, without damaging the pastry (La Cuisine, page 675).

Large silk brush

PASTRY BRUSH OR FEATHERS   Natural or nylon bristles, or feathers, work well both for brushing off excess flour from doughs and for glazing them (gourmet stores and the King Arthur catalogue, page 675).

ARTIST'S BRUSH   A small number 9 artist's brush is the perfect implement for brushing glaze on small pieces of pastry such as leaves and other decorations (art supply stores).

Pastry brush

RULER   An 18-inch-long transparent ruler is the perfect ruler for cutting even strips of dough for lattice crusts and other decorative pastries (art supply stores).

Pastry feather

FLOUR WAND   I use this device whenever I roll dough. It is essentially a coiled oblong spring with a handle that, when expanded, picks up flour, and, when waved over the dough, dispenses the finest dusting of flour over it (King Arthur catalogue, page 675).

Flour wand

KNIVES AND CUTTERS

BENCH SCRAPER   Metal bench scrapers are excellent for cleaning counters without scratching. They're also great for gathering up dough, keeping the edges of the dough even, and cutting dough. Plastic scrapers are also useful for other purposes because of their flexibility, such as scraping a bowl or scooping up filling. My friend Corby Kummer of the *Atlantic Monthly* showed me an excellent use of the scraper: He scrapes the outside of the pastry bag from the top toward the bottom to move all the filling toward the tube.

PIZZA CUTTER   The heavy-duty variety, with a large 4-inch wheel, offers steady, even pressure for cutting dough and is ideal for cutting croissant, puff pastry, and danish dough (La Cuisine, page 675).

ADJUSTABLE PASTRY DIVIDER   This is essentially a series of cutting wheels attached to an expandable gate that can be set at specific intervals, making it possible to cut identical parallel strips of dough quickly (La Cuisine, page 675).

FOURTEEN-INCH SERRATED KNIFE   A serrated knife with a long blade is invaluable for cutting tarts and pastries. Albert Uster Imports (page 675) carries a knife of this variety called a "wavy-edge slicer."

TART KNIFE   My favorite pie and tart server is an antique George Jensen blossom-pattern one, because it is so exquisitely lovely. But most of the time, I use my Wüsthof thin-bladed triangular tart knife, because it is ideal for cutting as well as serving. For a pie, a thin, flexible pie server such as the "Ultra-Flex Spatula" is ideal because it can bend and angle between the pie pan and the crust (King Arthur catalogue, page 675).

Bench scraper

Pizza cutter

Adjustable pastry divider

14-inch serrated knife

Tart knife

Ultra-flex spatula   *Nonstick razor knife*   *Pastry jagger*   *Vol-au-vent cutters*

NONSTICK RAZOR KNIFE   This is a knife like none other. It is the prize in my collection of over a hundred knives. Coated with a nonstick substance, it has an incredible thin sharp blade with a series of holes and a horizontal indentation that causes the blade, when dipped first in water, to sail through custard-type fillings without sticking. It comes from Japan and is called the Ito Chef, MO-V Steel. It's available with a 5½-inch or 8-inch blade (Katagiri, page 675).

PASTRY JAGGER   This little cutting wheel, with a zigzag blade, is used to cut lattice strips with a decorative edge that looks as if it was cut with pinking shears.

VOL-AU-VENT CUTTERS   This nested set of curved metal plates with finger holes in the center is designed for cutting discs of dough to specific sizes (La Cuisine, page 675). Pot lids work perfectly well, but these specialized cutters are handier than searching out the perfect-size pot lid.

PASTRY BLENDER   This utensil, made up of several curved wires attached to a handle, is used to cut flour into butter when preparing pie dough by hand.

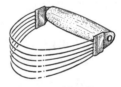

Pastry blender

ROSE LEAF CUTTER AND VEINER   For an illustration of a rose leaf cutter, see Designer Apple Pie (page 84). Of all the different leaf shapes, I find the rose leaf to be the most beautiful, so it is my usual choice for pastry cutouts. Using a special rose petal cutter with a vein imprint and a plunger to release the dough makes the task much speedier than shaping it free-form with a knife and then pressing it onto a veiner. Both the cutters (a set of varying sizes) and the veiner are available at New York Cake and Baking Distributors, page 675.

Pastry leaf veiner

GRATERS

ZESTER   A zester has a small metal head with a row of tiny rough holes in it. When scraped across a citrus fruit, it penetrates just deeply enough to remove the peel without removing the bitter pith beneath. For finely grated zest, first use the zester to remove the zest in strips, then use a chef's knife to chop it very fine. A vegetable peeler also works to remove the zest, but care must be taken so that it does not remove the pith as well. The strips of zest

Zester

can then be processed in a mini processor or placed in a food processor, along with some of the sugar in the recipe, and processed until fine. (The sugar keeps the zest from clumping and disperses it more evenly when added to the larger mixture.)

I prefer either of these methods to a box grater because the zest tends to get stuck between the grating holes. If using a box grater, a toothbrush reserved for this process works well to dislodge the zest.

"GREATER ZESTER" Cooking teacher and recipe developer Suzy O'Rourke has come up with the best tool of all for zesting citrus fruit. Its grating teeth are sharp and shallow, making it easy to remove the flavorful portion of the zest without touching the bitter pith beneath. She has also created a larger model with deeper grating holes that works so quickly and efficiently for grating chocolate and cheese, making such even, fluffy pieces, it makes grating a sensuous experience (Cooking by the Book, page 675).

"Greater zester"

Coconut grater

COCONUT GRATER Coconut, freshly grated, is the best it gets, but producing evenly grated coconut has always been tedious. A coconut grater from Williams-Sonoma (page 677) has a multibladed device with serrated teeth that fits into the hollow of a split coconut and, when turned by a crank, rapidly turns the coconut into a flurry of fine, perfectly grated flakes.

NUT GRATER If you don't use a food processor to grate nuts, a Mouli hand grater, which comes with three drums, works well, using the finest drum to grate nuts even and fine.

FOOD PROCESSORS

If I were asked to nominate the greatest unsung culinary hero who had the most influence or the way we cook, it would be Carl Sontheimer, who single-handedly introduced the food processor and made it possible to do a wide variety of kitchen tasks virtually without effort. One of the unrivaled uses of the food processor is the preparation of doughs. Cream puff pastry is easy beyond belief. Chocolate ganache, previously a tricky preparation, is child's play, and grating nuts or chopping chocolate is a joy.

Regrettably, Cuisinarts is no longer manufacturing the power strainer attachment to the super citrus juicer, which was the perfect device for puréeing raspberries, removing every last bit of fruit from the seeds without allowing the tiny seeds to pass through or crushing them in a way that released their bitterness. If you have one, treasure it. If you see one at a garage sale, keep your cool but be ready to pay whatever the asking price. It is worth its weight in gold. The only other device I know of that is fine enough to remove all the seeds from raspberries is the Pronto strainer from Villaware with optional berry screen (available through Fante, page 675), but the Cuisinarts model is all plastic and much easier to clean.

CUISINARTS MINI PROCESSOR   This smallest of all food processors is ideal for chopping small items that would otherwise elude the blades of larger models, such as ginger and citrus zest.

MIXERS

The KitchenAid K5M50P (5 quarts, 350-watt motor) and the Kenwood Major (7 quarts, 650-watt motor)* stand mixers are more a luxury than a necessity when it comes to pies and pastry. Everything in this book requiring a mixer can be accomplished with a good hand-held electric mixer. Even brioche dough can be made with a strong hand-held electric mixer, such as the Krups or Kitchen-Aid, which have dough hooks. Still, serious bakers will not want to be without a powerful stand mixer. It frees the hands for other tasks and for a baker becomes the heart of the kitchen.

Stand mixer with (from left to right) whisk, paddle, and dough hook attachments

For me, the KitchenAid is the symbol of baking. It is the mini version of the Hobart, found in commercial kitchens all over the world. But if I had to choose between one or the other, it's the Kenwood that would win for three reasons: its larger capacity; its conical-shaped bowl, allowing even small amounts to be beaten effectively; and its ability to tilt back, to make scraping the bowl easy.

Use the flat spade or paddle beater for general mixing and the whisk beater whenever the aim is to incorporate air into the mixture, such as for whipped cream and meringues.

If investing in a stand beater, it pays to buy an extra bowl and another set of beaters for the innumerable times egg whites need to be beaten after the rest of the ingredients have been mixed. As they require a spotlessly clean bowl and beaters, a second set comes in very handy. The K5 can handle up to 2 cups of egg whites (16 large whites), or any mixture that will not exceed 4 quarts in volume when beaten. The Kenwood can handle up to 2¾ cups of egg whites (22 large whites), or any mixture that will not exceed 6 quarts.

ICE CREAM MACHINES   The ultimate ice cream machine is one that has its own refrigerant and a fixed bowl. Though a removable bowl is convenient for cleaning, I don't recommend this model because it takes 30 to 40 minutes more for the ice cream to freeze. The Lussino model #4080 by Musser from Italy is my favorite of the fixed bowl type of machines. It is made of stainless steel and it is seamlessly constructed, making the bowl very easy to clean.

Fixed bowl electric ice cream maker

*The Kenwood is from England and in recent years has gone under the Rival name. A new distributor is presently in the works.

I also enjoy using the Donvier, a hand-crank machine with its own refrigerant, but it requires thorough chilling of at least 12 hours in a very cold freezer to work effectively.

OVENS   I use several ovens. The winner for even baking is my large electric Gaggenau oven, which can be used with and without convection. But even in this oven, the back bakes a little faster than the front. Only an oven with a turntable will bake totally evenly. No two ovens are alike, so get to know your own: how it bakes, where its hot spots are. In some ovens, where there are no coils at the bottom, it is possible to bake a pie or tart right on the floor of the oven, which results in a wonderfully crisp bottom crust.

Pastry basks in convection heat. It rises to its full advantage and is most evenly golden brown. Unlike cakes or soufflés, pies and tarts are very forgiving. They can be moved around during baking without harm. If the oven is uneven front to back, turn the pie partway through baking. If the top is not browning enough, raise it up higher toward the end.

Always preheat the oven at least 15 minutes ahead of baking; 20 minutes if the required baking temperature is 375°F. or higher.

BAKING STONE   This slab of quarry stone absorbs heat when preheated and helps to make the bottom crust evenly brown when a pie or tart is placed directly on it. I leave mine on the floor of the oven, as it seems to improve the evenness of all baking. I also cover it with foil to keep it from staining (King Arthur catalogue, page 675).

PIE PANS   Pie pans come in many different materials, all of which conduct and retain heat differently. I collect antique pie tins to decorate my country kitchen, but do not find the thin tin variety good for even baking. One of the treasures in my collection, however, is a rare tin-lined copper pie plate, which bakes very evenly, as does all heavyweight copper.

I prefer, in the following order: nonstick black steel, ceramic, Pyrex, and natural stoneware. Each has different advantages. A pie also bakes well in a cast-iron skillet. Avoid shiny pie pans, as they neither absorb nor retain heat well.

If making a pie to give as a gift, Pyrex pans can often be purchased for under $5, making it affordable to offer the pan with the pie. Alternatively, foil disposable pie pans can be used as liners. They are too thin and shiny to be used alone. E. Z. Foil, in packages of 6 deep pie pans 8¾ inches by 1½ inches deep, are just the right size for the standard pie.

Pyrex is great for enabling you to see the exact degree of browning. It can go from freezer to oven, but only if the oven is fully preheated, as a rising oven temperature may cause it to crack. Also, it cannot be set directly on a hot baking stone or oven floor if it has been in the freezer.

Wilton (page 676) carries an excellent 9-inch pie plate as part of its Excelle line. It is made of heavy-gauge dark steel with a double nonstick coating. As with any metal, it can go from freezer to hot baking stone without risk.

Mini pie pans have recently been produced in black steel (King Arthur catalogue).

I adore the Emile Henry ceramic pans, both mini and deep-dish. The fluted tops enable you to create a beautiful edge without effort. The surface releases perfectly for unmolding (Williams-Sonoma, page 676). They can go from freezer to oven—even directly to a preheated baking stone. Believe me; I've done it!

Superstone™, by Sassafras, makes a 9½-inch pie pan made of natural stoneware. Pies baked in this pan unmold perfectly, although the surface would not be damaged if the pie were cut in it. The natural stoneware draws some of the moisture from the pastry, thus producing a wonderfully golden crisp crust, except for the center section, which never gets as browned. The major drawback is that it cannot be taken from freezer to oven.

SIZES AND VOLUME   A 9-inch pie pan sometimes measures only 8½ inches across the inner edge of the top, so it is helpful to know the volume of the pan, should you need to adjust quantities.

> 9-inch Pyrex pie plate: 4 cups
> 9- by 2-inch Emile Henry ceramic pie plate: 6 cups
> 10-inch Pyrex pie plate: 6½ cups
> 9½-inch Pyrex deep-dish pie plate: 7 cups
> 4¼-inch mini pie pans: 14 tablespoons (7 fluid ounces)
> 4¼-inch deep-dish mini pie pans: 1½ cups
> 8- by 2-inch Pyrex square baking dish: 9 cups
> 9½-inch copper tarte Tatin pans: 5¼ cups
> 9- by 3-inch brioche pan: 8 cups

TART PANS

Two-piece removable-bottom tart pans are essential for ease in unmolding. The smallest two-piece tart pans at the present time are 4 inches in diameter.

As with pie pans, dark metal produces a better crust than shiny metal. My favorite fluted tart pans are produced by Gobel. They are dark metal and have an excellent nonstick surface that is slightly rough so that the pastry develops a nice texture. They also produce plain fluted tart pans that are shiny metal with a plain finish. The 2-inch-deep pans are not available in the dark nonstick finish. Gobel pans are carried by J. B. Prince (in large quantities only; page 675) and La Cuisine (page 675). (La Cuisine carries all sizes necessary for the wedding tart).

SIZES AND VOLUME   Tart pans are made in Europe, according to metric measure in centimeters. In converting to the inch measurement, I have rounded off to the nearest ½ inch. For ordering purposes, I also list the centimeter measurement where needed.

VOLUME OF ONE-PIECE TARTLET PANS

1-inch: 1 tablespoon
3- by ⅝-inch: 3½ tablespoons
3½- by ⅝-inch: 5 tablespoons

1-inch tartlet pans

VOLUME OF TWO-PIECE TART PANS
(WITH REMOVABLE BOTTOMS)

4- by ¾-inch: 6 tablespoons
4- by 1¼-inch: ¾ cup
4¾- by ¾-inch: ¾ cup
5½- by 1-inch: 1½ cups
7¾- by 1-inch: 3 cups
9½- by 1-inch: 4 cups
10- by 1-inch: 5½ cups
10- by 2-inch: 8 cups
11- by 1-inch: 7 cups
12½- by 1-inch: 9 cups

Gobel dark nonstick tart pans are currently available in the following sizes, measured in centimeters across the top: 12, 14, 20, 22, 24, 26, 28, 30, 32. Gobel plain metal two-piece fluted tart pans are available in the following sizes, measured across the top in centimeters (from 4 inches to 12½ inches in ¾-inch/ 2-centimeter increments): 10, 12, 14, 16, 18, 20, 22, 24, 26, 28, 30, 32. All are 2½-cm/1-inch deep except for the 10- and 12-cm ones, which are just under 2 cm/¾ inches deep. The 10-cm/4-inch tartlet pan is my favorite size for tartlets and is now available in two-piece.

Gobel also makes the extra-deep 4-cm/1½-inch tart pans in 15-cm/6-inch, 20-cm/8-inch, and 23-cm/9-inch sizes, and 5-cm/2-inch deep pans in 25-cm/almost 10-inch and 28-cm/11-inch sizes.

PIE CRUST SHIELD AND FOIL RINGS   Although it doesn't work for every size or shape of pie crust border, the Mrs. Anderson's Pie Crust Shield is a wonderful and inexpensive device to protect the edges of a pie from overbrowning. I do not advise placing it on the crust until after it has set, because if the dough is still soft, the shield will flatten the design slightly. This shield was invented by Georgette

Pie crust shield

Anderson of Portland, Oregon, who donated the design to the Challenge Center, a rehabilitation agency, which receives the proceeds from the sale (The Complete Kitchen, page 675).

I also designed a foil ring to use with pies or tarts when I was working on my first job in food, at Reynolds Metals Company, over thirty years ago. *To make your own foil ring:* Tear off a piece of heavy-duty foil a few inches larger than the diameter of the pie or tart pan. As a guide, use a pot lid or cardboard circle and a pencil to mark a cutout in the center that will expose the pie's top surface but not the decorative edge. With scissors, cut out the circle, leaving at least a 3-inch border, cut around the outside to form a ring. Shape it so that it will curve over the rim of the pie crust. This foil ring can be rinsed and reused several times. Disposable foil rings are also available in some specialty shops.

I do not recommend pie tape as an alternative to the metal or foil shield, as it presses against the crimped edge of the crust, flattening it slightly, and does not shield it well enough for pies that need to bake for more than 40 minutes.

FLAN RINGS, BAKING SHEETS, BLUE-STEEL PIZZA PANS, AND OTHER PANS
Flan rings come in many sizes and shapes. My favorites are the 8-cm (3-inch) flan ring and the heart-shaped flan rings. Round stainless steel flan rings come in sizes starting at 8 cm (3 inches) and increasing in 2-cm (¾-inch) increments up to 34 cm (13¼ inches). They are 2 cm (¾ inch) high.

EXPANDABLE FLAN RING   This black steel ring expands from 7 inches to 14 inches in diameter. I use it to cut perfect rounds of dough after rolling pie crust.

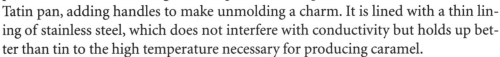

Expandable flan ring

TARTE TATIN PAN   The classic 9½-inch tarte Tatin pan is copper, lined with tin, for the most even caramelization of the apples. The only problem with this pan is that when the tart is unmolded, it is then very difficult to pry up the pan. Sur La Table has designed and produced the perfect Tatin pan, adding handles to make unmolding a charm. It is lined with a thin lining of stainless steel, which does not interfere with conductivity but holds up better than tin to the high temperature necessary for producing caramel.

BLUE-STEEL PIZZA PANS   These flat discs from France are the perfect pans for baking free-form tarts. I like the 9½-inch size for small tarts and the 12½-inch or 14-inch size for large ones (La Cuisine, page 675). With use, they become an attractive dark gray.

HALF-SIZE SHEET PAN OR BAKING SHEET   The 17- by 12-inch aluminum pan by Wearever has always been my favorite. It is sturdy enough not to torque or bend from the oven heat. Turned upside down, it can double as a cookie sheet (King Arthur). The AirBake insulated sheet is perfect for puff pastry that needs to bake longer than 30 minutes, as it keeps it from burning on the bottom. The largest size is 15½ inches by 20 inches, ideal for baking a long tart strip.

PAN LINERS   Reusable nonstick liners make cleanup easy. Food-service quality Silipat is not quite as nonstick as the Teflon-type liners available for home use, but it is a lot more durable. All the nonstick liners can be reused countless times.

PIE PAN OVEN GUARD   The 12-inch nonstick disc by Progressive International Corporation in Kent, Washington, designed to be placed under a pie pan to catch any spillovers, is the perfect answer to keep bubbling pie juices from sticking to the floor of the oven (King Arthur catalogue, page 675).

SAUCEPANS WITH NONSTICK COATING   Small and medium heavyweight saucepans with a nonstick lining, such as Anolon professional from the Meyer Corporation, or the more durable ceramic Titanium Scanpan 2001 professional nonstick cookware, from Denmark, is ideal for sugar syrups and reducing liquids because very little of the liquid sticks to the pan. Anolon pans are available at housewares stores. The Scanpan is available at Broadway Panhandler and through the Chef's Catalogue (page 675).

DECORATING AND PASTRY TUBES   Small tubes, referred to as decorating tubes, are used for small decorations. Larger tubes, referred to as pastry tubes, are used to pipe large festoons of whipped cream or pastry cream. For the recipes in this book, I have listed the numbers of the tubes and their diameters if they are not star tubes. The numbers apply to both Wilton and Ateco tubes, but tube numbers from other countries do not correspond to these, so it is best to check the diameters.

Wilton and Ateco produce nickel-coated pastry tubes, with welded, almost invisible, seams, that are sturdy enough to resist crushing (except underfoot). (Ateco also has a less expensive line in which the seams are visible, resulting in less precise piping). When tubes flatten and become deformed through much use, an inexpensive plastic tube corrector is all that is needed to put them back into shape.

Coupler

Plastic couplers make it possible to change tubes without emptying the pastry bag. French heavy-duty plastic tubes cannot be used with couplers but are absolutely impervious to distortion. (Stepping on one would hurt you more than it!)

I keep a separate set of tubes for working with meringue or royal icing, because even a trace of grease will break either of these down. Only hot water is needed to wash tubes encrusted with meringue or royal icing. Alternatively, the tubes can be well washed and soaked in a little vinegar to remove grease or detergent.

Reclosable freezer bag

PASTRY BAGS, PARCHMENT CONES, AND RECLOSABLE FREEZER BAGS   Pastry bags are useful not only for piping and decorating but also for filling small tart shells. Disposable plastic bags that can be cut to the desired size are available in all cake decorating supply stores and have all but replaced the traditional washable nylon bags. I also like to use reclosable quart-size and gallon-size freezer bags, because they are readily available and disposable. Because the top of the bag seals shut, the filling can't work its way out of the bag should your grip be too relaxed. Also, royal icing stays moist and pipable in the upper part of the bag, instead of drying and crumbling. Simply cut off a small piece from one corner of the bag and insert a tube (if you are using a large pastry tube) or a coupler first (if you are using a small decorating tube that would otherwise work its way back into the top part of the bag). Invert the bag over a blender container or large glass, fill the bag with the mixture, and close it securely.

TO MAKE A PARCHMENT CONE   For precise fine chocolate piping, nothing beats a parchment cone. It is preferable to using a plastic bag with a metal tube, because the chocolate often hardens in the tube. A parchment cone can also be used to pipe royal icing and, if made large enough, whipped cream, pastry cream, or other fillings.

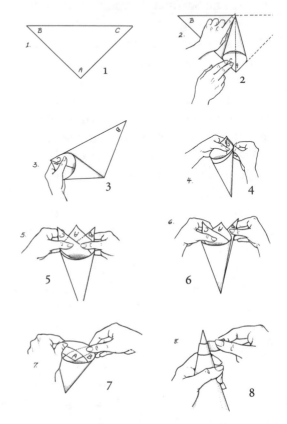

In these illustrations, the points of the triangle have been labeled A, B, and C. Place the triangle on a flat surface with A pointing toward you. (Figure 1) Curl C up and under, bringing it toward you until points A and C meet. The curled edge from C should lie on top of the edge between A and B. The parchment will curve more easily if you extend your right elbow while doing this. (Figure 2) Hold Points C and A together with your left hand while picking up B with your right. (Figure 3) Wrap B around to meet points A and C in the back, forming a cone. (Figure 4) Hold the bag with both hands, thumbs inside, and slide B and C in opposite directions to make a W formation. (Figure 5) Tugging point B slightly upward will help to form a sharp, closed point. (Figure 6)

Turn down the top and secure it with a staple. (Figure 7) Tape the outside seam of the bag. Use a small strip of tape near the point end. This will keep the cone from unfolding and the filling from coming out the side. (Figure 8)

If piping chocolate, cut off the tiniest amount possible from the tip. If piping icing, make an opening from the tube by clipping off ¾ inch from the tip. (Figure 9) Too large a hole will allow the tube to fall through; too small, and the parchment will cut off part of the tube's design. Make the cut slightly curved, so the opening will be round and icing will not creep out around the edges.

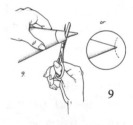

Drop the tube into the cone, narrow end first, and push it down firmly to make sure the tip is exposed. The weight of the filling will hold it securely in place.

To fill the cone, hold it near the bottom and use a long spatula to fill it with the piping mixture. (See Filling the Pastry Bag, pages 618–619.) Fill it half full, removing the filling from the spatula by pinching it between your thumb and fingers from the outside of the bag while withdrawing the spatula. Or, if using melted chocolate, simply pour it in.

Parchment cones must be closed tightly to keep the icing from escaping through the top. To close the cone, first smooth the top flat, using the side of your hand to force the icing toward the tip. Then fold in each side and roll down the top until it is close to the filling. Lock your thumb over the top with your remaining fingers curled around the side.

PASTRY CLOTH AND SLEEVE AND PLASTIC WRAP   A canvas pastry cloth and knitted cotton rolling pin sleeve are very helpful for rolling out dough while adding just the minimum amount of flour to prevent sticking. I don't use a pastry cloth with a hem when rolling the dough under ⅛ inch thick because the hemmed edge is thicker and raises the pin too high. Pastry cloths and sleeves are available at specialty stores such as Fante and from the King Arthur catalogue (page 675).

If rolling the dough between sheets of plastic wrap, I prefer the Saran brand of plastic wrap because it is very smooth and does not tend to get caught up in the dough. It is also ideal for wrapping things for storage because it is absolutely airtight.

MARBLE SLAB   No surface beats marble or granite for rolling out pie dough and pastry. Its coolness helps to keep the fat firm, which is essential to prevent it from being absorbed into the flour and thereby losing its flakiness or layering. On a very hot day, ice can be applied to a marble counter and then wiped dry. The marble will hold its coolness for a long while. An alternative and practical solution to a marble counter is to purchase a marble slab. Gourmet equipment stores often carry one that is 18 inches square, an excellent size for most pie crust and pastry. It is lightweight enough to lift easily and can be placed in the refrigerator to chill before using. Marble suppliers often have scraps that they will cut to size and finish for a reasonable price. Choose white or a light color that shows any dirt to make it easier to clean and prevent any foreign matter from ending up in the dough. Be careful not to allow citrus juice or alcohol to spill on the marble, as it will stain it and spoil the finish.

PIE BASKETS   The most beautiful, hand-woven maple pie baskets are made by Longaberger, in Ohio (page 675). They are woven double thickness for durability and are designed to be heirlooms. A pie presented in one of these baskets would make a memorable house gift. My favorite is the "small picnic" #11029, 12 inches by 12 inches by 6 inches.

NUTCRACKER   The "Perfect-a-Nut" Nutcracker is a unique Czech-designed nutcracker that easily cracks wal-

Nutcracker

nuts and pecans, leaving the nutmeat in whole pieces. It also functions as the ideal champagne opener.

CHERRY PITTER   I have tried many devices of varying prices and the one that works the best is the common old-fashioned metal hairpin! It ensures that every pit has been removed, as it is done one at a time, and it maintains the shape of the cherry. Purchase large sturdy hairpins. "Jumbo metal hairpins" are available through the Vermont Country Store (page 676). A great idea I learned when I worked at the famed chocolatier Bernachon, in Lyon, was to insert the ends of the hairpin into a cork. A champagne cork works especially well, as its rounded head fits right into the palm of your hand, making it more comfortable to use. Make the holes with a small awl or nail, insert the ends of the hairpin and press it in firmly.

POPPY SEED GRINDER   This adorable old-fashioned hand grinder looks like a miniature meat grinder. It is a luxury specialty item, but does it do the job! That is because it is designed expressly to grind poppy seeds uniformly into a fine fluff without risk of causing the oils to exude. If you are a lover of poppy seeds, this functional little item is a must (King Arthur catalogue and Miracle Exclusives, page 675).

Poppy seed grinder

PROPANE TORCH   Finally, fire for the pastry chef without making one feel like a welder on a construction site! The miniature torch from Williams-Sonoma (page 676) provides the professional way to caramelize crème brûlée, brown meringue, and heat the sides of tart pans for perfect unmolding.

Propane torch

PIE BIRDS   I have had one of these ceramic figurines for years and I have used it once. I'd rather collect them as decorations and, in fact, there are even pie bird collector clubs! The purpose of a pie bird is to create and maintain a fanciful opening in the upper crust of the pie for the steam and bubbling juices to vent. I find they are impractical, as they displace too much of the pie's filling, and slashing or cutting the dough will accomplish the same thing.

PRESENTATION PLATES   When I ordered a special acrylic tiered stand from the Van Horn–Hayward company in Texas (page 676), and told them my plan for it, they titled it the "Pie in the Sky" stand. The magic of this acrylic stand is that it all but disappears from sight, giving the tarts the illusion of floating in air. These stands can be custom-ordered in whatever size or shape one desires. The sizes needed for the Chocolate and Peanut Mousse Seven-Tier Holiday Tart (page 316) are: 4⅜ inches, 5 inches, 7⅜ inches, 8⅞ inches, 9¾ inches, 10½ inches, and

Seven-tier acrylic pie or tart stand

12⅛ inches. (This is the measurement of the bottom of each tart pan.) The spacers are 2¾ inches high.

RACKS   My favorite wire cooling racks are round wire racks from France. The wires are closer together than most, offering more support for smaller pastries.

Pie rack

ROLLING PINS   I have tried many rolling pins, including a hollow one designed to be filled with ice cubes to keep the pastry cold (it causes condensation on the outside of the pin) and a stainless steel one guaranteed not to stick to the dough (it sticks).

I collect rolling pins. Antique wooden ones, too warped to roll evenly, make wonderful wall decorations. One of my greatest prizes is a green bottle-glass rolling pin. But the rolling pin I reach for the most often is my solid white plastic pin from France. It is 1¾ inches in diameter and almost 20 inches long. The plastic makes it easy to wash without risk of warping (La Cuisine, page 675). I also enjoy using the *tutove* French rolling pin when rolling puff pastry (La Cuisine). Its ridges help to distribute the butter evenly throughout the dough.

ROLLING PIN SPACERS   One of my favorite and most used pastry gadgets is a simple clever device that slips onto a rolling pin and determines the exact thickness of the dough. Called Rolling Pin Rubber Rings, four pairs of rings slip onto each end of the pin, raising it from the counter a precise distance according to the thickness of the rings selected. The thickness of the dough is determined by the space between the pin and the counter.

Rolling pins

Available at specialty stores such as Fante and from the King Arthur catalogue (page 675).

SPATULAS AND STIRRING DEVICES   A small metal spatula with a narrow 4-inch blade and wooden handle is one of the most often used implements in my kitchen. It is perfect for leveling dry ingredients in measuring spoons and for dislodging crust from the sides of pans.

Small and large angled or offset spatulas are handy for spreading mixtures evenly in pans or for lifting small pastries.

Small spatula

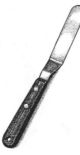

Offset spatula

High-heat spatula

I can't imagine doing without my array of small and large Rubbermaid spatulas. Nothing takes their place for scraping bowls, and they are also useful for folding together mixtures. As they retain odors, I have a separate set designated for baking. I adore the new high-heat spatulas for stirring hot mixtures up to 500°F. They are considerably thicker, so work less well for scraping and folding, but the handles stay cool to the touch and they can even be used for caramel. The white stirring blade makes it easy to see the color of the caramel (New York Cake and Baking Distributors and King Arthur catalogue, page 675).

PORCELAIN SPOONS   These spoons, made of French porcelain, are designed to be tasting spoons because they don't conduct heat and they don't absorb odors. These qualities also make them perfect for stirring hot liquids and for use in the microwave oven. I especially like to use porcelain spoons for making caramel. As with the high-heat spatulas, it's easier to see the true color of the caramel against the white of the porcelain (La Cuisine, page 675).

Porcelain spoon

SPUN SUGAR DEVICES   I have never seen a tool sold specifically for making angel hair. In France, pastry chefs make their own by cutting the loops of a whisk with wire cutters. I used to make one by bending the tines of a cake breaker, designed for cutting angel food cake, in opposing directions. More cumbersome, but also effective, are two forks held back to back.

WHISKS   I have whisks of all sizes and shapes, but there are only two I find indispensable: a balloon whisk, measuring 14¼ inches in circumference, for folding mixtures together with the least loss of air; and a small piano wire whisk, 10 inches long and 5 inches in circumference, which has at least 8 loops of fine wire that will reach into the corners of a saucepan, making it ideal both for preparing a smooth pastry cream and for evenly mixing together dry ingredients (La Cuisine, page 675).

STRAINERS   An extra-fine-mesh stainless steel strainer is indispensable for evenly dusting powdered sugar or cocoa onto pastries and for straining the solids from

Cut-off whisk

Balloon whisk

Piano wire whisk

clarified butter. Simply tap the side with a spoon or use
the spoon to press the powdered sugar or cocoa through
the fine openings. (A mesh tea caddy with a handle also
works well if only partially filled.)

THERMOMETERS

It is better not to use a thermometer at all than to use one
that is inaccurate and thereby gives false readings. Some
manufacturers state that a thermometer should be tested
in boiling water (212°F.), and if it is off, it should be
adjusted accordingly. The problem, however, is that at

*Extra-fine-mesh
strainer*

higher temperatures, the degree of inaccuracy will vary. It is for this reason that
several years ago I designed and started to produce Cordon Rose laboratory thermometers with one of the leading manufacturers in the industry, who produces
them to my specifications. There are now other good thermometers on the market, but when it comes to absolute accuracy and speed of response, nothing beats
the laboratory thermometers, which contain mercury and have an etched glass
stem with no metal touching it to throw off the reading.
When working with chocolate or a sugar syrup, a quick
response in a thermometer is imperative because the
temperature is continuing to rise even faster than the
thermometer may be capable of registering.

The Cordon Rose candy/deep fat thermometer has a
range of 20° to 500°F. in 2-degree increments. The
Cordon Rose chocolate thermometer has a range of 40°
to 130°F. in widely spaced 1-degree increments, accurate
to within 1 degree. They are both calibrated to standards
traceable to the National Bureau of Standards in
Washington, D.C.

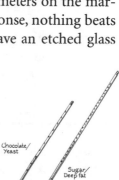

*Chocolate (left) and
candy (right)
thermometers*

My chocolate thermometer was favorably reviewed by a national magazine,
but in comparing it to another glass thermometer, they stated the "red mercury"
in the other thermometer made it easier to read. Mercury is a metal and is metallic
in color. It is never red. The red is dyed alcohol and is not reliable. These thermometers are available through Broadway Panhandler, J. B. Prince, La Cuisine,
and New York Cake and Baking Distributors (page 675).

HOW TO READ A MERCURY/GLASS THERMOMETER   Since many people hold a
thermometer with the left hand while stirring with the right, I designed the
Cordon Rose thermometers with two opposing scales so that they can be read left-
or right-handed.

A thermometer should be read at eye level, slanted slightly to one side. The
immersion level, indicated by an etched ring toward the base, is the point to which
it must be immersed to read most accurately. Thermometers should be immersed
up to this level when read, although one that is well made will still read with a fair

degree of accuracy despite the degree of immersion. If working with a small amount of liquid, tilt the pan slightly to increase the depth of the liquid when reading the thermometer. The highest accuracy of a thermometer is not at either extreme of its scale.

HOW TO CARE FOR A THERMOMETER   It is best to hang a thermometer out of harm's way, as rattling around in a drawer may cause mercury separation. This can also occur if the thermometer is handled roughly during shipping or if it is dropped. To reunite mercury into one solid column, all the mercury must either descend to its lowest point or rise to its highest. If the highest temperature is below the boiling point, this can be done by slowly immersing the bulb in boiling water and removing it as soon as the mercury is reunited. If the scale is higher, it must be returned to the manufacturer. Never place the bulb of the thermometer directly over an open flame.

To prevent breakage, avoid extremes in temperature. When removing the thermometer from a hot liquid, for example, do not place it on a cold drain board. Also, do not allow the thermometer to rest on a pan's bottom, because when it lies on its side, the uneven heat distribution could cause it to crack. Clips to attach thermometers to the side of a pan are prone to slipping, because they do not conform to a universal pan size or shape. I prefer to hold the thermometer, which is possible because glass does not significantly conduct heat.

PASTRY, BREAD, AND MEAT THERMOMETERS   Mercury glass thermometers are not practical for pastry, bread, or roasts, as it would be necessary first to make an indentation with a skewer. I find a high-quality probe thermometer more suited to the task. My favorite is the English battery-operated Thermapen 5F thermometer with a range of -50° to 550°F. (King Arthur catalogue, page 675).

Pastry, bread, and meat thermometer

OVEN THERMOMETERS   I use a laboratory cable thermometer from Omega (page 675), model #HH22. It is very expensive but far more accurate than any oven thermometer I have tested designed for home use, and it can be used for two ovens at the same time. It is important for an oven thermometer to be read without opening the oven, as the temperature would start to drop immediately.

Oven thermometer

The Polder Thermometer-Timer, designed with a probe and cable intended to be inserted in a roast, also works well to determine oven temperature (King Arthur catalogue, page 675).

For battery-operated thermometers, change the battery regularly. As the battery wears, accuracy decreases.

SOURCES

EQUIPMENT SOURCES

Many specialty-equipment stores have mail-order catalogues and will send them on request. *Note:* I have listed only long-established companies; however, over the years there may be changes, particularly in area codes and phone numbers. An asterisk (*) indicates that the store carries the Cordon Rose thermometers.

Albert Uster Imports, Inc.
9211 Gaither Road
Gaithersburg, MD 20877
(800) 231-8154

The Bridge Company
214 East 52nd Street
New York, NY 10022
(212) 688-4220

*The Broadway Panhandler
477 Broome Street
New York, NY 10013
(212) 966-3434

The Chef's Catalogue
P.O. Box 620048
Dallas, TX 75262
(800) 338-3232

The Complete Kitchen
118 Greenwich Avenue
Greenwich, CT 06830
(203) 869-8384

Cooking by the Book, Inc.
11 Worth Street
New York, NY 10013
(212) 966-9799

Dean & DeLuca
560 Broadway
New York, NY 10012
(800) 999-0306,
Monday–Friday, 9 A.M.–5 P.M.

Fante
1006 South Ninth Street
Philadelphia, PA 19147
(800) 878-5557

*J. B. Prince
36 East 31st Street, 11th floor
New York, N.Y 10016
(212) 683-3553
(food service quantity only)

Katagiri
224 East 59th Street
New York, NY 10022
(212) 755-3566

The King Arthur Flour Baker's
Catalogue
P.O. Box 876
Norwich, VT 05055-0876
(800) 827-6836

*La Cuisine
323 Cameron Street
Alexandria, VA 22314
(800) 521-1176

Lello Appliances Corporation
355 Murray Hill Parkway
East Rutherford, NJ 07073
(201) 939-2555
(call for distributors)

The Longaberger Company
One Market Square
1500 East Main Street
Newark, OH 43055
(740) 322-5163
(call for distributors)

Mettler Instrument
Corporation
350 West Wilson Bridge
Worthington, OH
(800) 786-0038

Miles Kimball
41 West 8th Avenue
Oshkosh, Wisconsin 54906
(800) 546-2255

Miracle Exclusives
64 Seaview Boulevard
Port Washington, NY 11050
(800) 645-6360

*New York Cake and Baking
Distributor
56 West 22nd Street
New York, NY 10010
(800) 942-2539

Omega
One Omega Drive
P.O. Box 4047
Stamford, CT 06907
(800) 826-6342

Scan Pan
49 Walnut Street
Norwood, NJ 07648
(201) 767-6252

Sur La Table
84 Pine Street
Seattle, Washington 98101
(800) 240-0853

Swissmar Imports, Inc.
35 East Beaver Creek Road
Richmond Hill, Ontario
L4B1B3, Canada
(800) 387-5707
(call for store in your area)

Van Horn-Hayward
P.O. Box 903
Bellaire, TX 77402
(713) 782-8532

The Vermont Country Store
Catalogue
P.O. Box 3000
Manchester Center, VT 05255
(802) 824-3184

Williams-Sonoma
Mail Order Department
P.O. Box 7456
San Francisco, CA 94120-7456
(800) 541-2233

Wilton Industries
2240 West 75 Street
Woodridge, IL 60517-0750
(800) 994-5866

INGREDIENT SOURCES

Many specialty-ingredient stores have mail-order catalogues and will send them on request.
Note: I have listed only long-established companies; however, over the years there may be changes,
particularly in area codes and phone numbers.

Alberto-Culver Company
2525 Armitage Avenue
Melrose Park, IL 60160
(800) 333-0005

American Spoon Food
P.O. Box 566
Petoskey, MI 49770
(800) 220-5886

Balducci's Mail Order Division
42-25 12th Street
Long Island City, NY 11101
(212) 225-3822

Cherry Marketing Institute
P.O. Box 30285
Lansing, MI 48909
(517) 669-4264

The Cherry Stop Retail Store
Orchards' Harvest
P.O. Box 4446
Traverse City, MI 49685
(800) 286-7209

Columbia Empire Farms
Seedless Preserves
P.O. Box 1
Dundee, OR 97115
(503) 554-9060

Dean & DeLuca
560 Broadway
New York, NY 10012
(800) 999-0306,
Monday–Friday, 9 A.M.–5 P.M.

Dillman Farms
4955 West State Road 45
Bloomington, IN 47403
(800) 359-1362

Dufour Pastry Kitchens
25 Ninth Avenue
New York, NY 10014
(212) 929-2800

Eggology
2899 Agoura Road
Suite 600
Westlake Village, CA 91361
(888) 669-6557

Fillo Factory
P.O. Box 155
Dumont, NJ 07628
(800) OKFILLO

Freida's Inc.
P.O. Box 58488
Los Angeles, CA 90058
(800) 241-1771

Friske Orchards
11027 Doctor Road
Charleboix, MI 49720
(888) 588-6185

Harrington's
Main Street
Richmond, VT 05477
(802) 434-4444

Hazy Grove Nuts
P.O. Box 25753
Portland, OR 97298
(503) 244-0593

Hellas International
35 Congress Street
Salem, MA 01970
(800) 274-1233

India Tree
4240 Gilman Place West #B
Seattle, WA 98199
(877) 665-5641
(call for distributors in your
area)

Keenan Farm
P.O. Box 299
Avenal, CA 93204
(209) 386-9516

The King Arthur Flour Baker's
Catalogue
P.O. Box 876
Norwich, VT 05055-0876
(800) 827-6836

Kojel Food Co.
137 Gardner Avenue
Brooklyn, NY 11237
(718) 821-5330

La Cuisine
323 Cameron Street
Alexandria, VA 22314
(800) 521-1176

Maison Glass Delicacies
725 Valley Brook Avenue
Lindhurst, NJ
(800) 822-5564

Master Chef (More Than
Gourmet)
115 West Bartges Street
Akron, OH 44311
(800) 860-9385

Mauna Loa Macadamia Nut
Corp.
Dept. G
H.C.01, Box 3
Hilo, Hawaii 96720
(808) 966-8612

New York Cake and Baking
Distributor
56 West 22nd Street
New York, NY 10010
(808) 942-2539

Nielsen-Massey Vanillas
1550 Shields Drive
Waukegan, IL 60085
(800) 525-7873

Penzeys, Ltd.
P.O. Box 933
Muskego, WI 53150
(414) 679-7207

San Saba
P.O. Box 906
San Saba, TX 76877
(800) 621-8121

Simpson and Vail
3 Quarry Road
Brookfield, CT 06804
(800) 282-8327

Sultan's Delight
P.O. Box 090302
Brooklyn, NY 11209
(800) 825-5046

Sunnyland Farms
P.O. Box 8200
Albany, GA 31706
(800) 999-2488

Taam-Tov Food, Inc.
188 28th Street
Brooklyn, NY 11232
(718) 788-8880

Williams-Sonoma
Mail Order Department
P.O. Box 7456
San Francisco, CA 94120-7456
(800) 541-2233

The Yorkville Packing House,
Inc.
1560 Second Avenue
New York, NY 10028
(212) 628-5147

FOOD SERVICE (MOSTLY LARGE-QUANTITY PURCHASE)

Albert Uster
(help line)
Susan Notter, corporate chef;
Andreas Galliker, executive chef
(800) 231-8154

Ambassador Fine Foods
(800) 272-8694

Gourmand
2869 Towerview Road
Herndon, VA 20171
(800) 627-7272

Harry Wils
182 Duane Street
New York, NY 10013
(212) 517-5370
(only to the trade)

Patisfrance
161 East Union Avenue
East Ruthford, NJ 07073
(800) PASTRY-1

Voilà
65 Porter Avenue
Brooklyn, NY 11237
(718) 366-1100

The White Lily Foods Company
P.O. Box 871
Knoxville, TN 37901
(800) 264-5459

ACKNOWLEDGMENTS

This book is a reflection of and belongs very much also to my treasured friend and associate David Shamah, whose heart and spirit is in so many recipes. Since *The Cake Bible,* ten years ago, he has opened his own restaurant, Back to Nature, in Brooklyn. He has adapted many of my recipes for restaurant quantity and production and I am very proud to see them on his menu. Despite the major full-time concerns of running a restaurant, he has stayed ever involved with my project, always insistent and uncompromising in his expectations and encouraging me to pursue and perfect concepts he encounters and admires. His taste has been utterly reliable and he rejoices and cares about every breakthrough and discovery as much as I do. It is thanks to him that these years of work have not been accomplished in solitude.

I also wish to acknowledge the devoted production team of this book: Susan Moldow, publisher; Roz Lippel, associate publisher; Beth Wareham, publicist extraordinaire; Matthew Thornton (Maria Guarnaschelli's assistant), who makes everything run smoothly; copy editor, fellow baker, and author Judith Sutton, whose suggestions were thoughtful and creative; senior copy editor M. C. Hald, whose eyes I trust more than my own, and her lovely assistants Jennifer Lynes and Laura Wise; Olga Leonardo, production director supreme; designer Barbara Bachman, whose talent proves that design is everything; art director John Fontana, who gave me the cover of my dreams; artist Laura Hartman Maestro, whose exquisite line drawings grace these pages; photographer Jerry Ruotolo, who provided Laura with the photos of me making strudel and the back cover photo; photographers Gentl & Hyers, artists and wonderful collaborators; stylist Roscoe Betsill, who performed miracles, and his assistants Jee Levin, Margarette Adams, Peter Occolowitz, and Michael Pederson; prop stylist Helen Crowther, whose sure and subtle touch completed the picture; and Paul Dippolito, text compositor, for his ingenuity. I am also grateful to my friends food writer Lee White and Chef Randy Eastman for cheerfully testing a sampling of the recipes.

The subject of pastry is a vast one, requiring extensive research. I am indebted to my many talented colleagues and friends for their contributions, influence, and encouragement: Marcia Adams, Stephen Schmidt, and Elizabeth Schneider (pumpkin pie); Jeanne Bauer (light custard rhubarb pie); Nancy Blitzer (plum flame tart); Chef Mark Bauer (temperature of baked pastry); Chef Wayne Brachman (nectarine pie); Shirley O. Corriher (escargot puffs); Chef Jim Dodge (banana cream pie); Nathalie Dupree (key limes versus Persian); Ray Farnsworth (steak and kidney pie); Keryl Fillers (angel biscuits); Helen Fletcher (Danish braid); Jane Freiman (apricot cheese tart, chocolate pecan blasts); Lynda Foster Gomé (designer apple pie decor); Chef Patti Jackson (currant scones); Mel and Sheryl London (pistachio baklava); Eleanor Lynch (frozen lime pie); Nicholas Malgieri (baking powder in pie crusts); Mark Moody (empanadas); Chef Stacie Pierce (panna cotta and Marionberry filling); Liz and Joe Reilly (fresh red currants); Chef Dieter Schorner (Danish snails); Chef Matthew Scully (bisteeya); Anita and Wayne South (wild Concord grapes); and to my friends and colleagues in Austria, Denmark, France, Germany, Hungary, and Switzerland.

There are a few special friends who also made valuable and unique contributions: Mark Kohut, who took a leap of faith ten years ago and helped put *The Cake Bible* on the culinary map; my lawyer, the late Arthur Ginsburg, who provided me with artistic freedom, and his associate Maura Wogan, who negotiated my contract, even testing two recipes in the process; Barbara Darnell, who generously volunteered her skills as scanner and typist; George Benson, who provided me with late-in-the-season persimmons, Fed-Ex'd from California; Angelica Pulvirenti and Guy Hirshout, who tasted and evaluated countless pastries; John Guarnaschelli, who, when called upon, unfailingly came through both cheerfully and brilliantly with the perfect turn of phrase; Soyoung Lee, Bachelor of Fine Arts student in the Textile/Surface Design Department of the Fashion Institute of Technology, under Zsuzsu Dalquist, who designed the apron I am wearing in the jacket photo; L. S. Colby, who provided continuous support over the years to keep me and my computer going; and the graceful and friendly Kempell typeface.

INDEX

When a recipe has more than one reference, the page number in **boldface** refers to the recipe itself; other page numbers refer to those recipes in which the main recipe is used.

~A~

agar-agar, 640
alligator, the, 507–9
all-purpose flour, 4, 5, 7, 8, 411, 633, 634
almond(s), 641
  cookie tart crust, sweet, **59–60**, 149–51, 157–60, 266–67
  cream filling (remonce), 485, 493–99, 502–6, **510–11**
    honey pecan, 507–9
  in gâteau Basque, 294–96
  hazelnut paste, in chocolate indulgence tartlets, 309
  ice cream tartlets, burnt, 230–31
  in Linzertorte, 283
  in Moroccan bisteeya triangles, 382–84
  paste, 642
  pastry cream:
    apricot tartlets with, 429–31
    blueberry or champagne grape tartlets with, 433
    pear tart with, 260–62
    in pears wrapped in fillo, 372–74
    red currant tartlets with, 431–33
  in Twelfth Night galette (galette des rois), 446–50
  in two miniature golden apple galettes, 434–36
angel butter biscuits, **355–57**
  ginger, 357
  in strawberry shortcake (with variations), 358–59
angel's hair (caramel for spun sugar), 602–3
appetizers:
  cheese straws, 463–64
  creamy and spicy crab tartlets, 343–44
  escargot puffs, 547–48
  Moroccan bisteeya triangles, 382–84
  spanakopita triangles, 380–81

appetizers (cont.)
  spring windfall morel quiche, 344–47
apple(s), 635
  dumplings, **141–43**, 641
  fruit pies, 74–77
    amount of cornstarch and sugar in, 76, 77
    best all-American, 79, **81–83**
    brandied raisin, 83
    crumb, 86–88
    crumb, crustless, 89–90
    open-faced designer, 84–86
    rosy cranberry, 91–93
  galettes, two miniature golden, 434–36
  pie, Gascon, **370–71**, 380
  strudel, 394–96
  streusel, 397–98
  tarts:
    galette, 278–80
    Tatin, 281–83
    with walnut cream, 263–65
    weincreme chiffon, 166–69
  turnovers, 134–37
apricot(s), 638
  Danish slips, 500–501
  dried, 639
  fruit pies, 76, 77
    open-faced, 120–21
  glaze, to moisture-proof the baked bottom crust, 20
  in honeycomb chiffon pie, 170–73
  lekvar, 138–40, 496, 500–501, 512
  poached, 208–09, **587–89**
  puff pastry:
    strip, 424–26
    tartlets with almond cream, 429–31
  tarts:
    cheesecake, 208–9
    weincreme chiffon, 166–69
  triangles, 496
Apricoture, 20, 638

Armagnac, in Gascon apple pie, 370–71
arrowroot, 650–51, 651–52
  glaze, 611, 612, 650, 652
artist's brushes, 658
Asiago cheese straws, 463–64
aurora blood orange tart, 177, **189–90**
Austrian buchteln, 522–24

~B~

bacon:
  and cabbage strudel, 408–10
  in quiche Lorraine, 337–38
Baker's Joy, 50, 252, 253, 624
baking, 65, 80, 366, 392, 414
  of flaky pie crust, 17–21
  of sweet cookie tart crust, 54–56, 252–54
  times, 19, 251–54
baking powder, 6, 8, 18, 350, 624–25
baking sheets, 413, 666
baking soda, 5, 350, 625
baking stores, 17, 663
baklava, pistachio, 367–69
balloons, Danish, 496
banana:
  cream pie, banner, 201–2
  split pie, 221, **223–26**
basic flaky pie crust, **22–26**, 350, 634
  buttermilk, **25**, 197–98
  in custard pies, 198–200, 201–2
  in fruit pies and turnovers, 102–11, 115–17, 120–21, 127–31, 134–38
  herb, 25
  in meringue pies and tarts, 178–81, 185–87, 189–93
  sour cream, 24–25
  sweet cream, **25**, 201–5, 276–78
  in tarts, 256–65, 281–83
  whole wheat, **24**, 333–36, 343–44
  yogurt, **25**, 187–89
Baumé scale, 648, 649

Bavarian filling, chiffon filling
    compared with, 144
beans, dried, as pie weights,
    18–19, 54, 251
bear claws (or cockscombs),
    497–99
beef:
    in baked empanadas,
        333–36
    in meat loaf in a flaky ched-
        dar crust, 331–33
    in steak and kidney potpies,
        326–28
    suet pie crust, flaky, **43–44,**
        326–28
    Wellington, 471–76
beeswax, 625
bench scrapers, 659
berry(ies), 635–36
    tart, fresh, 255–56
    see also specific berries
best all-American apple pie, 79,
    81–83
biscuits, 350–59
    butter, 351, **353–55,** 358–59
        angel, **355–57,** 358–59
        ginger, 354
    in strawberry shortcake,
        358–59
    touch-of-grace, 351–53
    see also scones
bisou, the, 177, **193–95**
bisteeya:
    larger (for a first course),
        384
    triangles, Moroccan, 382–84
bittersweet chocolate (semi-
    sweet chocolate), 626–27,
    628
    in the Boulders tart, 299–302
    in brownie puddle, 297–99
    in burnt almond ice cream
        tartlets, 230–31
    butter filling, in Danish
        braid, 490–93
    cookie tart crust *(pâte
        sucrée au chocolat)*
        50, **61–63,** 230–31, 252,
        254, 299–302, 314–16
        walnut, **62,** 311–13
    crème brûlée tartlets, 440–42
    croissants *(pain au chocolat),*
        483–84
    drizzle glaze, 453–55
    extra, 626–27, 628
    galettes, individual Twelfth
        Night, 450–52
    in hot fudge sauce, 596
    in light whipped ganache,
        559–60

bittersweet chocolate *(cont.)*
    mousse:
        eggless, Napoleons with, 460
        Napoleon, 453, **457–60**
    pastry cream, 562
    -speckled meringue, 576
    tartlets:
        dependence, 309–10
        flame, 310
        indulgence, 309
        oblivion, 308–10
        pecan blasts, 313–16
        soufflé, molten, 311–13
blackberry:
    pie, 14, 76, 77, 79, **115–17**
    turnovers, 136–37
Black Forest chiffon pie,
    173–76
blind baking, *see* prebaking
blueberry(ies), 635, 639
    fruit pies, 76, 77, **106–7**
        Internet deep-dish cran-
            berry/, 109–11
        open-faced fresh, 14, 73, 104,
            107–9
    tartlets with almond cream,
        433
    tart with lemon curd, 258–60
    turnovers, 136–37
borders:
    pie and tart, shaping of, 13
    piped, 620–21
bottom crusts:
    adding texture to, 9, 78
    baked, moisture-proofing of,
        20–21, 56
    fitting of, 12
    soggy, prevention of, 17–18, 78
    underbaking of, 21
bouchées, 412
    baking of, 415–16
    making of, 415
Boulders tart, the, 299–302
bourbon:
    butterscotch caramel sauce,
        223–26, 313–16, **598**
    whipped cream, 302–6, **551**
brandied:
    cherries, 173–76, 457–60, **594**
    mincemeat ice cream pie,
        228–29, 641
    raisin apple pie, 83
    raisins, 502–4, **514**
bread flour, 8, 386, 411
bread thermometers, 674
Brie fillo flowers, savory, 379
brioche, 515–27
    about, 362, 363, 515
    Austrian buchteln, 522–24
    master recipe for, 516–19

brioche *(cont.)*
    in snail buns, 525–27
    sticky buns, 519–21
brownie puddle (with caramel
    variation), 297–99
brusel, in strudel filling, 388–89
brushes, 658–59
buchteln, Austrian, 522–24
buns, sticky, 519–21
burnt almond ice cream tartlets,
    230–31
burnt orange caramel sauce, 598
butter, 629–30
    biscuits, 351, **353–55,** 358–59
        angel, **355–57,** 358–59
        ginger, 354
    clarified, 364, 366, 629–30
    filling, chocolate, in Danish
        braid, 490–93
    in flaky pie crust, 4, 5
    garlic, in snail buns, 525–27
    making of, 629
    in puff pastry, 411–12
buttermilk, 5, 350, 630
    chess pie, 197–98
    flaky pie crust, **25,** 197–98
    ice cream, 222, **233–35**
butterscotch:
    bourbon caramel, 223–26,
        313–16, **598**
    pastry cream, 561

~C~
cabbage and bacon strudel,
    408–10
cake flour, 4, 5, 7, 8
calcium acid phosphate, 6, 8,
    624
Camembert fillo flowers, savory,
    379
caramel(ized), 538–42, 649
    in the Boulders tart, 299–302
    brownie puddle, 299
    in crème brûlée tartlets,
        440–42
    for dipping, 600–601
    ice cream, **243–45,** 434–36
    onion tart, 338–40
        with custard, 340
    pastry cream, 562
    sauce, 434–36, **597–99**
        bourbon butterscotch,
            223–26, 313–16, **598**
        burnt orange, 598
        clear, 377–79, **599–600**
        ruby port, 598
    for spun sugar (angel's hair),
        602–3
    upside-down tarts (three
        Tatins), 280

caramel(ized) *(cont.)*
  apple, 281–83
  peach, 280, **283**
  pear, 280, **283**
  /walnut filling, in gâteau
      Engadine, 291–93
  whipped cream, 555–56
cassava, 650, 651, 652
  glaze, 611, 612, 652
Chambord, 222, 246–48, 358
Cheddar cheese, 631
  pie crust, flaky, **39–41**, 331–36,
      341–42
  puffs, spicy *(gougères)* 544–46
cheese:
  straws, 463–64
  see also Cheddar cheese;
      cream cheese; Gruyère
      cheese; mascarpone;
      Monterey Jack pepper
      cheese; mozzarella
      cheese; Muenster cheese
cheesecake tarts:
  apricot, 208–9
  Tahitian vanilla, 205–7
Chef Arthur Oberholzer's
      meringue pastry cream,
      561
cherry(ies):
  in Black Forest chiffon pie,
      173–76
  brandied, 173–76, 457–60
    Burgundy, 594
  cheese strudel, 399–401
    Fruit Perfect, 401
  dried, in walnut crostata,
      288–91
  in fruit pies, 76, 77, 79
    designer, 14, **95–96**
    Fruit Perfect, 95
    lattice, 93–97
    rhubarb lattice, 100–102
  pielets, 96
  pitters, 670
  turnovers, 136–37
Chiboust cream, 538–42, **565–67**
  and strawberry Napoleon,
      453, **455–56**
chicken:
  in Moroccan bisteeya trian-
      gles, 382–84
  potpies, deep-dish, 14, **323–26**
  stock, 653
chiffon pies, 144 76
  Black Forest, 173–76
  cranberry, 152–54
  frozen lime, 161–62
  honeycomb, 170–73
  lemon angel, 157–60
  pumpkin, 155–57

chiffon pies *(cont.)*
  raspberry, 149–51
  strawberry lover's, 146–48
  success pointers for, 144–45
chiffon tarts:
  apple weincreme, 166–69
  apricot weincreme, 169
  gingery pear, 162–65
chocolate, 625–28
  average mass and cocoa but-
      ter content of, 628
  in the bisou, 193–95
  chip whipped cream, 554–55
  compound, 615, 627–28
  cookie tart dough:
    baking, 252, 254
    testing for doneness, 54, 55
    see also bittersweet choco-
        late, cookie tart crust
  couverture, 627, 628
  cream pie, 202–5
  crumb crust, nut, 68–69
  curls, 202–5, 212–15, 299–301,
      617
    white, 201–2
  flurries, 616–17
  glaze, 20–21, 56, 536–38
  leaves, 617–18
  and peanut butter mousse
      tart, 63, **316–18**
  seven-tier, **318–21**, 670–71
  pies:
    cream, 202–5
    Grand Canyon, 190–93
    pecan (baked in a tart pan),
        304–6
  pure, 626
  sauce, 536–38
    hot fudge, 223–26, **596**
  storing of, 628
  techniques for, 613–18
    decorative, 616–18
    grating, 615
    melting, 613, 614
    tempering, 613, 615–16
  wafer crumb crust, **67–68**,
      228–29
    in chiffon pies, 146–48,
        152–54, 173–76
    deluxe, 65, **70–72**, 173–76
    in Grand Canyon pie,
        190–93
  see also bittersweet chocolate;
      ganache; milk chocolate;
      white chocolate
Christmas cranberry galette,
      286–87
cinnamon, 628
classic puff pastry, 411, **417–20**,
      426–29, 453–55, 538–42

Cobasan, 276–77, 550, 644
  in custard pies, 201–5
  in ice cream, 222–26, 233–42,
      245–46, 248–49
cockscombs (or bear claws),
      497–99
cocoa, 626, 628
  in brownie puddle, 297–99
  in light chocolate sponge
      cake layers, 585–87
  meringue, 177, 190–95,
      576
  whipped cream, 551
coconut, 643
  cookie tart crust, sweet, 50,
      57, **58**, 226–28, 272–74
  freshly grated, 226–28,
      591
  graters, 661
  ice cream pie (with crème
      fraîche variation), 49,
      226–28
coffee:
  custard sauce *(crème anglaise
      au café)*, 607–8
  ice cream, in burnt almond
      ice cream tartlets, 230–31
  pastry cream, 562
coffee filters, for prebaking,
      18–19, 54
Cognac, in Gascon apple pie,
      370–71
Concord grape pie, 76, 77, 79,
      127–29
convection ovens, 18, 663
cookie crumbs:
  for pie bottoms, 17
  standard sizes and weights
      for, 66
  see also crumb pie crusts
cookies, flaky pastry scraps,
      47–48
cooling procedures, 78, 80,
      254
cornstarch, 650–51
  in fruit pies, 20, 76, 77, 78,
      651
  glaze, 611, 612, 652
corn syrup, 646–47
Côte-Rôtie, in red wine ice
      cream, 248–49
coulibiac, 464–71
couscous and egg filling, in
      coulibiac, 464–71
crab tartlets, creamy and spicy,
      343–44
cranberry(ies), 636
  chiffon pie, 152–54
  in Christmas galette,
      286–87

cranberry(ies) *(cont.)*
  dried:
    in apple streusel strudel,
      397–99
    scones, 361
    walnut crostata, 288–91
  fruit pies, 76, 77
    Internet deep-dish blue-
      berry/, 109–11
    rosy apple, 91–93
    window, 129–31
cream:
  in egg glaze, 21
  fat in, 5, 48
  heavy, 630
  in ice cream, about, 222
  light, 630
  and peaches tart, 266–67
  piped decorations, 618–22
  in sweet cookie tart crust, 48
  see also pastry cream;
    whipped cream
cream cheese, 631
  cherry strudel, 399–401
  filling:
    fluffy, 401
    honey-stung, 504–6, **511**
  Fruit Perfect cherry, 401
  in open-faced double straw-
    berry pie, 104–6
  pie crust, flaky, *see* flaky pie
    crust, cream cheese
  in un-rugelach mini
    turnovers, 138–40
cream of tartar, 628
cream puff pastry *(pâte à
    choux)*, 528–48
  about, 528–29
  classic, **530–33**, 538–42
  Cordon Rose, 530, 534–36
  in gâteau St.-Honoré, 412,
    528, 530, 534, 538–42
  see also éclairs; profiteroles
cream puffs, **536–38**
  escargot, 547–48
  filling of, 532, 536, 543
  savory, **543–47**, 547–48
  shaping of, 531, 535
  spicy cheese, 544–47
  white truffle oil, 544, 547–48
crème anglaise (vanilla custard
    sauce), 372–74, 522–24,
    606–7
  au café (coffee custard sauce),
    607–8
  aux pistaches (pistachio cus-
    tard sauce), 457–60,
    610–11
  pralinée (praline custard
    sauce), 609

crème brûlée tartlets, 440–42
  chocolate, 442
crème fraîche, 141–43, 302–6,
    311–13, 358–59, **558**
  in apple Tatin, 281–82
  in custard pies and tarts,
    205–9, 217–220
  in ice cream pies and ice
    cream, 226–28, 232–33,
    241–42, 248–49
  in savory tarts, pies, and
    quiche, 322, 328–31,
    337–38
  in strudel, 394–96, 404–7
crème pâtissière, see pastry
    cream
crêpes, dill, in coulibiac, 464–71
croissants, 477–84, 633
  about, 362, 363
  chocolate *(pain au chocolat)*,
    483–84
  whole wheat, 477–83
crostata, dried cranberry (or
    cherry) walnut, 288–91
crumb pie crusts, 65–72, 632
  additions to, 65
  baked vs. unbaked, 65
  chocolate, 68
  chocolate nut, 68–69
  for 5-inch pielets, 66
  gingersnap, 67–68
  gingersnap nut, 68–69
  graham cracker, 65, **66**,
    178–84
  graham cracker nut, **67**,
    161–62
  nonchocolate, baking of, 65
  pan preparation for, 65
  standard cookie sizes and
    weights for, 66
  vanilla, *see* vanilla, nut crumb
    crust; vanilla, wafer
    crumb crust
crustless apple crumb pie,
    89–90
crustless peach ginger pie,
    126–27
crusts, 1–72
  commercial, 4, 65, 632
  walnut crostata, 288–90
  see also bottom crusts; crumb
    pie crusts; flaky pie crust;
    sweet cookie tart crust;
    top crusts
crystallized flowers and leaves,
    622–23
Cuisinarts, 661–62
  mini processor, 662
curd cream filling and topping,
    571–72

curls, chocolate, 202–5, 212–15,
    299–302, **617**
  white, 201–2
currant(s):
  in Paris Ritz pastry crisp,
    436–39
  scones, 359–61
  turnovers, 136–37
  see also red currant
custard:
  filling, in crème brûlée
    tartlets, 440–42
  pies, 196–208
    banner banana cream,
      201–2
    buttermilk chess, 197–98
    chocolate cream, 202–5
    cookie crumbs for bottom
      of, 17
    great pumpkin, 17, **198–200**
    persimmon, 217–220
    with rhubarb, 99
    rhubarb, light, 99
    shoofly, 215–17
    storing of, 21
  royale, milk rum strudel
    with, 404–7
  sauce, 606–11
    coffee *(crème anglaise
      au café)*, 607–8
    pistachio *(crème anglaise
      aux pistaches)*, 457–60,
      610–11
    praline *(crème anglaise
      pralinée)*, 609
    vanilla *(crème anglaise)*,
      372–74, 522–24, **606–7**
  tarts, 196, 205–15
    apricot cheesecake,
      208–9
    fig, with mascarpone
      cream, 210–12
    Tahitian vanilla cheesecake,
      205–7
    tiramisú black bottom,
      212–15
cutters and knives, 659–60

~D~

Danish pastry, 485–514, 633
  about, 362, 363, 485
  the alligator, 507–9
  bear claws (or cockscombs),
    497–99
  braid, 490–93
  dough, authentic
    (master recipe),
    486–90
  envelopes *(spandau)*, 493–97
  balloons, 496

Danish pastry *(cont.)*
   prune or apricot triangles,
      496
   triangle twists, 495–96
   filling for, *see* fillings, Danish
      pastry
   slips, apricot, 500–501
   snail buns, 502–4
   sugar glaze for, 493–97, 504–9,
      509–10
   twists, 504–6
      mini, 506
   waffle creams, 443–46
decorating and pastry tubes, 667
decorative techniques, decora-
      tions:
   for chocolate, 616–18
   cutouts, 14, 78, 118–19, 126–27
   piped, cream and meringue,
      618–22
deep-dish pies:
   blueberry/cranberry Internet,
      109–11
   chicken potpies, 323–26
   Marionberry, 118–19
defrosting of puff pastry, 414
deluxe chocolate wafer crumb
      crust, 65, **70–72**, 173–76
deluxe flaky pie crust, **26–29**
designer cherry pie, 95–96
dextrose, 648
dill crêpes, in coulibiac, 464–71
dip and sweep method, 8
dipping, caramel for, 600–601
double-crust, *see* two-crust
dough (prepared, store-
      bought), about, 632–33
dumplings:
   apple, **141–43**, 641
   golden, 524
duxelles, in beef Wellington,
      471–76

~E~
éclairs, 530, 534, **536–38**
   filling of, 532, 536
   shaping of, 531, 535
egg(s), 631–32
   white(s), 48, 631, 632
      glaze, 20, 56
   yolk(s), 48, 222, 632
      glaze, for top crust, 21
   quail, 347–49
elderberry flower concentrate,
      638
empanadas, baked, 333–36
equipment, 656–64
   brushes, 658–59
   food processors, 661–62
   graters, 660–61

equipment *(cont.)*
   knives and cutters, 659–60
   mixers, 662
   pans, 663–67
   thermometers, 673–74
   for weighing and measuring,
      656–58
   see also specific items

~F~
feta cheese, in spanakopita tri-
      angles (or pie), 380–81
fig(s), 652
   tart with mascarpone cream,
      210–12
filberts, *see* hazelnut(s)
fillings, Danish pastry, 510–14
   apricot lekvar, 496, 500–501,
      512
   brandied raisins, 502–4, **514**
   honey-stung cream cheese,
      504–6, **511**
   prune lekvar, 496, **513**
   remonce (almond cream),
      485, 493–99, 502–6, **510–11**
fillings and toppings, 549–94
   about, 549–50
   curd cream, 571–72
   food-processor poured fon-
      dant, 453–55, **581–82**
   fruit curds, 567–71; *see also*
      lemon curd; lime, curd;
      orange, curd; passion
      fruit curd
   poached apricots, 587–89
   praline powder, 564–65
   raspberry conserve, 283–85,
      589–91
   streusel, 86–88, 397–98,
      592–93
   sugar-glazed nuts, 593–94
   see also crème fraîche;
      ganache; meringue;
      pastry cream; sponge
      cake layers; whipped
      cream
fillo (phyllo), 362–84
   about, 362–66
   in chocolate mousse
      Napoleon, 457–60
   commercial, 392–94, 632
   flowers:
      panna cotta, 377–79
      savory Brie, 379
   frozen, 365, 366
   in Moroccan bisteeya trian-
      gles, 382–84
   pears wrapped in, 372–74
   in pistachio baklava, 367–69
   poppy seed roll, 404

fillo (phyllo) *(cont.)*
   in spanakopita triangles,
      380–81
   Syrian konafa, 375–77
flaky pastry scraps, **47–48**
flaky pie crust, 3–48, 251, 429–33
   baking, 17–21
      blind (prebaking), 18–19,
         251
      foil rings, 19
      frozen pies, 19
      moisture-proofing the
         baked bottom crust,
         20–21
      understanding, 21
   basic, *see* basic flaky pie crust
   beef suet, **43–45**, 326–28
   biscuits and scones compared
      with, 350
   browning of, 4–5, 6, 17, 19
   cheddar cheese, **39–41**,
      331–36, 341–42
   commercial, 4
   cream cheese, **29–32**, 74,
      323–26
      in custard pies and tarts,
         208–9, 215–17
      in fruit pies, turnovers,
         and dumplings, 81–88,
         91–102, 112–15, 121–25,
         132–38, 141–43
      in tarts, 278–80, 286–87,
         302–7
      whole wheat, **32–35**, 347–49
   deluxe, **26–29**
   goose fat, **45–46**, 323–26
   half-butter, half-shortening,
      38
   ideal, 4
   ingredients for, 5–6
   lard pie crust, miracle flaky,
      41–42, 333–42, 344–47
   making your own pastry
      flour for, 7
   mixing the dough for, 6
   resting the dough for, 7, 9
   rolling and shaping of,
      8–17
      borders, 13
      cutting the dough, 11
      decorative cutouts, 14
      fitting the bottom crust and
         placing the top crust, 12
      how to roll, 10–11, 251
      lattice crust, 16–17
      pan measurements, 8
      pan preparation, 9
      patching, 11
      rolling surface, 9–10
      scraps, 15

flaky pie crust *(cont.)*
    sizes of dough circles to cut
      for standard pans, 9
    steam vents, 14
    tarts, 251
    transferring dough to pan,
      12, 251
    in savory pies, tarts, and
      quiche, 337–49
    success pointers for, 8
    sweet cookie tart crust com-
      pared with, 48, 49
    tenderness of, 4, 5
    vegetable shortening, 36–39
flan rings, 666
    borders for, 13
    expandable, as guide for cut-
      ting dough, 11, 51
    large, transferring dough to,
      53
    sizes of dough circles to cut
      for, 49
    small:
      baking times, 19
      preparation, 50
      transferring dough to, 53
flour, 5, 633–34
    all-purpose, 4, 5, 7, 8, 411, 633,
      634
    cake, 4, 5, 7, 8
    freezing of, 4
    measuring of, 8, 623
    in pan preparation, 9, 78
    pastry, 4, 5, 7
    in puff pastry, 411
    self-rising, 634
    for strudel making, 38
    whole wheat, 5, 7, 634
flour wands, 659
flowers, 634–35
    crystallized, 622–23
    fillo:
      panna cotta, 377–79
      savory Brie, 379
flurries, chocolate, 616–17
foil:
    for easy oven cleanup, 18
    overbrowning prevented by,
      19, 78
    rings, 19, 665–66
fondant, food-processor
    poured, 453–55, **581–82**
food processors, 5, 6, 661–62
frangipane:
    in individual Twelfth Night
      chocolate galettes, 450–52
    in Twelfth Night galette
      (galette des rois), 446–50
freezer bags, reclosable,
    667–68

freezing:
    of baked pies and tarts, 21
    of cream, 630
    of crust, 7
    of Danish pastry dough, 485
    of egg glaze, 21
    of flour, 4
    of fruits, 638
    plastic wrap for, 15, 18
    of puff pastry, 413–14
    of scraps, 15
    of unbaked fruit pie, 17–18
frozen crusts, commercial, 4
fruit:
    about, 635–38
    curds and curd creams,
      567–72
    see also lemon curd; lime,
      curd; orange, curd; pas-
      sion fruit curd
    glazes, 611–12
    oils and essences, 638
    pies, 73–143, 651
      blackberry, 14, 76, 77, 79,
        115–17
      boiling down and concen-
        trating juices in, 74–75
      Concord grape, 127–29
      cornstarch and sugar quan-
        tities in, 76–77
      cranberry window, 129–31
      deep-dish Marionberry,
        118–19
      freezing of, prior to baking,
        17–18
      messing up with, 20
      open-faced apricot, 120–21
      quantities of ingredients in,
        76
      red currant, 112–13
      Shaker lemon, 132–34
      soggy, prevention of,
        17–18
      storing of, 78
      success pointers for, 78
      see also apple(s), fruit pies;
        blueberry(ies), fruit pies;
        cherry(ies), fruit pies;
        peach(es), fruit pies;
        raspberry(ies), fruit pies;
        strawberry(ies), fruit pies
    preserves glaze, to moisture-
      proof the baked bottom
      crust, 20, 56
    processed, 638–39
    turnovers (basic recipe),
      134–38
      variation of, 137–38
    see also specific fruits
Fruit Fresh, 638

Fruit Perfect:
    cherries, 639
    cherry/cheese strudel, 401
    cherry pie, 95
fudge sauce, hot, 223–26, **596**

~**G**~
galette:
    apple, 278–80
    Christmas cranberry, 286–87
    pear, 279
    puff pastry:
      making, 416
      Twelfth Night *(galette des
        rois)*, 446–50
      Twelfth Night individual
        chocolate, 450–52
      two miniature golden
        apple, 434–36
ganache:
    chocolate custard, in the
      Boulders tart, 299–302
    dark chocolate, in Grand
      Canyon pie, 190–93
    light whipped, 536–38, **559–60**
    quick, 559–60
    milk chocolate:
      in chocolate and peanut
        butter mousse seven-tier
        tart, 318–21
      in chocolate and peanut
        butter mousse tart, 316–18
    puddle, 297–99
garlic butter filling, for snail
    buns, 525–27
Gascon apple pie, **370–71**, 380
gâteau:
    Basque, 250, **294–96**
    Engadine, 250, **291–93**, 650
    St.-Honoré, 412, 528, 530, 534,
      538–42
gelatin, 639–40
    glaze, 612
ginger(y):
    butter biscuits, 354
      angel, 357
    cookie tart crust, sweet,
      56–57, **58**, 162–65
    ice cream, 241–42
    -peach pie, crustless, 126–27
    pear chiffon tart, 162–65
gingersnap(s):
    crumb crust, 67–68
      pecan, **68–69**, 155–57,
        217–220
      walnut, 68–69
    for pie bottoms, 17
glaze(d):
    about, 595
    caramel, for dipping, 600–601

glaze(d) *(cont.)*
chocolate, 20–21, 56, 536–38
egg white, 20, 56
fruit, 611–12
to moisture-proof the baked
bottom crust, 20–21, 56
raspberry pie, 103
currant, 103
strawberry pie, 73, **102–3**
sugar, 21, 493–97, 504–9,
509–10
for top crusts, 21
goat cheese fillo flowers, savory,
379
golden dumplings, 524
gold leaf, 640
gooseberry(ies), 636
pie, 76, 77
goose fat pie crust, flaky, **45–46,**
323–26
gougères (spicy cheese puff variation), 544–46
graham cracker crumb crust, 65,
66, 178–84
nut, **67,** 161–62
graham cracker crumbs, on
rolling surface, 17
Grand Canyon pie, 177, **190–93**
Grand Marnier and raspberry
cream cake tart, 276–77
grape(s):
pie, Concord, 76, 77, 79,
127–29
tartlets with almond cream,
champagne, 433
graters, 660–61
greasing of pans, 9, 50, 78, 252,
253
great pumpkin pie, 17, **198–200**
griottes, 639
Gruyère cheese:
in *gougères,* 544
in quiche Lorraine, 337–38
in roasted red pepper and
poblano quiche, 341–42

~H~
half-and-half, 630
half-butter, half-shortening pie
crust, 38
ham, in spicy cheese puff variation, 544–46
hand method, food processor
method compared with, 6
hazelnut(s) (filberts), 642
/almond paste, in chocolate
indulgence tartlets, 309
in individual Twelfth Night
chocolate galettes, 450
in Linzertorte, 283–85

hazelnut(s) (filberts) *(cont.)*
paste, 643
in praline powder, 564–65
sugar-glazed, 593–94
herb flaky pie crust, 25
Hiroko, the (raspberry and
Grand Marnier cream
cake tart), 276–77
honey(comb), 650
/almond pecan remonce,
507–9
chiffon pie, 170–73
-stung cream cheese filling,
504–6, **511**
hot fudge sauce, 223–26, **596**
Hungarian poppy seed strudel
(mákos kalácz), 401–4

~I~
ice cream, 221–49
buttermilk, 222, **233–35**
caramel, **243–45,** 434–36
ginger, 241–42
lemon-luscious, 235–36
peanut butter, 246–48
pineapple, 228, **239–40**
pistachio, 245–46
pure passion, 237–38
red wine, 248–49
standard base for, 223
tartlets, burnt almond, 230–31
triple vanilla (with crème
fraîche variation),
223–26, 228–29, **232–33,**
434–36, 536–38
understanding, 222–23
ice cream machines, 662–63
ice cream pies, 48, 221, 223–29
banana split, 221, **223–26**
brandied mincemeat, 228–29,
641
coconut (with crème fraîche
variation), 49, **226–28**
piña colada, 228
ingredients, 624–55
chocolate, 625–28
dairy and eggs, 629–32
dough, 632–33
flour, 633–34
fruit, 635–38
fruit and flavored oils and
essences, 638
fruit purées and processed
fruits, 638–39
gelatin, 639–40
measuring of, 623
nuts, 641–43
for pie crust, 5–6
stabilizers, 550, 644
substitutions for, 655

ingredients *(cont.)*
sugar and other sweeteners,
644–50
thickeners, 650–52
weights of, 654
see also specific ingredients
Italian meringue, 648
extra-light, 579–81
light, 578–79
in chiffon pies, 149–51,
157–60
topping, 178–84

~K~
kadaif, 632
"Key lime" pie, 177, **182–84**
with whipped cream topping,
184
kidney and steak potpies, 326–28
kirsch pastry cream, 436–39, **561**
kiss decorations, 620
kiwi tart with lime curd, 271–72
knives and cutters, 659–60
konafa, 632
Syrian, 375–77

~L~
lamb, in shepherd's pie, 328–31
lard, 5, 640–41
pie crust, miracle flaky, **41–43,**
333–42, 344–47
rendering of, 42–43, 640
La Smithereen *(millefoglie con
panna e crema chantilly),*
453, **456**
Latin American baked
empanadas, 333–37
lattice crusts:
egg glaze for, 21
making of, 16–17
lattice pies, 650
cherry, 93–97
cherry rhubarb, 100–102
pure rhubarb, 97–99
red currant-raspberry, 113–15
storing of, 78
leaves:
chocolate, 617–18
crystallized, 622–23
lekvar:
apricot, 138–40, 496, 500–501,
512
prune, 496, **513**
lemon(s):
-luscious ice cream, 235–36
Meyer, 637
Nadège tart, 185–87
poppy seed scones, 361
starch glaze, 612
yogurt cream, 358, **359**

lemon curd, 205–07, 639
  blueberry tart with, 258–60
  classic, 185–89, 258–60, **568–71**
  cream, 358, 359
    and raspberry Napoleon, 453, **456**
lemon pies:
  angel chiffon, 157–60
  meringue, 177, **178–81**
  pucker, 177, **187–89**
  Shaker, 132–34
lime:
  chiffon pie, frozen, 161–62
  curd, 568–69
    cream, 271–72
    kiwi tart with, 271–72
  pie, "Key," 177, **182–84**
Linzertorte, 250, **283–85**
liqueur:
  in chocolate dependence tartlets, 309–10
  pastry cream, 561
  see also specific liqueurs
liquids:
  in flaky pie crust, 5–6
  measuring of, 623
  in scones and biscuits, 350
  in sweet cookie tart crust, 48
love for three oranges (fresh orange tart), 267–71

~M~

macadamia nuts, 641, 642
  in the Boulders tart, 299–302
  sugar-glazed, 593–94
mákos kalácz (Hungarian poppy seed strudel), 401–4
mango(es), 637, 652
  passion tart, 272–74
maple:
  sugar glaze, 507–9, **509–10**
  walnut pie (baked in a tart pan), 306–7
marble, as rolling surface, 9, 50, 412, 669
Marionberry(ies), 635–36, 639
  filling, for shortcake, 358
  and passion cream Napoleon, 453, **456**
  pie, deep-dish, 118–19
marrow, rendering of, 44
mascarpone, 631
  cheese crust, 31
  cream, fig tart with, 210–12
  in tiramisú black bottom tart, 212–15
mashed potatoes, in shepherd's pie, 328–31
measurement:
  of dry ingredients, 623

measurement *(cont.)*
  of liquid ingredients, 623
  of pans, 8, 49
measuring cups and spoons, 658
meat loaf, in a flaky cheddar crust, 322, **331–33**
meat thermometers, 674
meringue:
  cocoa, 177, 190–95, **576**
  fillings and toppings, 572–81
    about, 572–74
    bitter chocolate-speckled, 189–90, **576**
    light Italian, 578–79
    pastry cream, Chef Arthur Oberholzer's, 561
    soft, 577–78
  in fluffy creamy cheese filling, 401
  pie shell or topping, crisp, 149–51, 157–60, **575–77**
  piped decorations from, 618–22
  for piping, 185–87
  spiral discs, 621–22
meringue pies, 177–95
  Grand Canyon, 177, **190–93**
  "Key lime," 177, **182–84**
  lemon, 177, **178–81**
  pucker, 177, **187–89**
  storing of, 21
meringue tarts:
  Nadège, 185–87
  orange:
    aurora blood, 177, **189–90**
    the bisou, 177, **193–95**
milk, 630
  in egg glaze, 21
  evaporated, 631
  goat's, 630
  in ice cream, 222
  rum strudel royale, 404–7
  sweetened condensed, 631
milk chocolate, 614, 625, 627, 628
millefoglie con panna e crema chantilly (La Smithereen), 453, **456**
mincemeat, ice cream pie, brandied, **228–29**, 641
mini pumpkin pielets, 200
mini turnovers:
  fruit, 137–38
  un-rugelach, 138–40
mixers, electric, 662
mocha:
  brownie puddle, 299
  filling, in chocolate pecan blasts, 313–16
  whipped cream, 551

molasses, 645, 646
  in shoofly pie, 215–17
molten chocolate soufflé tartlets, 311–13
Monterey Jack pepper cheese, in spicy spinach quiche, 347–49
morel(s), 641
  in beef Wellington, 471–76
  in deep-dish chicken potpies, 323–26
  quiche, spring windfall, 344–47
Moroccan bisteeya triangles, 382–84
mousse, chocolate:
  eggless, Napoleons with, 460
  Napoleon, 453, **457–60**
mousse, peanut butter:
  and chocolate tart, 63, **316–18**
  seven-tier, 318–20
mozzarella cheese, in spanako-pita triangles (or pie), 380–81
Muenster cheese, in spicy spinach quiche, 347–49
mushroom(s):
  velouté sauce, in coulibiac, 464–71
  see also morel(s); portobello mushrooms

~N~

Nadège tart, 185–87
Napoleon(s), 453–61, 639
  bite-size peanut butter, 453, **461–63**
  chocolate mousse, 453, **457–60**
  classic, 453–55
  with eggless chocolate mousse, 460
  La Smithereen, 453, **456**
  Marionberry and passion cream (or raspberry and lemon cream), 453, **456**
  strawberry and Chiboust, 453, **455–56**
nectarine(s), 638
  pie:
    amount of cornstarch and sugar in, 76, 77
    quantities of ingredients in, 76
    raspberry-, 121–23
    turnovers, 134–37
nonstick razor knives, 660
nougatine crumble, in Paris Ritz pastry crisps, 436–39

nut(s), 641–43
  cookie tart crust, sweet, *see*
    sweet nut cookie tart
    crust
  in crumb pie crusts, 65
  graham cracker crumb crust,
    67, 161–62
  pastes, 642–43
  sugar-glazed, 593–94
  vanilla, chocolate, or ginger-
    snap crumb crust, **68–69**
  see also specific nuts
nutcrackers, 669–70
nut graters, 661

~O~
oils:
  in crusts, 4
  fruit and flavored, 638
olives:
  in baked empanadas, 333–36
  in caramelized onion tart,
    338–40
onion tart, caramelized, 338–40
  with custard, 340
open-faced pies:
  apricot, 120–21
  designer apple, 84–86
  double strawberry, 104–6
  fresh blueberry, 14, 73, 104,
    107–9
orange(s):
  bitter Seville, 637
  blood, 637
  caramel sauce, burnt, 598
  curd, 193–95
    bitter Seville, 193–95,
      267–71, **569**
    blood, 189–90, **569**
    juice, 569–70
  flower water, 370–71, 375–77,
    638
  juice, in buttermilk ice cream,
    233–35
  pastry cream, 562
  tarts:
    aurora blood, 177, **189–90**
    the bisou, 177, **193–95**
    fresh (love for three
      oranges), 267–71
ovens, 17, 663
  convection, 18, 663
  easy cleanup of, 18
  temperature of, 18, 19
  thermometers for, 674

~P~
pains au chocolat (chocolate
  croissants), 483–84
PAM, 643

pan liners, 666
panna cotta fillo flowers, 377–79
pans, 17, 18, 78, 663–67
  ceramic, 17, 18, 78, 79, 663
  pie, 8, 9, 17, 18, 80, 663–64
  preparation of, 9, 50, 65, 78
  sizes of dough circles to cut
    for, 9, 49
  tart, *see* tart pans
  transferring of dough to, 12,
    52–54
parchment, for prebaking,
  18–19, 54
parchment cones, 667–69
Paris Ritz pastry crisps, 436–39
Parmesan cheese straws, 463–64
passion fruit, 637
  ice cream, pure, 237–38
passion fruit curd, 358, 359, **570**
  cream:
    mango tart, 272–74
    and Marionberry
      Napoleon, 453, **456**
pastis Gascon (Gascon apple
  pie), 370–71
pastry, 362–548
  about, 362–63
  see also brioche; cream puff
    pastry; croissants; Danish
    pastry; fillo; puff pastry;
    strudel
pastry, bread, and meat thermometers, 674
pastry bags, 667–69
  filling and use of, 618–20
pastry blenders, 660
pastry brushes or feathers, 658
pastry cloth, 9–10, 669
pastry cream (*crème pâtissière*),
  201–2, 504–6, 536–42,
  560–63
  almond:
    apricot tartlets with, 429–31
    blueberry or champagne
      grape tartlets with, 433
    in pears wrapped in fillo,
      372–74
    pear tart with, 260–62
    red currant tartlets with,
      431–33
  butterscotch, 561
  caramel, 562
  Chef Arthur Oberholzer's
    meringue, 561
  Chiboust, 538–42, **565–67**
    and strawberry Napoleon,
      453, **455–56**
  chocolate, 562
  coffee, 562
  kirsch, 436–39, **561**

pastry cream (*cont.*)
  liqueur, 561
  orange, 562
  peanut butter, 562
  praline crunch, 562
  praline paste, 562
  in puff pastry, 422–26,
    429–33, 437–39, 453–55,
    461–63
  in tarts, 255–56, 276–77,
    294–96
  whipped cream variation of,
    422–24, **562**
  white chocolate, 562
pastry dividers, adjustable, 659
pastry flour, 4, 5, 7
pastry jaggers, 660
pastry sleeves, 669
patching of crust, 11
pâte à Brique (warka), 365
pâte à choux, *see* cream puff pastry
pâte feuilletée, *see* puff pastry
pâte sucrée, *see* bittersweet
  chocolate, cookie tart
  crust; sweet cookie tart
  crust; sweet cookie tart
  crust, about; sweet nut
  cookie tart crust
peach(es), 638, 639
  filling, for shortcake, 359
  fruit pies, 76, 77, 79
    crustless ginger-, 126–27
    perfect, 124–25
  tarts:
    and cream, 266–67
    Tatin, 280, 283, **426–29**
  turnovers, 134–37
peanut butter:
  and chocolate mousse tart,
    63, 316–18
    seven-tier, **318–21**, 670–71
  cookie tart crust, sweet, 50,
    63–64, 316–21
  ice cream, 246–48
  Napoleons, bite-size, 453,
    461–63
  pastry cream, 562
peanuts, in Moroccan bisteeya
  triangles, 382–84
pear(s), 637–38
  chiffon tart, gingery, 162–65
  fruit pies, 76, 77
  pure, 83
  tarts:
    with almond cream,
      260–62
    galette, 279
    Tatin, 280, **283**
  wrapped in fillo, 372–74

pecan(s), 641–42
  in the alligator, 507–9
  in brownie puddle, 297–99
  chocolate blasts, 313–16
  cookie tart crust, sweet,
    59–60, 210–12
  gingersnap crumb crust,
    68–69, 155–57, 217–220
  halves, crunchy, 217–220
  pie (baked in a tart pan), 250,
    302–4
    chocolate (baked in a tart
      pan), 304–6
  remonce, almond/honey,
    507–9
  sugar-glazed, 593–94
  in vanilla, chocolate, or gin-
    gersnap nut crumb crust,
    68–69
peppers, *see* poblano peppers;
  red pepper
perfect peach pie, 124–25
perigueux sauce, with beef
  Wellington, 473, 476
persimmon, 638
  pie, 217–220
  purée, 638, 639
phyllo, *see* fillo
pie baskets, 669
pie birds, 670
pie crust, *see* crusts
pie crust shields, 665
pielets, mini pumpkin, 200
pielets, windfall fruit, 9, 47,
    78–80
  baking of, 80
  cherry, 96
  cooling of, 80
  filling amounts for, 79
  pie crust amounts for, 79–80
pie pan oven guards, 666
pie pans, 8, 9, 17, 18, 78, 80,
    663–64
pies:
  chiffon, *see* chiffon pies
  cooling of, 78
  custard, *see* custard, pies
  fruit, *see* fruit, pies
  Gascon apple, 370–71, **380**
  half, 80
  ice cream, *see* ice cream pies
  meringue, *see* meringue pies
  savory, 322–36
    baked empanadas, 333–36
    deep-dish chicken potpies,
      14, **323–26**
    meatloaf in a cheddar flaky
      crust, 322, **331–33**
    shepherd's, 328–31
    spanakopita, 380–81

pies *(cont.)*
    steak and kidney potpies,
      326–28
  single-crust, *see* single-crust
    pies
  storing of, 21
  two-crust, *see* two-crust pies
pie shells:
  borders of, 13
  testing for doneness of, 55
pie weights, 18–19
piña colada, ice cream pie, 228
pineapple, 638, 652
  ice cream, 228, **239–40**
piped decorations, cream and
    meringue, 618–22
  borders and sides, 620–21
  filling and use of pastry bag
    for, 618–20
  meringue spiral discs, 621–22
pistachio (nuts), 642
  baklava, 367–69
  blanched unsalted, 610–11
  custard sauce *(crème anglaise
    aux pistaches)*, 457–60,
    610–11
  ice cream, 245–46
  paste, 610–11, 643
pizza cutters, 659
pizza pans, blue steel, 666
plastic wrap, 78
  for freezing, 15, 18
  as rolling surface, 10, 15, 50,
    669
plum butter, 639
plum flame tart, 274–75
plum fruit pies, 76, 77
poached apricots, 208–09,
    587–89
poblano peppers:
  dried (ancho chiles), in baked
    empanadas, 333–36
  and roasted red pepper
    quiche, 341–42
poppy seed(s), 643
  grinders, 670
  lemon scones, 361
  roll, strudel dough or fillo,
    403–4
  strudel, Hungarian *(mákos
    kalácz)*, 401–4
portobello mushrooms, in steak
    and kidney potpies,
    326–28
Postilion mincemeat, 229, 641
potatoes, mashed, in shepherd's
    pie, 328–31
potpies, 322
  deep-dish chicken, 14, **323–26**
  steak and kidney, 326–28

praline:
  crunch pastry cream, 562
  custard sauce *(crème anglaise
    pralinée)*, 609
  paste, 643
  paste pastry cream, 562
  powder, 564–65
prebaking (blind baking), 18–19,
    54
  of puff pastry, 417
  of tarts, 251–53
presentation plates, 670–71
profiteroles, 530, 534, **536–38**
  filling of, 532, 533, 536
propane torches, 670
prune(s):
  lekvar, 496, **513**
  in shepherd's pie, 328–31
  triangles, 496
puff pastry *(pâte feuilletée)*, 280,
    411–84
  about, 350, 362–63, 411–17
  baking of, 414–17
    blind, 417
  in beef Wellington, 471–76
  in cheese straws, 463–64
  classic, 411, **417–20**, 426–29,
    453–55, 538–42
  commercial, 632–33
  in coulibiac, 464–71
  Danish waffle creams, 443–46
  defrosting of, 414
  fillo compared with, 364
  frozen, 413–14, 446–52,
    464–76
  galettes:
    individual, 449
    individual Twelfth Night
      chocolate, 450–52
    making, 416
    Twelfth Night *(galette des
      rois)*, 446–50
    two miniature golden
      apple, 434–36
  making a vol-au-vent from,
    414–15
  making bouchées from, 415
  in Paris Ritz pastry crisps,
    436–39
  quick, **420–22**, 426–29,
    436–39, 453–55, 463–64,
    538–42
  resting and relaxation of, 413
  rolling out, 412
  scraps of, 412, 413
  serving of, 414
  shaping of, 413
  storage of, 413–14
  taking the temperature of, 21
  tartlets, 429–33

puff pastry *(cont.)*
  apricot-almond cream,
    429–31
  blueberry or champagne
    grape-almond cream, 433
  crème brûlée, 440–42
  favorite sizes, 416
  making, 416
  red currant-almond cream,
    431–33
  tarts, 422–29
    apricot strip, 424–26
    making, 416
    strawberry strip, 422–24
    upside-down peach (peach
      tarte Tatin), 426–29
  see also croissants;
    Napoleon(s)
pumpkin:
  pie, 17
    chiffon, 155–57
    great, 17, **198–200**
    pielets, 200

~Q~
quail egg yolks, in spicy spinach
    quiche, 347–49
quiche, 322
  Lorraine, 322, **337–38**
  roasted red pepper and
    poblano, 341–42
  spicy spinach, 347–49
  spring windfall morel,
    344–47
quick puff pastry, **420–22,**
    426–29, 436–39, 453–55,
    463–64, 538–42

~R~
racks, 671
raisin(s):
  apple pie, brandied, 83
  in apple streusel strudel,
    397–99
  in baked empanadas,
    333–36
  brandied, 502–4, **514**
  in rosy apple cranberry pie,
    91–93
raspberry(ies), 636
  chiffon pie, 149–51
  conserve, 283–85, **589–91**
  filling, in Danish braid,
    490–93
  fruit pies:
    glazed, 103
    glazed currant, 103
    lattice red currant-, 113–15
    nectarine-, 121–23
  glaze, 20

raspberry(ies) *(cont.)*
  in Grand Canyon pie,
    190–93
  and Grand Marnier cream
    cake tart (the Hiroko),
    276–77
  jam, in Linzertorte, 283–85
  and lemon cream Napoleon,
    453, **456**
  in Paris Ritz pastry crisps,
    436–39
  sauce, 157–60, 308–10, 372–74,
    436–39, **603–4**
red currant:
  pie, 76, **112–13**
  -raspberry lattice pie, 113–15
  raspberry pie, glazed, 103
  tartlets with almond cream,
    431–33
red pepper, roasted, and
    poblano quiche, 341–42
red wine ice cream, 248–49
refiner's syrup, 646
remonce, 485, 493–99, 502–6,
    510–11
  almond/honey pecan, 507–9
rhubarb:
  fruit pies, 76, 77
    custard, 99
    custard, light, 99
    lattice, pure, 97–99
    lattice cherry-, 100–102
  and strawberry tart, fresh,
    256–58
rice, as pie weights, 18–19, 54, 251
ricotta cheese, in spanakopita
    triangles (or pie), 380–81
Ritz Hotel pastry crisps, 436–39
rolling, 10, 50, 251–54
  of flaky pie crust, 8–11, 251
  of puff pastry, 412
  surface for, 9–10, 50, 412
  of sweet cookie tart crust, 49,
    50, 252–54
rolling pins, 10, 412, 671
rose leaf cutters and veiners, 660
rosette decorations, 620
rose water, 375–77, 638
rosy apple cranberry pie, 91–93
ruby port caramel sauce, 598
rulers, 658
rum, milk, strudel royale, 404–7

~S~
salmon, in coulibiac, 464–71
salt, 643–44
saucepans with nonstick coat-
    ing, 667
sauces, 595–600, 602–11
  about, 595

sauces *(cont.)*
  perigueux, with beef
    Wellington, 472, 476
  raspberry, 157–60, 308–10,
    372–74, 436–39, 603–4
  strawberry, 436–39, **605–6**
  velouté, 464–71
  see also caramel(ized), sauce;
    chocolate, sauce; custard,
    sauce
savory cream puffs, **543–46,**
    547–48
savory dishes, 322–49
  about, 322–23
  baked empanadas, 333–36
  Brie fillo flowers, 379
  caramelized onion tart,
    338–40
  caramelized onion tart with
    custard, 340
  creamy and spicy crab
    tartlets, 343–44
  crust recommended for, 4
  meat loaf in a flaky cheddar
    crust, 322, 331–33
  potpies:
    deep-dish chicken, 14,
      323–26
    steak and kidney, 326–28
  quiche:
    Lorraine, 337–38
    roasted red pepper and
      poblano, 341–42
    spicy spinach, 347–49
    spring windfall morel,
      344–47
  shepherd's pie, 328–31
scales, 648, 649, 656–57
scones, 350
  currant, 359–61
  dried cranberry, 361
  lemon poppy seed, 361
  see also biscuits
scraps:
  flaky pastry, **47–48**
  puff pastry, 412, 413
  rolling and shaping of, 15, 51
  for windfall fruit pielets, 47,
    78–80
self-rising flour, 634
semisweet chocolate, *see* bitter-
    sweet chocolate
serrated knives, fourteen-inch,
    659
Shaker lemon pie, 132–34
sheet pans, half-size, 666
shell and shell border, 620–21
  sideways, 621
shepherd's pie, 328–31
shoofly pie, 215–17

shortcake, strawberry (with
    variations), 358–59
shortening, *see* vegetable short-
    ening
shrinkage of dough, 6–9, 412
side decorations, 620–21
silk brushes, large, 658
silver leaf, 640
single-crust pielets, 79
single-crust pies:
    prevention of overbrowning
        of, 78
    rolling and shaping consider-
        ations for, 8, 9, 49
    shaping the border for, 13
    soggy, prevention of,
        17
slips, apricot Danish, 500–501
snail(s):
    buns, 525–27
    canned, 633
    puffs, 547–48
snail buns, Danish, 502–4
sodium aluminum sulfate, 6, 8,
    624
soufflé tarts, molten chocolate,
    311–13
sour cream, 631
    in the Boulders tart, 299–302
    flaky pie crust, 24–25
    in open-faced double
        strawberry pie, 104–6
spanakopita triangles (or pie),
    380–81
spandau, see Danish pastry,
    envelopes
spatulas and stirring devices,
    671–72
spicy:
    cheese puff variation
        (*gougères*), 544–46
    and creamy crab tartlets,
        343–44
    spinach quiche, 347–49
spinach:
    quiche, spicy, 347–49
    in spanakopita triangles (or
        pie), 380–81
spiral discs, meringue, 621–22
sponge cake layers:
    light, 185–87, 189–93, 205–7,
        212–15, 272–74, 276–77,
        583–85
    chocolate, 585–87
    thick, 267–71
spoons:
    measuring, 658
    porcelain, 672
spring windfall morel quiche,
    344–47

spun sugar, 538–42, 625
    caramel for, 602–3
    devices, 672
squab, in Moroccan bisteeya
    triangles, 382–84
stabilizers, 550, 644
starches, 650–52
    glazes, 612, 650
star decorations, 620
steak and kidney potpies, 326–28
steam vents, cutting of, 14
sticky buns, 519–21
stock, veal and chicken, 653
storage:
    of baked pies and tarts, 21
    of chocolate, 628
    of eggs, 631–32
    of filled fillo, 366
    of flour, 634
    of fruit pies, 78
    of puff pastry, 413–14
    of suet or marrow, 44
    see also specific recipes
strainers, 661, 672–73
strawberry(ies), 636, 652
    and Chiboust Napoleon, 453,
        455–56
    fruit pies:
        glazed, 73, **102–3**
        open-faced double, 104–6
    lover's chiffon pie, 146–48
    and rhubarb tart, fresh,
        256–58
    sauce, 436–39, **605–6**
    shortcake (with variations),
        358–59
    strip, 422–24
streusel topping, 86–88, 397–98,
    592–93
strudel, 385–410
    about, 362, 363, 364, 385–86
    apple, 394–96
    apple streusel, 397–98
    cabbage and bacon, 408–10
    cherry cheese, 399–401
    cherry/cheese Fruit Perfect,
        401
    dough (master recipe), 387–92
    dough poppy seed roll, 404
    fillo as substitute for, 392–94
    fillo compared with, 365
    fluffy creamy cheese filling
        for, 401
    Hungarian poppy seed
        (*mákos kalácz*), 401–4
    royale, milk rum, 404–7
suet, rendering, 44
sugar, 644–50
    brown, 645, 646
    in fruit pies, 76, 77

sugar *(cont.)*
    glaze:
        for Danish, 493–97, 504–9,
            509–10
        maple, 507–9, **509–10**
        for top crust, 21
    -glazed nuts, 593–94
    granulations and forms of,
        647–48
    making of, 645–46
    spun, *see* spun sugar
    in sweet cookie tart crust, 48
    syrups, 648–50
swans, 530
    assembling of, 533
    shaping of, 531
sweet cookie tart crust (*pâte
    sucrée*), **56–58**, 430, 433
    chocolate, *see* bittersweet
        chocolate, cookie tart
        crust
    coconut, 50, 57, **58**, 226–28,
        272–74
    in custard pies and tarts,
        201–2, 205–7, 212–15
    ginger, 56–57, **58**, 162–65
    in honeycomb chiffon pie,
        170–73
    in tarts, 252–56, 267–72,
        274–75, 291–96
sweet cookie tart crust, about,
    48–56
    baking of, 54–55
        lining the dough for blind
            baking, 54
        moisture-proofing the
            baked bottom crust, 56
        tarts, 252–54
        testing for doneness, 54–55
    rolling and shaping of, 49–54
        cutting the dough, 51
        pan measurements, 49
        pan preparation, 50
        scraps, 51
        sizes of dough circles to cut
            for standard pans, 49
        tarts, 252–54
        transferring the dough to
            the pan, 52–54
    storage of, 55
sweet cream flaky pie crust, **25**,
    201–5, 276–78
sweet nut cookie tart crust (*pâte
    sucrée*), **58–60**, 430, 433
    tender, 58, **60**
    see also almond(s), cookie
        tart crust, sweet;
        pecan(s), cookie tart
        crust, sweet; walnut(s),
        cookie tart crust, sweet

sweet peanut butter cookie tart
    crust, 50, **63–64**, 316–21
Syrian *konafa*, 375–77

~T~

Tahitian vanilla cheesecake tart,
    205–7
tapioca, 650, 652
tarte Tatin pan, 666
tart knives, 659
tartlets, 308–16
    burnt almond ice cream,
        230–31
    chocolate, 308–16
        dependence, 309–10
        flame, 310
        indulgence, 309
        oblivion, 308–10
        pecan blasts, 313–16
        soufflé, molten, 311–13
    flaky vegetable shortening pie
        crust for, 36
    prebaked, baking times for, 19
    puff pastry, 429–33
        apricot-almond cream,
            429–31
        blueberry or champagne
            grape-almond cream, 433
        crème brûlée, 440–42
        favorite sizes, 416
        making, 416
        red currant-almond cream,
            431–33
    savory, creamy and spicy
        crab, 343–44
    sizes of dough circles to cut
        for, 9, 49
    testing for doneness of, 54–55
    unmolding of, 55, 251
tart pans, 79–80, 250–51, 664–65
    measurement of, 8, 49
    rolling and shaping consider-
        ations for, 8, 9, 49, 52–53
tarts, savory:
    caramelized onion, 338–40
    caramelized onion-custard,
        340
    see also quiche
tarts, sweet, 250–307, 316–21
    apple:
        galette, 278–80
        Tatin, 281–83
        with walnut cream, 263–65
    berry:
        blueberry, with lemon curd,
            258–60
        fresh (basic recipe), 255–56
        fresh strawberry and
            rhubarb, 256–58
        the Boulders, 299–302

tarts, sweet *(cont.)*
    brownie puddle (with cara-
        mel variation), 297–99
    caramelized-upside down, *see*
        Tatins, three
    chiffon:
        apple weincreme, 166–69
        gingery pear, 162–65
    chocolate and peanut butter
        mousse, 63, **316–18**
        seven-tier, **318–21**, 670–71
    Christmas cranberry galette,
        286–87
    dried cranberry (or cherry)
        walnut crostata, 288–91
    fresh orange (love for three
        oranges), 267–71
    gâteau Basque, 250, **294–96**
    gâteau Engadine, 250, **291–93**,
        650
    kiwi-lime curd, 271–72
    Linzertorte, 250, **283–85**
    mango passion, 272–74
    maple walnut pie, 306–7
    peach(es):
        and cream, 266–67
        Tatin, 280, 283, **426–29**
    pear:
        with almond cream,
            260–62
        galette, 279
        Tatin, 280, **283**
    pecan pie, 250, **302–4**
        chocolate, 304–6
    plum flame, 274–75
    puff pastry, 422–29
        apricot strip, 424–26
        making, 416
        strawberry strip, 422–24
        upside-down peach (peach
            tarte Tatin), 426–29
    raspberry and Grand
        Marnier cream cake (the
        Hiroko), 276–77
    shaping the border for, 13
    sizes of dough circles to be
        cut for, 9
    storing of, 21
    testing for doneness of, 55
    unmolding of, 55, 251
Tatins, three (caramelized
    upside-down tarts), 280
    apple, 281–83
    peach, 280, 283, **426–29**
    pear, 280, **283**
techniques, 613–23
    for crystallized flowers and
        leaves, 622–23
    for measuring dry ingredi-
        ents, 623

techniques *(cont.)*
    for measuring liquid ingredi-
        ents, 623
    see also chocolate, techniques
        for; piped decorations,
        cream and meringue
Teflon-type liner, 18, 54
temperature:
    of baking pie crust, 21
    of crust ingredients, 4, 8
    oven, for baking of crust, 18,
        19
    of puff pastry, 21
    for sugar syrup, 649–50
tempering method, classic, 615
tempering method, quick, 616
tender nut cookie tart crust, 50,
    60
testing for doneness, 54–55
thermometers, 673–74
thickeners, 650–52
thyme crêpes, in beef
    Wellington, 471–76
Tiptree lemon curd, 187
tiramisú black bottom tart,
    212–15
top crusts:
    decorative cutouts for, 14
    decorative openings for, 14
    glaze for, 21
    placing of, 12
touch-of-grace biscuits, 351–53
triangle(s):
    Moroccan bisteeya, 382–84
    prune or apricot, 496
    spanakopita, 380–81
    twists, Danish, 495–96
truffle oil, white, 328–31, 638
    cream puffs, **543–46**, 547–48
turnovers:
    baked empanadas, 333–36
    fruit (basic recipe), 134–38
    mini turnovers, 137–38
    un-rugelach mini turnovers,
        138–40
Twelfth Night galette (*galette des
    rois*), 446–50
    individual, 449
    individual chocolate, 450–52
two-crust pielets, 79–80
two-crust pies:
    fitting the bottom crust and
        placing the top crust for,
        12
    half, 80
    prevention of overbrowning
        of, 78
    rolling and shaping consider-
        ations for, 8, 9
    shaping the border for, 13

two-crust pies *(cont.)*
    soggy, prevention of, 17–18
    steam vents for, 14

~U~
un-rugelach mini turnovers,
    138–40, 512
upside-down tarts, *see* Tatins,
    three

~V~
vanilla, 52–53
    cheesecake tart, Tahitian,
        205–7
    custard sauce *(crème
        anglaise)*, 372–74, 522–24,
        606–7
    ice-cream, triple (with crème
        fraîche variation),
        223–26, 228–29, **232–33**,
        434–36, 536–38
    nut crumb crust, **68–69**
        walnut, **68**, 170–73
    wafer crumb crust, **67–68**,
        146–48, 152–54, 223–26
veal:
    kidney and steak potpies,
        326–28
    stock, 653
vegetable shortening, 4, 5
    nonstick, 78, 643
    pie crust, flaky, **36–39**
    in puff pastry, 41
velouté sauce, in coulibiac,
    464–71
vinegar, in flaky pie crust, 5–6
vodka, in ice cream, 222, 232–38,
    242–45
vol-au-vents:
    baking of, 415–16
    cutters, 660
    making of, 414–15

~W~
waffle creams, Danish, 443–46
walnut(s), 641, 642

walnut(s) *(cont.)*
    in apple streusel strudel,
        397–98
    in apple strudel, 394–96
    in banana split pie, 223–26
    /bittersweet chocolate
        cookie tart crust, **62**,
        311–13
    in Christmas galette, 286–87
    in cookie tart crust, sweet
        nut, **59–60**, 161–62,
        166–69, 308–10
    cream, apple tart with,
        263–65
    in crustless apple crumb pie,
        89–90
    in Danish snail buns,
        502–4
    dried cranberry (or cherry)
        crostata, 288–91
    in Gascon apple pie, 370–71
    in gâteau Engadine,
        291–93
    in individual Twelfth Night
        chocolate galettes, 450–52
    maple pie (baked in a tart
        pan), 306–7
    sugar-glazed, 593–94
    in un-rugelach mini
        turnovers, 138–40
    in vanilla, chocolate, or gin-
        gersnap nut crumb crust,
        68–69
warka (pâte à Brique), 365–66
water:
    in crust, 6, 21
    in egg glaze, 21
waxed paper, 10, 78
weighing equipment, 656–57
whipped cream, 141–43, 217–220,
    308–9, 394–96, 549–58
    about, 549–50
    bourbon, 302–6, **551**
    caramel, 555–56
    chocolate chip, 554–55
    cocoa, 551

whipped cream *(cont.)*
    mocha, 551
    pastry cream, 422–24,
        562
    perfect, 358–59, 536–38, **551**
    for piping, 152–57, 161–62,
        556–57
    real old-fashioned, 552–53
    rich, in Danish waffles,
        443–46
    stabilized, 184, **553**
    superstabilized, 557–58
    topping, "Key lime" pie with,
        184
whisks, 672
white chocolate, 614, 625, 627
    curls, 201–2
    as moisture-proof bottom-
        crust glaze, 21
    in open-faced double straw-
        berry pie, 104–6
    pastry cream, 562
whole wheat:
    cream cheese pie crust, flaky,
        32–35, 347–49
    croissants, 477–83
    flaky pie crust, basic, **24**,
        333–36, 343–44
    flour, 5, 7, 634
windfall fruit pielets, *see* pielets,
    windfall fruit

~Y~
yeast, 653–54
yogurt:
    cream, lemon, 358, **359**
    flaky pie crust, **25**, 187–89

~Z~
zest, citrus fruit, 637
zesters, 660–61
    "greater," 661